educational PSYCHOLOGY

for learning *and* teaching

kerri-lee krause   sandra bochner   sue duchesne

THOMSON

Australia · Canada · Mexico · Singapore · Spain · United Kingdom · United States

THOMSON™

102 Dodds Street
Southbank Victoria 3006

Email highereducation@thomsonlearning.com.au
Website http://www.thomsonlearning.com.au

First published in 2003
10 9 8 7 6 5 4 3 2 1
06 05 04 03

Copyright © 2003 Nelson Australia Pty Limited.

COPYRIGHT
Apart from fair dealing for the purposes of study, research, criticism or review, or as permitted under Part VB of the Copyright Act, no part of this book may be reproduced by any process without permission. Copyright owners may take legal action against a person who infringes on their copyright through unauthorised copying. Enquiries should be directed to the publisher.

National Library of Australia
Cataloguing-in-Publication data

Krause, Kerri-Lee Dawn.
    Educational psychology for learning and teaching.

    Bibliography.
    Includes index.
    ISBN 0 17 010351 X.

    1. Educational psychology. I. Bochner, Sandra. II. Duchesne, Susan. III. Title.

370.15

Editor: Glenys Osborne
Project editor: David Parnham
Publishing editor: Rebekah Jardine-Williams
Indexer: Fay Donlevy
Cover designer: Elizabeth Dias
Text designer: Leigh Ashforth @ watershed art & design
Technical illustrators: Shelly Communications and Xiangyi Mo
Photo and permissions researcher: Copper Leife
Typeset in Fairfield Light 11/13.5 by Leigh Ashforth
Production controller: Carly McCormack
Printed in China by C & C Offset Printing Co., Ltd.

This title is published under the imprint of Thomson.
Nelson Australia Pty Limited ACN 058 280 149 (incorporated in Victoria) trading as Thomson Learning Australia.

The URLs contained in this publication were checked for currency during the production process. Note, however, that the publisher cannot vouch for the ongoing currency of URLs.

KERRI-LEE:
To Rhoda and Milton for the gifts of life and a passion for learning

SUE:
To my father, whose wisdom and breadth of knowledge I will always miss

SANDRA:
To all the children I have known

Contents in brief

About the authors	xv
Authors' acknowledgements	xvi
Publishers' acknowledgements	xvii
Note to students	xviii
Note to instructors	xxi
Resources guide	xxii

MODULE I — The learner developing over time — 1

CHAPTER 1	Emerging skills	2
CHAPTER 2	Cognitive development	38
CHAPTER 3	Socioemotional and moral development	70

MODULE II — The learning process — 106

CHAPTER 4	Behavioural views of learning	108
CHAPTER 5	Cognitive explanations of learning	136
CHAPTER 6	Humanist approaches to learning	170

MODULE III — Individual difference in the inclusive classroom — 194

CHAPTER 7	Intelligence and motivation	196
CHAPTER 8	Learners with special needs	230
CHAPTER 9	Sociocultural factors in the learning process	262

MODULE IV — Educational psychology in the inclusive classroom — 302

CHAPTER 10	ICT in learning and teaching	304
CHAPTER 11	Assessment and reporting	338
CHAPTER 12	Managing behaviour and classrooms	372

Glossary	401
References	408
Index	445

Contents

About the authors — xv
Authors' acknowledgements — xvi
Publishers' acknowledgements — xvii
Note to students — xviii
Note to instructors — xxi
Resources guide — xxii

MODULE I The learner developing over time 1

CHAPTER 1 Emerging skills 2

Introduction. 3
Physical development over time 4
    Physical development in infancy 4
    Physical development in early childhood 5
    Physical development in middle childhood 5
    Physical development in adolescence. 7
    Variations in physical development 9
Brain development 12
    The brain's physical structures 12
    Brain development and the environment 14
Language development 15
    Language building blocks 15
    Language development during infancy. 16
    Language development during early childhood. 16
    Language development during middle childhood 18
    Language development during adolescence 19
    Adults' role in language acquisition 20
School-based skills 21
    Second-language development 21
    Literacy development. 24
    Numeracy development 28
Principles of development 32
    What contributes to development?. 33
Concluding comments 34
Chapter review 35
You make the connections 35
Key terms 36
Recommended reading 37

CHAPTER 2 Cognitive development 38

Introduction. 39
Piaget's theory of cognitive development 39
    Piaget's cognitive stages 41
    As children develop cognitively, what changes?. 53

What influences development? 55
Neo-Piagetians. 56
Strengths and limitations of Piaget's ideas 56
Vygotsky's sociocultural theory. 60
Sociocultural origins of cognitive development 61
Language as a mental tool 62
Zone of proximal development 63
Strengths and limitations of Vygotsky's theory 65
Linking Piaget and Vygotsky. 66
Concluding comments 67
Chapter review 68
You make the connections 68
Key terms 69
Recommended reading 69

CHAPTER 3 **Socioemotional and moral development** 70

Introduction. 71
Defining the self 71
Dimensions of the developing self. 71
Self-concept. 72
Self-esteem. 73
Self-efficacy 75
Self-concept, self-esteem and development. 76
Erikson's theory of psychosocial development 77
Theory overview 78
Stages of psychosocial development 79
Strengths and limitations of Erikson's theory. 83
The self across cultures. 85
The self developing emotionally and socially 86
Emotions and socioemotional development 86
Peer experiences and socioemotional development 88
The self developing morally. 94
Socialisation approaches to moral development 94
Cognitive-developmental theories of moral development. . . . 94
Further perspectives on moral development and values 100
Concluding comments 103
Chapter review 103
You make the connections 103
Key terms 104
Recommended reading 104

MODULE II **The learning process** 106

CHAPTER 4 **Behavioural views of learning** 108

Introduction. 109
Behavioural explanations of learning 110
Contiguity. 110
Classical conditioning 110
Pavlov's approach. 110
Watson and behaviourism 113

　　　　Strengths and limitations of classical conditioning 113
　Operant conditioning 114
　　　　Thorndike, trial-and-error learning and the law of effect 115
　　　　Skinner and operant conditioning 116
　　　　Principles of operant conditioning 117
　　　　Applied behaviour analysis 127
　　　　Strengths and limitations of operant conditioning and ABA . . 127
　Social learning theory and observational learning 128
　　　　Reciprocal determinism 128
　　　　Strengths and limitations of social learning theory 130
　Cognitive behaviour modification and self-regulation 131
　　　　Strengths and limitations of cognitive behaviour modification . . 132
　Concluding comments 133
　Chapter review 133
　You make the connections 134
　Key terms 134
　Recommended reading 135

CHAPTER 5 Cognitive explanations of learning 136

　Introduction 137
　Cognitive learning theory 137
　The information processing approach 137
　　　　The multistore model 138
　　　　The levels of processing model 139
　　　　The connectionist model 140
　　　　Why and how learners forget 140
　　　　Information and knowledge 142
　　　　Strengths and limitations of the information processing
　　　　　approach 143
　Metacognition: Managing cognitive processes 145
　　　　Metacognitive knowledge 145
　　　　Metacognitive experience 146
　　　　Metacognitive development 148
　　　　Metacognitive strategies and learning 148
　　　　Metacognitive strategies across culture 148
　Cognitive style 150
　　　　Perceptual style: Field dependence–independence 151
　　　　Conceptual tempo: Impulsivity–reflectivity 152
　　　　Deep and surface learning 153
　　　　Sociocultural factors and cognitive style 154
　　　　Approaches to learning in the classroom 154
　Constructivism 157
　　　　Forms of constructivism 157
　　　　Key principles of constructivism 158
　　　　Constructivism in the classroom context 158
　　　　Strengths and limitations of the constructivist approach 165
　Concluding comments 166
　Chapter review 167
　You make the connections 168
　Key terms 168
　Recommended reading 169

CHAPTER 6   Humanist approaches to learning   170

- Introduction 171
- What is humanism? 171
- Humanism and psychology 172
- Maslow and the hierarchy of human needs 173
  - Strengths and limitations of Maslow's hierarchy of needs 175
- Rogers: Non-directive teaching and 'freedom to learn' 176
  - Strengths and limitations of Rogers's educational ideas 178
- Humanism and education 178
  - Progressive education 179
  - The Dalton Plan 182
  - Cooperative learning 182
  - Strengths and limitations of humanism in the classroom 187
- Concluding comments 190
- Chapter review 190
- You make the connections 191
- Key terms 192
- Recommended reading 192

MODULE III   Individual difference in the inclusive classroom   194

CHAPTER 7   Intelligence and motivation   196

- Introduction 197
- Intelligence 197
  - Cultural influences on intelligence 198
- Models of intelligence 199
  - Spearman and 'g' 199
  - Thurstone and primary mental abilities 199
  - Guilford's structure-of-intellect model 200
  - Gardner's theory of multiple intelligences 201
  - Sternberg's triarchic model of intelligence 202
  - Strengths and limitations of models of intelligence 205
- Measuring intelligence 206
  - The Stanford-Binet test 206
  - Wechsler's intelligences scales 207
  - Administering intelligence tests 208
  - Interpreting IQ scores 208
  - The nature–nurture debate 210
  - Strengths and limitations of intelligence tests 211
- Learners with exceptional abilities 211
  - Concepts of giftedness, talent and creativity 212
  - Identifying gifted, talented and creative learners 212
  - Educational programs and provisions for gifted students 214
  - Strengths and limitations of programs for gifted, talented and creative students 215
- Motivation 216
  - Arousal, anxiety and motivation 217
  - Motivation in adolescence 218
  - Key concepts in motivation 219

Strengths and limitations of motivational factors in the
classroom.. 221
Theories of motivation.. 222
Behavioural explanations................................. 222
Cognitive explanations.................................... 223
Social learning theory explanations..................... 225
Humanist explanations..................................... 226
Strengths and limitations of motivation theories........ 226
Concluding comments... 228
Chapter review.. 228
You make the connections.. 228
Key terms.. 229
Recommended reading.. 229

CHAPTER 8 Learners with special needs — 230

Introduction... 231
What is special education?....................................... 231
Concepts of normal development................................ 231
Concepts of 'readiness' and preventative programs............. 232
Underachievers and supplementary programs............ 232
Compensatory programs.................................. 233
Learners with special needs...................................... 234
Learners with special support needs..................... 234
Learners with high support needs........................ 235
Learners with mild difficulties........................... 235
Learners at educational risk.............................. 236
Resilience and educational risk........................... 237
Concepts of impairment, disability and handicap......... 239
Special education in practice.................................... 247
Special education policies................................ 247
Special education services and programs................ 248
Integration, mainstreaming and inclusion................ 249
The integration–segregation debate...................... 251
The effectiveness of regular and special education programs.. 254
Controversial or alternative interventions and therapies..... 255
Concluding comments... 258
Chapter review.. 258
You make the connections.. 259
Key terms.. 259
Recommended reading.. 260

CHAPTER 9 Sociocultural factors in the learning process — 262

Introduction... 263
Bronfenbrenner's ecological systems theory..................... 263
Ethnicity, language and culture.................................. 265
Language and culture..................................... 266
Culture and beliefs about knowledge and learning........ 267
Cultural difference and misunderstanding................ 267
Racism... 268
Culture, advantage and disadvantage..................... 269
Resistance... 269
Gender.. 271

Sex and gender differences........................... 272
Gender identity formation........................... 272
Gender issues in schools............................ 273
Sources of gender difference in educational outcomes...... 274
Gender bias in classrooms........................... 276
Co-educational and single-sex schooling................ 279
Socioeconomic status (SES)............................. 281
Social class and SES................................ 281
Poverty and education............................... 282
School factors...................................... 286
Issues in education for indigenous learners............... 288
Achievement....................................... 288
Participation and attendance patterns.................. 290
Skills and strengths................................. 290
Issues in Indigenous Australians' education............. 290
Maori learners and New Zealand's education system...... 296
Effective teaching for indigenous communities........... 298
Concluding comments.................................. 299
Chapter review.. 299
You make the connections.............................. 300
Key terms... 300
Recommended reading.................................. 301

MODULE IV — Educational psychology in the inclusive classroom — 302

CHAPTER 10 — ICT in learning and teaching — 304

Introduction.. 305
Key concepts in ICT................................... 305
Technology.. 306
Educational technology.............................. 306
Information and communication technology.............. 306
Computer-mediated communication.................... 307
Computer literacy................................... 307
Information literacy................................. 307
How teachers use ICT in the classroom................... 309
ICT and theories of learning............................ 311
Behavioural learning theories and ICT.................. 312
Cognitive learning theories, constructivism and ICT........ 314
Humanist learning theories and ICT.................... 319
Strengths and limitations of different approaches to
learning with ICT................................. 320
Features of learning with ICT........................... 321
Learning to navigate using hypertext and hypermedia...... 322
Cognition and reading online......................... 323
Identity and the Internet............................. 323
Values and the Internet.............................. 324
ICT in the inclusive classroom........................ 325
Strengths and limitations of using ICT in the classroom.... 331
Concluding comments.................................. 335
Chapter review.. 336

You make the connections 336
Key terms 337
Recommended reading 337

CHAPTER 11 Assessment and reporting — 338

Introduction 339
Why do we assess? 339
Key terms in assessment 340
    Assessment 340
    Evaluation 340
    Measurement 341
    Test 341
Types of assessment 342
    Formative, summative and diagnostic assessment 343
    Interpreting assessment information 344
    Strengths and limitations of different types of assessment 347
How do we assess? 349
    Selecting assessment modes 349
    Gathering information for different modes of assessment 350
    Strengths and limitations of different assessment modes 357
Technical issues in assessment 358
    Reliability 358
    Validity 359
Assessment stakeholders 361
    Students 361
    Parents 362
    Teachers 362
    School psychologists, counsellors and guidance officers 362
    Schools and school administrators 362
    Employers 363
    Government 363
    Community 363
    Strengths and limitations of stakeholders' interest in assessment information 364
Recording and reporting assessment results 365
    Recording information 365
    Reporting information 366
Concluding comments 368
Chapter review 369
You make the connections 369
Key terms 370
Recommended reading 370

CHAPTER 12 Managing behaviour and classrooms — 372

Introduction 373
Classroom behaviour management 373
    Defining classroom management 374
    Behaviour management in practice 374
    Behaviour-management strategies: Alternatives to corporal punishment 379
    Strengths and limitations of classroom behaviour management 380

Models of effective classroom management ... 381
    The interventionist teacher ... 382
    The interactive teacher ... 384
    The non-interventionist teacher ... 387
    Strengths and limitations of classroom-management models ... 389
Managing conflict and problem behaviour ... 390
    Bullying ... 390
    Strengths and limitations of conflict- and problem-behaviour-management interventions ... 397
Concluding comments ... 398
Chapter review ... 398
You make the connections ... 399
Key terms ... 399
Recommended reading ... 399

Glossary 401
References 408
Index 445

About the authors

Kerri-Lee Krause, BEd, MA, PhD (Macquarie), is a Senior Lecturer at the School of Education, Australian Centre for Educational Studies, Macquarie University. Most recently she has been a Senior Fellow at the University of Melbourne's Centre for the Study of Higher Education, Faculty of Education.

Dr Krause has many years' experience teaching in high-school and tertiary-education settings, and has received a Macquarie University Outstanding Teacher Award in recognition of her contribution to promoting learning- and teaching-quality in educational psychology. She has a passion for supporting first-year students in their transition to university study. *Educational psychology for learning and teaching* stems from her desire to provide students with the best possible resources to enhance their learning and professional development.

As well as lecturing in educational psychology, Dr Krause conducts research in the area. She has a particular interest in cognitive processes and affective factors, and their relationship to literacy development. Her research interests extend to computer literacies and their role in effective learning and teaching. Dr Krause jointly edited the book *Cyberlines: The languages and cultures of the Internet* (2000), published by James Nicholas, and she co-edits the international refereed journal *Information Technology, Education and Society*.

* * *

Sandra Bochner, MA (Hawaii), MA(Hons) (Macquarie), PhD (Macquarie), is an Honorary Associate (formerly Associate Professor) in education at Macquarie University.

Dr Bochner has over 40 years' experience teaching and researching in the area of educational psychology and child development. Her specific interest is in aspects of special education, particularly the development of children who have special needs in the early childhood years. She convened a large introductory course in educational psychology at Macquarie University for five years, and continues to be a highly respected teacher and researcher in the area.

Dr Bochner has published over 30 articles in refereed journals and has also edited several books in the special education area. Her most recent book, written with Penny Price and Jane Jones, is *Child language development: Learning to talk* (1998), published by Whurr. She has a chapter in *Down syndrome across the lifespan* (2001), also published by Whurr.

Aside from writing and looking after her grandchildren, Dr Bochner enjoys sailing on Sydney's beautiful Pittwater.

* * *

Sue Duchesne, BADipEd(Hons), PhD (Macquarie), lectures in educational psychology at the School of Education, Australian Centre for Educational Studies, Macquarie University.

Dr Duchesne has extensive teaching experience in the primary-school and tertiary-education sectors, and has used her classroom teaching expertise to prepare preservice and inservice teachers in Australia and Nepal. She has a particular interest in promoting social justice in education. Her research areas include cross-cultural issues in educational psychology, as well as parental beliefs and behaviours, and in particular how these relate to schooling.

Dr Duchesne draws on her experience as the mother of three young children to inspire her students and to provide continued impetus for her research into the importance of parental involvement in education.

Authors' acknowledgements

This book is the result of the combined efforts, energies and encouragement of many of our colleagues, students, friends and family, not to mention a terrific team at Thomson Learning Australia. We would like to pay tribute to the support and expertise of Rebekah Jardine-Williams and Glenys Osborne, without whom this book would not be a reality. Thanks also to Lachlan McMahon, who played a pivotal role in the early stages of the project.

Early manuscripts were reviewed with care and insight. Our thanks go to the following reviewers, who provided incisive and helpful feedback:

- Dr Richard Berlach (Edith Cowan University)
- Dr Lise Bird (Victoria University, Wellington)
- Dr Esther Care (University of Melbourne)
- Mr Bill Foster (Australian Catholic University)
- Dr Heather Jenkins (Curtin University of Technology)
- Dr Judith MacCallum (Murdoch University)
- Dr Paul Newhouse (Edith Cowan University)
- Dr Chris Perry (Deakin University)
- Dr Reesa Sorin (James Cook University)
- Dr Richard Walker (University of Sydney).

Our colleagues in the School of Education at Macquarie University provided much encouragement and support. Thanks to Pamela Coutts and George Cooney for their expertise and assistance, and also to the many other members of staff who so willingly shared their skill and experience, and who provided feedback along the way.

We have consulted various classroom-teacher colleagues, whose practical classroom experience has made an important contribution to our text. We also thank our many friends and family members for their patience and good humour, and for not asking too many questions about when we would finally be done with the writing! Finally, we acknowledge all the students we have had the privilege of meeting in EDUC105. For your energy, inspiration, ideas, challenging discussions and fresh perspectives, we thank you.

Kerri-Lee Krause
Sandra Bochner
Sue Duchesne

Special acknowledgement from Kerri-Lee and Sue

This project represents years of combined teaching and research experience on the part of the author team. Our teaching partnership on a first-year educational psychology unit has extended over a significant time period. We would like to pay tribute to Sandra Bochner's mentorship, her support of us in the early parts of our academic careers, and her belief in this project. Sandra's energy, optimism and wisdom in this writing journey have meant a great deal to both of us. Thank you, Sandra.

Publishers' acknowledgements

The publishers would like gratefully to credit or acknowledge the following sources.

Images

APL/ Corbis/ © AFP, p. 198 (middle)/ © Bettmann, pp. 40, 111/ © Corbis, p. 173/ © Rufus F. Folkks, p. 198 (left)/ © Lindsay Hebberd, p. 198 (right)/ © Stephanie Maze, p. 265/ © Richard T. Nowitz, p. 177 (bottom)/ © Roger Ressmeyer, p. 177 (top)/ © Ted Streshinsky, p. 78; Pieter Breugel the Elder, *Children's Games* (1560), 118 × 161 cm, oil on wood panel, Kunsthistorisches Museum, Vienna, Austria, p. 6; Digital Vision, p. 273; Courtesy of the Disability Museum, p. 243; Getty Images/ Tony Stone, p. 352; Gould League for *Ollie Saves the Planet*, p. 317 (bottom); David Hancock/ Skyscans, p. 85; Harvard News Office, © 1987, President and Fellows of Harvard College, p. 96; Image Addict, pp. 62 (left), 87; LaTrobe Picture Collection, State Library of Victoria, p. 243 (top); National Library of Medicine, pp. 116, 207, 385; J. Philp for illustration, *Mike's Five Mice*, used with permission, p. 28; Royal Australian Navy, p. 62 (right); Sport. The Library, p. 216; Courtesy of Professor Robert Sternberg, p. 203; Bill Thomas, p. 373; William Glasser Institute, p. 387.

Text

M. Andrews, Gordon Arthur Andrews obituary, *The Australian*, 31/1/01, p. 172; 'Participation in organised sport and physical activities, 1995–1996', ABS Cat. No. 4177.0, 1997, p. 11/ 'Should definitions of disability incorporate indigenous perceptions of disability?', *Indigenous disability data: Report on proceedings of the Canberra workshop*, April 1998, ABS Cat. No. DIS 10, p. 240/ 'Relationship among conditions, impairment, disability and handicap', *Disability, aging and carers: Summary of findings*, ABS Cat. No. 4430.0, 1993/ 'Females as a proportion of Australian teachers, 1998 & 1999', *Australian Social Trends*, ABS Cat. No. 4102.0, p. 276. ABS data used with permission from the Australian Bureau of Statistics, www.abs.gov.au; 'How to include women and girls in sport, recreation and physical activity: Strategies and good practice', © Australian Sports Commission, 1999, reproduced by permission, pp. 11–12; D. L. Ball & H. Bass, 'Making believe: The collective construction of public mathematical knowledge in the elementary classroom', *Constructivism in education: Opinions and second opinions on controversial issues*, The National Society for the Study of Education, Chicago, 2000, reprinted by permission of D. L. Ball & H. Bass and the Association for Childhood Education International, 17904 Georgia Ave., Suite 215, Olney, MD, 20832, © 2000 by the Association, p. 161; Breen et al., *Literacy in its place*, Edith Cowan University, WA, 1994, © Commonwealth of Australia, reproduced by permission, p. 282; M. Cole & S. R. Cole, *The development of children*, Worth Publishers, New York, 2001, p. 13 (top); *Technology for learning: Students with disabilities*, Ministerial Advisory Committee, 2000, © Commonwealth of Australia, reproduced by permission, pp. 328–9; H. Cowie, P. Smith, M. Boulton, & R. Laver, *Cooperation in the multi-ethnic classroom: The impact of cooperative groups' work on social relationships in middle schools*, London, Fulton, 1994, p. 394; P. Foreman (ed.), *Integration and inclusion in action*, Thomson Learning Australia, p. 126; J. Hattie, *Self-concept*, Lawrence Erlbaum Associates Inc., 1992, p. 74; 'Bush talks in South Headland WA', 20 May 1999, *Rural and remote education inquiry briefing paper E*, HREOC, p. 292; R. Kruse for models, p. 312; J. Leonard & K. McElroy, 'What one middle school teacher learned about cooperative learning', *Journal of Research in Childhood Education*, 14:2, 2000, reprinted by permission of Leonard & McElroy and The Association for Childhood Education International, 17904 Georgia Ave., Suite 215, Olney, MD 20832, © 2000 by the Association, p. 162; NSW Teacher's Federation for cartoon, p. 179; J. Ogborn, G. Kress, I. Martins & K. McGillicuddy, *Explaining science in the classroom*, Open University Press, 1996, reproduced by permission of McGraw Hill Education, p. 18; J. Piaget, *The moral judgment of the child*, trans. M. Cook, The Free Press, New York, 1965, p. 95; D. Roberts et al., 'Growth and morbidity in children in a remote Aboriginal community in north-west Australia', *MJA* 1988; 148: 68–71, © 1988, *The Medical Journal of Australia*, reproduced with permission, p. 10; J. Sattler, *Assessment of children*, San Diego, p. 209; J. Slee, 1996, 'A behavioural approach to a behavioural disorder', in J. Izard & J. Evans (eds), *Student behaviour: Policies, interventions and evaluations*, p. 124/ K. Rigby, 'Forms of bullying experienced often during the school year', 'Incidence of reported victimisation among school children' and 'Gender of the bully or bullies: Percentages in each category', *Bullying in schools: What to do about it*, 1996, pp. 391–2, reproduced by permission of ACER, Melbourne; B. Wadsworth, *Piaget's theory of cognitive development*, © 1996, Allyn and Bacon, Boston, MA, © 1996 Pearson Education, reprinted by permission of the publisher, p. 52; M. Wood, 'Boys' own adventure', *Sun-Herald*, 21/4/02, pp. 279–80.

Every attempt has been made to trace and acknowledge copyright holders. Where the attempt has been unsuccessful, the publishers welcome information that would redress the situation.

Note to students

For many students using this book, the field of educational psychology – or 'ed. psych.', as you may soon call it – will represent uncharted waters. You may have chosen this area because you have always been interested in psychology, or perhaps you are studying to be a teacher and educational psychology is a compulsory subject. Whatever your reason for using this text, we encourage you to take a few minutes to read these introductory comments before you go further. These notes may help you to better understand the subject and to make links to other aspects of your experience and study.

What is educational psychology?

Some students ask: 'Why not just simplify and call it *psychology*?' The reason is that **educational psychology** is a discipline in its own right, and connects the disciplines of education and psychology (Walberg & Haertel, 1992). It involves not only scientific research on the various dimensions of learning and teaching, but also the investigation of ways to apply psychological principles to educational contexts with the aim of enhancing learning and teaching quality.

One of the things students enjoy most about this subject is that by studying theories of learning and development they learn a lot about their own development and what influenced it. Most if not all of the effective teaching practices you experienced at school could be traced back to some element of educational psychology. As you read this book, you will begin to understand your own learning processes and how to improve them. You will also be challenged to think about ways that teaching could be improved to cater for student differences and particular student needs.

> **educational psychology**
> A branch of psychology concerned with studying how people learn and the implications for teaching.

Who studies educational psychology?

The discipline of educational psychology can be applied in many contexts. Many who use this book will do so because they plan to be teachers, and must study educational psychology as a foundation unit. Other readers may be psychology students who are interested in working with children or adolescents, whether in professional practice or as a school counsellor in a school setting. Others may be preparing to be educational psychologists – qualified psychologists who specialise in applying their expertise in educational contexts, and who work in schools or other institutional settings (for example, university, government or corporate settings) where education takes place. Still others may be reading this text so as to better understand their own learning and the education process.

We recognise that the majority of this book's readers will be planning a teaching or related career. For this reason, our examples focus on school-aged children and youth.

Why study all those theories?

It is true that when you first start studying educational psychology you are introduced to many theories. Some educational psychology students have been heard to say: 'Ed. psych. is just a lot of theory … I came to uni to learn how to teach kids!' Our advice to you is to not lose heart and to remember that theories have an important purpose.

You will discover that theories form the foundation for understanding many critical issues that face learners and educators in the 21st century. Throughout this book, particularly in the first half, we link theory to practice and encourage you to do the same. You will find that theories help us answer questions like: What are the best ways of studying? How can I improve motivation – both mine and others'? Why do some young people give up on themselves, and what can I do about it? How can technology be used to enhance learning? Is education redundant in the Information Age?

Educational psychology and the theories of development and learning covered in this text will:

- help you understand your own development and factors that have contributed to it
- provide strategies to enhance the quality of your learning and motivation
- guide your understanding of how learners learn and how educators can become more effective in their teaching practice
- contribute to your personal philosophy of learning and teaching.

0.1 More about educational psychology

How to get the most from this book

The material we cover in this book will be most meaningful to you if you see connections between theories and issues in the real world. The book contains four modules of three chapters each. The first two modules introduce you to theories of development and learning, which we encourage you to think about in relation to your own development and learning processes so as to understand practical applications. The remaining two modules draw on these theories as the basis for discussing issues related to the learning–teaching process.

As you start reading, prepare to learn many new terms, especially in the first half of the book. Students often become discouraged because they forget what they have read and feel overwhelmed. The key is to deal only with small chunks of new information at a time. Talk with fellow students and with your lecturer or tutors about the most effective ways to learn and revise this material. Usually, as students become more familiar with educational psychology and with discussing its application in classroom or other contexts, they start to see connections.

Each chapter in this book has the following features:

- **Concept maps** at the start of each module and chapter illustrate the connections between key concepts.
- **Objective lists** at the start of each chapter provide a broad outline of chapter content. After you study each chapter, you can return to the list to check your understanding of each topic.
- **Critical reflection** panels throughout the text enable you to reflect critically on the processes of learning and teaching, and on your beliefs about these processes.
- **Activities** at the end of many boxed items give you the opportunity to apply your new knowledge.
- **You make the connections** sections at the end of each chapter allow you to test yourself to see if you can connect theoretical concepts and real-world contexts. Here, tutorial activities, essay-type questions and many other activities will help you consolidate your understanding and apply what you have learned.
- **Weblink** icons throughout the book indicate where there are links to additional material on the *Educational psychology for learning and teaching* companion website. You can find the Weblink material for this book under 'student resources' at the website <www.thomsonlearning.com.au/krause>.

Developing a personal philosophy of learning and teaching

Critical reflection involves analysing your own and others' thoughts and beliefs. It involves thinking about why people – yourself and others – behave in certain ways. When you reflect critically, you analyse and question existing knowledge and assumptions.

Studying educational psychology provides an ideal opportunity to develop the ability to reflect critically, and in so doing to develop a personal philosophy of learning and teaching. A philosophy is like a personal mission statement: it guides your choices, behaviours, thoughts and feelings. Whether you plan to teach in classrooms, work as a school counsellor, support your own children's learning or simply be a responsible and informed member of society, your personal philosophy will be central to what you believe, how you think and behave, and how you relate to others.

Throughout this book, we raise issues for you to consider as you determine your beliefs and understandings about what it means to learn and teach in the 21st century. The companion website also provides a helpful guide for further developing your philosophy of learning and teaching.

You will notice that the term 'learning' comes before 'teaching' throughout this book. This reflects our philosophy that teaching is about learning and that all teachers are learners. Our hope is that this text will challenge your thinking as you learn and transform this learning in your own contexts.

---

critical reflection
Analysing what we are thinking and learning by questioning assumptions, perspectives and values related to our thoughts or to new information.

Note to instructors

This book grew from our passion for learning and teaching. It grew from our belief that educational psychology is a powerful vehicle for challenging students' thinking and for engaging students in critical reflection about their own learning, their own development and about ways they might enhance the learning and teaching experiences of new generations.

We have written this book with university students and their teachers in mind. The text is divided into four modules of three chapters each, with an emphasis on the connections among and within chapters. Each module focuses on connections between theoretical explanations of human learning and their practical applications. We have selected key theories and material with a view to providing students new to the discipline with a foundational introduction to the field. Additional readings are suggested for those who wish to pursue further study or research on particular topics.

The companion website, which can be found at <**www.thomsonlearning.com.au/krause**>, is a significant dimension of the text. It provides research examples and commentary designed to add to students' understanding, and may prove useful for tutorial and lecture discussions. Instructors' supplementary material includes an Instructor's Manual and PowerPoint® slides CD-ROM, as well as an ExamView® testbank on CD-ROM.

As teachers, we understand the value of students applying their knowledge. Our primary aim is to create opportunities for students to develop their skills as critically reflective learners and practitioners. To this end, the text contains the following features:

- **Case studies** and **Classroom links** within boxed material throughout the text provide real-world examples of theories in action, while **Research links** highlight the pivotal role of research in educational psychology.
- **Critical reflection** panels appear throughout the text. These contain questions designed to problematise the content and encourage students to consider issues from different perspectives.
- **You make the connections** sections at the end of each chapter contain activities and questions designed to help students make connections between theoretical concepts and real-world contexts. The questions may be used for self-testing, as the basis for tutorial discussions, as essay writing exercises or as action research activities.

Resources guide

For the student

As you read this text you will find a wealth of features in every chapter to help you learn the theory of educational psychology and then link it to what actually happens in the classroom. Please take note of the following features:

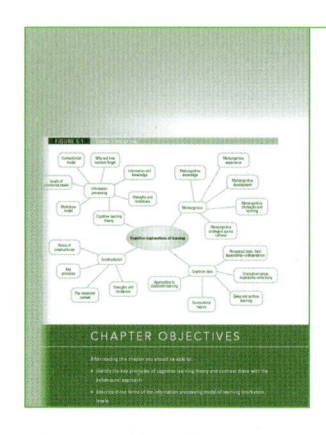

Module and chapter maps at the start of each module and chapter provide you with a visual overview of the key concepts to be covered and how these concepts connect to each other.

Core questions at the start of each module help you to connect the theory you will learn to real-world issues.

Chapter objectives let you know what you will learn in each chapter.

Definitions of key terms are included in the margins to reinforce your understanding of key concepts in each chapter.

Key terms are listed at the end of each chapter.

Weblink icons in the margins direct you to additional content on the text's companion website at http://www.thomsonlearning.com.au/krause

Research links throughout the chapters highlight educational psychology research and help you to understand the role of research in teaching and learning.

Case studies and 'implications for educators' boxes throughout the chapters help you to link the theory your have learnt to real-world situations.

Activities throughout the chapters encourage you to apply the theory you have just learnt and to check your understanding.

Critical reflections sections throughout the text give you the opportunity to solve problems by thinking critically and to analyse and question important concepts covered from different perspectives.

Leading contemporary and historical psychologists and their theories are highlighted throughout in boxed features.

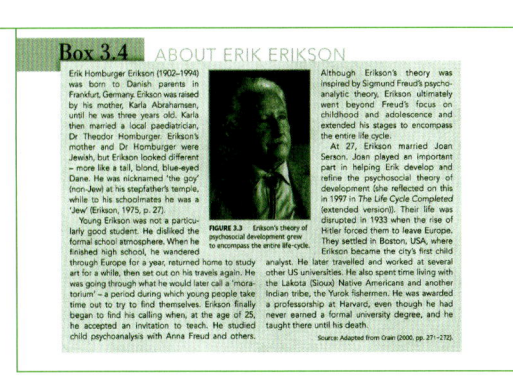

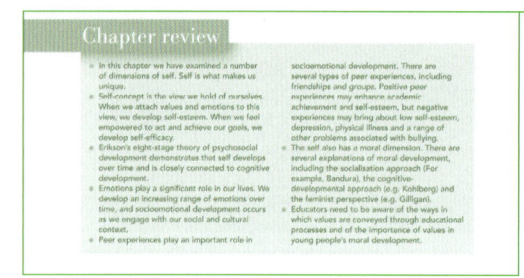

Chapter review sections at the end of each chapter provide valuable summaries of key concepts and issues.

You make the connections: Questions and activities for self-assessment and discussion allow you to test your comprehension of key concepts at the end of each chapter and also to promote group discussion and debate.

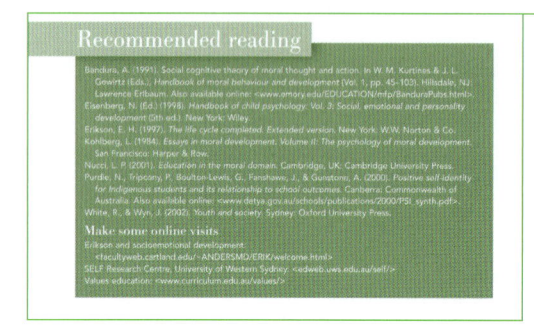

Recommended reading sections at the end of each chapter list useful additional references and websites where you can find more information.

To supplement your reading of *Educational psychology for learning and teaching*, and further expand your study of educational psychology, you can utilise the following online resources:

http://www.infotrac-college.com

Included with this text is a passcode that gives you a four-month subscription to **InfoTrac® College Edition**. This online library will provide you with access to full-text articles from hundreds of scholarly and popular periodicals, including the *Australian Journal of Early Education*, the *Journal of Educational and Psychological Measurement* and the *Australian Journal of Education*.

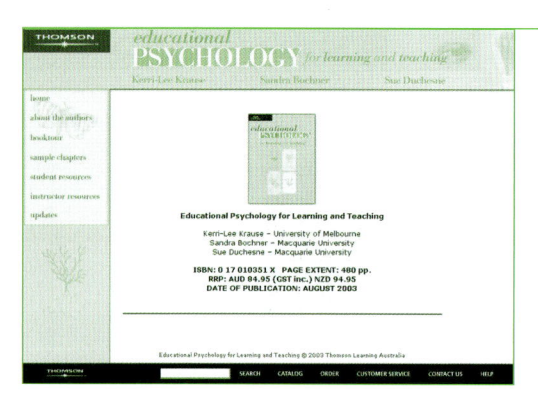

For additional resources, updates and news relating to *Educational psychology for learning and teaching* please go to the companion website and visit the student resources section.

For the instructor

Thomson Learning is pleased to provide you with an extensive selection of electronic supplements to help you lecture in educational psychology. These resources have all been specifically developed to supplement *Educational psychology for learning and teaching*.

ExamView® Testbank ISBN 0 17 010492 3

Helps you create, customise and deliver tests in minutes – both print and online. The *Quick Test Wizard* and *Online Test Wizard* guide you step by step through the test-creation process, while the unique WYSIWYG capability allows you to see the test you are creating on the screen exactly as it will print or display online. With **ExamView's** complete word-processing capabilities, you can add an unlimited number of new questions to the bank, edit existing questions and build tests of up to 250 questions using up to 12 question types.

Instructor's Manual and PowerPoint® presentation on CD-ROM, ISBN 0 17 010491 5

The **Instructor's Manual** provides you with a wealth of content to help you set up and administer your educational psychology course. It includes learning objectives and explanations, chapter summaries, teaching tips and warm-up activities.

Also included on the CD-ROM is a PowerPoint presentation that includes images and figures from *Educational psychology for learning and teaching*. You can use this presentation as is or edit it to your own requirements.

To request copies of these instructor resources please contact Thomson Learning:

Phone 1 800 654 831
Fax 1 800 641 823
Email customerservice@thomsonlearning.com.au

THOMSON

FIGURE MI Module I concept map.

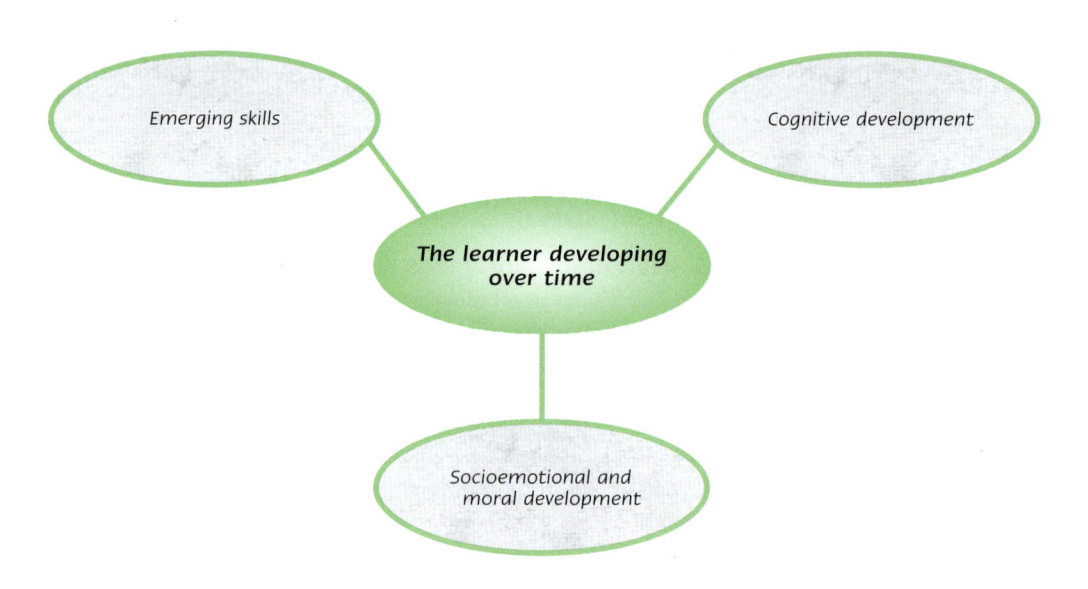

- Emerging skills
- Cognitive development
- The learner developing over time
- Socioemotional and moral development

MODULE CONTENTS

- **Chapter 1** Emerging skills
- **Chapter 2** Cognitive development

MODULE 1

The learner developing over time

Core question: *Can theories of development enhance the understanding of learning and teaching?*

Human development occurs in many areas: physical, cognitive, social, emotional and moral, to name a few. None of these aspects of development occurs in isolation. To understand the learner as a whole person, you need to see the interconnections between the different facets of development and the ways these contribute to the emergence of a complex but integrated individual.

While genetic influences on development are significant, the role of social and cultural factors is receiving increasing attention. In this module you will notice the use of the prefix 'socio' to highlight social influences on development in words such as 'socioemotional', 'sociocultural' and 'sociomoral'.

The three chapters in this module highlight the learner's complex, multidimensional nature. In Chapter 1 we explore the physical and linguistic dimensions of development and how these relate to learners developing the basic skills of literacy and numeracy. Chapter 2 focuses on the learner's mind and the ways in which thinking and reasoning develop over time. Chapter 3 examines what makes the learner unique – the self – and how thinking about the self and others develops as cognitive-processing abilities become more complex. We also examine the relationship between cognitive and emotional development, the capacity for moral reasoning and the development of values and beliefs.

Recognising how developments in one dimension support and contribute to developments in other areas helps teachers consider all aspects of their students' lives in order to design appropriate learning and teaching experiences. In each chapter of this module we encourage you to consider how teachers can adapt their teaching to cater for students' varying developmental needs.

FIGURE 1.1 Chapter 1 concept map.

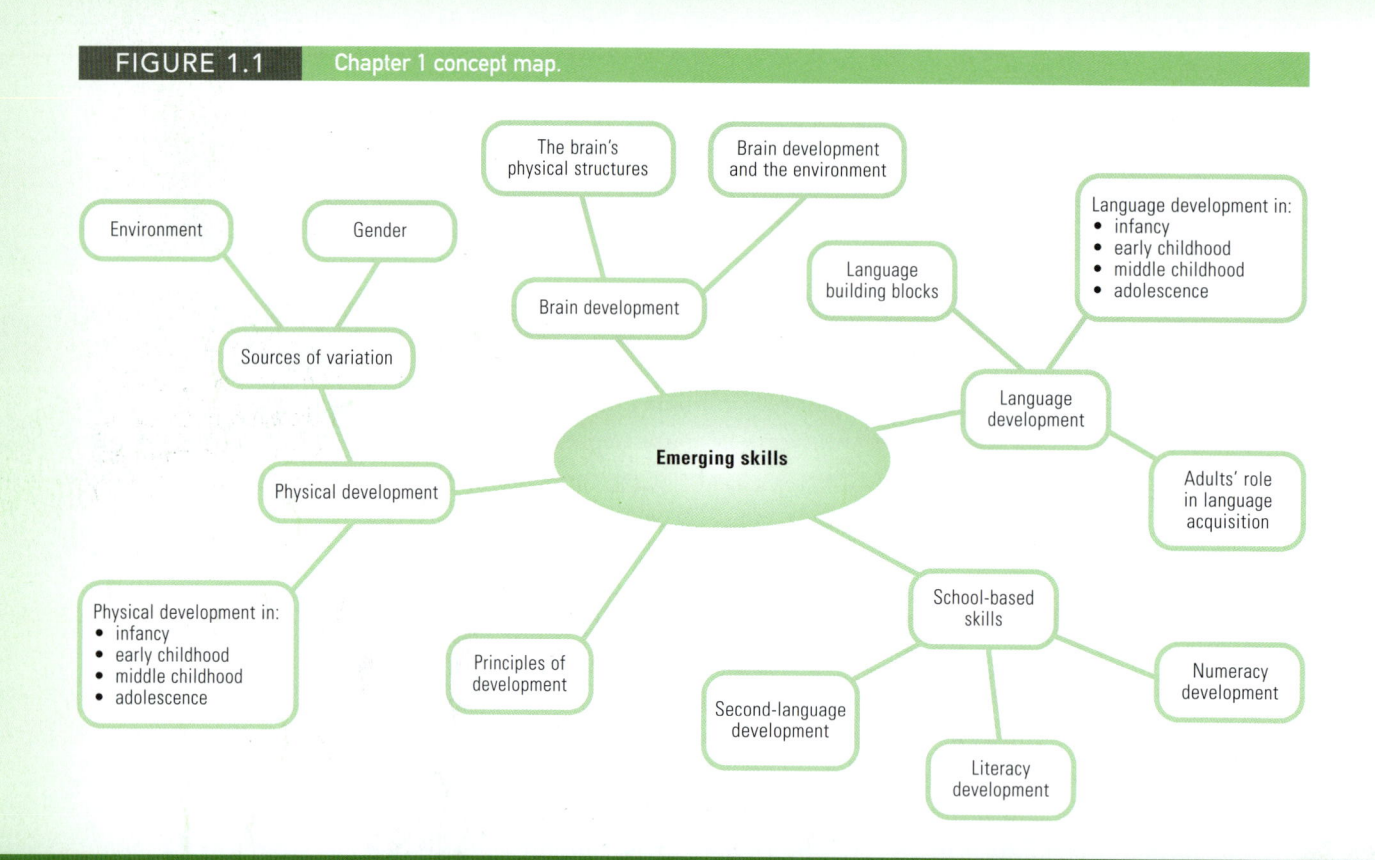

CHAPTER OBJECTIVES

After reading this chapter you should be able to:

- describe the broad course of physical development from early childhood to adolescence

- give examples of links between physical, cognitive and emotional development

- broadly describe the course of language acquisition

- list some similarities in language and mathematics development

- identify and comment on some key principles of development.

CHAPTER 1

Emerging skills

Introduction

Can you remember how any of your skills developed? Compare yourself as you are now to someone starting high school, someone starting primary school and someone starting preschool. List some of the typical skills you associate with people in each of those age groups. You may have possessed some skills in a less developed form when you were younger; some you may have consciously worked on; while others may seem to have appeared spontaneously.

FIGURE 1.2
Our skills develop through a combination of innate and environmental factors. What aspects of these skills do you consider learned? What aspects of these skills might be inherited or automatic?

In this chapter we consider some of the skills that emerge as children and adolescents mature, act on the world and are influenced by their environment. One of the enduring debates in theories of development – the 'nature–nurture debate' (see Chapter 7) – concerns the relative contributions of innate factors and environmental factors. This chapter explores a number of skills that develop as a result of both types of influences. The relative contribution of nature and environment to each skill varies, with some skills (such as physical and brain development) having a strong biological basis, other skills (such as language) being a mixture of biology and environment, and still other skills (such as literacy and numeracy) being predominantly school-based.

Physical development over time

As we explore development in this chapter and throughout Module I, we look at four phases of the child's life: 'infancy' (the first 2 years), 'early childhood' (from 2 years old until the child enters school), 'middle childhood' (from 5 years old to adolescence) and 'adolescence' (around 12 years old to adulthood). Development does not stop at adolescence, of course, but continues throughout the lifespan. This text focuses on the school years: middle childhood and adolescence.

Physical development in infancy

Physical development sometimes seems to happen without our noticing. Yet the physical developments of childhood – changes in growth, in motor skills, and in the body and brain's structures – form an important basis for developments in cognition (thinking) and emotion.

Consider a newborn baby. Right now she has no control over her movements, yet within 18 months she will be walking, in another year running, and soon after jumping and throwing and kicking balls. In the first 2 years, children develop physically at a faster rate than at any other time in their lives. While we do not describe infants' physical development here in any detail, it forms an important basis for children's development – not just physical, but also social, emotional and cognitive – in later years.

1.1 Infant development

Physical development, cognition and emotion

Physical developments in infancy are connected to developments in the infant's cognition (thinking) and emotion. Children who learn to crawl earlier tend to develop earlier 'object permanence' (see Chapter 2), which is the understanding that objects continue to exist when out of sight. They also learn to find hidden objects (Bai & Bertenthal, 1992) and to perceive depth on a visual cliff (Bertenthal, Campos, & Barrett, 1984) earlier than their peers who are not yet crawling.

It is likely that the development of these skills is related to children's increased physical ability to explore their environment, although it may also be linked to changes in brain organisation. Research on the changing structure of infants' brains reveals that crawling appears to strengthen the neural pathways associated with vision, planning of movement and understanding of space (Bell & Fox, 1997). Thus not only the physical crawling behaviour but also the associated experience and mental activity are related to these changes in brain structure. Evidence from studies of children with severe visual impairment also points to a relationship between motor and cognitive development (Fraiberg, 1977).

The onset of crawling also affects children's relationships with their caregivers, and helps children develop emotional understanding. It is usually the period when parents start to say 'no', helping children to realise that their actions affect others' emotions (Campos, Kermoian, & Zumbahlen, 1992). In infancy, children are already developing the physical, cognitive and emotional bases for the skills they will use at school.

1.2 Studies of the development of blind infants

Physical development in early childhood

While the rate of physical growth slows in early and middle childhood, age brings further increases in children's size, strength and coordination. This development of children's muscle strength, plus improved balance and coordination along with a lower centre of gravity, all support the development of children's motor skills (Berk, 2003).

Motor-skill development in early childhood

Gross motor skills are those skills involving large muscle groups and often whole-body movements such as rolling, jumping, clapping, throwing and running. **Fine motor skills** are skills involving smaller muscle movements, usually of the hands and fingers, which include grasping and manipulating pencils or scissors. As children's development progresses and their control becomes increasingly refined, they move from requiring large pieces of paper on which to work, and large implements with which to write, to being able to write with a variety of pens and pencils between ruled lines on a page.

gross motor skills
Movement skills using large muscle groups

fine motor skills
Movement skills using small muscle groups

Acquisition of motor skills is one of the main developmental tasks of early childhood, and for this reason most preschool and early-school programs in Australia and New Zealand attach great importance to it. Climbing over obstacle courses; rolling, throwing and catching balls; and running, jumping, hopping and skipping all help to develop gross motor skills. Likewise, using dough, clay, crayons and paint, and activities that involve crumpling or tearing paper, all contribute to fine motor-skill development. Parents also contribute to motor-skill development at home through undertaking everyday activities with children, such as going to the park for a swing, drawing, and doing puzzles. In some communities, motor skills are developed through community or traditional activities as well as in formal preschool contexts. In the Torres Strait region of Australia, for example, Indigenous children's motor skills are developed through involvement in community dances from the time they can walk. The dances are taught more formally at school, which refines these skills (Davis, 2001, personal communication). Likewise, Maori communities in New Zealand develop *te reo kori* (the language of movement) within *ngā mahi a rēhia* – Maori recreational and leisure activities such as *poi*, *rakau* and *whai* (Ministry of Education, 1999).

Children's spontaneous activity also contributes to their motor-skill development. The seemingly constant movement of preschoolers has a purpose in developing their gross motor skills, strength, coordination and sense of balance. Children also benefit from such activity in other ways, since as we have seen, motor and cognitive development are related. The contribution of motor activity to cognition continues beyond the early years, influencing later academic skills such as reading and number. Berninger, Abbott, Abbott, Graham and Richards (2002) found a relationship between children's fine-motor skill in handwriting and the reading-and-writing-related skills of spelling, word recognition, reading comprehension and writing composition.

Physical development in middle childhood

Continued increases in size, strength, flexibility and coordination during the school years enable children to master the skills involved in sports. However, rather than learning entirely new skills – as occurs in early childhood – the task now is to refine and recombine existing skills to suit new challenges. Consider as an example the running, turning and kicking involved in playing soccer; or the running, throwing and catching required in netball. The jumping and chasing games and ball throwing and kicking done in early childhood are precursors of the advanced skills that are combined in specialised ways to play each sport (see Figure 1.3 on page 6). While younger children may be able to jump, hop, run, turn, and throw a ball in isolation, being able to combine these skills is a new achievement of the middle-childhood years. The ability to coordinate motor skills, such as in eye–hand and foot–hand coordination, is a significant development of middle childhood.

FIGURE 1.3
A shift in the centre of gravity, together with increased coordination and flexibility, contribute to improvements in running skill that occur with age.

Motor-skill development in middle childhood

Children's playground games (see Figure 1.4) such as hopscotch, skipping, elastics, chasing, handball and jacks all contribute to the development of motor skills during the middle-childhood period.

Swimming, riding bikes and scooters, and similar activities enjoyed by children in their leisure hours are also important. Once again, there is evidence of a link between motor skill and cognition. One Italian study found that children's sports activity contributed to their learning capacity (Mengheri & Tubi, 1989). One of the concerns expressed about the amount of time children spend watching television or playing computer games is the time taken from more active pursuits. The Australian Broadcasting Authority (1996) estimated that, on average, Australian children spend a third of their leisure time watching television.

FIGURE 1.4
How might the activities these children are engaged in contribute to their motor development?
(Source: *Children's Games*, Breugel the Elder, 1560.)

Physical development in adolescence

During adolescence, physical growth resumes the rapid pace of that in infancy. The hands, feet and legs are the first to increase in size, which sometimes results in a 'coltish' look and in clumsiness. The trunk of the body lengthens last, bringing adolescents to adult body-proportions (Berk, 2003). These developments are accompanied by significant muscle growth – although this is greater in boys than in girls, for whom there is a 40 per cent increase in body fat. These sex differences result in the different body shapes of adulthood, with men generally leaner and more muscular than women.

Sex differences in adolescent development

Often the terms 'puberty' and 'adolescence' are used synonymously, but they are not the same thing. The period of **adolescence** is usually associated with the teen years (from ages 13 to 19) but may be defined as the period between childhood and adulthood. Thus in Western societies adolescence can stretch from 11 to 21 years and is typically defined in terms of age and social circumstances. **Puberty**, on the other hand, is defined by physical changes, specifically the physical and biological changes associated with sexual maturity. Puberty generally occurs during adolescence, but may start some years earlier than the age of 13, particularly in Western girls. Puberty tends to be completed within 4 years; adolescence, however, may last from 6 to 10 years and tends to be longer in industrial societies, where young people are often engaged in education for long periods before they are truly independent of their parents (Cote & Allahar, 1996).

adolescence The period between childhood and adulthood

puberty The biological changes associated with sexual maturity

In girls, puberty is signalled by rapid increases in height and weight, which trigger the onset of 'menarche', or first menstruation. This is accompanied by other physical changes that are related to reproduction, including breast development (which precedes menarche), and the enlargement of the uterus and the appearance of pubic hair (which usually follow menarche).

In boys, sexual maturity starts with changes to the testes and scrotum, followed by the appearance of pubic hair and then growth of the penis. Increases in height generally occur later in boys' developmental patterns than in those of girls, which explains why girls may be taller than boys in the early years of high school. 'Semenarche' (or first ejaculation) commonly follows the height spurt in boys, just as menarche does in girls. Other changes associated with the later stages of puberty for boys include the growth of facial and body hair, and the deepening of the voice as the larynx lengthens. This can initially cause boys some embarrassment as the voice 'breaks' with sudden changes in pitch.

Connections among physical, cognitive and socioemotional development in adolescence

The dramatic physical changes of puberty are accompanied by social, cognitive and emotional changes. One of the most significant results of physical changes is a concern with body image. A feeling of 'not fitting' the new taller body, bigger hands and feet may bring self-consciousness for boys; while girls may become dissatisfied with their increased weight and body fat that do not match the 'ideal' body image promoted in the media (Rosenblum & Lewis, 1999). Australian studies of body image and dieting behaviour have shown that dieting and dissatisfaction with body image are widespread, and greater among girls than boys. In one study, dieting was reported by over half the female high-school students surveyed, and by only 16 per cent of the male students. Extreme weight-loss strategies such as fasting and crash dieting were reported as being used 'at least sometimes' by 47 per cent of girls in the study, and weekly by 12 per cent (Maude, Wertheim, Paxton, Gibbons, & Szmukler, 1993).

A second corollary of puberty is the emotional highs and lows commonly observed in adolescents. While hormonal changes may contribute to these (Brooks-Gunn & Warren, 1989),

1.3 Research into adolescent mood changes

adolescent egocentrism
The tendency in adolescence to assume that others share one's thoughts and feelings

there are also psychological and environmental influences. Adolescence can be a stressful time, with changes in roles and responsibilities.

An increased cognitive capacity for self-reflection and introspection also means that adolescents are aware of and thinking about what is happening to them in more complex ways than before. **Adolescent egocentrism** – a term referring to adolescents' tendency to focus on themselves and their needs while ignoring others' perspectives – may be a result of the cognitive and emotional demands made by increased self-reflection as adolescents process the physical, social, emotional and cognitive changes associated with this period of development.

CRITICAL REFLECTION

- What might you observe in the classroom as a result of adolescents adjusting to the changes of puberty? What support could you offer as a teacher?

Transitions in relationships with family members during adolescence can be particularly difficult for parents and adolescents alike. Conflict with parents tends to peak during puberty, generally in the 6 months before and after menarche for girls (Holmbeck, 1996). These conflicts are generally mild – although they may not seem so at the time – and rarely have long-term consequences for the parent–child relationship. Conflicts between parents and adolescents commonly centre on issues of control, and concern topics such as curfews, dating, financial independence and responsibility in areas such as household chores (Holmbeck, 1996). The adolescent's transition from childhood to adulthood is at the root of these issues. Parents are involved in this transition just as much as their adolescent children. Furthermore, conflict may have a role to play in helping adolescents to separate from their parents and become their own people (Steinberg, 1999).

The frequency and intensity of parent–adolescent conflict tend to decline when an adolescent is around 14 or 15 years old, at which time adolescents' relationships with their parents tend to improve again, and they spend less time at home and more time with friends or in the community (Larson, Richards, Moneta, Holmbeck, & Duckett, 1996). Peers commonly take a more prominent place in the adolescent's priorities, which we explore in Chapter 3. Risk-taking behaviours such as experimentation with drugs, alcohol, sex and driving represent adolescents' exploration of their new adult status and help them bond with peers (Lightfoot, 1997).

The timing of puberty appears to affect how adolescents cope with developmental changes as well as with others' reactions to these changes. Early-maturing boys and late-maturing girls tend to fare the best, exhibiting higher levels of self-confidence and a more positive body image. Body image plays a critical role in adolescents' self-concept (discussed in more detail in Chapter 3). Early-maturing boys and late-maturing girls tend to fit the stereotype for beauty in Western cultures – muscular for boys and thin for girls. Not surprisingly, these adolescents tend to be evaluated by adults and their peers as attractive, independent, confident and popular. In contrast, late-maturing boys and early-maturing girls are generally less popular than their peers, lack self-confidence and are often anxious or stressed. Research indicates that late-maturing boys may be described by others as attention-seekers; while early-maturing girls are more likely to be involved in the risk-taking behaviours described previously, and tend to have lower academic achievement (Brooks-Gunn, 1988; Ge, Conger, & Elder, 1996; Stattin & Magnusson, 1990).

Social context can help modify some of these effects. Caspi (1995) found that early-maturing girls at a single-sex high school in New Zealand were less likely to exhibit delinquent behaviours and had higher achievement-levels than girls at a co-educational school. Another

FIGURE 1.5 The timing of puberty varies from individual to individual.

study found that early-maturing Year 6 girls in K–6 primary schools had more positive views of themselves than those at K–8 schools, perhaps because they were not pushed into adolescence before they were ready (Blyth, Simmons, & Zakin, 1985). Some studies show that the effects of early or late maturation persist into adulthood, largely because people have to live with the consequences of their adolescent behaviour – consequences that can include early parenthood and poor academic results (Stattin & Magnusson, 1990). Other research suggests that the difficulties develop more resilient, independent and flexible individuals (Livson & Peshkin, 1980). The link between physical and emotional development here is evident but complex: there is considerable scope for individual difference in outcomes depending on context, level of support and personality factors.

In this section we have looked at variation *within* groups of boys or girls. In the next section, we consider variations in physical development *among* groups.

Variations in physical development

Individual differences in the rate of physical development and the timing of major milestones such as puberty occur between males and females, and across different social and cultural groups (see Figure 1.5 above). These differences attest to the combination of environmental and inherited factors involved in development.

Environmental influences

Adolescent girls in industrial societies tend to experience menarche earlier than those living in countries with widespread poverty. As the onset of menarche is associated with increases in body fat, nutritional factors are likely to be responsible for this difference. Girls who participate in rigorous exercise programs – such as those for athletes in training – also tend to experience menarche later than their peers (Rees, 1993). In industrial societies, and in some developing nations, the age for menarche onset has declined steadily over the past century or more, probably as a result of improvements in nutrition and general health (Tanner, 1990).

Differences in growth rates and eventual height have also been observed among people from different countries (Evelyth & Tanner, 1990). While there may be genetic factors involved in these differences, it is likely they are also related to diet and to health issues such as the prevalence of disease in particular countries. People from countries with widespread poverty tend to be smaller on average than those from developed nations such as Australia and New Zealand, although there is also variation within populations. Indigenous Australians living in remote communities tend to have poorer health than the Australian population in general, with higher levels of infectious disease, poor sanitation and housing, malnourishment and limited access to clean water. A study by Roberts, Gracey and Spargo (1988) that compared the growth of Aboriginal children in the Kimberley region of Western Australia

FIGURE 1.6 Mean weights of Kimberley Aboriginal boys who were undernourished at 5 years of age (●——●) compared with those of Aboriginal boys whose weight was adequate at 5 years of age (○——○), plotted from birth to 5 years and compared with National Center for Health Statistics (USA) reference values (x——x). (Source: Roberts, Gracey, & Spargo, 1988, Figure 3.)

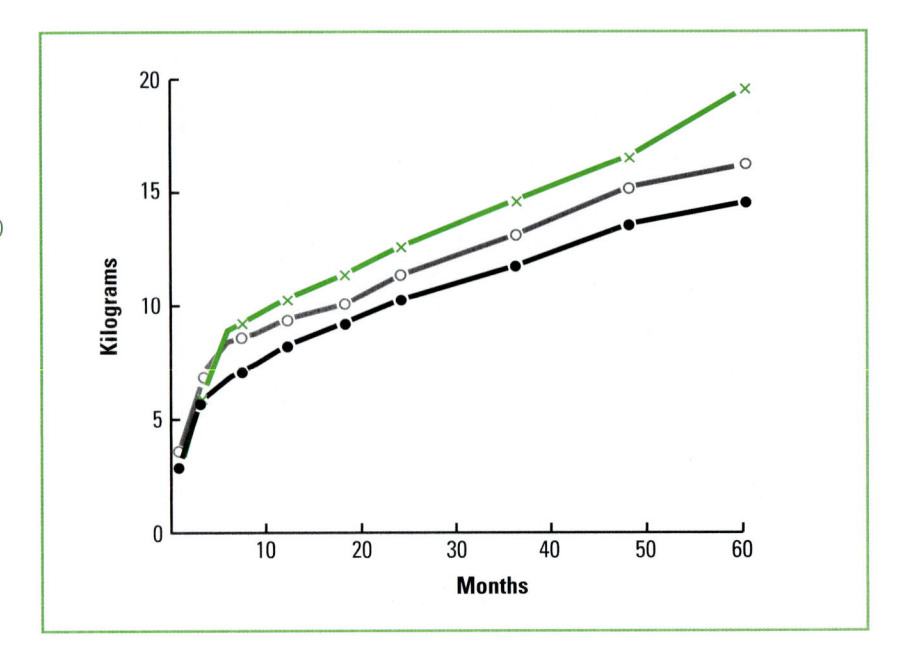

with international norms showed the influence that environmental factors can have on infant growth (see Figure 1.6), and showed that low birth-weight was significantly related to later growth. The pattern shown in Figure 1.6 is similar to that of malnourished infants in the Third World – thriving in the first 3 months and then faltering in height and weight.

Other areas of physical development are also influenced by environmental factors. Some of these are associated with a child's development in the womb; for example, pregnant mothers' consumption of alcohol and tobacco (as well as less widely available drugs) is associated with abnormal physical and brain development (Berk, 2003). Other influences may be felt later in the child's life; for example, high levels of family conflict are associated with earlier onset of menarche (Moffit, Caspi, Belski, & Silva, 1992). Environment is a significant force throughout the course of development.

Gender differences

You have probably heard it said that girls mature faster than boys. Physically this tends to be true, with girls reaching some milestones several weeks ahead of their male counterparts during infancy, and the gap widening through childhood so that girls may reach the end of puberty as much as 2 years ahead of boys (Tanner, 1990). Boys are generally taller and heavier than girls throughout childhood, with the exception of a brief time in early puberty (around 11 years old) when girls go through the pubertal growth spurt about 2 years ahead of boys.

Sex differences in motor-skill development are increasingly evident from early childhood through to adolescence. In early childhood tests of motor ability, girls perform better on balance tasks, while boys have better hitting and ball skills (Hands & Larkin, 1997). Later, boys tend to be better at sports involving force and power, while girls are more skilled in fine motor tasks and activities requiring agility (Malina, 1998). These differences are partly a result of boys' greater muscle mass and heart-and-lung capacity, but can also be attributed to the societal roles apportioned to males and females. Boys tend to be encouraged to play ball sports, while girls are steered towards dance and gymnastics. While a 5-year-old boy might be given a football or basketball as a gift, a girl is more likely to receive (and to ask for) a skipping rope. In addition, boys tend to be admired by peers for sporting prowess, something that tends to be far less important to girls and that is probably related to the relative significance placed by the media and society on men's versus women's sport. Similarly, boys are more likely than girls to play computer games.

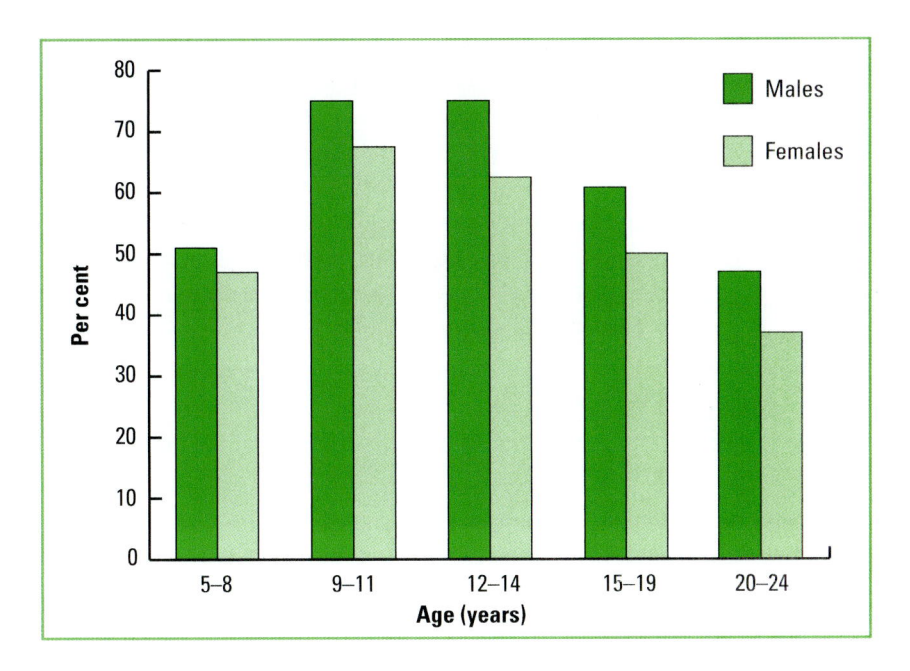

FIGURE 1.7
Participation in organised sport in Australia 1995–1996 by age and gender.
(Source: Moon, Rahman, & Bhatia, 1999, Figure 14.3, from data in the ABS Population Survey Monitor 1995–1996.)

Gender differences in physical activity and exercise involvement are more widespread than this, however. Girls from 5 to 24 years old are less likely than boys to be involved in organised sport or physical activity, and participation rates decline with age from 12 years (see Figure 1.7) (Moon, Meyer, & Grau, 1999; Moon, Rahman, & Bhatia, 1998). Reported exercise levels for girls are similarly lower than those for boys, with boys more likely to exercise at vigorous and moderate levels, and girls more likely to exercise at low levels or to be sedentary (Moon, Rahman, & Bhatia, 1998). Given the links between physical activity and learning discussed earlier, as well as the demonstrated relationship between physical exercise and the risk of disease, these differences are of widespread concern, which has been taken up by schools. Box 1.1 looks at some Australian Sports Commission (1999) strategies and examples of successful programs that were designed to address the need for girls to be more active.

Box 1.1 CLASSROOM LINKS

Freeing-up the curriculum, Newton Moore Senior High School, Bunbury, Western Australia

In 1997 extensive research tracking Newton Moore Senior High School students' progress in health and physical education showed a significant decline in girls' participation between year 8 and year 10. Acting on this information, the school council endorsed and funded a 'Girls' Physical Activity Outcomes' proposal. The proposal included research, planning and program implementation. The distribution of a needs analysis survey, combined with a focus-group test of girls considered to be high achievers, underachievers, and 'conscientious objectors', and other research data, helped the school draw up a list of issues that it felt it could deal with.

These included:
- identifying students' needs and interests
- de-emphasising competition for students at risk
- providing activities that are fun and have a social component
- providing activities with low entry-level skill requirements
- providing non-traditional activities
- reducing the opportunities for girls to be observed by boys
- providing links with community sport so that girls have an easier transition to community activities
- ensuring uniforms make all girls feel comfortable
- providing curriculum time for body-image education, and
- celebrating the successes of girls at all levels of activity. As a result, the school has implemented a 'freeing-up the curriculum' program, in which girls

have greater choice in activities. The school also encourages students to help plan their class unit of physical education, to learn fundamental skills and play a season of competition in the same team, and to take responsibility for all aspects of the competition. Other successful programs include the 'meet you in the middle' program, actively involving players and officials from sporting groups in students' physical education lessons, and 'psychology of involvement', where students participated in a seven-week course that focuses on material related to exercise values, goal setting, assertiveness and reward.

The school has also tackled the issue of body image by providing more privacy in changing rooms and removing athletics from the compulsory physical education program, among other strategies. Anecdotal evidence now shows there are very few girls in the target group who don't participate in physical activity. In 1998 the school won the Active Australia Education Award for its work in this area.

Source: Australian Sports Commission (1999).

Activity

Visit a primary-school playground and note the play patterns of boys and girls.
1. Do boys and girls play together or separately?
2. What sorts of games do you notice?
3. How much space is used for different activities?
4. In your tutorial, discuss your observations and how they relate to the current call to encourage girls to be more active.

Brain development

One dimension of physical development that is particularly important in the learning and teaching processes is brain development. The brain directs the course of overall development and responds to environmental stimuli to promote its own growth. In this section we consider how the brain's physical structures develop, and how this development is related to visible changes in thinking and behaviour.

The brain's physical structures

The brain is made up of billions of nerve cells, or **neurons**, which store and transmit messages to other cells. When a cell is activated, or 'fired', information travels as an electrical impulse along the **axon**, and then crosses a gap called the **synapse** by means of a chemical **neurotransmitter**. The synapse thus forms a junction between neurons. The branchlike **dendrites** from the neighbouring cell receive the message (see Figure 1.8).

Over the course of development, neurons develop in size and complexity, growing more dendrites and growing axon branches that connect to other cells (see Figure 1.9). This enables the networks of cells to be connected as more synapses are formed. Many neurons are connected with thousands of other neurons, organised in networks that interact with further networks. In addition, a process of **myelination** occurs, in which the axon is insulated in a fatty sheath that improves the speed of transmission by up to a hundred times. This enables different parts of the brain to be connected more efficiently.

How are these processes reflected in the developments we observe in children? First, remember that one of the patterns of development is an increase in skill complexity and coordination, which relates in part to the increase in networks of nerve pathways. Second, growth spurts in the brain coincide with major achievements in cognitive development (Fischer & Rose, 1995). For example, as myelination increases throughout childhood and adolescence, it may contribute to increases in children's abilities to think of more than one thing at once, and to their ability to coordinate perspectives. Chapter 2, which deals with cognitive development, gives further examples of advances in thinking that can be explained by brain growth.

---

neuron
A nerve cell

axon
The long 'arm' of a neuron that carries messages to other cells by means of electrical impulses

synapse
The gap between the axon and dendrites of two neurons

neurotransmitter
A chemical substance that carries messages between neurons across the synapse

dendrites
Branch-like protrusions from a neuron that receive messages from other cells

myelination
The process whereby axons are insulated with a sheath of fatty cells, which improves the speed and efficiency of message transmission

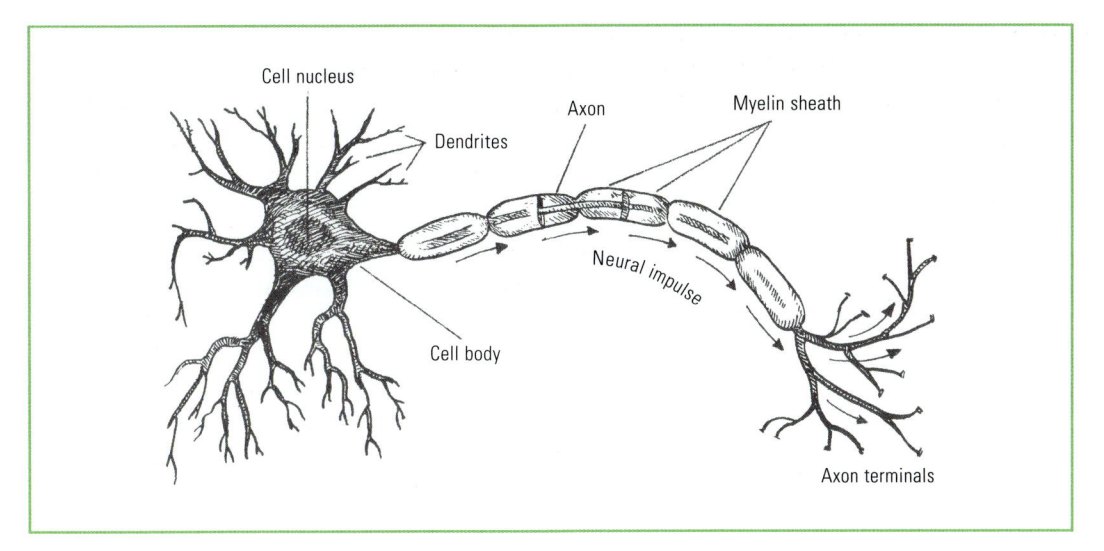

FIGURE 1.8
The neuron receives messages through its dendrites and passes messages along its axons and across the synapse to other cells.
(Source: Cole & Cole, 2001, Figure 4.1.)

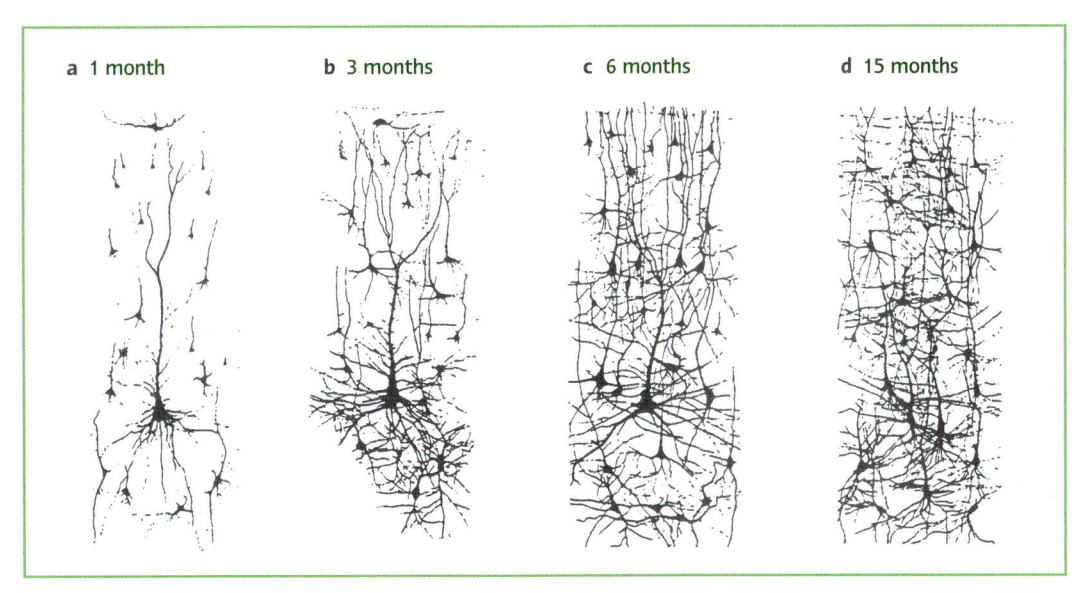

FIGURE 1.9
Neurons grow in size and complexity with brain development, increasing the connections between networks of cells, and resulting in greater coordination and complexity of thought and action.
(Source: reprinted by permission of the publisher from *The postnatal development of the human cerebral cortex* (vols 1–8), by Jesse LeRoy Conel, Cambridge, MA: Harvard University Press, Copyright © 1939, 1975 by the President and Fellows of Harvard College.)

The cerebral cortex

Like the rest of the body, different parts of the brain develop at different rates. The **cerebral cortex** (see Figure 1.10 on page 14) is one of the last areas of the brain to develop and is considered the most important contributor to children's cognitive functioning. It is also the area of the brain that appears to be most affected by the environment.

Development of areas of the cerebral cortex parallels development in corresponding functions: for example, the area of the brain that controls language shows most development in infancy and early childhood, when children are acquiring language. The cerebral cortex is divided into two hemispheres, which are the so-called 'left and right sides' of the brain. Each hemisphere controls the side of the body that is opposite to it, and specialises in certain types of functions – a process known as **lateralisation**.

Within the cerebral cortex, various regions have been associated with different bodily functions. Broadly, the left hemisphere controls language, while the right hemisphere controls spatial abilities. Emotion is also divided between the two hemispheres, with positive emotions centred in the left hemisphere and negative emotions in the right. In addition, most people are dominant in one of the hemispheres: right-handed people tend to be dominant in the left hemisphere, and some left-handed people are dominant in the right. This dominance mainly relates to motor activity, although other functions may also be affected. About 60 per cent of left-handed people have less strongly lateralised brains

cerebral cortex
The outer layer of the brain, which is responsible for human intelligence

lateralisation
The specialisation of functions in the two hemispheres of the cerebral cortex

FIGURE 1.10
The cerebral cortex. While particular functions are localised in specific areas of the cortex, most skills involve the coordination of messages from a number of areas.
(Source: Cole & Cole, 2001, Figure 4.3.)

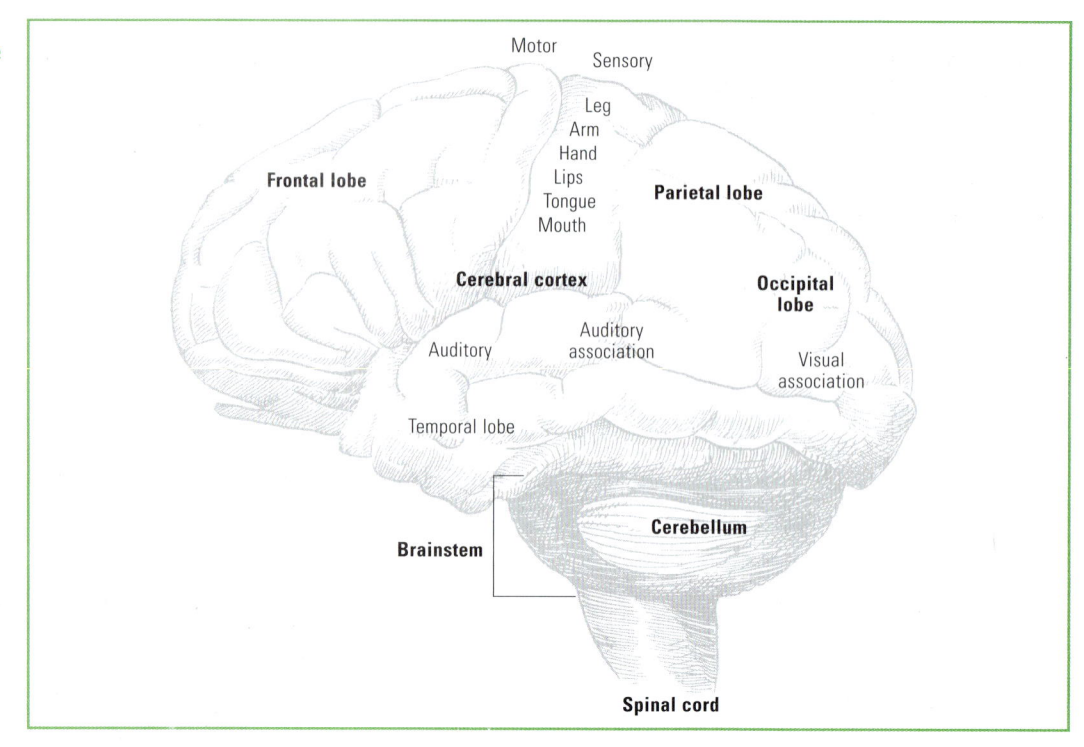

than do right-handed people, with language shared between left and right hemispheres (Dean & Anderson, 1997). Left-handed people are also more likely than right-handed people to show superior skills in mathematics and verbal language (Flannery & Liederman, 1995). One explanation of this is weaker lateralisation in the brains of some left-handed people, which may enable them to coordinate messages from both hemispheres more effectively than can people with strongly lateralised brains.

Brain development and the environment

Some of the changes that take place in the brain are a matter of physical maturation. However, stimulation from the environment and the child's activity also play a critical role. In the first year of a child's life, the brain produces many more synapses than it will need: thus, the infant brain is readied for experience. Synapses that are not used – that do not receive stimulation – are 'pruned' over time, while those that receive use through environmental stimulation are strengthened. This is one explanation of how patterns of individual difference in learning (discussed in Module III of this book) come about. The phrase 'neurons that fire together wire together' expresses the idea that neural 'networks' are formed when connections are made between various parts of the brain. Some of the links between language and thinking discussed later in this chapter are good examples of neural networks, since neurons in the language and cognitive-reasoning areas appear to 'fire together', creating connections between the two domains.

Box 1.2 discusses the impact of developmental factors in the classroom.

Box 1.2 IMPLICATIONS FOR EDUCATORS

Physical development and the classroom

- The connections observed between physical development and developments in cognition and emotion suggest that opportunities for a range of physical activities should form part of schooling.
- Motor-skill development is an important part of the curriculum in preschool education in Australia and New Zealand, while health and

physical education is a Key Learning Area in the National Goals for Schooling in Australia (Curriculum Corporation, 1989) and in the New Zealand Curriculum Framework (Ministry of Education, 1993).
- The New Zealand Health and Physical Education Curriculum (Ministry of Education, 1999) adopts the Maori philosophy of health and well-being, or *Haviora*, which recognises the interconnection of *taha tinana* (social well-being) with *taha hinengaro* (mental and emotional well-being), *taha whanao* (social well-being) and *taha wairua* (spiritual well-being).
- Breaks for morning tea and lunch offer informal opportunities for children to be active. In Taiwan and Japan, where the school day is longer than in many other countries, students have regular breaks for formal and informal physical activity, spending a quarter of their day in recess and lunch breaks as well as being given opportunities for extra-curricular activities including sport (Stevenson, 1992). Stevenson (1992) suggests that these regular breaks contribute to students being more attentive and having more positive attitudes to school.
- Physical exercise can contribute to academic learning in terms of attention and motivation as well as cognition.
- Encouraging girls to be more active remains a challenge for secondary schools in particular, something recognised worldwide (Australian Sports Commission, 1999; see also Box 1.1 on page 11).
- Some educators have used brain lateralisation to explain children's academic strengths and weaknesses, or as a basis for programs that seek to tap into the skills of one or other side of the brain (see, for example, Edwards, 1981). Bruer (1999) warns against such simplistic applications of brain lateralisation research, pointing out that most skills involve the coordination of messages from both sides of the brain. While research into brain structure has been prolific over the last decade, work investigating the application of this new understanding of how the brain works is still in its infancy.

1.4 Misapplication of brain research to education

Language development

Language expresses our intentions and desires, allows us to frame and express our thoughts, helps us to achieve our goals, and is fundamental to our relations with others. It is central to our cognition and social interaction, but its development is also influenced by cognitive, social and emotional development. Unlike physical development, language development does not occur without social interaction or the child's interaction with the environment. Language develops in context, and with a particular set of purposes.

Language building blocks

In describing the process of language acquisition, linguists have divided language into a number of 'systems'. We can think of these systems as the building blocks of sounds that are combined into words, then combined into phrases or sentences with the addition of meaning and usage in context.

Four systems comprise the components of language. **Phonology** refers to the sound systems of a language. The **semantics** of a language are the relationships between words and their meaning: you know what the words 'cat' and 'dog' refer to because of your semantic knowledge. **Morphology** describes the way words are made up according to tense, gender, number and so on; for example, the difference between the forms *write*, *writes*, *wrote* and *writing* are aspects of morphology. **Syntax** refers to the grammatical systems that combine words into phrases and sentences. **Pragmatics** is concerned with the appropriate use of language in social settings; for example, while 'Give me some cake now' is syntactically correct, it is an impolite way to phrase a request in English. Knowing how to achieve your aims using language, and how to express yourself appropriately, are part of your pragmatic knowledge of language. Linguists tend to describe the four systems as separate, but of course they interact and work together to form the larger language system.

phonology
The sound system of language

semantics
The system of meanings associated with language

morphology
The combination of units of meaning in words, e.g. listen + ed = past tense of 'listen'

syntax
The grammatical system that orders the construction of sentences

pragmatics
Rules for the appropriate use of language in social contexts

Children develop the key features of language in the first 3 to 4 years of life. Knowing the early processes of language development can help us understand later developments in literacy and second-language learning.

Language development during infancy

In the first days after birth there are signs that language is developing. Infants' early cries use sound to communicate emotion, and infants discriminate between speech and other sounds, and between their mother's and others' voices (Sachs, 1997). They also learn the rules of taking turns in conversations in these first months, with 'visual conversations' observable in exchanges of eye contact between mothers and their babies. These early 'conversations' affect the rate of language development – a clue that social interaction is an important influence in language acquisition – and are complemented by verbal turn-taking conversations at around 3 months. Games such as peek-a-boo also contribute.

The sounds made by infants progress from cooing (mainly vowels) at around 2 months, to babbling (strings of consonants and vowels such as 'dadadada') about 2 months later. By around 7 months, the babbling starts to sound more like language, and by the end of the first year, when the first words appear, they have the intonation and other sound patterns of the child's native tongue.

Children comprehend language long before they produce it, and this priority of comprehension over production continues throughout the course of language acquisition. The production of language-forms appears closely linked to developments in cognition.

The first words appear around the first birthday and tend to be limited in number, to be simple in pronunciation, and to refer to familiar, concrete objects or important people – 'Mummy', 'dog', 'juice'. Towards the end of the second year, the child's vocabulary increases rapidly to about 50 words, and words start to be combined to produce **telegraphic speech** of two words – usually to ask for more ('more milk'), to say no ('no bath'), or to notice the presence or absence of something ('all-gone milk'). With time, the range of meanings expressed broadens, although children are still constrained while in the two-word stage to talking about the here and now. Aspects such as tense, gender and number appear as the length of children's utterances grows.

There are links in this early development to cognitive and emotional development. The spurt in vocabulary that occurs at the end of the second year has been associated with a number of changes in the nature of children's thought (Bloom, 1998). We have already noted that children first learn words referring to people or objects that are important to them. Infants' early words are also usually related to their actions: they first learn the names of objects that move ('car', 'ball'), and words relating to actions themselves ('up', 'gone', 'more'). With the development of object permanence (see Chapter 2), terms like 'all gone' appear; and with early understanding of causality, terms such as 'oh dear' and 'uh oh'. One explanation of the link between cognition and this aspect of language is that children's vocabulary is acquired around the particular cognitive problems they are solving (Gopnick & Meltzoff, 1997).

Language development during early childhood

Between 2 and 3 years old, children start to speak in three-word sentences, and with the word order of their native language (subject–verb–object in English) (Maratsos, 1998). Grammar also develops, with categories such as nouns, pronouns and verbs appearing in sentences as adults would use them. Thus, preschoolers' speech begins to resemble more closely that of adults.

The kinds of errors children make as they acquire language reveal the process of problem solving in which they are engaged. Very young children 'underextend' and 'overextend' meanings of words as they work to define the limits of a category. That is, they may use the word

---

telegraphic speech
Communication using two-word sentences, leaving out smaller words

'dog' to refer to all animals (an example of **overextension**) or to refer only to their own dog (an example of **underextension**). They may also develop their own expressions for words they do not know by combining words; for example, Jake, who is 4 years and seven months, said:

> You can't touch his head because there's a hole and you might hurt his *thinking thing*

while Eloise, 2 years and 4 months old, said:

> Don't *fall me down* [drop me].

Overregularisation of grammatical forms occurs at the preschool stage as children recognise a particular rule and attempt to apply it. Initially they tend to ignore irregular forms and apply the rule universally, for example:

> I goed to the zoo with Nana and we seed a baby giraffe

and

> He did it well-ly, Mummy.

It is a measure of children's understanding of the language system that such overregularisations are limited to the appropriate part of speech (verbs, in 'I goed … we seed') and tense (the past, in this case). Some of these kinds of errors are also made by learners in the process of acquiring a second language, and by children learning to spell.

As children begin to form more complex sentences, joining phrases together, another sequence is evident that appears to parallel cognitive development. The first joining word is 'and', followed by 'then' or 'when' and 'because' or 'so'. Children learn in a similar way about concepts: first that things can be grouped together ('and'), then that they can be sequenced ('then'), and finally that relationships may be causal ('because') (Bloom, 1998). Bloom reminds us that the same sequence is seen in children's storytelling and understanding of stories. As an example, compare the joining words used in the two stories in Box 1.3.

> **overextension**
> Inappropriate use of a word for a class of things rather than for one particular thing
>
> **underextension**
> Inappropriate use of a word for one thing rather than for a class of things
>
> **overregularisation**
> Application of a grammatical rule, ignoring its exceptions

Box 1.3 CLASSROOM LINKS

Connectives in children's storytelling

The following example of Jacob's storytelling when describing a film in the *Star Wars* series is typical of his age (5 years and 3 months):

> Luke does fight Darth Vader and he cuts Darth Vader's hand off and it exploded and Luke was dragging him, pulling his hand and it was dead and he said, 'Let me see you with my own eyes,' and he said: 'Take my mask off.' 'But you will die. I have to rescue you.' 'You already have Luke, take off my mask. Only for once.' And then 'OK.'

Compare Natalie's story, describing a school excursion, at 7 years and 10 months:

> Yesterday my class (2C) went to the Field of Mars. To get there my class went on the bus with 2B. When we got there we went down to the mangroves but we didn't stay there long because we did have to go to the eucalypt upstairs. It was a lot of climbing to do. When I got there it looked a lot drier than downstairs because upstairs it had harder ground … In the eucalypt field I saw some long grass with a humungous flower in it and we knew there was a bushfire because when there's a bushfire the flower's seeds fall onto the ground and it grows (but only when there's a bushfire).

Activities

1. What differences do you notice in the ways events are linked in the two stories?
2. How might this be related to each child's understanding of time and causality?
3. What kinds of experiences might contribute to the development of children's storytelling ability, apart from reading, listening to and telling stories themselves?

The pragmatics of child language also develop throughout the periods of infancy and early childhood, as the child's use of language moves from simple expressions of emotion to a realisation that language can be used to direct and control others. Children as young as

Language development during middle childhood

While the majority of children's language development is complete by the time they enter school, there are some further developments in middle childhood. Children's vocabulary increases from 50 words at eighteen months old, to around 10 000 words in the first year of school, to 20 000 words by Year 3, and to 40 000 words as the child enters adolescence (Anglin, 1993). A more complex grammar develops in order to deal with the increasing number of words used, and there is a close relationship between vocabulary size and grammatical complexity (Bates and Goodman, 1999).

These changes are accompanied by a greater awareness of language itself, which we refer to as **metalinguistic awareness**. Children's awareness progresses from appropriate use of phonology, morphology, syntax, semantics and pragmatics to specific knowledge of the rules being followed and the ability to express these rules. Such awareness is particularly important as children learn literacy skills. It may be that the school context itself focuses children's attention on the nature of language (Gombert, 1992). Bloom (1998) suggested that children's language develops around and in response to the meanings and intentions of the child's activity. In the early years, the first words tend to refer to the important people, events and objects in the child's world. Then as the child's context changes from home to school, the activities on which the child focuses attention also change. Quite a bit of time is spent in classrooms talking with children about what language does and how it works (see Box 1.4). The meanings talked about are often to do with language itself, which helps children develop their cognitive understanding of language.

metalinguistic awareness
Awareness of and understandings about language

Box 1.4 CLASSROOM LINKS

Sound waves

Read the following classroom interaction about sound waves.

Alan: As the sound goes [*speaking in a low pitch voice*] lower, what happens?

Student: They get wider.

Alan: They get spread out. Now then, what measurement can we make on those waves? What can we actually – let me put it in a different way. You drew out a wave. OK? You said that the distance between a peak and a peak or between a trough and a trough had a certain name. Can anyone remember what that name is? Yes.

Student: [*Inaudible*] wavelength.

Alan: The wavelength – the distance between two peaks or two troughs or any two corresponding points on the wavy lines. If the sound is going to get higher we've already said that the waves are going to get squashed, closer together, so what is actually happening to the wave length? Is it increasing or decreasing?

Student 1: They're increasing.

Student 2: [*Inaudible*] decreasing.

Alan: The distance between two peaks?

Student 1: Decreasing.

Alan: OK. Good. I thought you knew the answer to that. So the wavelength is decreasing as the frequency or pitch is increasing.

Source: Ogborn, Kress, Martins and McGillicuddy (1996, pp. 128–129).

> **Activity**
>
> Write down the ways students' attention is focused on language in this interaction.

Children's language play reveals a developing metalinguistic awareness. Early play with language tends to focus on phonological (sound-related) features; for example (from Harry, 4 years old):

> Hello Jacob Wacob.
>
> Jacob wacob cacob macob.

This kind of play with the sounds of language contributes to later developments in reading. It can be supported with nursery rhymes and stories that make use of repetition and rhyme (Bryant, Bradley, McClean, & Crossland, 1989).

As children become more aware of other features of language, they move from being concerned with purely phonological features to an interest in playing with semantics and syntax; for example, Jack (aged 6) said of his baby brother:

> Harry will be good at basketball when he grows up, because he dribbles a lot

or Jacob (aged 5) said when he learned his cousin's name:

> I'm not going to call him Henry, I'm going to call him Chickenry.

This shift is displayed through an interest in riddles when children are around 6 to 8 years old. Once again there is a link between the ability to understand riddles, and reading ability (Ely & McCabe, 1994). The metalinguistic skills involved in interpreting riddles are the same as those involved in making sense of a text.

In late middle childhood and adolescence, with increasing awareness of the rules for language use, children can become pedantic about what is said and how (and delight in picking up their teachers or parents on errors!); for example:

> 'Can you take the garbage out?'
>
> 'Yes I can. ... Oh, do you want me to? I thought you were just asking if I was strong enough. Ha, ha!'

Language development during adolescence

Increases in vocabulary during adolescence include the wider use of a variety of forms such as connectives ('although', 'however', 'nonetheless') and further developments in syntax, with mastery of complex forms such as the passive ('it was taken by him' rather than 'he took it')

FIGURE 1.11 Adolescence brings increased metalinguistic awareness. As a result, older students show greater ability to edit their work.

and nested clauses ('the man who was riding the elephant's camera'). Correct use of subtle distinctions in word use, as in the use of 'can' and 'may' in the garbage example just given, are probably learned through formal instruction (McDevitt & Ormrod, 2002).

Development of abstract thinking in adolescence is reflected in language (see Figure 1.11 on page 19). The ability to compare what is said to the underlying reality allows adolescents to go beyond the literal. This ability shows itself in increased use and understanding of figurative speech, sarcasm and multiple meanings (McDevitt & Ormrod, 2002). Such developments are also related to further increases in metalinguistic awareness, with some students enjoying debating, arguing for the sake of arguing, and using language to think through ideas.

Adults' role in language acquisition

Joint attention

When parents and children both focus on an object or activity in **joint attention** sessions, language learning is more rapid when parents do not interrupt or change the focus but instead talk about the object of the child's attention (Carpenter, Nagell, & Tomasello, 1998). In these interactions, adults are supporting children's language development by labelling their environment for them.

Rogoff (1990) showed that children play an important, active role in such situations, directing much of their interaction with adults and initiating conversations or joint attention sessions. By being in charge, children can direct the focus to an issue of concern to them, keeping learning at an appropriate level. Implied in this is the assumption that children attend to their environment selectively, learning from the experiences they are interested in and can make sense of.

joint attention When carer and child together attend to a stimulus, such as when reading books or playing peekaboo games

1.5 Adult–child interaction across cultures

CRITICAL REFLECTION
- How might we let individual children control the focus and pace of their learning in the school context?

Child-directed speech

Adults worldwide adjust their language when talking to children, producing a special register of speech termed 'motherese', or **child-directed speech**. This type of speech tends to be higher in pitch than other speech, simple in grammar and vocabulary, and characterised by exaggerated expression and enunciation of words. It appears to help children separate the flow of speech into words, and to attend to the key words in a communication (Snow, 1995). Even children adjust their speech in this way when talking to babies. Infants show a preference for child-directed speech compared to other adult talk (Cooper & Aslin, 1994), and its use in the first year is positively related to infants' language comprehension at 18 months (Murray, Johnson, & Peters, 1990).

child-directed speech A type of speech directed to young children, characterised by high pitch, short and well-spaced sentences, simple vocabulary, and exaggerated intonation

Expansion and recasting

As well as simplifying what they say, parents may *amplify* what the child says, repeating the child's statement with an **expansion**, and **recasting** errors in grammar. For example, the child's phrase 'Daddy work' may be responded to with 'Yes, Daddy's gone to work in his car, hasn't he?', *expanding* the information by adding 'in his car', and *recasting* the phrase into correct grammar: 'Daddy's gone to work.' Children repeat adults' recasts, but the contribution that expansions and recasts make to children's language acquisition is a matter of debate (Nicholas, Lightbown, & Spada, 2001).

expansion Parents' tendency to respond to young children's utterances by restating them in a more elaborate form

recasting Parents' tendency to respond to children's utterances by restating them in the correct grammatical form

Language input

While investigators debate the nature of the contribution adult language makes to children's language development, it is clear that the amount of language in the home affects the rate at which children acquire vocabulary. This is one explanation for differences in language observed between people of various social classes. Hart and Risley (1995) found significant differences in the amount of language directed at children in different socioeconomic groups. Particularly affected were children of families in situations of poverty: these children had a third of the interaction and experience with language than children in families from higher socioeconomic strata. Acquisition rate also links to later achievements. In the same study, Hart and Risley found a positive correlation between children's language experience before 3 years old, and verbal intelligence scores at ages 9 to 10. Other researchers have likewise suggested that conversation is important to children's cognitive development (Peterson & Siegal, 1999). Ginsberg, Klein and Starkey (1998), discussing differences in mathematics achievement, suggested that children in situations of poverty do not lack the thinking skills, but rather the language needed for school mathematics learning. In Chapter 9 we explore the contribution of socioeconomic factors to individual differences in more depth, including the variability observed within and among different social and ethnic groups.

In the section that follows Box 1.5, we discuss how children's prior experiences in language and other areas contribute to their understandings and to their learning in school. Being aware of the interests and activities for which children use language (including playing with language itself) can help us as teachers to make learning relevant for students.

Box 1.5 IMPLICATIONS FOR EDUCATORS

Language development and the classroom

Imagine you are walking past two very different classrooms. One is silent, with children engaged individually in their work. The other is very noisy, with children talking and arguing with one another while the teacher has a discussion with a group in the corner. Which process is more effective?

From our discussion of language development, we have seen that input from others makes a difference to children's language development, and that language development does not end when the child reaches school. Children's activity also directs their language development. Exposure to a wide range of language models, and to activities that prompt children to discuss and explore verbally, are important to both cognitive and linguistic development – all of which suggests that totally silent classrooms are not conducive to effective learning.

School-based skills

Children do not arrive at school without knowledge or skills. Physical and language skills developed in infancy and early childhood form an important basis for the skills that are the focus of schooling. In this section we discuss second-language learning – for many children an essential skill necessary to access education – and the skills of literacy and numeracy. In each case, children's knowledge develops from very early in life and is built upon by formal teaching in schools.

Second-language development

We described the process of first-language acquisition earlier, but for many children in Australia and New Zealand, English is not their first but their second (or maybe even third or fourth) language. For these children, acquiring a second language is an essential skill for success at school. But is a second language acquired in the same way as a first language?

There are some similarities in the ways first- and second-language learners use language, which seem to be related to the nature of the language-learning process. There are also important differences arising from the differing contexts in which people learn first and second languages. The focus in this discussion is on learning English as a second language (ESL), something that confronts non-English-speaking migrants and some Indigenous children in Australia and New Zealand. Foreign-language learning (for example, speakers of Standard Australian or New Zealand English who learn French or Vietnamese in classrooms in Australia or New Zealand) is a different although related process.

Comparing first- and second-language acquisition

Similarities between first- and second-language acquisition include an early dependence on routine phrases such as those in telegraphic speech. Young children may use phrases such as 'allgone' for all situations where an absence of something is indicated, later recognising that these phrases can be combined with other language units to make phrases like 'allgone milk', or separated to make phrases like 'Mummy gone'. Second-language learners at early stages similarly depend on remembered language chunks – formulaic phrases that have not been separated into their component parts, and that cannot therefore be applied flexibly or adapted and expanded upon. Some common examples are the questions: 'Where is it post office?', 'How are you your father?', 'Who is she this man?' The constraint at this early stage may be one of memory, since when confronted with a large, unfamiliar system, people commonly start with a small sample of language and build from there. The overgeneralisation of grammatical rules is another feature of both first- and second-language acquisition. The problem-solving nature of the language-development task is evident here.

Why is it that learning our first language sometimes seems effortless and automatic, while learning a second language can be a long and difficult process? The contextual features of second-language acquisition make it a more difficult task than learning a first language. In first-language acquisition children tend to be supported by their parents, with intense one-to-one interaction focused at the child's level and on the activities the child is engaged in. Second-language acquisition rarely occurs with this level of intense support. In addition, as we have seen, the child's emotional, social and cognitive development is progressing in tandem with language development, supporting and being supported by it. When second-language acquisition happens later this match does not occur, and the child has often quite complex thoughts, ideas and emotions to express in the new language. There are emotional and motivational differences, too. As we saw earlier, first-language acquisition is an intrinsically motivating task for the child due to parents being involved in the process. There are many rewards for success – and even for failure – when parents respond to the child's requests and attend closely to clarify meaning. Second-language learning can be frustrating and anxiety-producing, particularly for a newly arrived non-English-speaker in an Australian or New Zealand school. When second-language acquisition occurs in the school context there is also the double demand of learning about other curriculum areas through the second language (Gibbons, 1991).

CRITICAL REFLECTION

- How might the school context be shaped to support second-language acquisition?

In addition, it seems that there is a sensitive period – or 'window' – for language acquisition, beyond which the neurological process is different and the task more difficult and less automatic. Children exposed to a language before about 6 years of age are more likely than older children to acquire it completely. Further, the later a child is exposed, the less complete their acquisition of the language tends to be in terms of phonology and syntax (Long, 1990).

It is important to note that younger children's superiority over older children in language acquisition is not a matter of the first language 'confusing' the second. Indeed, the strength of the first language may support the learning of a second, with considerable knowledge about language and the way it works already in place (Gibbons, 1991). This has been one argument in favour of programs that support first-language maintenance for Aboriginal, Maori and other bilingual children in Australian or New Zealand schools (Makin, Campbell, & Jones Diaz, 1995). Children for whom English is the second language tend to learn English and other subjects more effectively when their first-language skills are strong (Cummins, 1979; Thomas & Collier, 1999).

Learning ESL in schools

ESL learners may be of any age, with differing levels of cognitive development and skill in their first language. In addition, they may differ in their experience of English prior to starting school (McKay & Scarino, 1991). Thus, effective evaluation and teaching programs are marked by flexibility. Rather than being guided by a specific developmental path, teachers focus on students' needs.

ESL programs in Australian schools are currently of two types: intensive English programs for newly arrived migrants, and support programs in mainstream schools. The latter may be within classes, where specialist and general classroom teachers support the development of English while studying the curriculum; or in withdrawal situations, where English may be the sole focus (Scarino, Vale, McKay, & Clark, 1988). In New Zealand, bilingual classes are provided for Maori students, in which the development of spoken and written fluency in their first language is encouraged, and a chance is given to explore tasks in the first language before moving between the two languages. For migrants, there are intensive English classes, with some immersion in mainstream English classrooms, to ready these students for mainstream classes once the intensive class ends (Ministry of Education, 1994). Box 1.6 contains some classroom strategies for supporting ESL learners.

1.6 Research on the importance of first-language in learning

Box 1.6 CLASSROOM LINKS

Supporting ESL learners in mainstream classrooms

Strategies teachers use to support learners of ESL in the mainstream classroom can include:

- modelling (or demonstrating) language by using whole phrases and natural intonation when speaking to ESL learners
- using visual aids and gestures to assist comprehension
- accepting errors and responding naturally – as in first-language acquisition – with recasts and expansions (see page 20)
- focusing on the message rather than its form
- accepting children's choice to be silent, as this can be an important time of learning (consider how many new experiences are thrust on a new-language learner in an English-speaking classroom)
- communicating in real ways about real situations that are related to students' interests and needs
- making the classroom an interactive environment, where children constantly talk together and with the teacher
- recognising that children may feel safer talking in pairs or small groups rather than during whole-class activities
- allowing children to continue learning in familiar ways (which may include observation, rote learning and individual or collaborative work)
- supporting the maintenance of the child's first language by involving parents in the classroom, particularly in other curriculum areas such as mathematics
- encouraging other children to use the child's first language, and if possible using it yourself with the whole class in a range of contexts (this may require you to learn some of the language and teach it to the class)

- teaching about language differences explicitly, comparing across languages; for example, teaching about the different use of questions in English and some Aboriginal languages, and teaching that the phrase 'Once upon a time' indicates a fairy story.

Source: Adapted from Makin, Cameron, & Jones Diaz (1995) and Gibbons (1991).

Literacy development

literacy
The ability to read and use written information, and to write appropriately in a range of contexts

Traditionally, **literacy** has been conceptualised in terms of the written language skills of reading and writing. The Commonwealth Language and Literacy Policy (DEET, 1991) defines literacy as 'the ability to read and use written information and to write appropriately, in a range of contexts'. More recent conceptions of literacy are much broader than this, recognising the link between written and spoken language (Garton & Pratt, 1998), literacy as a social construct (Jones Diaz, Arthur, Beecher, & McNaught, 2000) and literacy in other media. The New Zealand literacy and numeracy strategy defines literacy as 'the ability to use and understand those language forms required by society and valued by individuals and communities' (Ministry of Education, 2002). Literacy is a critical skill for learning and life, across a broad range of contexts. In this chapter we focus on reading and writing, keeping in mind social contexts that contribute to the development of these skills. (Two other forms of literacy – computer literacy and information literacy – are discussed in Chapter 10.)

We have seen a number of features and practices in language development that later contribute to literacy development. While children commonly learn to read and write once they are at school, many precursors of these skills are developed in the preschool years.

Emergent literacy

emergent literacy
Understandings about and attitudes towards reading and writing, which are the precursors of acquiring those skills

Early awareness of literacy has been termed **emergent literacy** (Clay, 1991). This includes understandings about conventions of print, such as the left–right, top–bottom ordering of print on a page in English, and the knowledge that letters represent sounds and are combined to form words separated by spaces. It also includes attitudes about the purposes and value of reading and writing.

Activities such as looking at books, reading environmental print such as street signs or the title of a favourite television show, and simple rhymes and songs all contribute to reading, as does writing. Similarly, writing is developed through reading, as well as through such activities as drawing, telling stories, and adult-supported writing such as writing a letter, a birthday 'wish list' or a story dictated by the child.

A child's home environment is an important contributor to emergent literacy, both in terms of direct literacy support from parents, and indirectly. For instance, a relationship has been demonstrated between children's reading ability and such features of the home environment as length of family mealtimes (Anderson, Wilson, & Fielding, 1988), number of books in the home, library membership and the amount parents (particularly fathers) read (Share, Jorm, Maclean, Matthews, & Waterman, 1983), as well as more direct activities such as parents or other family members reading books with the child (Griffin & Morrison, 1997).

CRITICAL REFLECTIONS

- A number of activities have been identified in the previous paragraphs, including looking at books, singing rhymes and songs, and drawing. Can you identify the range of skills that each of these activities might help develop in young children?

- How could you use such activities to help a child who is having difficulty learning to read or write?

Differences in the nature of the home environment have been one explanation of differences in reading ability observed between children of various social classes (Share et al., 1983). A number of intervention programs focus on the home environment as one contributor to children's reading progress. An example is given in Box 1.7.

Box 1.7 RESEARCH LINKS

Bridging the gap: Improving literacy outcomes for Aboriginal students

Developed by Louella Freeman and Sandra Bochner at Macquarie University in New South Wales, and working with the Indigenous Catholic Education Unit at Parramatta, this project aimed to introduce Aboriginal families in Parramatta, Sydney, to techniques for shared book reading and other literacy activities. Its aims were to improve children's experiences and parents' confidence, skills and involvement in their children's education.

Each fortnight, Aboriginal education assistant/community liaison officers based in Parramatta schools visited the homes of the 20 families involved in the project. They brought a book, the book's story recorded onto tape by a volunteer from the Aboriginal community, some games and some reading-related activities. In the course of an hour-long visit, they discussed how parents could use the materials with their kindergarten-age children. Other family members were also encouraged to be involved. The book and other materials then became the property of the family, who were asked to use them during the ensuing fortnight.

Project outcomes included:
- improvements in children's pre-literacy and literacy skills over the time of the project, and related increases in self-confidence at school
- fostering of child–family interactions with literacy, with many parents and children continuing to use strategies learned in the program
- increased links between home and school for Indigenous families – in particular, the positive first contact with families meant that parents were more likely to be actively involved in school activities.

Source: Adapted from Bochner and Freeman (2002).

Learning to read and write

Reading and writing are complex skills that involve the coordination of a number of individual skills.

For expert readers, reading tends to be automatic, but for children the process is demanding and a little like solving a puzzle in code. Readers must simultaneously decode individual letters as sounds, group strings of letters together to form new sounds, and check the word formed against their vocabulary – and that is just to read one word! As readers continue the process with subsequent words in a sentence, they must keep each word in their working memory so as to combine it with the other words in a meaningful way, and attend to punctuation to obtain clues about intonation and stress. It is little wonder that comprehension is often set aside as children tackle the complexities of decoding (see Box 1.8). The information-processing approach (see Chapter 5) describes reading as an information-processing problem that makes demands on working memory. The individual skills must become automatic in order for working memory to operate efficiently, or reading performance will be affected (Perfetti, 1997).

Box 1.8 CLASSROOM LINKS

Beginning to read

Read this transcript of a beginning reader. The child's speech is given in *italics*. The author's speech and observations are in roman font.

This book is called 'Colours'.
Colours.
This colour is black.
This fire engine is red.

> How did you know that said 'fire engine'?
> *Because there's a picture.*
> Come back to this page and read it to me again.
>
> This car is black.
> *This fire engine is red.*
> *This b–boat is blue [pauses to check the picture].*

Activity

Identify the particular skills the child has acquired, and those he is having difficulty with.

Once reading becomes more automatic, attention is increasingly focused on a variety of purposes, so that rather than 'learning to read', children start to 'read to learn' at around 9 years old (Ely, 1997). In primary school, children progress from reading aloud to silent reading, and show increases in 'sight vocabulary' (the number of words they can recognise automatically) that affect fluency. Going into adolescence there are further increases in fluency and in the ability to read complex, unfamiliar and abstract texts. Learners' ability to go beyond the literal meaning and consider multiple viewpoints and draw inferences from a text also improves with the development of abstract reasoning (see Chapter 2) (McDevitt & Ormrod, 2002).

Similarly, in writing, children progress from focusing on form to using writing as a tool. For example, Jacob enjoys playing 'cafés' with his family, taking down each person's order on a notepad. To begin with, when Jacob is 4 years old, the orders are a series of scribbles on the page. Later, Jacob progresses to writing strings of letters and numbers. By 6 years old, his letters approximate the sounds they are meant to make, and others can read what he has written.

With further formal instruction at school, children's spelling and punctuation become more standard (see Figure 1.13 on page 27). There is a wide age range in children's development of these skills: in the same kindergarten class there may be one child still writing in unrecognisable scribbles, while another is writing elaborate stories.

In parallel with developments in their reading, children in middle childhood start to use writing as a learning tool to help make sense of information or events (Daiute & Griffin, 1993). Instruction becomes focused on writing for different purposes (genres) as children become more proficient and their understanding of other perspectives improves.

In adolescence, writing shows more complex syntax, better planning and editing, and an increasing depth of topic. The earlier focus on the mechanics of the writing process is replaced in these older learners by the ability to phrase things in their own words and to adapt their writing for a variety of purposes and audiences (McDevitt & Ormrod, 2002).

Teaching literacy in schools

There are two main approaches to teaching reading and writing. The 'whole-language' approach to reading instruction uses the process of language acquisition as a model, arguing that children who are exposed to print in all its forms, and who are encouraged and supported as they experiment with reading, will develop the necessary skills and understandings just as they did when learning to speak (Cambourne, 1988). The emphasis in this approach is on the purpose of reading, which is to make meaning. Children are urged to draw from all the clues available in the text – 'graphophonic' (letters representing sounds), picture, and context – to make predictions about meaning and individual words, and to verify such predictions (see Figure 1.12). It is argued in this perspective that the skill of reading should not be divorced from its context, and that the context itself can support the reading process. This is the essence of **top-down approaches** to learning and teaching, of which the whole-language approach to literacy instruction is one example.

---

top-down approaches
Teaching approaches (such as the whole-language approach) that emphasise task presentation and skill development within real contexts that involve whole-skill development

CHAPTER 1 EMERGING SKILLS   27

FIGURE 1.12
Children's attention is drawn to cues to meaning in the pictures and text, helping them make predictions about words. What cues can you identify in this page that might help children decode the text?
(Source: McHalick, 1996.)

FIGURE 1.13 Children explore print in drawing and attempts at writing. Through invented spelling, children experiment with and develop their understanding of spelling rules.

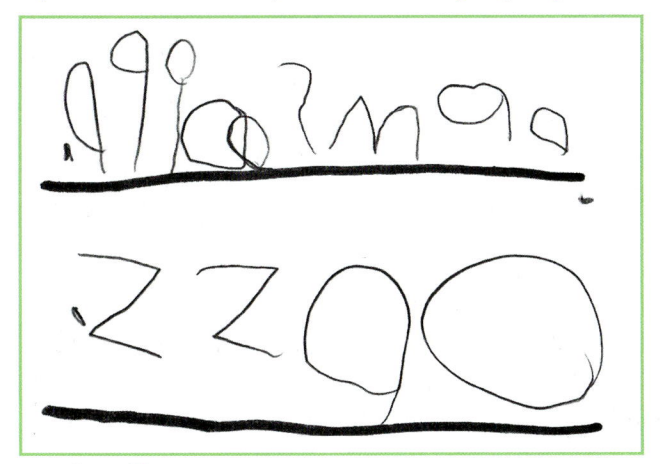

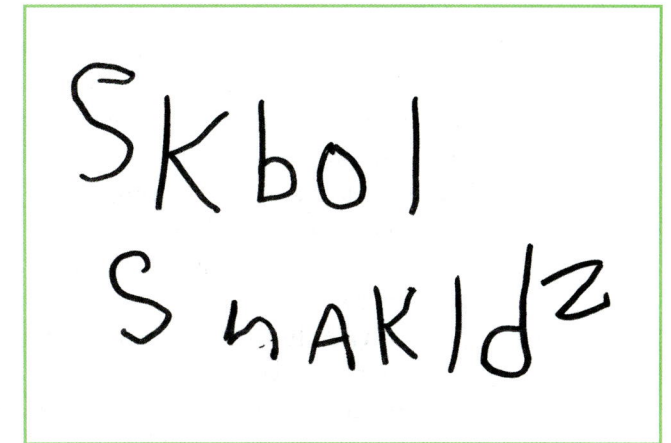

a Strings of letters

b Invented spelling

c Conventional spelling

Similarly, in writing, children are encouraged to experiment by 'writing' stories that progress from scribbles on the page, to strings of letters and symbols, to approximations and then to increasingly accurate English spelling. Writing develops out of children's explorations with print (Garton & Pratt, 1998) (see Figure 1.13).

Bottom-up approaches emphasise the teaching of component skills such as phonics. Children are taught the component skills of reading, which are built up progressively towards the total reading process. Texts are graded according to the length and complexity of sound strings, sentences and meanings. This also reflects what happens as children learn to speak and parents simplify language for them. In writing, children are taught to form letters and to spell words, with an emphasis on developing accuracy. As they are being taught, letters or words are grouped with those with similar features to facilitate learning the rules (see Figure 1.14 on the next page).

bottom-up approaches
Teaching approaches that emphasise the development of individual skills that can be built up towards competence in the overall task

FIGURE 1.14 The similar sounds focus children's attention on particular phonic rules. (Source: Center & Freeman, 2000. Illustration by J. Philp. Used with permission.)

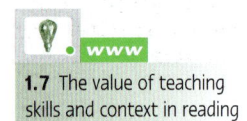

The five mice like to slide down the pipes and fall into the pile of rags. Mike smiles at the white mice while they hide in the rags.

1.7 The value of teaching skills and context in reading

numeracy
The ability to use mathematics effectively and with confidence in a range of contexts

Each of the two approaches contributes to reading and writing in important ways. There is evidence that children switch between top-down and bottom-up learning in their reading development (Chall, 1983), and that the most effective approach is to combine the two (Pressley, 1994). Children need help in gaining the skills to approach the complex task of reading, but they also need to combine lower-order skills of decoding (translating letter symbols into sounds and words) with higher-order comprehension skills. Clearly, the optimum approach to teaching reading and writing involves a balance between top-down and bottom-up approaches.

More recently a third approach, called the 'explicit' or 'functional' approach to literacy, has been adopted in Australian schools. It combines the approaches already described by explicitly teaching features of the language, but doing this in the context of real tasks. Students are exposed to a range of genres – or 'text types' – and taught explicitly about the purpose, structure and linguistic features that define each one. Students' efforts to write using particular text types are supported by modelling and guided practice (Gibbons, 2002).

Numeracy development

Numeracy is often used as a partner term to literacy. It is defined by the Australian Association of Mathematics Teachers (AAMT) as the capacity and disposition 'to use mathematics effectively to meet the general demands of life at home, in paid work, and for participation in community and civic life' (AAMT, 1997), a definition similar to that adopted by the New Zealand Ministry of Education (2001). It involves mathematics, but goes beyond the mathematics of the classroom to be involved in all curriculum areas. A distinction between numeracy and school mathematics is implied in the definition, which is a reminder that schools need to focus on the application of mathematical thinking and strategies beyond the maths classroom.

Just as literacy is thought to be intrinsic to everyday functioning in our society, numeracy is also recognised as a key skill for learning and life. In 1999, the Australian federal government set goals for literacy and numeracy that included: 'every student should be numerate, able to read, write and spell at an appropriate level' (MCEETYA, 1999).

Emergent numeracy

As with language, awareness of mathematical principles seems to be biologically determined. Research with infants shows that they are aware of quantity from the first days after birth, recognising changes in numbers of small sets of objects (Antell & Keating, 1983). By 2 years, children also show expectations that adding something will increase amount, and that taking something away will decrease it (Sophian & Adams, 1987).

These early understandings are built upon by the developing child's experiences in the physical and social world. Look around you: almost unconsciously, you may notice that the level of tea in your cup is lower than it was earlier, that there is more text on this page than on the last, that the hands on the clock have moved from four towards five. We operate in and are surrounded by a world of quantities, measurements and spaces. Children's daily experiences habituate them to think about mathematical constructs.

Learning to be numerate

The child's role

As in language acquisition, children are active in developing mathematical understandings and strategies for operating in their world. These strategies increase in complexity and effectiveness with age (Baroody, 1987). For example, by around 4 years of age, children use a counting strategy to combine groups of objects: 'one, two … three, four (2 + 2)' (Ginsburg, Klein, & Starkey, 1998). Such strategies for addition and subtraction appear spontaneously before the child starts school. These strategies are later extended by combining counting and the use of memorised number-facts ('one and one is two … three, four, five (1 + 1 + 3)'), then by more sophisticated strategies such as recombining or restructuring numbers to simplify a problem ('nine and one are ten and six are sixteen (9 + 7)'). Children are able to apply strategies first with concrete objects they can see, then with invisible objects ('doing it in your head'). You may see why this is so in the description of Piaget's theory in Chapter 2.

The role of culture

Culture contributes to the process of dealing with the world of quantity by providing the child with tools for the task. (You will see in Chapter 2 that Vygotsky talked about mathematics – as well as language – as a cultural tool that helps to shape children's thinking). These tools may include language and the society's counting system, as well as formal strategies for addition, subtraction and other operations. Counting systems vary from one culture to another. While English and many other languages use a base of 10, another common counting base is 5, seen for example in most Aboriginal and Islander languages (Harris, 1987). Each of these bases probably has its origin in the number of fingers on one hand (5 fingers) or two hands (10 fingers). In some languages, the link to the hand is clear in the number-words used. For example, Harris (1987, p. 33) describes the Martu Wangka counting system, from Jigalong in Western Australia, as follows:

one	*kuja*	
two	*kujarra*	
three	*kujarra kuju*	
four	*kujarrakujarra*	
five	*marakuju*	(hand-one)
ten	*marakujarra*	(hand-two)

1.8 Comparing children's mathematics abilities across countries

Across cultures, however, objects are counted according to the same principles of **order** ('two' comes after 'one' and before 'three'), **cardinality** (when counting a group of objects, the last number counted represents the amount), and **one-to-one correspondence** (each member of a group must be counted once and only once) (Gelman & Gallistel, 1978). Although young children have difficulty applying these principles in practice, they recognise them from as young as 4 years of age (Gelman & Meck, 1983).

order
The principle that numbers are counted in a fixed order

cardinality
The principle that when counting, the last number counted represents the total

one-to-one correspondence
The principle that each item in a group is counted only once

Numeracy in the classroom

Children's exposure at school to more formal systems, with written rules and procedures, parallels learning to read and write, and the formal systems of language. The informal mathematics developed before school provides children with an important base on which to build new understandings. As with reading and writing, the challenge for teachers is to help children connect their informal understandings with new ways of thinking about and representing mathematics.

Children are faced at school with the task of learning formal systems for representing number: for example, that 24 is written as '24' and not as it is said ('20–4'). Children also learn formal ways of carrying out operations with number, such as in the procedure for long division or for multiplying numbers with more than two digits. Just as we saw with literacy, effective instruction in numeracy involves a balance between the drill of facts and operations, and an understanding of the processes involved. Using strategies without understanding can result in misapplication of those strategies to new problems. Box 1.9 gives an example of this kind of difficulty.

Box 1.9 CLASSROOM LINKS

Parsid

Consider the following description, by a teacher, of a student who has knowledge without understanding in mathematics.

> She had moved into Year 4 (8–9 year olds). By this time, Parsid had learned her times tables and could reel them off by rote but could not pick out individual number facts at all. Even the question 'What are five sixes?' floored her, although she could recite the six-times table perfectly. A simple multiplication sum (46 × 6) revealed that her knowledge of tens and units was sketchy in the extreme, as she constantly (but not invariably) 'carried' the wrong digit.
>
> At this point we went back to the blocks and started to look at 10 + 6 = 16. This was easy enough, but 9 + 6 = 15 and 11 + 6 = 17? Not a chance, even with the blocks in front of us. In the end I decided that these were the facts I was going to concentrate on, and we repeated, by rote, addition facts with the blocks in front of us. I also put a number (less than 10) in a circle and we wrote addition facts round the edge. An early breakthrough was when, having written (for example) 5 + 3 = 8, Parsid immediately wrote 3 + 5 = 8. We always finished the session with some times-tables work, as she was proud of her achievement here and so left each session on a good note.
>
> I would never say that this girl will have a warm and wonderful feeling for number, but sheer determination and rote learning have had their place. Parsid is now confident that arithmetic is within her grasp, and is willing to try. I am sure confidence is the key to success.
>
> Source: Kate Wylie-Carrick (personal communication, 2001).

Activity

Describe the development in Parsid's understanding of number:
1. How might her teacher's activities and the rote learning Parsid favours have contributed to this development?
2. Would you do anything differently with a child like Parsid?

Current approaches to teaching numeracy aim that students develop understandings about number and the processes they apply to numbers, estimating and checking as they work (see Figure 1.15). The use of concrete materials such as fingers, counters and base 10 blocks aids this process of developing understanding. Drill and practice are also important in making automatic the retrieval of number facts and use of operations, so that working-memory space can be freed for more complex operations.

Box 1.10 (see page 32) looks at the classroom implications of skills development. Vygotsky's work, described in Chapter 2, may help you in thinking about how to assess children's abilities and how to take account of these in your own teaching. Chapter 11, which deals with assessment, contains further strategies that might be helpful.

CHAPTER 1 EMERGING SKILLS   31

FIGURE 1.15 Current approaches to mathematics teaching utilise a combination of focusing on understanding, using concrete materials, and drill and practice. (Source: Doyle, 2003, p. 60.)

Measuring Area

Date: _____

You will need: Centicubes

Find the approximate area of each island. For each island:
- Place Centicubes on the island and count them.
- Convert the Centicubes to square kilometres using this scale:
  1 Centicube = 1 square kilometre (sq km).
- Record the area.
- Then list the area of each island, from smallest to largest.

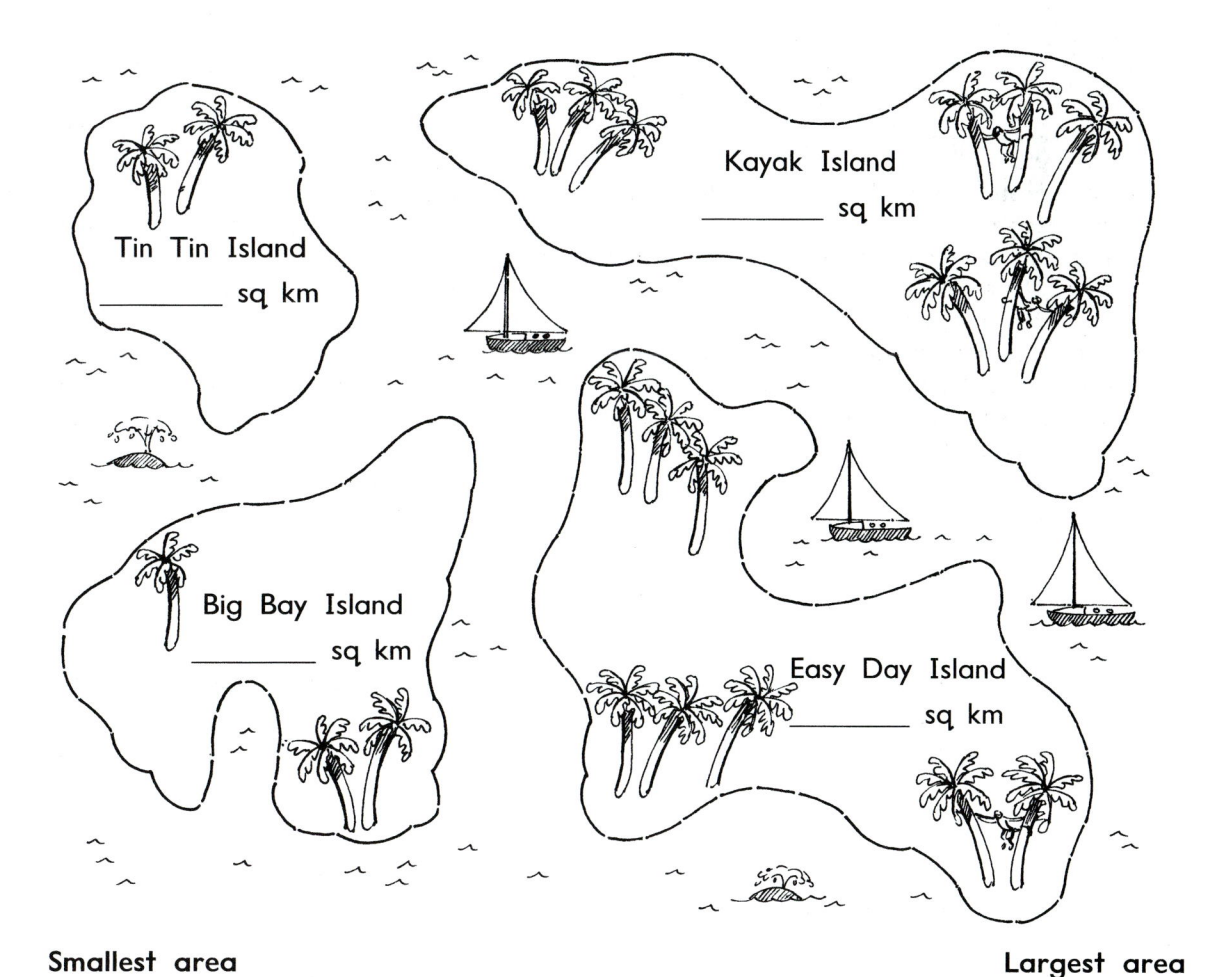

Tin Tin Island
_____ sq km

Kayak Island
_____ sq km

Big Bay Island
_____ sq km

Easy Day Island
_____ sq km

Smallest area   Largest area

_____   _____   _____   _____

Unit 21 Area (See *Teacher's Resource* pp. 84–86.)

60

CSF II *Measuring and estimating*   **3.1** Make increasingly accurate estimates of measurements using informal units and standard units.
3.2 Measure and compare using appropriate informal units.

Box 1.10 — IMPLICATIONS FOR EDUCATORS

Developing skills

- Supporting ESL learners is important to their success not only in English, but also across the curriculum.
- Encouraging children to think and talk about new concepts in their native language can help them acquire the concepts and learn to express those concepts in English.
- Involving parents in the classroom and encouraging them to talk to children in their own language can help facilitate the process of acquiring and expressing concepts in English.
- Students bring important skills and knowledge to their learning, as well as attitudes about particular subjects or skills and about learning itself.
- Recognising students' past experiences is important for accurately matching teaching to students' abilities.
- Current approaches to teaching language, literacy and numeracy take account of what the student already knows, in order to build new knowledge. (One example of this is the Count Me In Too project, developed in New South Wales and widely adopted in Australia and New Zealand, which aims to help teachers match teaching to students' number strategies in the early years of school.)
- There have been debates about the best way to teach literacy and numeracy, and even about what the content of instruction should be. The research reviewed here suggests that the most effective approach includes a focus on skills (bottom-up) and context (top-down).

Principles of development

In this chapter we have examined the acquisition of a number of different skills in the domains of physical development, language, literacy and numeracy. Despite the range of domains and skills, some principles of development can be deduced that also apply across the cognitive and socioemotional domains discussed in chapters 2 and 3. The principles are as follows:

- *Development involves a series of progressive and orderly changes leading to maturity.* Development involves change of a particular type, and is generally orderly (we learn to crawl first, then to walk, then to run). It is also directional: the changes, at least in childhood, tend to lead towards more complex, effective ('mature') behaviour. This trend towards complexity and more organisation is seen in all aspects of development, and reflects brain development.
- *Development is continuous but uneven.* Different areas of the body and brain develop at different times, as do different functions. One example is in language, where syntax development follows vocabulary acquisition.
- *Development is a lifelong process.* Although we develop at different rates in different areas, we can be said to be developing throughout the lifespan. Commonly, children's development is described as occurring in a number of stages: infancy (0–2 years), early childhood (3–7 years), middle childhood (8–11 years) and adolescence (12–20 years). You will recognise the age-ranges associated with these stages in the descriptions of Piaget's theory in Chapter 2, and in Erikson's theory in Chapter 3. A number of researchers have noted the shifts that occur in children at around 2 to 3 years old, 7 to 8 years old and 11 to 12 years old – not only in cognitive development, but also in the social and personal areas. Growth spurts have also been observed in the brain at these ages. The shifts can be attributed to changes in both maturation and environment. While there are physiological changes that occur across cultures, the precise age at which the shifts occur varies due to environmental factors such as diet or cultural practices.
- *Development can vary from one individual to another.* The most obvious developmental variations occur between males and females, with girls tending to lead boys in physical development. Other group variations can be observed among different racial groups.

There are many other sources of variability too. The chapters in Module III of this book examine a number of these sources in detail. In general, the variability in development can be explained by looking at the forces affecting that development.

What contributes to development?

This question of what contributes to development has been a major source of controversy for developmental psychologists. Theorists argue about the roles of maturation, learning, environment and culture. Yet while the controversy continues about each aspect's relative contribution, few would argue for an extreme position that relied on or entirely excluded any one of these forces. The following points review some examples of each kind of influence from the domains discussed in this chapter:

- *Development results from both maturation and learning.* This position represents the nature–nurture debate mentioned at the start of this chapter and discussed in Chapter 7. As we have seen, both innate and environmental forces combine to influence development across the physical and language domains. Other chapters in this book similarly illustrate the influence of a mixture of innate and environmental forces in development.
- *Development occurs in context and is influenced by environment.* There are environmental influences on language development, in the social interaction children hear and are involved in. In terms of physical development, family and community activities and the formal activities of school contribute to children's motor skills.
- *Children are active in development.* Far from being something that simply 'happens' to children, development grows out of children's activity. For example, crawling produces changes in brain structure that support physical, perceptual and cognitive changes. Children actively try to make sense of language and of mathematics. These attempts, while they may result in errors, are testimony to the important role children play in their own development in all domains.
- *Development is cumulative.* One change provides a basis for further change. In this chapter we have seen a number of examples of the close interaction between different dimensions of development. As one area develops, it changes the kinds of activities children engage in and their relationships with those around them, providing new opportunities for development in other areas. One example is adolescents' capacity for abstract thinking, which changes the way they deal with their emotions. This in turn affects their friendships and influences their thoughts and behaviours.

Box 1.11 (see page 34) looks at a number of implications for educators of considering the developmental principles.

Box 1.11 — IMPLICATIONS FOR EDUCATORS

Considering development in the classroom

- Because development is orderly and progressive, teaching must be tailored to children's developmental level (that is, there is no point teaching calculus to preschoolers, or basketball to babies). This involves teachers being aware of the course of development across a number of domains. This chapter and others in Module I should help you develop such knowledge.
- Stages in development coincide with stages of schooling, in that middle childhood roughly coincides with the primary years, and adolescence with secondary schooling. Recognising developmental shifts that occur with age, some states in Australia further break these broad groupings into stages of 2 years each. The aim is that teachers plan learning and teaching strategies to match students' developmental stage, and that students develop skills appropriate to their developmental level.
- Developmental variations are important for teachers to consider. One explanation of gender differences in literacy outcomes is the relatively slower development of language in boys. It has been suggested (House of Representatives Committee, 2002) that boys should receive a different kind of literacy instruction to cater for this developmental difference. Chapter 9 explores this and other gender issues in greater depth.
- Because development occurs in context, what happens around children influences their development. It is important for teachers to consider not just *what* is taught, but *how* it is taught. Other environments children are involved in also influence children's development through the experiences and knowledge they provide. Teachers therefore need to know about children's home environments in order to effectively consider children's needs. Chapter 9 explores this issue in relation to poverty.
- That children are active in development suggests that students should be mentally and physically active in their learning, too. For example, learners can be encouraged to make sense of how new and old experiences and knowledge fit together.
- Since development is cumulative, it is important when teaching skills to build up from what students can do first, and towards the final goal. Identifying a number of steps or component skills in a complex task can help in this process. Task analysis, described in Chapter 4, is one approach to this strategy. Designing tasks that draw on skills from a number of areas can help students consolidate earlier achievements, as well as integrate and coordinate their skills.

Concluding comments

Development is influenced by genetics, environment and the activity of individuals themselves. Effective teaching therefore recognises each of the possible influences on a student's development. This chapter has explored these influences on physical and language development, and on the development of some school-based skills. In Chapter 2 we look at some theories of cognitive development.

Chapter review

- There are connections between physical, cognitive, language, social and emotional development throughout the lifespan.
- Maturation, parents, the community and school, and the child's own activity all contribute to motor-skill development. The development of fine and gross motor skills is important in early childhood, while middle childhood sees increased coordination and combining of motor skills.
- Puberty is the major physical development in adolescence, presenting challenges to adolescents' self-image and family relationships. Individual differences in the timing of puberty affect adolescents' ability to adapt successfully to these changes.
- There are group differences in development due to environmental factors such as nutrition, and sociocultural factors such as gender-typed activity.
- Brain development also shows complementary influences from genetics, environment and the child's activity.
- Developmental increases in complexity and coordination of thoughts, feelings and behaviours are associated with structural neurological changes such as increases in neuronal size and complexity; and myelination, which improves efficiency of message transmission.
- The course of first-language acquisition is remarkably consistent across cultural and language groups. It shows children's active involvement in their acquisition of language.
- Adults make important contributions to language development, which continue into a child's school years.
- The school-based skills associated with second-language learning, literacy and numeracy all build upon early developments in physical, motor and language skills, as well as the cognitive, social and emotional developments discussed in chapters 2 and 3.
- Children's active involvement in making sense of their world shows itself in their understandings about language and number from the first days after birth. In schools, we build upon these early understandings and so need to be aware of and recognise them.
- Approaches to teaching literacy and numeracy tend to vary in focus on skills (bottom-up) or strategies (top-down), with research evidence suggesting that the most effective approach involves a combination of these.
- Development is a series of progressive and orderly changes leading to maturity, which shows both consistency across humanity and also individual difference. Development is lifelong, with each change providing a basis for future changes.

You make the connections:

Questions and activities for self-assessment and discussion

1. Copy the table below and list examples of connections between physical, cognitive, emotional and language development that have been mentioned in this chapter. You can add to your table as you study later chapters in this module.

Physical development	Cognitive development	Language development	Socioemotional development
Crawling	Object permanence	'No more'	Parents say 'no'; frustration
Puberty			

2. Identify some sociocultural influences on development. Skip forward to Chapter 9 to see what impact these differences might have on children in classrooms.

3. Describe the main features of language in each of the following samples from children of different ages:

   13 months: Da da [pointing to or calling to father];
   Mo? [requesting water or milk]

   24 months: Mummy nere [there] [used for 'Mummy is there'/'Mummy, sit there'/ 'Mummy, take me there']

   26 months: Mummy read book

   36 months: Mummy, he gived me a smile when I comed out [playing peekaboo under a blanket with a baby]

   5 years: Mum, can we make something? Like some pikelets or pancakes or something? Like those kind of things?

   8 years: Mum, I don't like this dinner … I LOVE it!

   13 years: Just listen to me, Mum. If you buy me this Gameboy, then I can get the shirt, and I'll still have $17 left over. No, no, just listen. That way I'll be able to save up for Christmas. You're always telling me I have to save my money, and if you buy me the Gameboy, then I can!

4. How does children's activity contribute to their development? Give examples of this in the school context.

5. Describe how students' ideas and experiences influence their learning. How can students' existing ideas and understandings be utilised in teaching new content?

Key terms

gross motor skills	lateralisation	child-directed speech
fine motor skills	phonology	expansion
puberty	semantics	recasting
adolescence	morphology	literacy
adolescent egocentrism	syntax	emergent literacy
neuron	pragmatics	top-down approaches
axon	telegraphic speech	bottom-up approaches
synapse	overextension	numeracy
neurotransmitter	underextension	order
dendrites	overregularisation	cardinality
myelination	metalinguistic awareness	one-to-one correspondence
cerebral cortex	joint attention	

Recommended reading

Berk, L. E. (2003). *Child development* (6th ed.). Boston, MA: Allyn & Bacon.
Berko Gleason, J. (2001). *The development of language* (5th ed.). Needham Heights, MA: Allyn & Bacon.
Bloom, L. (1998). Language acquisition in its developmental context. In D. Kuhn & R. S. Siegler (Eds.), *Handbook of child psychology: Vol. 2* (5th ed., pp. 309–370). New York: Wiley.
Cole, M., & Cole, S. R. (2001). *The development of children* (4th ed.). New York: Worth.
Garton, A., & Pratt, C. (1998). *Learning to be literate: The development of spoken and written language* (2nd ed.). Oxford: Blackwell.
Ginsburg, H. P., Klein, A., & Starkey, P. (1998). The development of children's mathematical thinking: Connecting research with practice. In I. E. Sigel & K. A. Renninger (Eds.), *Handbook of child psychology: Vol. 4* (5th ed., pp. 401-476). New York: Wiley.

Make some online visits

Visit your local education-department website to look at their approach to teaching physical education, literacy and numeracy.

Australia: <www.dest.gov.au>
NSW: <www.schools.nsw.edu.au>
ACT: <www.decs.act.gov.au>
Victoria: <www.deet.vic.gov.au/deet/>
Queensland: <education.qld.gov.au>
South Australia: <www.dete.sa.gov.au/decs_home.asp>
Western Australia: <www.eddept.wa.edu.au>
Tasmania: <www.education.tas.gov.au>
Northern Territory: <www.education.nt.gov.au>
New Zealand: <www.minedu.govt.nz>
<www.tki.org.nz>

FIGURE 2.1 Chapter 2 concept map.

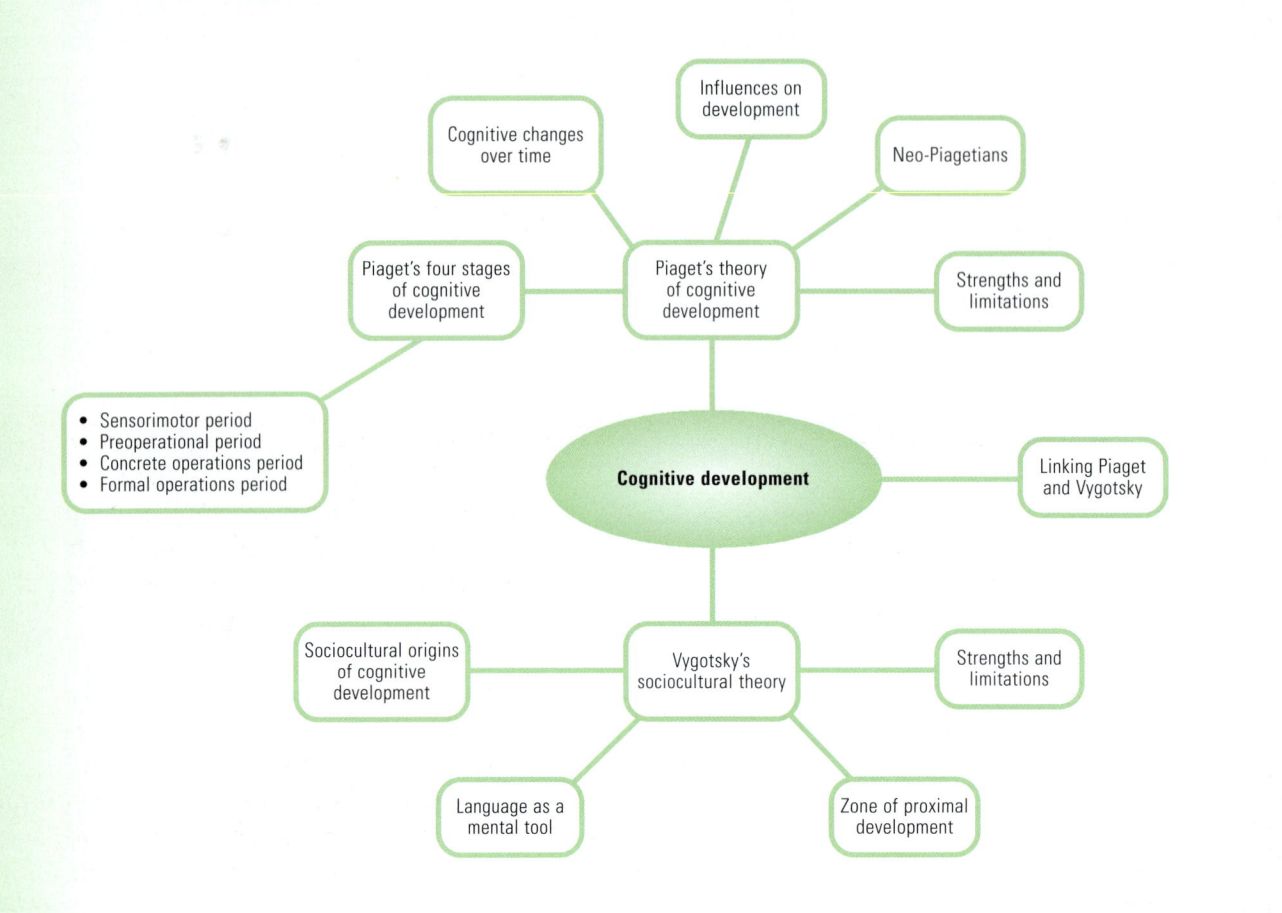

```
                    Influences on
                    development
  Cognitive changes                    Neo-Piagetians
  over time
                    Piaget's theory
  Piaget's four stages  of cognitive          Strengths and
  of cognitive       development              limitations
  development

• Sensorimotor period
• Preoperational period
• Concrete operations period        Cognitive development        Linking Piaget
• Formal operations period                                        and Vygotsky

  Sociocultural origins    Vygotsky's              Strengths and
  of cognitive             sociocultural theory    limitations
  development

              Language as a       Zone of proximal
              mental tool         development
```

CHAPTER OBJECTIVES

After reading this chapter you should be able to:

- identify the four factors that, according to Piaget, influence children's thinking from early childhood to adulthood
- explain key developmental milestones in Piaget's sensorimotor, preoperational, concrete operations and formal operations stages of cognitive development
- discuss issues educators need to consider when working with those in the sensorimotor, preoperational, concrete operations and formal operations stages
- comment on the role of social and cultural influences in Vygotsky's ideas about children's cognitive development
- critically evaluate the theories of Piaget and Vygotsky and what they offer educators in the 21st century.

CHAPTER 2

Cognitive development

Introduction

Have you ever played hide and seek with a group of children that includes a 3-year-old? When everyone else runs to find a place to hide, the 3-year-old will stand in the same spot and cover her face with her hands, thinking this makes her invisible. According to Piaget, 3-year-olds are egocentric in the way they see the world. They know if they cover their eyes, then everything around them becomes invisible. They have not yet reached a stage in their thinking whereby they are able to see the world from another person's point of view.

Cognitive development is concerned with our ability to think, to reason, and to understand and remember the world around us. It involves mental processes that are associated with taking in, organising and making sense of information – processes that include perceiving, attending to, understanding and recalling information. These mental functions are part of what is referred to as **cognition**. In this chapter, we look in some detail at the work of two of the most important and influential theorists in this area: Jean Piaget and Lev Semanovich Vygotsky.

cognition
The mental processes involved in perceiving, attending to, understanding and recalling information

Piaget's theory of cognitive development

When you consider the skills of a 6-month-old infant compared with the skills of a 3-year-old, a 6-year-old or a 13-year-old, it becomes apparent that children's knowledge increases with age. More importantly, the *way* children think – the strategies they use to solve problems and to make sense of new experiences – also changes. It is not just that children accumulate more information as they mature: how they think and the way they interact with the physical and social world also change.

In his studies of children's thinking, the theorist Jean Piaget (see Box 2.1 on page 40) was interested not so much in what or how much children know, but in how they think, how they see the world around them, and the language they use to explain what they see. In observing his own children, Piaget was interested in what changes as children's thinking develops, and in what influences these changes.

Box 2.1 ABOUT JEAN PIAGET

Jean Piaget (1896–1980) was born in Neuchâtel, Switzerland, to well-educated and professional parents (Brainerd, 1996). His childhood was not happy – his mother had mental health problems and this led Piaget, like his father, to spend his time in scientific study rather than pursuing more conventional leisure activities. It also stimulated an interest in psychology.

Piaget showed early promise of intellectual ability. At the age of 7 he began to study molluscs, carrying out very detailed observations in the lakes around Neuchâtel. By 10 years old he had published his first scientific article, and at 14 years old was offered a curator's position at the Geneva Museum of Natural History but was too young to take up the position (Wadsworth, 1996). At the age of 18, he gained a Bachelor's degree from the University of Neuchâtel, then a PhD, and by the age of 21 had published twenty-five scholarly papers.

Apart from his study of science, Piaget was also interested in philosophy and in the origins and nature of human knowledge. His dual involvement in the biological sciences and philosophy was highly influential in his later work on children's intellectual development.

Piaget's interest in how people acquire knowledge led him in 1919 to study psychology at the Sorbonne in Paris. While there, he worked in the laboratory of Alfred Binet, who was interested in measuring intelligence (see Chapter 7). Piaget assisted in standardising a French version of a reasoning test, his task being to identify norms for the average French child as compared with those for an English child. This was a rather dull, mechanical task, and Piaget's interest was captured by the wrong answers that children gave to items on the test. Using interview techniques he had learned at the Sorbonne, Piaget asked the children to explain their answers and found their explanations of errors were much more interesting than explanations of correct answers. During these interviews, Piaget noted that 6-year-olds, 8-year-olds and 13-year-olds made different types of errors. He also noticed that children of roughly the same age not only got the same items wrong but also made the same kinds of errors. He became convinced that children think in ways that are qualitatively different from the ways adults think.

Piaget held chairs of psychology, sociology and related areas at universities in Switzerland during 1925–1964, and was director of the International Centre for Genetic Epistemology in Geneva from 1955 until 1980. He continued to publish scholarly works until just before his death in 1980 at the age of 84. His enormous productivity over a 60-year period is one of the reasons he is so well regarded.

FIGURE 2.2 Piaget observed children and questioned them about the way they solved problems. His work changed the way we think about cognitive development.

It is sometimes said that Piaget is the one name people remember from studies in educational psychology. Introductory courses almost always include reference to Piaget, and most textbooks contain a chapter on his work (Siegler & Ellis, 1996). Why is this theorist so important? The answer is that Piaget was one of the first theorists to attempt to comprehensively describe the process of cognitive development in children. Aspects of his work have been disputed over the years, but his ideas remain influential. More importantly, subsequent theories of cognitive development have had to address many of the issues Piaget initially raised. In particular, his method of questioning children about how they make sense of their experiences – probing to understand their errors and then following up with further questions – is one of his most significant contributions.

2.1 Piaget's free conversation or clinical method

In reviewing some of the main questions that interested Piaget, and in looking at the implications of his ideas for educators, it is important to be aware that Piaget's language can be confusing. The meaning of some of the words he used is different from that in common usage, such as when he used 'conservation', 'assimilation', 'accommodation' and 'egocentrism' (defined later in this chapter). This can be attributed in part to Piaget's background as a biologist, and to his use of biological terms to explain cognitive development.

Piaget's cognitive stages

Piaget believed that rather than being continuous, children's cognitive development is discontinuous, proceeding sequentially through a series of distinct 'stages' from birth to adulthood, with thinking at one stage being qualitatively different from thinking at the next (see Figure 2.3). A stage-based concept of development can be likened to climbing stairs:

FIGURE 2.3 Piaget's stages of cognitive development.

Sensorimotor stage
Main achievements:
- object permanence
- goal-directed action
- deferred imitation

Dominated by motor and sensory activities:
- hearing • seeing
- touching • tasting
- smelling

Birth to 2 years

Preoperational stage
Main achievements:
- language acquisition
- symbolic thought

Thinking still limited; appearance dominates perceptions and understanding

2 to 6 or 7 years

Concrete operations stage
Main achievements:
- ability to represent events mentally
- ability to operate logically on surroundings
- classifying objects mentally
- reversing actions
- compensating for changes
- seeing from another's viewpoint

7 to 11 or 12

Formal operations stage
Main achievements:
- abstract thought
- some achieve hypothetical reasoning in secondary school

From around 12 years

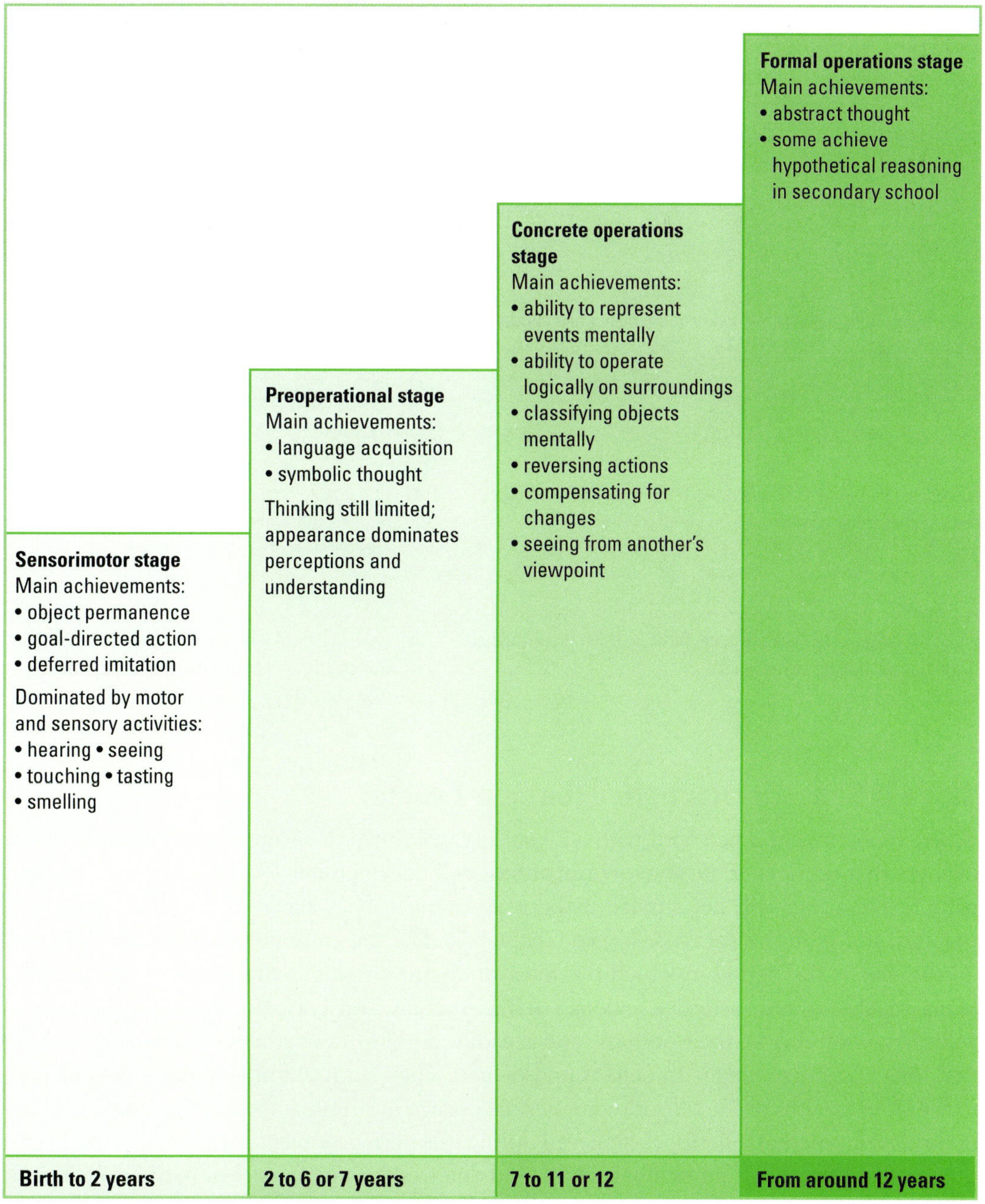

each step (or stage) in the hierarchical sequence of development involves the progression to a more advanced level of functioning, which is followed by a period of consolidation before an individual proceeds to the next step. Piaget believed that the stages he identified had two very important properties: first, they are *universal* (that is, they apply to everyone); second, they are *invariant* (that is, unchanging), meaning that the order in which children pass through the stages cannot be varied. Children must progress through them in sequence, beginning with the sensorimotor stage, although some may never reach the final stage of formal operations.

For each of his stages of cognitive development, Piaget identified what he called 'developmental milestones' – key achievements that have to be attained by a child at each cognitive level. A number of developmental milestones have been identified for each of Piaget's four stages, and selected examples from each level are in Table 2.1.

TABLE 2.1 Main developmental milestones at each cognitive stage

Cognitive stage	Developmental milestones	Developmental milestones in action
Sensorimotor:		
Object permanence	Knowing that something continues to exist even when it is out of sight	▪ Looking for a lost ball
Goal-directed or intentional action	Actions that are produced consciously for the purpose of achieving a desired end	▪ Hitting a musical toy to elicit a sound
Deferred imitation	Repeating an action observed on a previous occasion	▪ Making a sweeping action with a broom after watching someone sweep the floor
Preoperational:		
Symbolic thought and language	Using gestures, signs, sounds and words to represent and convey meaning	▪ Pointing to something of interest ▪ Waving goodbye ▪ Saying 'brm' while pushing a toy car ▪ Asking for 'mo' (more)
Concrete operations:		
Conservation	Understanding that objects or quantities remain the same despite changes in physical appearance	▪ Understanding that the amount of juice remains the same whether it is in a tall thin glass or a short fat glass (see Box 2.3)
Formal operations:		
Abstract thought and propositional reasoning	Attaining the capacity to think abstractly; that is, using propositional and hypothetical, deductive reasoning	▪ Solving logical problems like 'If Jo is fatter than Sue and thinner than Eve, who is the fattest?' (see Box 2.4)

Stage 1: Sensorimotor period (birth to 2 years)

When you compare a newborn with a 2-year-old, you become aware of the enormity of the changes that occur over the **sensorimotor stage** of development. Newborn infants are basically helpless and will not survive without assistance. They have no language, very little mobility, and primitive social skills (see Chapter 1). The sensorimotor stage usually lasts only 2 years but is the period in which the most dramatic developmental changes occur. From being capable of only reflexive actions such as sucking and grasping, infants begin to gain voluntary control over their actions, and steadily develop new strategies and schemes for exploring and interacting with objects and people. They learn to imitate others' actions and, in the latter months of the sensorimotor period, engage in simple forms of pretend play. Three of the developmental milestones achieved during this period – object permanence, the beginning of goal-directed or intentional action, and deferred imitation – are of particular interest.

sensorimotor stage
The earliest of Piaget's developmental stages, characterised by object permanence, intentional or goal-directed behaviour, and deferred imitation

Until they reach about 4 months old, infants do not fully understand that concrete objects have a permanent existence (Lutz & Sternberg, 1999, p. 279). However, by approximately 8 months (see, for example, Baillargeon, 1991; Spelke, Breinlinger, Macomber, & Jacobson, 1992) they have attained **object permanence**: that is, if a toy drops out of sight babies will look for it, even if they cannot reach out to search for it.

From around 6 months of age, infants become capable of **goal-directed or intentional action**, meaning that they begin to use their own actions and vocalisations to influence others' actions in order to achieve a desired goal such as attention, comfort or food (see, for example, Coupe & Goldbart, 1988; Halliday, 1975).

Deferred imitation refers to children's ability to reproduce actions they have seen and remembered, such as when towards the end of the sensorimotor stage children begin to copy actions, speech sounds and facial expressions they have seen previously.

Piaget's Stage 1 in education

For those working with infants and toddlers in the age-range from birth to around 2 years of age, the skills likely to be of most interest include imitation (immediate or deferred), social interaction and play (appropriate use of objects) (Bochner & Jones, 2003). Most children acquire these skills as a natural outcome of their daily experiences, although children who have an intellectual disability or who are at risk of delay in some aspect of their development may need extra help. (These issues are discussed more fully in Chapter 8; see also Box 2.2.) Successful progression through Stage 1 is evident in children's play and in the emergence of age-appropriate language and communication skills that facilitate progress to the next stage.

> *object permanence*
> Piagetian term used to refer to children's understanding that objects continue to exist even when they are out of sight
>
> *goal-directed or intentional action*
> A sequence of acts produced intentionally to achieve a desired outcome
>
> *deferred imitation*
> Actions copied from models no longer present, the actions having previously been observed and remembered
>
> **2.2** An observation of intentional action reported by Piaget

Box 2.2 CASE STUDY

A cognitive approach to delayed language development

Joe, who had delayed language development, was aged 5 years and five months when he was referred to the Learning Centre by a school counsellor. He was the youngest child in his family. His parents spoke very little English but his three siblings were bilingual and fluent in both English and their parents' language.

According to the initial referral, Joe was mildly intellectually disabled (developmentally, he was at the 2–3-year level), with a delay in general development and language. His language-age was assessed as being at 9 months (with an expressive language age of 3 months, and a receptive language age of 16 months). He did not speak, nor did he appear to understand either English or his parents' language. At school he made no attempt to communicate. There appeared to be no physical cause for his slowness in development.

During Joe's first days in the support class at the Learning Centre, the teacher observed him carefully. Joe presented as a very shy, tense and silent child. He kept his gaze lowered and generally did not respond when called by name. He showed no curiosity about the classroom or the activity of the children around him.

Joe did not appear to be frustrated by his lack of speech, but it confused his teacher, who could not be sure that Joe understood any language directed to him. Early screening showed that Joe could follow directions if a visual cue was provided. If offered a choice of toys to play with, he would reach for the preferred object or shake his head to indicate 'no'. He could imitate actions but would only mouth, not voice, sounds in imitation. He responded to different voice tones: he beamed when praised and became visibly upset when scolded.

Working one-to-one, the teacher tried to test Joe's recognition of concrete objects and pictures, but Joe did not respond appropriately. It was decided to see what language would emerge if the classroom atmosphere was totally relaxed and a warm, reassuring bond developed between teacher and child. This became the first goal of the program. Joe did as he wished at school – wandering about the room, examining objects, and watching and sometimes playing with other children. He was observed using gestures to communicate (he tugged at the teacher's skirt), and he vocalised unintelligibly, imitated some utterances and spoke a few words spontaneously. The initial recognition task was repeated using three objects (ball, book, car), but it was clear that Joe was confused by the teacher's language.

Joe's performance on Piagetian-based tasks (Mehrabian & Williams, 1971) showed he could point to or touch objects he could see, but lacked the concept of object permanence – he would not search for objects or people that were out of sight. It was decided that Joe needed help in understanding and expressing the concepts of presence ('there'), recurrence ('more'), disappearance ('where?'), non-existence ('gone') and cessation ('stop'). He also needed to learn to use language to express needs ('I want') and protest ('no' or 'don't do that'). Weekly samples of Joe's language were collected to document changes in his skills. These samples showed that the most dramatic gains were made in the early stages of the program, with increases in expressive language-age from 3 to 30 months over a four-month period, though receptive language-age increased by only 4 months (to 20 months).

Joe's language program was implemented during daily 15-minute sessions in the classroom, using his own possessions and other relevant materials. Sometimes teaching took the form of a game. Peers were often included to encourage Joe to interact verbally. Piaget (1971) interpreted play as a child distancing himself until he has differentiated the word from the actual object/event/action, and play had an important place in Joe's language development. Early screening showed that Joe was at the level of manipulating concrete objects. Over time, he progressed to using models, then pictures, and finally drawings and imaginative games. A vivid example of this progression was recorded early in Joe's days at the Learning Centre when, in imitation of the teacher, Joe was selecting fish pictures and putting them on a magnet board. The teacher drew a pond on the board to represent water and continued to model the task – demonstrating the appropriate behaviour for the boy by putting the fish on the board – adding that she was 'putting the fish in the water'. After an interval, Joe filled a cup with water from the sink and threw it onto the fish on the board.

After 4 months at the Learning Centre, Joe was able to indicate the presence of objects and people verbally (for example 'there'), rather than just by touching. He also searched more readily for hidden objects or people, and by the time he had been in the class for 12 months, could denote absent objects or people both verbally and with gestures ('gone', 'no'). He learned to express his needs using words ('I want') rather than by crying and whimpering, and to protest – first by whispering 'no' and later by using 'don't', 'no' and 'not' in two-word phrases (for example 'no drink', 'not there').

Initially, Joe responded only occasionally to his own name, but after 4 months he responded readily when addressed and referred to himself as 'I', 'me' and 'Joe'. When Joe left the Learning Centre after 12 months, his expressive and receptive skills language skills were consistent with his general developmental level, and probably reflected his general level of functioning in the mildly intellectually disabled range.

Source: Adapted from Bochner, Price, Salamon, Yeend, & Orr (1980).

Activities

1 Identify the aspects of this case study that are consistent with Piaget's theory.
2 Using a Piagetian framework, what other strategies could have been used to assist Joe in the classroom?

2.3 Operations

operations
Actions that are governed by rules and logic, and that are performed mentally rather than physically

preoperational stage
Piaget's second stage, in which a child is not yet able to 'operate' or carry out logical physical actions mentally, but is reliant on manipulating real materials

Stage 2: Preoperational period (2 years to 6 or 7 years)

Piaget used the word **operations** to refer to actions that are performed in the mind and governed by rules and logic (Singer & Revenson, 1996). He argued that the young child's thinking at the **preoperational stage** precedes the ability to perform actions mentally rather than just physically, and to think logically.

Over the period from around 2 years of age to the first years of formal schooling, some astonishing changes occur in communication and language skills. From an infant who has no intelligible speech there emerges a 6-year-old with a vocabulary of at least 10 000 words and a functional knowledge of the pragmatics and grammatical structures of language. **Symbolic thought** is a critical milestone for the preoperational stage. This is typically demonstrated in the acquisition of language (see Chapter 1 for a discussion of language acquisition).

FIGURE 2.4   At the sensorimotor stage, children's drawings are largely scribbles. By the preoperational stage, children are able to represent human figures in their drawings

The emergence of symbolic (or representational) thought is probably most evident in children's play over the preoperational period. At the simplest level, a toddler learns to pretend that Teddy is drinking from a cup or having a bath. Stones become cakes and a broom is a horse. Play is very important at this stage. It is a platform for demonstrating a child's understanding of symbols and the ways in which symbols can be used to represent objects and events. (Types of play and their development are discussed in Chapter 3.) Language during play is limited, initially, to performative sounds ('brm' for a car, 'sh-h-h' for pouring tea), then single words appear ('car', 'Mum', 'all gone', 'more'), with the sounds and words being added to expanding concepts such as 'ball', 'car', 'drink' and so on. Simple sentences are formed by combining words ('car gone', 'more drink'). Later, games that involve role-taking (Mummy and Daddy, the doctor, Batman, a princess) are played, and imaginary friends appear. During this period, children begin to create their own stories and to draw representational pictures (see Figure 2.4). Earlier, in the sensorimotor stage, children draw largely random scribbles; but gradually they begin to attempt to draw realistically. These developments are dependent on the emergence of representation or the use of symbols.

One characteristic of Piaget's theory, in relation to children at the preoperational stage, is that he emphasised the limitations of children's thinking, rather than what they can actually do (Beilin, 1992; Donaldson, 1978). Here, Piaget identified three related issues: egocentrism; centration, or a tendency to be perception-bound; and animism.

Egocentrism, or the tendency for children to think and talk about things from their own immediate perspective, is most evident in children's use of language. For example, a child may talk to a stranger about familiar people or events and be surprised that the stranger does not share the child's knowledge of those people and events. Piaget used a task known as the 'three-mountains problem' to explore children's egocentrism. This involved showing children a model of three mountains: one snow-capped, the second with a Red Cross, and the third with a small house on top. The children were then shown some photographs and asked to choose one that represented what a doll sitting at the opposite side of the table would see (see Figure 2.5 over the page). Most 4-year-olds did not realise that theirs was not the only possible view of the model. They could not imagine what another person, looking from a different angle, would see. They could only describe what another person might see in terms of what they themselves saw. Their thinking was egocentric. Does this remind you of the development of writing in Chapter 1?

symbolic thought
The ability to represent objects and events mentally

egocentrism
An individual's belief that everyone sees the world in exactly the same way as that individual

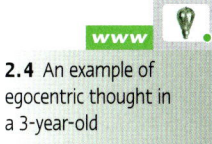

2.4 An example of egocentric thought in a 3-year-old

FIGURE 2.5
What does the doll see?

centration
Concentrating attention on one aspect of a stimulus while ignoring other features

2.5 Illusions

2.6 Examples of Piaget's observations of animism in children's thought

Centration refers to children's inability to focus on more than one or two conspicuous aspects of a situation, and their tendency to not notice other, less dominant features. A characteristic of children at the preoperational stage is that they are 'perception-bound', meaning that they attend to the physical appearance of objects and situations, and that they believe what they see. If one object looks taller than another, they will say the taller object is the bigger of the two. If one object looks wider, they will say that object is bigger (see Box 2.3 on the opposite page).

Another characteristic of preoperational children is 'animism', or the tendency to think of inanimate objects as being alive and capable of thinking and feeling like humans (Piaget, 1929). Some argue that the animism Piaget observed in children's thinking at the preoperational stage is learned, rather than being characteristic of this developmental stage. Adults often talk in animistic ways to children, and children's books and cartoons often include animism (for example, the stories of Peter Rabbit, or Walt Disney cartoons). So it is possible to claim that adults teach or at least encourage children to think in this way. However, there is also evidence that when the tasks given to them involve more familiar materials, 3–4-year-olds are less egocentric and animistic in their thinking than Piaget thought. Children eventually come to distinguish themselves from objects, and also realise that words are not part of the objects they represent, but are 'situated in the head' (Piaget, 1929, p. 251).

Piaget's Stage 2 in education

Those caring for children in Piaget's preoperational stage must give them opportunities to explore their physical world during play and problem-solving activities. It is through such activities that children's existing concepts are challenged and modified, or new concepts formed. 'Hands on' experiences are needed, involving the many different types of materials generally available in early-childhood settings such as preschools, crèches or long-day-care centres. For most children, the need for access to 'hands on' activities continues beyond preschool years, and in this Piaget foreshadowed 'constructivism' (see, for example, Driver, 1983; Duckworth, 1987; Kamii, 2000), with its emphasis on children constructing knowledge through direct experience (see Chapter 5).

For teachers, the egocentric and perception-bound characteristics of the preoperational child are the most relevant. Such children have difficulty understanding others' actions. Some assistance could be given to help children understand that others see the world differently. They also need opportunities to talk both with peers and with adults about activities they are engaged in, as a way of extending their understanding and language skills. For older children, introduction to early reading and number skills will contribute to this process (these topics were introduced in Chapter 1).

Transition between stages

In thinking about children's progress through the four stages, Piaget realised that there are periods of transition as children move from one stage to another. He acknowledged, for example, that between the ages of 5 and 7 there is a period sometimes called the '5 to 7 shift'. This is interesting in relation to children's entry to school and the commencement of what can be described as 'formal schooling'. Across many education systems – not just in Australia and New Zealand, but elsewhere – it is rare for formal instruction in the basic skills of literacy and numeracy to begin much before the age of 7. If you think about what is in the curriculum in the first year at school (such as at Kindergarten, or in Prep, Reception or Year 1), and compare it with the curriculum in the following year, there is often material that functions as a foundation for later learning in the areas of reading, writing and mathematics. Much of this introductory material is consistent with the characteristics of the preoperational child, with the emphasis being on play, symbolism and language development. The introduction of more structured material, in content as well as presentation, does not usually start until the second year at school. By this time, most children have reached the concrete operations stage and have the cognitive skills needed for the more formal curriculum of the primary school.

Stage 3: Concrete operations period (7 years to 11 or 12 years)

The developmental milestones for the child at the **concrete operations stage** are many, but there is one that is particularly significant: **conservation**, or the child's acquisition of the ability to see that certain characteristics (such as height or weight) of an object or entity do not change when the object's physical appearance changes. There are a number of logical principles involved in conservation at the concrete operations stage, but in this chapter we focus on the following five principles – identity, reversibility, compensation, seriation and classification – which can be demonstrated readily in Piaget's conservation tasks (see Box 2.3).

> **concrete operations stage**
> Piaget's third stage, in which a child is able to mentally manipulate and think logically about objects that are present
>
> **conservation**
> The ability to see that certain characteristics (size, height, length, amount) of an object do not change with changes in the object's physical appearance

Box 2.3 RESEARCH LINKS

Examples of Piaget's conservation tasks

The following four conservation tasks are examples of those used by Piaget in his studies of children's thinking. Notice that the materials used in each task are presented in two ways. The first presentation represents the way the task is initially given to children – that is, the first question that is asked and the way the materials are initially set out in front of the child. The second presentation shows the way Piaget changed or rearranged the materials before he asked the second question.

1 Number

First presentation
'Are there the same number of Smilies in each row, or does one row have more than the other?'

Second presentation (transformation)
'Now are there the same number of Smilies in each row, or does one row have more?'

2 Substance (mass)

First presentation
'Is there the same amount of clay in each ball, or does one ball have more than the other?'

Second presentation (transformation)
'Now does each ball have the same amount of clay, or does one have more?'

3 Area

First presentation
'Does each of these two cows have the same amount of grass to eat, or does one have more than the other?'

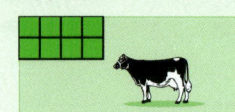

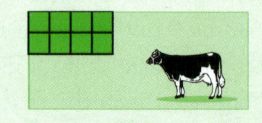

Second presentation (transformation)
'Now does each cow have the same amount of grass to eat, or does one cow have more?'

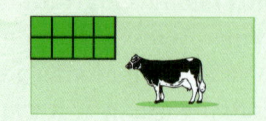

4 Liquid volume

First presentation
'Is there the same amount of water in each glass, or does one have more than the other?'

Second presentation (transformation)
'Now is there the same amount of water in each glass, or does one have more?'

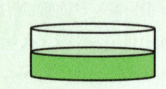

Activity

Present one or two of the tasks shown above to children in the 4–12-plus age range. Try to find at least three children, one from each of the 4–5 years, 8–9 years and 12-years-plus age groups. You should use real materials, not the diagrams shown here. Remember to ask the children to explain their answers to your questions.

1 Tape-record your conversation with each child while doing the tasks.
2 Compare the responses of younger and older children.
3 Can you identify which children have achieved conservation in the areas covered by the tasks you used (for example, conservation of number, substance or area)?
4 Were the results what you expected in terms of the age and developmental level of the children? If not, can you explain any anomalies?

2.7 A few more conservation tasks

---

reversibility
The ability to mentally reverse thought, such as adding back something that has been taken away or remoulding something to its original shape

compensation
The ability to see that an increase in one dimension (such as height) is compensated for by a decrease in another dimension (such as width)

seriation
The ability to mentally arrange objects or elements in terms of a dimension such as length, weight or volume

---

Three of the conservation principles – identity, reversibility and compensation – underlie successful performance of the conservation tasks. All three principles are linked to the very first property of matter children have to understand: that is, object permanence. Children must learn that things have a relatively permanent 'identity' or existence. For example, a quantity of water is still the same even though its height changes when you pour it into a flat saucer or into a tall glass. A quantity of playdough is still the same whether you have it in one lump or break it up into 100 little pieces and spread the pieces over a larger space (see Figure 2.6 opposite). See Wadsworth (1996) for more information on the Piagetian tasks and how to administer them.

Children also learn that any changes made to objects and materials can be reversed and the materials changed back into their original form. That is, the water can be poured back into the glass and the little bits of playdough rolled back into one big lump. This is **reversibility**. Similarly, children learn that change in any one part of a closed system or situation will lead to **compensation**, or complementary changes in another part. For example, if you have six marbles – three in one hand and three in the other (3 + 3 = 6) – and you drop a marble from one hand, in order to still have six marbles you will need to compensate by picking up an extra marble in the other hand (2 + 4 = 6). These principles are acquired very slowly. If you ask a 4-year-old 'Do you have a sister?' and she says 'Yes, her name is Sarah', you might ask her next 'Does Sarah have a sister?' and find she answers 'No'. As yet, the 4-year-old has not come to understand the principle of compensation.

Seriation is concerned with the ability to order objects according to a dimension such as length or thickness. A child's game of nesting boxes is a good example of seriation: each

CHAPTER 2 COGNITIVE DEVELOPMENT

FIGURE 2.6 This child has not yet understood that the amount of playdough does not vary with changes in its shape. What experiences might contribute to the development of such an understanding?

2.8 Sequence and age at which different conservation tasks are achieved

box must be fitted into the next by size so that at the end of the game all the boxes disappear inside the largest one. **Classification** occurs when objects are grouped together according to a criterion such as shape, colour, function or size. It includes, for example, the knowledge that dogs, cows and donkeys are all 'animals', and that stamps, envelopes, computers and words are all 'tools for communication'. Seriation and classification are among the most important achievements of the concrete operations stage. They develop late in this period and indicate that the child has developed 'logical operations', or the ability to apply logical reasoning to a problem-solving task such as that in Box 2.4.

classification
The ability to mentally group objects in terms of similar characteristics; for example, pansies, daffodils and roses are all 'flowers'

Box 2.4 RESEARCH LINKS

An example of Piaget's logical operations tasks

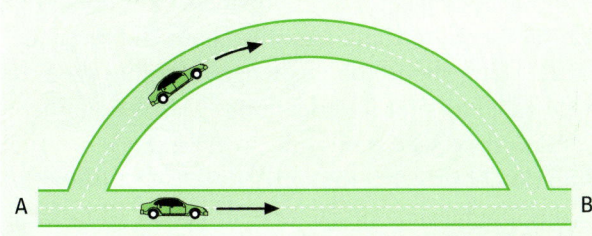

In this task, children are told: 'Two cars leave point A at the same time. They both arrive at point B at the same time but they travel by different routes.'

Research indicates that when asked 'what happened?', children at the preoperational stage think only about the point of arrival. At around 8 years of age they begin to think about the relationship between time and distance travelled. Children usually do not understand the concept of velocity (time/speed) until they are about 10 or 11 years old (Wadsworth, 1996).

Activities

1. Try this task with some children aged around 8 and 10 years.
2. Document and report your findings.
3. Do you get the same results as described here? If not, can you explain why?

2.9 More logical operations tasks: seriation and classification

One of the key aspects of classification is **class inclusion**, or the understanding that a number of small collections can be combined in different ways to form a larger collection. This is sometimes called 'multiple classification', such as occurs when a preoperational child recognises that something can be a flower *or* it can be a rose. 'Simultaneous multiple classification' occurs at the concrete operations stage and is demonstrated when a 5- or 6-year-old looks at his mother quizzically and asks 'Mummy, when you are at school being a

class inclusion
Understanding that a number of small collections can be combined in different ways to form a larger collection

teacher, are you still my mummy?' (WJF, personal communication, October 2001). You can try this yourself. Ask a 5-year-old 'How many boys are coming to your party?' The child may answer 'Eight.' Now ask the child 'How many girls?' and the reply might be 'Two.' 'Are there more boys or more girls?' 'More boys.' 'Will there be more boys or more children at your party?' The child is likely to reply 'More boys.' This last response is not related to the child not knowing what 'children' means, because if you ask the child a separate question, 'What are children?', the answer will be 'Children are boys and girls.' The problem is that the child is focused on only one dimension (in this case, the larger group 'boys') and does not understand there can be subgroups (that is, 'boys and girls') that can be combined into a bigger, single class (in this instance 'children').

At the concrete operations stage, children may seem to use words such as 'some' and 'all' appropriately, but their understanding of these terms is not yet fully consistent with adult usage. Once children realise that objects can be classified in terms of more than one dimension (that is, the children can solve a class-inclusion problem), they seem amazed if you ask questions such as 'Are there more boys or more children?', and can then respond very quickly to the question. Consider how much of our education system depends on this type of understanding: you can see why these cognitive skills are so important and why children need to master them.

The main limitation in children's thinking at the concrete operations stage of development is that their understanding of mental operations is restricted to concrete situations. They are concerned with the present and are not yet able to think hypothetically, in the abstract. However, their thinking is no longer dominated by what they see: they can now carry out tasks that require logical or mathematical reasoning; for instance, arranging objects in terms of a dimension such as length or weight (seriation), or grouping objects in terms of similar features such as shape or colour (classification).

Piaget's Stage 3 in education

The main characteristic of children at the concrete operations stage is their inability to think in abstractions, so one of their main needs is for teaching to be carried out in contexts that provide plenty of concrete experiences. Opportunities should be provided for students to experiment with materials, to test ideas and to begin to think logically about the problems they encounter. Students' current ways of thinking should be challenged, forcing them to extend and expand their existing knowledge as a basis for later learning. This is congruent with the constructivist principles of instruction discussed more fully in Chapter 5.

It is important to remember that children do not progress through the stages at the same rate in all areas of experience. Students do not achieve concrete operations on all tasks at the same time. Conservation of number is usually achieved before conservation of density and mass, and before the more complex concepts of time and speed (see Box 2.4 on page 49), but all are gradually attained within the concrete operations stage. Piaget referred to this as **horizontal decalage**. The term **vertical decalage** is used to refer to students who move from one stage to the next only in selected areas of their experience, such as in mathematics, science or music. For example, vertical decalage might occur in a 9-year-old girl who has been learning the violin very successfully for several years. Most of her thinking will be at the concrete operations level, but she may have reached the formal operations stage in music as a result of the advanced level of her studies. This effect can become apparent as students move into the stage of formal operations, with more abstract thinking being achieved gradually, and in areas where students have been exposed to more stimulating experiences (Sutherland, 1992, p. 24).

For educators, the most important aspect of the concrete operations stage is concerned with its upper limits and with students' transition to the next stage of formal operations. At this point, students are no longer dependent on concrete experiences to solve their

horizontal decalage
Gradual development within a cognitive stage, as demonstrated in the gradual attainment of the different aspects of conservation within the concrete operations stage

vertical decalage
Unevenness in cognitive development, as demonstrated by advanced development in one area compared to development in other areas

problems, and can begin to think hypothetically. There is evidence that not all adults reach the stage of formal operations (Keating, 1980; Neimark, 1981). This failure to progress can be an outcome of cultural and educational factors, as in contexts (for example) where there is little emphasis on the use of symbolic skills (Capon & Kuhn, 1979; Gardner, 1982). Piaget (1972) argued that educational experiences emphasising symbolic thought can promote the emergence of higher-order thinking skills. One of the tasks to be addressed by teachers and others working with students at the concrete operations level is therefore to provide experiences that will promote or stimulate more advanced ways of thinking.

It is also worth noting that there is controversy about the effectiveness of attempts to 'teach' children concepts such as the conservation of liquid or mass (Hutt, Tyler, Hutt, & Christopherson, 1990; Rutter & Rutter, 1992). Children cannot be moved onto a higher stage through instruction alone, but teachers can build on the skills and understandings that children have achieved, and in this way guide them towards more advanced ways of thinking (Sutherland, 1992; Wadsworth, 1996).

Stage 4: Formal operations period (11 or 12 years to adulthood)

The key characteristic of the **formal operations stage** is that the young person who has reached this level of cognitive development demonstrates a capacity to think – not just about concrete realities, but about abstract possibilities or 'an infinite number of imaginable realities' (Siegler, 1998, p. 43). The main developmental task for this stage is attainment of the capacity for abstract thought, and for propositional and hypothetical reasoning.

Adolescents are able to reason logically, speculate and hypothesise far more readily than concrete-operational children, who are more dependent on what they see, hear and experience. Adolescents no longer need a reference to real-life situations in order to do a task. Ideas can be formulated, tried out mentally and later tested in real-life situations. Reasoning is now **deductive reasoning**, meaning that rules or general principles are used to form hypotheses about possible solutions to specific problems, with these hypotheses then being tested to see if the predictions are true. This can be contrasted with **inductive reasoning**, or the ability to induce general principles or rules from knowledge of specific examples, then apply the rules to predict new instances (see the discussion of discovery learning in Chapter 5). Ideas about infinity, humanity, democracy or compassion can now be conceptualised. The key developmental milestones to be achieved in the period of formal-operational thinking are therefore:

- 'propositional thinking', or reasoning that is 'logical, abstract and systematic' (Wadsworth, 1996, p. 120)
- 'hypothetico-deductive reasoning', or the ability to form hypotheses and argue from them.

Not surprisingly, in view of his background in science, Piaget used mathematical and scientific-type tasks that involved propositional and hypothetico-deductive thinking in the studies he conducted into formal-operational thinking (Inhelder & Piaget, 1958). Examples of the logical reasoning tasks used include:

> Edith is fairer than Susan. Edith is darker than Lily. Who is the darkest?

and

> A > B and B > C. Is A > or < C?

Examples of the scientific-type tasks Piaget used with older children include a problem that involves a pendulum (see Box 2.5 over the page) and one that involves a colourless liquid (chemical combination). In the pendulum problem, students are asked to identify the variables that influence the rate of oscillation in a pendulum's swing. Is it the attached weight, the height from which the weight is released, the length of the string, the amount of pressure exerted to set the pendulum swinging, or some other factor that affects the

---

formal operations stage
Piaget's fourth stage, in which the individual is now able to think abstractly and logically, to form hypotheses and to solve problems systematically

deductive reasoning
Using rules or general principles to find general solutions to specific problems

inductive reasoning
Inducing general rules or principles from observation of specific examples

2.10 The meaning of 'form' in the word 'formal'

oscillation rate? Children at the concrete operations stage usually consider all possible factors at the same time and 'have great difficulty in excluding the weight factor' (Piaget & Inhelder, 1969, p. 148). Older children who have reached the formal stage in thinking are able to separate the factors and establish that the rate of the pendulum's swing reflects the length of the string and is unaffected by other factors (see Figure 2.7).

FIGURE 2.7 Students benefit from group work when completing activities such as the pendulum task. Piaget proposed that peer collaboration could provoke disequilibrium, as peers explain their own and challenge one another's ideas.

Box 2.5 RESEARCH LINKS

Examples of Piaget's formal operations tasks
The pendulum problem

A weight, suspended on the end of a string and then set in motion, acts as a pendulum. Children are provided with strings of varying lengths and different weights and asked to determine and explain what controls the pendulum's rate of movement and oscillation. Factors usually considered by the children are the length of the string, the weight at the end of the string, the height from which the weight is dropped to start the motion and the force or push in starting the pendulum in motion. The single factor that controls the rate of oscillation or movement of the pendulum is the length of the string. The problem is to isolate this factor from the other possible factors.

Source: Wadsworth (1996, pp. 116–117).

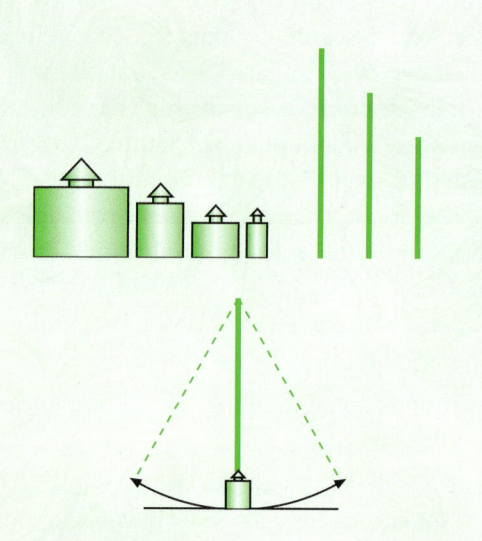

Activity

Present the pendulum problem to some students in the 11–18 age range. Try to find younger and older students, as you are then more likely to see different patterns of response.
1. Keep a record of what the students do and any explanations they give.
2. Do the students solve the problems in the way you expected?
3. Can you explain any unexpected outcomes?

2.11 A few more examples of formal operations tasks

In the chemical-combination problem, the child is presented with five jars, each containing a colourless liquid. A yellow colour is obtained when three of the liquids are combined. The child is shown the coloured liquid and asked to find the combination of liquids that produced it. The concrete-operational child usually works through combinations of two of the liquids, while the child who has reached formal operations methodically tests all possible combinations, eventually solving the problem (Inhelder & Piaget, 1958).

Solving problems such as that of the pendulum – which involves considering two or more variables – requires the ability to be systematic, to form hypotheses and to make deductions from findings. Many adults find such tasks exceedingly difficult. Even Piaget (1974) conceded that most people only reach a formal-operational level of thinking in the area of their greatest expertise. For many people it is much easier, or less challenging in a cognitive sense, to function at a concrete operations level. Interestingly, it has been suggested that Piaget's formal operations stage may not be the final stage of cognitive development. According to this view, adult thinking – when compared with the thinking of children and adolescents – is characterised by greater flexibility, and sensitivity to ambiguity and the impact of social, political and moral influences (Basseches, 1984; Labouvie-Vief, 1980; Lefrancois, 1997).

Piaget's Stage 4 in education

Teachers need to provide opportunities for more advanced students to be challenged cognitively, as in the curriculum areas of science and mathematics where students can be encouraged to find creative solutions to unusual problems that can later be tested in real-life contexts. Students can be grouped into teams to work on problems, with each team including students who think at both concrete- and formal-operational levels. This would allow the more advanced thinkers to challenge and stimulate the thinking of the less advanced students. Implementing the best plans would provide the 'formal' thinkers with opportunities to test their ideas in real-life situations, while also giving the more 'concrete' thinkers the opportunity to operationalise or work out their ideas in practical ways.

Opportunities for challenging students' thinking at both concrete and formal levels can be identified in most teaching situations. For example, the plot in one of Shakespeare's plays can be studied in terms of a sequence of events that follows logically from beginning to end. At the same time, attention can be directed to the more abstract themes that overlie the action: compassion, jealousy, pride, desire. Hypothetical situations can be identified from the plot, and a sequence of events identified as being possible had alternative actions been taken or different motives followed. Here, the main focus is to encourage and provide opportunities for students to begin to think abstractly about possibilities, divergent solutions and so on. These thinking patterns are most likely to be achieved in areas of activity in which students are 'experts'. Teachers at the secondary level who want to stimulate more advanced patterns of thinking in their students can begin by capturing students' interest and creating enthusiasm for the curriculum area in which they are working. Teachers cannot assume that all high school students are able to reason hypothetically, as would be expected if they had attained formal operations. Many will still reason at the level of concrete operations.

As children develop cognitively, what changes?

Piaget argued that across the age range *how* we think remains basically the same. We all eat, sleep and breathe in the same way at every age. So, too, the act of thinking remains the same for everyone, across all age groups. What changes, particularly during childhood and adolescence, is the *way* we organise our thoughts into what Piaget called 'schemes' (or 'schemas').

A **scheme** is an abstract concept or mental image – a cluster of ideas about a particular object or experience – that is used to organise existing knowledge and make sense of new experiences. The idea of a scheme as an organised collection of thoughts or ideas associated with a particular topic or experience is a useful device for thinking about how children accumulate information about specific aspects of their experience. It can be helpful in understanding their behaviour and in guiding our responses to them.

scheme
A mental image or cluster of related ideas used to organise existing knowledge and to make sense of new experiences

disequilibrium
Cognitive imbalance resulting from inconsistency between what is known and expected, and something strange and unexpected

adaptation
The process of adjusting to new situations and experiences through the modification of existing schemes (assimilation) or the creation of new schemes (accommodation)

assimilation
Adjusting an existing mental model or scheme to fit a new experience

accommodation
Using fresh information to form a new mental model or scheme

2.12 What do you do when you see or hear unfamiliar words?

How do children modify the schemes they have developed? Under what circumstances does such modification occur? The need for modification arises when children experience **disequilibrium**; that is, when an inconsistency arises between what is known and expected, and something strange, unexpected and new. This is where the process of **adaptation** takes place. Here, Piaget draws a parallel between the natural sciences and intellectual development: just as animals adapt to their environment, so too must human organisms respond to the unexpected and to new situations and experiences by modifying existing schemes and adapting to changing conditions.

Think about the following scenario: 3-year-old Gina uses the word 'bird' to refer to something flying in the air. It is one of the words most children learn fairly early. One day she sees a dragonfly and hesitates because it is different from other things she has seen flying in the air. It looks like a leaf. It looks like a ball flying through the air. However, although the dragonfly is different in a number of ways from a bird, it is closer to 'bird' than to any of Gina's other schema for flying things. So the dragonfly is fitted into the 'bird' schema, which gradually becomes more effective for detecting 'birdness' (WJF, personal communication, October 2001).

Piaget used the biological terms 'assimilation' and 'accommodation' to identify the two processes involved in adaptation. **Assimilation** refers to the adjustment of an existing scheme to fit a new experience. The account of Gina looking at a dragonfly and deciding it is a 'bird' is an example of seeing something new and adjusting an existing scheme to include it. It is an example of assimilation.

Aaron's word for anything that has four legs and walks around is 'dog'. One day he sees a horse. While a horse has four legs, it is quite different from a dog. The horse does not quite fit Aaron's existing scheme for 'dog', and he feels confused. Rather than just saying 'dog', he asks 'dog?' with rising intonation, looking at his father. Recognising Aaron's uncertainty, his father says 'No, not dog. Horse.' For the child, accepting this new information involves creating a new scheme for 'horse'. This is an example of **accommodation**, where new information is used to establish a new model or scheme. Aaron now has two schemes for four-legged animals: if the animal is not too big, it is 'dog'; if it is very big, it is 'horse'. This works well until Aaron goes to the zoo and encounters another four-legged animal such as an elephant or a giraffe, neither of which fits easily into the 'dog' or 'horse' schemes. Perhaps Aaron's father will help his son create more 'four-legged animal' schemes during their next visit to the zoo.

With more varied experiences, a child is able to refine existing schemes so that they fit more closely a specific class of objects (for example, dogs), while also establishing new schemes for novel instances that cannot be fitted into existing schemes. The concept map at the beginning of this chapter (see Figure 2.1 on page 38) illustrates the way in which individual cognition is structured by the interconnections between different schemes.

The process of adaptation, involving either assimilation or accommodation, occurs regularly in daily life, and with great frequency in the lives of young children. Another mental process – 'organisation' – is also under way, although we are not conscious of it happening. As new ideas and information are identified and processed mentally, we organise this material in terms of existing schemes, or create new schemes. This organisational process is essential so that we can store and later retrieve information.

There is one proviso – particularly relevant to education – that needs to be made when thinking about the organisational process involved in assimilation and accommodation. When we attend to new material (such as an unfamiliar insect or a maths formula) and the process of adaptation is about to be triggered, the concepts of 'readiness' and 'closeness of the match' become relevant. In teaching anything to a child, the new material must be close enough to what is already known by the child in order for a link to be made between old and new. If such a link is made, the process of either assimilation or accommodation can begin. The term 'readiness' is used to describe a child who has the prior knowledge or experiences needed to make a link between the known and the unknown. The phrase 'closeness of the match' (sometimes called 'goodness of fit') refers to the relative distance, in terms of the child's experience and understanding, between what is already known and new information. These concepts have important implications for those working with children.

The mental processes of adaptation and organisation described here continue throughout the lifespan, but they are most obvious in childhood because change occurs most rapidly during this period. This is why examples of these processes are largely taken from the childhood years, although these phenomena are also common in adults.

CRITICAL REFLECTIONS

- Think of your first few weeks of university. Did you have to develop new schemes in order to adapt to your new context?
- Can you identify examples of adaptation, assimilation and accommodation in your thinking in the past six months?

What influences development?

In the introduction to this first module, we defined development as a series of progressive and orderly changes leading to maturity; and maturation as genetically determined biological changes associated with growth over time. Piaget suggested that there are four main factors that work together to influence the development of children's thinking over the years from early childhood to adulthood. The first factor ('maturation') is innate or biological in origin, and is discussed in Chapter 1. The second factor ('activity') and third factor (**social interaction**, sometimes called **social transmission**) are associated with the physical and social world in which children develop. According to Piaget's perspective, children actively exploring their world are acting as 'miniature scientists', learning by experimenting through physical and mental activity. Social interaction is particularly important because children are interacting with their peers — that is, those who think in similar ways and who have had similar experiences, but who have a slightly different perspective that challenges the children's thinking and stimulates cognitive development. The fourth factor ('equilibration') is concerned with the way children respond to conflicts and inconsistencies between what they already know and what they experience in daily life.

The concept of equilibration, probably the most important influence that Piaget said drives cognitive development, can be traced to Piaget's background as a scientist. In the example of an infant seeing an elephant for the first time, the child's response might be to dismiss the huge animal as 'just another (very big) dog' (assimilation). Alternatively, the elephant might be accepted as totally unfamiliar, and a new scheme for 'elephant' created (accommodation). Either way, disequilibrium or cognitive discomfort is replaced by equilibrium.

Just as our physical body has to be in balance for us to function properly, Piaget claimed we also need to have cognitive or mental balance. When we encounter objects or events that are unfamiliar, our cognitive balance is upset. We become confused and uncertain about how to think or act. **Equilibration** is the process of seeking to restore the balance between what is familiar and known — or the child's existing cognitive system — and new information or the external world (Siegler, 1998). Balance is regained through the processes of assimilation and accommodation.

The notion of equilibration, or cognitive balance, is very important in Piaget's theory. He believed that the way in which a child interprets a new or unfamiliar experience will depend on two factors. One factor concerns information that is already available to the child, or

social interaction (social transmission)
The interactions with others (parents, peers, teachers etc.) that contribute to children's learning experiences

2.13 Early infant visual perception

equilibration
Achieving cognitive balance between what is familiar and known, and what is new or unfamiliar, through the processes of assimilation and accommodation

what is already known (that is, readiness). In the case of the elephant, the child may have already seen a huge dog or a picture of a very big animal that his father called 'elephant', so the experience is not totally unfamiliar. The other factor concerns the child's level of cognitive development, or stage of reasoning. According to Piaget, how you interpret something new or unfamiliar will depend on the particular stage of reasoning you have reached. Intuitively, parents, teachers and other carers come to recognise a child's stage of development from a very early age. For example, parents know that there is no point trying to teach a 3-year-old that the sun does not go to bed as they do when it disappears at night. At this stage, it is easier to accept the child's idea that the sun goes to bed at night and gets up in the morning. This is a matter of matching information given to children to their current level of understanding or reasoning.

Neo-Piagetians

Researchers such as Biggs (Biggs & Collis, 1982), Case and Okamoto (1996), Halford (1982) and Pascual-Leone (1970), who came to be known as **neo-Piagetians**, focused on explanations of cognitive development that were more concerned with children's information-processing capacity than with their logical competence. These researchers studied aspects of children's cognition – such as short-term and working memory, speed of information processing, and metacognitive processes – that were outside a Piagetian framework, and were more concerned with analysing the requirements of tasks used with children than with the children's logical structures. This approach was developed into a set of cognitive-based theories, which are reviewed in Chapter 5.

Overall, the neo-Piagetians retained many of Piaget's core ideas, but conceptualised children's thinking in terms of information-processing structures – that is, likening them to 'a computer that processes information', rather than seeing them as 'solitary scientists'.

Strengths and limitations of Piaget's ideas

Strengths

Piaget taught us to listen to children and to appreciate the intelligence they bring to the task of attempting to make sense of their world. Piaget was interested in how children think and how they come to understand concepts such as time, space, movement and self. The types of tasks and the procedures he used to collect data stimulated new ways of thinking about children's cognitive development. Probably Piaget's most important contributions to the study of child development concern the way we think about children and the methods we use to study them (Flavell, 1996; Siegler & Ellis, 1996). Piaget's focus on analysing the errors children make when they solve problems was also significant (see, for example, Gelman & Gallistel's 1978 work on children's understanding of number concepts).

Piaget viewed children's cognitive development as a gradual process of change, with new mental schemes emerging from pre-existing structures. This view has resulted in a general recognition by educators that it is the *stage* of development a child has reached that is important – not the age. The term 'developmentally appropriate education' is sometimes used to refer to this idea. The 'stage not age' concept, or the idea of matching instructional strategies to children's current level of understanding, means that teachers need to be aware of their students' level of reasoning, and plan accordingly. For example, younger students who still need concrete experiences in their learning need real objects, diagrams and the written word, not just verbal instruction. At the secondary level, teachers cannot assume that students are thinking hypothetically: adolescents may need considerable assistance not only to begin to reason at this level but also to reason at this level consistently.

One aspect of Piaget's theory that has not been challenged is the idea that children actively

---

neo-Piagetians Theorists who retained many of Piaget's ideas while conceptualising children's thinking in terms of information processing

2.14 A neo-Piagetian conservation task

2.15 Piaget's contribution to psychology

create their own learning (that is, the idea of the 'solitary scientist') and that direct experience is essential for such learning to occur. Constructivism, discovery learning, cooperative learning and other related approaches (see chapters 5 and 6) are extensions of this principle. Piaget's theory also reminds us that children's thinking is not the same as that of adults. It is both different and less efficient. Teachers need to be aware of the process of thinking, not just the outcome. It is not just a question of children getting a problem right or wrong, but how they do the task, the types of errors they make and the processes they use to reach an answer.

Limitations

Anyone who strives to develop a grand theory is likely to be criticised, and this is true of Piaget. The length of time that elapsed between his first publications in the area of children's cognitive development (in the 1920s) and his last (in 1981), the amount of data he collected and the very large number of his major publications make such criticism inevitable (Lourenco & Machado, 1996). While there was remarkable coherence in Piaget's work over these six decades (Brainerd, 1996), there was also variability as his ideas and research methods changed direction and new interpretations and emphases emerged (Beilin, 1992). However, much of the criticism that has been levelled at Piaget's theory has stimulated further research that in turn has expanded our understanding of how cognitive development occurs. In this sense, criticism can be seen to have had a positive effect on the field of educational psychology as a whole.

Ages and stages

One of the first criticisms often made of Piaget's theory concerns his ideas about the timing of children's attainment of developmental milestones within the different stages. For example, studies have shown that he overestimated what the average 12-year-old could do, and underestimated what the preoperational child could do. However, Piaget himself commented that the ages at which different stages are attained are highly variable, depending on the child's experiences and social environment (Piaget, 1972). The important issue here is the *sequence* of changes that occur in the way children think, rather than the ages at which such changes occur.

Stage concept

Doubts have been raised about Piaget's notion of stages. It is argued (see, for example, Bryant, 1974; Goswami, 1991; Rutter & Rutter, 1992; Siegler, 1998) that failure at a particular task, such as understanding analogies, may be more a matter of memory failure than lack of ability. Other variables that have been identified as contributing to performance on Piagetian tasks include the child's verbal ability, attention span, the type of language used by the adult during testing, and the complexity and/or familiarity of test materials (Miller, 1993). Questions have also been asked about the possibility of training children to function at a more advanced stage than they might reach without such training. While there is some evidence that this kind of training can be effective (see, for example, Beilin, 1978), it is also accepted that children who are given instruction with the intention of accelerating their level of cognitive functioning encounter much greater difficulties in achieving that goal than children who are left to progress at their own rate. Overall, while many studies have been reported that question aspects of Piaget's ideas, the underlying concept of developmental stages remains irrefutable. 'No amount of training will cause, say, a four-month-old to walk or talk, or a six-year-old to learn differential calculus' (Rutter & Rutter, 1992, p. 195).

Absence of skills

A related criticism concerns the very negative view of development that Piaget presented, particularly in relation to the thinking of young children, who are described in terms of what they *cannot* do, rather they what they can do. For example, Piaget saw the preoperational child as incapable of thinking logically and lacking any understanding of seriation, conservation, reversibility and so on. Here, his focus was on a transition from absence to presence of a particular type of understanding rather than on the quite remarkable cognitive capacity that the preoperational child has already achieved. In Piaget's defence, it is claimed he did not see children at the sensorimotor or preoperational stage as lacking specific abilities, but rather as being capable of certain types of understanding that are gradually transformed over time into new schemes or cognitive structures (Smith, 1993). That is, he did not see development at these stages as a progression from absence to presence of particular cognitive structures, but rather as a gradual progression towards cognitive competence.

Role of social context

Some critics of Piaget's theory claim that Piaget's explanation of cognitive development pays insufficient attention to the role of others or to the child's social environment. In fact, Piaget did acknowledge the contribution of social interaction with others to children's intellectual development. He was particularly interested in peer interaction as a means for children to expand their ideas, to overcome conflicts (disequilibrium) and to achieve shared solutions (equilibrium) that are more mature than individual efforts (Brown, Metz, & Campione, 1996). The place of peer interaction is particularly evident in Piaget's work on moral development (see Chapter 3). On the other hand, within a Piagetian-based curriculum, the role of the teacher is primarily concerned with assessing the level of children's thinking and providing appropriate experiences rather than teaching students directly.

Additional factors in development

Other limitations often attributed to Piaget's model, particularly by theorists interested in information-processing and motivation (see Chapter 7), are that he did not sufficiently take into account memory, motivation and emotion (that is, feelings or 'affect'). However, arguments can be made to counter this criticism. For example, Piaget perceived memory as part of the process whereby children create schemes to represent aspects of their experience, such as with the concept of a 'dog', and then reactivate these schemes when retrieving (remembering) information at their next encounter with a dog. Motivation is seen as an element in the process of disequilibrium, in that the experience of cognitive conflict motivates children to strive to resolve their uncertainty and to regain equilibrium. Cognitive development occurs as an outcome of this process. Emotions (feelings, or affect) contribute to development by influencing the selection of what is attended to. Children are most likely to become involved in an activity if their interest (and emotion) is roused.

Individual differences

Finally, criticisms of Piaget have included claims that he paid insufficient attention to individual differences among children; for example, differences in gender or cultural background, or the presence of a disability. Piaget did not report any differences in the way males and females develop intellectually (see, for example, Sutherland, 1992; Wadsworth, 1996). Dasen (1977) notes that Piaget never asserted that his theory had universal application, although it has been described as 'idiographic', meaning that it is concerned with the intensive psychological study of individual cases. In fact, Piaget's studies have been successfully replicated in many different contexts involving children with a range of disabling conditions and from a variety of cultural backgrounds. Studies using Piagetian tasks have been reported – particularly in the sensorimotor, preoperational and concrete operations stages – involving samples of children from many different cultural backgrounds (see, for example, Dasen, 1973; Goodnow, 1962). Piaget's associate, Barbel Inhelder, conducted research on reasoning in children with intellectual disabilities (Inhelder, 1968). Results have supported the contribution of cultural and environmental influences to cognitive development, and also to the need to focus on 'stage, not age'.

Box 2.6 contains some issues relevant to classroom applications of Piaget's ideas, as well as some suggestions for classroom activities derived from Piaget's theory of cognitive development.

Box 2.6 IMPLICATIONS FOR EDUCATORS

Applying Piaget's ideas in the classroom

Some of the issues relevant to classroom instruction that are highlighted by Piaget's theory (see also Table 2.2 below) include the need for teachers to:

- listen to children and observe what they do, in play and in other activities
- take into account the critical factors that influence children's cognitive development, including maturation or biologically based changes associated with growth; children's role as miniature scientists and the learning that results from their physical and mental activity; and children's interaction with adults and other children
- ensure that children maintain equilibration or cognitive balance between new experiences and what is already known, challenging their thinking by providing opportunities for them to find links between the unfamiliar and existing knowledge, which may involve creating new schemes or adjusting existing ones
- ensure that information given to children is close enough to their current level of understanding so that linkages can be made between the old and the new.

TABLE 2.2 Summary of Piaget's ideas for classroom application

Stage	Classroom activity	Example of activities
Sensorimotor (birth – 2 years)	Turn-taking; imitation of actions and sounds; appropriate play	• Play peekaboo; roll a ball or toy car back and forth; build a tower of three blocks and knock it over, saying 'uh-oh', child to do the same • Sit beside child in front of a mirror, imitate actions (smile, poke out tongue, touch nose); sing songs like 'Everybody do this' and 'Old MacDonald had a farm'; look at books together, naming objects and making appropriate sounds ('cow, duck, dog' or 'moo, quack, woof-woof') • Provide a variety of materials for play; model appropriate behaviour
Preoperational (2 years to 6 or 7 years)	Hands-on experiences that allow child to 'construct' own knowledge; group activities involving peers; variety of activities to encourage symbol development and language (early literacy and number)	• Provide practical experiences with a variety of concrete materials (sand, water, blocks; see free-play areas in early-childhood programs) • Keep in mind children's egocentrism; encourage activities that increase awareness of other's point of view, such as 'pretend' (imaginary) games; play turn-taking games such as lotto and board games • Sing nursery rhymes; play word games (I spy); read alphabet books; play rhyming and counting games; do sorting, matching, pattern-making and counting activities in play and during daily routines
Concrete operations 7 years to 11 or 12 years	Concrete experiences to allow for experimentation, for testing ideas, for beginning to think logically; situations that challenge existing ideas, create disequilibrium, expand vocabulary; opportunities to explore new areas, expand experience and develop a wider knowledge base; work in groups	• Provide concrete resources to support learning • Provide opportunities for problem-solving and logical thinking using a variety of materials • Encourage students to discuss problems, share ideas, identify possible solutions, plan alternatives, implement plans and revise, finding solutions as needed (e.g. make a matchstick bridge to cross a gorge) • Encourage group work, with students challenging each other's ideas; give a range of experiences to expand knowledge base and vocabulary
Formal operations 12 years to adulthood	Think hypothetico-deductively; understand and appreciate irony, satire, fantasy and paradox	• Provide opportunities for students to extend their knowledge and ideas, challenge current assumptions, express their ideas in written forms through a variety of different genres (including poetry and prose) and express their ideas orally by engaging in discussions and debates on hypothetical and theoretical topics

Vygotsky's sociocultural theory

2.16 Links between Piaget and Vygotsky

Lev Semanovich Vygotsky (see Box 2.7) was a contemporary of Piaget's for a short period, from when Piaget began publishing in 1920 to Vygotsky's death in 1934. Vygotsky was certainly aware of Piaget's work, and read some of his books. In Vygotsky's first collection of writings (*Thought and language*, 1934), he criticised some aspects of Piaget's theory, such as Piaget's concept of egocentrism and in particular egocentric language.

Box 2.7 — ABOUT LEV SEMANOVICH VYGOTSKY

Lev Semanovich Vygotsky (1896–1934) was born into an intellectual Russian-Jewish family that lived within the restricted territory (the Pale) in the southern Byelorussian town of Gomel, close to the Ukrainian border (Dixon-Krauss, 1996). His father was a bank manager and his mother was a teacher. Lev was the second-born of eight children.

Intellectually gifted and with an extraordinary memory, Vygotsky was educated at home and, at the secondary level, at the local gymnasium (a European secondary school that prepares students for university). As a Jew, his access to education was severely restricted; there were strict limits on the number of Jews who could undertake university studies (Bodrova & Leong, 1996). However, Vygotsky won a place at the University of Moscow in 1913, receiving a degree in law, with a specialisation in literature, in 1917. He was widely read in literature, poetry and the arts (Miller, 1993).

Returning to Byelorussia after his graduation, Vygotsky taught a range of subjects to adults and children, including language and literature, logic and psychology, and art history and theatre (Dixon-Krauss, 1996, p. 2). He also became interested in children with learning difficulties and intellectual disabilities, and established several research clinics that conducted research into the problems of such children. He was particularly interested in devising ways to assess children's intellectual abilities and to evaluate the efficacy of intervention strategies (Wertsch, 1985).

In 1924 Vygotsky was invited to join the Institute of Psychology in Moscow. He moved there with his family and began a collaboration with two other Russian psychologists, Alexander Luria (1902–1977) and Alexei Leontiev (1903–1979). Together, they developed a 'cultural-historical' or 'sociohistorical' view of human development that emphasised cognitive activities such as thinking, memory and reasoning (Miller, 1993). The three worked together until Vygotsky's death in 1934. Political pressures in the Soviet Union at that time resulted in Vygotsky's work being banned from 1936 to 1956 (Miller, 1993). By the 1960s, when Piaget's theory was becoming more widely known in the West, interest in Vygotsky's work and access to his writings outside Russia began to increase. An English translation of *Thought and language* was published in 1962, and the first of six volumes of Vygotsky's collected writings appeared 15 years later (Miller, 1993).

FIGURE 2.8 Vygotsky emphasised the social nature of children's learning and the contribution of social interaction to this process.

In many ways there was significant overlap between Piaget's and Vygotsky's work, but there were also major differences in their ideas, which reflected, in part, the differences in their social and cultural backgrounds. Piaget focused on the individual, paying little attention to the social environment. In contrast, and largely as a result of the social and political system operating at that time in the Soviet Union, Vygotsky's concern was with learning and development occurring within a sociohistorical and sociocultural context. This orientation was an outcome of the particular society, period of history and culture in which he worked.

Vygotsky argued very strongly that the child and the environment interact to mould cognition in culturally appropriate ways. This view is evident in the themes that distinguish Vygotsky's ideas, including the sociocultural and sociohistorical origins of cognitive development, language as a mental tool, the role of private speech, and the 'zone of proximal development'.

Sociocultural origins of cognitive development

Vygotsky's ideas about the way in which our social, cultural and historical background and experiences shape cognition are demonstrated in descriptions of children's behaviour in early infancy (see, for example, Bruner, 1975; Kaye, 1982; Lock, 1978). According to Vygotsky, infants are born with an inherited capacity for specific patterns of action. They have also had prenatal experiences. But from the time of birth, their task is to acquire a sequence of skills and competencies that are uniquely human, with language being probably the most important of these skills. This acquisition, or learning, is achieved through social interaction. As carers interact with infants, they unconsciously structure the baby's experiences in ways that reflect the carers' own social, cultural and historical background.

Vygotsky described humans' mental abilities as:

- 'lower mental functions' (meaning inherited, involuntary capacities such as vision, hearing and taste) that are controlled by external objects and events
- 'higher mental functions' (meaning those developed through social interaction, including logical and abstract thinking, and language) that operate internally (that is, 'in the head') and are used to control lower mental functions, to think and to solve problems concerning external objects and events.

In reviewing Vygotsky's ideas about adults' role in structuring infant cognitive development, Lock, Service, Brito and Chandler (1989) highlight his notion that the developmental process is primarily concerned with the infant gaining control over lower mental functions, such as hearing and vision, that are present at birth. A child has to learn which stimuli, among the myriad of stimuli in the environment, are considered (by carers) to be important and should be attended to. For example, Dad points to Mum getting into the car and says 'Wave goodbye to Mum', but the baby finds Dad's eyes much more interesting to look at and to touch. Dad turns the baby's head towards Mum, points and says 'Look!' Vygotsky argued that children learn to control lower mental functions and begin to acquire higher-level functions through such interactive experiences.

In their 'peekaboo' study, Bruner and Sherwood (1975) gave a fine example of the emergence of early communicative behaviour in mother–infant pairs. They cited data from observation of one mother–infant pair who were seen, over a period of time, to play peekaboo twenty-two times, the first time when the baby was 10 months of age, and the last when the baby was aged 15 months. The game always began with face-to-face contact between mother and child, and sometimes included a vocalisation by the mother to attract the child's attention. The mother initiated almost all of the episodes observed (19 out of 22), her face being hidden almost as often as the child's face was hidden. In the few instances when the game was initiated by the child, her face was hidden, not the mother's face. Peekaboo is a good example of the 'social-structuring' process described by Vygotsky. Here, the helpless newborn is gradually transformed, through recurring interactive experiences with familiar partners, from passive respondent to active participant, with increasing control of cognitive functions. The skills learned have been internalised. Note that in thinking about these exchanges, Vygotsky recognised that what is passed from adult to child includes aspects of current and past experience, knowledge, attitudes, and the beliefs and values of the child's social group, as represented by the carer. This explains the use of both 'sociocultural' and 'sociohistorical' to refer to Vygotsky's model.

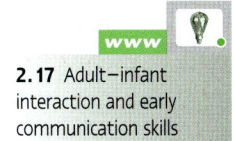

2.17 Adult–infant interaction and early communication skills

2.18 More about the Peekaboo study

Language as a mental tool

In thinking about Vygotsky's assertion that cognitive development is an outcome of interaction between human infants and their carers, his ideas about language and other cognitive skills being psychological tools (Bodrova & Leong, 1996) begin to emerge. The mental tools passed from adults and peers to children during social interaction include language, but these tools also include 'various systems for counting; mnemonic techniques; algebraic symbol systems; works of art; writing; schemes, diagrams, maps, and mechanical drawings; all sorts of conventional signs, and so on' (Vygotsky, 1981, p.137; cited by Cole & Wertsch, 2000).

If Vygotsky had lived into the 21st century, he would no doubt have included telephones, typewriters, word-processors and computers on his list of mental tools. Computers exemplify the way in which a mental tool can shape thinking (see Chapter 10). Miller (1993) used the invention of and access to paper to illustrate changes in the mental tools needed by children growing up in earlier centuries or in more primitive societies with oral rather than written traditions. A similar example can be found in the impact of maps and other technologies on navigation at sea. The southern continents of Australia and New Zealand were located by navigators such as Captain James Cook using primitive charts, a compass and a sextant. In contrast, the island of Tahiti had earlier been located by people from the Hawaiian Islands travelling in large canoes, their navigators reading the waves, stars, the flight of birds, and charts made of sticks and knotted twine (Lewis, 1972) (see Figure 2.9). In the 21st century, these earlier methods appear very primitive. Navigators now work with computers and satellite technology to plan their routes. Imagine how varied the mental maps of the Pacific Ocean would be for these different groups of navigators. These examples illustrate Vygotsky's claim that the mental tools acquired by individuals are the product of their social, cultural and historical background. One of the responsibilities of adults, including parents and teachers, is therefore to give children the mental tools or cognitive strategies they will need to function effectively and independently within their own cultural and social environment.

For Vygotsky, language is the most important mental tool. Initially, it has a social function, providing a means for interacting with others. However, as children's language skills increase, it begins to serve an intellectual function, as a tool for problem solving and self-regulation. The change is reflected in a shift from reliance on external devices for solving problems (for example, counting on fingers or tying a knot in a handkerchief to remember something) to speech that is 'internalised' (that is, 'in the head'), or **private speech**. With very young children, self-instructional language – egocentric speech, in Piaget's terms – is

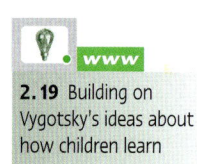

2.19 Building on Vygotsky's ideas about how children learn

private speech
Silent speech used by adults to guide their thinking and actions

FIGURE 2.9   Could modern seamen navigate using the methods employed by these people in seagoing canoes?

often spoken out loud. Piaget thought this self-talk was just a primitive way of using language, since it drops out as children develop. But Vygotsky thought such language was actually helping children to think. He used tasks with increasing levels of difficulty to explore the use of self-talk (see Box 2.8), finding that as thinking became more sophisticated, this type of speech ceased or the children became silent (see also the discussion of verbal self-instruction in Chapter 4).

Box 2.8 RESEARCH LINKS

An example of self-talk reported by Vygotsky

In one of our experiments, a child of five-and-a-half was drawing a picture of a tram. While drawing a line that would represent a wheel, the child put too much pressure on the pencil and the lead broke. The child attempted, nonetheless, to complete the circle by pressing the pencil to the paper. But nothing appeared on the paper other than the imprint of the broken pencil. As if to himself, the child quietly said, 'Broken.' Laying the pencil aside, he took a paint brush and began to draw a broken tram car that was in the process of being repaired after an accident, continuing to talk to himself from time to time about the new subject of his drawing. This egocentric utterance is clearly linked to the whole course of the child's activity. It constitutes a turning point in his drawing and clearly indicates his conscious reflection on the situation and his attendant difficulties. It is so clearly fused with the normal process of thinking that it is impossible to view it as a simple accompaniment of that thinking.

Source: Vygotsky (1987, p. 70; cited by Newman & Holzman, 1993, p. 116).

Activities

1. Sit quietly beside a 4- to 5-year-old who is engaged in a practical activity such as drawing and painting, or building in a sandpit or with blocks.
2. Listen for any self-talk. Keep a note of what the child says and does.
3. Think about what was happening as the child talked. Is the language simply an accompaniment to the activity, or is it more closely involved in the child's thought processes?

Vygotsky suggested that private speech has an intellectual function, being an important tool for structuring intellectual activity. Children often model (or replicate) the process of moving from external language to inner speech when they learn to read. In the early stages, printed symbols are recognised and sounded aloud, initially in a social context such as a classroom, or with a tutor. As word-recognition skills increase, the reader becomes more confident and the need for social support diminishes. Reading aloud is replaced by 'mumble reading' (Dixon-Krauss, 1996, p. 11), and then by silent reading. The shift from dependence on external and social processes to internalised (or purely mental) functioning has been achieved. Reading has become a tool for use in intellectual activities.

CRITICAL REFLECTION

- How can teachers support students' use of private speech in the classroom?

Zone of proximal development

In thinking about the social context in which children learn, Vygotsky identified what he called the **zone of proximal development**, or the distance between what children can do by themselves and what they can do with others. Think about this. If you give a series of

zone of proximal development
The distance between children's current level of competence on a task and the level they can achieve with support or guidance

tasks to two children and they perform at the level of the average 8-year-old, most people would say the children were performing at the same level. This represents their unassisted level, or what they can do by themselves. Now, imagine a situation where you give both children the same amount of assistance to do the task. You might give a series of hints or prompts, or structure the task to make it easier – such as setting out the materials in the order they should be used, or simplifying the instructions. After getting this help, one child performs like a 12-year-old and the other like a 9-year-old. Given this outcome, can you claim that the two children are at the same level? Vygotsky argued that what differs between the two children is their zone of proximal development. One child is able to benefit much more from your assistance than the other. The one who progresses further is in some way more advanced in relation to the required area of knowledge than the other child. ==This difference between what children can do by themselves and what they can do with the help of others is very important, and gives educators and other experts a significant role in assisting learners to progress== (see Figure 2.10).

CRITICAL REFLECTIONS

- Identify the people who have had the most impact on your learning. Why do they stand out in your memory?
- What were some of the methods they used?

FIGURE 2.10 In Vygotsky's view, adults play important roles in the development of children's thinking. What are some of the contributions this mother might be making as she helps her daughter do her homework?

Vygotsky argued very strongly that it is in interaction with others that we learn how to think. A study that explored this issue (Wertsch, McNamee, McLane, & Budwig, 1980, p. 1219) looked at how mothers interacted with their 3-year-old when the child was presented with a simple shape-puzzle. The researchers found that mothers structured the task, giving assistance rather than just letting the child do it randomly. The type of assistance given is important. A mother would direct attention to relevant pieces:

'Look, what are you trying to make?'
'It's a truck.'
'What part of the truck would be easy to find?'
'A wheel.'
'So, what is a wheel?'
'Round.'

The mother would then point to a wheel piece. What is happening here? The mothers are **scaffolding** the task (Wood, Bruner, & Ross, 1976): breaking it into small parts, directing the child's attention and giving strategies to solve the problem. The more expert person in the relationship – the mother – is giving lessons in 'how' to learn. Her directions are not just concerned with how to do this particular little task. Rather, she gives general lessons, directing attention to whole–part relationships or finding small pieces to make up a whole, and so on. Educational terms associated with this type of learning are 'active learning', 'assisted learning', 'reciprocal teaching' and 'assisted discovery' (see Chapter 5).

A similar situation as that in the previous example occurs when a child cannot remember where some homework has been put, and the child's mother says: 'Where did you last have it? Was it in your school bag? Did you put it on the table? Did you leave it at school?' After a number of such suggestions, the child will say: 'I remember: I left it in my desk at school.' What is happening here? Who does the remembering? To begin with, the mother does not know where the homework is, and the child cannot remember; but between them they co-construct the memory and find out where the homework was left. This is an example of what Vygotsky meant when he said thinking can actually be a social activity. This is quite different from Piaget's ideas about the child as 'solitary scientist'. It also suggests a more active role for educators and teachers.

> **scaffolding**
> The support provided to learners to enable a task to be done successfully and a student to work more independently

2.20 Alternative strategies for scaffolding learning in a classroom

---

CRITICAL REFLECTION

- Can you describe an example of scaffolding in your own learning? You might like to think back to the time you were first learning to write an essay or doing a science experiment. Think about questions and hints given by the teacher, or perhaps the way the task was presented.

Strengths and limitations of Vygotsky's theory

Strengths

One of the most interesting of Vygotsky's ideas is that cognitive development is essentially a social process. Ways of thinking and acting are first acquired through social interaction and then gradually internalised, or processed silently in the mind, so that learning proceeds from the 'outside in' (Lutz & Sternberg, 1999, p. 292). Vygotsky's focus on the social nature of children's learning, and the extent to which social experiences structure the way children think – and in particular the meaning they attribute to language concepts – is one of the most influential of his ideas for psychology and education (Duveen, 1997; Wells, 2000).

Vygotsky's work underpins much of the group work and interactivity that is characteristic of learning spaces in the 21st century (see Chapter 6). Thus it may be said that one of the key strengths of his approach to cognitive development is its wide-ranging applicability to learning and teaching, particularly in classrooms with a diverse social and cultural mix. These advantages are highlighted in chapters 5 and 6, where we discuss practical applications of Vygotsky's ideas.

Limitations

As with Piaget, criticisms of Vygotsky's ideas are frequently associated with the vagueness or very general terms in which the ideas are expressed (Miller, 1993). This can lead to problems when practitioners attempt to apply them. Some of the problems associated with Vygotsky's concept of the zone of proximal development concern the vagueness of the concepts involved. For example, is the width of a child's zone the same across all areas of learning? Does it vary at different times of the day, with different levels of motivation in the child or the partner in a tutoring situation? Is it generally stable? Is it wider if a child is unfamiliar with a particular curriculum area or tutor, and narrower if the child has already received some help or is familiar with the tutor? Is there always a gap between what a child can do alone and what can be done with assistance? Commenting on the concept of the zone of proximal development, Bryant (1990) suggested there is no direct evidence to prove that children's cognitive skills develop as a result of help from a parent or tutor.

There are also questions about the relevance of Vygotsky's ideas – developed in 1920s and 1930s Soviet Russia in the context of Marxist-Leninist ideology – for Western education systems in the 21st century (Lambert & Clyde, 2000). Other criticisms concern Vygotsky's failure to acknowledge the role of developmental influences (such as physical maturation), and his overemphasis on the role of language in intellectual development.

You will notice that this critique of Vygotsky's work is much briefer than that of Piaget's work. One reason for this is that Vygotsky's views of cognitive development were not developed as extensively as Piaget's stage theory; nevertheless, Vygotsky's ideas offer a very useful, socially oriented perspective on cognitive development (see Box 2.9) that complements Piaget's individualistic model.

Box 2.9 IMPLICATIONS FOR EDUCATORS

Applying Vygotsky's ideas in the classroom

In interpreting Vygotsky's ideas for classroom application, teachers need to do the following:
- In assessment, take account of what children can do independently and also what they can do with assistance or social support. This is sometimes referred to as 'dynamic assessment' (see Beasley & Shayer, 1990; Feuerstein, Rand, & Hoffman, 1979) (see also Chapter 11), and is linked to the notion of 'readiness'.
- Focus instruction not on what children can already do independently (they will become bored very quickly), but on tasks that are within the zone of proximal development or the range that children can achieve with some assistance from a more advanced partner.
- Centre instruction at the point between what the child can do without support and what can be achieved with assistance from an adult, a more advanced peer or even an interactive computer program (see Chapter 10) (Renshaw, 1998).
- Recognise that Vygotsky's approach potentially assists all learners, but is possibly most appropriate for children experiencing problems resulting from learning difficulties or intellectual disabilities, on the grounds that much of Vygotsky's work was in the area of 'defectology or mental abnormality' (Lambert & Clyde, 2000, p. 26) (see Chapter 8).
- Take advantage of existing strengths, 'amplifying' these while also working with behaviours that are on the edge of emergence (Zaporozhets, 1986, as cited by Bodrova & Leong, 1996, p. 42).
- Structure tasks by breaking them into manageable parts, repeating instructions, limiting the number of components presented at one time or providing appropriate resources (Rogoff, 1990). This is sometimes called 'guided participation'.
- Create a 'construction zone' where the teacher is aware of the goal, what the child understands and what is expected to be achieved, while the child must struggle to identify what the adult wants to be done (Newman, Griffin, & Cole, 1989).

Linking Piaget and Vygotsky

Shayer (1997) provides an example of a research project in which the ideas of both Piaget and Vygotsky were used in a school program to promote formal-operational thinking in 12- to 14-year-olds in the areas of science and mathematics. The aim of the study was to ensure that students reached formal operations during secondary school, this level of cognitive functioning being a prerequisite for success in science at the major examinations held at the end of Year 9. To achieve this goal, a set of Piagetian-type activities was devised and implemented over a 2-year period, using a Vygotskian framework that included a combination of discussion and individual work. Results suggested that the program was successful in increasing the achievement level of the students involved – not only in the target curriculum area, but also more generally (Shayer, 1997).

A further significant application of Vygotskian theory is the recognition of the role social interaction plays in promoting cognitive development. Social interaction may occur in various forms in the classroom. ==Using group work and encouraging children to learn from each other in pairs within larger groups is one application of Vygotsky's theory.== Social interaction in productive, carefully organised groups can promote cognitive development, while group work allows students to use language as a tool for learning and for scaffolding the learning of others. It also allows students to experience 'cognitive apprenticeship' (Roth & Bowen, 1995) – a related application of group work that recognises the value of social interaction in the use of 'experts' to scaffold novices' learning in the classroom. In the early years, this process occurs at home, where parents and family members – the 'experts' – communicate with and scaffold the infant's or novice's cognitive development. In the school context this can continue when parents and community helpers are invited into the classroom to assist teachers and to work with individuals or small groups to develop skills such as reading. In a multicultural classroom it is particularly helpful if these 'expert' assistants represent a range of multicultural backgrounds, as this helps to recognise and validate the contribution of individuals from a range of cultures within the sociocultural context (see Figure 2.11). Chapters 5 and 6 of this book expand on the use of group work in teaching and learning.

2.21 Case study of a maths lesson using Piagetian and Vygotskian principles

FIGURE 2.11 Many different 'experts' can contribute to classroom programs.

Concluding comments

Probably the most important contribution that Vygotsky and Piaget made to understanding how children's thinking develops is not in their theoretical models of cognitive development, but in the questions they raised and in the research stimulated by their ideas about how children think and why children behave as they do. Piaget and Vygotsky's influence on teachers' ideas about instruction has also been profound. In particular, the two theorists highlighted the need for teachers to observe children carefully, to match learning experiences to level of cognitive development and to recognise the contribution to the learning process of factors within the learner's social and physical environment.

Chapter review

- Cognitive development is concerned with how our capacity to think, reason and remember develops over time.
- Two of the most influential theorists in the area of cognitive development are Piaget and Vygotsky. Piaget viewed the child as a 'little scientist', whereas Vygotsky saw cognitive development as occurring within a social context that is framed by the child's social, cultural and historical background.
- Piaget identified four universal and invariant stages of cognitive development: the sensorimotor stage (birth to 2 years), the preoperational stage (approximately 2 years to 6 or 7 years), the concrete operations stage (approximately 7 years to 11 or 12 years), and formal operations (approximately 11 or 12 years to adulthood).
- Piaget identified four factors that together influence the development of children's thinking from early childhood to adulthood, these being maturation, activity, social interaction and equilibration.
- Neo-Piagetians' work arose out of criticisms of Piaget's ideas and methods. Neo-Piagetians have extended Piaget's theory with an information processing framework while retaining many of his core ideas.
- The strengths of Piaget's ideas concern his focus on children's thinking, the questions he raised and the research methods he pioneered in this field of study. Doubts have been raised about Piaget's notion of stages, particularly in terms of his failure to take into account the impact of contextual factors on children's performance of his tasks.
- Vygotsky was interested in the way in which our social, cultural and historical background shapes our thinking. He argued that infants and children interact from birth with carers, who scaffold the child's experiences in ways that reflect the carer's own background.
- Vygotsky saw language as a mental tool that can be used to control intellectual activity. Initially its function is social, but it is gradually internalised as inner or private speech and is used for self-regulation.
- Vygotsky identified the zone of proximal development as the distance between what a child can do alone, without help, and what the child can do with assistance from a more experienced partner.
- The notion of dynamic assessment reflects an approach to assessment that focuses on identifying what a child can do with and without help, leading to instruction that can take the form of assisted learning, reciprocal teaching and assisted discovery.

You make the connections:
Questions and activities for self-assessment and discussion

1. Define Piaget's concept of 'scheme' and give an example of how a scheme develops.
2. According to Piaget, what are the four main factors that influence development?
3. Compare and contrast the ideas of Piaget and Vygotsky concerning the role of social interaction in children's development.
4. What are the main implications of Piaget's work for teachers and others working with children across the years prior to school and through to adulthood?
5. Discuss the implications of Vygotsky's ideas for assessment and instruction.
6. Both Piaget and Vygotsky began writing in the 1920s. How relevant are their ideas for the 21st century? Which aspects of their ideas should be abandoned and which retained? Why?

2.22 More activities for you to do

Key terms

cognition	concrete operations stage	inductive reasoning
sensorimotor stage	conservation	scheme
object permanence	reversibility	adaptation
goal-directed or intentional action	compensation	assimilation
deferred imitation	seriation	accommodation
operations	classification	social interaction (social transmission)
preoperational stage	class inclusion	equilibration
symbolic thought	horizontal decalage	private speech
egocentrism	vertical decalage	zone of proximal development
centration	formal operations stage	scaffolding
	deductive reasoning	

Recommended reading

Bodrova, E., & Leong, D. J. (1996). *Tools of the mind: The Vygotskian approach to early childhood education.* Englewood Cliffs, NJ: Prentice-Hall.

Dixon-Krauss, L. (Ed.) (1996). *Vygotsky in the classroom: Mediated literacy instruction and assessment* (pp. 7-24). White Plains, NY: Longman.

Miller, P. H. (1993). *Theories of developmental psychology* (3rd ed.). New York: W. H. Freeman.

Newman, F., & Holzman, L. (1993). *Lev Vygotsky: Revolutionary scientist.* London: Routledge.

Siegler, R. S. (1998). *Children's thinking* (3rd ed.). Upper Saddle River, NJ: Prentice-Hall.

Singer, D. S., & Revenson, T. A. (1996). *A Piaget primer: How a child thinks* (Rev.). New York: Penguin.

Sutherland, P. (1992). *Cognitive development today: Piaget and his critics.* London: Paul Chapman.

Wadsworth, B. J. (1996). *Piaget's theory of cognitive and affective development* (5th ed.). White Plains, NY: Longman.

Make some online visits

Search on the World Wide Web and databases such as ERIC and the Australian Education Index (AEI) using terms like 'Piaget', 'neo-Piagetians', 'Vygotsky' and 'cognitive development'.

FIGURE 3.1 Chapter 3 concept map.

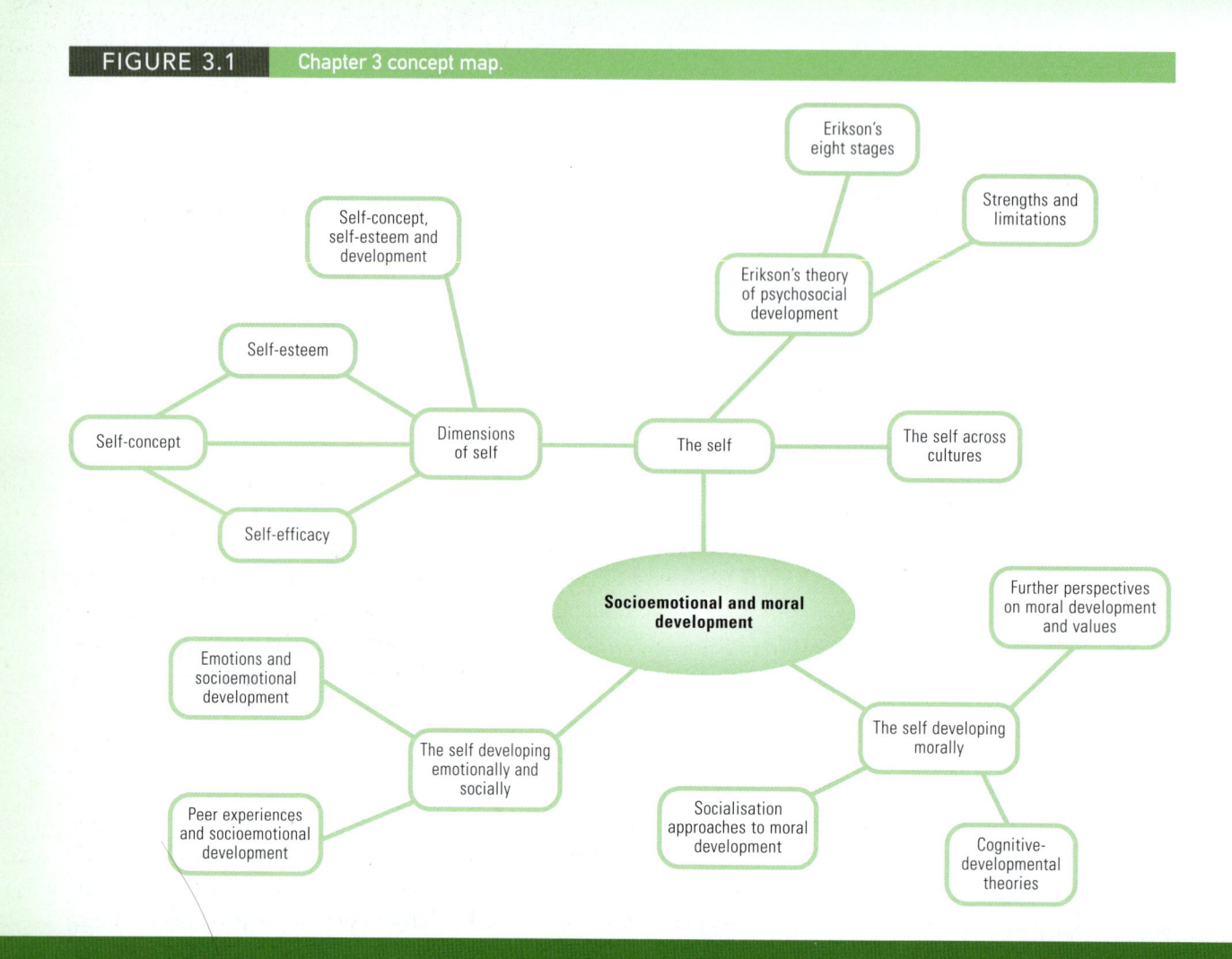

- Socioemotional and moral development
  - The self
    - Dimensions of self
      - Self-concept, self-esteem and development
      - Self-esteem
      - Self-concept
      - Self-efficacy
    - Erikson's theory of psychosocial development
      - Erikson's eight stages
      - Strengths and limitations
    - The self across cultures
  - The self developing emotionally and socially
    - Emotions and socioemotional development
    - Peer experiences and socioemotional development
  - The self developing morally
    - Further perspectives on moral development and values
    - Socialisation approaches to moral development
    - Cognitive-developmental theories

CHAPTER OBJECTIVES

After reading this chapter you should be able to:

- explain from a psychosocial perspective how the self develops over time
- distinguish between self-concept, self-esteem and self-efficacy, and discuss their role in learning
- describe the role of peer experiences in socioemotional development
- discuss the differences between socialisation approaches to moral development, and cognitive developmental views
- comment on the role of values in 21st century learning and teaching.

CHAPTER 3

Socioemotional and moral development

Introduction

Our view of self is closely connected to our emotional development, our relationships with others, and our values and moral judgements. This chapter is concerned with personal development. It focuses on the gradual emergence of concepts of self, and looks at Erik Erikson's theory of psychosocial development as a framework for understanding identity development, particularly in adolescence. This chapter also explores issues associated with socioemotional development, the role of peer relationships, the moral dimensions of self and the development of values in sociocultural contexts such as classrooms.

Defining the self

self
Who we are, what makes us unique and who we believe ourselves to be

The way you stand, your haircut, the clothes you wear, the way you decorate your room – all are expressions of your 'self'. They are a way of saying: 'This is who I am!' The **self** differentiates each person as a unique individual and separates us from one another. It lies at the core of who we are. According to Gordon Allport, one of the early researchers in the area, the self is that 'central, private region of our life' (1961, p. 110). It is who we are as individuals – what makes us unique and who we believe ourselves to be. The word 'self' is most commonly attached to other words, as in 'self-concept', 'self-esteem', 'self-control' or 'self-help'. A common view is that the self is not a single entity: rather, we are made up of many 'selves' and dimensions (Barrett, 2000; Fogel, 1995). These dimensions of self become more complex as we develop and interact with the world over time.

Dimensions of the developing self

Do our views of the self have a role to play in development? How are beliefs about the self linked to our thoughts, feelings and actions? Here we focus on three dimensions of self – self-concept, self-esteem and self-efficacy – and their role in learning and teaching.

Self-concept

A concept is an abstract cognitive structure. It is abstract because while it exists in our thinking it is not a concrete reality. A concept helps us categorise and group information or ideas on similar topics. **Self-concept** refers to the collection of knowledge, ideas, attitudes and beliefs we have about ourselves. It is formed through interaction with our environment and the people in it. Self-concept is particularly influenced by how significant others evaluate us (Marsh, 1990). It has no concrete reality but it plays an important part in our thoughts and feelings about ourselves.

Contemporary research generally confirms that our self-concept is multidimensional, or multifaceted (Byrne, 1996; Marsh, Craven, & Debus, 2000; Shavelson, Hubner, & Stanton, 1976). Self-concept is like a filing cabinet with many drawers, and many folders within those drawers. We each have a single self-concept – a filing cabinet for all the information we have about ourselves – but within it we develop categories of information, these being attitudes and feelings about different parts of ourselves. Information is filed away within each of the categories as we develop a 'self' in a variety of contexts. As we file information and develop more dimensions of self, the self-concept becomes more differentiated, with increasing dimensions and parts. For example, in the family setting we may conceive of ourselves as an obedient son or daughter; in a social setting we may be the 'life of the party'; in university tutorials we may contribute well to discussions or be rather quiet observers; and in the classroom with our students we may be firm but compassionate. These different dimensions of self may vary from setting to setting and will also be influenced by factors such as age, race and gender (Crain, 1996).

Figure 3.2 (see opposite page) illustrates several aspects of self-concept that can be divided into three main categories: general (or global), academic and non-academic. 'General (or global) self-concept' refers to the broad characteristics of the self, such as self-confidence and self-assertiveness. These are overarching views of the self that filter down to the self-concept in the academic and non-academic domains (Marsh, 1993). The global self-concept is not directly linked to a specific curriculum area at school.

'Academic self-concept', on the other hand, is derived from views of personal achievements in curriculum areas such as mathematics and reading (see Figure 3.2). Later revisions of this model include academic areas such as economics, foreign languages and the arts (Marsh, Byrne, & Shavelson, 1988; Vispoel, 1995; see also Byrne & Gavin, 1996). Academic achievement and perceptions of self are closely related (Hay, 1997; Marsh, 1992; Marsh, Kong, & Hau, 2000; Marsh & Yeung, 1998). Students develop their academic self-concept in two ways: first, through social comparison with peers; and second, through internal comparison, by relating their own ability in one subject with their ability in another (Marsh, 1986). In schools where academic streaming occurs (that is, where students are grouped in separate classes according to their ability), social comparison plays a significant role in students' perceptions of their academic abilities. Studies indicate that students who believe themselves to be academically competent and attend lower-ability streamed classes typically have more positive perceptions of their academic competence than peers of similar ability who attend higher-ability streamed classes (Ireson, Hallam & Plewis, 2001; Wong & Watkins, 2001) (see Box 3.1 opposite). The matter is complicated in the case of high-ability students who attend academically selective schools, since they face more demanding comparisons with classmates, yet also enjoy the pride of attending what may be perceived as more prestigious schools (see, for example, Kong, 2000). There are trade-offs between academic and social-pressure-and-prestige factors, which obviously differ for each individual. Nevertheless, students' differing perceptions of self highlight the link between academic self-concept and contextual factors such as type of class or school.

---

self-concept
A collection of information, ideas, attitudes and beliefs we have about ourselves

3.1 Dimensions of self-concept

CHAPTER 3 SOCIOEMOTIONAL AND MORAL DEVELOPMENT 73

Box 3.1 RESEARCH LINKS

Big-fish-little-pond effect

A study of 7997 students in 44 high schools in Hong Kong (Marsh et al. 2000) found that when a high-ability student who is achieving well in a school with lower academic achievement levels moves to a school with higher average levels of achievement, that student's academic self-concept is negatively affected and self-esteem typically decreases. This is known as the big-fish-little-pond effect (BFLPE). As children move from relative success in one school, where they are like big fish dominating a little pond, to a school where the academic competition and pressure is more rigorous, academic self-concept tends to suffer as self-esteem decreases. This effect on self-concept and self-esteem is generally linked to academic self-concept only and has not been found to have the same effect on general self-concept. (For more research on this see Marsh, Chessor, Craven, and Roche (1995); Marsh et al. (2000); Wong & Watkins (2001).)

'Non-academic self-concept' is derived from perceptions of physical appearance, skills, abilities and the self in social situations such as peer and family relationships (Marsh, Hey, Roche, & Perry, 1997; see also Berndt & Burgy, 1996; Byrne & Shavelson, 1996.). Non-academic self-concept is our perception of who we are in social situations and relationships. It plays a key role in friendships and peer relationships, which are discussed later in this chapter. Non-academic self-concept is also connected to academic achievement, since children who are socially accepted and popular tend to achieve higher grades (Wentzel & Erdley, 1993). The interrelationships between the global, academic and non-academic aspects of self-concept are illustrated in Figure 3.2 below.

3.2 Case study: big-fish-little-pond effect

3.3 Measuring self-concept

FIGURE 3.2 Hierarchical self-concept.

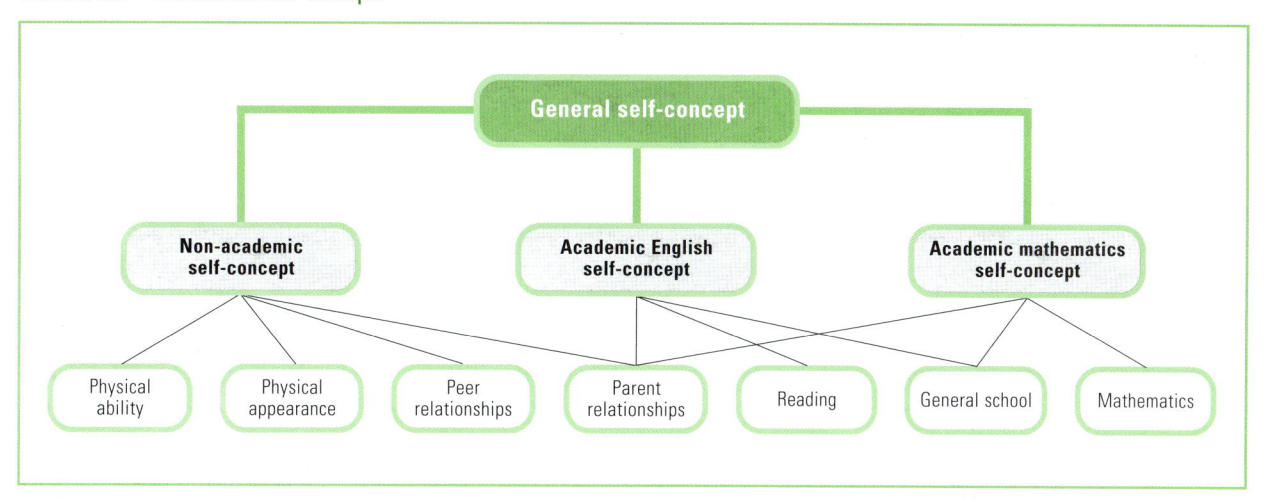

```
                    General self-concept
          ┌────────────────┼────────────────┐
    Non-academic      Academic English    Academic mathematics
    self-concept      self-concept        self-concept
   ┌─────┬─────┐    ┌──────┬──────┐     ┌──────┬──────┐
Physical Physical Peer    Parent  Reading General Mathematics
ability  appearance relationships relationships   school
```

Self-esteem

Self-esteem and self-concept are closely connected and the terms are often used interchangeably, which can cause confusion (Strein, 1995). Our self-concept depends on what we value and consider important, and influences self-esteem. Early in life we develop a concept of who we are – our self-concept – and then attach **affect** (which refers to attitudes and feelings we experience) to that concept. **Self-esteem** is therefore the 'affective' dimension of self-concept: it consists of the feelings we have about who we believe ourselves to be. Our self-esteem may be high (positive) or low (negative) – that is, a general approval or disapproval of who we think we are (Brown, 1993). Hattie (1992, p. 54) provides the following example:

affect
Attitudes and feelings, such as happiness or resentment

self-esteem
The level of satisfaction and pride that individuals have in the self

I may be an extremely capable mountain climber and have a remarkable knowledge of carabineers, ropes, loads, and New Zealand mountain geography. If these technical aspects of mountain climbing are not important then my self-esteem will probably not be affected. Only if [they] were important would it have a bearing on my self-esteem as a mountain climber.

Self-esteem plays a powerful role in our lives. For example, promoting positive self-esteem has been proposed as a way to remedy personal and social problems (Leary, Schreindorfer, & Haupt, 1995). Research indicates a connection between low or negative self-esteem and adolescent drug-and-alcohol abuse (Finke & Williams, 1999; Irving, Wall, Neumark-Sztainerm, & Story, 2002), depression and suicide (Leslie, Stein, & Rotheram-Borus, 2002; Raab, 2001), eating disorders (Ross & Ivis, 1999), and crime and violence (Ackard & Neumark-Sztainer, 2002). Low self-esteem is also regarded as a barrier to participation in activities such as sport (Perry-Burney & Takyi, 2002). It also plays a role in teenage pregnancy (Klerman, 2002; Lipovsek, Karim, Zielinsky Gutierrez, Magnani & Gomez 2002; Smith & Grenyer, 1999), although the results on this are equivocal, with some studies showing pregnant adolescents exhibiting comparatively high self-esteem levels (Corcoran & Franklin, 2002). This finding highlights the need for caution in making generalisations about trends such as those mentioned already.

Research also indicates a positive correlation between self-esteem and school achievement, but the relationship varies with age. For example, Bergstrome (2002) found the relationship strongest among pre-adolescents and adolescents in the early years of high school. Similarly, Alves-Martins, Peixoto, Gouveia-Pereira, Amaral and Pedro (2002) found a positive relationship between self-esteem and achievement among Grade 7 students, but this was not apparent among Grade 8 and Grade 9 students. Self-esteem is connected to students' perceptions of their academic abilities and how they compare with friends (see Box 3.1 on page 73). If students feel they compare negatively with others and have lower ability, they will feel inferior and have a lower self-esteem. The reverse is also true. This has been demonstrated in numerous studies, including a study of Hong Kong secondary school students, where higher self-esteem was reported by students who perceived their academic performance as higher and who attended lower-ability-stream classes (Wong & Watkins, 2001).

School-based programs aimed at enhancing students' self-esteem have been found to increase positive feelings about self, decrease absenteeism and enhance students' success at school (Walz & Bleuer, 1992). Some theorists, however, have cautioned that isolating individual factors for attention in such programs is an unbalanced approach (Kohn, 1994) and suggested that attention should be given to increasing students' academic competence rather than altering their self-beliefs (Pajares & Schunk, 2001). Nevertheless, some research indicates that targeted programs may contribute to changing for the better young people's views about illicit drug use, alcohol abuse or risk-taking sexual behaviours (Donnelly, Ferraro, & Eadie, 2001; Taranowski, 1995). Box 3.2 provides a case study demonstrating one teacher's approach to enhancing adolescents' self-esteem and addressing drug-related issues.

Box 3.2 CASE STUDY

Self-esteem and drugs

Self-esteem plays a role in many areas of our lives. It influences how we feel about ourselves, our relationships with others, and the types of activities we get involved in. In Australia and overseas there is concern about the role of low self-esteem in drug-taking behaviours and in suicidal tendencies among adolescents (Fuller & Pawsey, 1994; Martin, 1995; McDowell & Ziginskas, 1994; Rivers, 1995; Western Australian Health Department, 1994).

In Victoria, Creating Conversations is one example of a program designed to encourage young people to interact with their parents about issues — particularly drug-related issues — that are real and relevant for them. The program uses a peer education model to teach Year 9 and Year 10 students to facilitate an interactive parent evening. Teachers assist students to plan activities designed to share attitudes and values about drug issues with parents, teachers and other adolescents. Parents, teachers and students who have been involved report positively on the benefits of the program, including:

- increased self-esteem and confidence among adolescents, as the program provides them with an opportunity to feel important in front of their peers, teachers and parents
- development of cooperative team building skills and communication skills
- exploration of drug-related situations and issues that are real and relevant
- increased understanding of harm-minimisation strategies and knowledge of drug issues
- promotion of responsible decision-making.

Source: Adapted from State of Victoria (Department of Education and Training) (2002)

Activity

To find out more about how the Creating Conversations program works, visit the webpage <www.sofweb.vic.edu.au/wellbeing/druged/creating.htm>.

Self-efficacy

A third dimension of self relates to individuals' beliefs about their ability to perform tasks successfully. This is known as **self-efficacy**, which influences how people feel, think and act (Bandura, 1995). Like self-concept, self-efficacy is domain- or context-specific. This means that we may have high self-efficacy in a sport, like tennis or basketball, but low self-efficacy in maths. Our self-efficacy is determined by our skill levels in a particular domain, as well as by our prior achievements and experiences, both positive and negative. Typically, individuals with a strong sense of efficacy are self-confident about their ability to cope with demanding challenges and stressors in a particular domain or range of contexts (Klassen, 2002; Pajares, 1997; Schwarzer & Fuchs, 1995). Learners with high self-efficacy beliefs tend to feel confident about doing challenging tasks and believe that their actions make a difference and can result in successful outcomes. Such learners generally have a greater sense of control over their work and may even select more difficult tasks if given the choice. A strong sense of competence facilitates cognitive processes and performance, including quality of decision-making, and academic achievement (Greve, Anderson, & Krampen, 2001; Higgins, 2000; Licht, 1992; Schwarzer, 1998).

On the other hand, learners with low self-efficacy beliefs often feel powerless and incompetent. These negative feelings have a far-reaching effect on thoughts, behaviour and motivation. Low self-efficacy may be associated with depression, anxiety and feelings of helplessness (Bandura, 1994). Learners in this category tend to have low self-esteem and are pessimistic about their accomplishments and personal development (Brophy, 1998; Lane, Jones, & Stevens, 2002).

The sense of enablement that comes with high perceived self-efficacy is particularly important to adolescents, who find themselves managing major biological, educational and social-role changes concurrently (Bandura, 1997; Crockett & Crouter, 1995; Graber & Archibald, 2001; Greve et al., 2001). In the school context, adolescents experience major environmental changes as they move from primary school to the high school environment. They experience new social arrangements, as they may have six or seven different classes with a different peer group in each. During this period, young adolescents may experience some loss of personal control, become less confident in themselves and experience lower levels of self-efficacy (Bandura, 1997; Eccles & Wigfield, 1995; Jacobs, Lanza, Osgood, Eccles, & Wigfield, 2002). On the other hand, adolescents with higher self-efficacy beliefs develop a stronger sense of personal competence. This link between self-efficacy and student

self-efficacy
An individual's sense of being able to manage a task effectively and successfully in a particular domain

outcomes is powerfully illustrated in a study of Indigenous Australian students, in which self-efficacy beliefs were found to play an important role in school outcomes (Purdie, Tripcony, Boulton-Lewis, Fanshawe, & Gunstone, 2000).

CRITICAL REFLECTIONS

- Think about your own self-efficacy beliefs. Do they vary depending on the context? Can you trace these variations? How do they affect your approach to your work in a particular domain?
- What are your self-efficacy beliefs regarding your teaching? How do you think these beliefs might influence your relationships with students?

3.4 Self-efficacy in the classroom

Self-concept, self-esteem and development

Self-concept, including the affective dimension of self-esteem, develops gradually and changes over time. These changes are influenced by several factors, such as the developing cognitive capacity for abstract thinking. In young children the concept of self is related to concrete characteristics such as physical appearance and possessions. As the child develops, self-concept is increasingly based on abstract psychological conceptions of self (see Table 3.1).

TABLE 3.1 Development of self-concept over time

Developmental stage	Self-concept statement	Characteristics of the statement
Early childhood	'I am a boy. I like soccer'	Concrete concept based on appearance and favourite activity
Middle childhood	'I am clever because I get good English marks'	Abstract concept of cleverness is combined with concrete concept of marks
Adolescence	'I am an empathetic and compassionate person'	Abstract psychological concepts of empathy and compassion illustrate more sophisticated concepts of self

In early childhood, children's beliefs about the self tend to be positive – sometimes unrealistically so – since they have a relatively small social circle with whom to make comparisons. With age, children compare themselves with school peers and measure their strengths and weaknesses against their peers (Marsh, 1990; Witt, 2000). Self-esteem tends to decline during pre-adolescence (Jacobs et al., 2002), but begins to increase during early or middle adolescence and increases further during late adolescence and early adulthood (Rosenberg & Owens, 2001). Thus, self-esteem tends to be at its lowest during the preadolescent years of 10 to 12, although this is partly due to the often unrealistically high self-concepts typical of young children. As children develop cognitively and become less egocentric, they begin to engage more in social comparison and their self-concept becomes more realistic.

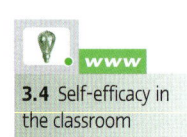

Gender differences in self-concept are not easily summarised, as the research findings are equivocal. Nevertheless, the most consistently significant gender difference across age groups is in the area of physical ability, where boys regularly express more positive views of their physical abilities than do girls (Jacobs et al., 2002; Kramer, 1996). These gender differences, while relatively small, continue to adolescence, and may be explained by the great emphasis placed on boys' participation in sports and games; the relatively greater variety of sports activities available to them; and the large number of male role models in the sports domain.

The physical-appearance dimension of self-concept also changes over time. Girls aged 5 to 8 years tend to have more positive views of their physical appearance than do boys, but this is reversed in adolescence, with boys in early adolescence expressing more positive views in relation to their physical appearance than girls. This gender difference is attributed to the importance girls are encouraged to attach to physical attractiveness (Fox, 1997). They tend to become increasingly self-conscious and dissatisfied with their physical appearance as they develop. The link between perceived physical appearance and self-concept continues into adulthood (Harter, 1990).

Box 3.3 discusses programs and strategies that relate to building self-concept and enhancing self-esteem in the classroom.

Box 3.3 IMPLICATIONS FOR EDUCATORS

Building self-concept and enhancing self-esteem

Enhancing learners' self-esteem is central to teaching. Many helpful programs have been developed for enhancing self-esteem; for example, Kiwi Can in New Zealand (see <www.kiwican.telecom.co.nz/>), and Education Queensland's Body Image and Eating Issues program, which addresses self-esteem issues relating to body image (see <education.qld.gov.au/tal/equity/bodyimg/index.html>). A common theme in these programs is valuing individuals for who they are and what they bring to the learning context. Suggested strategies include:

- Be aware of your students' self perceptions, particularly when these are negative and may interfere with their learning, peer relationships and general wellbeing.
- Help learners to set goals and link sustained effort with success.
- Celebrate students' abilities and achievements as members of the learning community.
- Respect students' inborn strengths and the experiences they bring to the classroom. Look for opportunities to encourage and develop these strengths.
- Examine the values you are promoting, bearing in mind that self-esteem is grounded on what the learner values.
- Value differences, whether they be of ethnicity, race, language, ability, gender, sexual orientation or appearance.
- Encourage peer-support programs and 'buddy programs' where older students team up with younger students to offer them support. These focus on developing communication skills, self-confidence and self-esteem, and can help students resist peer-group pressure that may be harmful to them.

CRITICAL REFLECTIONS

- From your experience, what are the connections between self-concept, self-esteem and academic achievement?
- What will you do in your classroom to enhance students' self-esteem?

Erikson's theory of psychosocial development

Erik Erikson (see Box 3.4 over the page) studied the interrelationships between psychological development and the way individuals interact socially and with their environment. He argued that psychological and social facets of development occur concurrently and are interdependent. Like Piaget (see Chapter 2), Erikson viewed development as occurring in stages, with development in each stage dependent on development in previous stages. According to this theory, the stages of development are invariant and build progressively on one another, yet they are qualitatively different.

Box 3.4 ABOUT ERIK ERIKSON

Erik Homburger Erikson (1902–1994) was born to Danish parents in Frankfurt, Germany. Erikson was raised by his mother, Karla Abrahamsen, until he was three years old. Karla then married a local paediatrician, Dr Theodor Homburger. Erikson's mother and Dr Homburger were Jewish, but Erikson looked different – more like a tall, blond, blue-eyed Dane. He was nicknamed 'the goy' (non-Jew) at his stepfather's temple, while to his schoolmates he was a 'Jew' (Erikson, 1975, p. 27).

Young Erikson was not a particularly good student. He disliked the formal school atmosphere. When he finished high school, he wandered through Europe for a year, returned home to study art for a while, then set out on his travels again. He was going through what he would later call a 'moratorium' – a period during which young people take time out to try to find themselves. Erikson finally began to find his calling when, at the age of 25, he accepted an invitation to teach. He studied child psychoanalysis with Anna Freud and others.

FIGURE 3.3 Erikson's theory of psychosocial development grew to encompass the entire life cycle.

Although Erikson's theory was inspired by Sigmund Freud's psychoanalytic theory, Erikson ultimately went beyond Freud's focus on childhood and adolescence and extended his stages to encompass the entire life cycle.

At 27, Erikson married Joan Serson. Joan played an important part in helping Erik develop and refine the psychosocial theory of development (she reflected on this in 1997 in *The Life Cycle Completed* (extended version)). Their life was disrupted in 1933 when the rise of Hitler forced them to leave Europe. They settled in Boston, USA, where Erikson became the city's first child analyst. He later travelled and worked at several other US universities. He also spent time living with the Lakota (Sioux) Native Americans and another Indian tribe, the Yurok fishermen. He was awarded a professorship at Harvard, even though he had never earned a formal university degree, and he taught there until his death.

Source: Adapted from Crain (2000, pp. 271–272).

Theory overview

psychosocial development
Psychological development in a social context

psychosocial crisis
A 'turning point', where individuals experience a temporary state of conflict and disequilibrium

Erikson proposed that we move through a series of eight **psychosocial development** stages in which our selfhood, independence, identity and self-worth may be developed or crushed, depending on how we resolve issues and interact with others along the way. Each stage is characterised by a **psychosocial crisis**, or 'turning point' (see Table 3.2 opposite). During these turning points we experience a temporary state of conflict and disequilibrium that must be resolved before we may move to the next stage of psychosocial development.

According to Erikson, in each psychosocial stage individuals face a choice between two ways of coping. One way is to resolve crises in a positive way, which leads to healthy personality development. The alternative is to resolve crises in a negative way, which leads to difficulties and problems in later stages if issues are unresolved. As individuals resolve crises they develop psychosocial strength, which in turn helps them move to the next stage. Erikson believed that those who fail to resolve particular conflicts may continue to struggle with these conflicts later in life. He saw the tension between negative and positive polarities as necessary for healthy psychosocial development. The ways in which individuals interact with others helps to determine how each crisis will be managed. Table 3.2 identifies the significant social relations that are typical of each stage.

Stages of psychosocial development

Erikson's theory accounts for development across the lifespan, from birth to death. The main focus of this text is the school years addressed by Stage 3 (ages 3–6 years) and stages 4 and 5 (middle childhood and adolescence).

TABLE 3.2 Erikson's stages of psychosocial development

Stage (age)	Psychosocial crises	Significant social relationships
1 Infancy (0–1 year)	Basic trust vs. basic mistrust	Close carer(s) – mother/father
2 Early childhood (2–3 years)	Autonomy vs. shame and doubt	Parental person(s)/parents
3 Play age (3–6 years)	Initiative vs. guilt	Family
4 School age (7–12 years)	Industry vs. inferiority	Neighbourhood, school
5 Adolescence (12–18 years)	Identity vs. role confusion	Peer groups, role models
6 Young adulthood (the 20s)	Intimacy vs. isolation	Partners, friends
7 Adulthood (late 20s to late 50s)	Generativity vs. stagnation/self-absorption	Household, workmates
8 Old age (60s and beyond)	Ego integrity vs. despair	'Humankind', 'my kind'

Source: Adapted from Erikson (1982, pp. 32–33).

Infancy and early childhood

Stage 1: Basic trust versus basic mistrust

Stage 1 covers approximately the first year of life. This stage is an opportunity for infants to learn to trust others to provide for basic needs such as for food, warmth and love. The infant learns that the world, especially the social world, is a safe place to be and that parents and carers are reliable and loving. However, if parents and carers are unreliable or if they reject or harm the infant in some way, the baby will become mistrustful, apprehensive and suspicious around people. Erikson argued that a certain measure of mistrust is a healthy part of development and that the primary aim in this stage is for the child to achieve a balance between trust and mistrust (Erikson, 1963). While issues of trust occur throughout life, Erikson theorised that they are most central during the early stage of life.

Stage 2: Autonomy versus shame and doubt

Stage 2 covers the early-childhood period spanning 2 to 3 years of age. In Stage 2, the child's task is to start developing autonomy while minimising shame and doubt. Young children at this stage experiment with newfound independence and the ability to exercise their will. For example, they are able to walk and run on their own and they have many more choices available to them than before. With a child's increased mobility and the ongoing development of thinking processes comes a desire to be independent and to 'do it myself'. If children are allowed to explore and manipulate their environment, they will develop a sense of autonomy. On the other hand, if children are constantly discouraged from expressing themselves and from following their interests, they will learn to feel ashamed and doubt their own abilities. Erikson (1964) argued that the capacity to feel some shame and doubt can be beneficial, since children must learn self-control and self-discipline in order to participate effectively in society. The aim is a healthy balance between autonomy and feelings of shame and doubt.

The preschool and primary school years

Stage 3: Initiative versus guilt

Stage 3 covers approximately the 3-to-6-years age group. Remember when you were 4 years old and feeling very independent? Perhaps you remember the time you decided to give yourself a haircut and you hacked off bits of your fringe, to your parents' horror! Or perhaps you took the initiative in the kitchen by trying to make your own breakfast, but in the process the milk spilled and cornflakes went flying. Were you punished and made to feel guilty for being naughty, or were you praised for taking initiative and being independent? Erikson suggests that the central task of this stage is to learn initiative without feeling too much guilt. Initiative builds on the autonomy developed in the previous stage. It involves acting independently, taking on responsibilities, learning new skills and feeling purposeful.

Children in Stage 3 tend to be inquisitive and have a desire to explore their world. They are also developing the cognitive capacity for setting goals and for planning and initiating activities. They begin to take responsibility for their actions. At the same time, a growing sense of moral responsibility means they are capable of feeling guilt, such as when they misbehave or have ideas they believe to be wrong or unacceptable in the eyes of parents or significant others. A parent or carer may also promote feelings of guilt through punishing misbehaviour. Once again, Erikson argued for a balanced approach. If children experience excessive guilt, they may become inhibited and afraid to try anything for fear of making mistakes. However, growing up with no sense of responsibility is an unhealthy alternative. Encouraging children to take the initiative and to think for themselves while considering the consequences of their actions helps to promote a healthy personality in preparation for the next stage of psychosocial development.

Stage 4: Industry versus inferiority

Stage 4 spans the ages of approximately 7 to 12 years. During Stage 4 most children are at school and industriously engaged in activities related to acquiring basic skills and the social and cultural tools that enable them to participate in society. The dominant task for children at this stage is to appreciate the value of industry and productive activities while avoiding an excessive sense of inferiority. In indigenous societies, children may be educated within the wider family group, learning to track, find food or make utensils (Crain, 2000), while in Western cultures children typically attend school and learn basic literacy and numeracy skills.

FIGURE 3.4 Teacher feedback contributes to students' sense of industry or inferiority.

Children need to experience feelings of success, whether at home or in a wider learning environment; whether academically (see Figure 3.4) or socially. If they experience repeated failure, they are likely to develop a sense of inferiority or incompetence. Additional sources of inferiority mentioned by Erikson include racism, sexism and other forms of discrimination. If children believe that success is related to 'who you are' rather than to how hard you try, they will begin to think 'Why try?' Teachers play a particularly important role (Erikson, 1959), as they can encourage talent and a sense of competence among learners.

While children at this stage are seeking a balance between industry and inferiority, the conflicts of earlier stages do not disappear. For example, young children starting school must develop trust in teachers and a sense of autonomy in their new school environment in order to develop as successful learners. Each stage of the theory builds on the conflicts resolved in previous stages: people often revisit the conflicts of earlier stages as they encounter new social situations and contexts.

High school years

Stage 5: Identity versus role confusion

Stage 5 describes the period of adolescence, beginning with puberty and ending around 18 or 20 years of age. The primary task during adolescence is to develop an identity, which lays the foundation for adulthood. Identity means knowing who you are and how you fit into the larger society. Marcia (1980, p. 159) defined **identity** as an internal self-structure in which we organise our beliefs, abilities, needs and self-perceptions. A healthy identity is flexible and open to change. It is a dynamic structure with elements constantly being added or taken away over time. While the identity-forming process is lifelong, it is most intense during adolescence (see also Erikson, 1997). White and Wyn (2002) document some interesting developments and changes in the ways Australian young people are experiencing adolescence in the 21st century (see also Wyn and White, 1997). Similar trends are evident in other developed countries such as New Zealand. Despite sociocultural and technological changes, the primary task of identity formation remains central for adolescents in this millennium.

'Role confusion' may result when adolescents have difficulty deciding which roles to play in life, and may stem from uncertainty about their place in the world. Think about all the roles you played as an adolescent: sibling, son or daughter, good mathematics student, naughty student in geography class, popular sportsperson, member of the choir, and many more. How did you resolve the tension between all of your roles? Did one dominate, or were you able to adapt from situation to situation? Were you satisfied with your identity or did you long to be someone else? This is all part of resolving the identity-versus-role-confusion conflict.

Adolescents confronted by role confusion are said by some to be experiencing an 'identity crisis'. The term 'crisis' should be used with caution, however. Some people have the perception that adolescence is, by definition, a tumultuous period characterised by rebellion, and that it is traumatic for parents, teachers and teenagers alike. You may know of some adolescents who fit this stereotype, but equally there are many adolescents who resolve identity issues in a healthy way with little difficulty (Bandura, 1997). The 'crisis' of adolescence, therefore, is often not as problematic as it sounds. Nevertheless, dramatic social and economic changes pose new challenges for adolescents – particularly those in Western countries – and have had an impact on adolescents' attitudes towards issues such as health, relationships and career prospects (Dwyer & Wyn, 2001).

identity
An internal self-structure in which we organise our beliefs, abilities, needs and self-perceptions

3.5 Adolescents and sexual identity: supporting gay and lesbian students

FIGURE 3.5 What issues of identity might these students face over the next few years? What approaches could they take to dealing with identity?

> **identity achievement**
> Occurs when adolescents explore several identity roles, but resolve conflicts and feel comfortable with who they are and who they hope to be
>
> **identity foreclosure**
> Describes adolescents who typically form their identity by adopting the occupational and ideological goals of significant others, often their parents
>
> **identity diffusion**
> Occurs when young people have little direction, their life and career goals are unclear, and they do not know who they are or who they want to be
>
> **moratorium**
> Refers to the state of adolescents who postpone making a definitive commitment to a single identity or set of values

The attempt to resolve identity issues may be exacerbated by rapid physiological changes that are characteristic of puberty (see Chapter 1). Social factors, including pressure from peers, adults and the media, also play a significant role (see, for example, Crain, 2000; White & Wyn, 2002; see Figure 3.5 on page 81). Several researchers have extended Erikson's seminal work, including Marcia (1980, 1993), who expanded on adolescent identity development. Marcia identified four identity statuses – **identity achievement**, **foreclosure** and **diffusion**, and **moratorium** – which describe the ways adolescents attempt to resolve the identity-versus-role-confusion conflict. These four statuses are outlined in Table 3.3.

TABLE 3.3   Marcia's four identity statuses

Identity status	Describes young people who:
Identity achievement	■ Resolve the psychosocial conflicts of Erikson's Stage 5 ■ Successfully negotiate decisions about identity ■ Pursue self-chosen occupations or studies and ideological goals ■ May have explored several identity roles, but have resolved the conflicts and generally feel comfortable with who they are and who they hope to be
Identity foreclosure	■ Avoid the dilemma of role confusion by adopting the occupational and ideological goals of significant others such as parents, but also religious cults, militaristic organisations, or groups divorced from mainstream society ■ Foreclose on the psychosocial crisis of Stage 5 and follow in the footsteps of others without working through identity issues for themselves
Identity diffusion	■ Have no direction for the future ■ Are unclear about their goals and do not know what occupation to pursue ■ Have not made any decision about their identity and may feel confused and frustrated
Moratorium	■ Postpone a definitive commitment to a single identity or set of values ■ Choose to take time out between childhood and adulthood before making a commitment about who they want to be ■ Experiment with different roles in areas such as gender, occupation and family

Source: Adapted from Marcia (1980, p. 161).

Post-school and adult years

Stage 6: Intimacy versus isolation

Stage 6 spans young adulthood, which lasts from approximately 20 to 30 years of age. During this stage the individual's psychosocial task is to achieve some degree of intimacy, as opposed to remaining in isolation. 'Intimacy' is the ability to be close to others – as a lover, a friend, and as a participant in society. Young adults must somehow resolve the tension between intimacy – which, if taken to excess, leads to promiscuity – or remaining emotionally and socially isolated.

Stage 7: Generativity versus stagnation/self-absorption

Stage 7 typically spans the late 20s to the late 50s. Generativity involves a concern for the next and future generations. The raising of children is the most common example of generativity, but there are many other ways to accomplish this, including teaching, writing, inventing, the arts and sciences, social activism, and generally contributing to the welfare of future generations (Erikson, 1964). Stagnation, on the other hand, is self-absorption – caring for no one. The stagnant person ceases to be a productive member of society. Those who achieve a balance at this stage generally maintain an appropriate balance between productive activity and rest. Such balance contributes to preparation for the later years of life.

Stage 8: Ego integrity versus despair

Stage 8 was originally the final stage in Erikson's theory. It is said to begin around retirement, at approximately 60 or 65 years of age. The individual's task at this stage is to develop 'ego integrity' with minimal despair. Ego integrity involves coming to terms with the past, the present and the end of life. There are many sources of despair during this stage. For example, some people retire from jobs they have held for years, other people find their duties as parents coming to an end, and many people may feel detached from society. Typically, the body undergoes significant physical changes and there are concerns about illness and death. More recently, Joan Erikson, the theorist's widow and co-researcher, proposed a ninth stage depicting a period of later adulthood beyond the age of 80. This proposal points to an important characteristic of psychological theories: they are constantly evolving and open to change, amendment and further discoveries.

CRITICAL REFLECTIONS

- Before reading further, review each of Erikson's stages.
- Looking back, can you identify with elements of the first five or six stages?
- Do you think your adolescence is best described by identity achievement, by identity foreclosure, by identity diffusion or by moratorium, or did you perhaps experience several identity statuses?
- When you look at older family members and friends, can you see evidence of stages 7, 8 or (proposed stage) 9 in their lives?

Strengths and limitations of Erikson's theory

Erikson's theory has much to offer the classroom teacher, but the theory's benefits and utility should always be interpreted in light of its possible limitations.

Lifespan approach

Erikson's theory illustrates that psychosocial development continues through life. The theory also demonstrates interrelationships between earlier and later stages of our lives. However, some theorists have criticised Erikson's theory, arguing that despite its claim to be a lifespan theory, more attention is paid to infancy and childhood than to adult life.

A stage theory

Erikson's stage approach is helpful because it provides a framework for interpreting psychosocial development. If you divide the average human lifespan into two sequences of four stages, you can see that the first four stages of Erikson's theory address child development, while the remaining stages cover adolescent and adult development. However, stage theories have limitations (see Chapter 2). For example, Erikson describes a single central conflict in each psychosocial stage, whereas in reality individuals confront many conflicts that may not be restricted to particular stages. Questions have also been raised about the universal applicability of the order of stages and the relevance of this theory's lock-step approach to development. For this reason, some theorists prefer the terms 'phases' or 'transitions' rather than 'stages'.

The role of society and culture

A useful aspect of Erikson's theory is his emphasis on the role of social relationships in development. This is especially important for classroom teachers, as they need to understand their students' development in social and cultural contexts. However, Erikson's theory is primarily Western in orientation, and many argue that his stages do not apply across cultures and across historical contexts. Barrett (2000) questions whether Stage 2 (autonomy versus shame and doubt) holds true for collectivistic cultures (see the next section, 'The self across cultures'), where autonomy and independence are not valued as highly as they are in individualistic cultures. Erikson and other researchers have argued that the general stage pattern and characteristic psychosocial crises do hold across cultures (Wang & Viney, 1996), although social and cultural factors play a significant role in shaping identity (see, for example, Comunian & Gielen, 2000).

Links with Freudian theory

A controversial aspect of Erikson's work is his assumption (in agreement with Freud) that personality differences between the sexes are biologically based. Erikson believed that we are genetically programmed to proceed through stages of development and that our biological makeup interacts with social and cultural factors to contribute to development. Some theorists have challenged this view, seeing it as deterministic and problematic.

Gender differences

Critics of Erikson's theory say the theory is more applicable to males than to females. Gilligan (1982) argues that Erikson's focus on autonomy, independence and industry is more characteristic of males than of females, who tend to consider themselves in terms of relationships rather than in terms of separateness and individuality.

In balance, Erikson's theory offers several important insights into the interrelationships between physical, psychological and emotional development in a social context. Erikson's theory has inspired ongoing research, particularly in the area of identity development and his work has many practical implications for classroom teachers.

The table in Box 3.5 gives guidelines and examples for activities with students in stages 3 to 5.

Box 3.5 IMPLICATIONS FOR EDUCATORS

Erikson's theory of psychosocial development has several implications for classroom practitioners. Table 3.4 below presents guidelines and sample activities for classroom application.

TABLE 3.4 Erikson's theory (stages 3–5) in the classroom

Stage	Guidelines for teachers	Examples of activities for each stage
Stage 3: Initiative vs. guilt (preschool and early primary years)	Foster initiative and creativity; encourage responsibility; balance punishment for wrongdoing with encouragement of individuality	■ Encourage students to make decisions about a group project or about how a game will be played ■ Allocate free-choice time where learners select their activity ■ Be flexible and listen to students' ideas. If they suggest inappropriate or dangerous activities, discuss ways of reworking their suggestions in acceptable ways rather than discouraging and ignoring them
Stage 4: Industry vs. inferiority (primary school years)	Value hard work and industry; encourage individuals to do their best no matter what their ability; while some competition is healthy, discourage excessive competition, which may lead to feelings of inferiority and low self-worth	■ Set tasks to match students' ability levels, being aware of each learner's abilities and trying to develop activities accordingly ■ Provide choices to allow for different interests and abilities ■ Help students to set learning goals for themselves to encourage a sense of achievement ■ Be patient when students make mistakes. Avoid public humiliation. When students feel they are not keeping up with their peers, they will want to give up, so develop individual learning programs and encourage students to work at their own pace

Stage	Guidelines for teachers	Examples of activities for each stage
		■ Acknowledge successes outside the classroom in sport or other endeavours
Stage 5: Identity vs. role confusion (high school years)	Provide opportunities to explore and discuss different identities and viewpoints; be aware that adolescents will experiment with different roles; be observant regarding potential risk-taking and harmful behaviours; encourage open communication with parents, teachers, peers and significant others; be supportive, especially during students' times of uncertainty	■ Invite guest speakers to discuss relevant life issues such as the dangers of drug-taking. Provide role models, such as sportspeople who discuss the value of healthy life choices ■ Provide a forum for students to discuss problems and share ideas. This should be done in a safe classroom environment. Adolescents appreciate the opportunity to express themselves in writing: they may also use online technologies or some other medium ■ Acknowledge students' interests: learn a bit about their sports, magazines or music, and provide for this in assignments; e.g. one wide-reading assignment topic could be based on a hobby or sport magazine of their choice (which you have approved!)

The self across cultures

As Erikson's theory suggests, self should be understood in light of our relationships with others and our environment. Culture plays a critical role in determining how we view ourselves, how we relate to others, and what we value. Until the late 20th century, most of the documented theories of self came from Western researchers, but crosscultural research indicates that views of self differ across cultures (see, for example, Purdie et al., 2000). One way of explaining these differences is to categorise cultures into 'individualistic' and 'collectivistic' cultures, and to contrast them (although conclusions that arise from such a generalised approach should be treated cautiously).

In **individualistic culture**s the focus is on the individual self, which is autonomous and unique. The successful pursuit of individual goals is most highly regarded in such cultures. **Collectivistic culture**s, on the other hand, tend to be group-centred, viewing individuals in terms of their relationships with others in a cohesive community group.

In collectivistic cultures, focusing on individual goals may even be a cause for embarrassment or shame (Shweder & Haidt, 2000), as individuals are typically defined in terms of their roles, responsibilities and relationships within their community. For example, research indicates that Indigenous Australian youth base their identity on factors such as kinship group, sense of communal history, language, traditional practices and place (Purdie et al., 2000) (see Figure 3.6). The individual and society are interdependent (Biggs, 1996;

individualistic culture
Focuses on the self as an autonomous individual; successful pursuit of individual goals is valued

collectivistic culture
Typically group-centred, viewing individuals in terms of their relationships, roles and responsibilities in the community

FIGURE 3.6
A sense of belonging to a cultural group stems from communal activities and rituals, shared values and common goals.

Marjoribanks, 1997; Triandis, McCusker, Betancourt, Iwao, Leung, Salazar et al., 1993). Some examples of collectivistic cultures include Confucian-heritage cultures, such as those of Mainland China, Hong Kong and Singapore; Polynesian cultures, such as those of the New Zealand Maoris; and Australian Aboriginal cultures. The nature of the culture in which we live and work powerfully influences our sense of self in a sociocultural context (see Greenfield and Suzuki, 1998).

One shortcoming of categorising cultures is that escalating globalisation means boundaries between the views and values of different cultures are increasingly blurred (see, for example, Cha, 1994). For example, New Zealand combines the typically individualistic cultures of Western societies with the collectivist values of the Maori cultures. Similarly, in Australia, Western individualistic cultural values exist beside collectivist values such as those of Australian Indigenous cultures or Confucian-heritage cultures. These cultural groups influence one another as they interact.

Another limitation of the individualist–collectivist dichotomy is that cultures comprise complex social and cultural subgroups. Nevertheless, the individualist–collectivist categorisation provides general principles that may help you to better understand the young people you work with.

The self developing emotionally and socially

So far we have learned that the self has several dimensions and that its development is influenced by many factors, including those of a social and cultural nature. We now consider the emotional dimension of the self and the role of peers and friends in this development.

Emotions and socioemotional development

Emotional development is a key piece of the jigsaw puzzle of development. Increasingly, educational psychologists and researchers acknowledge that emotions are central to learning and teaching, and that an understanding of their role in the learner's experience is essential (Schutz & Lanehart, 2002). An **emotion** expresses an individual's attempt to establish, maintain or change a relationship with their environment on a matter of importance to that person (Saarni, Mumme, & Campos, 1998). We typically experience emotion when we evaluate an event as being relevant to our concerns or goals (Fridja, 1986). Emotions tend to be positive if we believe that we can meet our goals, and negative if we perceive that our goals are impeded. We usually experience emotions as a type of mental state that is closely connected to our actions and sense of wellbeing. Emotions influence and are influenced by thinking and behaviour. Similarly, emotions also have strong ties to our social interactions. **Socioemotional development** examines the way emotions develop in a social context. Others may infer our emotions from facial or vocal expressions, by listening to our conversation or by observing our body language.

Human beings are born with a biological capacity for experiencing emotions, but emotions are also shaped by cultural and social forces (Fischer, Wang, Kennedy, & Cheng, 1998; Menon, 2000). Research has found a link between emotions, intelligence and cognition (Mayer, 2001; LeDoux, 1995). The **functional-organisational approach** to emotions draws attention to the function of emotions in directing, shaping and organising thoughts and behaviours (see Barrett & Campos, 1987; Fischer et al., 1998; Lazarus, 1991). One example of shaping is the well-established link between the emotion of anxiety, and academic achievement (Beidel, Turner, & Taylor-Ferreira, 1999; Durbrow, Schaefer, & Jimerson, 2001). Research indicates that high levels of anxiety interfere with academic

---

emotion
Occurs when we evaluate an event as relevant to our concerns or goals. Usually experienced as a mental state, emotion is closely connected to behaviour

socioemotional development
Emotional development in a social context

functional-organisational approach
An approach that views emotions as shaping and organising thoughts and behaviours

performance on a range of tasks, including essay writing (Boice, 1994; Krause, 1997; Reeves, 1997), mathematics (Wither, 1998) and computer use (Bradley & Russell, 1997).

Types of emotions and their development

Researchers generally agree that babies are born with the ability to express **basic emotions** such as happiness, sadness, anger and fear (Campos, Barrett, Lamb, Goldsmith, & Stenberg, 1983; Izard, Fantauzzo, Castle, Haynes, Rayias, & Putnam, 1995; Saarni et al., 1998) (see Figure 3.7). These emotions are most often expressed in the early years through facial expressions such as frowns or smiles, vocal expressions such as crying or laughter, or body language such as kicking the legs or turning away the head.

Over time, the capacity for **self-conscious emotions** develops (Lewis, 1993b; Saarni, Mumme, & Campos, 1998). These are known as 'higher-order' emotions because they require higher-order cognitive processing (see Chapter 1) and because they depend on our capacity to reflect on our self. Self-conscious emotions are associated with our core values, such as the valuing of good academic results, or the valuing of others' opinions of our honesty or trustworthiness (Turner, Husman, & Schallert, 2002). To experience self-conscious emotions we require an awareness of our self and of the ways in which that self might be harmed or enhanced. Higher-order emotions develop with adults' encouragement. For example, we experience the emotion of pride when we feel positive about ourselves for doing a good job. Thus, if a teacher praises a student for doing well on a test, the student feels proud of his achievement. Conversely, that student may feel shame if he fails a test and his parents are disappointed or even angry. The student's sense of self is harmed and he feels negative about himself for his failure.

Self-conscious emotions vary with age. They first appear between 18 and 24 months, when babies are capable of experiencing pride, shame and embarrassment. By about 3 years old, children are able to experience emotions of envy and guilt (Lewis, 1993a; Sroufe, 2000). In the early years, these emotions are evoked primarily through adults' influence, such as when adults' praise for a job well done evokes pride in a child. Alternatively, parents punish children for lying, making them feel shame and guilt for being deceitful (Zahn-Waxler & Robinson, 1995). Later in life, as a sense of self develops, external agents are no longer necessary in order to arouse these emotions. We feel proud of our accomplishments, or ashamed of our weaknesses, usually no matter what others think.

Self-conscious emotions may vary across cultures. For example, the emotion of shame takes on particular significance in Confucian-heritage cultures such as in China or Japan when compared with its importance in Western cultures. Chinese parents introduce shame-oriented experiences to children at an early age, with the result that shame becomes an organising influence on development; while in Western cultures parents tend to minimise shame experiences for children from an early age (Fischer et al., 1998, p. 24).

Social emotions develop as children are socialised within their culture and learn to interact with others. Social emotions demonstrate the link between individuals and their sociocultural context, and are cultural constructions that direct our feelings and how we express them (Menon, 2000). Children soon learn about the appropriateness of public displays of emotion by watching role models. Examples of this can be seen in the different ways grief is expressed across cultures.

---

basic emotions
Babies are born with the ability to express basic emotions such as happiness, sadness, anger and fear

self-conscious emotions
Higher-order emotions (such as pride and shame) that require advanced cognitive processes and a capacity to understand how the self might be harmed or enhanced

3.6 Emotional development in the first three years of life

FIGURE 3.7
This young child's emotions are clearly expressed through facial expressions, body language and crying.

social emotions
Cultural constructions determining what individuals feel and how they should demonstrate these feelings in public

Emotional and cognitive development

Emotional development is closely linked to cognitive development. As infants move beyond egocentrism to recognise the social world around them, they learn that others have feelings different from their own. By the age of 4 or 5, children are able to explain why a friend is sad ('He is sad because he lost his bike'). Young children generally believe that people experience only one emotion at a time (Arsenio & Kramer, 1992). In middle childhood, as children become capable of more complex cognitive operations, they learn that emotions are more complicated and that it is possible to experience more than one emotion simultaneously (Wintre & Vallance, 1994). Adolescents, with their capacity for abstract reasoning, are increasingly able to consider multiple viewpoints and emotions, and the possible outcomes of those emotions.

Cognitive development determines children's ability to interpret and understand their own and others' emotions. Sympathy is the capacity to feel for others, while empathy is the ability to detect others' emotions, take their perspective and understand how they might be feeling (Saarni, Mumme, & Campos, 1998; Zahn-Waxler & Radke-Yarrow, 1990). Empathy promotes **prosocial behaviour**, which is voluntary behaviour intended to benefit others (Eisenberg & Fabes, 1998).

Perspective-taking is the ability to imagine oneself in another's position. This ability begins to develop at the age of 2 or 3 when young children become aware of others' feelings (Eisenberg & Fabes, 1998). The capacity to understand others' feelings is facilitated by the ability to think abstractly. Not until late childhood or early adolescence do children develop more sophisticated perspective-taking skills. Adolescents can typically move beyond concerns with individuals close to them and the immediate situation, to a wider range of people. They become more concerned with whole groups of people and with larger issues such as poverty in the Third World, or the greenhouse effect and its impact on world population.

We have seen that emotional and cognitive development are closely linked and that these combined aspects of development play a significant part in social interactions. Emotions never occur in isolation: they are based on our appraisals of situations within a social context and are influenced by cultural beliefs and norms (Ratner, 2000). We next examine the role of peers and friends in socioemotional development.

Peer experiences and socioemotional development

Peer experiences are an important part of healthy socialisation and the socioemotional development of children and adolescents. In Chapter 2 we learned that peer interactions provide a context for cognitive development. They also foster emotional development, as we see in this section.

Types of peer experiences

Think about your own peer experiences over time. Do you remember the names of your friends in Year 3? Were they mainly male or female, or a mixed group? Now that you are at university, do you tend to have close friends on campus, or are they mainly acquaintances or study partners? Can you think of any changes in the way you have interacted with your peers through the course of your development?

Social interaction with peers forms a significant part of our lives from an early age. There are three main ways we engage socially with our peers as we develop and mature over time. These types of peer exchange are categorised according to the depth of interaction and relationship we have with our peers and have been called **interaction**s, **relationship**s and **group**s (Rubin, Bukowski, & Parker, 1998). Table 3.5 outlines the characteristics of these peer exchanges.

---

prosocial behaviour
Voluntary behaviour intended to benefit others

perspective-taking
The ability to imagine the self in another's position and to understand others' feelings

interaction
A first-order (or superficial) social exchange between two or more individuals, with little emotional commitment

relationship
An exchange between two or more people, resulting from several interactions and taking on emotional significance

group
An exchange involving several interacting individuals who have formed a relationship and who have some degree of reciprocal influence over one another

TABLE 3.5	Characteristics of peer exchanges
Type of peer exchange	**Characteristics**
Interaction: first- (lower) order exchange	■ Social exchange between two or more individuals
Relationship: second- (higher) order exchange	■ A series of significant interactions between two individuals ■ Characterised by stronger emotions and more frequent contact than interactions, and by a commitment to the exchange (Hinde, 1995) ■ Predominant emotions in relationships are affection, love, attachment or enmity ■ Require a shared culture in terms of accepted patterns of communication and appropriate behaviour ■ Friendship is a type of relationship ■ Friendship is voluntary, positive and characterised by reciprocal affection (Rubin et al., 1998)
Group: third-order exchange	■ A collection of interacting individuals who have formed a relationship and who have some degree of reciprocal influence over one another ■ Groups tend to be: – formed spontaneously, though they may be established formally, as in a class group at school – cohesive, in that there is unity among members, who usually have common interests – hierarchical, in that there is often a leader or subgroup of leaders in a group – homogeneous in one or more observable characteristics such as sex, race, attitudes to school, clothing and socioeconomic status – characterised by distinctive group norms or patterns of behaviours and attitudes that distinguish group members from others

Source: Adapted from Rubin, Bukowski and Parker (1998, pp. 633–644).

The role of peer experiences

Peer relationships perform several functions, including assisting in:
- emotional support
- socioemotional development
- self-esteem
- identity development
- cognitive and moral development.

Emotional support

Close **friendship**s provide affection, intimacy, and a sense of reliability and loyalty (Erdley, Nangle, Newman, & Carpenter, 2001) (see Figure 3.8). Intimacy develops when friends feel it is safe to share secrets and personal aspects of themselves. Trust develops, and friends' loyalty promotes feelings of security. Peers also give emotional support by providing nurture and companionship.

Socioemotional development

Peer relationships also promote socioemotional development. Among younger children, play provides an opportunity for children to experiment with emotions in a safe context where they are 'allowed' to be angry or afraid; for example, because they are 'just pretending'.

FIGURE 3.8
Friendship plays important roles in development.

friendship
A voluntary relationship, characterised by reciprocity of affection

Children learn to manage and self-regulate their emotions among their peers; for example, if they want a game to continue, they need to learn to control their anger and to compromise or negotiate. Social self-concept – our perception of who we are in a social context – also develops as children interact with others and understand themselves as social beings (Berndt & Burgy, 1996).

For adolescents, peer interactions provide a source of emotional support and a context for talking about sensitive emotional issues.

Self-esteem

Peer relationships play a part in enhancing self-esteem. If children and adolescents feel included and accepted, particularly by the larger peer group, they are more likely to feel positive about themselves (Berndt, 1992; Hartup, 2000).

Identity development

Peer interactions assist in identity development by supporting adolescents as they develop their identity; experiment with different roles; develop attitudes, values, and ideological and belief systems; and determine sexual attitudes and sex-role behaviours (Berndt, 1998).

Cognitive and moral development

The quality of the relationship between peers contributes to cognitive growth and promotes thinking and problem-solving skills. Peers also play a part in moral development, in that they help children develop an understanding of abstract concepts such as loyalty and honesty in relationships.

Friendship provides a safe environment for experimenting with new thoughts and ideas. Friends may also argue with or challenge each other, causing disequilibrium within the relatively stable friendship and so enhancing cognitive development (Azmitia & Montgomery, 1993; Hartup, 1998).

Peer experiences over time

The nature of peer interactions changes over time (Hartup, 2000), as summarised in Table 3.6. Early experiences play a significant role in how we adjust as adolescents and adults (Bagwell, Newcomb, & Bukowski, 2000), and at each developmental stage a young person builds on the social skills and experiences of previous stages.

TABLE 3.6 Development of peer interactions over time

Developmental stage	Developments in interactions	Developments in relationships	Developments in group experiences
Infancy and toddlerhood (0–2 years)	■ Ability to coordinate own behaviour and that of play partner ■ Helping and sharing behaviours ■ Imitation of peer's activity ■ Limited turn-taking ■ By age 2, approximately 10% of social interaction involves peers	■ Friendships exist, but only with those who initiate positive social interaction ■ Friendships tend to be short-term relationships	■ Small groups may form (e.g. with day-care friends) but these are unstable
Early childhood (2–5 years)	■ Frequency of peer interactions increases ■ Peer interactions occur mainly in the home ■ Play dominates and becomes increasingly interactive (see Table 3.7 for types of play)	■ Children distinguish between friends and non-friends ■ Children engage in more prosocial behaviours and more conflicts with friends than with non-friends ■ Perceptions of friendship are anchored in the here and now	■ Groups form and are strongly influenced by group hierarchy ■ Groups are hierarchically structured and tend to be dominated by those more skilled at manipulating their peers or meeting their interpersonal goals

Developmental stage	Developments in interactions	Developments in relationships	Developments in group experiences
Middle childhood/ preadolescence (6–12 years)	■ Approximately 30% of social interaction involves peers ■ Interactions are less supervised by parents ■ Interactions occur mainly at school or in social settings (e.g. friend's home, shopping mall, movies) ■ Gossip plays a big role in reaffirming the child's membership in same-sex social interactions, as well as confirming shared attitudes, beliefs and behaviours ■ Bullying and victimisation increase	■ Friendships become more exclusive and individualised ■ Same-sex friendships are most dominant ■ Close friends increase in number up to age 11 ■ Friendships are more stable ■ Loyalty, trust and self-disclosure are highly valued	■ Groups are stable and polydyadic (that is, several individuals in close dyadic (two-member) friendships form a group) ■ Groups tend to be smaller in size (called a 'clique') ■ Same-sex cliques dominate the group interactions ■ Peer-group acceptance is important
Adolescence (13–19 years)	■ Far less adult supervision of interactions than in middle childhood ■ Interactions with the opposite sex increase	■ Friendships are more stable and enduring ■ Adolescents have fewer friends than do younger children ■ Same-sex friends account for the largest proportion of friendships, but friendships with the opposite sex increase ■ Adolescents are less possessive of friends – they recognise others' need for independence and autonomy	■ Intimacy and self-disclosure in friendships are highly valued ■ Cliques remain important, but are not as consolidated as in earlier years; clique boundaries tend to blur ■ Isolated single-sex cliques build ties with opposite-sex cliques to permit new social activities; these cliques then dissociate as dyadic dating relationships evolve ■ Crowds may form, being larger groups who do not necessarily spend time together but who share similar attitudes or activities and tend to be stereotyped accordingly (examples of adolescent crowds include the school 'nerds', 'punks', 'techos' or 'brains')

Source: Adapted from Hartup (2000); Kindermann (1995); Leaper (1994).

Early childhood and primary years

For younger children, play is a context in which to practise emotions without fear of failure. There is evidence that following new play activities children attend more carefully to unfamiliar than familiar experiences and are more likely to express emotion (Lifter & Bloom, 1998). Play has several key characteristics, in that it is:

- *intrinsically motivated* – it is enjoyed for its own sake, and brings satisfaction
- *voluntary* – children choose to play
- *valued as an end in itself* – it is fun, pleasurable and enjoyable without having specific goals
- *nonliteral, or pretend* – there are certain elements of make-believe, particularly in symbolic play, where children experiment with new roles
- *active* – children actively engage physically, and/or psychologically (Rubin, Fein, & Vandenberg, 1983, pp. 698–699).

Researchers have identified several subtypes of play, which include rough-and-tumble play (horseplay), constructive play (making things for fun), formal games (games and sports with designated rules) and pretend play (portraying imaginary roles) (Gray, 1991). Several key types of play are exemplified in Table 3.7 over the page.

TABLE 3.7	Types of play
Types of play	**Examples**
■ Solitary play: children play alone	Playing with blocks, water and sand, puzzles, computer and video games for one person, dolls, models (cars and planes)
■ Parallel play: children play beside but not with other children	Bouncing a ball, playing with blocks or a doll in close proximity to other children, but not engaging with them
■ Cooperative play: children play in pairs or in groups	Playing soccer, hide and seek, building a tree-house
■ Pretend or imaginary play: children assume roles or play with imaginary objects or people – Solitary pretend play: imaginary play alone	Feeding dolls or teddy bears, pushing toy trains around a track while saying 'chuff chuff'
– Sociodramatic or cooperative pretend play: imaginary play with other children, often involving role-play (a form of drama)	Adopting different family roles; eating breakfast with other children; using real or pretend bowls, glasses, and cups; playing 'Cowboys and Indians'

As children develop through the primary years their play becomes increasingly sophisticated as cognitive and motor skills develop (see chapters 1 and 2). Peers play a critical role in helping children develop in all dimensions, and the value of time for play and social interaction should not be underestimated.

Pre-adolescent and adolescent years

As children move into late primary and early adolescent years, the nature of their peer interactions changes. Dunphy's (1963, 1990) research with Australian students focuses on peer interactions from early to late adolescence. His five-stage model of peer interaction (Dunphy 1990) is as follows, with particular emphasis on changes in male–female interactions over time:

- *Stage 1 – precrowd stage:* During early adolescence, isolated same-sex **clique**s form exclusive friendships.
- *Stage 2 – beginning of the crowd:* Same-sex cliques interact but the separate cliques remain intact, providing stability and relative protection for individual members.
- *Stage 3 – transitional crowd:* High-status members from separate same-sex cliques form a heterosexual clique. Individuals may date across cliques but they retain their membership of the same-sex clique.
- *Stage 4 – fully developed crowd:* Same-sex cliques now interact more openly. The same-sex clique boundaries blur and heterosexual cliques re-form and interact with other heterosexual cliques.
- *Stage 5 – disintegration of the crowd:* In late adolescence many of the heterosexual clique members form couples. The large crowd and smaller cliques begin to disintegrate as more intimate heterosexual relationships form.

While this model illustrates structural changes in peer-group interactions during adolescence, it does not take into account the development of homosexual relationships within same-sex cliques as adolescents come to terms with their sexual orientation and develop intimate relationships.

> **clique**
> A group whose members associate regularly on the basis of affection, common interests and shared identity

> **3.7** Dunphy's stages of group development during adolescence

CRITICAL REFLECTIONS

■ Can you identify Dunphy's five stages in your peer experiences?

■ Why do you think teachers should be aware of how peer experiences develop? Do you think peer interactions have an impact on how students learn?

Peer experiences across cultures

As noted in our discussion of cultural differences, generalisations about the characteristics of particular cultural groups should be used only as guides to promote understanding and cultural awareness. Nevertheless, research indicates that cultural values and socialisation do play a role in children's peer relationships. A study comparing Chinese and Canadian 5-year-olds (Orlick, Zhou, & Partington, 1990) found that Chinese children engaged in more prosocial behaviours, such as sharing toys or helping each other, than did their Canadian peers. Canadian children, on the other hand, displayed less cooperative behaviour, and 78 per cent of their interactions involved conflict of some kind. Research also indicates that in cultures where the sense of community is strong and extended families are the norm, children may form strong friendship ties among family and extended-family members (Schneider, 2000).

However, in support of the earlier caution about making generalisations, Dong, Yang and Ollendick (1994) have noted that as Chinese children move from primary school into the more competitive Chinese high school settings, where selection procedures determine the type of education they will receive, helping, sharing peer interactions may be replaced by increasingly independent, self-controlling and competitive behaviours in light of the academic pressures to perform as individuals.

Peer experiences and academic achievement

Peer acceptance plays a significant role in academic adjustment and achievement. Children rejected by their peers tend to be perceived by teachers and peers as weak and lacking in self-assurance (Eisenberg, 1998; Wentzel & Asher, 1995). The antisocial behaviour that often leads to these children being rejected by their peers tends to make it difficult for such children to adjust to the classroom context. This often leads to poor academic performance on their part, and the results may be ongoing academic difficulties and perhaps dropping out of school.

One longitudinal study (Ollendick, Weist, Borden, & Greene, 1992) found that children who were actively disliked by their peers were up to seven times more likely to fail an academic year of school than better-liked and accepted peers. Ollendick et al. found that 18 per cent of rejected children drop out of school by the end of Year 9, compared with only 5 per cent of more popular children (see also Hymel, LeMare, Ditner, & Woody, 1999). DeRosier, Kupersmidt and Patterson (1994) also found that peer rejection was highly correlated with absenteeism. On the other hand, children who feel accepted by their peer group tend to feel happier at school, see their classmates as supportive and have generally positive attitudes towards school (Ladd, Kochenderfer, & Coleman, 1996).

Box 3.6 gives some strategies for fostering child and adolescent peer interactions.

Box 3.6 IMPLICATIONS FOR EDUCATORS

Strategies for fostering peer interactions

- Be aware of children or adolescents who have no friends or who are rejected by peers (Eisenberg, 1998). Chronic peer rejection in middle childhood is associated with depression and loneliness (Burks, Dodge, & Price, 1995).
- Look for reasons for poor behaviour or inattention. Rejected children may be more likely to experience behaviour problems, display aggression and attentional difficulties, and may report higher levels of substance abuse and more delinquent offences than their more popular or average peers (Ollendick et al., 1992; Rubin, Booth, Rose-Krasnor, & Mills, 1995).
- Consider a combination of social-skills development for children and instruction for parents on how to manage their children's behaviour in order to enhance children's prosocial behaviour (Kazdin, Siegel, & Bass, 1992; MacMullin, 1998; see also Bierman & Greenberg, 1996).

- Develop students' conflict-resolution skills. Since many conflicts occur at school in the playground, often out of sight of adults (Cunningham, Cunningham, Martorelli, Tran, Young, & Zacharias, 1998), empowering students through student-mediated conflict resolution is another way in which peer relations may be improved (Irving, 1998; Schneider & Blonk, 1998).

3.8 Conflict resolution in the classroom

CRITICAL REFLECTIONS
- From your experience, what is the link between peer interactions and self-esteem?
- What role do you think social and cultural factors play in peer interactions?

The self developing morally

As children's sense of self develops, they encounter situations that extend and challenge their thinking about what is 'moral'. **Morality** is concerned with fundamental questions of right and wrong, justice, fairness and basic human rights. Moral issues are mediated by sociocultural factors, since cultural values and norms have a strong bearing on how individuals think and act. Nevertheless, attitudes towards such issues as lying, stealing, murder and the value of justice are generally considered to be shared across cultures (Nucci, 2001).

morality
The fundamental questions of right and wrong, justice, fairness and basic human rights

Socialisation approaches to moral development

Like other dimensions of development, moral development progresses gradually. There are several views about how this occurs. One approach argues that children develop morals as a result of gradual immersion and socialisation into the adult world (Leman, 2001). This view adopts the principles of social learning theory (see Chapter 4). Social learning theorists such as Bandura (1977) contend that we learn to behave in moral or immoral ways primarily by observing others – particularly parents, caregivers and significant others such as teachers and peers. The view that moral development is moulded by society's values has been supported by Durkheim (1961) and Freud (1930/1963), who both claimed that the quality of children's relationships with their parents greatly influences moral development.

Cognitive-developmental theories of moral development

An alternative to the socialisation approach is the argument that children actively construct their own ways of understanding the world, including what is right and wrong, good and bad. As you learned in Chapter 2, Piaget viewed children as 'little scientists' interested in exploring and making sense of their world. His theory of cognitive development extends to the moral domain and provides the foundation for the cognitive-developmental approach to interpreting moral development.

Cognitive-developmental approaches emphasise moral reasoning rather than moral behaviour alone, yet they do not rule out the impact of social context. Similarly, the socialisation approach to moral development does not ignore the influence of cognitive development (see, for example, Bandura, 1991). The distinguishing features of the different approaches to moral development lie in the emphasis and relative importance they attach to contributing factors. Moral reasoning involves analytical thinking about why we respect and follow 'moral rules' (Piaget, 1932). A moral rule is a generally accepted rule about human behaviour within a particular society; for example, 'You should not murder' is a moral rule in most Western communities (Langford, 1995).

Piaget proposed that cognitive development is connected to the individual's ability to reason morally. Lawrence Kohlberg (see Box 3.8 on page 96) was inspired by Piaget's work, and particularly his method of observing and interviewing children. Piaget and Kohlberg are considered cognitive developmental theorists. They argued that children's ability to reason morally depends on the level of their general thinking abilities, but they also acknowledged the important role of social forces.

Piaget and moral reasoning

Piaget developed carefully constructed stories, or **moral dilemmas** about issues such as clumsiness, stealing and lying that are relevant to the lives of children and adolescents (see Box 3.7 below). The stories were designed to provoke a judgement about the level of guilt or naughtiness of the young people in the story. Piaget's findings led him to describe two types of moral reasoning, which are closely aligned with cognitive development: 'heteronomous morality' and 'autonomous morality'.

Heteronomous morality is typical of younger children (age 4 to 10 years). It focuses on following rules unswervingly and obeying authority figures such as parents, whose moral authority is supreme. Children who reason about moral issues using heteronomous morality do not consider the motives or intentions behind actions. While heteronomous morality is most typical of children, the ages given are only a guide, since some adults are thought to operate at this level of moral reasoning.

The ability to reason about moral issues at a deeper level is known as **autonomous morality**, which is characterised by a capacity for appreciating the perspectives of others and the motives behind words and actions. The development of autonomous morality parallels the development of formal operations and abstract thought, which typically occurs at approximately 10 or 11 years old and continues through to adulthood.

moral dilemma
A moral problem requiring individual judgements and moral reasoning

heteronomous morality
Moral decisions based on the rules of authority figures such as parents

autonomous morality
Moral reasoning that appreciates the perspectives of others and the motives behind their words and actions

Box 3.7 RESEARCH LINKS

A Piagetian moral dilemma

Here is an example of a moral dilemma Piaget used on the subject of stealing. Try to predict how children of different ages might respond before checking on Piaget's findings.

Stealing dilemmas

A Alfred meets a friend who is very poor. This friend tells him that he has had no dinner that day because there was nothing to eat in his home. Then Alfred goes into a baker's shop, and since he has no money, he waits until the baker's back is turned and steals a bread roll. Then he runs out and gives the roll to his friend.

B Henriette goes into a shop. She sees a pretty piece of ribbon on a table and thinks to herself that it would look very nice on her dress. So, while the saleslady's back is turned, she steals the ribbon and runs away at once.

Question: Are these children equally guilty? Which of the two is naughtier, and why?

Source: Adapted from Piaget (1932, p. 119).

What the research found: Sample response typical of heteronomous morality	What the research found: Sample response typical of autonomous morality
Alfred is naughtier than Henriette because a bread roll costs much more than a ribbon.	Henriette is naughtier than Alfred because she is being deceitful. She steals the ribbon while the lady's back is turned and she knows she's done the wrong thing. Alfred has good intentions and is trying to help his friend.

Activities

1 What differences do you observe in the two responses?

> **2** Piaget argued that younger children (using heteronomous morality) tend to make judgements based on the material result and consequences (rather than motive), while older children (using autonomous morality) judge wrongness in terms of the motives behind the act. Can you think of more current moral dilemmas that are appropriate for the age group you plan to work with?

Kohlberg's theory of moral development

Like Piaget, Kohlberg believed that moral reasoning was closely linked to cognitive development, and he used a methodology similar to Piaget's to collect his data (see Box 3.8). Kohlberg proposed a complex six-stage sequence of moral development taking place within three broad levels (see Table 3.8 opposite). Progress from one stage to the next comes about through a combination of cognitive development and socialisation. As we interact with others, learn to appreciate differing viewpoints and have our own views challenged, our mental processes are stimulated and we develop new ways of interpreting the world and making moral judgements.

Box 3.8 ABOUT LAWRENCE KOHLBERG

Lawrence Kohlberg (1927–1987) grew up in New York and attended Andover Academy, an academically demanding private high school in Massachusetts. He did not go straight to university but instead joined the Israeli army. In 1948, Kohlberg enrolled at the University of Chicago, where he scored so high on admission tests that he only had to take a limited number of courses to earn his Bachelor's degree, which he completed in one year. He stayed on at Chicago for graduate work in psychology. At first he planned to become a clinical psychologist but he soon became interested in Piaget's work and began interviewing children and adolescents on moral issues. Kohlberg taught at the University of Chicago from 1962 to 1968 and at Harvard University from 1968 until his death in 1987.

Kohlberg was an unassuming man. When he taught, he frequently went to class dressed in a flannel shirt and baggy pants – as though he had thought it was his day off. He usually began by asking questions in an off-the-cuff manner. In the first days of the university year, students did not always know what to make of him, but they soon realised they were in the presence of a true scholar, a man who had thought long and deeply about critical issues in philosophy and psychology. Unfortunately, Kohlberg suffered from a tropical disease and bouts of depression that caused him intense pain during the last 20 years of his life. At the age of 59, he ended his life by drowning himself.

FIGURE 3.9 Kohlberg believed that moral reasoning was closely linked to cognitive development.

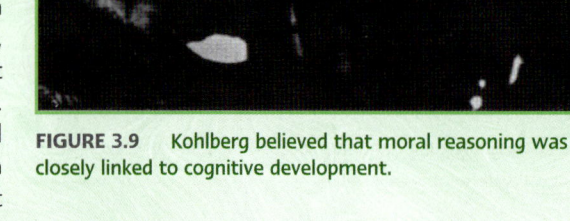

Source: Adapted from Crain (2000, pp. 147–148).

TABLE 3.8	Kohlberg's stage theory
Level I: Preconventional morality	
Stage 1	**Heteronomous morality** ■ Avoidance of breaking rules for fear of punishment ■ Obedience for obedience's sake
Stage 2	**Individualism, instrumental purpose and exchange** ■ Acting in accordance with individual interests – fairness is an equal exchange based upon motivations of self-interest
Level II: Conventional morality	
Stage 3	**Mutual interpersonal expectations, relationships and interpersonal conformity** ■ Living up to what is expected of you ■ Mutual relations of trust and respect should be maintained provided they conform to your expected social role
Stage 4	**Social system and conscience** ■ Rules are to be upheld except when they conflict with other social duties ■ Right is contributing to society and fulfilling social duties
Level III: Postconventional morality	
Stage 5	**Social contract or utility and individual rights** ■ Awareness of the social contract between individuals, but also of the different moral perspectives of others ■ Some individual rights, however, transcend the different perspectives of others and therefore should be upheld
Stage 6	**Universal ethical principles** ■ Following self-chosen ethical principles ■ When such principles conflict with existing moral standards, these principles should be upheld regardless of majority opinion

Source: Adapted from Weiten (2001, p. 455, Figure 11.16).

In Level I (**preconventional morality**), children do not yet see themselves as members of society, and understand morality as a set of rules handed down by adults. As children move from Stage 1 to Stage 2 they begin to see that there may be different views on a single issue. However, they are still self-focused and reason in terms of what will benefit them. In Level II (**conventional morality**), older children and adolescents start to see themselves as conventional members of society. In Stage 3, being a good person and helping those close to you, such as family and friends, is a priority. As the individual moves to Stage 4, the reasons for behaving morally revolve around obeying society's laws in order to maintain law and order.

In Level III (**postconventional morality**), the focus is on what is best for society and on ways of promoting justice. While in Level II the smooth functioning of society is paramount, in Level III people begin to ask: 'How can we improve society?' 'What is just and fair for all?' In Stage 5, for example, individuals may argue that it is appropriate to break some laws if this means protecting the rights of all. An example of this occurred in South Africa during apartheid (a government policy of racial segregation), when Nelson Mandela broke laws that prohibited not only free speech but particularly criticism of the White government. Mandela broke the laws of the country because the basic human rights of Black South Africans were being ignored. As a result he was imprisoned, but was later freed and ultimately became the President of South Africa, the laws of which changed dramatically in the process. It could be argued that Mandela was reasoning at Stage 6; however, due to

preconventional morality
Morality is seen as a set of rules handed down by adults

conventional morality
Being a good member of society and helping those close to you is a priority

postconventional morality
Individuals move beyond the conventional rules of their community to focus more broadly on what is best for society at large, and on ways of promoting justice in society

difficulties with scoring responses at this highest stage, Kohlberg eventually labelled it a 'theoretical' stage and collapsed Stages 5 and 6 in his later analyses (Colby, Kohlberg, & Kauffman, 1987).

Box 3.9 gives an example of a Kohlbergian dilemma, which formed the basis of much of Kohlberg's research on moral reasoning.

Box 3.9 RESEARCH LINKS

The Heinz dilemma

In Europe, a woman was near death from a special kind of cancer. There was one drug that the doctors thought might save her. It was a form of radium that a druggist in the same town had recently discovered. The drug was expensive to make, but the druggist was charging ten times what the drug cost him to make. He paid $200 for the radium and charged $2000 for a small dose of the drug. The sick woman's husband, Heinz, went to everyone he knew to borrow the money, but he could only get together about $1000 which is half of what it cost. He told the druggist that the wife was dying and asked him to sell it cheaper or let him pay later. But the druggist said: 'No, I discovered the drug and I'm going to make money from it.' So Heinz got desperate and broke into the man's store to steal the drug for his wife. Should the husband have done that?

Source: Kohlberg (1963, p. 19).

Activity

Present the Heinz dilemma to a person from each of the following age groups:
- age 6–10
- age 11–15
- age 16–24
- age 25 or older.

1. Record each person's responses and report back to your tutorial/study group.
2. Can you find age differences in your interviewees' moral reasoning?
3. Does Kohlberg's theory help you interpret the responses? If so, how? If not, what weaknesses do you see in Kohlberg's theory?

3.9 More about the Defining Issues Test (DIT)

Neo-Kohlbergians

While some theorists have rejected Kohlberg's view of morality, neo-Kohlbergians contend that his theory is still valid, although some elements require modification. Recognising the limitations of a stage theory, Rest (1979, 1986) built on Kohlberg's work and proposed the Four Component Model for describing moral behaviour. Rest presents moral judgement as one of four interactive psychological processes, the other three being moral sensitivity, moral motivation and moral character.

Rest emphasised that moral judgement is a process of deciding what is a moral thing to do in a moral dilemma. According to Rest and other neo-Kohlbergians, moral judgements reflect a person's underlying organisation of thought about matters of right and wrong. Rest (1986; Rest & Narvàez, 1994) has developed an instrument – the Defining Issues Test (DIT) – that highlights the role of moral judgement in moral development (see also Rest, Thomas, & Edwards, 1997). Neo-Kohlbergians like Rest have responded to the limitations of Kohlberg's theory by examining the role of factors such as age and education trends, cross-cultural issues and educational interventions in moral development.

Strengths and limitations of Kohlberg's theory

Kohlberg's theory provides a comprehensive guide for understanding how moral reasoning progresses, and represents one of the most coherent attempts to chart the development of moral reasoning over time. Kohlberg's theory places moral reasoning in a sociocultural context, emphasising that we are influenced by and in turn influence those around us by our actions. However, his theory has several limitations.

Moral reasoning versus moral behaviour

Since Kohlberg's theory is concerned with moral reasoning, and not moral behaviour, some have argued that this limits the theory's practical applicability because advanced moral reasoning does not necessarily translate into moral behaviour. Kohlberg himself (1987) acknowledged the limitations of verbal responses as a way of gauging someone's level of moral development.

Gender bias

Kohlberg's initial research was exclusively with males aged 10 to 16 years who came from middle- and lower-class families in Chicago. Moreover, Kohlberg's moral dilemmas are predominantly male-oriented. Kohlberg, Levine and Hewer (1983) argued that later studies of females and males showed negligible differences between their scores on moral-dilemma tasks.

Sociocultural bias

Kohlberg's theory of moral development has been criticised for its Western bias. Kohlberg (1987) argued, however, that his theory holds true across cultures, based on research in such countries as India, Taiwan, Kenya, Japan and Israel. These findings were supported by the research of others (for example, Power, Higgins, & Kohlberg, 1989; Snarey, 1985), many of whom were Kohlberg's contemporaries. Such cross-cultural studies provide some evidence for the fundamental stage sequence of moral development in different cultural contexts. More recent research, however, has considered in greater depth the elements of cultural difference in the way people reason and develop morally. Cultural variations do exist, and Kohlberg's theory has been criticised for failing to take account of the impact of cultural differences, social conventions and contexts on the development of moral reasoning (Miller & Bersoff 1992; see also Nucci, 2001). His theory appears to suggest that moral judgements are context-independent, but Nucci argues strongly for interrelationships between morality, social conventions and the sociocultural contexts in which individuals live. There is some evidence, for example, that people holding predominantly individualistic cultural values (such as those dominant in Australia or in the United Kingdom) interpret moral questions differently from people in typically collectivistic cultures (such as those of Japan or India) (Markus & Kitayama, 1991). Kohlberg's theory tends to attach greatest importance to individuals and their capacity to make rational, ethical decisions in the highest stages of the theory. Yet this focus on the individual and the attainment of individual goals tends to be a predominantly Western orientation, typical of individualistic cultures (Krause & O'Brien, 2001). The concern with such generalisations is that these cultures are far from homogeneous in nature; nevertheless, the research highlights trends that are worth noting.

Problems with stages

We have learned (see Chapter 2) that stage theories can be problematic, and a number of criticisms have been levelled at Kohlberg's theory in this regard. First, the stages are not universal: there is evidence that children respond in different ways to different issues. Personal, social and cultural factors play a role in their reasoning and decision-making on moral issues. Second, the stages are not self-contained: children may be predominantly in one stage, but may reason at a different stage depending on the situation. Finally, Kohlberg has been criticised for being idealistic and unrealistic in expecting that individuals will make moral judgements based on cooperation with others as equals.

Despite these limitations, Kohlberg's theory has inspired ongoing research and debate in the field of moral development. Neo-Kohlbergian theorists are a good example of this.

CRITICAL REFLECTIONS

- Kohlberg argued for a connection between emotional development and moral reasoning. Can you explain this connection from your own experience?
- Should principles such as telling the truth be taught as absolute principles (that is, as being always the case) or as qualified principles (that is, as being sometimes the case)? Defend your view. (Adapted from Leming, 2000.)

Further perspectives on moral development and values

There are ongoing debates about what is of value in moral terms, whether there is a universal core set of values that binds individuals across cultures, and whether or not educators play a role in moral development. We cannot examine all these questions here, but we encourage you to consider them carefully for yourself and in your class discussions. In addition to the neo-Kohlbergian approach to moral development, several other theories have been proposed.

Moral development in a social context

The term 'sociomoral development' is increasingly used as theorists recognise the social and cultural dimensions of moral development (Nucci, 2001). Smetana (1995) and Turiel (1983, 1998) proposed a social domain theory of moral development, arguing that children construct social knowledge, including morality, through their social experiences with adults (including parents and teachers), peers and siblings. Morality is constructed through children's reciprocal social interactions. Smetana (1995) attributes particular importance to the role of parents in children's moral development.

Gilligan's feminist voice

Another perspective is that of Carol Gilligan, a former student and co-researcher of Kohlberg's at Harvard University. Gilligan (1982) argued that the primarily male orientation of Kohlberg's theory centres on concerns about justice, rules and rights as reasons for acting morally. Her research on women's morality found that women considered interpersonal relationships, connections between people, compassion and care for others as important reasons for behaving morally. Gilligan contended that, because males and females reason differently about moral dilemmas, females tend to score lower than males on Kohlberg's scoring system.

Gilligan's views have been challenged (Crain, 2000; Walker, 1984; see also Evans, Forney, & Guido-DiBrito, 1998) but there is general acceptance that there are two different moral orientations – one focusing on justice and one motivated by care and compassion. While studies show that the care orientation tends to be more apparent among women and girls (Garmon, Basinger, Gregg, & Gibbs, 1996), another approach is to realise that both the justice and the care-and-compassion orientations may exist in females and males. Gilligan (1982) herself acknowledged that as people progress in their moral development, the two orientations become more closely connected and integrated in both sexes (see also Walker, DeVries, & Trevethan, 1987).

Tronto (1987) suggested that Gilligan's care orientation in moral reasoning may be more representative of many indigenous societies and collectivistic cultures who value the community and the welfare of the group above the individual. Those who value community are typically categorised as falling within Kohlberg's Stage 3, yet Gilligan argues that the valuing of interdependence and relationships should be acknowledged as more advanced moral reasoning.

Values in the education process

A concept closely associated with moral development is that of values. **Values** are ideals that individuals hold regarding what is of worth, and what is good or bad. These ideals in turn guide thoughts and actions, and help us make judgements about what is worthwhile and valuable. Values that most individuals and societies share include respect for self and others, concern for the common good, honesty, fairness and an appreciation of the company of others.

Values are closely connected to the sociocultural context in which they are held. Values do not develop in isolation, but as part of the socialisation process and the interaction between individuals and their communities. A range of social forces operates to shape the development of values. These social agents include parents, the extended family, school, teachers, peers, and the media in all its forms including electronic media such as the Internet.

Values are integral to the learning–teaching process, and you will find they shape the curriculum documents that will guide your future practice. For example, in Western Australia five core values have been identified as part of that state's curriculum framework (Curriculum Council, 1998):

> The minimum set of core values comprises those that are considered generally to be held by members of Australia's multicultural society, taking into account certain shared values which are distinctive to Aboriginal culture. The core values can be summarised as follows:
> - a pursuit of knowledge and a commitment to achievement of potential;
> - self-acceptance and respect of self;
> - respect and concern for others and their rights;
> - social and civic responsibility;
> - environmental responsibility.

Another example of values in the curriculum is found in the New South Wales K–10 Curriculum Framework (New South Wales Board of Studies, 2000b), where core values are as important as core knowledge, skills and understanding in students' learning. For instance, in the New South Wales Geography syllabus for Years 7 to 10, the aim of the course is to help students develop values in the form of a commitment to ecological sustainability, a just society, intercultural understanding and lifelong learning (New South Wales Board of Studies, 2000a).

The role of educators

As you can see, values form an important part of curriculum and classroom practice. Your understanding of how moral development takes place will influence your views about the role of educators in promoting moral development among young people. Those who argue that children develop morally as a result of society moulding children's values promote **character education**, an approach based on the philosophy that values can be conveyed through discipline and modelling, thus developing children's characters and enhancing their moral development. On the other hand, those who adopt the view that children are active participants in their own moral development will provide opportunities for children to examine and critically evaluate moral matters, and encourage them to approach moral issues as problems that require careful analysis and thought (Turiel, 2001).

As an educator, it is impossible for you to stay out of the values arena, since everything you do and say conveys your values to your students. The challenge is to develop ways of enhancing your students' capacity for critical moral reflection and debate within the safety and support of your classroom (see Figure 3.10 over the page) (Nucci, 2001). Research indicates that a classroom characterised by predictability, trust, emotional warmth and reciprocal respect is conducive to the development of the moral self (Arsenio & Lover, 1995). Some strategies to guide your practice are outlined in Box 3.10 (see over page).

---

values
Ideals that individuals hold regarding what is of worth

character education
An approach to education based on the philosophy that values can be conveyed to students through discipline and modelling

3.10 Values in action

Box 3.10 IMPLICATIONS FOR EDUCATORS

Fostering moral development and values

- Develop an attitude of respect for children and young people. This respect is expressed in your classroom organisation, in classroom management, in activities, and in your interactions with learners.
- Make time to learn about your students' interests, feelings, values and ideas.
- Expose learners to different viewpoints. Encourage class discussions about current news items. Give learners opportunities to think about moral problems.
- When discussing sensitive moral issues, let students know ahead of time what is appropriate behaviour. For example, all voices will be heard unless they are deliberately offensive and contravene basic human rights. Respect for each other both inside and outside the classroom is essential. Manage the classroom environment by using reasoning and positive emotions. Be proactive rather than reactive.
- Social experiences stimulate mental processes and help to promote development. Consider excursions or guest speakers to encourage social interactions and exposure to different viewpoints.
- Debates challenge students' positions on topics and further stimulate mental processes.
- Role-playing opportunities help learners imagine what it would be like to be someone else. As young people discuss issues and try to work out how to deal with their differences, they begin to come to terms with the concepts of fairness and justice.
- Identify disciplinary issues with moral content – that is, those that relate to moral values. Develop cases, problems or scenarios that involve these values so students can discuss them.
- Provide opportunities for students to discover how various cultural groups reason about moral issues.
- Every subject – even disciplines such as mathematics that may appear to lack obvious moral content – offers opportunities for helping students develop their skill in moral reasoning. Every group can become a learning community where values of mutual respect, sensitivity to others' needs and cooperation are emphasised and discussed.

Source: Adapted from Crain (2000, p. 156).

FIGURE 3.10 Debates and discussions challenge students' positions on topics.

Concluding comments

There are important connections between how young people develop socially and emotionally, and how they develop their system of values and understandings of what is moral. Like other dimensions of development, these facets of the self remain with children and adolescents throughout adulthood. To ensure healthy development in these areas, young people need to be supported as they come to terms with who they are, how they fit into their sociocultural context, and how to deal with complex sociomoral issues.

Young people need to be active agents rather than passive listeners when grappling with moral issues and dilemmas. The challenge for educators is to provide opportunities for learners to become independent thinkers who are self-aware, critically reflective and conscious of their role in the broader social and cultural contexts in which they live.

Chapter review

- In this chapter we have examined a number of dimensions of self. Self is what makes us unique.
- Self-concept is the view we hold of ourselves. When we attach values and emotions to this view, we develop self-esteem. When we feel empowered to act and achieve our goals, we develop self-efficacy.
- Erikson's eight-stage theory of psychosocial development demonstrates that self develops over time and is closely connected to cognitive development.
- Emotions play a significant role in our lives. We develop an increasing range of emotions over time, and socioemotional development occurs as we engage with our social and cultural context.
- Peer experiences play an important role in socioemotional development. There are several types of peer experiences, including friendships and groups. Positive peer experiences may enhance academic achievement and self-esteem, but negative experiences may bring about low self-esteem, depression, physical illness and a range of other problems associated with bullying.
- The self also has a moral dimension. There are several explanations of moral development, including the socialisation approach (for example, Bandura), the cognitive-developmental approach (for example, Kohlberg) and the feminist perspective (for example, Gilligan).
- Educators need to be aware of the ways in which values are conveyed through educational processes and of the importance of values in young people's moral development.

You make the connections:

Questions and activities for self-assessment and discussion

1. Define and explain the relationship between self-concept and self-esteem.
2. What is self-efficacy? Comment on the role of self-efficacy during the period of adolescence.
3. Outline Erikson's stages of psychosocial development.
4. Define emotion and explain the functional approach to emotional development.
5. Identify three types of peer experiences and explain their importance in the lives of children and adolescents.
6. Draw a concept map illustrating what you have learned about the connections between cognitive, psychosocial, emotional and moral development.

Key terms

self	individualistic culture	relationship group
self-concept	collectivistic culture	friendship
affect	emotion	clique
self-esteem	socioemotional development	morality
self-efficacy	functional-organisational approach	moral dilemma
psychosocial		heteronomous morality
psychosocial crisis	basic emotions	autonomous morality
identity	self-conscious emotions	preconventional morality
identity achievement	social emotions	conventional morality
identity foreclosure	prosocial behaviour	postconventional morality
identity diffusion	perspective-taking	values
moratorium	interaction	character education

Recommended reading

Bandura, A. (1991). Social cognitive theory of moral thought and action. In W. M. Kurtines & J. L. Gewirtz (Eds.), *Handbook of moral behaviour and development* (Vol. 1, pp. 45–103). Hillsdale, NJ: Lawrence Erlbaum. Also available online: <www.emory.edu/EDUCATION/mfp/BanduraPubs.html>.

Eisenberg, N. (Ed.) (1998). *Handbook of child psychology: Vol. 3: Social, emotional and personality development* (5th ed.). New York: Wiley.

Erikson, E. H. (1997). *The life cycle completed: Extended version.* New York: W.W. Norton & Co.

Kohlberg, L. (1984). *Essays in moral development. Volume II: The psychology of moral development.* San Francisco: Harper & Row.

Nucci, L. P. (2001). *Education in the moral domain.* Cambridge, UK: Cambridge University Press.

Purdie, N., Tripcony, P., Boulton-Lewis, G., Fanshawe, J., & Gunstone, A. (2000). *Positive self-identity for Indigenous students and its relationship to school outcomes.* Canberra: Commonwealth of Australia. Also available online: <www.detya.gov.au/schools/publications/2000/PSI_synth.pdf>.

White, R., & Wyn, J. (2002). *Youth and society.* Sydney: Oxford University Press.

Make some online visits

Erikson and socioemotional development:
　<facultyweb.cartland.edu/~ANDERSMD/ERIK/welcome.html>
SELF Research Centre, University of Western Sydney: <edweb.uws.edu.au/self/>
Values education: <www.curriculum.edu.au/values/>

FIGURE MII Module II concept map.

- Behavioural views of learning
- Cognitive explanations of learning
- Humanist approaches to learning
- The learning process

MODULE CONTENTS

- Chapter 4 Behavioural views of learning

MODULE II

The learning process

Core question: *Can theories of learning enhance the understanding of learning and teaching?*

As children develop they learn. Changes that come about through learning can relate to such things as knowledge, skills, beliefs, attitudes, habits and feelings. Such changes are enduring. They can result from instruction or be an unintended outcome of experience.

This module focuses on ways of understanding the learning process. It explores different theoretical explanations of how we learn, and the implications these explanations have for teachers in how they view their role, relate to learners, arrange their classrooms, deliver content and assess students' work.

Chapter 4 presents behavioural explanations of learning, which are concerned with learners' observable behaviours, and where the quality and extent of learning is measured by what learners can show or do to demonstrate what they have learned. Chapter 5 explores cognitive and constructivist explanations of learning, which draw attention to the learner as an active participant in learning and as a constructor of meaning, and which view learning as a collaborative partnership in which social interaction is particularly important. Chapter 6 discusses humanistic approaches to learning, which draw attention to personal, social and qualitative aspects and which are concerned with the whole learner and with developing learners' full human potential.

Each chapter of this module encourages you to consider different theories of learning and what these can teach you about the learner's and the teacher's role in the classroom and in learning. Teachers often enhance their effectiveness by being eclectic – that is, by using elements of different theories to achieve the best possible results for their students. You may wish to keep this in mind as you study this module and consider your developing philosophy of learning and teaching.

FIGURE 4.1 Chapter 4 concept map.

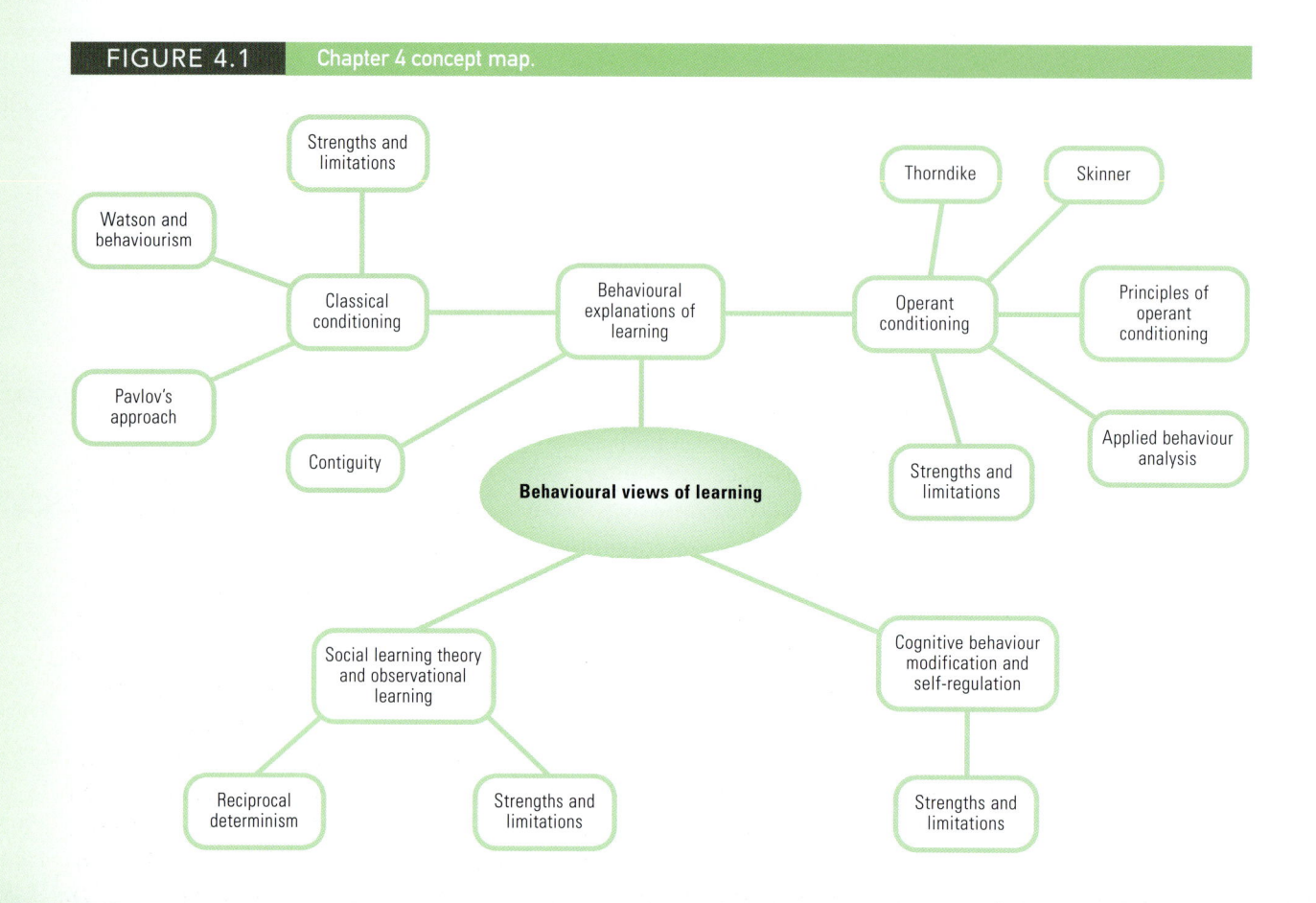

CHAPTER OBJECTIVES

After reading this chapter you should be able to:

- identify some of the main characteristics that distinguish classical conditioning from operant conditioning

- describe the Premack principle and give an example of its use in everyday life

- explain why poker machines are so effective in holding players' attention

- describe how a teacher can use antecedent-behaviour-consequence (A-B-C) information to manage behaviour

- give an example of applied behaviour analysis (ABA) in the classroom

- review the main theories discussed in the chapter and identify the common threads that connect them.

CHAPTER 4

Behavioural views of learning

Introduction

Have you ever tried to teach a dog to do tricks? Have you ever attempted to teach a cockatoo to talk, or mice to turn a wheel by running up the rungs, or a child to swim? If you have tried any of these things, then you will most probably have used behavioural techniques. Every time you say 'good dog', 'good swimming' or give some other form of praise, you are giving your pupil what behaviourists call 'reinforcement'.

This chapter is about the principles that underlie behavioural explanations of learning, sometimes called 'behaviourism'. According to behavioural views of learning, actions that are reinforced (or rewarded) are more likely to be repeated. When you praise a pupil for doing the right thing, you are enhancing the likelihood that the actions you are rewarding will be repeated, and that learning – or permanent changes in behaviour resulting from experience – will occur. Behavioural explanations of learning are concerned with the effect of external events, such as reinforcement or punishment, on changes in behaviour. The example of mice learning to turn the wheel is a little different, however. You might be responsible for the mice having a wheel in their cage, but you probably do not teach them (through using planned rewards) to make it turn. In this case, the mice will initially turn the wheel by accident when they run across it. Having made the wheel move, and liking the effect, they will repeat the original action and in doing so turn the wheel intentionally. You can then reinforce this behaviour by rewarding them with food each time the wheel is turned. However, running on the wheel is self-reinforcing for the mice, and they quickly learn how to keep the wheel moving without any help from you.

Some aspects of behavioural principles and their application in specific situations are controversial. For example, instead of using rewards or reinforcements to encourage learning you can also use punishment to change behaviour or achieve a learning objective. Examples are given later in the chapter of situations where punishment rather than praise may be the most appropriate way to change behaviour and achieve desired learning. Here, **behaviour** is defined as any actions that are observable and measurable.

The strategies identified in behavioural approaches to learning provide educators with very powerful tools to use as part of instruction. Examples of such uses, such as praise to encourage good behaviour or the use of Grandma's rule (see 'The Premack principle' later in this chapter) to help a child finish a task, will help you understand why teachers need to learn about behavioural theories as part of their preparation for teaching.

behaviour
Actions that are observable and measurable

Behavioural explanations of learning

Do you associate the smell of baking bread with eating fresh bread – a pleasant experience for most people? If you have learned this association, the smell of baking bread will trigger thoughts in you about eating bread and, perhaps, memories of holidays when Mum or Dad baked the bread at home or there was a good bakery close to where you were staying. Similarly, learning to recite the alphabet or to count to 10 involves building associations: saying 'a, b, c, d' or '1, 2, 3' triggers even quite young children to recite the next letters or numbers in these sequences.

Contiguity

At the most simple level, behaviourists see learning as an outcome of **contiguity**, or the connections or associations that link a **stimulus (S)** (something that affects the senses) and a **response (R)** (a reaction to a stimulus). Contiguity assumes that whenever two events or sensations occur often, and at the same time, an association develops so that at other times when only one of the events or sensations occurs, the other is also remembered.

Contiguity provides a simple principle that can be used to help learners develop associations between specific stimuli (objects, events, sensations) that often occur at about the same time or that are closely paired in terms of similarity and contrast. Examples include learning the alphabet and learning to associate concepts such as 'hot–cold', 'good–bad', 'big–little'. Instances of applied contiguity in learning include the use of drill and rhyme to teach simple facts such as the spelling of irregular words (for example, '*i* before *e* except after *c*') or number facts (for example, '$5 \times 5 = 25$'). The principles of contiguity are also used to help children remember the details of their name, address and telephone number.

Tabula rasa

The principle of contiguity can be traced back to the Greek philosopher Aristotle (384–322 BC). He described the mind of an infant as a blank slate, or what the English philosopher John Locke (1632–1704) called a *tabula rasa* (Latin for 'scraped tablet'). 'I imagine the minds of children are as easily turned, this way or that way, as water itself' (from *John Locke on education*, Gay, 1964, p. 20). According to this 'associationist' view of learning, the newborn knows nothing but has the potential to learn from experience as a result of an innate ability to perceive sensations and to build associations among them. Particular sensations are remembered if they are associated in memory as a result of contiguity (that is, they occur in the same time and place), similarity (they are alike) or contrast (they are dissimilar, or opposites). However, while associationism's principles of contiguity can be used to explain simple learning that involves stimulus-response (S-R) linkages, most learning cannot be adequately understood in such terms, and more complex explanations are needed. These gradually emerged, over time, as a result of more systematic study of the learning process in children and animals.

Classical conditioning

Pavlov's approach

Probably the most important contribution to our understanding of the process of **classical conditioning** was made by a Russian physiologist, Ivan Petrovich Pavlov (see Box 4.1 opposite). As part of a wider study of digestion and the production of saliva in dogs, Pavlov (1928) attempted to study the relationship between a dog being fed, and the dog's salivation and digestion.

---

contiguity
The association of two events that are always closely paired or that repeatedly occur at about the same time

stimulus
An environmental condition or event that activates the senses

response
An observable reaction to a known (or unknown) stimulus

4.1 Locke's concept of *tabula rasa*

classical conditioning
The association of an automatic response with a new stimulus

Box 4.1 ABOUT IVAN PETROVICH PAVLOV

Ivan Petrovich Pavlov (1849–1936) was born in Ryazan, a rural village in central Russia. His father was the village priest and the family hoped the boy would follow his father into the priesthood. Pavlov attended the church school, and later the seminary in Ryazan. However, after reading translations of the scientific work of Charles Darwin and others, he left the seminary and enrolled at the University of St Petersburg, where he studied chemistry and physiology, gaining a doctorate in 1879. In 1883 he completed medical studies at the Imperial Medical Academy. His early research was concerned with the physiology of the heart and the nervous system (Nobel lecture, 2002).

In 1881, Pavlov married Seraphima, who was a teacher and the daughter of a doctor in the Black Sea fleet. They had three sons and a daughter.

Pavlov is best known for his studies of the digestive system in dogs, exploring as he did the relationship between salivation and digestion. As a result of his research into the relationship between the brain and the body's physiological processes, he identified a set of basic principles concerning the brain's role in relation to organisms' overall functioning. As result of this work, Pavlov was awarded the Nobel Prize for Physiology and Medicine in 1904.

FIGURE 4.2 Pavlov (second from right) contributed to our understanding of classical conditioning through his studies of salivation and digestion in dogs.

One of the more interesting research techniques devised by Pavlov involved the use of his surgical skills to create permanent openings in the body that could be used to directly observe processes such as digestion (Nobel lecture, 2002).

If you want to know more about Pavlov, use his name to search the World Wide Web.

Salivation triggers digestion in the stomach, and if salivation does not occur, then digestion does not begin. Pavlov argued that salivation is not innate, but rather is a 'conditioned' (or learned) response (as opposed to an innate or involuntary response like blinking) that originates in the brain's cerebral cortex and that is governed by the central nervous system (Nobel lecture, 2002).

For the purposes of Pavlov's study, a small operation was performed on a dog to alter the flow of saliva to an opening (or fistula) on the outside of the dog's cheek. A glass funnel was attached to the opening to collect the flowing saliva and the dog was taught to stand quietly on a table while loosely harnessed (see Figure 4.3 over the page). Pavlov experimented with stimuli other than food to find out if these could trigger salivation and hence digestion. Using a bell as the new stimulus, he began to sound the bell at the same time food was presented to the dog and found that whereas the dog had initially salivated only at the sight of food, it now began to salivate at the sound of the bell. In addition, while he was working with the dog, Pavlov noticed that whenever the assistant who regularly fed the dog came into the room, the dog began to salivate as though it had been given food. Intrigued by this unexpected development, Pavlov changed the focus of his study from digestion to the process by which a dog salivated at the sight or sound of the person who fed him rather than solely at the sight or smell of food (Hilgard & Marquis, 1961).

In his study of the way in which the dog learned to salivate at the sound of a bell rather than at the food, Pavlov implemented the following procedures using a tuning fork instead of a bell.

FIGURE 4.3
Pavlov's arrangement for the study of salivary conditioning.
(Source: Yerkes and Morgulis, 1909, reproduced in Hilgard & Marquis, 1961, Figure 3.1.)

1 Unconditioned stimulus and response

First, a tuning fork was sounded for 7 to 8 seconds before a small amount of food was moved close to the dog's mouth. At this stage, the sound of the tuning fork was a **neutral stimulus (NS)** – that is, a stimulus that does not excite or provoke activity – and the dog did not respond to it. There was no salivation. However, the dog salivated copiously while eating the food, the food being an **unconditioned stimulus (US)** or natural, unlearned, primary stimulus that elicited the uncontrollable response of salivation in the dog. In this case, the dog's salivating was an automatic or **unconditioned response (UR)** – that is, no prior training or **conditioning** was needed to elicit salivation from the dog in response to food.

2 Conditioned stimulus and response

Pavlov then sounded the tuning fork just *before* food was presented to the dog. His aim was to train or 'condition' the dog to salivate to the sound of the tuning fork. Initially, salivation occurred after the tuning fork had been sounded for 18 seconds, but on later tests salivation occurred within 1 to 2 seconds. The previously neutral sound of the tuning fork had become a **conditioned stimulus (CS)**. The dog now salivated, or gave a learned or **conditioned response (CR)**, to the sound of the tuning fork.

3 Discrimination, generalisation and extinction

Subsequently, Pavlov achieved stimulus **discrimination** by teaching the dog to respond to one specific tone from the tuning fork while ignoring other tones. Pavlov was also able to 'generalise' the learned responses by teaching the dog to respond to a range of different sounds, not just a single tone of the tuning fork. Finally, he 'extinguished' the learned behaviour after he repeatedly presented the conditioned stimulus (the sound of the tuning fork) *without* producing the food. Here, the learned or conditioned response (salivation) gradually disappeared as the association between the two events (sound and food) weakened and disappeared.

Pavlov's influence

Pavlov's research into classical conditioning had a tremendous impact on ideas about learning. In particular, his use of precise observation and measurement, derived from his work as a physiologist, established an invaluable framework for future research into human learning and behaviour. His work attracted the interest of American psychologists, who adopted Pavlov's terminology as well as his research strategy, which involved carrying out a number of related experiments to explore one topic with great precision (Hilgard & Marquis, 1961).

---

neutral stimulus (NS)
An event or happening that has no effect on an organism

unconditioned stimulus (US)
An object, event or happening in the physical environment that causes spontaneous activity in an organism

unconditioned response (UR)
An action triggered spontaneously by a stimulus

conditioning
The establishment of a new association between a stimulus and a response

conditioned stimulus (CS)
A previously neutral stimulus that elicits a conditioned response after pairing with an unconditioned stimulus

conditioned response (CR)
A response evoked by a conditioned stimulus

discrimination
Learning that it is appropriate to respond to some stimuli but not to others

Watson and behaviourism

Pavlov's behavioural principles were developed further by John B. Watson (1878–1958). Watson was an American psychologist who introduced the term 'behaviourism' into US psychology. Like Pavlov, Watson worked with animals. He believed that behaviour could be explained not in terms of instincts and other inherited mental characteristics, but rather in terms of S-R associations and, in particular, conditioned reflexes and responses. He argued that it was not necessary to study thoughts, feelings, intentions or meanings – which was common practice at the time – in order to understand behaviour.

According to Watson's view of early development (1913, 1919, 1925), infants are born with innate reflexes and emotional reactions such as fear, love and anger. As they develop, other S-R associations are formed. In this way, the newborn infant's limited range of innate responses is gradually extended and expanded as a result of experience.

4.2 Unconditioned responses in early behavioural research

Little Albert and the rat

Watson is best known for an experiment in which he and Rosalie Rayner used Pavlov's classical conditioning principles to induce fear in Little Albert, who was a healthy infant about 9 months old (Watson & Rayner, 1920).

When first shown a white rat, Albert reached out to touch it. At this stage, the rat was a neutral stimulus (NS), but as Albert again tried to touch it, Watson and Rayner made a loud sound (US) behind Albert's head by striking a hammer on a steel bar. As expected, Albert began to cry (UR). After a number of trials in which the loud sound was made each time Albert reached out to touch the rat, even just the *appearance* of the rat (CS) caused Albert to cry (CR). He had been conditioned (or had learned) to fear the rat. Subsequently, Albert's fear extended or 'generalised' spontaneously to objects that resembled the rat, such as a white rabbit, cotton wool and a Father Christmas mask.

A few years later, classical conditioning was used to extinguish fear in a young boy called Peter, who was fearful of white rabbits (Jones, 1924). In this study, Peter was seated in a high chair and given food he liked. While he was eating, someone brought a white rabbit in a small cage as close as possible to Peter without distracting him. This process was repeated, with the white rabbit (CS) always presented at the same time as Peter's favourite food (US) until Peter's fear response (CR) decreased.

Strengths and limitations of classical conditioning

Strengths

Pavlov's studies of classical conditioning had an impact on research methodology, both in terms of the value placed on precise observation and measurement, and the use of a number of experiments to explore one topic with great precision.

At a more practical level, therapists and others often use classical conditioning principles to reduce fearful or irrational behaviour in children and adults. Many irrational fears and phobias are formed as a result of the pairing of neutral stimuli with stimuli that trigger an involuntary response (such as pleasure, anxiety or panic). For example, throwing a child who cannot swim into deep water on the assumption that this will make the child learn to swim is likely to result in the child developing a fear of water. Therapists often use procedures derived from classical conditioning to help us overcome such problems (Alberto & Troutman, 1999).

Limitations

Not all behaviour follows the model identified in classical conditioning, since some actions are initiated by an organism as a result of an impulse or a conscious intent that is not under the direct or immediate control of an external stimulus. It is not possible to trigger such actions in the way Pavlov triggered salivation in his dog.

On the other hand, it is sometimes difficult to find responses that can provide a starting point for instruction, such as when a child is mute at the time when speech should be emerging. As a result, formal instructional procedures based on classical conditioning principles are not often used, although classical conditioning can come about inadvertently, and many irrational fears and phobias as well as negative or inhibiting responses to daily experiences are formed in this way.

The implications of classical conditioning for teaching practice are explored in Box 4.2.

Box 4.2 IMPLICATIONS FOR EDUCATORS

Classical conditioning in classrooms

Instances of classical conditioning in classrooms and even in daily life are easy to find. For example, the very common fear of dentists can easily be explained in terms of Watson and Rayner's 1920 study with Little Albert.

Examples of classical conditioning in schools and classrooms include:

- feelings of embarrassment or extreme anxiety associated with classes taught by teachers who use shaming and ridicule to make students conform, leading to continuing negative feelings about the subject matter taught by these teachers or about schools in general, and to avoidance of further study
- the use of existing behaviour by forming associations between involuntary responses and specific stimuli that are neutral in their effect until paired closely with a particular stimulus; for example, using children's tendency to stop and look when they hear a loud sound in order to teach students to respond immediately to a teacher's call for attention (this can be done by pairing the teacher's call with a sound like a bell or a gong: over time, the bell or gong can be phased out as the teacher's voice alone captures the students' attention).

CRITICAL REFLECTION

- Can you think of examples from your own experience that might explain any uncomfortable feelings you have about your experiences at school?
- What can teachers do to ensure that their students feel positive about school? How can they avoid creating negative feelings about learning in some students?
- How might you begin to teach a child to talk if the child is not making sounds that resemble speech? How might you begin to teach writing if the child has never used a crayon or a pencil?

4.3 More about classical conditioning

Operant conditioning

Answers to some of the problems identified in the use of classical conditioning (such as the need to find an automatic response as a starting point for instruction) are provided by 'operant conditioning', which is concerned not with unintentional or automatic responses to environmental stimuli, but with behaviour that is conscious, intentional or voluntary.

A toddler will look for a toy in a play box out of curiosity or boredom, a dog will sniff around a tree to find out if other dogs have passed by recently, and a kookaburra will swoop down to catch a lizard because of hunger. These actions are not responses to external stimuli. A model explaining the occurrence of these types of behaviour was provided initially in the theory of learning proposed by E. L. Thorndike (1874–1949), an influential psychologist and a contemporary of Watson; and by B. F. Skinner (1904–1990). Their contributions to theories of learning were concerned with the field of **operant** (or instrumental) **conditioning**, where the learner's behaviour is instrumental in triggering a sequence of events that leads to a positive or negative outcome, and to learning. The term 'operant' refers to individuals being autonomous and free to 'operate' in their own way on the environment.

Thorndike, trial-and-error learning and the law of effect

Thorndike's (1911, 1931) main contribution to the development of behaviourism was his work on the effect of rewards on behaviour. His explanation of learning as involving the formation (or 'stamping in') of associations or connections between stimulus and response came to be known as **associationism**.

Cats and the puzzle box

In a series of now-famous studies, Thorndike (1911) trained cats to escape from a 'puzzle box' to obtain food. The box used in the studies had vertical slats so that once the cat was in the box it could see but not reach food that had been placed outside (see Figure 4.4). To open the door of the box and reach the food, the cat had to perform an action such as pressing a latch or pulling a cord. If a hungry cat was put into a puzzle box, it became very active – clawing, scratching and moving around the box in its eagerness to get to the food. During this random activity, the cat would accidentally trigger the door to open and was immediately rewarded with the food. If the cat was put into the box again, it would again begin to claw, scratch and push, but this time its movements would be concentrated in the area from where the latch had previously been released. After more trials, during which the cat would direct its activity towards the latch mechanism, other actions would gradually drop out as the correct act was learned or 'stamped in'. By this stage, the cat would perform the correct action as soon as it was put into the box.

Thorndike described this process as trial, error and accidental success (Thorndike, 1898) and called the cat's actions **trial-and-error learning**. He explained the processes involved in terms of the **law of effect** – that is, responses that have a satisfying outcome (such as when the cat reached the food) are likely to strengthen and be repeated, whereas those that are followed by discomfort or annoyance are likely to weaken or not be repeated. Over time, the terms 'satisfaction' and 'annoyance' were replaced by words such as 'reward', 'reinforcement' and 'punishment'. Thorndike also expressed his belief that the connections between actions and new outcomes are strengthened the more often they are repeated, which is known as the **law of exercise**.

operant conditioning
The use of positive and negative consequences to strengthen or weaken voluntary behaviour

associationism
An explanation of learning as the formation of connections between stimuli and responses

trial-and-error learning
An explanation of learning that states when an individual is placed in a problem-solving situation, the correct response will be learned through being reinforced

law of effect
Responses that have a satisfying outcome are likely to be strengthened and repeated

law of exercise
Connections between actions and new consequences are strengthened the more they are repeated

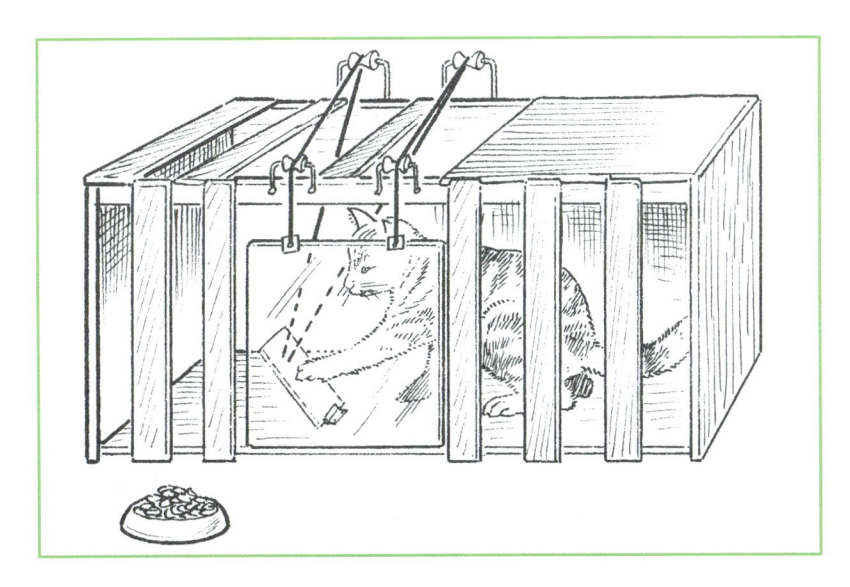

FIGURE 4.4
The cat has to find a way to escape from the puzzle box in order to reach the food.

FIGURE 4.5
How would the law of effect be used to train this dog?

Thorndike showed that trial-and-error actions resulting in the delivery of a reward need not be associated just with mechanical acts such as stepping on a latch or nudging a lever. For example, he taught a cat to lick itself in order to get food. The key factor is that the action results in receipt of the reward. An everyday example of the law of effect is a dog putting out a paw to 'shake hands' (see Figure 4.5). This trick has been taught through the law of effect, by giving the dog a reward such as food or a pat every time it carries out the action. If the trick is practised often, the law of exercise is also being applied. Can you think of other everyday examples of this type of learning?

Box 4.3 discusses the classroom implications of Thorndike's work.

Box 4.3 CLASSROOM LINKS

Trial-and-error learning

Thorndike's work is significant because of his studies of trial-and-error learning. Teachers need to be aware of:
- the *effects* of behaviour on learning, and the idea of learning as the establishment of connections between stimuli and responses
- the relationship between individuals' behaviour in problem situations and subsequent learning, represented in the law of effect and the law of exercise, which provided a basis for Skinner's studies of operant learning.

Skinner and operant conditioning

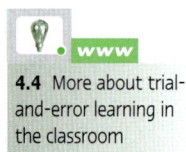

The early research of Harvard psychologist B. F. Skinner (see Box 4.4) was mainly concerned with white rats. In these studies, a rat would be placed in a cage-like box. The box could be opened with a device, such as a lever, that the rat could operate to obtain food. Later, having observed some pigeons flying, and noting their excellent vision and ability to manoeuvre, Skinner began to use pigeons in his studies, again placing them in boxes that were totally under his control (see Figure 4.7 opposite).

www
4.4 More about trial-and-error learning in the classroom

Box 4.4 ABOUT B. F. SKINNER

Burrhus Frederick Skinner (1904–1990) was born in Susquehanna, a small Pennsylvanian railroad town close to the New York State border. The family lived in a comfortable two-storey wooden house with a yard that was 'strewn with debris, the garden overgrown' (Bjork, 1993, p. 3), a paradise for an enterprising boy with a vivid imagination and an interest in construction. From an early age, Skinner enjoyed making gadgets from junk lying around the yard. For example, after frequent scolding by his

FIGURE 4.6
Skinner's work on the principles of operant conditioning and the relationship between behaviour and its consequences had a major impact on learning and teaching in classrooms.

mother for forgetting to hang up his pyjamas, Skinner built a device involving a hook, nails and a string that led to the bedroom door with a sign 'Hang up your pyjamas'. When the pyjamas were on the hook, the sign lifted out of sight. When they were off the hook, the sign came down as a reminder to put them away (Bjork, 1993, p. 13).

At school and at college, Skinner was interested in literature and biology and considered becoming a poet and novelist. However, he became interested in psychology after reading books by Pavlov and Watson. He enrolled at the psychology department at Harvard University, gaining a PhD in psychology in 1931. In 1948 he returned to Harvard to work in the psychology department, remaining professionally active until his death in 1990 (Skinner Foundation, 2002).

Skinner is remembered for three specific initiatives, which involve pigeons he attempted to train as navigator-bombardiers during World War II; a thermostatically controlled, enclosed 'baby box' he designed for his second daughter and that he tried to commercialise without success; and 'teaching machines' that gave immediate feedback and reduced the time wasted by students who worked more quickly than their peers.

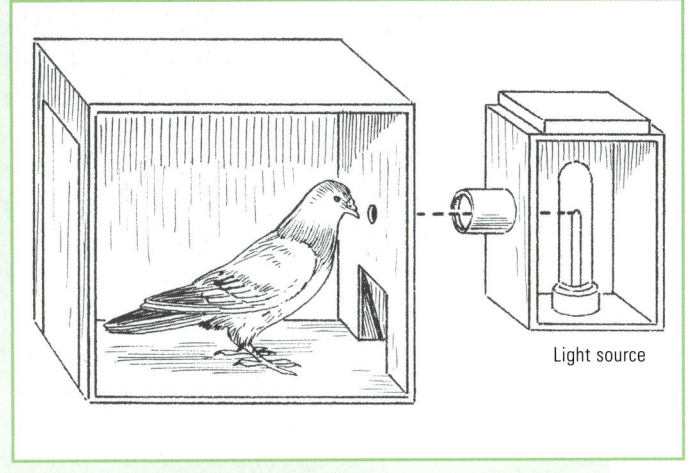

FIGURE 4.7 A typical Skinner experiment. The pigeon in the 'Skinner box' is reinforced by a flashing light after pecking a key.
(Source: Guttman and Kalish, 1958; reproduced in Hilgard & Marquis, 1961.)

4.5 More about B. F. Skinner

From the 1930s and, more particularly, during the 1950s to the 1970s, Skinner (1938, 1948, 1957, 1968 1971) was, and remains, the most famous name in the field of operant conditioning, and has been a major influence in the fields of education and psychology. His main interest was in the relationship between behaviour and its consequences.

Skinner acknowledged the principles of classical conditioning demonstrated by Pavlov and Watson. However, he argued that the principles of classical conditioning were incomplete and did not account for the much larger number of behaviours that individuals initiate spontaneously. He called these self-initiated behaviours **operants** because they involved actions that are produced or emitted voluntarily by the individual as an operator in the environment. Operant behaviours were contrasted with **respondents**, these being elicited or reflex reactions produced when an individual responds (often involuntarily) to recognised stimuli in the environment.

When children are placed in strange situations, such as trying to operate a new toy or find their way to some swings, their first actions will be more or less random. However, a pattern of action very quickly emerges in response to the feedback – or **reinforcement** – received. In trying to operate a new toy, initial unsuccessful attempts are abandoned and new ways tried – and, in the case of the swings, alternative routes are attempted – until a successful outcome results. The child's actions in trying to make the toy work or to find the swings in a park are operants. Getting the toy to work, or finding the swings, is a reinforcement. Learning occurs as the correct actions are reinforced. The child's performance response has been strengthened and will recur more quickly in future encounters with similar situations.

operants
Voluntary actions, usually goal-directed

respondents
Elicited or reflex reactions to a specific stimulus

reinforcement
Increasing or strengthening the likelihood of a behaviour recurring through use of contingent feedback

Principles of operant conditioning

Antecedents and consequences

The word 'behaviour' was defined earlier as the actions or activities of a living organism that are observable and measurable. Such activities do not occur in isolation, but are part of an ongoing string of actions, reactions, responses and initiations. For example, if you take a specific action produced by a child sitting in a classroom and examine it carefully, you will see that the action you have observed is embedded in an extraordinarily complex array of ongoing events. It may involve other people (the teacher, other children), the classroom setting (furniture, books, pencils and so on) and all the child's previous experiences (breakfast at home, the trip to school on the bus, games in the playground before class, something that happened last week or last year). It may also involve expectations and thoughts about what will happen next (in the playground or on the way home from school). It is impossible to isolate a single act from all the events and influences that have preceded it and that will follow it. So in any attempt to study an instance of a single act (such as a rat pressing a lever or a child reaching out to touch a white rat), it is important to take account of what precedes it ('antecedents') and what follows it ('consequences').

Behaviourists believe that all voluntary (intentional) behaviour is controlled by antecedents and consequences. Both types of information are important in understanding humans' and animals' actions. In behavioural research, the ongoing chain of activity that is behaviour is represented symbolically as **antecedent-behaviour-consequence (A-B-C)** (see Table 4.1 in Box 4.5 for an example of an A-B-C record from a disruptive classroom situation). A-B-C is a strategy used by teachers to specify the exact nature of problem behaviour and any contextual factors that may be contributing to its occurrence. It involves the teacher or other observer recording the behaviour of a particular 'target' child in terms of the events that immediately precede the behaviour and that follow it.

antecedent-behaviour-consequence (A-B-C)
Behaviour represented as an ongoing chain of activity involving events that immediately precede the behaviour and that follow it

Box 4.5 CLASSROOM LINKS

An A-B-C situation

In the following example, a teacher is concerned about one boy, Darren, who displays a range of inappropriate behaviours. The teacher wants to pinpoint specific behaviours in Darren that need to be changed, as well as any classroom events that may be contributing to the problem. An aide has agreed to observe Darren's behaviour during a mathematics lesson. These are her notes.

TABLE 4.1 A-B-C record of a disruptive classroom situation

Time	Antecedent behaviour	Behaviour (target child)	Consequent behaviour
9.16	1. Teacher (T.) 'Get out your workbooks and get ready to write answers to these problems'	Darren (D.) did not listen to T. [C]ontinued to talk to child next to him	T. repeated the instruction to Darren
	2.	D. walked over to pencil sharpener, bumped another child's desk – all the books fell to the ground	Child hit Darren
	3. Child hit Darren	D. hit child and swore at him	T. 'Stop that, D.! [O]r you'll have to leave the room'
	4.	D. continued to fight	Other child now crying
	5. T. 'D., I said stop it immediately. Go to your own desk'	D. went to pencil sharpener	T. 'I'm nearly ready to start now. Just waiting for D.'
9.25	6.	D. sharpen[ed] 3 pencils	T. 'Hurry up, D.'
	7.	D. return[ed] to desk, trie[d] to find workbook	
9.30	8. T. 'Are you ready?'	D. 'No, I can't find my book'	

Source: Ward, Bochner, Center, Outhred, & Pieterse (1987, p. 164).

Activities

1. Can you identify the precise nature of the inappropriate actions that annoyed Darren's teacher, the antecedent conditions that triggered these actions and the consequences that followed to increase or decrease the actions' rate of occurrence?
2. What changes could Darren's teacher introduce to reduce Darren's inappropriate actions?
3. What appropriate behaviour could be encouraged? How might this be done?

When a child makes a rude sign to another child who reacts by hitting and spitting, it is the initial actions of the child making the sign that trigger the behaviour of the other. The **antecedent**s of behaviour, or the conditions that precede particular actions, contribute to the action's occurrence. **Consequence**s are conditions or events that immediately follow actions and that can *increase* the likelihood of a specific behaviour recurring. Consequences can also *decrease* the likelihood of recurrence, such as when you rebuke a child for walking on a clean floor with muddy feet. Sometimes a consequence has no effect on the behaviour it follows – that is, it is neutral in its impact on the behaviour – such as when a child ignores a reprimand.

antecedent
An event that precedes a behaviour

consequence
An event that follows a behaviour

Observing antecedents

Harry is an 8-year-old with normal intelligence who always seems to be in the middle of every disturbance. To find the antecedents of his involvement in a fight, and to achieve planned instructional outcomes, his teachers need to watch what is happening before these fights erupt. They also need to understand the effect of the consequences that immediately follow these disturbances. This will help them to learn how to decrease undesirable behaviour (in Harry's case, fighting) and increase the rate of occurrence of more appropriate activity.

The effect of consequences

Documentaries made on the topic of behaviourism often include short segments from Skinner's studies with rats and pigeons (see, for example, Zimbardo, 1987). Typically, such segments show a rat turning a wheel or pressing a bar, or a pigeon pecking an illuminated disc, pulling a string or turning circles in order to receive a reward of food pellets. Receipt of the reward ensures that the actions are repeated. However, in some studies, aversive (undesirable) rewards such as a loud noise are given, and these have the effect of reducing or eliminating the target actions. In thinking about operant conditioning a distinction needs to be made between two types of consequences: reinforcements, which act to strengthen a behaviour or increase the likelihood of its being repeated; and 'punishments', which have the opposite effect, in that they weaken a behaviour or reduce the likelihood of it recurring.

Types of consequences: reinforcement and punishment

Reinforcement

A student studies hard for a test and gets a good mark. A swimmer wins a race and receives a cheer from the watching crowd. Both the student and the swimmer have been 're-inforced' for their efforts, and this will motivate them to try harder next time. A **reinforcer** is any consequence that has the effect of maintaining a specific behaviour or increasing the rate at which the behaviour occurs and the probability that it will occur again. The consequence may take the form of a lolly, a hug, a push on a swing, good marks, or cheers from a crowd. The main point is that reinforcement maintains or increases the behaviour that it follows. It also has **contingency**, being dependent on the individual fulfilling the conditions that have been set, meaning that it is given only when a particular, identified

reinforcer
Any event that strengthens the behaviour it follows

contingency
Reinforcement that is only given when the target behaviour is produced

behaviour occurs, such as good marks on a test or the fastest time in a race. Reinforcement must occur *immediately* after the identified behaviour occurs, or be clearly linked to the target behaviour, since any delay or uncertainty may result in the wrong behaviour being reinforced (see Alberto & Troutman, 1999, Malott, Whaley, & Malott, 1993; Porter, 2000; Schloss & Smith, 1998; and Sulzer-Azaroff & Mayer, 1977).

When a specific behaviour, such as finishing a page of sums, is immediately followed by the delivery of a desirable consequence, such as a jellybean or a smile, then **positive reinforcement** has occurred (see Box 4.6 on page 122). All reinforcement has the effect of increasing the frequency of the behaviour it follows, and most reinforcement delivered by teachers is positive, in that it involves contingent presentation of a rewarding object or activity immediately following the target behaviour. Examples of common reinforcers that usually have a positive effect on behaviour include praise, points towards something special, and money. However, it is important to realise that what functions as a positive reinforcer for one person may not have the same effect for someone else. For example, a Smarty is a strong positive reinforcer for a child who loves chocolate, but not for a child who hates chocolate!

In some situations, the frequency of a target behaviour is increased by the contingent removal or withdrawal of an aversive consequence; for example, 'If you finish piano practice you will not have to clean out the bird's cage.' Here, the individual is rewarded for desirable behaviour by being allowed to escape from an unwanted object or experience. This process is called **negative reinforcement**.

While teachers mainly use positive reinforcement, in some situations negative reinforcement may be appropriate. For example, a teacher might allow students who finish their work on time to escape the task of cleaning up the classroom after a messy art activity.

Selecting reinforcers

A pat on the head or a smile may be positively reinforcing for many children; however, such behaviour is not acceptable for some cultural groups and may be negatively reinforcing for children from such groups, and for those who do not like to be touched or who do not like the person giving the pat or touch. Similarly, most children like ice-cream and are motivated to complete a task if such a treat is offered as a reward; while others have different, unexpected preferences, such as to be given a smack (for some children, a smack is positively reinforcing because it is associated with gaining attention). It is important to remember that objects and actions usually considered to be positive or negative reinforcers may not function in the expected way for particular individuals. So when designing a program that includes positive and negative reinforcers, it is essential to check that the reinforcers used have the required effect on the person for whom they are selected.

Primary and secondary reinforcers

The reinforcers used to reward behaviour can be of two types: primary and secondary. **Primary reinforcer**s include naturally occurring or 'unconditioned' (unlearned) stimuli that are innately rewarding for the individual. They are usually associated with the satisfaction of basic needs such as those identified by Maslow (1970) (see Chapter 6); for example, food and drink are classed as primary reinforcers. Typically, primary reinforcers are used with younger children or with those who have moderate-to-severe intellectual disabilities, and might include small edible items (such as Smarties, jellybeans, Coco Pops), fruit juice or gold stars (see Figure 4.8 opposite). These types of reinforcers can be very effective in establishing new behaviours rapidly. However, over time, the strength of their effectiveness can wear off, and alternatives have to be found. **Secondary reinforcer**s are 'conditioned' (learned) rewards, such as a smile, praise, good grades and applause. Initially, they are usually paired with a primary reinforcer, such as when a teacher says 'good girl' (secondary reinforcer) while giving a jellybean (primary reinforcer) to a child. Eventually, the jellybean can be phased out, and praise alone becomes an effective reinforcer.

---

positive reinforcement
Increasing the likelihood of a behaviour occurring, by contingent presentation of a reward immediately following it

negative reinforcement
Increasing the likelihood of a behaviour being repeated by contingently removing an aversive object or activity

4.6 More about selecting reinforcers

primary reinforcer
An unconditioned (unlearned) stimulus that is innately rewarding

secondary reinforcer
A conditioned (learned) stimulus that functions as a reward

The Premack principle

Everyone will be familiar with 'Grandma's rule': first eat your vegetables and then you can have your dessert. In Grandma's terms, this means 'Do what I want and then you can do what you want.' The key principle here is that activities individuals enjoy and do often can be used contingently as positive reinforcers for activities that do not occur often and that are less enjoyable. Otherwise known as the **Premack principle**, Grandma's rule is a very useful strategy for increasing the performance frequency of undesirable, dull or difficult tasks.

Punishment

As with the term 'reinforcement', most people have some idea of what the word 'punishment' means. However, this word also needs to be understood within the context of behavioural theory. **Punishment** functions as an aversive (unpleasant or negative) experience that individuals will strive to avoid or remove. The most important aspect of this definition concerns the effect of punishment on the likely recurrence of the behaviour that it follows. The main effect of punishment is to weaken (and eventually eliminate) a behaviour by presenting an aversive object or event immediately after the behaviour occurs. Punishment involves establishing a contingency that has the effect of decreasing the likelihood of a target behaviour recurring. Consequences that have the effect of reducing a behaviour's occurrence or eliminating it altogether are referred to as 'punishers'.

As with reinforcement, punishment can take the form of *giving* something unpleasant, such as a smack on the hand, a reprimand, or a ticket for exceeding the speed limit in a car. Alternatively, punishment can also involve *taking away* something pleasant, such as when points are lost in a contest or privileges are withdrawn (for example, the use of a car) (see Box 4.6 over the page). Punishers also parallel reinforcers, in that they are either primary (that is, unconditioned (unlearned or innate)); or secondary (that is, conditioned (learned)). The feel of a very hot kettle to a child who touches it could be classed as an unconditioned punishment, in that the heat of the kettle acts as a punisher to the child even if the child has never before touched something hot. The child does not need to have had a prior experience of touching a hot kettle in order to experience the sensation of touching one as unpleasant or painful. The effect of the experience is that the child learns (is conditioned) to avoid touching hot kettles – and hopefully other hot objects – in the future.

Distinguishing between negative reinforcement and punishment

People are generally familiar with the word 'reinforcement' and understand its meaning when it is used in a positive way. However, there is usually much more confusion about the meaning of the concept of 'negative reinforcement' and how to distinguish it from punishment (see Box 4.6). One undergraduate student (Heather M, EDUC 105 student, Macquarie University, 2001), in trying to distinguish between the different forms of reinforcement and punishment, summed them up in the following way:

> A reward is to give them something they want (positive reinforcement) or to take away something they don't want (negative reinforcement). Punishment, on the other hand, is giving them what they don't want or taking away what they want.

Box 4.6 gives some examples of positive and negative reinforcement and punishment being used to increase or decrease behaviour.

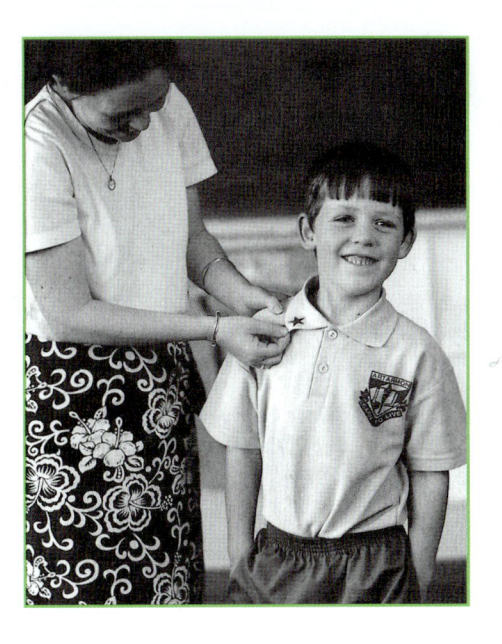

FIGURE 4.8
How might the reinforcement of a gold star influence this student's future behaviour? What conditions need to be met for the star to be an effective reinforcer?

Premack principle (Grandma's rule)
Any behaviour that is enjoyed and that occurs often can be used to reinforce behaviours that are not enjoyed and that do not occur often

punishment
Weakening or reducing behaviour through contingent use of aversive objects or events

4.7 Examples of primary and secondary reinforcers
4.8 Using praise in the classroom
4.9 More about the Premack principle

Box 4.6 CLASSROOM LINKS

Reinforcement and punishment

Reinforcement and punishment are powerful tools that can be used in practical situations to change behaviour (see Table 4.2 below).

TABLE 4.2 Types of reinforcement and punishment

Action	Aim	
	To increase behaviour (i.e. use reinforcement)	**To decrease behaviour (i.e. use punishment)**
Give something	Positive reinforcement, e.g. 'Good girl!'	Punishment, e.g. give a smack
Take something away	Negative reinforcement, e.g. 'You've finished your homework, so you don't have to do the dishes!'	Punishment, e.g. 'You can't play football this week'

Activities

1 What is the distinction between the four categories of rewards and punishments shown in the table?
2 Think of some examples of rewards and punishments, and situations where these might be used.

Extinction, time out and 'fair pair'

Undesirable behaviour can also be weakened and eliminated by **extinction**. Extinction occurs if all reinforcement is withdrawn. This is usually done by ignoring a behaviour until the behaviour stops. The procedure is difficult to carry out, in part because the target behaviour usually gets worse before it is extinguished. In a classroom situation, an alternative to ignoring an offending child while she remains in the usual place is to move her to another part of the classroom – or in an extreme case to a designated place outside the classroom – for a set period such as 3 minutes. During this time, the child is denied access to attention (or reinforcement), a process called 'time out' or 'time out from reinforcement' (see Figure 4.9).

extinction
Reduction and cessation of a response following the withdrawal of reinforcement

4.10 Example of the use of time out

FIGURE 4.9
How might time out help to extinguish this child's inappropriate behaviour?

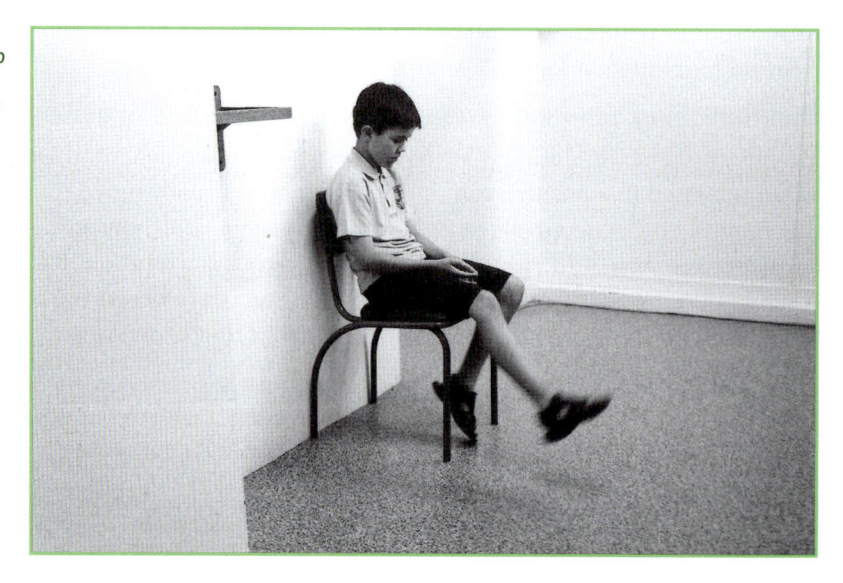

When trying to decrease or eliminate undesirable behaviour, it is a good idea to keep in mind the concept of a 'fair pair'. A fair pair is when at the same time as you use punishment or negative reinforcement to reduce the occurrence of one behaviour, you also find another behaviour that can be rewarded and increased, since it is important that learners have positive as well as negative experiences.

Maintenance and generalisation

Once a skill as been learned, issues such as 'maintenance' and 'generalisation' need to be considered to ensure that what has been learned is not forgotten, and that newly acquired skills are used outside the context in which they were taught.

When teaching an individual a new skill or behaviour, one of the teacher's most important goals is to ensure that learning outcomes are maintained, or continue, long after instruction has ceased. With much new learning, **maintenance** is assured after instruction stops because the newly learned skill is incorporated into a more complex set of skills that are in regular use. Examples of skills that are incorporated in this way are the subskills that contribute to early reading or numeracy, such as learning to identify the letters in your name and learning to count to 10. However, skills or behaviours that are not embedded into more complex hierarchies may extinguish over time if reinforcement is withdrawn. For example, learning how to make a bird in origami will be forgotten if this new skill is not practised for a long while. Intermittent 'maintenance checks' are sometimes included in a unit of instruction as a way of ensuring that the skills learned in the unit are durable and not lost through lack of practice and attention.

Generalisation refers to the process whereby individuals learn to respond to stimuli that are similar to but not the same as those that triggered the original response. For example, a newly acquired skill or behaviour learned in one context and with one teacher has generalised if it is reproduced in another setting and with different people. In designing an instructional program based on behaviourist principles, provision must be made to ensure that both maintenance and generalisation occur. Such provision may involve checks of previously mastered material to ensure that skills have been maintained, and allowing for newly acquired behaviours to be practised in (that is, generalised to) different settings and with different people.

maintenance
The continued performance of a learned action after instruction has ceased

generalisation
Learning to respond to stimuli that are similar to but not the same as those that previously triggered a response

Reinforcement schedules

One of the decisions that must be made when planning a behavioural program concerns the selection of an appropriate 'reinforcement schedule'. For example, when you first introduce a new task for a student to acquire, it may be appropriate to reinforce the target behaviour every time it occurs.

4.11 More about reinforcement schedules

Continuous reinforcement

When you are working with very young children or children who have disabilities, continuous reinforcement is useful, particularly in the early stages of teaching a new skill. The problem with continuous reinforcement is 'satiation', when the reinforcer being used loses its appeal as a motivator. There is a limit to how many Smarties a child can eat during one teaching session and still continue to respond to the same reinforcer. For this reason alternative schedules, or different reinforcers, need to be used in order to maintain the momentum of learning.

Intermittent reinforcement

Once a new behaviour has been established, it is usually appropriate to systematically reduce the rate at which rewards are given, using a schedule that involves 'intermittent reinforcement'. Some, but not all, correct responses are now reinforced. This is useful when an individual is at risk of satiation, or is losing interest in a particular reward such as food. It is also useful in maintaining a behaviour.

ratio schedules
When a reward is given in a predetermined ratio to the number of responses

interval schedules
When a reward is given after a set period of time

4.12 Example of a token and a contract system

Intermittent reinforcement can take two forms. **Ratio schedules** refer to when a reward is given in a predetermined ratio to the number of responses. The ratio used can be 'fixed' (preset), such as with a reward for every fourth response; or 'variable' (changeable), such as with a reward for correct responses at an average rate of one in four. **Interval schedules** refer to when a reward is delivered after a predetermined period of time. As with ratio schedules, interval schedules can be fixed or variable. In thinking about the relative effectiveness of these different ways of giving reinforcement, it is useful to remember the power of poker machines, with their variable-interval reinforcement schedule, in holding the attention of some punters. Other strategies you can use to achieve behaviour change include systems of tokens and contracts (see Box 4.7).

Box 4.7 CASE STUDY

Implementing a contract system

The following account is from research reported by Slee (1996, p. 278), which took the form of a case study of selective mutism in a 6-year-old girl:

> The child, Anna, spoke at home but did not speak at school. An intervention program was designed that aimed to have the child speak to one person in one setting, and then gradually generalise this behaviour by speaking to other people in different settings. One of the first procedures introduced in Anna's program was a type of *contract* system: contingency contracting.

> Anna enjoyed colouring and cutting out so we gave her a book with a drawing of a different pet on each page that could be cut out to form a stand-up model. She was allowed to complete one each day, contingent on her identifying the pet. (I dreaded the thought of day three where there was a squirrel). In the presence of my co-worker she ... eventually said 'bird' to describe the pet on the first page.

Slee reported that the intervention plan proved to be effective in helping Anna begin to speak out loud at school.

Activities

1. What is the rationale behind the procedures used in this case study?
2. What other strategies might have been effective in helping Anna overcome her mutism?

Shaping, chaining, cueing, prompting, modelling and task analysis

When teaching a new behaviour involving actions that are new or unfamiliar to a student, the techniques known as 'shaping', 'chaining', 'cueing', 'prompting', 'modelling' and 'task analysis' are invaluable tools for helping the student learn. Early behaviourists such as Pavlov and Watson, in their studies of dogs salivating and babies being scared by white rats, were concerned with controlling or conditioning actions and innate or involuntary responses to stimuli. Later behaviourists – like Thorndike with his trial-and-error studies of cats escaping from boxes, and Skinner in his work with rats and pigeons spontaneously acting to obtain food – focused on behaviours that were already in animals' repertoires and that were emitted with high frequency. But what about teaching a *new* skill to an individual – a skill that involves the individual producing totally unfamiliar actions?

If you have to wait until an action is produced spontaneously, new learning may never occur, so in order to teach new behaviours you may need to use the techniques of shaping, chaining, cueing, prompting, modelling and task analysis, reviewed here.

Teaching new behaviours

shaping
Reinforcement of gradual approximations of the target behaviour

Shaping involves the reinforcement of gradual approximations to the desired or target behaviour. To shape a new behaviour, you need to look for an instance of a behaviour that approximates, or has features in common with, the behaviour you want to teach. Over time, you can selectively reinforce the actions that approximate your goal so that these gradually take the form of the final target behaviour. When a mother responds to a baby's 'm–m–m' by saying 'Mum' and smiling, she is shaping what she sees as the baby's first attempts to communicate. Similarly, when trying to teach a child to dive into a swimming pool, you can begin by getting the child to roll into the water from a squatting position at the edge of the pool. Then you begin to selectively reinforce those parts of the rolling action that form the first step in learning to dive, such as tucking the head between outstretched arms and gradually moving to a standing position before 'diving' into the water. Over time and with practice, the child will learn to dive.

Chaining occurs when a 'chain' of behaviours is created, with each behaviour in the chain functioning both as a reinforcer for the preceding act and as a stimulus for the next. Actions in the chain can be taught in any sequence; for example, beginning in the middle of the chain and working backwards to the beginning of the task ('backward chaining'), or working forwards to the completion of the task ('forward chaining') (see Box 4.8).

chaining
When one action functions both as a reinforcer for the previous action and as a stimulus for the next

Box 4.8 CLASSROOM LINKS

Examples of chaining

Backward chaining: Learning to get dressed to go outside on a cold day

The following is an example of backward chaining, or teaching the last action in a sequence first. Yasmin's mother taught her to:

Put on hat → Put on coat → Pull on long pants → Put on jumper → Put on shirt → Put on shoes → Put on socks → Pull on underpants

Forward chaining: Learning to do homework tasks

Here is an example of forward chaining, where actions are taught in sequence from first to last. Fidele's teacher taught him to:

Get books from schoolbag → Find set homework tasks → Clear rubbish off desk → Find pen, calculator, ruler etc. → Choose first task → Do first task → Get next task → Do next task

Activities

Devise examples of either a forward or a backward chain for doing some of the more complex activities that young people sometimes get involved in, such as:
1 catering and cooking for a group of 100 adolescents at a youth camp
2 organising a church or school fete
3 producing a school play
4 completing a project on the flora and fauna of the Antarctic.

Cueing, prompting and modelling are additional forms of stimulus that increase the likelihood of a target response occurring. **Cueing** is when a specific stimulus is used as a 'cue' to elicit a desired response. For example, when asking a child to recall a word in a poem, the teacher can provide a cue by saying the preceding line of the poem. **Prompting** is when an additional stimulus (or hint) is used to assist the child in discriminating the relevant features of the stimulus; for example, a teacher can prompt the child's recall of a word by saying 'It is an *a–*' (with mouth wide open and shaped to say 'a' for 'apple') so as to help the child

cueing
Using a specific stimulus to elicit a desired response

prompting
Providing an additional stimulus to elicit a desired response

modelling
A form of prompting that involves demonstrating a desired response for someone to imitate

task analysis
Breaking a task into a series of manageable steps so as to assist learning

remember the correct word. **Modelling** is a form of prompting that involves demonstrating a desired response for a learner to imitate. For example, a teacher can model the word 'apple' while touching the picture of an apple, and encouraging the child to imitate the model. Cues, prompts and models are gradually faded as the learner becomes more able to complete the task without help.

Task analysis entails breaking a task down into a sequence of more manageable steps, and can be used to help students acquire a new skill. When linked together, the steps form a sequence that becomes a more complex behaviour. For example, the task of learning to write your own name involves:

1 holding a pencil correctly
2 using a pencil to make a mark on paper
3 drawing shapes of characters that are similar to a model
4 drawing character shapes without a model
5 writing characters of the correct shape and size to form a word.

FIGURE 4.10 Learning to tie a shoelace may involve cueing and shaping. What steps could you take to cue and/or shape the skill for this student?

Scope-and-sequence charts associated with curriculum areas (such as early literacy and numeracy) are examples of task analysis drawn from the educational field. Steps in a sequence such as that for the attainment of early numeracy can be used in the initial stages of instruction to assess what students know and do not know (see Chapter 11). Each of the steps can be broken down further – or task analysed – to make a set of more manageable steps for students who are having difficulty with learning tasks at a particular level.

Box 4.9 gives an example of task analysis being used in a classroom situation.

Box 4.9 CLASSROOM LINKS

Example of task analysis

Using a calculator to check four-digit addition problems

Prerequisite skills: Fine motor control in order to grasp and activate the calculator, and to press appropriate keys.

Steps in task analysis
1 Turn calculator on.
2 Read through the written problem on the sheet, including the solution.
3 Key in the first number.
4 Press +
5 Key in the next number.
6 Press +
7 Key in the next number.
8 Press =

Compare totals on the written sheet and on the calculator display.

Source: Adapted from Foreman (1996, p. 127).

Activity

Task analyse a complex behaviour you may want to teach one day, for example:
1 riding a bike
2 looking up a train timetable
3 using a catalogue
4 getting onto the Internet
5 making a pavlova.

Applied behaviour analysis

The term **applied behaviour analysis (ABA)** refers to the use of behavioural learning principles to change behaviour in settings such as classrooms and play areas. The procedures associated with implementing behaviourist principles form the basis of ABA (Alberto & Troutman, 1999; Schloss & Smith, 1998). The primary focus is on behaviour (academic, communicative, social, motor, vocational, self-help) that is observable and quantifiable. The goal is to change behaviour that is socially important (not trivial) (Baer, Wolf, & Risley, 1968).

The main features of ABA, as it is used in classrooms, include:

- clearly specifying the target behaviour and goals; that is, describing the behaviour to be changed, and identifying the behavioural goals – or **behavioural objective**s – in terms that are observable and measurable
- developing and implementing an intervention plan, taking account of antecedents and consequences as appropriate
- monitoring the results of intervention and instituting changes in intervention procedures as required (the 'test-teach-test' cycle).

> **applied behaviour analysis (ABA)**
> The use of behavioural principles to change behaviour
>
> **behavioural objectives**
> An instructional goal stated in terms of observable and measurable behaviour
>
> **4.13** Ethics and behavioural programs in classrooms

Strengths and limitations of operant conditioning and ABA

Strengths

The main strengths of behavioural approaches to learning are that they provide educators with simple but effective strategies that can be used quite easily to teach new skills and behaviours quickly and efficiently, particularly to young children and to students with intellectual disabilities and behaviour problems. Such strategies are especially useful for teaching action sequences that need to be performed at an automatic level, such as tying shoelaces, cleaning teeth or even the mechanical aspects of driving a car. These methods are also effective for managing the many forms of undesirable behaviour, often minor in nature, that disrupt most classrooms at some time during the day. Teachers using behavioural methods to manage such behaviour can respond to student disruptions quickly, consistently and without emotional involvement.

Limitations

A major criticism of behavioural approaches is that they neglect the contribution of cognition, or cognitive skills, to the learning process. This is particularly relevant for more complex forms of behaviour, such as problem solving, for which other approaches may be more appropriate (see chapters 5 and 6). Additional problems that have been identified include concerns about the impact of long-term dependence on extrinsic rather than intrinsic forms of reinforcement (see Kohn, 1993), and ethical issues concerning the use of some types of punishment and aversive techniques (see Alberto & Troutman, 1999; Schloss & Smith, 1998).

Box 4.10 discusses the classroom implications of operant conditioning and ABA.

Box 4.10 IMPLICATIONS FOR EDUCATORS

Operant conditioning and ABA in the classroom

If you observe a classroom for a while, you will see many examples of operant conditioning and ABA procedures being used. For example, depending on the students' age and the subject matter being taught, you should see:

- the impact of antecedents and consequences on particular students' behaviour
- instances of both positive and negative reinforcement, as well as forms of punishment that involve giving something unpleasant or taking away something pleasant
- situations where time out or a student's removal from an activity for a set period of time occurs,

- and use of a 'fair pair' or strengthening one behaviour while at the same time reducing another to ensure students have good as well as bad experiences in a classroom
- evidence of techniques such as shaping, chaining, cueing, prompting, modelling and task analysis being used to elicit and support learning; there may also be examples of Grandma's rule being used
- some indication that the teacher is using the key elements of ABA, with initial observation and assessment of student behaviour to identify objectives for instruction, development and implementation of an intervention plan, followed by frequent evaluations of progress, which lead (if necessary) to current intervention procedures being modified (the test-teach-test cycle).

4.14 More about ABA
4.15 A case study of applied behaviour analysis
4.16 Precision teaching, mastery learning, direct instruction and DISTAR

Social learning theory and observational learning

As the research focus of behaviourists shifted from animals to human beings, questions began to be asked about the adequacy of extreme behavioural models to explain more complex human behaviour such as reading or problem solving, and enduring behavioural patterns such as friendliness or aggression. However, the main criticism of extreme behaviourism was that it neglected the influence of cognition and cognitive skills, such as self-assessment and self-monitoring, on the learning process. It was in this context that Albert Bandura developed his 'social learning theory' (also known as 'social cognitive theory') (Bandura, 1977). Social learning theory was an extension of behavioural explanations of learning, and recognised the contribution of personal (mental or psychological) factors to the learning process, providing an explanation of human behaviour in terms of cognitive, environmental and behavioural influences.

Reciprocal determinism

A key aspect of Bandura's model is that behaviour is not just the outcome of direct internal (cognitive and personal) influences and external influences (such as instructional procedures and physical settings). Rather, it is the product of complementary interaction between these two aspects, together with the influences of behaviour itself (for example, actions and utterances). Bandura (1977, p. 9) stated: 'It is largely through their actions that people produce the environmental conditions that affect their behaviour in a reciprocal fashion.' Explanations that attempt to account for behaviour solely in terms of external influences are therefore inadequate in that they ignore the contribution made by personal factors and behaviour itself. This interactive, complementary system is termed **reciprocal determinism**.

Bandura (1986) identified three key aspects that contribute to the interactive process inherent in his ideas about human behaviour and cognitive functioning: observation ('vicarious learning'), language ('symbolic processes') and self-talk ('self-regulation'). An interesting aspect of Bandura's work was his demonstration of links between the vicarious learning associated with watching violence depicted in films and on television (and now perhaps in video games), and aggression in children (see Box 4.11 opposite).

reciprocal determinism
The interactive, complementary system formed by people and environments

Box 4.11 RESEARCH LINKS

Bandura's studies of children and aggression

Albert Bandura and his team conducted a series of studies that explored the extent to which children's behaviour could be influenced by exposure to adults modelling aggressive behaviour. Many of the studies involved three groups of children: an experimental group that observed a film of a person acting aggressively, a contrast group that watched an adult behaving in a non-aggressive way, and a control group who did not watch any film.

In one study (Bandura, Ross, & Ross, 1961), the experimental group of children watched an adult directing verbal and physical aggression in relatively novel ways towards an adult-sized inflated plastic Bobo doll that righted itself each time it was hit, while the contrast group watched an adult behave in a subdued and inhibited way towards the same doll. The third group saw the aggressive adult but did not see the doll. Half the children watched an adult model who was the same gender as their own and the other half watched an opposite-gender model. After exposure to the different models, all the children were left alone in a playroom with a few toys that included a Bobo doll. They were then tested for aggressive and non-aggressive behaviour. Results showed that the children who had observed an aggressive model showed almost twice as much aggression as did the children in the non-aggressive and the control groups. In contrast, the behaviour of the children in the non-aggressive group was inhibited, like the model they had watched, and they showed even less aggression than the children in the control group who had seen the adult behaving aggressively.

The effect of the model's gender was that the aggressive male model was more influential than the female model, with some children commenting that the aggressive female model was inappropriate: 'That's no way for a lady to behave' (Bandura, 1969, p. 282). Other findings were that the children who had observed an aggressive model imitated, quite precisely, some of the actions they had observed the model using, whereas children in the other two groups rarely produced such actions.

These findings were replicated using film and cartoon versions of the real-life situations. Bandura (1969) noted that according to psychoanalytic theory (for example, Freud, 1933), children's vicarious participation in aggressive situations functions as catharsis, allowing the 'drainage' of suppressed or 'pent-up' aggression. In contrast, Bandura and Walters (1959) argued that studies in which young people view films including models of aggression have established that 'vicarious participation in aggressive activity increases, rather than decreases, aggressive behaviour' (Bandura, 1963, quoted by Pronto, 1969, p. 282).

Moreover, a later study involving preschool children (Bandura, Ross, & Ross, 1961) showed that children could discern that aggressive behaviour was wrong, but saw it as successful and to be imitated when the child who acted aggressively was rewarded by gaining control of 'all the good toys'. Similarly, children who knew they would be punished as part of reproducing an aggressive act were willing to reproduce the act when they were offered an attractive reward, contingent on them imitating the act. Later studies showed that this effect was most likely to occur when an appropriate stimulus and instruments necessary for performing the action were present, together with the prospect of 'sufficiently attractive positive rewards contingent on the successful execution of the behaviour' (Bandura, 1963, quoted by Pronto, 1969, pp. 284–5).

Activities

1. Do you agree with Bandura's findings? Why?/Why not?
2. Have you any personal experience of children imitating aggressive actions they have viewed in films, on television or while playing video games? Which children are most likely to imitate such actions?
3. What are the implications of Bandura's findings for television shown during the hours that children are likely to be watching?
4. How long do you think the effects, if any, of watching aggression on film, television or video are likely to last?

In extending his ideas about learning beyond the behaviourists' simple S-R model so as to include acknowledgement of the contributions of mental or cognitive factors to human activity, Bandura provided a bridge to later, more cognitive-based explanations of behaviour and learning (see also Chapter 5). Note also that there are links between the place of observation and imitation in Bandura's social learning theory and Piaget's studies of the place of imitation and modelling in children's learning (see Chapter 2).

Strengths and limitations of social learning theory

Strengths

Bandura extended behavioural theories of learning to encompass the broad range of factors – internal (cognitive and personal) and external (environmental or contextual) – that influence learning. This broader behavioural explanation of learning, with its recognition of the learner's active contribution to behaviour change, is evident in subsequent developments in this field, including the cognitive behaviour-modification model by Meichenbaum (1977). Bandura's focus on the place of observation and imitation in learning meant that his work served to heighten awareness of the possibility of 'calculated manipulation and control of people' (Bandura, 1977, p. 208) through such sources as film and television. Vicarious learning through observation and imitation can have positive outcomes, but students need to be aware that some sources can have a persuasive and possibly negative influence on their own behaviour.

Limitations

The conditions under which vicarious learning occurs have been questioned. Why do children imitate some of the behaviours they observe but ignore others? How can educators be sure that desirable behaviours modelled in learning situations have an impact on learners, while undesirable behaviours are ignored and forgotten? Research studies in this field (such as Bandura, Ross, & Ross, 1961) were concerned with children's responses to observed aggression in the time period immediately following exposure to a model. How long after this experience would the children remember and imitate what they had seen? What would happen when the children observed models in similar situations behaving differently? Considering the myriad situations that developing children experience, it is difficult to accept that specific observational experiences will have a long-term impact on the viewer, although repeated exposure to instances of aggressive behaviour may have a continuing influence on young observers' behaviour.

Box 4.12 explores some classroom implications of social learning theory.

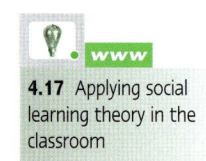

4.17 Applying social learning theory in the classroom

Box 4.12 IMPLICATIONS FOR EDUCATORS

Social learning theory in the classroom

Teachers need to be aware of the impact that all aspects of a classroom situation, including internal (cognitive and personal) factors, have on learning. They also need to take account of the place of observation and modelling in the learning process. Such awareness might include:

- that teachers are constantly being observed by students who may model their own behaviour on what they see
- teaching children to be aware of the impact on their own behaviour of what they observe (this may include children developing critical thinking skills in relation to what they see, hear and read about, whether through television, radio or newspapers, and including advertisements and other types of information about public affairs)
- the recognition that using some children in a class as models of appropriate behaviour, such as in 'Watch Gerry do this task' or 'Look at Suzie's good work' may have unintended consequences, either on the models ('teacher's pet') or because the children attend to inappropriate or undesirable aspects of the modelled behaviour.

Cognitive behaviour modification and self-regulation

Instruction based on cognitive behavioural techniques shares with social learning theory the view that learning involves environmental factors and also – more importantly – cognitive and personal factors. **Cognitive behaviour modification** is concerned with the use of behaviour-modification strategies that emphasise behavioural and also cognitive aspects of the learning process. The major focus of the cognitive behavioural model of learning that distinguishes it from other behavioural models is its concern with both observable behaviour and unobservable cognition and cognitive activities (Ashman & Conway, 1993; Cole & Chan, 1990). Donald Meichenbaum (1977) is a key exponent of these ideas, which can also be traced back to the Russian psychologist Alexander Romanovich Luria (1961). For example, Luria (1963) reported a study in which children with a particular type of brain dysfunction had learned to focus on a task and reduce errors by using self-instruction techniques such as saying 'press' as they pressed a balloon, to do a task that had previously been too difficult. (Prior to instruction, the children had been required to press the balloon when a light flashed.) Subsequently, Meichenbaum and Goodman (1971) published an influential study in which a five-step instructional program was described that had been designed to help impulsive second-grade students to use self-control techniques as a way of increasing their attention to a task and reducing errors. An early example of Meichenbaum's ideas is the Turtle Technique, which uses a self-instruction procedure to help children control aggression. More recent examples include Stop Think Do (Petersen, 1994; Petersen & Gannoni, 1989), which was designed to help children experiencing problems with relationships; and Talk Sense to Yourself (Wragg, 1989), a program designed to help students comply with teacher demands in the classroom.

Some suggestions for self-managing behaviour are set out in Box 4.13.

> **cognitive behaviour modification**
> Use of behavioural strategies and cognitive processes to change behaviour

4.18 More about Meichenbaum, a description of the Turtle Technique, steps from *Stop Think Do* and *Talk sense to yourself*

4.19 About process-based instruction

CRITICAL REFLECTION

Could you use the principles of cognitive behaviour modification to change some aspect of your own behaviour?

Box 4.13 RESEARCH LINK

Learning to self-manage behaviour

Sometimes researchers carry out studies using themselves as subjects. Cognitive behaviour modification, using a self-management program, provides an example of such research. The research project described below is based on the work of Meichenbaum (1977), but also draws on Vygotsky's ideas (see Chapter 2) about the role of inner speech in self-instruction.

Research plan

You first need a research plan. Think of an aspect of your own behaviour you would like to change. You might want to eat less, quit smoking, spend less time daydreaming, watch less television, or stop moaning about lack of time, money, friends, fun, and so on.

Procedure

You then need a procedure. To set up a self-management program to control some aspect of your own behaviour, you will need to think about the following issues:

- *Set yourself a goal.* Identify an action or activity that you would like to see changed or improved.
- *Define the target behaviour operationally, using concrete examples.* For example, 'daydreaming' might be defined as 'staring into space, not engaged in any activity'.
- *Decide if you are going to keep a record of the target behaviour, and if so, how.* Record-keeping

gives you useful feedback about the frequency of the behaviour. Tally instances of the behaviour over an hour, a day or a week. Record instances in a notebook as they occur, or on a strip of masking tape on your wrist, and later transfer the data to a chart or graph as a cumulative record of the behaviour. Alberto and Troutman (1999, p. 442) note that simply tallying instances of behaviour such as daydreaming reduces its frequency.

- *Identify any strategies that you are already using, or have used, in attempting to achieve your goal.* Were any of these strategies effective? You may decide to incorporate these into your plans.
- *Carefully analyse the cognitive operations involved in performing the activity you want to change.* For example, if the problem concerns overeating or smoking, what is going on in your head when you are involved in these activities? Can you think of an alternative pattern of thought that would help you change the behaviour?
- *Try to identify an intervention strategy that is as close as possible to your normal routine.* Make sure you are comfortable with any proposed procedures and that there is no conflict between aspects of the intervention plan and your current ways of thinking and acting.
- *Make sure that any self-instructions you plan to use are as specific as possible to the target activity.* Specificity will maximise your chances of success. Broad self-instructional statements may appear to be appropriate, but have been shown to be ineffective in improving target behaviour.
- *Anticipate failures and include strategies for coping with such failure in your plan.*
- *Continue to follow your self-instructional plan until it is evident that it has been effective.* Then check your behaviour from time to time to ensure you are not relapsing!

Results

To report your results, write a report using the data you have collected. Identify which strategies were most effective and why.

Good luck!

Source: Adapted from Alberto & Troutman (1999, Chapter 12); Cole & Chan (1990, Chapter 9).

Activities

1. Plan and carry out a research project like the one outlined above.
2. How effective were the self-management techniques for changing your own behaviour? What other strategies might be more effective?
3. What are the limitations of this approach to changing behaviour? How might these be overcome?
4. Can you think of classroom or similar situations where cognitive behaviour modification might be appropriate? Give examples.

Strengths and limitations of cognitive behaviour modification

Strengths

Cognitive behaviour modification's biggest contribution to behavioural explanations of learning is its emphasis on the importance of cognition in the learning process. This is evident in the use of cognitive or self-regulated behavioural strategies in programs that are designed to modify or change unwanted or undesirable behaviours (see Box 4.13 above) such as smoking, alcoholism and even addiction to chocolates or television.

Limitations

A major limitation in the use of self-regulation to control behaviour is that such strategies require commitment and self-discipline if they are to be implemented successfully. In addition, support is usually needed from an experienced psychologist or therapist who has the skills required to design, implement and monitor such a program, and to support the individual during the intervention period and beyond. As with all behaviourist methods of behaviour change, there are concerns regarding programs being implemented in accordance with ethical principles and general community norms, beliefs and practices.

Box 4.14 discusses issues to consider when using cognitive behaviour modification in the classroom.

Box 4.14 IMPLICATIONS FOR EDUCATORS

Cognitive behaviour modification in the classroom

Cognitive behavioural techniques can be a powerful tool for teachers seeking to change aspects of a student's behaviour where those aspects are interfering with student learning. Issues to consider when designing and implementing such a program include:
- students' ability to follow procedures (this includes the motivational and cognitive skills needed to behave as required (see Chapter 7))
- the teacher's need to have the competencies necessary to plan and implement a program using cognitive-behaviour-modification techniques; assistance may have to be sought from more experienced colleagues or other experts
- provision to ensure that any intervention is congruent with other aspects of the classroom program and that it does not involve the teacher spending excessive time planning the intervention, preparing resources or attending to the student.

Concluding comments

While there have been some criticisms of behavioural theories and the methods of teaching derived from them, behavioural approaches are useful for teachers. They are relatively easy to use, are effective in teaching new skills and behaviours quickly, and can be implemented with a variety of learners in a range of contexts. The basic principles can be learned through self-instruction programs or in short courses for teachers, parents and others who work with children and adults. Indeed, behavioural principles are widely used in everyday settings by people who may be unaware of the underlying learning principles. As with other approaches to learning and teaching, when correctly implemented, behavioural methods provide a valuable pedagogical tool for educators.

4.20 Table of main learning theories

4.21 Time line for the emergence of behavioural theories

Chapter review

- Behavioural explanations of learning focus on learners' behaviour, observable actions or activity.
- Contiguity, or a close association in meaning or time between two events or sensations, can lead to learning so that the occurrence of one event triggers recall of the associated event.
- Classical conditioning (Pavlov) is concerned with learning that is produced when involuntary or automatic responses are triggered by specific stimuli in the environment.
- Operant conditioning is concerned with actions that an organism initiates, and includes trial-and-error learning and the law of effect (Thorndike), and the learning that occurs when behaviours are rewarded or reinforced (Skinner).
- Applied behaviour analysis (ABA) refers to the application of behavioural principles in the classroom, with clear specification of the target behaviour and goals, development and implementation of an intervention plan, and monitoring of results with changes implemented as required (the test-teach-test cycle).
- Social learning theory and observational learning (Bandura) assert that behaviour is the outcome of complementary interactions among internal (personal), external (environmental) influences and behaviour, a process known as 'reciprocal determinism'. Learning occurs not only by doing, but also by observing. Language and self-regulation (self-talk) are key elements of the learning process.
- Cognitive behaviour modification focuses on cognition or thinking processes, using strategies derived from cognitive behaviour modification in self-instruction programs for teaching academic and social skills.

You make the connections:
Questions and activities for self-assessment and discussion

1. Describe two behaviours that change over time and that can be called examples of learning. Describe two other behaviours that also change over time but that are not instances of learning.
2. Give an example of contiguity learning from your own experience.
3. Can you think of any fears or anxieties you have learned as a result of unplanned classical conditioning?
4. In what circumstances would using ABA procedures be most appropriate? Describe a situation you have encountered where such strategies would have been useful.
5. Does viewing violence on film and/or television have an effect on children's behaviour? Give reasons for your answer.
6. How could Bandura's ideas about vicarious learning be used to teach moral values to children?
7. a What are some common threads linking the different theoretical models of learning discussed in this chapter?
   b Can you recall situations in your own life where one or more of these models influenced your actions?
8. Think about your personal philosophy of teaching. Does it contain elements that you would describe as 'behavioural'? If so, what are they?
9. Answer the following questions (note that you might also find answers to these questions later in this module):
   a Have you developed your ideas about handling difficult or inappropriate classroom behaviour?
   b Which groups of students are most likely to engage in inappropriate classroom behaviour?
   c Would you use behavioural methods to control such students?
   d What other approaches might you use?

Key terms

- behaviour
- contiguity
- stimulus
- response
- classical conditioning
- neutral stimulus (NS)
- unconditioned stimulus (US)
- unconditioned response (UR)
- conditioning
- conditioned stimulus (CS)
- conditioned response (CR)
- discrimination
- operant conditioning
- associationism
- trial-and-error learning
- law of effect
- law of exercise
- operants
- respondents
- reinforcement
- antecedent-behaviour-consequence (A-B-C)
- antecedent
- consequence
- reinforcer
- contingency
- positive reinforcement
- negative reinforcement
- primary reinforcer
- secondary reinforcer
- Premack principle (Grandma's rule)
- punishment
- extinction
- maintenance
- generalisation
- ratio schedules
- interval schedules
- shaping
- chaining
- cueing
- prompting
- modelling
- task analysis
- applied behaviour analysis (ABA)
- behavioural objectives
- reciprocal determinism
- cognitive behaviour modification

Recommended reading

Alberto, P. A., & Troutman, A. C. (1999). *Applied Behaviour Analysis for teachers* (5th ed.). London: Prentice-Hall International.

Cole, P., & Chan, L. (1990). *Methods and strategies for special education.* Sydney: Prentice-Hall.

Foreman, P. (Ed.) (1996). *Integration and inclusion in action* (Chapter 9). Marrickville, NSW: Harcourt Brace.

Gordon, C., Arthur, M., & Butterfield, N. (1996). *Promoting positive behaviour: An Australian guide to classroom management* (Chapter 5). Melbourne: Nelson.

Herbert, M. (1997). *ABC of behavioural methods.* Melbourne: Australian Council for Educational Research.

Journal of Applied Behaviour Analysis. See research reports and articles in this journal.

Lefrancois, G. R. (1997). *Psychology for teachers* (5th ed.) (Chapter 4). Belmont, CA: Wadsworth.

Malott, R. W., Whaley, D. L., & Malott, M. E. (1993). *Elementary principles of behaviour* (2nd ed.). Englewood Cliffs, NJ: Prentice-Hall.

Porter, L. (2000). *Behaviour in schools: Theory and practice for teachers.* St Leonards, NSW: Allen & Unwin.

Schloss, P. J., & Smith, M. A. *Applied behaviour analysis in the classroom.* Needham Heights, MA: Allyn & Bacon.

Make some online visits

Search on databases such as ERIC and the Australian Education Index using terms like: 'behaviour modification', 'operant conditioning', 'token economy', 'social learning theory' and 'cognitive behaviour modification'.

FIGURE 5.1 Chapter 5 concept map.

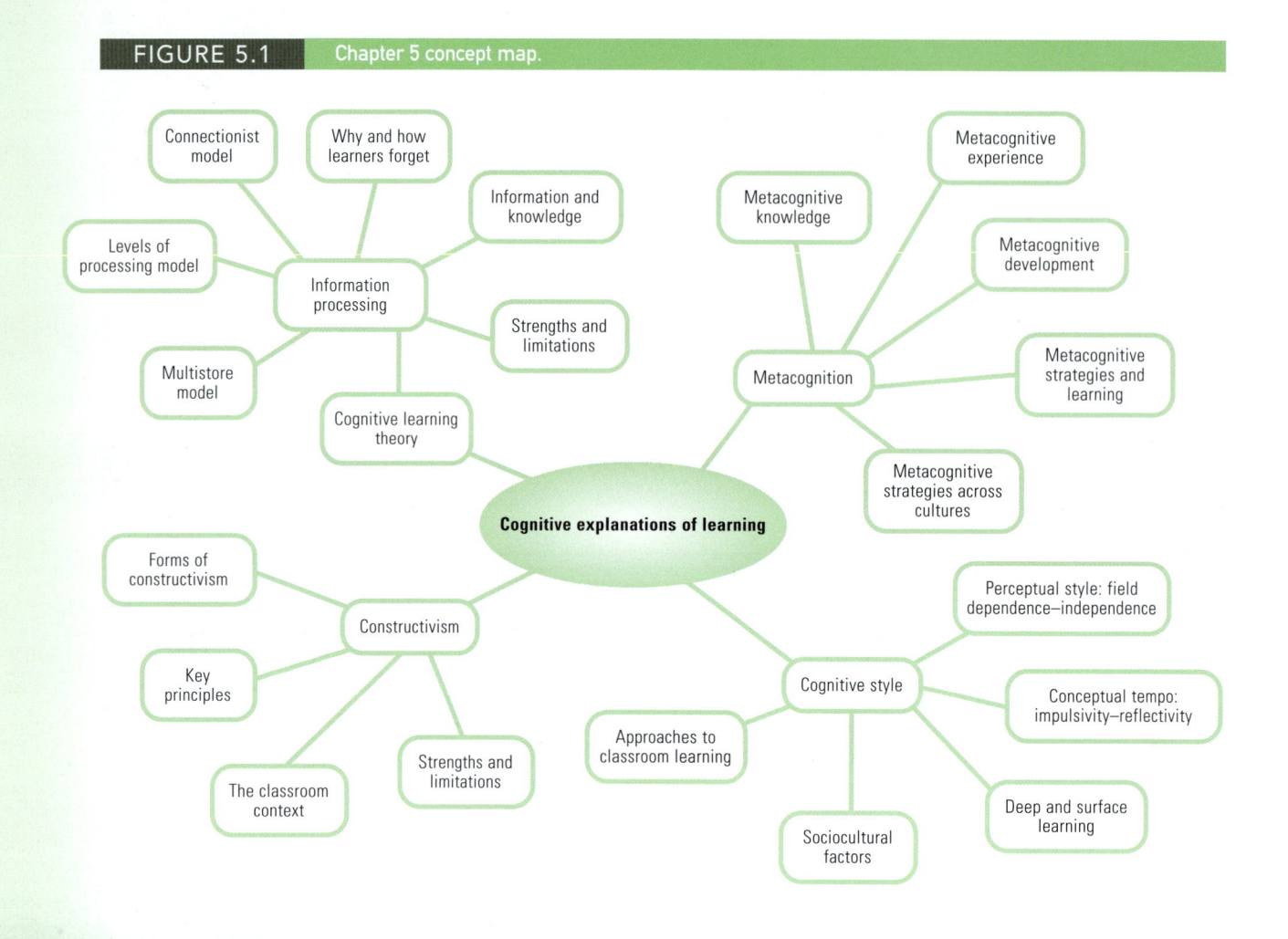

Concept map centred on "Cognitive explanations of learning" with the following branches:

- **Cognitive learning theory** → Information processing
  - Connectionist model
  - Why and how learners forget
  - Information and knowledge
  - Strengths and limitations
  - Levels of processing model
  - Multistore model
- **Metacognition**
  - Metacognitive knowledge
  - Metacognitive experience
  - Metacognitive development
  - Metacognitive strategies and learning
  - Metacognitive strategies across cultures
- **Cognitive style**
  - Perceptual style: field dependence–independence
  - Conceptual tempo: impulsivity–reflectivity
  - Deep and surface learning
  - Sociocultural factors
  - Approaches to classroom learning
- **Constructivism**
  - Forms of constructivism
  - Key principles
  - The classroom context
  - Strengths and limitations

CHAPTER OBJECTIVES

After reading this chapter you should be able to:

- identify the key principles of cognitive learning theory and contrast these with the behavioural approach
- describe three forms of the information processing model of learning (multistore, levels of processing and connectionist)
- distinguish between a range of cognitive styles and comment on their impact on learning
- explain the role of metacognition in learning and memory
- identify four key principles of constructivism and discuss ways of putting these into practice in the classroom.

CHAPTER 5

Cognitive explanations of learning

Introduction

cognitive learning theory
Concerned with internal mental processes and how learners manipulate information during learning

information processing model
Likens the human mind to a computer that interprets, stores and retrieves information

This chapter's theme is cognitive approaches to learning. In Chapter 4 we looked at learning from a behavioural point of view, focusing on learners' observable behaviours and their responses to external stimuli. In this chapter we shift our focus from external processes to internal mental processes in order to examine what happens in the mind when we learn. Unlike the behavioural perspective, cognitive explanations view learners as active constructors of their own learning. The emphasis is on how learners make meaning and remember what they learn.

Cognitive learning theory

Cognitive learning theory focuses on internal mental processes and their role in learning. Its primary concern is with making meaning out of information and experience (Bruner, 1990) and with how learners manipulate both new and familiar information. According to this approach, learning involves acquiring new ways of processing information and revising existing processes (Vosniadou, 1995). As you learned in Chapter 2, cognition describes the mental processes that transform the information we take in through our senses, and that code it, store it in memory and later retrieve it for use.

The information processing approach

The **information processing model** is one way of depicting how mental processes operate. This approach to cognitive processing evolved in the 1950s and 1960s, coinciding with the development of computer technologies. Proponents of this view liken the human mind to a computer – an information processing device that interprets information from external sources, and that stores and later retrieves that information. Information processing accounts were developed in reaction to behaviourist theories, which were seen as substantial oversimplifications of how humans learn (Eysenck, 1998). While behaviourists focus on observable responses to stimuli, information processing accounts attempt to explain how the brain actually deals with information, and, therefore, how we learn. Learners are viewed as 'bundles of knowledge structures that become increasingly sophisticated and hierarchical as they gain experience' (Gallagher, 1994, p. 172). Thinking is portrayed as a highly rational process. Memory lies at the heart of the information processing accounts, which generally do not take account of the role of emotions or imagination in thinking. There are several information processing models detailing cognitive processes and how the mind works. Three of these are the 'multistore' model, the 'levels of processing' model, and the 'connectionist' model.

The multistore model

The **multistore model** of information processing (Atkinson & Shiffrin, 1968) has been called the 'boxes-in-the-head' approach. It is also known as the 'stage' model, since it depicts information processing as a sequence of discrete stages equivalent to the serial processing that takes place in computers. This model relates to how information is processed and stored in memory. It views the information input you receive moment by moment as being processed and stored in three locations, or 'boxes', which are known as 'sensory register', 'short-term memory' and 'long-term memory' (see Figure 5.2). Each 'box' has a different processing function, with the sensory register being the first location.

multistore model
Depicts how information is processed and stored in memory in a sequence of stages

FIGURE 5.2
The multistore model of information processing.
(Source: Eysenck & Keane, 2000, Figure 6.1.)

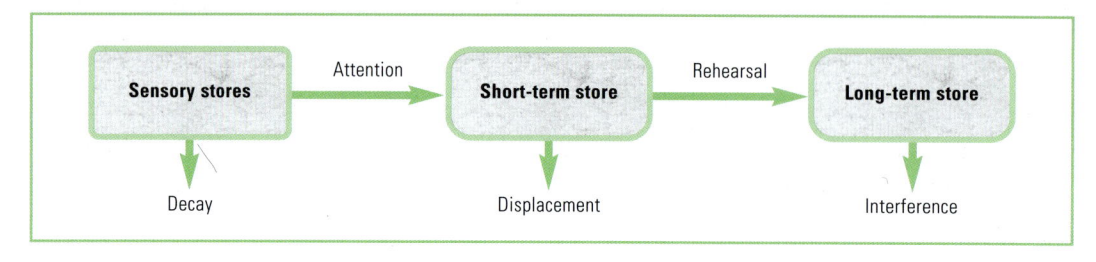

Sensory stores → Attention → Short-term store → Rehearsal → Long-term store
↓ Decay   ↓ Displacement   ↓ Interference

Sensory register

The **sensory register** is the first compartment, or storage box, for information input. New information enters the sensory register through the five senses and is stored for less than one second (Schneider & Bjorklund, 1998). Visual information goes into the visual store, auditory information into the auditory store and so on. The number and range of stimuli that constantly bombard us exceed the amount we can process, and since we cannot process everything, we must be selective. The central process associated with this stage is attention. When we focus on certain information with the aim of remembering it, we are said to be 'paying attention'. If we attend to information, it moves to the next storage box, the short-term memory, for further processing. If we do not pay attention, the information decays and disappears.

sensory register
New information enters the sensory register through the five senses and is stored for less than one second

5.1 Example of information processing in action

Short-term memory

Short-term memory (STM), or 'working memory' (Baddeley, 1986), is a temporary storage place with a limited capacity to store approximately seven items of information at a time (Miller, 1956). Short-term memory only stores information for a few seconds: in order to remember the information in short-term memory we may either rehearse it or 'chunk' it. 'Rehearsal' involves us repeating and practising information to help ourselves remember it. 'Chunking' occurs when we group related pieces of information into a single meaningful unit. You may have used chunking to remember a list of numbers. For example, if your student number is quite long, you may chunk the nine digits as '925–231–378'. Thus, nine pieces of information are reduced to three bundles, which makes the number easier to remember. The rhythm of this grouping may also help you remember the sequence. The more effectively material is chunked and rehearsed, the more likely it is to be transferred to long-term memory. Unrehearsed items are usually displaced by new information and are soon forgotten.

short-term memory
A temporary storage place with a limited capacity to store approximately seven items

Long-term memory

The third component of the process and a permanent storage facility for information, **long-term memory** is, as far as anyone can tell, unlimited in capacity and storage time. Memories may remain in long-term memory indefinitely, and long-term memories take many forms. Three main types of long-term memory are 'episodic', 'semantic' and 'procedural' (Tulving, 1985).

Episodic memories are the memories we have for events that have happened to us personally, like a school concert where you played the lead role, or your first kiss. **Semantic memory** is concerned with language and the world around us; for example, knowing that chopsticks are implements used for eating, or that December and January are summer months in the southern hemisphere. Semantic memories generally lack the specific information about time and place that characterises episodic memories. If you remember something that happened to you while you were eating with chopsticks at your favourite Chinese restaurant last summer, this would be an episodic rather than a semantic memory. **Procedural memory** helps us recall steps or procedures for performing a skill; for example, you need procedural memory to help you use the chopsticks for eating. While episodic, semantic and procedural memories differ in content and function, these types of long-term memory are often interconnected. For instance, your semantic memory of chopsticks may be connected to your episodic memory of the first time you tried to eat with them – and perhaps failed miserably! At times, long-term memories may interfere with one another, making it difficult to recall information. This process is discussed in the next section.

As with short-term memory, rehearsal helps us remember information stored in long-term memory. 'Elaboration' is another important strategy, which involves linking new information to something already stored in the long-term memory. This makes the new material more meaningful because we connect it to something familiar, thus increasing our likelihood of remembering it in the future. Elaboration strategies are positively associated with academic performance, particularly in reading (Sturrock & May, 2002).

long-term memory
A permanent storage facility for information

episodic memory
Memory for personal events in our lives

semantic memory
Memory about language and the world around us

procedural memory
Memory about steps or procedures for performing a skill

CRITICAL REFLECTIONS

- How well does the multistore model describe the way you have processed information during your reading of the previous one or two pages?
- What types of external stimuli did you try to *avoid* storing in your sensory register while you read these pages?
- What techniques did you use to enhance your short-term and long-term memory while you read the pages?
- How might the multistore model improve the way you teach your students?

The levels of processing model

As the name suggests, the **levels of processing model** (Craik & Lockhart, 1972; Lockhart & Craik, 1990) focuses on the *depth* of information processing and how this affects our ability to recall information. 'Deep processing' means that information is attended to, fully analysed, enriched by association with existing knowledge, and is thus remembered because of the extent of the processing that has occurred (see Figure 5.3 on page 140). 'Shallow processing' occurs when information is not given full attention, and is analysed only superficially. It is most likely that information analysed at a surface level will soon be forgotten.

levels of processing model
A process-oriented approach that attaches most importance to the type and depth of processing taking place

FIGURE 5.3 Deep processing will help this student remember the material.

The amount of attention allocated, the type of information and its meaning for us, and the time available for processing the new materials all contribute to depth of processing. In a later version of their theory, Lockhart and Craik (1990) pointed out that they originally envisaged processing as sequential, proceeding from shallow to deeper processing. More recently, however, their research has indicated that processing at different levels may occur simultaneously or that deep processing may precede shallow processing depending on several factors such as the learner's familiarity with the information being processed and the type of task (Lockhart & Craik, 1990, p. 95).

The connectionist model

Recent information processing accounts have tended to focus on how the human brain functions and the role of neural networks in cognitive processing and memory. This focus has led to **connectionist model**s, in which information is seen as being stored in multiple locations throughout the brain, forming networks of connections; that is, the brain is depicted as a complex network of interconnected units of information (Ellis & Humphreys, 1999). In Chapter 1 you learned about brain development and the increasingly complex networks that develop with age (see Figure 1.9 on page 13). This development of connectivity and complexity in brain networks helps explain why a young child's memory capacity is smaller than an adult's.

According to the connectionist model, there is no such thing as an isolated memory, since one memory is connected to many others as in a vast computer network. McLelland and Rumelhart (1986) have developed one of the more widely accepted connectionist models. They extended the levels of processing model, arguing that information is stored in multiple locations throughout the brain, in the form of networks of connections.

> **connectionist model**
> Views the brain as a complex network of interconnected units of information, with information stored in patterns of connectivity

Why and how learners forget

How can the three models of information processing and storage we have examined help the teacher who is trying to ensure that students learn and remember important information? The information processing model in all its forms helps us to understand how we process and store information cognitively. It also seeks to explain the flipside of remembering – that is, forgetting.

Much of what happens in the learning process relies on students' ability to recall necessary information and put stored knowledge into action quickly. The most common reason for forgetting in the short term is that we fail to pay adequate attention to information that is processed through the sensory register and short-term memory. Another reason for forgetting is that – as mentioned earlier – short-term memory is limited in the number of items it can hold at any given moment, and new information tends to bump old information out of short-term memory store (Engle & Oransky, 1999). Other factors may be lack of motivation to remember certain information, or failure to develop adequate memory skills

(Guenther, 1998, p. 148). But what about when we forget information we thought we had stored in long-term memory?

Cognitive learning theorists draw on the information processing model to explain why we forget such information. Some cognitive learning theorists argue that we forget because long-term memory 'decays' and disappears over time, but there is little direct support for this view (Eysenck & Keane, 2000). A second explanation is the 'interference' approach, which argues that we forget because long-term memories interfere with one another (see Figure 5.2 on page 138). Old memories interfere with storing new ones, while new memories may make it difficult to retrieve old ones. Thus, forgetting occurs when we cannot access a memory effectively, not because the memory has disappeared. The more information we memorise and the more memories we develop over time, the greater the possibility of interference.

Another explanation for why we forget is 'cue-dependent forgetting' (Tulving, 1974). According to this explanation we do not lose information: it is held in storage, but we cannot retrieve it because we do not have the right cues. The process of remembering is an interconnected one. Information is recalled, which cues other information, which in turn cues other information, and so on (Nuthall, 2000). For example, a cue for remembering compass points might be the phrase '**N**ever **E**at **S**our **W**atermelons', where the first letter of each word corresponds to a compass point. These letters cue long-term memory for individual compass points, and remind us of the order of the points in a clockwise direction. Thus, one piece of information cues another. Table 5.1 contains more information on memory principles and strategies. Table 5.2 (see page 142) gives some examples of mnemonic devices, which help us to remember information by associating new information with meaningful images or contexts.

5.2 Social interaction and memory

TABLE 5.1	Memory principles and strategies for classroom application
Principles	**Strategies**
Focus attention	■ Use cueing signals: 'Are you listening carefully?'; 'Let's concentrate on this' ■ Emphasise important information: 'There are three important ideas in this passage. Can you find them?'; 'This is a key point' ■ Model how to identify important ideas: write them on the board, highlight them on paper and distribute them
Use prior learning and background knowledge	■ Review previous lessons ■ Brainstorm ideas on the board or on paper to trigger memory and focus thinking ■ Invite students to talk about their experiences (such as those in another culture, or in a sport or hobby area) to make new information meaningful
Present information in an organised manner	■ Show a logical sequence to ideas to help students store information in an organised way ■ Move from simple to complex when presenting new material ■ Use 'advance organisers' (Ausubel, 1977, 1978; Griffin, Malone, & Kameenui, 1995): – first, orient learners by directing them to familiar material … this gives them a framework for acquiring new knowledge meaningfully – next, help students organise the knowledge they already have and combine it with new information to be processed – use concept maps, structured overviews and outlines
Teach cognitive and memory strategies	■ **Chunking:** Demonstrate how to chunk related information by presenting it in categories and showing learners how they might organise items into categories rather than memorising a list in serial order ■ **Elaboration:** Help learners to link new information to existing knowledge. For example, when teaching a new concept such as 'osmosis' in Biology, use a familiar real-world example – such as why pot plants or flowers wilt, then bloom when watered – to help students make connections between new and existing material. The greater the elaboration, the more deeply the concept will be processed, and the better it will be remembered ■ **Mnemonic devices**: Use mnemonic devices to associate new information with meaningful images or contexts (see Table 5.2 over the page)
Review and practise	■ Repeat important principles to assist short-term memory and prevent decay (Rosenshine, 1997) ■ Review previous lessons

(Continued over page.)

Principles	Strategies
	■ Provide opportunities for practice by encouraging 'distributed' or 'spaced' practice, where learners distribute their study effort over many sessions. This is more meaningful than 'massed practice' (or 'cramming'), where students try to memorise material quickly and rote learn (Caple, 1996; Donovan & Radosevich, 1999; Hall, 1992)
Monitor student progress	■ Be aware of students' level of understanding. Can they remember and apply the basics? Are they ready for new learning? ■ Monitor motivation levels (see Chapter 7) ■ Consider and cater for differences between students in their learning preferences.

TABLE 5.2 Mnemonic devices for the classroom

Mnemonic device	Example
The 'loci' or 'place' method *Strategy:* Use familiar locations and visual imagery to remember items	To remember four unrelated items – elephant, car, milk, CD – visualise a familiar location such as your home. 'Place' each item in a location around the house and 'pick it up' as you take a mental walk around the house: 'The elephant arrives home by car. First she walks into the kitchen to put the milk away, then she walks into the living room to play her new CD'
Peg method *Strategy:* Remember sequences of unrelated items in the correct order using familiar peg words (common peg-word sequences are numbers, and letters of the alphabet)	To remember the names of the three largest New Zealand cities in the correct order, use the familiar peg words '1', '2' and '3': 1 is A1 – A is for Auckland 2 – 2 'l's in Wellington 3 – 3 'c's in Christchurch
Rhymes *Strategy:* Use rhyming sounds to assist memory	'The First Fleet landed in Botany *Bay* on a 1788 January *day*'
Acronyms *Strategy:* Remember lists of words by chunking or reorganising information to make a word or phrase that is easy to remember	In an acronym, the first letter of each word in a list forms a key word, name or sentence. For example, in music theory, to remember the notes that occupy the lines on the treble clef (E, G, B, D, F), you may remember that 'Every Good Boy Deserves Fruit', while the acronym 'FACE' represents the notes that occupy the spaces on the treble clef

Information and knowledge

So far in this chapter we have focused on models that attempt to explain how humans process information. But when does information become knowledge? 'Knowledge' is information that is acted upon cognitively. In other words, knowledge refers to what we do with the information we process and how we make meaning from it. Knowledge is broader, deeper and richer than information. Three main types of knowledge are 'declarative', 'procedural' and 'conditional'.

Declarative knowledge is concerned with *knowing that* something is so. For example, knowing that chopsticks are implements for eating is declarative knowledge. When you commit that knowledge to memory it becomes semantic memory (as discussed earlier). **Procedural knowledge** refers to *knowing how* to perform an action or action sequence for solving problems (Rittle-Johnson & Alibali, 1999). It is knowledge you can demonstrate, like knowing how to type, how to use a computer, how to drive a manual car or how to perform long division. **Conditional knowledge** is *knowing when and how* to use different types of knowledge for different purposes.

In teaching, the three types of knowledge are particularly important for teachers and learners. For example, you may be a skilled mathematician who can perform long division

---

declarative knowledge
Knowing that certain facts, information and experiences exist and are real

procedural knowledge
Knowing how to perform an action or sequence of actions

conditional knowledge
Knowing when and how to use different types of knowledge

in your head without any trouble – that is, you have the *procedural knowledge*. But can you explain the steps in long division to your students – that is, do you have the necessary *declarative knowledge* to be able to show others how to perform the skill? Further, do you have the *conditional knowledge* to know when to put the other forms of knowledge into practice? While this discussion distinguishes between three main types of knowledge, it is not easy to distinguish them so clearly in practice, since they are interconnected and different types of knowledge overlap. Box 5.1 highlights how we use different kinds of knowledge to interpret and access information within a particular context.

5.3 The role of knowledge in learning

Box 5.1 CLASSROOM LINKS

Knowledge needed in the classroom

Kate is a Year 1 student who is learning the basics of addition. The teacher provides the following information in the form of a problem:

> I have three pears and two apples. How many pieces of fruit do I have?

Kate needs certain kinds of knowledge to solve the problem. (Try to list these before you read any further.)

Kate needs to know that:

- Each word in the problem has a particular meaning. A rudimentary knowledge of how to decode words (see Chapter 1 for details on language development) and knowledge of numbers (for example, how many '3' refers to) are therefore required.
- Pears and apples are two types of fruit.
- The word 'and' is important because it indicates a connection between two pieces of information.
- To solve the problem, the words must be transformed into an equation (for example, '3 + 2') to arrive at the correct answer.

Activities

1 Compare your list of the types of knowledge Kate needs with the list above. Are there any differences?
2 Can you think of any other knowledge Kate might need in order to process the teacher's information effectively?
3 Kate wonders: 'Should I call out in the class, put my hand up, write the equation in my workbook or perhaps walk up to the blackboard and write the answer there when the teacher asks for a response?' What type of knowledge is Kate demonstrating as she considers how she might behave?

Strengths and limitations of the information processing approach

The information processing account of how we process and remember information is widely accepted in the field of cognitive psychology. There are several models of information processing, each with its own merits and limitations. In contrast to the behaviourist focus on observable behaviours, the information processing approach attempts to depict the complex mental processes that occur between the stimulus and response, and how these contribute to learning and remembering.

Strengths

Using the computer as a metaphor for the human mind, the information processing models help us understand the complexity of cognitive processing and the many stages and processes involved in storing and recalling information. This approach facilitates close study and analysis of cognitive processes – something particularly beneficial for educators seeking to understand how best to assist young people to learn and recall important information. The multistore model draws attention to different dimensions of memory (such as sensory, short-term and long-term memory) and to the value of strategies such as rehearsal and elaboration in enhancing recall. Levels of processing models are advantageous since they distinguish between type and depth of processing and the subsequent effect on quality of memory storage and recall. Connectionist models, which draw upon research into the brain's neural networks, are valuable because they provide insights into the connectedness and interdependence of cognitive processes and stored memories.

Limitations

The information processing approach is limited in several ways. Some models of information processing (such as the multistore model) suggest the mind processes information sequentially. This depiction is idealised and is unrepresentative of the complexity and interconnectedness of the brain's neural networks (see Ellis & Humphreys, 1999). The information processing approach has also been criticised for an over-reliance on the computer as an analogy for how the mind works. The brain is not constructed like a standard computer (Klahr & MacWhinney, 1998): computers are built of hardy electrical components, and individual items can be reliably stored in discrete locations and accessed in predictable ways when needed (Kanerva, 1993). 'Neural hardware', on the other hand, is made out of 'noisy, unstable components', and it is not always possible to guarantee information retrieval (Klahr & MacWhinney, 1998, p. 651). In using computer modelling, most information processing models fail to take account of environmental, genetic and cultural differences in the ways individuals process information. Such models tend to decontextualise information processing, ignoring situational and personal factors – such as emotional state, time of day and level of ability – that may influence how an individual responds to and processes information.

The models are nevertheless intended as abstract representations that enable researchers to predict behaviour and test hypotheses. Seen in this light, information processing models draw our attention to several important principles of cognitive processing and are particularly helpful in examining the learning process.

Box 5.2 presents some implications of the information processing approach for classroom practice.

Box 5.2 IMPLICATIONS FOR EDUCATORS

Applying information processing in the classroom

The information processing model draws attention to the complex mental operations involved in processing information. To apply this model in your teaching you may do the following:
- Teach students to pay attention to important information from the earliest moment of impact in the sensory register.
- Model how to select and pay attention to the most important information.
- Provide opportunities for students to rehearse and repeat information in short-term memory, to ensure that the information moves into the long-term memory store.
- Give learners opportunities to elaborate on information and to link it to existing information so it will be meaningful and thus easier to recall.
- Adapt teaching methods to cater for an individual's cognitive style (Grigorenko & Sternberg, 1995).
- Provide students with learning strategies that will enable them to cope with situations where their preferred style is not the most appropriate (Riding & Rayner, 1998).
- Consider how your own cognitive style and preferred teaching styles affect classroom activities and the quality of students' learning (Ferrari & Sternberg, 1998; Sternberg & Grigorenko, 1995).
- Encourage students to process information deeply so as to transform it into meaningful knowledge they can use for different purposes and contexts.
- Teach and model memory skills (see tables 5.1 and 5.2 on pages 141 and 142).

Metacognition: Managing cognitive processes

So far, we have learned that cognition describes the mental processes involved in transforming, coding, storing and retrieving information. But how do we know which mental processes to use, and when, and how, and why? The answer lies in our capacity for **metacognition**, which literally means 'thinking about thinking' or 'knowledge about knowledge' (Weinert, 1987). It is cognition about one's own cognitive processes (Flavell, Miller, & Miller, 1993) and refers to our ability to monitor, control and organise our own mental activities. Metacognition is known as an 'executive control' process that monitors and regulates our thought processes (Davidson, Deuser, & Sternberg, 1994).

Since we cannot process all information to the same depth, we need an 'executive' function to oversee the process of encoding, transforming, processing, storing, retrieving and utilising information. This executive function involves both self-monitoring and self-regulation. **Self-monitoring** is a broad monitoring activity that helps us keep track of our progress in understanding and remembering. **Self-regulation**, on the other hand, is concerned with central executive processes that comprise several specific functions such as planning, directing and evaluating our cognitive behaviour (Nelson & Narens, 1994; Schneider & Bjorklund, 1998). Self-regulated learners regulate their actions, cognitions, beliefs and motivations by selecting their own approach to learning and processing information (Shin, 1998). When faced with a task, a self-regulated learner will typically:

- analyse the task and interpret task requirements
- set task-specific goals that aid successful task completion
- self-monitor progress and provide 'self-feedback'
- adjust strategies and goals throughout the process
- use self-motivational strategies to ensure task completion.

Metacognition thus involves planning, monitoring, regulating, questioning, reflecting on and reviewing our cognitive processes. Figure 5.4 illustrates the executive control function of metacognition.

Metacognition comprises 'metacognitive knowledge' and 'metacognitive experience' (Flavell, 1987; Flavell, Miller, & Miller, 1993), which are discussed in the following sections.

5.4 The difference between cognition and metacognition

metacognition
Knowledge about knowledge

self-monitoring
A metacognitive activity that involves monitoring how well we are understanding and remembering

self-regulation
A metacognitive activity that involves planning, directing and evaluating one's cognitive processes

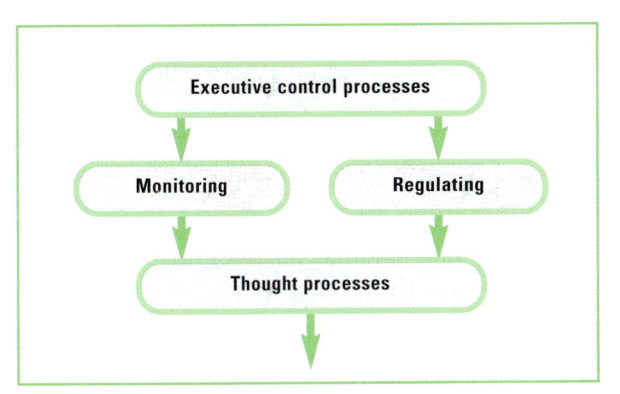

FIGURE 5.4 Metacognition is like a company executive overseeing (monitoring and regulating) the workers (thought processes) of the company.
(Source: Adapted from Kluwe, 1982, pp. 201–224.)

Metacognitive knowledge

Learners develop three forms of metacognitive knowledge: of person, of task and of strategy.

'Person knowledge' is the knowledge you have about your own cognition and your understanding of others as cognitive processors. For example, we describe some people as 'reflective' or 'thoughtful'; we describe others as 'good with mathematical problems' or as having a 'bad memory'. These descriptions reflect an awareness of individuals' cognitive characteristics.

'Task knowledge' is the metacognitive knowledge that different tasks require different approaches and different types of skills (Pintrich, 1996). With experience, we learn more about task demands and how we can meet them under different circumstances. For example, we learn that a textbook like this one is densely packed with information, and that we need to proceed slowly and carefully in order to process the information effectively.

We also develop 'strategy knowledge' over time. There are many types of metacognitive strategies, which can be broadly said to belong to one of three categories: planning, monitoring or evaluating (Pintrich & DeGroot, 1990; Pintrich & Schunk, 1996; Wittrock, 1991) (see Table 5.3 for some examples of metacognitive strategies). Strategy knowledge involves knowing which metacognitive strategies to use and when in order to accomplish a set task. For example, if you want to know whether a book will be useful for your assignment, strategy knowledge would prompt you to skim-read, or check the table of contents, rather than read the book from cover to cover. Strategy knowledge helps learners to be efficient and effective by giving them the means to select the most appropriate metacognitive strategies for their purpose.

5.5 Metamemory: Learn more about how memory works

TABLE 5.3 — Examples of metacognitive strategies

Metacognitive strategy	Examples of self-questions
Planning	What type of task is this?
	What skills and resources do I need?
	What are my task goals?
	How long will the task take to achieve?
Monitoring	How are my motivation levels?
	How well am I going?
	Do I need to change my approach?
	Do I need to adapt my task goals?
Evaluating	How well did I do?
	What did I do well?
	What did not work too well?
	What should I change next time?

Source: Adapted from Pintrich & Schunk (1996) and Wittrock (1991).

Metacognitive experience

We also have 'metacognitive experiences', which include feelings related to particular cognitive activities (Flavell, 1987; Flavell, Miller, & Miller, 1993). For example, you may feel anxious when you realise you do not understand something important your lecturer is explaining to the class. This is a metacognitive experience because you are reflecting on how poorly you are processing the information being shared and you are concerned because you do not understand it. Metacognitive experiences are connected to self-esteem and self-efficacy: if we feel capable of controlling and regulating our cognitive processes, we will feel more positive about ourselves and our abilities (Borkowski, Carr, Rellinger, & Pressley, 1990). The interrelationships between the different aspects of metacognition are presented in Figure 5.5. Box 5.3 presents an example of the role of metacognition in the classroom.

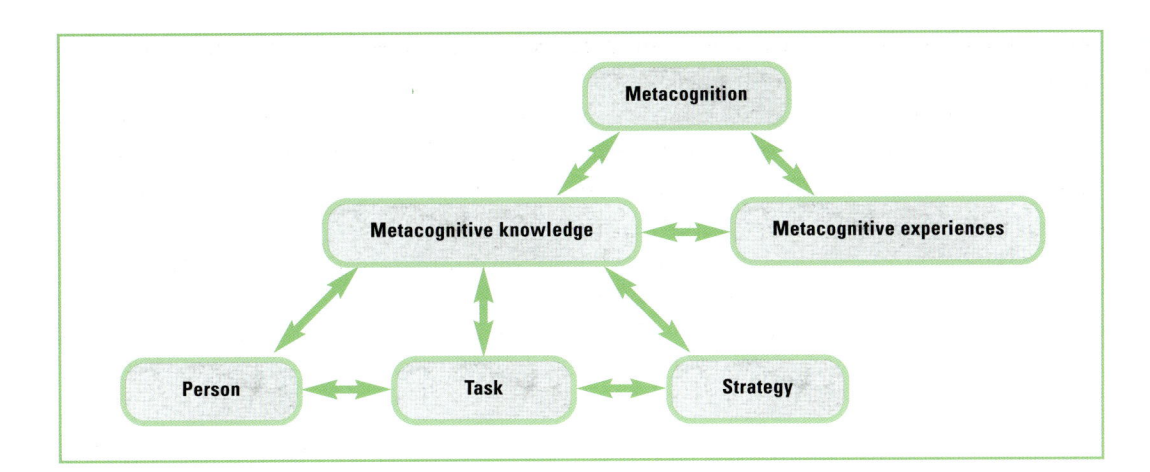

FIGURE 5.5 Dimensions of metacognition.

Box 5.3 CLASSROOM LINKS

Metacognitive knowledge and experiences

Shiori is a diligent Year 12 student who is sitting at her desk with a pile of homework. Before Shiori commences work, she plans the order in which she will complete the tasks. She decides to do her mathematics homework on integral calculus first, because she needs a clear head to work through the calculations. She decides to do her chapter summaries for *Tomorrow, When the War Began* last. She shifts all unnecessary books to the floor so she has fewer distractions.

The calculus problem concerns the concept of area under a mathematically defined curve and requires Shiori to find the area under a rollercoaster track. Shiori knows how to calculate the area of a rectangle, and understands how she can use what she knows to find the total area under the track. Unfortunately, the rollercoaster example has reminded Shiori of last summer's holiday on the Gold Coast, and memories of the fun she had on a rollercoaster interfere with her ability to focus on the calculus problem. She realises that for the last 5 minutes she has been staring at her textbook and reminiscing about her Gold Coast holiday. At the same time, Shiori is distracted by her little brother crying in the next room. She knows she is easily distracted when tired, so closes her door and decides to focus her concentration even more to filter out the noise. She then also realises she can use her memories of the rollercoaster to help her visualise the calculus problem.

Shiori visualises the superstructure that supported the rollercoaster and draws a sketch on scrap paper to see if this will help to solve the calculus problem. Her concentration is broken again when she remembers her teacher mentioning a short quiz that is to be held on this material in the next Maths class. Shiori's stomach sinks. She knows she does not fully understand how to solve the calculus problem and apply the equations she has learned, which means she will need to wake up early tomorrow morning and try to get the teacher's help before school commences.

Identifying examples of metacognition

There are several examples of metacognition in the scenario above. These include metacognitive knowledge in the form of:

- *Person knowledge.* Shiori knows she is easily distracted when tired. She decides to focus her concentration even more.
- *Task knowledge.* Shiori has a number of homework tasks, but decides to do her Maths homework first because she needs a clear head. Near the end of the scenario, Shiori assesses her understanding of the calculus concept and realises she does not know the material well enough for a quiz being held in her next Maths class. In this case, she has metacognitive knowledge of what she does *not* know.
- *Strategy knowledge.* Shiori consciously uses her memories of the rollercoaster to help her. She uses visual images and sketches to try and solve the calculus problem.

Shiori also has metacognitive experiences:

- Shiori has the metacognitive experience of frustration when she realises she is reminiscing about the summer holiday rather than completing the maths problem.
- Shiori experiences the sinking feeling that she is not ready for the Maths quiz because she does not fully understand the material. This experience is the result of her self-monitoring and self-regulating her thought processes.

Source: Adapted from Hacker (1998, pp. 1–2).

> **Activities**
>
> 1. Can you find any other examples of metacognition in this scenario?
> 2. How could you use Shiori's experience to teach your students about the role of metacognition in their own thinking and learning?

Metacognitive development

When does metacognition begin to develop? In Chapter 2 we learned that according to Piaget's theory, young children are cognitively egocentric. They generally do not reflect on their own thinking and do not seem to realise that other people have thoughts or preoccupations. 'Theory of mind' research explores the ways in which children develop theories and understandings of their own mental world and that of others (Flavell, 1999). Like Piaget, John Hurley Flavell contends that children develop an increasingly complex theory of the mind and mental processes. This development is enabled by their increasing capacity for abstract thought.

Since metacognition requires self-reflection and the awareness of mental processes we cannot see or touch, it requires the ability to reflect on abstract processes. While research has found some evidence of metacognition in younger children (Fang & Cox, 1999), this skill is most evident among adolescents. It develops over time as cognitive skills increase (Kuhn, 2000).

5.6 Theory of mind and metacognition in younger children

Metacognitive strategies and learning

A significant body of research indicates that students benefit from learning about and using metacognitive strategies. In particular, research suggests a positive relationship between performance on academic tasks and the level of metacognitive awareness. In a study of 155 Year 5 mathematics students, Lucangeli, Coi and Bosco (1997) found that poor problem-solvers had lower metacognitive awareness than average or good problem-solvers. The same authors argued the case for a link between the use of metacognitive strategies and academic performance (see also Carr, Alexander, & Folds-Bennett, 1994). Students of lower ability have been found to benefit significantly from direct instruction in metacognitive strategies (Cardelle-Elawar, 1995; Spence, Yore, & Williams, 1999). In an Australian study of poor readers in upper primary school, Bruce and Robinson (2001) found that direct instruction in metacognitive word-identification strategies and metacognitive awareness-raising contributed to improved word identification and reading-comprehension skills in poor readers within a regular classroom setting. Studies of students with learning disabilities have also found that metacognitive strategy instruction enhances such learners' thinking and social skills (Powell & Makin, 1994; Rosenthal-Malek, 1997). A recent study of very able students found that computerised metacognitive strategy instruction proved beneficial in raising students' performance levels in both reading and writing (Kaniel, Licht & Peled, 2001).

Metacognitive strategies across cultures

Vygotsky (discussed in Chapter 2) drew attention to the impact of culture and social interactions on thinking. These sociocultural influences have been found to influence the ways in which individuals think about themselves and their own thinking (Kurtz, 1990). Research in this area is equivocal, however, and there is no simple connection to be made between metacognition and culture. Some studies find few cross-cultural differences; for instance, a study of Australian, Japanese and American students showed that similar metacognitive strategies were used across these three cultures (Jones & Davenport, 1996; Purdie & Hattie,

1996). There is some research evidence, however, to indicate differences in the ways learners from different cultures use metacognitive strategies; for example, a study of 94 Zulu children aged six to thirteen years found that they were similar to an American sample in terms of metacognitive knowledge of person and task, but lagged behind the American sample in their metacognitive knowledge of strategy (Sharratt & van den Heuvel, 1995). Sharrat and van den Heuvel argued that there are possible cultural and educational reasons for these differences.

As you may have noted, cross-cultural studies pose many problems and their results need to be considered with caution. The dangers of oversimplifying results should be taken into account, and questions should arise about the difficulties of comparing students from different cultural and educational backgrounds. Results will depend, for example, on the ways in which data are collected, how the sample is selected and so on. Nevertheless, it can be extrapolated from the study of Zulu children that subtle cross-cultural differences might emerge in the area of metacognition within your own teaching contexts. You need to be aware of the ways in which such differences may impact on the quality of students' learning experiences.

Box 5.4 discusses some classroom implications of metacognitive strategies.

Box 5.4 IMPLICATIONS FOR EDUCATORS

Metacognitive strategies in the classroom

Research suggests that educators have a significant role to play in raising students' awareness of their own thinking (Paris & Winograd, 1990) and in teaching them how to monitor their strategic behaviour and performance (Borkowski & Muthukrishna, 1992). However, an important first step is for teachers to become more self-aware and develop their own metacognitive skills (Zohar, 1999). Once you develop the skill of reflecting on your own cognitive processes and develop metacognitive strategies, you will be better equipped to model these for your students and to support their learning.

Here are some strategies to use with your students:

- Teach and model metacognitive strategies explicitly (Boekaerts, 1997), particularly in the basic skills of literacy and numeracy (Maqsud, 1997; Moely, Santulli, & Obach, 1995).
- Demonstrate a procedure and encourage students to follow you step by step (Wilen & Phillips, 1995), as demonstrated in Table 5.4 below.
- Journal writing – on paper or online – encourages students to reflect on their learning without worrying about assessment.
- Provide sample questions to encourage self-reflection:
  – What went well in this class today?
  – Did I get distracted? When and why?
  – What will I do next time to keep my attention focused?

This type of reflection encourages students to self-monitor and self-regulate.

Table 5.4 provides an example of how to foster metacognition through modelling.

TABLE 5.4 Modelling essay-writing techniques: Strategies for promoting metacognition

Instructions to use when modelling	Commentary
Students, ask yourselves: ■ What is the essay question asking me to do? ■ What do I know about this topic? ■ What else do I need to know? ■ Where will I go to get information?	■ Teachers' aim is to model the self-questioning technique so students can employ this strategy on their own when they have to write an essay
Spend time planning: ■ Break the task into small steps ■ How many paragraphs am I going to write? ■ What will be the topic of each paragraph?	■ Students benefit from planning before they commence the essay, and hopefully soon learn to plan without being prompted by the teacher ■ Teachers help students believe in their own ability to accomplish a task by breaking it into small, manageable steps ■ Teachers demonstrate planning strategies so students learn to implement these for themselves

(Continued over page.)

Instructions to use when modelling	Commentary
During the writing process: Stop and go back to your plan to make sure you are on track: ■ How am I going? ■ What am I doing well? ■ What do I need to change or add? ■ Am I answering the question? ■ Am I using the appropriate style? ■ How am I going for time?	■ Encourage students to self-monitor throughout the writing task: students need to become aware of what they are thinking as they write and direct their cognitive resources appropriately
At the end: ■ How did I go? ■ Did that plan work? ■ What might I change next time? ■ What was successful? ■ Do I need to proofread the essay and check spelling?	■ Promote evaluation and self-reflection ■ Encourage students to evaluate their strengths and weaknesses and to set goals for improving their execution of the task next time

Activity

Complete the following steps:
1. Select a subject area and age group that best applies to your interests.
2. Plan a lesson involving the modelling of metacognitive strategies.
3. List the strategies you will model and questions you will ask.
4. Ask your peers to give you feedback.

5.7 Approaches to teaching metacognitive strategies

CRITICAL REFLECTIONS

■ Can you recall being taught metacognitive strategies when you were at school? If so, how did you benefit? If not, how did you learn these strategies?

■ How do you think your own experience will impact on your approach to teaching metacognition?

■ Consider the range of subject areas you may teach: mathematics, science, languages, art. Are there some subject areas where metacognitive strategies are more important than others?

Cognitive style

Models of information processing attempt to depict how learners mentally manipulate information. The way we process and respond to information varies considerably from one learner to another. Have you ever tried to complete a task with another student and found that it was difficult because the way each of you approached the task was completely different? You preferred to organise everything before you started, while the other person thought it was better just to begin with something interesting and work out what was missing along the way. You needed to write down all the decisions that were made, while your partner was happy to remember everything without making notes. You worked steadily, finishing everything in plenty of time, while your partner preferred to work in bursts, often leaving everything until the last minute. These differences can be described as differences in cognitive and learning styles. The term 'style' refers to 'habitual patterns or preferred ways of doing something (e.g., thinking, learning, teaching) that are consistent over long periods of time and across many areas of activity' (Sternberg, 2001, p. 2). Styles are not abilities, but rather choices and preferences about how to use abilities (Sternberg, 1997b).

5.8 Thinking styles and mental self-government

Cognitive style refers to the characteristic ways of thinking and perceiving that individuals use to process and remember information (see also Ferrari & Sternberg, 1998; Riding & Rayner, 1998). **Learning style** is the way students interact with and respond to information in learning contexts – their preferred ways of learning (Jonassen & Grabowski, 1993; Keefe & Ferrell, 1990). The two terms are often used interchangeably in the professional literature (see Kogan, 1994), which can cause confusion. We use the broader term 'cognitive style' to include learning style (the ERIC Thesaurus (1980) adopts this approach), and discuss learning style preferences later in this section.

Cognitive style is linked to cognition and intelligence (see Chapter 7), to personality (Biggs & Moore, 1993; Jackson & Lawtyjones, 1996; Sternberg & Grigorenko, 1997), and to the way we interact with others (Saracho, 1998). As mentioned in the earlier section on metacognition, it is also influenced by cultural factors (Biggs & Moore, 1993; Engelbrecht & Natzel, 1997; Park, 2000; Willcoxson & Prosser, 1996). Cognitive styles are relatively enduring, although research has demonstrated that they may vary across settings (for instance, in classroom versus sports-field contexts (Coker, 1995), see Box 5.6, on page 154) and that characteristics like 'conceptual tempo' ('impulsivity–reflectivity', discussed later) can be modified (see, for example, Jonassen & Grabowski, 1993, Chapter 9).

Three topics that have attracted considerable research interest are concerned with specific aspects of cognitive style. These are perceptual style, conceptual tempo and approaches to learning, which are discussed in the following sections.

> **cognitive style**
> The way an individual tends to perceive and process information

> **learning style**
> Learner preferences for types of learning and teaching activities

Perceptual style: Field dependence–independence

When shown a picture of a rural landscape containing a cow, a pig, some sheep and a dog (see Figure 5.6 over page), one child might describe the picture in broad terms, as 'in the country'. Another will see the picture in terms of details such as a cow, a pig, some sheep and a dog in a large field, describing it as 'cows and sheep and pigs and a dog in a paddock'. In the first case, the overall scene in the picture dominates the child's perception (field dependence); when describing the picture, the child pays attention to the *overall impression* of the scene rather than the details. On the other hand, the second child's interest is in the *detail* of the picture (field independence), rather than the background scene. The way we perceive the world is an important element of cognitive style. The terms **field dependence** and **field independence** are used to describe two extreme dimensions of human perception of visual stimuli. The more a learner is able to separate relevant material from its context (or 'field'), the more 'field independent' they are said to be.

Research into the impact of field dependence–independence on perception suggests that these are stable traits that affect individual responses in a variety of situations. For example, people who are field dependent are likely to see problems as a whole and have difficulty separating component parts (Riding & Cheema, 1991; Witkin & Goodenough, 1981). They are typically more intuitive in their perception, and tend to be socially oriented, enjoying situations that allow for interaction and group work (Jonassen & Grabowski, 1993). In contrast, field-independent learners tend to be more analytical and prefer analysing visual stimuli and breaking down problems into component parts. They tend to be more efficient than field-dependent learners in processing information (see, for example, Davis & Cochran, 1989), are better readers, are highly task-oriented and prefer structured, impersonal situations. Field-dependent learners tend to do better in the humanities, while field-independent learners do better in mathematics and the sciences (Witkin & Goodenough, 1981).

In learning contexts, field-dependent learners have been shown to be more likely than their field-independent peers to use rehearsal strategies, repeating information mentally, orally or in writing (Frank & Keene, 1993). Field-independent learners, on the other hand, tend to rely more heavily on elaboration strategies. This is consistent with their greater tendency to be analytical in their approach to learning (Tinajero & Paramo, 1998). Research

> **field dependence**
> A cognitive style related to perceiving items, events or information as an integral part of a broader context (or 'field')

> **field independence**
> The tendency to perceive individual items, events or pieces of information analytically, and as distinct from the broader context (or 'field')

FIGURE 5.6   Example of an embedded figures task. Can you find a gargoyle, a key, a hat, five dwarves, a fairy?

indicates that field-independent children learn new computer languages more quickly and make fewer errors than do their field-dependent peers (Easton & Watson, 1993; Watson & Brinkley, 1992). Field-independent individuals are also more likely to learn as a result of intrinsic motivation and are influenced less by social reinforcement (see Chapter 7 for more on motivation). In a study of 239 Canadian primary school children (Baillargeon, Pascual-Leone, & Roncadin, 1998), field-dependent learners were less efficient in their mental processing and attentional capacity on a set task than were field-independent learners. However, as ever, generalisations should be treated cautiously.

There is some evidence (see, for example, Armstrong, 2000) that the methods of assessment used in educational institutions tend to favour students who are field independent. Such assessments usually focus on written work involving systematic analysis of information and the development of well-structured, logical arguments. The field-dependent tendency to focus on global aspects may be a problem for tasks that require learners to be more analytical in their approach (Tinajero & Paramo, 1998b). Somewhat predictably, studies have demonstrated a positive association between field independence and performance on intelligence tests (Sternberg & Grigorenko, 1997), since the skills measured by most intelligence tests cover the types of learning included in the traditional academic studies in which field-independent people excel (see Chapter 7 for more on intelligence). In contrast, there has been little effort to design tests that are more congruent with the cognitive style of field-dependent learners. Such tests might include elements of dance, art, music, drama, video and film production, and other, non-traditional forms of visual and oral presentation.

Conceptual tempo: Impulsivity–reflectivity

Another dimension used to distinguish between learners' cognitive styles is concerned with the speed of their responses to a task, or the degree of 'impulsivity' or 'reflectivity' demonstrated in their responses. When presented with a task, some students react very quickly, sometimes without much thought. Others in a similar situation respond more slowly, pausing to consider possibilities (see Box 5.5). These distinctions, first defined by Kagan

(1958, 1966), have been the subject of considerable research. Much of this research has involved the Matching Familiar Figures Test (Kagan, 1966), which consists of a set of pencil and paper tasks and involves selecting, usually from a set of very similar drawings, a drawing that exactly matches a model. Individuals with rapid response times are termed as having **impulsivity** and those who respond more slowly are described as having **reflectivity**.

impulsivity
Having a cognitive preference for rapid problem solving

reflectivity
Having a cognitive preference for taking time to solve problems and to analyse oneself and the context

Box 5.5 CLASSROOM LINKS

Impulsive versus reflective behaviour

It is generally assumed that, in classroom contexts, reflective behaviour is more closely associated with learning than is impulsive behaviour. But is this always so? While administering the Matching Familiar Figures Test to a group of 4th graders, the examiner was surprised by one student's pattern of responses. The task involved the student choosing, from six drawings of a teddy bear, the drawing that was identical to a model. In every case, the student pointed to the matching picture so quickly that the examiner hardly had time to press the stopwatch on and off. The surprising aspect of this student's performance was that all her choices were correct. Later, the tester was intrigued to see the student's name and realised she was the daughter of a local artist.

Activities

1. Can you think of learning situations where very rapid response times are desirable?
2. In what situations can the introduction of a program to change conceptual tempo (that is, from impulsive to reflective) be justified?
3. What other factors might need to be present to justify such an intervention? Can you give any examples?

Various studies have reported on the impact of conceptual tempo on children's learning (see, for example, Smith & Caplan, 1988; Smith & Nelson, 1988; Wagner, Cook & Friedman, 1998). In general, reflective children take longer to complete tasks but are often more accurate than their more impulsive peers (Entwistle, 1991). They are also often better readers (Kogan, 1983; Smith & Caplan, 1988). The value of helping impulsive learners to become more reflective has also been demonstrated. For example, Navarro, Aguilar and Akalde (1999) reported success in a training program that aimed to help children in the third grade solve arithmetic problems by becoming more reflective. Not surprisingly, the intervention program had no impact on the performance of reflective students.

Deep and surface learning

Studies of the ways in which children approach a learning task, such as reading text, suggest that from an early age all learners try to self-regulate and have distinct motives and strategies for learning (Zimmerman, 1998). Students with a 'deep approach' to learning are intrinsically motivated to study, and are interested in satisfying their curiosity about a topic or understanding the meaning of a text. They approach learning tasks using problem-solving strategies (such as questioning, planning, evaluating) to maximise their understanding, as shown in the statement: 'I try to relate what I have learned in one subject to what I already know in other subjects' (Biggs & Moore, 1993, p. 316). On the other hand, students with a 'surface approach' to learning typically have extrinsic motives and simply want to avoid failure. They tend to do as little work as possible and use memorisation as a key strategy during study, as evidenced in the statement: 'I tend to study only what's set; I usually don't do anything extra' (Biggs & Moore, 1993, p. 316). Deep and surface approaches to learning are closely linked to deep and surface processing, as depicted in the levels of processing model earlier in this chapter. A learner's approach to learning will influence the way that person processes information.

In addition to deep and surface approaches, learners may demonstrate an 'achieving approach' to learning (Biggs, 1987a). Learners in this category are typically intrinsically motivated by a desire to do well at school, and adopt study techniques such as efficient use of time and resources to maximise their chances of success, as exemplified in the statement, 'I regularly take notes from suggested readings and put them with my class notes on a topic' (Biggs & Moore, 1993, p. 316). In a review of research on deep and surface approaches to learning, Zhang and Sternberg (2000) concluded that the evidence did not appear to support the existence of Biggs's third category (achieving approach) although there were data to confirm both deep and surface styles.

Sociocultural factors and cognitive style

Vygotksy and neo-Vygotskian accounts of cognitive development (see Chapter 2) emphasise the importance of social and cultural factors in cognitive development. It follows, then, that sociocultural factors may have an impact on learners' preferred ways of thinking, processing and remembering. Social structures and processes influence the types of activities we engage in and value, and these activities have a powerful impact on cognitive development (Herbert, 2000; Meadows, 1998). Meadows argues that, just as teaching and learning do not occur independent of culture and history, so they cannot be studied 'irrespective of the cognitive and affective history of the individual learner' (Meadows, 1998, p. 6).

A study of East Asian learners found them to be holistic and field dependent in their preferences, compared with Westerners whom the researchers described as more analytic and field independent in their cognitive styles (Nisbett, Peng, Choi, & Norenzayan, 2001). Biggs (2001), on the other hand, argues that the research focus should not be on cognitive style, but on the teaching and assessment methods used and the types of cognitive styles they encourage. He cautions against stereotyping learners from particular cultures and emphasises the importance of considering cognitive style in a cultural context. This advice is very valuable because it guards against false generalisations. In contrast to the view that there are differences in cognitive styles across cultures, another body of cross-cultural research argues that cognitive style is a universal phenomenon that is not culturally bound (Kubes, 1998; Riding & Al-Sanabani, 1998) (see Box 5.6).

Box 5.6 RESEARCH LINKS

Cognitive style, culture and sport

The issue of cognitive style is not limited to the classroom setting, but applies across a range of contexts, including that of sport. A New Zealand study by Williams, Anshel and Quek (1997) set out to investigate whether there were cultural differences and personal factors in the cognitive styles that competitive adolescent athletes used in approaching their sport.

The study sample included 395 Australian, 167 New Zealand and 411 Singaporean competitive athletes aged 11 to 17 years old. The study investigated internal factors such as perception, personal dispositions and affect; and external factors including social needs, behavioural tendencies and environmental features. The researchers concluded that while athletes' cognitive style in a competitive-sport setting is partly dependent on their culture and gender, there are more similarities than differences among genders and cultures – at least in the case of adolescent athletes.

Approaches to learning in the classroom

A study of cognitive styles highlights that students learn in different ways. Some are 'visual learners', taking cues from the teacher's body language and facial expressions along with visual displays like diagrams or images to help them learn. Others are 'auditory learners' who learn best by listening and talking with peers in groups. Another approach to learning is tactile or 'kinesthetic learning', where learners prefer a hands-on approach and like to explore for themselves. These are just three of many learning styles identified in the professional literature. An Australian researcher has identified 'chaotic learning' (Lee, 2001) – a relatively new learning style associated with the way learners interact with and search the World Wide Web. The relationship between computer use and choice of learning style is a growing research area (see, for example, Lewis, 1996; Liu & Reed, 1994; Vincent, 2001). There is also strong research interest in the connections between learning styles and Gardner's (1983) theory of multiple intelligences (Franzen, 2000; Howell, 2001; Simpson, 2001), a theory depicting intelligence as occurring in different domains (you will understand more about these connections after you study Chapter 7).

Teaching strategies to cater for learner differences have received much attention in Australia and New Zealand. There is general agreement that students approach learning in diverse ways, using a variety of styles, and that all students should have the opportunity to demonstrate their skill level in ways that best suit their individual learning style (Victorian Government, 2002). Attention has also been given to the connection between culture and the learning styles of Indigenous peoples of Australia and New Zealand, and to the development of curriculum practices that reflect students' preferred learning styles and cultural experiences (Education Department of Western Australia, 1999; Sturrock & May, 2002).

One outcome of research into students' preferred learning styles has been the proposal that learning may be enhanced if a match is made between a student's dominant learning style and the methods of instruction used. This association has been labelled **aptitude–treatment interaction** (Snow, 1991). Information about students' learning styles is gathered through tests such as the Learning Style Inventory (Dunn, Dunn, & Price, 1989), the Myers-Briggs Type Indicator (Briggs, Myers, & McCaulley, 1985), and the Learning Process Questionnaire (Biggs, 1987b).

The elements tapped by these inventories include factors such as the preference for visual or aural models of learning, for group size, for early or late study time, for being seated or moving about the classroom, for bright or subdued lighting, for quiet or noisy environment, and for hot or cold classroom temperature. There is some evidence to suggest that the attitudes and learning of low-achieving students and students with special learning needs are enhanced if teachers cater for preferred learning styles during instruction (see, for example, Braio, Beasley, Dunn, Quinn, & Buchanan, 1997). Similar results have been reported for gifted students (see, for example, Baum, Renzulli, & Hebert, 1995). Learning styles have also been linked to achievement in specific skill areas such as reading (Oglesby & Suter, 1995; Sturrock & May, 2002). Children's reading skills have been found to improve when teaching methods, resources and assessments are adapted to their preferred learning styles.

While several studies support the value of matching students' learning styles to classroom practices, some have questioned this approach as simplistic and potentially limiting for students (see, for example, Curry, 1990). Problems are also associated with confusion over the distinction between terms such as 'cognitive style', 'learning style' and 'thinking style', and the bewildering array of similar, often overlapping, definitions that have been proposed (Suedfeld, 2000; Zhang & Sternberg, 2000). There are also questions about the validity and reliability of some of the inventories developed to measure cognitive and learning styles (Burns, Johnson, & Gable, 1998; Stellwagen, 2001; Wright, 1992). The inventories typically contain self-report items that provide only one perspective on learning-style preferences. Questions also arise regarding the multidimensional nature of cognitive and learning styles, and whether or not the inventories are capable of reliably measuring particular constructs. In addition, difficulties have been reported with interventions designed to take advantage of students' preferred cognitive styles (for example, field independence versus field dependence), to enhance preferred approaches to learning (for example, encourage deep rather

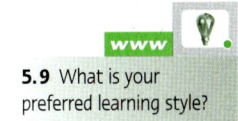

5.9 What is your preferred learning style?

aptitude-treatment interaction
The relationship between learner characteristics and the characteristics of the learning situation

than surface learning), and to match teaching and learning styles (Curry, 1990; Kavale & Forness, 2000; Stellwagen, 2001). These findings suggest that teachers should focus on how students learn and process information, but evidence on the efficacy of attempts to change individual cognitive styles and on the success of aptitude–treatment interaction remains equivocal, and these approaches should not replace proven methods of instruction.

Box 5.7 explores some classroom implications of students' cognitive and learning styles.

CRITICAL REFLECTIONS

- Identify the key characteristics of your preferred cognitive style. How do you think it will impact on your teaching?
- Discuss the issue of cognitive styles with your tutorial group, commenting on the advantages and potential limitations of trying to identify and cater for your students' styles.

Box 5.7 IMPLICATIONS FOR EDUCATORS

Cognitive and learning styles in the classroom

- Make time to learn about your students' cognitive style and preferred learning styles. Provide opportunities for students to learn about how they learn best (see Callan, 1996). A learning-styles inventory – see, for example, Dunn, Dunn and Price (1989) – is a useful tool.
- Recognise the diversity of students in your classes and adapt your teaching by using a variety of teaching methods, resources and assessments to suit different students' preferred learning styles. Allow for multiple 'style-shifts' (Suleiman, 1996), noting that:
  - students from some cultural groups may prefer learning in non-competitive, sharing environments; for example, see Charter (1996) on integrating traditional Aboriginal teaching and learning approaches in education
  - it is wise to consider the linguistic differences of students for whom English is not the first language, making use of multimedia and online learning environments to individualise instruction where necessary.
- Expose students to a range of learning approaches and encourage them to experiment with different styles so as to broaden their learning-skills repertoire. This includes using a combination of individual and group work, abstract and concrete examples, and visual and aural learning resources.
- Be aware of your own cognitive style and preferred learning styles, and how these affect the way you teach and assess student learning. Grasha and Hruska-Reichmann (Grasha, 1996) identified six learning styles and associated classroom practices to support those learning preferences (see Table 5.5 below). You may find these a useful starting point for considering ways of adapting your teaching style to support student learning.

TABLE 5.5 The Grasha-Reichmann student learning styles

Learning style	Learner characteristics	Suggested classroom activities
Competitive	Competes with other students; likes to be the centre of attention and to receive recognition for accomplishments	▪ Provide opportunities for group leadership ▪ Praise individuals for doing a good job
Collaborative	Shares ideas with others, cooperates with teacher and enjoys working with others	▪ Foster small student-led groups, group projects and group assessment ▪ Give students responsibility for developing aspects of the subject or lesson
Avoidant	Unenthusiastic about learning; a non-participant, who may be overwhelmed by what happens in class	▪ At times, provide an anonymous environment in which the student is not asked to participate in group activities ▪ Develop individualised tasks to motivate such learners

Learning style	Learner characteristics	Suggested classroom activities
Participant	Eager to participate and generally enjoys class	■ Encourage group work with plenty of discussion opportunities
Dependent	Shows little intellectual curiosity, learns only what is required and sees the teacher as an authority figure	■ Provide clear instructions with little ambiguity ■ Teacher-centred focus
Independent	Prefers to think for herself; confident in her learning abilities; prefers to work alone than in groups	■ Offer independent, individualised study and projects ■ Adopt a learner-centred approach

Source: Adapted from Grasha (1996, p. 128).

Constructivism

We have established that cognitive learning theories focus on internal mental processes and their role in learning and remembering. The information processing explanation of how we learn is one way of depicting these cognitive processes, and metacognition plays an important role in self-regulating and monitoring such processes. A related explanation of learning, also from the cognitive perspective, is constructivism.

Constructivism focuses on cognition as a collaborative process (Rogoff, 1998) involving social processes, interactions with the environment and self-reflection. It is an approach to learning that owes much to the work of Piaget and Vygotsky (see Chapter 2) and to such philosophers as John Dewey, Thomas Kuhn and Karl Marx. Constructivists believe that knowledge is 'constructed', that the thinker is both mentally and physically active in this construction, and that the sociocultural context in which knowledge construction occurs provides the thinker with invaluable resources, support and direction (Fosnot, 1993; Phillips, 2000a; Wells & Chang-Wells, 1992).

Essentially, constructivists argue that young children learn by developing increasingly complex cognitive structures, or schemas, and that they use new information to progressively add to these (Byrnes, 1996; Yager & Lutz, 1994). As learners interact with their environment, they link information learned through experience to previous knowledge, and so construct new understandings and knowledge. Constructivism encourages educators to recognise the value of the knowledge and experience students bring to learning, and to provide experiences that help students build on their current knowledge of the world (Duit & Confrey, 1996; Kearney & Treagust, 2001). An important part of the constructivist philosophy is that learning is supported by social interaction with peers and adults.

constructivism
An explanation of learning that views it as a self-regulated process that builds on learners' existing knowledge and in which learners are active participants

Forms of constructivism

Constructivism takes several forms. Two of these are 'psychological constructivism' and 'social constructivism' (Palincsar, 1998; Phillips, 2000a). While they share a focus on individuals constructing their own learning, each has a different emphasis: one on the individual, the other on the social context.

Psychological (or individual) **constructivism** is concerned with individual learners and how they construct their knowledge, beliefs and identity during the learning process. Piaget's theory of cognitive development, with its emphasis on the individual's progression through a series of stages, forms the foundation for psychological constructivism. Like Piaget, psychological constructivists acknowledge the importance of the social environment, but see the role of the individual learner in constructing the learning environment as central.

Social constructivism draws heavily on Vygotsky's belief that social processes are integral to learning. This approach rejects the view that the locus of knowledge lies within the individual. Rather, the social constructivist view is that social interaction shapes cognitive

psychological constructivism
Focuses on individual learners and how they construct their own knowledge, beliefs and identity

social constructivism
Emphasises the role of social and cultural factors in shaping learning

development and is an essential component of the learning process (Cobb & Yackel, 1996; Prawat, 1996).

There is some debate regarding the merits of distinguishing between psychological and social constructivism and the various ways of applying it (see, for example, Phillips, 1997), but in the classroom you will see a combination of these forms of constructivism at work.

Key principles of constructivism

You will find much on constructivism in the classroom in educational psychology literature and research. The following principles may help to guide your reading and practice in this area:

- Learners are *active participants* in their learning. 'Learning by doing' is central to constructivism in practice (Howe & Berv, 2000).
- Learners are *self-regulated*. They construct and monitor their own learning, and meta-cognition plays an important role in facilitating this self-regulation.
- *Social interaction* is necessary for effective learning. Both Piaget and Vygotsky acknowledged the role of social interaction with peers and significant others (such as parents and teachers) in cognitive development.
- Constructivism encourages individuals to make sense of information for themselves (Bruner, 1990). This means that knowledge may be relative and may differ for each learner (see Matthews (2000) for a discussion of this issue in the context of mathematics and science education). And just as individuals construct their own meaning within a social and cultural context, knowledge and understanding may differ across learners and contexts.

Constructivism in the classroom context

The constructivist principles already outlined have many implications for classroom practice, and resulting strategies tend to fall into one of three broad categories, in that they:

1 encourage learner-centred experiences and activities
2 provide opportunities for learners to work together
3 assist novice learners to develop expertise.

This section looks in detail at these three categories of constructivist learning, which, while discussed separately, clearly overlap and share a common focus on the learner.

1 Encourage learner-centred experiences and activities

The constructivist approach is learner-centred and the teacher's starting point should be the knowledge, attitudes and interests that learners bring to the learning context. These shape the meaning students make of learning. Because of constructivism's focus on the value of students' background experiences and prior learning, the approach welcomes multiculturalism and the development of personal ideologies (John-Steiner & Mahn, 1996; Solomon, 2000). 'Discovery learning' is one way of putting this learner-centredness into practice.

Discovery learning

Bruner (1966) argued that if students discover the connections between their learning in a meaningful context, they will be able to make sense of and remember and apply what they have learned. He called this **discovery learning**. In this approach, the learner manipulates materials or ideas in the learning environment and discovers connections among them. By actively engaging in problem solving, learners are more likely to remember what they have learned, will have increased motivation to continue learning and will be able to apply their learning to solve new problems in new learning contexts.

'Guided discovery' learning is problem solving accompanied by teacher directions for each step, while 'open discovery' is problem solving without close monitoring by the teacher. Each method has its advantages and limitations. Guided discovery is more commonly used

> *discovery learning*
> The learner actively manipulates materials or ideas in the learning environment and discovers connections between them

CHAPTER 5 COGNITIVE EXPLANATIONS OF LEARNING

in classrooms because it provides students with a framework for learning and at the same time allows students a sense of autonomy within the guidelines provided by the teacher.

2 Provide opportunities for learners to work together

In a constructivist classroom, learning needs to be experiential, and group work features prominently as students are encouraged to discuss ideas and learn from one another. Knowing how to work with others, and how to build on the knowledge and experiences of diverse people who bring different perspectives to the thinking and reasoning process, can help students expand their thinking and explore new approaches to learning (Caudron, 1997).

There are several ways of enabling students to work together. These include cooperative learning, collaborative learning and peer-assisted learning. Because of the student-focused nature of these strategies, they also illustrate key principles of the humanist perspective of learning (see Chapter 6). For this reason, cooperative learning is outlined in more detail in the next chapter. In this section we focus on a range of strategies and their role in helping students to actively construct their knowledge and learning.

'Cooperative learning' refers to the organisation of classroom activities so that students must work together in order to gain rewards for themselves and their group. Box 5.8 presents strategies for fostering cooperative learning in your classroom. The teacher plays an important role in organising and managing the learning activity (see Chapter 12). 'Collaborative learning' also involves students working in groups (see Figure 5.7); however, in this approach students tend to have more autonomy, as the teacher is not as actively involved in managing the group activity. Research indicates that learners in either cooperative or collaborative learning contexts gain academically and socially as a result of their peer interactions. Rothschild (1999) found that when a group of primary school students worked collaboratively on a problem-solving task, they learned by discussing results with their partners and receiving feedback on their ideas. Davenport and Howe (1999), however, caution against making generalisations about the benefits of students working together, arguing that factors such as gender and ability may affect the outcomes (see also Fuchs, Fuchs, Hamlett, & Karns, 1999).

5.10 Cooperative learning in the classroom

FIGURE 5.7 In order for collaborative learning to be effective, students need good communication skills and teacher support.

Box 5.8 CLASSROOM LINKS

Strategies for fostering cooperative learning

Prior to the class

Devise activities designed to develop students' ability to help one another while working on the problems.

Preparatory activities in class

1 Provide students with 'getting to know you' activities to break the ice.
2 Teach communication skills, such as guidelines for interaction:
 • Develop a handout that summarises the techniques students could use to help one another learn in cooperative learning groups.

- Provide strategies for generating discussion and explanations (see Webb & Farivar, 1999).
3 Assign students to groups.

Groupwork activities
1 Explain the outcomes that students are to achieve, and provide clear directions about the group task.
2 Explain how individual students' learning will be assessed.
3 Remind students of your expectations of them and the cooperative goal structure.
4 Provide students with necessary resources such as space within the room, or butcher's paper and some pens for recording their learning experiences.
5 Move around the room to monitor group activities and learning. Make notes of matters you will need to deal with once the group sessions have finished. Do not interfere: allow the groups time to deal with problems themselves as much as possible.

Concluding activities
1 Conclude the lesson by drawing the groups together and summing up in some way.
2 Evaluate student achievement and help students assess how well they collaborated with one another.

Source: Adapted from Webb & Farivar (1999) and Killen (1998).

Activity

Use the sets of steps given above to plan a lesson for the subject area and age group most applicable to your teaching.

Remember: To be successful, cooperative learning needs careful planning and time. As the teacher, you need to select tasks carefully, make sure there are appropriate group incentives to motivate students, and use the strategy over an extended period of time so students develop the necessary skills.

'Peer-assisted learning' is another form of student-centred learning that encourages social interaction and gives learners opportunities to construct their learning and support their peers in doing the same. As the name suggests, peer-assisted learning occurs when peers help one another to learn and, in turn, learn by teaching. There are several ways peer-assisted learning can take place. Peers may give each other feedback during learning; for example, Johnson and Ward (2001) found that peer feedback and assessment assisted Year 3 students with the development of motor skills. Another study of middle-school learners (that is, years 5 to 7) with reading disabilities found that when these students assisted each other in paired reading groups that teachers structured and monitored, all students registered significant gains in reading performance. Additional benefits were that students enjoyed tutoring more than their traditional instruction, appeared to see the value and benefits of the tutoring, and wanted to include tutoring as part of their other classes such as science and social studies (Mastropieri, Scruggs, Mohler, Beranek, Spencer, Boon, & Talbott, 2001).

Another approach may be to ask more-competent students in the class to guide and teach less-competent peers in a group or in pairs (Coenen, 2002). Alternatively, 'cross-age tutoring' may be used, where younger students are tutored by older students. This form of tutoring may take place in several ways. In one study, a group of Year 5 to 7 students who had been identified as struggling readers were invited to peer-tutor Year 1 and 2 students (Fisher, 2001). The experience was beneficial for both younger and older students; in the case of the older students, tutoring gave them an authentic reason for developing their literacy skills and they had regular feedback on their own reading (for more examples see Newell, 1996; Nixon & Topping, 2001).

The social interaction that occurs in each of these learner-centred contexts allows for cognitive conflict (see Box 5.9 opposite) as learners challenge and defend different viewpoints within a supportive environment (Wadsworth, 1996; Yager & Lutz, 1994; see also Chapter 3 on the importance of peer relationships in cognitive development). 'Social negotiation' is another feature of students learning together, particularly if the teacher fosters group work and allows learners to establish their own group rules. Groups may interact face to face, but computers also provide a useful means of fostering cooperative learning groups online (see Chapter 10), particularly if students have to share a small number of computers in a classroom (Holden, 1992; Male, 1992; Mevarech & Light, 1992; McInerney, McInerney, & Marsh, 1997).

Box 5.9 CLASSROOM LINKS

Encouraging students to construct their learning

Read the following example (from Ball & Bass, 2000) of a Year 3 class interacting with their teacher on the concept of evenness and oddness in mathematics. Sean claims that the number 6 could be even and odd at the same time. This challenges the group's cognitive equilibrium on the topic of odd and even numbers, and the interaction provides a worthwhile example of how the students construct their mathematical knowledge. The class reasons about Sean's claim as follows:

Riba: [*to the class*] So, Sean is saying that some even numbers, in a pattern, can be even *and* odd and some can't. Four can't, because it's two groups. Six can. Eight can't. Ten can. [*Pointing at the number line above the chalkboard, she uses a pointer to mark off consecutive even numbers.*] Can't. Can. Can't. Can …

Ofala: Well, I just think that just because twenty-two is eleven groups, that doesn't mean it's an odd number. My conjecture, I think it's always true, is that if all twos are circled in a number, then it's an even number.

Sean: What conjecture?

Ball: Ofala, tell him what you're talking about when you talk about your conjecture. He's not sure what you're referring to.

Ofala: That conjecture I already …

Sean: That's not a conjecture. That's a *definition*.

Source: Ball and Bass (2000, p. 193).

Activities

1. As a teacher in this Year 3 classroom, what kinds of group-interaction rules or guidelines would you need to put in place before the discussion commenced?
2. In your tutorial discussion group, identify a scenario in which Year 9 or 10 students might have the opportunity to construct their learning. What concept would you discuss? How would adolescents' level of reasoning differ from that of Year 3 students?
3. What are the advantages and disadvantages of teaching important concepts in the manner illustrated here?

If you want to adopt learner-centred approaches, there are several points to bear in mind. Not all groups collaborate successfully (Cohen & Lotan, 1995). For example, minority students may be excluded from group activities because they are seen by the rest of the group as being less competent (Blumenfeld, Marx, Soloway, & Krajcik, 1997). Substantial time may be needed to eliminate biased attitudes within the class group (Killen, 1998). Teachers play a central role by treating students as collaborators in the learning process, by giving students opportunities to collaborate (Forman, Stein, Brown, & Larreamendy-Joerns, 1995; Rogoff, 1998), by arranging groups (Mulryan, 1995) and by providing students with the skills necessary to function effectively in groups. Students need clear instructions before participating in group activities (Chan, Burtis, & Bereiter, 1997; Webb & Farivar, 1999). An example of instructions that one teacher in a Japanese classroom used are shown below. The instructions were placed on the classroom walls as constant, tangible reminders to guide student interaction, particularly in group-work settings (Toma, 1991, pp. 3–4):

Instructions for:
- agreeing with someone else: 'I agree with [name]'s opinion. This is because …'
- disagreeing: 'I disagree with [name]'s opinion. This is because …'

- requesting clarification: 'I would like to ask [name]. Did you mean to say …?'
- extending an argument: 'Does anyone have another idea [opinion]?' or 'I would like to add … to [name]'s idea'.

As you can see from this example, while being learner-focused, this approach is carefully framed by the teacher. Teachers also need to take care when selecting group tasks. For example, tasks that have more than one solution strategy and that require explanations tend to be more successful because they give students opportunities to interact and to reveal their thinking in a group context (Slavin, 1996; Stein, Grover, & Henningsen, 1996).

Box 5.10 presents a case study illustrating cooperative learning in a Year 6 classroom.

Box 5.10 CASE STUDY

Cooperative learning in a Year 6 mathematics class

The following case study illustrates how a teacher manages cooperative learning in a Year 6 mathematics class. Students in the class have been given the task of building a physical structure that will hold the weight of at least one textbook. The structure is to be made out of index cards and tape. Study the ways in which the students interact with one another and their teacher. Can you identify key principles of cooperative learning?

Extract 1

Brad: Okay. They [*the index cards*] have to be low to the ground and thick, but not too thick though because we still have to make it high.

Calvin: Yes.

Tina: [*Takes possession of the cards.*] There.

Teacher: What did you get? Oh, index cards.

Calvin: We have to make a building strong enough.

Teacher: I know.

Calvin: Hold up! Let me get an idea. [*Places finger on head.*] We have to do some cutting of the index cards because we already have 13, and you can't get it up one more building. Think of the capacity!

Tina: Calvin, calm down!

Calvin: Can we cut the cards?

Teacher: How tall is the card?

Calvin: Almost 13 centimetres, and that's almost half of 20 centimetres.

Teacher: It's more than half.

Calvin: Ah man, this is hard. Imagine making a building! You could go like that and tape like that. [*Shows with hands.*] [*The other students ignore Calvin's comments.*]

Did you notice how the teacher helped the group get under way at the outset by offering support and validating ideas? Calvin's peers ignore his suggestions, but look at the way the group reaches a consensus in the next excerpt.

Extract 2

Brad: If we had a bunch of cards, it would be easy. [*Tries to take cards.*]

Tina: Hold on! No! …

Calvin: [*Takes cards from Tina.*] What if we did this? [*Shows stairstep-like structure with hands.*]

Teacher: Try it.

Tina: It's got to hold a maths book.

Teacher: Get a maths book out.

Calvin: Let's see if that can hold. Of course it's not going to be that. [*Holds cards as pillars with no support or tape.*] …

Tina: Should we make it like a box and build it up?

Brad: They would collapse.

Tina: No they wouldn't!

Brad: Yes they would!

Tina: If you cut them down far enough, they wouldn't collapse.

Teacher: You do that. Try it. …

Calvin: Hold up before you cut. I'll measure this. Yes, it goes all the way to the table. You know, supports itself. [*Brad and Tina cut cards to make a lattice structure.*]

Gretchen: Will it hold up anything? Try it. [*Gets maths book.*]

Tina: No, let's see if it will hold up this. [*Gets pencil box.*]

Calvin: Now let's see if it will hold this. [*Gets book.*]

Tina: But that's not all of it though.

Brad: Don't crush it. Please, don't crush it. [*Cards collapse.*] It crushed.

Source: Leonard & McElroy (2000, pp. 241–242).

Think about the features of this cooperative learning experience:
- The teacher plays an important role in setting up the activity and in commenting as the discussion proceeds.
- Most students are highly engaged in the activity.
- There are opportunities for students to disagree, experiment and try different solutions.
- The group members are interdependent. Each plays an important role; for example, Calvin provides suggestions, Gretchen's role is to record the group's ideas and procedures on paper, and so on.

Activities

1 How does what happens in this case study differ from some of your own group work experiences?
2 Can you think of classroom contexts in which cooperative learning may not be appropriate? Why?

3 Assist novice learners to develop expertise

A primary aim of constructivism is to help novices develop expertise in a particular area of knowledge so that they may become more independent, autonomous and self-regulated learners. The 'apprenticeship' concept provides a useful metaphor for the way in which a young learner or novice is guided by an expert.

Cognitive apprenticeships (Rogoff, 1990) describe how 'apprentice' (or novice) learners are guided by an expert who provides scaffolding (see Chapter 2) so that eventually the novice will be able to perform tasks and work through problems autonomously. This approach illustrates the value of social interaction in cognitive development and learning (see Figure 5.8). The learning process is seen as a partnership. Hogan, Nastasi and Pressley (2000) found that teacher-guided discussions – where, without providing direct information, teachers acted as catalysts in prompting students to expand and clarify their thinking – were an efficient means of fostering higher levels of reasoning and better-quality explanations. The teacher or more expert adult or peer gives guidance and assistance in joint problem-solving activities and is responsive to the novice learner's current level of understanding. Apprenticeship occurs in practical activities such as children learning to feed or dress themselves, but it can also be applied in classroom contexts with learners of all ages. One example of cognitive apprenticeships is 'reciprocal teaching'.

cognitive apprenticeship
An 'apprentice' learner or novice is guided by an expert

reciprocal teaching
Adopts the principles of collaborative learning, where peers assist each other under the guidance of an expert who facilitates group thinking processes

FIGURE 5.8 Peers can be involved formally in cognitive apprenticeship through peer teaching programs, or informally.

Reciprocal teaching

Reciprocal teaching was pioneered by Palincsar (1982) and her colleague Brown (1984, 1989; Brown & Palincsar, 1989; Palincsar, Brown, & Campione, 1993) to assist learners with their reading comprehension. Since then, it has been adapted for a range of contexts and cultures (see, for example, Coley, DePinto, Craig, & Gardner, 1993; Roh, 1997; Taylor & Cox, 1997). Reciprocal teaching combines teacher intervention and student-directed learning (Palincsar, 1998). It adopts the principles of collaborative learning, in that peers assist each other but learning takes place under the guidance of an expert – usually the teacher – who helps the group with understanding the content matter and with group thinking processes (Brown & Palincsar, 1989; Rogoff, 1998). Cole (1996) found that, by encouraging student interaction, reciprocal teaching improved students' engagement with learning by enhancing their opportunities to make meaning out of their learning in a social context.

Reciprocal teaching involves four strategies – 'predicting', 'questioning', 'summarising' and 'clarifying' – with the aim of helping readers to construct the meaning of a text and to monitor their comprehension of it (see Box 5.11). Teachers explicitly model each of the four strategies, with the intention of increasing students' responsibility for their own strategy use by asking them to take turns leading the discussion of the text (Palincsar, 1998). As students lead discussions, teachers provide support to assist them as they practise predicting what will happen next or practise clarifying the meaning of a text portion. A similar approach has been used to teach writing, where the four strategies of reciprocal teaching were used to help 7- to 9-year-olds develop their story-writing skills. Peer collaboration combined with teacher guidance resulted in more mature forms of writing than children had produced when working alone (Daiute & Dalton, 1993). Box 5.11 further discusses results from research into reciprocal teaching.

Box 5.11 RESEARCH LINKS

Reciprocal teaching

Findings from several studies of primary and of high school students confirm the positive effects of reciprocal teaching on reading comprehension. Palincsar (1986, 1987) and associates (see Brown & Palincsar, 1989; Palincsar & Brown, 1987; Palincsar & Herrenkohl, 1999) experimented with reciprocal teaching in several ways, as:

1. whole-group instruction
2. small-group instruction
3. one-to-one tutorials
4. small-group sessions led by peers.

Reading comprehension improved in each situation.

Reciprocal teaching has been particularly effective for improving the reading comprehension skills of students with learning disabilities (Klingner & Vaughn, 1996; Lederer, 2000; Little & Richards, 2000). Often, reciprocal teaching is combined with other approaches discussed elsewhere in this chapter. For example, Koutselini and Hadjiyianni (1999) report on the success of an intervention program designed to help Year 3 students become conscious of their own deficiencies in reading comprehension, and to assist them develop metacognitive strategies and improve their reading comprehension. The program combined reciprocal teaching and cooperative learning, and explicit teaching of metacognitive strategies. Wilson's (1994) research with children from years 4 and 5 in a middle-sized rural school in Australia found that reciprocal teaching was a major contributor to building students' confidence in their abilities as problem solvers.

Rosenshine and Meister (1994) reviewed 16 studies on reciprocal teaching and additional related studies, and found that students who had been engaged in reciprocal teaching achieved significantly higher reading-comprehension scores than students who had not engaged in such activity. Similar findings were reported in a New Zealand study of Grade 8 adolescents who had reading comprehension deficits (Westera & Moore, 1995). Greenway (2002) found that reciprocal teaching enhanced the autonomy and self-regulation of a group of Year 6 students who followed the teacher's example and gradually adopted the teacher's role and style of questioning (as used in the reciprocal teaching method) as they became more confident in their learning (see also King & Johnson, 1999).

5.11 Promoting higher-order thinking through constructivist-style questioning

Skilful questioning and self-questioning are important in reciprocal teaching and in other constructivist approaches (Henson, 1996; Yager & Lutz, 1994). Constructivist educators pose thought-provoking questions to stimulate thinking, reflecting and problem solving. Reflection is central to constructivist learning and teaching (Tobin, 2000). Students need to be encouraged to reflect on their construction of knowledge. Teachers, too, need to reflect on their practice and their own construction of knowledge and the learning context. Constructivist questioning and self-questioning help promote reflective learning and teaching.

Strengths and limitations of the constructivist approach

Strengths

Constructivism has many benefits for student learning. Constructivism acknowledges that learners are 'constructors' of meaning, actively seeking to discover and learn. In constructivist classrooms, students are encouraged to participate in their learning, rather than being passive recipients of information transmitted by the teacher. Constructivism also attaches importance to students' prior learning and the background knowledge they bring to the learning environment.

Students' social and cultural heritage plays an important part in learning and is valued in the constructivist approach. Social networks are seen as important in constructivist learning environments, with value attached to dialogues and interactions among students and between students and teachers. There is also scope for parent and community-member involvement as 'experts' who can support students in cognitive apprenticeships. These are just some of the many benefits the constructivist approach offers learners and teachers.

Limitations

Constructivism has its limitations, however. One limiting factor is that allowing students to construct their own learning takes a lot of time and may be complicated to set up (Bevevino, Dengel, & Adams, 1999). Teachers need to ensure that they provide sufficient scaffolding and support structures to facilitate constructivist learning. If students have questions, they need to feel safe enough to ask them. It may take time to develop a safe and supportive learning environment so that this can happen.

There are also many potential disadvantages to group work (Killen, 1998; Tiberius, 1990). It takes time to set up the groups. Teachers need to equip students with the necessary group work skills in order for those students to be able to manage their work and their relationships within the groups. Teachers may also need to monitor the groups closely, depending on the task and the students involved.

Discovery learning, too, has limitations. It may work well for self-motivated students, but it can be very frustrating for those who do not feel confident or have not had sufficient experience at discovering information for themselves. The uncertainty of this type of learning environment, where the teacher does not supply the 'answers', may frustrate and discourage some learners. The discovery process can also be time-consuming, as students may venture down thinking pathways that teachers have neither anticipated nor planned for. Brown and Rose (1995) found that teachers they surveyed were knowledgeable about constructivist principles, yet did not adopt the approach widely in their teaching. The reasons given were that they lacked the sufficient time and often did not feel confident about managing discovery learning along with all the other curriculum demands.

Box 5.12 (see page 166) presents a summary of the constructivist approaches that have been discussed throughout this section, as well as some related strategies for classroom use.

CRITICAL REFLECTION

- Do you see yourself as a constructivist educator in the making? Why or why not? Discuss your views with your tutorial or study group.

Box 5.12 — IMPLICATIONS FOR EDUCATORS

Constructivist approaches in the classroom

Constructivist approaches focus on learners actively engaging with making meaning for themselves, supported by peers, teachers, parents and community members. Such approaches place value on the background knowledge and experiences learners bring to the learning environment.

Table 5.6 (below) summarises the main constructivist approaches to learning, and offers some constructivist strategies for classroom use.

TABLE 5.6 Constructivist approaches and classroom strategies

Teaching aim	Constructivist approach	Strategy
1 Encourage learner-centred experiences and activities	**Discovery learning:** The learner works with materials and ideas, discovering connections between them; uses active problem solving	■ Facilitate discovery by developing task-appropriate resources, activities and classroom organisation ■ Provide opportunities for students to develop problem-solving skills ■ Encourage students' active involvement in learning ■ Promote students' confidence in their ability to learn and discover new concepts, by creating a safe, supportive learning environment
2 Provide opportunities for students to work together	**Cooperative learning:** Group work, with the teacher managing and organising activities; cooperation required for group rewards (see Box 5.8 on page 159) **Collaborative learning:** Group work, with greater student autonomy and less teacher involvement **Peer-assisted learning:** Peers teach one another; may be same age or cross-age partnerships	■ Develop and implement guidelines for group and pair work ■ Negotiate activities and assessments to encourage student involvement ■ Arrange the classroom to promote group interaction ■ Capitalise on learner strengths and abilities by establishing peer-assisted learning experiences
3 Assist novice learners to develop expertise	**Cognitive apprenticeships:** Experts guide novice apprentice learners with the aim of developing learners' autonomy and expertise **Reciprocal teaching:** Combines collaborative learning with expert guidance and modelling to achieve progressively greater learner autonomy and understanding	■ Encourage learner–teacher interaction as a learning partnership ■ Make time for dialogue – listen and respond to student questions and comments ■ Draw on the expertise of parents and community members or more able students to develop cognitive apprenticeships in your classroom

Concluding comments

Cognitive learning theories attach importance to the cognitive processes that occur as we learn. Different approaches emphasise different aspects of these processes. We began this chapter by examining the information processing account of how learners acquire and organise information in memory. Inspired by the inner workings of computers, the information processing approach provides various models of how the mind processes, stores and retrieves information. In contrast, the constructivist view of learning focuses on the role of social interaction and the impact of sociocultural factors on one's ability to process information cognitively. Learning is viewed as a process of acquiring socially derived forms of knowledge that are not only internalised over time but also manipulated and influenced by processes of interaction and collaboration (Billet, 1995; Palincsar, 1998). Each of these explanations contributes to our understanding of how students learn. Further, such explanations share a focus on the learner's centrality, the complexity of the learner's cognitive processes, and the value of providing learners with opportunities to make meaning and be active participants in the learning–teaching experience.

Chapter review

- The information processing model likens the human mind to a computer, and learning is depicted as the processing of information.
- The multistore model of information processing describes three memory-storage areas in the brain: the sensory register, the short-term memory and the long-term memory.
- The levels of processing approach distinguishes between deep and shallow information processing. According to this model, depth of processing determines how information is processed and remembered.
- Connectionist models focus on the connectivity between pieces of information that are stored as memories. They depict the brain as a vast computer network with all information interconnected.
- Cognitive learning theory offers several explanations of why we forget. Three reasons for forgetting are that (i) memory decays over time, (ii) long-term memories interfere with each other and inhibit remembering, and (iii) we do not always have the necessary cues to retrieve stored information.
- Knowledge is information that is acted upon cognitively in an effort to make meaning and connect new and existing pieces of information. The three main types of knowledge are declarative, procedural and conditional.
- Cognitive styles depict learner differences in the processing of information and may be understood in terms of perceptual style (field dependence–independence), conceptual tempo (impulsivity–reflectivity), and approach to learning (for example, deep, achieving or surface learning).
- Metacognition is the executive control process that directs our thinking. Learners develop metacognitive knowledge about how they and others process material (person knowledge), about particular tasks and the metacognitive skills they demand (task knowledge), and about a range of metacognitive strategies and how best to use them (strategy knowledge).
- Constructivist approaches focus on the role of social interaction and on the impact of sociocultural factors on our ability to process information cognitively.
- Four key principles of constructivism are (i) learners are active participants in learning, (ii) learners are self-regulated, (iii) social interaction is necessary for effective learning, and (iv) learners' knowledge may be relative, since learners construct their own meaning depending on individual factors such as prior knowledge and sociocultural context.

You make the connections:

Questions and activities for self-assessment and discussion

1. Identify and explain the key concepts associated with the following information processing models:
   a. multistore model
   b. levels of processing model
   c. connectionist model.
2. Why and how do learners forget? Draw on at least three explanations to formulate your answer.
3. Argue for the importance of metacognition in learning.
4. Identify and discuss the key principles of constructivism.
5. Observe a classroom teacher in action and record the number of occasions when the teacher:
   - employs group work or pairwork
   - encourages students to discover new information for themselves instead of giving them answers
   - uses questioning to promote higher-order thinking skills such as moving beyond content to deeper analysis, and critical thinking
   - raises students' awareness of their metacognitive strategies by asking why or how they reached a particular solution.

   a. When you meet with your tutorial group, discuss your findings.
   b. Do you think teachers' use of strategies depends on age group, lesson topic, student ability or any other factors?
   c. Would you classify this classroom as primarily teacher-centred or learner-centred?
   d. Identify at least three activities that make it so.

Key terms

cognitive learning theory	connectionist model	impulsivity
information processing model	declarative knowledge	reflectivity
multistore model	procedural knowledge	aptitude–treatment interaction
sensory register	conditional knowledge	constructivism
short-term memory	metacognition	psychological constructivism
long-term memory	self-monitoring	social constructivism
episodic memory	self-regulation	discovery learning
semantic memory	cognitive style	cognitive apprenticeship
procedural memory	field dependence	reciprocal teaching
levels of processing model	field independence	

Recommended reading

Byrnes, J. P. (1996). *Cognitive development and learning in instructional contexts*. Boston, MA: Allyn & Bacon.

Cobb, P., & Yackel, E. (1996). Constructivist, emergent, and sociocultural perspectives in the context of developmental research. *Educational Psychologist, 31*(3–4), 175–190.

Cowan, N., & Hulme, C. (Eds.) (1997). *The development of memory in childhood*. Hove, East Sussex: Psychology Press.

Eysenck, M. W. (Ed.) (1998). *Psychology: An integrated approach*. Harlow, Essex: Longman.

Eysenck, M. W., & Keane, M. (2000). *Cognitive psychology: A student's handbook* (4th ed.). Hove, East Sussex: Psychology Press.

Greenway, C. (2002). The process, pitfalls and benefits of implementing a reciprocal teaching intervention to improve the reading comprehension of a group of year 6 pupils. *Educational Psychology in Practice, 18*(2), 113-137.

Grigorenko, E., & Sternberg, R. J. (1995). Thinking styles. In D. H. Saklofske & M. Zeidner (Eds.), *International handbook of personality and intelligence* (pp. 205–229). New York: Plenum Press.

Metcalfe, J. & Shimamura, A. P. (Eds.)(1994). *Metacognition: Knowing about knowing.* Cambridge, MA: MIT.

Phillips, D. C. (Ed.) (2000). *Constructivism in education: Opinions and second opinions on controversial issues*. Chicago: The National Society for the Study of Education.

Make some online visits

Biggs' Revised Study Process Questionnaire (1987), a sample report:
<celt.cityu.edu.hk/inventory/student_report_sample_spq.htm>

Constructivism: <library.trinity.wa.edu.au/teaching/construct.htm>

Learn about your own learning styles:
<www2.ncsu.edu/unity/lockers/users/f/felder/public/ILSdir/ilsweb.html> and
<snow.utoronto.ca/Learn2/mod3/index.html>

Memory techniques: <www.learnline.ntu.edu.au/studyskills/ex/ex_ep_re_me_me.html>

FIGURE 6.1 Chapter 6 concept map.

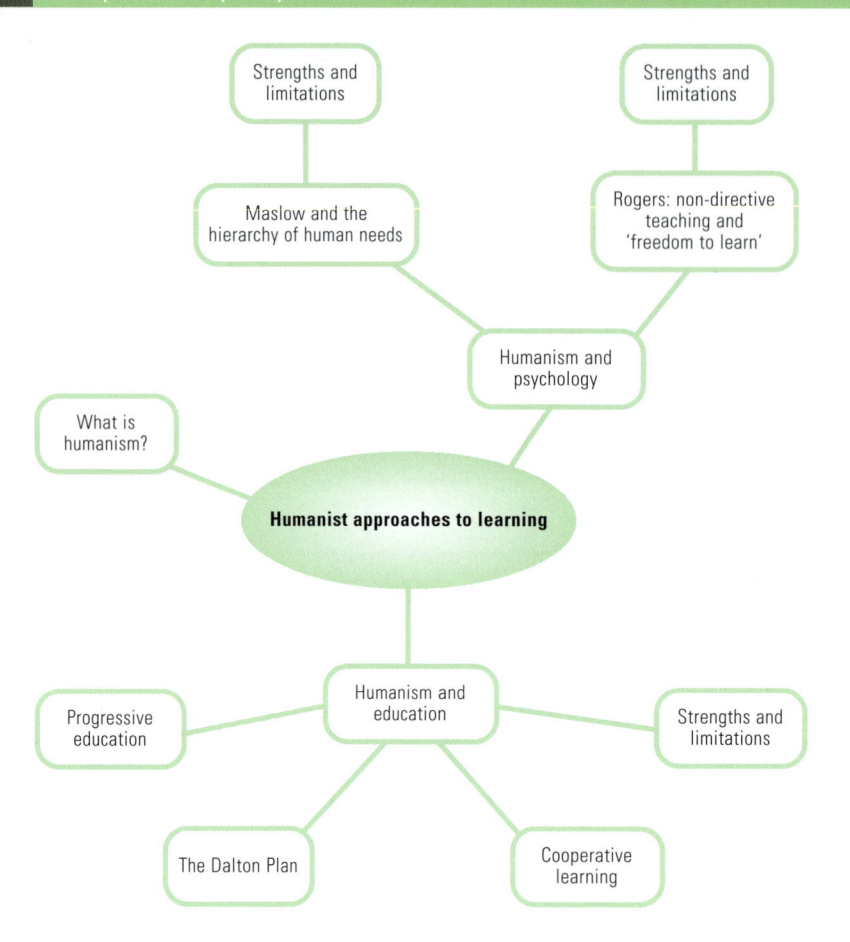

- Strengths and limitations
- Maslow and the hierarchy of human needs
- Strengths and limitations
- Rogers: non-directive teaching and 'freedom to learn'
- Humanism and psychology
- What is humanism?
- **Humanist approaches to learning**
- Humanism and education
- Progressive education
- The Dalton Plan
- Cooperative learning
- Strengths and limitations

CHAPTER OBJECTIVES

After reading this chapter you should be able to:

- explain Maslow's concept of human needs

- identify some of the main factors that distinguish traditional education from progressive education

- identify some of the ways in which humanist ideas have influenced current practices in primary and secondary education

- discuss the links among behavioural, cognitive and humanist approaches to education

- explore the elements of humanism that are present in your own philosophy of teaching and learning.

CHAPTER 6

Humanist approaches to learning

Introduction

If you walked into a classroom today, what would you expect to see? Would the students be sitting in pairs at desks, in straight rows, with the teacher standing at the front of the room? Would the room be bare and silent apart from the teacher's voice? This is most probably the type of scenario your parents and grandparents would have known when they were at school.

Throughout the 20th century, but more particularly in the latter half of the century, there was a steady change in patterns of classroom organisation and management in most school systems, particularly at the primary level. Students now rarely sit in neat rows and are not often expected to be silent. The teacher's role is no longer that of an autocrat but rather that of a democratic manager, in control of the situation and responsive to students' needs and interests, and also to students' various social, cultural and environmental backgrounds. Classroom activities, particularly in the years prior to the secondary level, are no longer dominated by a rigid curriculum. They are much more likely to be shaped in terms of the level of children's development, and their individual needs and learning styles.

Such changes became increasingly evident after World War II, following the growth in popularity of 'child-centred', 'activity-centred' or 'progressive' models of education. Terms such as 'open classroom', 'free school' and 'new education' were used to refer to these new approaches to learning. Such approaches were child-oriented rather than subject-oriented, and focused on children's 'educability' or the level of their development and the extent to which they were ready to begin learning at school (see the discussion of 'readiness' in Chapter 2). This can be contrasted with more traditional 'lock-step' teaching models. Child-centred views of education can be traced back to the influence of humanistic thinkers such as Jean Jacques Rousseau, Friedrich Froebel, Johann Pestalozzi, Maria Montessori; and, more recently, to the ideas of Abraham Maslow, Carl Rogers and John Dewey. The ideas of Piaget and Vygotsky (discussed in Chapter 2) and Erikson (discussed in Chapter 3), have also been influential in this area.

What is humanism?

Have you ever thought about why some students do well at school, while others are turned off, become bored and drop out as soon as they are old enough to leave? What has happened to cause these different responses to the experience of going to school? Is the problem something to do with the individual student, or has it something to do with what happens at school?

Humanists would explain the alienation of some school students in terms of the traditional idea of a school as a place where students must learn to conform to a specific set of expectations and requirements. One outcome of pressures to ensure that children learn to conform at school is the risk that some become 'increasingly alienated from learning and from almost anything else related to school' (Postman & Weingartner, 1973, p. 8) (see Box 6.1).

Box 6.1 CASE STUDY

Study of a school failure

Obituary: Gordon Arthur Andrews, designer, born Sydney, January 10, 1914, died Sydney, January 17, aged 87.

Gordon Andrews was saddened a few years ago when the last of the decimal currency bank-notes he designed was replaced. Andrews may not have been a well-known figure. But every last Australian was touched by the artistic efforts of this designer. The original decimal currency banknotes were his best-known creations. But he also designed the coat of arms for the House of Representatives chamber in Canberra's Parliament House. And there were sculptures in civic centres such as Top Ryde in Sydney and Cowra in central NSW.

Right up to his death, Andrews was still creating unique pieces of furniture and sculptures for fun and to ensure that his mind was kept active.

He had been a failure at school, the butt of sneering criticism from one particular teacher. 'During reading, writing and arithmetic, I was cruelly pointed out as the school idiot,' he explained. 'The fact that I was the best at drawing, modelling and woodwork was completely overlooked or dismissed.

'One day the teacher stood me in front of the class and declared "This boy is so stupid he'll never find a job better than night-soil collection".' Young Andrews was so devastated, he took a length of rope and climbed the old camphor laurel tree beside the family home in suburban Ashfield and tried to hang himself. Suddenly, he slipped, became entangled in the rope and hung upside down by a leg for about a quarter of an hour until he was discovered by his father. 'What do you think you're doing?' his father said. The irony is that Andrews became a thousand times more successful than the teacher.

Source: Obituary by Malcolm Andrews, *The Australian*, Wednesday, 31 January 2001, p. 12.

---

humanism
An orientation or philosophy that is primarily concerned with human rather than spiritual matters

Most dictionaries define the term **humanism** as any system of thought that is predominantly concerned with human experience and reasoning rather than with spiritual aspects of life (see, for example, the *Macquarie Dictionary*). Humanism can be traced back to ancient Greece to thinkers such as Aristotle and Epicurus, who were both interested in everyday life and the real world rather than in religious beliefs and the gods. Humanistic thinking also shows evidence of Chinese and Indian influences through some of the writings of Confucius and Buddha (Brockett, 2000; Misiak & Sexton, 1973). The word 'humanist' is used to describe a general orientation to life or a personal philosophy that recognises the uniqueness of human beings and the qualities of life that contribute to our humanity, in art, literature, music and all aspects of daily living.

Humanism and psychology

Throughout the first half of the 20th century, psychology was strongly influenced by two theoretical approaches: behaviourism, represented by B. F. Skinner (1957) (see Chapter 4), and psychoanalysis, represented by Sigmund Freud (1933). Psychoanalytic explanations of behaviour are derived from Freud's work (Freud lived from 1856 to 1939) and are concerned with psychosexual development and the way in which individuals resolve conflicts between biological drives (or basic needs) such as sexual desires and aggression, and social expectations and values. Humanist psychology began to emerge in the 1950s as a reaction against behaviourists' 'over-scientific' or 'de-humanising' methods, and psychoanalysts' pessimistic obsession with mental illness and disturbance.

Two theorists who contributed most to the development of humanistic ideas in psychology and education in the 20th century were Abraham Maslow and Carl Rogers. Both emphasised the essential goodness of human beings and the need for each individual to achieve 'self-actualisation' (or self-fulfilment). Maslow (1969) described humanist psychology, with its focus on the healthy person, as the 'third force' (the other two forces being behaviourism and psychoanalysis). These ideas – particularly Maslow's theory of human motivation and the hierarchy of needs, and Rogers's (1951) model of client-centred therapy and the concept of 'freedom to learn' – have continued to influence professional practice in both psychology and education throughout the 20th century and beyond.

Maslow and the hierarchy of human needs

The most basic of human needs are physiological, as in newborn infants' need for food and warmth. Later, infants begin to need safety, social contact and love. During childhood and adolescence, needs extend to include esteem (from the self and others) and finally, in maturity, there is the need for self-actualisation or the achievement of one's full potential. Maslow's early interest in human beings' basic needs arose from his work as a psychotherapist helping people who were psychologically disturbed (see Box 6.2). Through this work, Maslow came to believe that human activity is motivated by an urge to satisfy a set of basic needs and growth needs.

Box 6.2 ABOUT ABRAHAM MASLOW

Abraham Maslow (1908–1970) was born on 1 April 1908 in New York, the eldest of seven children. He remembered his childhood as being very unhappy (Boeree, 2000), and described himself as being 'extremely shy, nervous, depressed, lonely and self-reflecting' up to the age of 20 (De Carvalho, 1991, p. 19). The family lived in a non-Jewish area in New York, and Maslow (who looked Jewish) encountered anti-Semitism there. Unhappy at home and isolated at school, he spent many hours in the library (De Carvalho, 1991).

As a student, Maslow did well and his parents encouraged him to study. He spent a brief period studying law in New York, as advised by his father, but this did not interest him. He then married, and enrolled in psychology at the University of Wisconsin. At this time, he was interested in the work of John Watson and the behaviourists (see Chapter 4), and his early research was concerned with emotional and social relationships in dogs and apes. Later, Maslow worked with Harry Harlow (Harlow & Zimmerman, 1959), who is known for his studies of attachment behaviour in infant rhesus monkeys.

Returning to New York, Maslow worked first in the area of social psychology with E. L. Thorndike (see Chapter 4) at Teachers College, Columbia University. During this period, he came to know a number of German psychologists who had escaped to the USA during World War II. One outcome of Maslow's contact with these European psychologists

FIGURE 6.2 Maslow believed that humans are essentially good, but that this inner goodness can be suppressed if their basic human needs are denied.

was his interest in mental health and the potential of human beings. He began to take notes about successful individuals and the way they behaved, finding it significantly different from the behaviour of mentally 'ill' people who were his main focus of attention at the time. Maslow now began to argue that human beings were essentially good, but if their basic needs were frustrated or denied, this inner nature could be suppressed, leading to undesirable or bad reactions. He proposed that these basic human needs could be viewed in terms of a pyramidal hierarchy, the base of which consists of the most basic human survival needs (see Figure 6.3), ranging to the need for self-actualisation at its apex. Maslow saw motivation as a means for the satisfaction of basic needs.

Maslow had a successful career in psychology. He taught at Brooklyn College, was chair of the Psychology Department at Brandeis University and in 1968 was President of the American Psychological Association. He died in 1970.

6.1 More about Maslow

basic needs
Lower-level or deficit needs, such as the need for food, safety, love and respect

growth needs
Higher-level, or 'being' needs, such as the need for self-actualisation

self-actualisation
The achievement of one's full potential

Maslow (1968, pp. 199–200) described humans' **basic needs** and **growth needs** in terms of five ascending levels (see Figure 6.3), which are as follows:

1 *food, shelter, clothes* – sometimes referred to as 'physiological needs'; the most urgent basic elements needed for survival
2 *safety, protection, security* – once basic physiological needs are satisfied, we seek a sense of security and stability
3 *belongingness, love* – such as that in a family, a community, a clan, a gang, friendships; involving feelings of affection
4 *respect, esteem, approval, dignity, self-respect* – involving two sets of needs:
   a respect from others, including status, public recognition and acclaim, even fame and in some instances dominance
   b self-respect and feelings about the self, including a sense of competence, self-confidence, independence and freedom
5 **Self-actualisation** – freedom for the fullest development of one's talents and capacities, or the achievement of one's full potential.

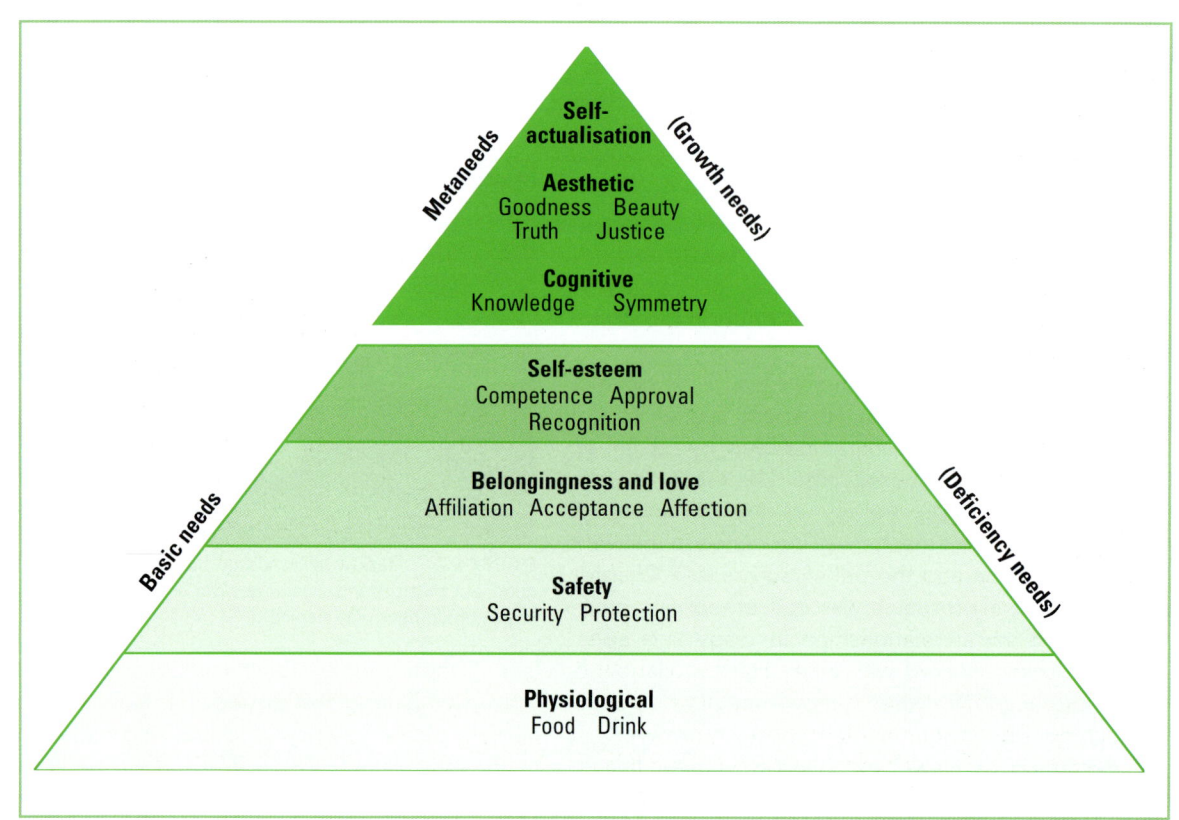

FIGURE 6.3
Maslow's hierarchy of human needs.
(Source: LeFrancois, 2000, Figure 11.3.)

Maslow referred to levels 1 to 4 in the hierarchy as **deficit (D-needs)** and the fifth and highest level as representing **being needs (B-needs)**. He believed that only a small percentage of individuals (less than 1% of adults (Maslow, 1968, p. 204)) truly reached the fifth level of development, identifying as examples of such achievement historical figures such as Mahatma Gandhi, Albert Einstein, Abraham Lincoln and Eleanor Roosevelt.

According to Maslow, children whose basic material needs are satisfied (see Figure 6.4) and who are assured of safety, love and a sense of belonging are able to cope with some frustration and disappointment provided these are not overwhelming. Such challenges strengthen the individual and lead to healthy self-esteem that is based not only on the approval of others, but on a realistic view of the self, an awareness of personal success and an intrinsic motivation towards achievement and growth.

Box 6.3 (see page 176) discusses the implications of applying Maslow's ideas in the classroom.

FIGURE 6.4
Maslow's hierarchy of needs reminds us of the importance of considering children's basic needs before their academic needs. Breakfast programs in schools ensure that hunger does not hamper students' concentration.

deficit needs (D-needs)
Basic needs that motivate individuals to action in order to reduce or eliminate the need

being needs (B-needs)
Growth needs that motivate individuals to achieve personal fulfilment and self-actualisation

Strengths and limitations of Maslow's hierarchy of needs

Strengths

Maslow's ideas about human needs and self-actualisation have had a continuing impact on education: the 'needs' hierarchy is mentioned in most educational psychology textbooks. Also significant is the focus on students' needs in a learning situation, rather than those of the teacher or curriculum. Attention is on children's basic needs for food, safety and belonging; on the affective or emotional aspects of their development (feeling, interest, attitudes and values); and on motivation rather than academic achievement.

Limitations

One of the main criticisms of Maslow's work concerns the hierarchical nature of his human-needs model. Critics have argued that the sequence of Maslow's human needs does not always apply, as in the example of the hero who 'may sacrifice his life for honour' (Patterson, 1973, p. 67). In this case, the hero's need for self-actualisation is stronger than his more basic need for safety. Other criticisms of Maslow's work concern the vagueness of terms such as 'self-actualisation', and uncertainty about measuring its achievement (for example, when it can be said to have been achieved, and under what conditions).

CRITICAL REFLECTIONS

- Reflect on Maslow's hierarchy of needs as it applies in your life. Can you identify with each of the needs? Are there any that don't apply to you?
- What role do you think Maslow's hierarchy of needs has in the 21st century classroom?
- Do you think teachers can contribute to prompting a student's need for self-actualisation? Can you think of any teachers in your experience who played a part in satisfying this need?

Box 6.3 — IMPLICATIONS FOR EDUCATORS

Applying Maslow's ideas in the classroom

The implications of Maslow's ideas for education mainly concern the place of basic needs and motivation in the learning process. For example:

- Children's basic physiological needs must be met before they can be motivated to learn. School breakfast programs for children who are from economically disadvantaged homes are based on Maslow's human-needs model.
- Strategies that are designed to enhance children's self-esteem and develop positive feelings in children about their own competence and effectiveness (see Chapter 3) reflect Maslow's ideas about the importance of motivation in learning and achievement.
- Children should be provided with opportunities to develop their understanding and appreciation of affective aspects of human achievement as exemplified in music, art, poetry and literature, since for many individuals these provide a means of achieving self-fulfilment.

Rogers: Non-directive teaching and 'freedom to learn'

During his years as a psychologist, Carl Rogers worked first with delinquents, then with people who had psychiatric disturbances, and finally with healthy people. His ideas changed over the years (see Box 6.4 opposite). As a psychology student, he assisted in behavioural experiments with rats (see Chapter 4). Later, as a clinical psychologist using psychoanalytic (or Freudian) strategies with disturbed children, he was concerned with how to treat individuals who had psychological disorders. Eventually, he realised that psychotherapists had to stop trying to 'cure' people. Rather, he argued, their task is to provide a supportive relationship within which individuals can begin to heal themselves. Rogers's view was that human beings have an inner drive towards self-fulfilment and maturity: the therapist's role is therefore to help people achieve health and wellbeing by providing a positive psychological climate. Therapists have to become good listeners.

For Rogers and other humanists, **active listening**, sometimes called 'reflective listening' (Gordon, Arthur, & Butterfield, 1996; Porter, 2000), involves more than simply hearing individuals describe their difficulties. It involves attending purposefully to the meaning and intention of what is said, and reflecting or paraphrasing content and emotion as a way of demonstrating that the message has been received and understood. This response strategy encourages the individual to continue talking. It is also an opportunity to release any tensions or emotions, and to clarify aspects of the communication that might have been misunderstood. Active listening helps teachers build more effective relationships with their students. An example of active listening would be:

Alex:	Ben spat at me. I hate him.
Mrs Burnett:	Wow. That's pretty bad. Ben spat at you. You must be feeling angry.
Alex:	He's always doing bad things to me in the playground.
Mrs Burnett:	You would be angry about that.
Alex:	I hate him. He makes me mad. I don't think I'll play with him any more.
Mrs Burnett:	You think you might stop playing with him?
Alex:	Maybe I could try to keep away from him during recess.
Mrs Burnett:	That sounds like a good idea! Keep away from him during recess.
Alex:	Yes, I will. I'm mad at that boy!

active listening
Attending purposefully to the meaning and intention of what another person is saying

Box 6.4 — ABOUT CARL ROGERS

Carl Rogers (1902–1987) was born in Chicago, the fourth of 6 children, to a well-to-do and very religious family that emphasised the value of hard work. His father was a civil engineer. The young Carl was a quiet child who spent much time reading. When he was about 12 years old, the family moved to the country so the children could escape the temptations of the city. Rogers became interested in agriculture, choosing to study in this area when he left school, but he soon changed to history as a preparation for later entry to the ministry.

After graduating from the University of Wisconsin-Madison, Rogers married and then moved to New York to enter the very liberal Union Theological Seminary. At about this time, he attended a World Student Christian Federation Conference in China. This experience led him to see that people could sincerely hold very divergent religious viewpoints, and he began to question the strict religious views he had been taught, developing his own philosophy of life (Carl Rogers, 2000). He decided to abandon his plans to join the ministry. An interest in child guidance led him to enrol at the Teachers College, New York, where he specialised in clinical and educational psychology.

Initially, Rogers worked as a psychologist with delinquent children, becoming increasingly involved in child guidance and therapy. He proposed that therapy should be non-directive, or 'person-centred' (Rogers, 1939; 1942), and concerned not with finding a 'cure', but rather with setting up a supportive climate and relationship within which a disturbed or disordered person can find self-acceptance, understanding and personal growth (Carl R. Rogers Collection, 2003).

Rogers is best known for his non-directive form of psychotherapy, which came to be widely used as an alternative to psychiatry and psychoanalysis. Later in his career, he began to encourage teachers to become more personal, innovative and non-directive in their teaching, arguing that their goal should be to nurture students rather than control their learning (Rogers, 1969; De Carvalho, 1991).

FIGURE 6.5 Rogers believed that a supportive, non-directive relationship helps individuals begin to heal themselves.

Rogers promoted these ideas at a time when psychologists were 'heavily experimental, "rat-oriented", distrustful of clinical psychology and sceptical of his [Rogers's] views' (De Carvalho, 1991 p. 23). Later, through his work with encounter groups – groups in which participants can express their feelings free from the usual social constraints (see Figure 6.6) – Rogers became interested in education. Both he and Maslow emphasised the importance of freedom and choice for mental and emotional health. Education was seen to contribute to these goals by providing a nurturing environment where learners could follow their interests to reach their full potential. Similar goals could not be achieved through traditional educational programs, with their emphasis on the delivery of a fixed curriculum. A new, **non-directive teaching** approach was needed that would free students to develop their talents through self-directed activity.

non-directive teaching
Teaching in which the teacher is a facilitator, guiding students and nurturing their learning

FIGURE 6.6 Encounter groups are designed to create a supportive, trusting atmosphere in which participants can express their feelings without inhibitions.

Strengths and limitations of Rogers's educational ideas

Strengths

The strength of Rogers's ideas is in his emphasis on the value of each individual, on the importance of teachers having a positive view of children and on the need for teachers to actively listen to children. Also significant is his concern that teachers create in their classrooms a climate of trust to support and enhance children's social, emotional and cognitive development.

Limitations

The main limitation of Rogers's ideas is that he presented no guidelines to help teachers who lack the personal or professional skills needed to implement a non-directive program. There are also few suggestions for helping students who lack motivation and are underachieving, or for coping with disruptive behaviour. In addition, the procedures Rogers described may not be appropriate for students who lack the language or cognitive skills needed to negotiate effective classroom arrangements (Kohn, 1996; Porter, 2000).

Box 6.5 discusses the implications of applying Rogers's ideas in the classroom.

6.2 More about Rogers's ideas on education
6.3 About encounter groups

Box 6.5 — IMPLICATIONS FOR EDUCATORS

Applying Rogers's ideas in the classroom

The major impact of humanist psychology on educational practice has been felt through the work of Rogers (1969, 1983) and his belief that positive human relationships provide children with a context within which they are free to grow. He criticised the traditional approach to education, with its '*prescribed curriculum, similar assignments for all students, lecturing* as almost the only mode of instruction, *standard tests* by which all students are externally evaluated, and *instructor-chosen grades* as the measure of learning' (Rogers, 1983, p. 21). Rogers argued that:

- Teachers should be non-directive, focusing on their role as a facilitator, guiding students, nurturing their learning and developing student–teacher partnerships, rather than being primarily concerned with subject matter and instructional objectives.
- The key to effective education lies not in the curriculum, but in the development of a positive and supportive relationship between learner and teacher.
- The role of the non-directive teacher is to nurture the learner as a person, rather than to instruct.
- Rather than talking, the teacher needs to listen actively or reflectively.
- The key to achieving effective education is in the quality of the relationship between the learner and teacher.

Humanism and education

People who advocate teacher-dominated approaches to instruction criticise humanist models of education on the grounds that these lack the structure needed to ensure that desired learning outcomes are achieved. Such structure can include a formal course of study, clearly stated teaching objectives, procedures for regular progress assessment, and defined instructional methods and materials (Center, Ward, Ferguson, Conway, & Linfoot, 1989; Cole & Chan, 1990). This view is in conflict with that promoted by humanists, who are more concerned with children's personal and emotional development within a caring and supportive environment than with ensuring that set topics are covered and that students achieve prescribed goals in basic skills such as reading, writing and mathematics. Choosing between these differing positions is a dilemma that must be resolved by parents and anyone planning to become a teacher. The increasing demand for schools to be more accountable in terms of learning outcomes achieved by students can be seen as a reaction against the influence of humanist principles on school practices (see Chapter 11).

CRITICAL REFLECTIONS

- How do you plan to balance in the classroom the goal of teaching content with the goal of meeting students' personal needs?
- Can you think of situations when these two goals might be in conflict?

While Maslow and Rogers contributed to the emergence of a humanistic view of education, the ideas of philosophers such as John Dewey (1916, 1937) and the movement that is referred to as 'progressive education' are also relevant.

Progressive education

In the first half of the 20th century, when educators emphasised subject mastery in the context of a traditional classroom, humanists such as John Dewey (1859–1952) began to advocate 'experience-based', 'child-oriented' or **progressive education** that was based on a commitment to democratic ideals. The different forms of progressive education that developed in response to these ideas – usually referred to as 'child-centred' education in Britain, **open education** in the USA (Darling, 1990, p. 43) and 'progressive education' in Australia (Barcan, 1980; see also Figure 6.7) – involved classrooms that provided a warm, caring climate and that built on children's interests and experiences. Greater emphasis was placed on children's thinking, feelings and effective communication than on their acquisition of knowledge 'that may soon be obsolete or forgotten' (Walberg, 1986, p. 226). Students were encouraged to develop personal values and a clear sense of self. The teacher's task was to provide a stimulating environment where children would be actively involved in the learning process. Strategies included using small groups, individual instruction, flexible timetabling, mixed-ability groups and a reduced emphasis on grading. School would be fun and students would be motivated to learn.

progressive education
A child-centred approach to education based on a commitment to democratic ideals

open education
A model of learning and teaching that provides a warm, caring environment, and that builds on children's interests and experiences and actively involves them in the learning process

FIGURE 6.7 The New Education Fellowship Conference on Education for a Progressive Democratic Australia provided a new educational ideology that was welcomed by some educationists discontented with established patterns. The journal of the New South Wales Teachers' Federation, which published this cartoon in June 1939, gave its own slant to the new doctrines.
(Source: Barcan, 1980, p. 275.)

6.4 Case studies of a traditional and a humanist classroom

6.5 Four types of schooling for lower primary students

6.6 About progressive education and setting up a progressive school

The most important characteristics of progressive education reflect the humanist concern with the unique characteristics of each child, and a belief in the capacity of each individual to realise full potential. Darling (1994) identified some of the critical features of child-centred approaches to learning in terms of the following:

- Development in childhood is seen as a natural progression; children are not miniature adults.
- Children are naturally active; education involves them in mental (creative) and physical activity.
- Children are respected for their individual talents and needs. Different needs are recognised, diversity is valued and conformity is avoided.
- The curriculum is determined in terms of each child's needs and interests. The classroom atmosphere is relaxed and children are responsible for their own learning; they are 'free to learn'.

Descriptions of humanist education, or what came to be called progressive education, can be found in Dennison (1969), Kohl (1968, 1969), Neill (1968; see Box 6.6) and in accounts of those who attempted to establish such schools in the 1970s (see, for example, Conroy, 1980). Other developments in the provision of educational services that reflect humanist principles include **British Infant Schools** (Darling, 1994). The National Curriculum, introduced in Britain in 1989, continues to advocate the benefits of children working in groups, and this emphasis has been reinforced more recently by moves to place greater emphasis on citizenship in the British primary school curriculum (Lewis, Maras, & Simonds, 2000). The curricula in most early childhood programs and lower-primary classrooms in Australasia follow similar principles.

British Infant Schools
Classes for children aged 5 to 8 years in British schools, usually providing an informal, open approach to learning with student-selected activities

6.7 More about Summerhill

Box 6.6 CLASSROOM LINKS

Summerhill

Summerhill is a progressive coeducational boarding school and was founded as a 'free' school in 1921 by the British educator A. S. Neill. Born in Scotland in 1883, Neill was the son of a puritanical village schoolmaster who used the strap on his students and expected his son, a pupil-teacher at the age of 15 years, to do the same.

After taking a degree in English at the University of Edinburgh, A. S. Neill worked as a journalist before becoming principal of a small school in Gretna Green. It was here, and later during a visit to a community for delinquent adolescents, that he began to develop his ideas about the importance of children's freedom and emotional wellbeing, and about self-government in schools. In 1921, Neill founded a school, based on his principles of freedom in education, in a suburb of Dresden in Germany. Subsequently, following complaints from local citizens about unorthodox curriculum and teaching methods, the school was moved to Austria, and then (following similar complaints) to a house called Summerhill in Dorset, England. In 1927, the school moved to its present site in Suffolk.

Over the years, Neill's ideas have stimulated considerable debate among educators about alternative or non-traditional forms of education. One of the key features of Summerhill is its democracy. The school functions as a self-governing community, with decisions about its operation being decided at a weekly meeting that is attended by the teachers and other staff, and by the students, who number over sixty and who are aged between 6 and 16. Another feature of the school that has stimulated considerable interest is its flexible curriculum and the prominence given to students' motivation to learn. Attendance at lessons is optional.

In 1999, Summerhill was threatened with closure by the Office for Standards in Education following a negative report by government inspectors about the school's standards. Their major concern was about the freedom of students not to attend lessons, which had led to some students 'not attending maths lessons for two years' (BBC News, Thursday 27 May 1999). Representatives of Summerhill argued, in defence of the school, that students' attendance at lessons should not be the only basis for determining the adequacy of instruction at the school. The threatened closure was eventually averted, with the Minister of Education acknowledging that, as an international 'free' school, Summerhill was entitled to follow Neill's philosophy (BBC Education, Thursday, 23 March 2000).

Humanist principles are evident in classroom programs that are described as 'open' or 'open-space' (Bennett, Andreae, Hegarty, & Wade, 1980; Doyle, 1986; Sharples, 1990). Also exemplifying these principles are the **Reggio Emilia** approach to early education, which was developed in the northern Italian city of Reggio Emilia and which uses a constructivist project-based approach with a particular focus on children expressing their ideas in many different language modes (such as drawing, sculpture, dramatic play, writing, etc.) (Edwards, Gandini, & Forman, 1998; New, 2000). Examples of non-traditional or alternative schools include 'Preshil', the Margaret Lyttle Memorial School in Melbourne; the Brisbane Independent School (Anonymous, 2001); and the Ananda Marga River School in New South Wales (Anonymous, 2000). Schools based on the educational philosophy of Rudolf Steiner (1865–1925), who was an Austrian-born philosopher and educationalist concerned with the physical, spiritual and mental aspects of children's development; and Maria Montessori (1870–1952), who was an Italian physician and educator who believed in nurturing children's natural love of learning, can also be described as humanistic in orientation.

More traditional educators who are critical of the progressive education movement argue that it is simply a fad that leads to 'watering-down the traditional curriculum and coddling students' (Richards & Combs, 1993, p. 256). However, a synthesis of research on open (or progressive) education reported by Walberg (1986) concluded that, provided the programs were not extremely radical, students in open education programs were not academically disadvantaged when compared with other students. Moreover, they did substantially better on educational goals that were highly valued by educators, parents and students, such as co-operation, critical thinking, self-reliance and constructive attitudes. The more effective programs did not stress multi-age grouping, open space and team teaching, but did emphasise 'the role of the child in learning, use of diagnostic rather than norm-referenced evaluation, individualised instruction, and manipulative materials' (Walberg, 1986, p. 226) (see also Chapter 11).

In the years after the 1970s, the popularity of progressive schools diminished. In part, this was a result of the difficulties that some groups had experienced in establishing such schools. However, the more open approaches to schooling stimulated educators in general to think about new ways of teaching. Instructional models derived from or strongly influenced by humanistic principles give greater primacy to the student's role in the learning process. In contrast to the behavioural models discussed in Chapter 4, where the teacher is seen as controlling all aspects of instruction, the teacher's role in a humanist classroom is more indirect.

The humanist teacher is expected to be 'open' and honest with students as a way of setting up an 'authentic' humanist relationship with them. Such teachers are responsible for planning what happens in the classroom and for providing an array of intellectual activities that will develop creativity and critical-thinking skills. They should strive to value students' ideas, culture and language, and nurture students' emerging sense of identity and self-esteem. The humanist teacher's role is to facilitate learning, although humanist teachers have no direct control over how and what students learn, which is instead controlled by students. In the humanist teaching situation, the teacher needs to ensure that students are motivated to learn (see Chapter 7). This is where one of the main characteristics of humanistic approaches to teaching becomes evident. Humanist teachers take advantage of children's natural activity, curiosity and interest in learning, ensuring that students are not 'turned off' by negative experiences at school or by a mismatch between what students want to learn and what teachers want them to learn (Darling, 1990). Students are encouraged to use their inner resources in order to become fully functioning individuals (Rogers, 1969).

Reggio Emilia
A system of education for the early childhood years (under 6 years of age)

6.8 Case studies of open plan classrooms

6.9 A class of their own

> **CRITICAL REFLECTIONS**
>
> ■ What difficulties can you see in trying to implement the principles of progressive education in mainstream classrooms?
>
> ■ What are the potential benefits of progressive education principles?

Examples of teaching strategies that share common elements with humanist ideas and that have been widely used and evaluated include 'cooperative learning', 'problem-based learning', 'peer tutoring', 'team teaching', 'the Dalton plan', 'family-based groups', 'ungraded schools' and 'open-plan schools'. Many of these approaches, such as cooperative learning and peer tutoring, are also the domain of cognitive learning theory (see Chapter 5). Some of them are described in the following sections of this chapter.

The Dalton Plan

The Dalton Plan was devised in the early 20th century as a response to growing discontent among progressive educators about the inadequacies of traditional educational practices. The Plan was based on an individualised, child-centred approach to learning that sought to introduce the features of a democratic community within the framework of a progressive school. It was first implemented in 1920 by Helen Parkhurst in a high school at Dalton, a small town close to New York.

Within the Dalton Plan, each curriculum area is divided into a set of monthly contracts and daily assignments. Students are free to plan their own work timetables, although they are also responsible for finishing one assignment before they begin another. Group work is encouraged (Edwards, 1991; Semel, 1992). The Dalton Plan continues to be used in Australian schools; for example, Ascham in Sydney and Walford Church of England Girls' Grammar in Adelaide adopted these methods in 1920 and 1937 respectively, and were still using them in 1980 (Barcan, 1980, p. 284).

Cooperative learning

6.10 Examples of cooperative learning

In Chapter 5 we discussed the centrality of cooperative learning in the constructivist classroom. Along with constructivist theorists, humanists value the importance of student-centred classrooms that emphasise student interaction as a way of encouraging learners to make learning meaningful.

There are many ways in which classrooms may be organised to facilitate student learning. Some approaches encourage individualistic and competitive work habits, while others encourage cooperation among students who learn from one another in groups. The way in which you organise your classroom will depend on a number of factors, including your level of expertise and familiarity with the group, what and how you would like the students to learn, and your philosophy of learning and teaching. Johnson, Johnson and Holubec (1994, pp. 1–3) identify three ways in which teachers can organise their lessons and classrooms. Each of these approaches achieves different outcomes, as listed below:

1 Students may work *competitively* to do better than their peers on norm-referenced tests (see Chapter 11). Those who know they have a chance of success are highly motivated to work as fast and as accurately as they can, while the rest of the class loses interest.

2 Students may work *individually*, at their own speed, to achieve personal goals on criterion-referenced tests. Students are encouraged to focus on their own learning, to ignore others and to see their own achievements as unrelated to the progress of others.

3 Students may work *cooperatively* in small groups to achieve shared goals that benefit the

FIGURE 6.8
Group work has benefits for developing tolerance and acceptance among students from various backgrounds.

student and other members of the group. Group members develop an interdependence and a pride in one another's achievements, recognising that group goals will only be reached if everyone collaborates on each task.

Cooperative learning, the most humanistic of these three alternatives, refers to learning situations where small groups of students are encouraged and motivated to co-operate and help each other learn in order to gain contingent rewards (see Figure 6.8). Success is dependent on all working together to achieve a common goal. There is a shared-incentive system, with students' work evaluated in terms of personal and group outcomes.

Cooperative groups can operate formally, with students working on a set task or parts of a task during regular class periods (such as the Friday mathematics class), or over a brief or an extended period of time (for example, for three weeks in Term 1 or across the school year). Groups can also be informal, created as appropriate in a lesson to fulfil an immediate need, such as when students are asked to turn to their neighbours and spend 5 minutes clarifying their ideas about a particular topic. Before working cooperatively, students are usually taught specific social skills to ensure that the group achieves its particular goals. Assessment is often criterion-referenced (see Chapter 11) and based on the performance of the group as a whole.

Two critical features of cooperative learning concern task structure and the use of contingent rewards (Stallings & Stipek, 1986). Students can work on a task cooperatively as a group, or individual students may undertake separate components of a common task. Rewards can be contingent on the group's successful completion of a task, or on the average achievement of the group's individual members.

Some form of cooperative activity occurs in all types of group learning, but the use of a system of rewards that are contingent on group performance or on the sum of individual performance within the group is unique to cooperative learning. Teachers often encourage students to share their ideas with others when they are working on a task, arguing that this is a form of cooperative learning (see Model 1, Box 6.7 on page 184). However, this type of arrangement does not use contingent rewards and so does not satisfy the criteria for cooperative learning. Models 2 and 3 in Box 6.7, which involve students working individually on elements for a joint outcome (Model 2) and working together for a joint outcome (Model 3), are examples of cooperative learning in practice.

cooperative learning
The organisation of classroom activities so that students must cooperate in order to gain contingent rewards

Box 6.7 CLASSROOM LINKS

Alternative models of group learning

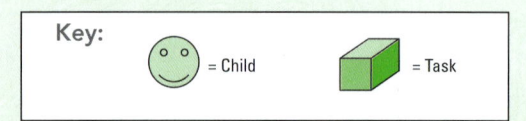

Key: ☺ = Child   ▣ = Task

Model 1: Working individually on identical tasks for individual products

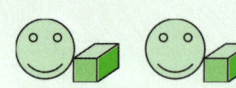

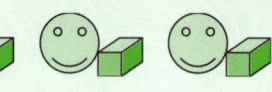

This appears to be a group of students working independently on a task. However, the students may share ideas and contribute to others' interest and motivation if the teacher builds such elements into the task. Otherwise, the students are simply working individually, since the task does not demand cooperation.

Model 2: Working individually on 'jigsaw' elements for a joint outcome

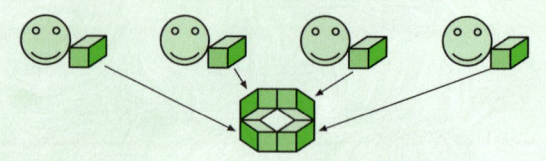

Each student works on one element of the task and parts are eventually fitted together, as in a jigsaw. No student can leave her part of the task incomplete and not jeopardise the group's task completion. With the jigsaw method of working, cooperation is built into the task, together with individual accountability.

Model 3: Working jointly on one task for a joint outcome

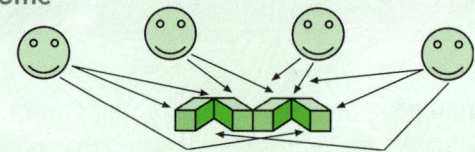

Here, students work cooperatively, since there is only one task. The contribution of each student is important for task completion.

Source: Adapted from Cowie, Smith, Boulton and Laver (1994, pp. 96–98).

While there is considerable debate about which of the different forms of cooperative learning implementation is the most effective (see, for example, Abrami, Chambers, Poulsen, De Simone, D'Apollonia, & Howden, 1995), there is general agreement that these approaches can produce positive gains in academic learning (Abrami et al., 1995; Cohen, 1994; Stahl, 1997; Tomlinson, Moon & Callahan, 1997). However, there is some disagreement about which areas of the curriculum are most conducive to cooperative approaches. For example, there is evidence that cooperative learning has a positive impact on mathematics achievement and on conceptual understanding in physics (Howe, Tolmie, Greer, & McKenzie, 1995; McCaslin & Good, 1996; Peklaj & Vodopivec, 1999; Webb & Farivar, 1994; Whicker, Bol, & Nunnery, 1997) (see also Box 5.9 on page 161). Graybeal and Stodolsky (1985) reported that the greatest gains were in the area of social studies and with activities that involved higher-order cognitive skills, although Robinson (1990) and Stallings and Stipek (1986) questioned claims that cooperative methods had the most impact on activities involving higher-order skills. However, in a review of relevant research, Bossert (1988) concluded that cooperative methods stimulated higher-order cognitive information-processing skills.

A cooperative learning environment, coupled with a problem-solving approach, has been shown to increase achievement in computer-based instruction (Sussman, 1998). It is particularly effective in language studies and in helping students who are learning English as a second language (Calderon & Slavin, 1999; Gillies & Ashman, 1998; Johnson & Johnson, 1989; Sharan, 1990; Sharan & Shachar, 1988; Winitsky, 1991). Overall, tasks that require creative thinking and problem solving appear to be particularly suited to cooperative learning methods (Duren & Cherrington, 1992; Johnson & Johnson, 1991). Good and Brophy (1997) concluded that the most significant aspect of the gains associated with cooperative learning methods is in the affective domain, or in students' feelings, interests, attitudes and values.

The impact of cooperative learning on prejudice

Sharan (1980, 1990) presented evidence to confirm claims that cooperative learning not only enhances children's academic progress, but also has a positive impact on interpersonal relationships in classrooms with students from different ethnic backgrounds (see also Duran, 1994, and Box 6.8 below). The approach has also been found to be effective in enhancing the social acceptance of students with disabilities (see, for example, Jacques, Wilton, & Townsend, 1998). Walker and Crogan (1998), in a comparison of the relative effectiveness of a cooperative learning environment and the Jigsaw strategy (see Box 6.9 on page 186), confirmed these findings, although they also demonstrated the importance of training in appropriate social skills as a prerequisite for success. Walker and Crogan reported that introducing tasks involving simple cooperation in the classroom can exacerbate existing ethnic tensions and **prejudice** (that is, preconceived, uninformed opinions) within the classroom, whereas the **Jigsaw** strategy, which involves both cooperation and interdependence, leads to improved academic performance and liking of peers, and reductions in racial prejudice. The observed effect on interpersonal relations in classrooms is consistent with Gordon Allport's (1954) identification of the basic conditions needed to overcome prejudice, which are that:

- contact is direct and involves students from different ethnic (or disability) groups
- students are equal in status
- contact is concerned with common interests and goals.

prejudice
A preconceived, uninformed opinion

Jigsaw
A form of cooperative learning where each group member works individually on components of the one task

Box 6.8 CASE STUDY

A collaborative-learning-group experience for a student from a minority ethnic background

Cowie et al. (1994) reported a case study from some research that explored the impact of introducing cooperative group-learning strategies ('cooperative group work', or 'CGW') to classes for 8- to 9-year old students in ethnically mixed (Asian and White) middle schools in northern England. The aim of the research, which extended over 2 school years, was to improve ethnic and social relationships in the classes. Teachers participating in the study were encouraged to use cooperative techniques for at least 1 hour each day. In-service training was given and additional support was provided in the form of back-up visits from members of the research team. Diary records were kept by teachers as a means of documenting the extent to which cooperative methods were used.

The following case study is based on material reported by teachers, together with the results of quantitative and qualitative assessment of students' academic achievement, and social and ethnic attitudes and experiences. (Another case study from Cowie et al's 1994 research appears in Box 12.11, on page 394).

Sudha: A victim

Sudha was a very quiet, unusually small child, and easily overlooked in class. When her teacher asked children to choose partners, Sudha was seldom chosen. She was often alone. At the beginning of the project, 63% of the children in her class nominated her as a 'victim'. The most she could expect was to 'be tolerated, not chosen'.

Sudha could never be sure that anyone would play with her at playtime and on the few occasions she tried to join games she was often violently rejected by domineering children. She had certain strategies that sometimes stopped the worst of the aggression against her in the playground ('I give them some of my snack') and in the classroom ('I don't be in fights. I just carry on with my work'). However, these strategies only worked sometimes, and Sudha was very vulnerable to exploitation.

Two girls spoke of Sudha with disdain in her presence:

Lara I don't know much about her. I hardly see her. She's quiet.
Susan You can't see her, she's so small. She lets you use things you want 'cause she's too shy to say 'no'.

Sudha chose to say nothing about Lara and Susan, reverting to her withdrawn, silent behaviour.

By the end of the second year of participating in cooperative group work, Sudha became more involved with the other children in her group. They were now supportive of her, behaving in a kind and friendly way, and she was able to contribute more to group activities. While still not popular, she had begun to form friendships within the group. As her teacher said at the end of the study period:

Sudha is not left out in cooperative group work so she gets involved. ... They'll give her something to do and she'll join in. So if they're made to be in a group then she is involved, but if they're allowed to chooose partners she won't usually be chosen.

Sudha was cautiously in favour of cooperative group work provided there were no boys in the group and there was no fighting. The positive impact of the cooperative arrangements was that her nomination as a victim decreased quite markedly over this time period.

Source: Adapted from Cowie, Smith and Laver (1994, pp. 177–183).

Activities

1 How would you evaluate the impact of cooperative group work on Sudha?
2 If you were Sudha's teacher, would you recommend that the cooperative approach be continued in the next school year? Why/why not?
3 What other strategies could be used to help address the isolation of children like Sudha? (You may find some ideas for this in Chapter 4.)

CRITICAL REFLECTIONS

- Has cooperative learning featured in your educational experiences? If so, what did you like or dislike about it?

Many forms of cooperative learning have been described in the literature (see, for example, Cowie & Rudduck, 1990; Dunne & Bennett, 1990). Examples of cooperative learning in practice can be found in programs such as Group Investigation (Sharan & Sharan, 1992); Learning Together (Johnson & Johnson, 1999); Student Team Learning, which includes Student Teams and Achievement Divisions (STAD) (Slavin, 1994) and Teams-Games-Tournaments (TGT) (De Vries & Slavin, 1978); and Jigsaw (Aronson, Blaney, Stephen, Sikes, & Snapp, 1978; Slavin, 1994) (see Box 6.9).

6.11 Group investigation and student team learning

Box 6.9 CLASSROOM LINKS

About the Jigsaw strategy

The Jigsaw strategy (Aronson et al., 1978) was initially devised in the USA during the mid-1970s to help black and white students to interact positively in desegregated classrooms. Research had demonstrated that simply bringing groups of children into contact with other groups only heightened any conflicts that already existed between them (Sherif, 1967). One of the conditions that could be used to ensure that such contact was successful was the presence of a shared activity, particularly one that involved positive interdependence and cooperation (Allport, 1954; Brown & Turner, 1981; Sherif, 1967). It was on the basis of these research findings that Aronson and his colleagues devised the Jigsaw strategy.

The Jigsaw strategy was designed for use with pre-adolescent students (Years 5 and 6) but has been used across all age groups. To implement the procedure, students are formed into small heterogenous Jigsaw groups. The task and any necessary resources are also sub-divided ('jigsawed', Abrami et al., 1995, p. 143) and one person in each group is allocated a part of the task to be studied. Individuals who have been given the same sub-task then re-form into 'expert' groups to study the specific topic they have been allocated. Once this study process is completed (about 30% of lesson time), students return to their Jigsaw groups and teach what they have learned to the other members of their group (about 60% of lesson time).

> In this way, each member of a Jigsaw group becomes an expert in one part of the learning task and is instructed in the remaining parts of the task by other experts in the group. At the end of the learning period, students are assessed individually. The Jigsaw procedure requires that students are *interdependent* and work *cooperatively* to complete the set task.

Strengths and limitations of humanism in the classroom

Since its development in the mid-1970s, considerable evidence has accumulated about the effectiveness of cooperative learning methods. The results are generally positive, although some problems have been reported, particularly in regard to implementation.

Strengths

Richards and Combs (1993, pp. 266–267) summarised the impact of ideas promoted by the humanist psychologists and educators such as Maslow, Rogers and Dewey as:

- recognition of each human being's uniqueness, and support for individualised instruction
- recognition of the importance of a positive self-concept and self-esteem in the objectives of education (see Chapter 3)
- reduction in dependence on whole-class methods of instruction coupled with more widespread use of small-group and cooperative strategies, an increased emphasis on the teacher's role as facilitator and helper rather than as director and manager, and increased efforts to include students in decision-making in schools
- attempts to make schools pleasant and caring places, with warm or positive relationships between teachers and students
- widespread provision of school-based guidance and counselling services.

Summarising the results of studies into the efficacy of cooperative learning, Good and Brophy (1997, p. 277) concluded that:

- Cooperative learning methods can realistically be implemented in many classroom situations and are likely to have positive effects.
- Positive effects seem to result from the use of group rewards rather than from the cooperative nature of the activities employed.
- The gains associated with cooperative learning strategies appear to be primarily motivational rather than cognitive, and associated with a need to help individual team members achieve their goals in order for the team to do well.
- Effects are greatest when there are group rewards, and when students are accountable not only for their own mastery of the task, but also for their team-mates' mastery.
- When used with mixed-ability groups in mathematics, cooperative learning methods have also been shown to be effective in reducing the gap that develops, over time, between high- and low-achieving students, with the performance of intermediate- and low-level students improving and a negligible impact on more competent students' progress (Linchevski & Kutscher, 1998).

Limitations

Much of the criticism directed at humanistic education has resulted from the humanist focus on affective aspects of development rather than on more objective and quantifiable aspects of learning. Because of the qualitative nature of the outcomes of humanistic teaching models, relatively little research as been reported on their effectiveness. Most accounts of humanistic classrooms have tended to be subjective descriptions of program implementation. Quantitative evaluations have tended to indicate a risk of poor progress in basic skills such as reading and writing within humanistic programs, since attention is focused on affective rather than academic outcomes. A further source of difficulty in evaluating humanistic approaches to learning is that teachers often lack the knowledge and skills needed to implement humanistic ideas (Antil et al., 1998; Rich, 1992). In addition, school systems may be unsympathetic to such instructional models, particularly when comparisons can be made between schools on the basis of widespread basic skills testing (see Chapter 11).

At a more practical level, while there is considerable debate about the effectiveness of cooperative methods for enhancing student achievement and promoting students' **interpersonal skills** (awareness of and sensitivity to others) and self-esteem, there is also evidence that students and teachers can experience problems when cooperative learning strategies are introduced into a classroom. Some of the issues that may need to be considered when cooperative methods are implemented include the following:

- *Interpersonal skills.* Students do not always have the interpersonal skills needed to function effectively in a small group. Some training in effective communication (listening, trying to understand another's point of view, giving feedback), as well as in sharing, resolving conflicts, and learning to accept, support and trust others in the group may be needed prior to the commencement of a cooperative activity (see Goodwin, 1999).
- *Task completion.* Students may also lack the skills needed to complete a set task within a cooperative group setting. The task itself should be carefully structured, with the final goals clearly stated and, in the case of the Jigsaw strategy, the task and any resources designed so they can be broken into roughly equivalent parts. Students need to learn how to get help from other group members (such as by asking questions or watching what others do), how to pace what they do to fit with others in the group, and the particular strengths (and weaknesses) of each group member.
- *Experiences in cooperative groups.* Efforts may need to be made to ensure that students' experiences in cooperative groups are positive – not negative. This will include checking that more-competent students are not overworked or bored, and that less-competent students are not ignored or made to feel 'dumb' or 'useless'.
- *Student cooperation.* It is almost inevitable that some students will not cooperate in the group activity, either through contributing nothing or by acting disruptively. Positive intervention is needed to avoid this outcome (Bower, 1989; Ellis & Whalen, 1992).
- *Rivalry among groups, and misbehaviour.* This can disrupt the function of groups. Changing group membership at the end of a unit of work, or after regular periods of time, can help to reduce this effect, but difficulties may still be experienced in classes with a small number of disruptive, difficult, unpopular or non-cooperative students (Cowie et al., 1994). Teachers need to have clear expectations concerning the behaviours required for successful classroom functioning, and need to use a group-based positive reward system and appropriate classroom-management techniques (Kagan, 1992; Slavin, 1994). Training in conflict-resolution techniques may be helpful (see Chapter 12).
- *Size of group.* Group size can have an impact on the success of a cooperative learning program. Groups need to be small enough to facilitate interaction and interdependence. Fuchs et al. (2000) reported that students working in pairs achieve superior levels of collaboration and higher performance scores than students working in small groups, but the level of cognitive functioning (an outcome of cognitive conflict; see Chapter 2) is higher in the small groups.
- *Arrangement of furniture in the classroom.* Furniture arrangement can influence the success of cooperative learning. The teacher needs to have easy access to each group and there should be space for students to move around as required (see Chapter 12).
- *Teacher commitment and classroom-management skills.* Teachers implementing cooperative strategies need to be committed to using cooperative learning methods, but they also need reasonably high-level classroom-management skills and/or training before the new

---

interpersonal skills
Awareness of and sensitivity to others' attitudes, intentions, feelings, needs and motivations

methods are implemented. It is also important that, where necessary, there is provision for an aide, volunteer parent or student tutor to provide additional assistance to individuals and groups. This is particularly important when there are disruptive students in the class (Cowie et al., 1994). Participation in a teaching team or teachers' learning community (Calderon & Slavin, 1999) and ongoing support from colleagues, administrators and students have been shown to have a positive influence on long-term use of cooperative learning strategies (Ishler, Johnson, & Johnson, 1998).

- *Cooperative learning strategies should complement rather than replace existing classroom practices.* Team-based methods can be used for follow-up learning after whole-class instruction, and for practical application of new material. However, cooperative learning strategies should not replace whole-class instruction by the teacher where new subject matter is being introduced, or when the learning tasks are not suited to cooperative activity (such as in routine computation practice).

Evidence on teachers' use of cooperative methods suggests that many regularly use some form of cooperative activity in their classrooms (see, for example, Antil, Jenkins, Wayne, & Vadesky, 1998). In most primary classrooms, students spend much of the day learning in supportive groups sitting at a table with other students, rather than in individual activities at a single desk or listening to whole-class 'teacher talk'. However, few of the teachers Antil et al. (1998) surveyed used a recognised form of cooperative learning, primarily because they did not link individual accountability to group goals. Interestingly, the increasing availability of computers in classrooms may contribute to greater use of cooperative learning strategies, since computers have been demonstrated to provide an effective platform for cooperative learning activities among students of varying ages and ability levels (McDonald & Ingvarson, 1997; Sussman, 1998; see also Chapter 10).

Box 6.10 details the implications of humanism in the classroom.

Box 6.10 IMPLICATIONS FOR EDUCATORS

Humanism in the classroom

The key elements of humanism, or progressive education, in classroom practice include:
- an emphasis on *experience-based instruction* – or 'learning by doing' – building on students' interests and experiences, and involving them in mental and physical activity (see chapters 2 and 5)
- concern with *students' thinking, feelings and communication skills*, together with respect for their needs and talents
- encouragement for students to develop *personal values and self-awareness* (see Chapter 3)
- provision of a *stimulating environment* to actively involve students in learning, giving them 'freedom to learn'
- provision of *progressive education* as exemplified in the programs of A. S. Neill, Rudolf Steiner, Maria Montessori, the Reggio Emilia early childhood education model and non-traditional or alternative schools
- application of *individualised, child-centred teaching strategies*, as used in the Dalton Plan and in the different forms of cooperative learning.

Key elements of cooperative approaches to learning include:
- *positive interdependence*, where students are linked to others in their group in such a way that if one fails, all fail and none can succeed unless the whole group succeeds; and where tasks and resources are shared and each group member is responsible for completing a task and for ensuring that others in the group complete their tasks
- *face-to-face facilitative interaction*, where students aid group success by listening to and helping one another, by sharing information and resources, by resolving differences, by giving feedback, and by encouraging and motivating one another to participate fully and to achieve shared goals (Gillies & Ashman, 1998)
- *individual accountability and personal responsibility*, where the assessment results of each student's work are reported to both the student and the group as a whole ('students learn together and then perform alone' Johnson, Johnson, & Holubec, 1994, p. 31), with each member of the group contributing a 'fair share' to the task

- *interpersonal and small-group skills*, where students learn academic subject matter and small-group social skills in order to function effectively within a team – getting to know the others in their group, learning to trust them, and to communicate clearly with them, support them and resolve conflicts successfully; training may need to be given to ensure that students have these skills

- *group review (processing)*, where students reflect on how effectively their groups have operated, giving positive feedback about actions that are helpful and those that are not helpful. Research cited by Johnson, Johnson and Holubec (1994, p. 34) indicates that group review of activities is most effective (that is, it contributes to higher student-achievement levels) when teacher and students all participate in the review process.

Concluding comments

The humanists' most important contribution to the debate about effective education has been to heighten our awareness of teaching as an art to be undertaken by caring individuals committed to helping their students to succeed in the difficult process of growing up. Education is not just a mechanical process. While highly structured teaching methods and related technologies are very important in the learning process, the humanity of teachers and others who contribute to children's learning should also be recognised.

Chapter review

- Humanism is a philosophy of life that emphasises human experience rather than spiritual matters. Its origins can be traced back to ancient Greece, but it has continued to be evident in the writings of philosophers over the centuries.
- Humanists Abraham Maslow and Carl Rogers are known for their work on motivation and the hierarchy of human needs, and on the need for teachers to nurture rather than instruct, allowing children the freedom to grow and learn.
- Humanism in education emphasises children's thinking and feelings, and effective communication rather than the acquisition of information that will quickly be forgotten or become obsolete. The teacher's task is to believe in the potential of every child, and to provide a stimulating environment where children can be happy, motivated to learn and actively involved in learning.
- Progressive education strategies that are used in humanistic classrooms include small groups, individual instruction, flexible timetabling, mixed-ability groups and a reduced emphasis on grading. Examples of the application of humanist ideas in education include individual schools such as A. S. Neill's Summerhill, British infant schools, most early childhood and lower-primary classrooms in Australasia, and other alternative or non-traditional schools.
- Examples of teaching methods that incorporate humanist principles include cooperative learning, team teaching, peer-tutoring, family-based groups, ungraded schools, open-plan schools and the Dalton Plan.
- Critical features of cooperative learning include students working cooperatively in small groups to achieve shared goals that benefit individuals within the group and the group as a whole. Results of evaluation of these methods demonstrate the efficacy of cooperative learning across a range of age groups and curriculum areas, and in developing positive interpersonal relationships within classrooms.
- Problems noted in cooperative learning have included students' lacking the personal and social skills needed to participate successfully in a cooperative group, tasks that are poorly designed, and the lack of necessary planning and management skills among teachers.
- Critics of humanistic education identify the 'watering-down' of the curriculum and 'coddling' of students as major concerns. However, research has suggested that, provided the programs are not extremely radical, students in child-centred or non-traditional schools are not disadvantaged

- academically when compared with those in more mainstream schools.
- Most teachers use cooperative activities to complement other, more traditional classroom practices, but these methods often lack the key cooperative-learning elements of individual accountability linked to the achievement of group goals.

You make the connections:
Questions and activities for self-assessment and discussion

1. Can you describe the main features of humanism? What are its strengths? What are its limitations?
2. If you were appointed to a teaching situation where humanist principles were followed, what steps might you take to ensure that the potential limitations of humanist teaching strategies were avoided?
3. Think of a classroom that is very familiar to you. If this was your class, when might you use cooperative learning techniques? Why? What difficulties do you anticipate might occur? What steps would you have to take to ensure the success of this method of instruction?
4. Are traditional structured teaching programs inevitably in conflict with humanist progressive education? Answer this question and then do the following activity. When you have finished the activity, see if your answer is still the same.
    a. Think of a school level you are familiar with (early childhood, lower or upper primary, lower or upper secondary). Make a three-column table.
    b. In column 1, list the different elements of a school program and the types of arrangements different schools make reflecting the underlying philosophies of traditional and progressive education. You might include the various aims, types of assessment, curriculums, types of classes, teaching methods, types of timetable and discipline methods. You may need to consult material in other chapters to compile this list.
    c. Label columns 2 and 3 'Traditional' and 'Progressive'.
    d. In columns 2 and 3, briefly note the key characteristics of each school type in relation to each element listed in column 1.
    e. What characteristics do the two types of school have in common? In what ways are they different?
5. What was the dominant philosophy of education when you were at school? Would you describe the classrooms you remember as humanistic in orientation? Think about the most effective teacher you have had. How would you describe that teacher's personal philosophy of teaching?
6. Think about your own philosophy of teaching and learning. Can you identify elements that could be described as humanist? Are there also behavioural and constructivist elements? In what aspects of classroom experience are humanist ideas likely to be influential? Where would behavioural and constructivist ideas be more appropriate?

6.12 More activities for you to do

Key terms

- humanism
- basic needs
- growth needs
- self-actualisation
- deficit needs (D-needs)
- being needs (B-needs)
- non-directive teaching
- progressive education
- open education
- British infant schools
- Reggio Emilia
- cooperative learning
- prejudice
- Jigsaw
- interpersonal skills

Recommended reading

Abrami. P. C., Chambers, B., Poulsen, C., De Simone, C., D'Apollonia, S., & Howden, W. (1995). *Classroom connections: Understanding and using cooperative learning.* Toronto: Harcourt Brace.

Good, T. L., & Brophy, J. E. (1997). *Looking in classrooms* (7th ed.). New York: Longman.

Johnson, D. W., & Johnson, R. T. (1991). *Cooperative lesson structures.* Edina, MN: Interaction Book Company.

Joyce, B., & Weil, M. (1996). *Models of teaching* (5th ed.). Boston, MA: Allyn & Bacon.

Killen, R. (1998). *Effective teaching strategies: Lessons from research and practice* (2nd ed.). Katoomba, NSW: Social Science Press.

Reid, J. (2002). *Managing small-group learning.* Newtown, NSW: Primary English Teaching Association.

Slavin, R. E. (1990). *Cooperative learning: Theory, research and practice.* Englewood Cliffs, NJ: Prentice-Hall.

Slavin, R. E. (1994). *A practical guide to cooperative learning.* Boston, MA: Allyn & Bacon.

Make some online visits

Information about progressive education can be located on the World Wide Web under terms such as: 'alternative schools', 'non-traditional schools', 'free schools', 'open education', 'open classrooms', 'open-plan schools', 'Summerhill' and 'Reggio Emilia'.

FIGURE MIII Module III concept map.

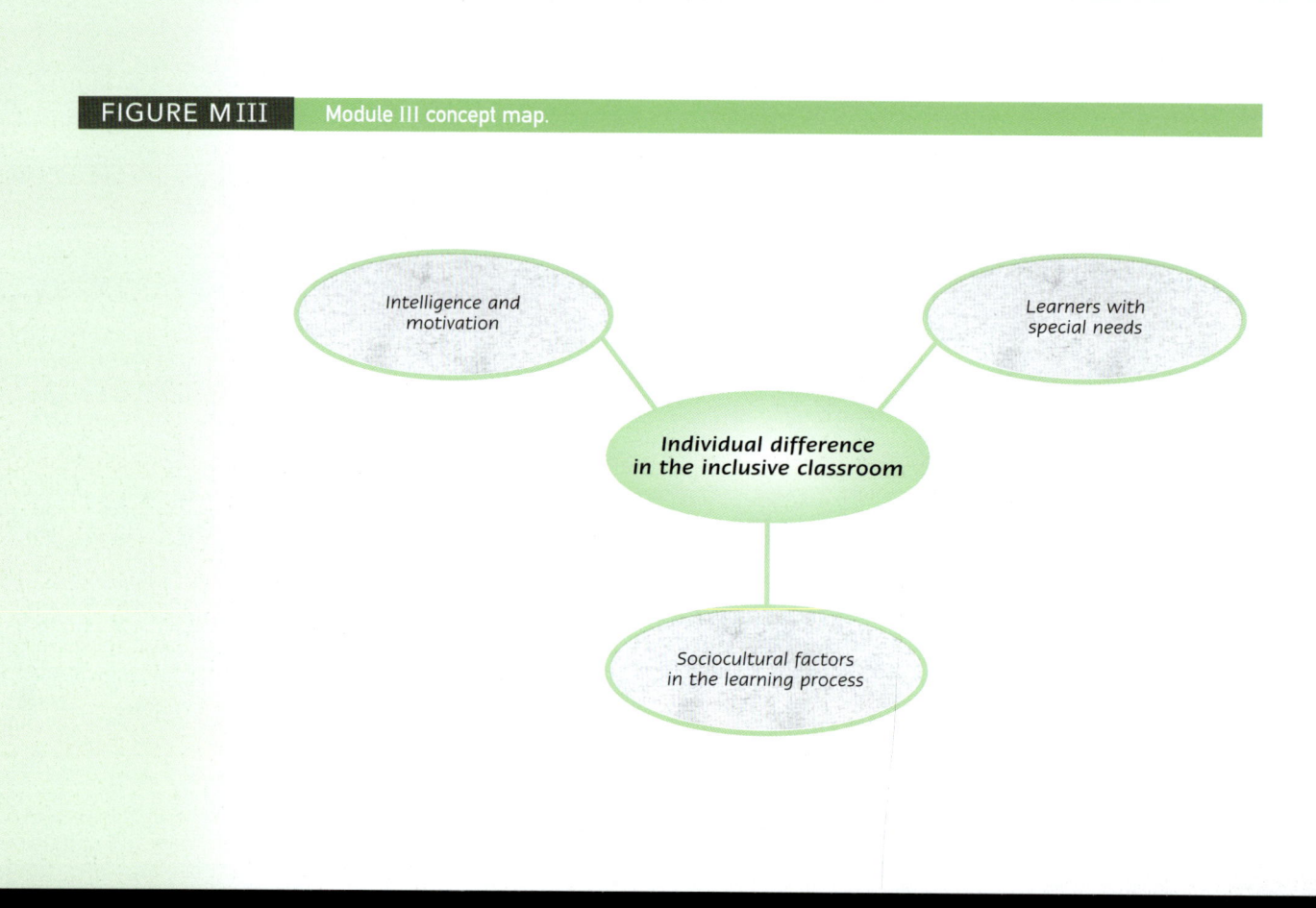

- Intelligence and motivation
- Learners with special needs
- Individual difference in the inclusive classroom
- Sociocultural factors in the learning process

MODULE CONTENTS

- Chapter 7 Intelligence and motivation

MODULE III

Individual difference in the inclusive classroom

Core question: *How does educational psychology help us understand learner differences?*

Each student comes to the learning environment with a different set of experiences, values, interests, needs and abilities. In an inclusive classroom, teachers recognise difference, devising ways to address students' differing needs and also taking into account what each learner brings to the learning process.

School systems and individual teachers also play a significant role in addressing sources of educational disadvantage and in taking steps to ensure that all learners are catered for and that background factors affecting learning are taken into account. Teachers need to be aware of sources of 'cumulative' disadvantage, and of issues facing students whose cultural backgrounds differ significantly from the dominant culture of the society in which they live.

Chapter 7 examines intelligence and motivation – factors intrinsic to all children and that affect school learning and contribute to differences among students. Chapter 8 considers the challenges of teaching and supporting students who have a range of special learning needs associated with disabilities and learning difficulties. Chapter 9 addresses the complex sociocultural factors that contribute to student difference – factors that are particularly important in understanding equity in education.

Your understanding of and response to the issues discussed in this module should be central to your development as a critically reflective educator and to your developing philosophy of learning and teaching. As you consider sources of student difference, reflect on how teachers might cater for individual differences to maximise the learning of all their students.

FIGURE 7.1 Chapter 7 concept map.

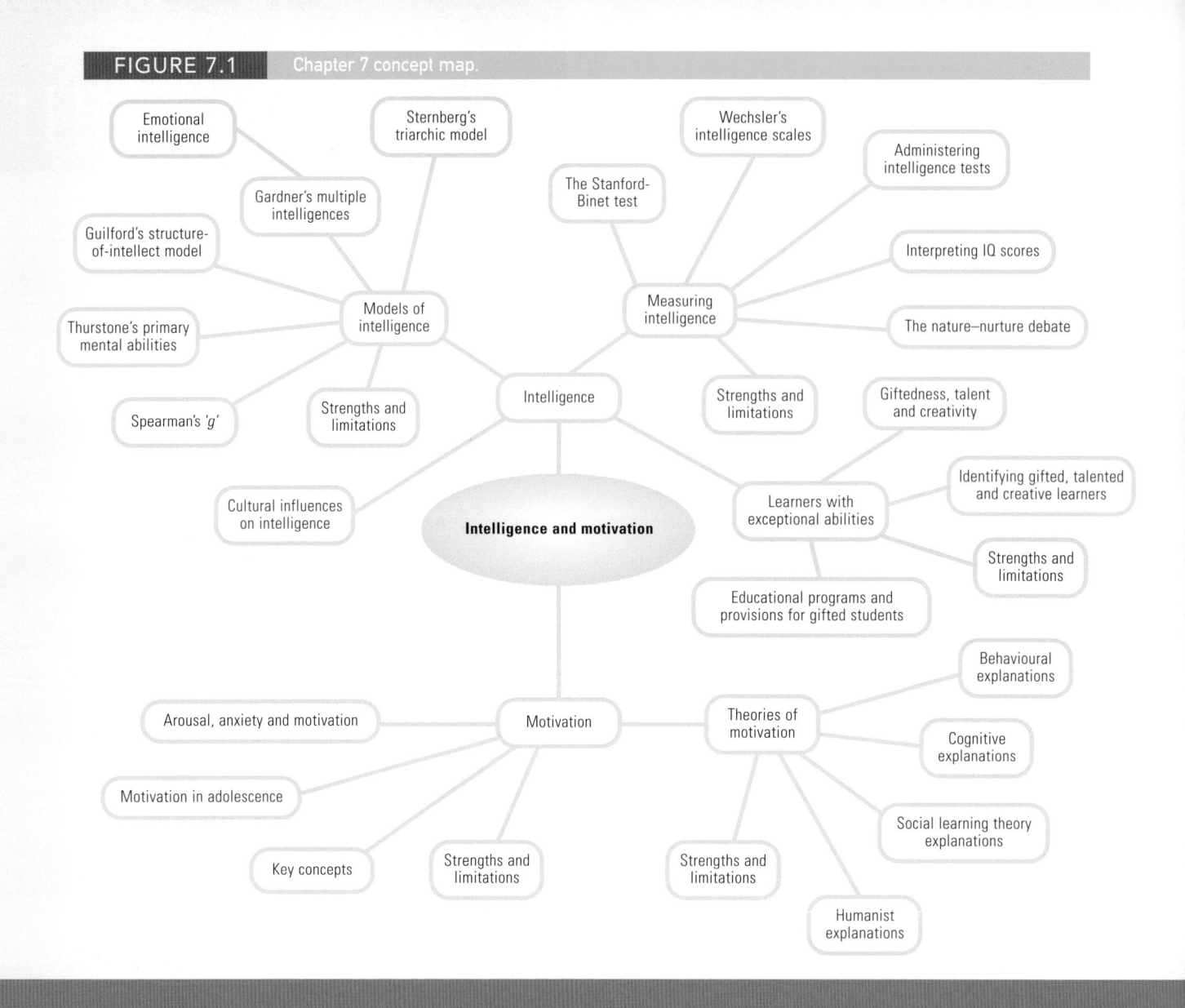

- Intelligence and motivation
  - Intelligence
    - Models of intelligence
      - Emotional intelligence
      - Sternberg's triarchic model
      - Gardner's multiple intelligences
      - Guilford's structure-of-intellect model
      - Thurstone's primary mental abilities
      - Spearman's 'g'
      - Strengths and limitations
    - Cultural influences on intelligence
    - Measuring intelligence
      - Wechsler's intelligence scales
      - The Stanford-Binet test
      - Administering intelligence tests
      - Interpreting IQ scores
      - The nature–nurture debate
      - Strengths and limitations
    - Learners with exceptional abilities
      - Giftedness, talent and creativity
      - Identifying gifted, talented and creative learners
      - Strengths and limitations
      - Educational programs and provisions for gifted students
  - Motivation
    - Arousal, anxiety and motivation
    - Motivation in adolescence
    - Key concepts
    - Strengths and limitations
    - Theories of motivation
      - Behavioural explanations
      - Cognitive explanations
      - Social learning theory explanations
      - Humanist explanations
      - Strengths and limitations

CHAPTER OBJECTIVES

After reading this chapter you should be able to:

- define intelligence and identify some of the characteristics usually included in such definitions
- identify the models of intelligence proposed in scientific studies of intellectual ability
- describe ways in which contemporary models of intelligence are applied in classrooms
- outline examples of strategies educators can use to ensure that students with exceptional gifts, talents and creative abilities realise their full potential
- define motivation and explain its impact on behaviour.

CHAPTER 7

Intelligence and motivation

Introduction

When children come to school they bring with them an array of qualities, including personal characteristics and prior experiences, that will inevitably have an impact on what happens at school, what they learn, which friends they make, what interests they develop and so on. In a class situation it is often difficult for teachers to recognise the influence of such factors on individual children's behaviour and learning, although most teachers understand the importance of these elements in children's development. This chapter looks at intelligence and motivation: two factors intrinsic to all children, which affect school learning. Also considered are issues associated with identifying and educating highly gifted and talented children, and highly creative children.

Intelligence

intelligence
A general aptitude and capacity for understanding and learning

What is intelligence? What is meant when someone is described as 'smart', 'bright', 'clever' or 'intelligent'? It is easy to assume that these terms mean much the same to everyone. But is this so? Think about what is meant by a word like 'beauty'. Everyone can identify examples of beauty in daily life, although it can be very difficult for people to pinpoint the specific characteristics that make one person appear beautiful and another person appear plain. Moreover, perceptions of beauty differ across social groups and over time. Think of the rounded curves of Mona Lisa, painted in an earlier century by Leonardo da Vinci, in comparison with the almost anorexic appearance of current fashion models. Concepts of intelligence are similar. While the term **intelligence** can commonly be taken to mean a general aptitude and capacity for understanding and learning, different people mean different things when they talk about intelligence, as a result of historical and cultural factors (see Figure 7.2 over the page).

In everyday usage, intelligence is usually conceived as a mental ability that is present in individuals in differing amounts: 'Jack is clever; Arnold is a bit dumb.' Words like 'bright', 'brilliant', 'smart' or 'wise' are used to refer to examples of human activity thought to be indicative of high ability or intelligence. For most people, intelligence is valued in terms of 'the more the better'. Some views of intelligence even seem to imply that it has a physical existence in the human skull. However, few people can give a definition of intelligence, although most can cite examples of intelligent behaviour. More interestingly, as suggested earlier, definitions and examples given will differ from individual to individual, from culture to culture, and across time.

Cultural influences on intelligence

The idea of intelligence as mental agility or mental speed is a very Western notion. In some non-Western cultures, speed of thinking and finding solutions to problems is not regarded as a particularly important attribute (Biesheuvel, 1969). In such cultures, wisdom can mean the ability to listen, observe, reflect, learn from others, and think through the short- and long-term consequences of an action. Those growing up in communities with such beliefs would be unlikely to give quick, accurate responses to questions in a standard Western intelligence test.

FIGURE 7.2 Which is 'beautiful'?

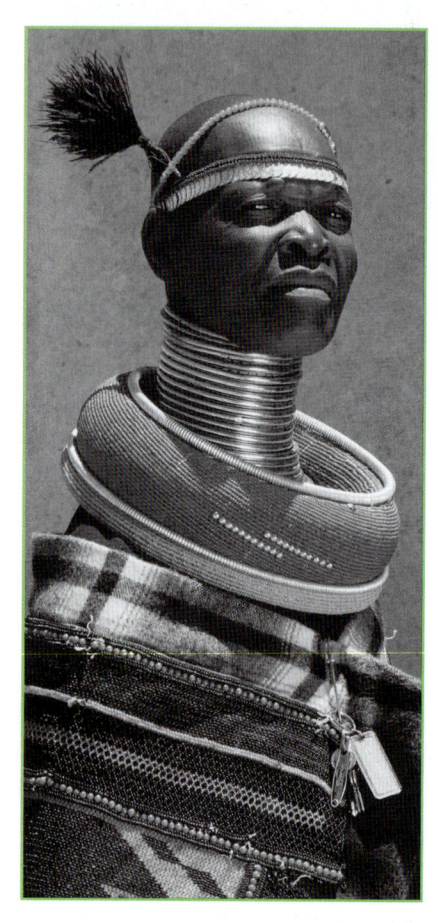

The skills valued by particular societies are likely to represent the skills that are useful in that society (think about this in terms of Vygotsky's sociocultural theory; see Chapter 2). For example, in some Pacific Island communities where the skills of navigation (the ability to read the waves, clouds and stars) are regarded as indicative of intelligence, mental agility in a Western sense is irrelevant. For example, Heyerdahl (1950) and Lewis (1972) found that navigators from these societies develop complex 'mental maps' of their region and use this knowledge to move from island to island. If these notions were applied in our society, very few of us would be regarded as 'intelligent'.

In technologically developed societies, intelligence is generally seen as involving high levels of competence in literacy, numeracy and, increasingly, technological skills. Children are expected to acquire such skills from an early age. The types of paper-and-pencil tasks used in Western-based intelligence tests are typical of the types of instruction that children encounter at school and at home. Even the way we conceptualise an abstract idea such as 'intelligence' is strongly influenced by cultural and social factors.

Models of intelligence

Is intelligence simply an innate capacity or general mental ability that enables individuals to complete the types of tasks that are included in intelligence tests? People often appear to do well on intelligence-test tasks (such as verbal reasoning, abstract and visual reasoning, vocabulary knowledge and sentence comprehension), while others do poorly, and these results would seem to suggest the existence of a general mental capacity, or 'g'. However, closer examination of test results often reveals a consistent pattern in individual responses to different types of items in a test. One person might answer most of the items involving vocabulary, general comprehension, arithmetic and reasoning correctly, but have more difficulty in completing mazes, copying block designs or arranging pictures to tell a story. Another might struggle to get any correct answers on the test, achieving the best scores in digit span (repeating a sequence of digits) and coding (pairing symbols and digits using a key). These different response patterns suggest that intelligence comprises not only a general, over-arching mental capacity, but also some specific abilities.

There are a number of different models of intelligence, including models proposed by Charles Spearman and L. L. Thurstone, both early researchers in the area of intelligence; and those devised by later researchers such as J. P. Guilford, Howard Gardner and Robert Sternberg. Early researchers tended to conceptualise intelligence as a general mental ability that could be measured by verbal and non-verbal reasoning tasks. The broad concept of intelligence as a general mental ability that, umbrella like, overlies a multifaceted cluster of abilities has continued to interest researchers in this field (for example, see Anderson, 1999; Carroll, 1996). Examples of this idea can be found in Guilford's structure-of-intellect model (1967), in Gardner's theory of multiple intelligences (1983) and in Sternberg's triarchic theory of intelligence (1985).

Spearman and 'g'

Charles Spearman (1904, 1927), an English psychologist, was among those who supported the concept of intelligence as comprising a **general mental capacity**, or 'g'. He argued that some people are highly intelligent because they are 'well endowed with g' while others are less intelligent because they are 'low in g' (Howe, 1997, p. 27). However, Spearman also observed that there is often considerable variability in the way individuals perform on the different types of items used in intelligence tests (such as in naming objects, recalling strings of letters and mentally manipulating three-dimensional shapes). One person may be particularly gifted in language-related activities and poor in recalling lists of digits, while another can visualise three-dimensional shapes easily but cannot name objects quickly. Spearman explained these individual variations in terms of **specific mental abilities** ('s') that are overlaid by the general mental capacity of the individual. General intelligence, or g, reflects the speed and efficiency of the brain's processing, while s represents the specific mental abilities tapped by particular tasks.

Spearman's ideas are sometimes described as a 'two-factor theory of intelligence', the two factors comprising g, or general mental capacity; and s, or the specific mental abilities tapped by different items in an intelligence test (see Box 7.6 on page 209).

general mental capacity (g)
Basic intellectual capacity

7.2 More about Spearman's ideas

specific mental abilities (s)
A collection of distinct intellectual abilities

Thurstone and primary mental abilities

The debate about whether intelligence can be adequately explained in terms of g led to a search for alternative explanations, spearheaded by an American psychologist, L. L. Thurstone (1938). Using data similar to Spearman's, but a different method of statistical analysis, Thurstone came to the conclusion that intelligence comprises a number of distinct

7.3 Thurstone's primary mental abilities

mental faculties rather than a single *g*. Based on his analysis of results derived from a battery of tests measuring many different aspects of mental activity, Thurstone proposed a model of intelligence that involved a set of specialised intelligences or **primary mental abilities (PMA)**. By 1941, Thurstone had identified seven abilities: numerical, verbal comprehension, word fluency, space, reasoning, memory and possibly perceptual speed. Intelligence tests based on Thurstone's model provided a profile of the individual's performance on each of the seven PMAs Thurstone had identified rather than a single score as proposed by Spearman.

primary mental abilities (PMA)
The separate abilities that comprise intelligence

Guilford's structure-of-intellect model

J. P. Guilford (1967) identified a large number of distinct abilities that he conceptualised in terms of three basic dimensions:

- the processes or mental *operations* performed (that is, thinking, evaluating and recalling)
- the *content* or the kind of stimulus material that is involved (that is, words or symbols, pictures, sounds, feelings and actions)
- the form of the *products* being processed (that is, units, classes, relationships, systems and implications).

Guilford's concept of the structure of intellect is usually represented in terms of a three-dimensional model (see Figure 7.3). Each of the 120 cells in the model depicts a specific ability that can be conceptualised in terms of the three basic dimensions: operation, content and product. Much of Guilford's work was concerned with designing tasks that could be used to tap the abilities represented within each cell. He eventually completed 100 tests (Gardner & Sternberg, 1994). Guilford's model has been extensively criticised (see, for example, Brody, 1992), but it provided researchers with a comprehensive framework for conceptualising intelligence.

Guilford's structure-of-intellect model
Classification of intellectual abilities as mental operation (process), type of stimulus material (content) and form (product)

FIGURE 7.3 Guilford's structure-of-intellect model is represented in a three-dimensional cube, with each side of the cube depicting one of the three dimensions: operations, content and **products**. (Source: Guilford, 1959; reproduced in LeFrancois, 1997, Figure 7.7.)

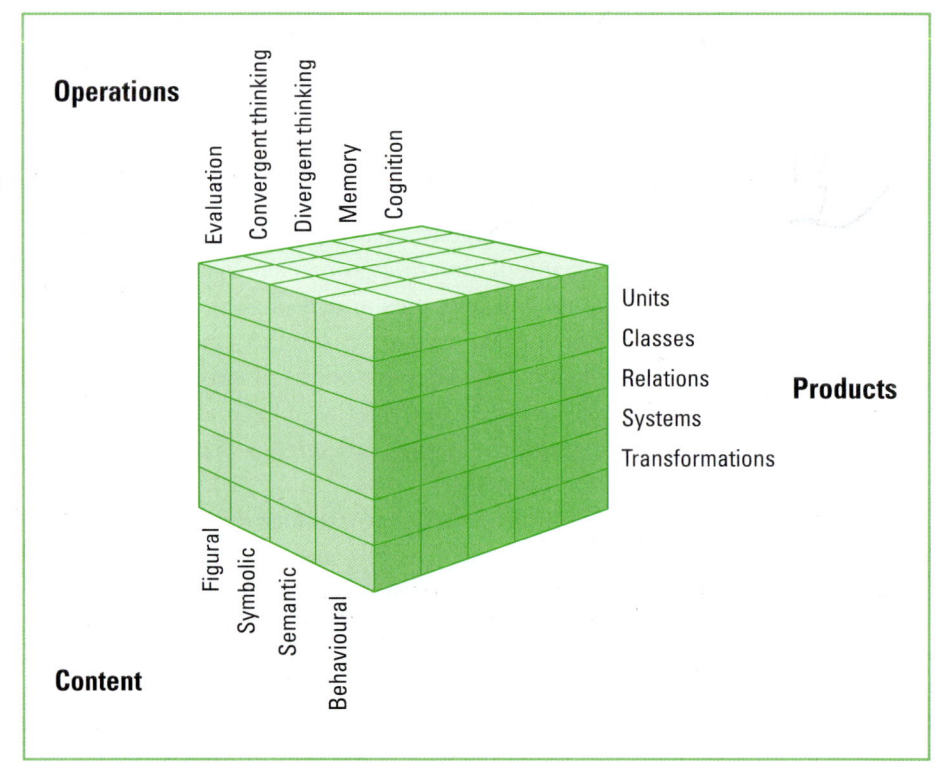

Gardner's theory of multiple intelligences

Howard Gardner's (1983) model of intelligence extended traditional ideas about intelligence to include a wider range of abilities, or **multiple intelligences (MI)**. Gardner dismissed traditional intelligence tests, arguing that they are based on a narrow view of human intelligence that is dominated by Western ideas. According to Gardner, intelligence comprises a set of separate intelligences, each of which is specialised for acquiring knowledge and solving problems in different areas of cognitive activity. He identified at least seven (later eight) domains of intellectual functioning, each of which is quite distinct, in that how we perform in one area is quite separate from how we perform in another (see Box 7.1). Interestingly, the intelligences identified by Gardner represent distinct areas within our cultural experience, and include language, music, mathematical comprehension and reasoning, spatial awareness, physical movement, and social understanding.

> **multiple intelligences (MI)**
> Seven or more domains of intellectual functioning
>
> **7.4** More about Gardner's model of intelligence

Box 7.1 RESEARCH LINKS

Gardner's theory of multiple intelligences

Gardner identified eight distinct domains, or areas, within his model of multiple intelligences, which are set out in Table 7.1 below.

TABLE 7.1 Gardner's eight domains of intelligence

Domain (area) of intelligence	Description of content	Example of occupation	Representative individuals
Linguistic	Ability to perceive or generate spoken and written language	Poet Lawyer Journalist	T. S. Eliot, Patrick White, Judith Wright, Henry Lawson
Musical	Sensitivity to pitch, rhythm and timbre; the ability to create, communicate and understand meaning in sound; the ability to discern sound patterns	Musician Music critic Auto-mechanic Cardiologist	Igor Stravinsky, Percy Grainger, Dame Kiri Te Kanawa
Logical-mathematical	Use and appreciation of numerical, causal, abstract or logical relations	Mathematician Scientist Engineer	Albert Einstein, Howard Florey, Douglas Mawson, Frank Macfarlane Burnet
Spatial	Ability to perceive visual and spatial information, and to transform or modify this information and re-create visual images	Visual artist Draftsperson Navigator	Pablo Picasso, Albert Namatjira, Frida Kahlo, Kay Cottee
Bodily-kinaesthetic	Control of all or parts of one's body to solve problems or create products	Dancer Athlete Hiker	Martha Graham, Vaslaw Nijinsky, Ian Thorpe, Cathy Freeman, Sir Edmund Hillary
Intrapersonal	Capacity to form a mental model of oneself and use the model to make informed decisions about possible actions	Psychoanalyst Psychologist	Sigmund Freud, Melanie Klein, B. F. Skinner
Interpersonal	Capacity to recognise, distinguish between and influence in desired ways others' feelings, beliefs and intentions	Religious leader Politician	Martin Luther King, Nelson Mandela, Mahatma Gandhi
Naturalist	Ability to understand and work effectively in the natural world	Biologist Zoologist Naturalist	Charles Darwin, Jane Goodall, David Attenborough

In 1999, Gardner considered the possibility of two more domains: 'spiritual intelligence' and 'existential' intelligence, but these are still under investigation, and research continues to collect data on these and other potential intelligences not yet identified.

Source: Adapted from Gardner (1993, 1999); Granott & Gardner (1994, p. 174); and Torff & Gardner (1999, pp. 143–144).

Activities

1. Can you identify a range of intelligences that you possess?
2. How did you identify your intelligences? What indicators did you look for?
3. How would you identify intelligences among the students in your class?
4. Do you notice any cultural bias in the examples of people provided in Gardner's list of intelligences? Can you substitute examples of historic or current figures from within your own country and culture?

Emotional intelligence

Following from Gardner's extended notions of intelligence, a number of writers have argued for the categorisation of 'social intelligence', or 'emotional intelligence', as a form of intelligence. According to Mayer, Caruso and Salovey (1999, p. 267) **emotional intelligence** is defined as 'an ability to recognise the meanings of emotions and their relationships, and to reason and problem-solve on the basis of them'. It involves the skills of reflectively regulating emotions, understanding emotions, assimilating emotion in thought, and perceiving and expressing emotion.

Daniel Goleman brought the concept of emotional intelligence to popular attention with the publication of a bestselling book, *Emotional Intelligence*, in 1995. In it, Goleman argued that emotional intelligence – including such skills as empathy, delayed gratification, impulse control and persistence – is at least as important in guiding behaviour as the cognitive skills tapped by traditional measures of intelligence. Further, Goleman suggested that emotional competence can be taught to children and adults. In Chapter 3 earlier, we examined the development of emotion and its importance to cognition and social interaction. The question is whether these skills constitute an 'intelligence' or something else. Research into emotional intelligence has been hampered by the lack of a clear definition of the concept and by difficulties in its measurement (Pfeiffer, 2001), but some studies have shown emotional intelligence to have positive correlations with verbal intelligence (Mayer et al., 1999), self-esteem, sociability and life satisfaction (Mayer, Salovey, & Caruso, 2000).

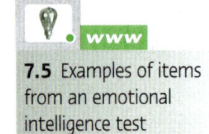

emotional intelligence
The ability to recognise and understand emotions

7.5 Examples of items from an emotional intelligence test

Sternberg's triarchic model of intelligence

One of the most prolific writers about intelligence is Robert Sternberg (1985) (see Box 7.2 opposite). Like Gardner, Sternberg rejected the traditional idea of intelligence as a relatively narrow set of abilities closely associated with academic learning. However, whereas Gardner is primarily interested in the *content* of the different intelligences he has identified (for example, linguistic, mathematical, musical and spatial), Sternberg is more interested in the *application* of these intelligences. He has argued that individuals who are more intelligent display their abilities through their ability to learn and process information very rapidly. Such people are also able to respond appropriately in novel situations and to adapt to the demands of everyday life by modifying their needs and changing their goals when necessary. Sternberg's theory is called the **triarchic model of intelligence** because he identified three key aspects of intelligent behaviour (Sternberg, 1997, p. 344), which are:

triarchic model of intelligence
Intelligence defined as thinking (analytic), responding to new experiences (creative) and coping with everyday situations (practical)

- *analytic*, or the mental aspects of an individual's cognitive activity, as in information-processing skills and metacognition (see Chapter 5). Examples include the critical dissection of ideas by a literary reviewer or mathematician.
- *creative*, or an individual's ability to respond to events in the light of previous experience. This is often evident in responses to unusual or novel situations, or in learning new skills. Examples include the accomplishments of poets, composers or engineers.
- *practical*, or how an individual copes with everyday environments, as in the adaptation of existing skills in response to the demands of particular situations. Examples include the applied skills and expertise of a computer operator, nurse or carpenter.

Box 7.2 ABOUT ROBERT STERNBERG

Robert Sternberg (1949–) was born in New Jersey, on the US east coast. He was a bright student who became interested in intelligence and intelligence testing when as a 6th-grade student he was forced to retake an intelligence test with students in the 5th grade. Sternberg recalled in 1995 that his poor results (due to nerves) on intelligence tests resulted in his teachers having low expectations about what he could achieve at school, which led to him trying to please his teachers by meeting those expectations (Miele, 1995). When he overcame his test anxiety and did well on an intelligence test, teachers' expectations for him increased and he began to do well at school. In 7th grade, he designed the Sternberg Test of Mental Ability for a science project and administered the test to his classmates along with the Stanford-Binet Intelligence Scales he had found in the local library.

Later, while at college, Sternberg had summer jobs working at the Educational Testing Service in Princeton, which produced many of the standardised tests used in schools throughout the world. He went to Yale University as an undergraduate and majored in Psychology, graduating in 1972 with a BA summa cum laude (the US equivalent to first-class honours), and gaining a PhD at Stanford University in 1975.

FIGURE 7.4 Sternberg's ideas about intelligence challenge existing ideas about the relationship between intellectual abilities, and learning and teaching.

Sternberg has been awarded many honours in the field of psychology, including the Distinguished Scientist Award for an Early Career Contribution to Psychology. His major research interests are human intelligence, human creativity, thinking styles, learning disabilities and love. He is IBM Professor of Psychology and Education in the Department of Psychology at Yale University.

If you want to know more about Robert Sternberg, look at his webpage: <www.yale.edu/pace/team members/personalpages/bob.html>.

Sternberg (1997a, p. 359) discussed how the triarchic theory might be applied in curriculum areas such as literature, mathematics, history, biology and art. He suggested that when teaching and evaluating learning, one might:

- emphasise *analytical* abilities by asking students to compare and contrast, analyse, evaluate, critique, explain why, explain what caused …, or evaluate what is assumed by …
- emphasise *creative* abilities by asking students to create, invent, design, imagine, imagine what you would do if …, show how you would …, suppose that, say what would happen if …
- emphasise *practical* abilities by asking students to apply, show how you can use …, implement, demonstrate how …

An example of the classroom application of Sternberg's ideas is set out in Box 7.3.

Box 7.3 — CLASSROOM LINKS

Applying Sternberg's triarchic theory in the classroom

Sternberg, Torff and Grigorenko (1998) described a study in which the triarchic theory of intelligence was applied in a classroom situation. The study's aim was to create links between students' specific abilities, and modes of instruction and assessment.

A social studies unit on communities was taught over 10 weeks, four days per week, 45 minutes per day, to students in nine 3rd-grade classes that each comprised 20–25 students (213 students in all). The regular teacher in each class taught the unit using an instructional method based on one of three models: *traditional*, with no change in the usual method of instruction; *critical-thinking*, with critical-thinking or analytical-thinking skills added to the usual method of instruction; and *triarchic*, with instruction based on Sternberg's triarchic model of intelligence.

It was predicted that the triarchic model would improve achievement because students would be encouraged to think, learn and remember in three different ways: analytically, creatively and practically. The triarchic model would also allow students to take advantage of their cognitive strengths and compensate their weaknesses. Assessments used in the study included tests designed to identify how much the students had learned (memory) and if they could use what they had learned (performance).

Prior to the intervention, the nine participating teachers were trained in the instructional model they were to use. For instance, all classes were taught a unit on the public service. Using the traditional model, students simply memorised the titles and functions of different public-service roles. With the critical-thinking model, students learned the titles and functions of different public service roles, comparing and contrasting these different functions. With the triarchic approach, students were able to do something like design a public-service system, describe its aims and how it operates, and compare their new model with the one operating in their local area.

Results of the assessments used in the study showed that the classes using the triarchic model achieved consistently better results than the classes using the traditional or the critical-thinking models. While differences in results may have reflected a higher level of motivation among students who used the more exciting triarchic model, Sternberg et al. concluded that the students who received instruction based on the triarchic model learned more than the students who received instruction based on either of the other two models. The students benefited from an instructional approach that provided for a broad range of student abilities, with better performance in both memory and in analytic, creative and practical skills.

Source: Adapted from Sternberg, Torff, & Grigorenko (1998).

Activity

Make a grid with columns (see below) for Sternberg's three categories: analytical, creative and practical. Identify three topics within a curriculum area familiar to you and suggest a way in which each topic could be approached using the three areas identified in Sternberg's triarchic theory.

Curriculum area:

Topic	Analytic	Creative	Practical
1			
2			
3			

Sternberg noted that most instruction and evaluation in schools is concerned with what students know. Teachers tend to focus on instructions such as: 'Who said …?', 'Summarise', 'Who did …?', 'What happened?', 'How did it happen?', 'Repeat back' and 'Describe'. In pointing out the limitations of this type of questioning, Sternberg reminded us that while what you know is important, knowing how to use what you know is even more important (Sternberg, 1997, p. 360).

Strengths and limitations of models of intelligence

Strengths

One of the main strengths of the different models of intelligence proposed by Spearman, Thurstone, Guilford, Gardner and Sternberg is that they provide us with ways of conceptualising intelligence (see, for example, Figure 7.3 on page 200). The different models also provide guidelines for collecting evidence on intelligence in activities as diverse as reasoning, problem solving, dance, music and art. They draw attention to the need for educators to cater for children's different needs and interests.

Limitations

Limitations of these models include a lack of empirical research-based evidence to support the specific abilities identified as comprising intelligence, a lack of clarity in the way these abilities are defined, and a lack of agreement about which of the different models of intelligence is the most useful for educators.

Table 7.2 summarises the models of intelligence – and their strengths and limitations – proposed by Spearman, Thurstone, Guilford, Gardner and Sternberg. Box 7.4 (see over page) briefly discusses these models' implications for classroom practice.

TABLE 7.2 Models-of-intelligence summary

Theorist	Concept of intelligence	Measurement	Strengths	Limitations
Spearman	General mental ability, or g; plus specific abilities, or s	Single intelligence score	Intelligence score a useful predictor of school performance	Doubts that intelligence is a single general mental ability
Thurstone	A set of primary mental abilities	Profile of individual performance	Test scores provide a useful profile of an individual's strengths and weaknesses	Identification of distinct abilities is simply an outcome of data-analysis method
Guilford	A structure-of-intellect model built around three dimensions: operations, content, products	Multiple tasks tap three dimensions of ability (120 cells in a 3 × 3 model, see Figure 7.3)	Useful reminder of the variety of abilities that can be conceptualised as dimensions of intelligence	Can intelligence be meaningfully represented by such an extensive list of abilities?
Gardner	A set of separate, specialised multiple intelligences	Individual tests designed to tap a specific intelligence	Helpful in drawing attention to the need to understand and nurture children's special talents	Are Gardner's intelligences just special talents?
Sternberg	A triarchic model of intelligence comprising analytic, creative and practical aspects	Specific tests designed to tap each aspect	Emphasises the practical aspects of intellectual skills and their application in everyday life	Can Sternberg's model be applied successfully to classroom practice? (See Box 7.4)

CRITICAL REFLECTIONS

- Among the different models of intelligence covered so far, which is closest to your personal concept of intelligence?
- Can you recall factors in your own life that influenced your ideas about the nature of intelligence?

Box 7.4 — IMPLICATIONS FOR EDUCATORS

Models of intelligence in the classroom

The models of intelligence discussed in this chapter visualise intelligence as a complex, multi-faceted cluster of abilities associated with every aspect of human activity, not just academic learning. This has major implications for classroom practice, and indicates that:

- school curriculums should be broadened to cover the range of activities represented in profiles of student abilities and interests
- teachers should consider matching student abilities to the forms of instruction and assessment used in the classroom, since there is evidence that such matching leads to improvements in student performance (see, for example, Sternberg, 1997; Sternberg, Torff, & Grigorenko, 1998)
- teachers need to be aware of each child's particular abilities and ensure that appropriate experiences are provided to promote each child's potential (such experiences can be derived from a particular model of intelligence or from any program that provides a varied curriculum).

Measuring intelligence

Can we measure intelligence? People generally think of intelligence as a score on an IQ test, so if you ask a person what they know about intelligence they usually tell you something about IQ scores. But what is an 'IQ score'? Such scores are no longer used very much in school systems, but they provide a valuable insight into the history and development of intelligence measurement.

At the beginning of the 20th century, as the principle of universal education became more widely accepted, it became apparent that many children of school age could not cope within the regular school system. There was something 'different' about these children when compared with their peers: intelligence tests seemed to provide a means for identifying and explaining these differences.

The Stanford-Binet test

The first effective tests of intelligence were devised by Alfred Binet (see Box 7.5) and his colleague Theodore Simon. The tests were designed to measure general mental ability, and were used to screen children in order to identify those who were thought to be capable of benefiting from school education, and those who were slow learners and needed extra help (Brody, 1992) (see also Chapter 8).

Box 7.5 — ABOUT ALFRED BINET

Alfred Binet (1857–1911) first became interested in measuring intelligence by measuring the volume of people's skulls. After collecting data on skull size from several hundred children, he found the differences in skull size were very slight, and the measurements unreliable (Gould, 1981). He subsequently abandoned 'craniology'.

After studying attention span in his two daughters, Binet began to devise a set of activities that would tap the diverse range of 'thinking' abilities that, it was hypothesised, constituted 'intelligence'. The tasks and puzzles Binet created covered everyday reasoning and comprehension problems such as counting coins, pointing to parts of the body and naming items in a picture. Learned skills, such as reading, were not included. Binet was aware that age was a major determinant of children's capacity to complete tasks, and so included in each set of tasks examples appropriate for children at different age levels. Children able to complete tasks that could be done by most children of the same chronological age were judged to have 'normal' intelligence. However, children who failed tasks that most children of their chronological age could do, or who completed more tasks than expected for their age, were judged respectively as 'backward' or 'advanced'. From these tests, Binet developed the concept of 'mental age'. The concept continues to be used, and provides a basis for the concept of 'intelligence quotient', or IQ, which was eventually defined as:

$$\frac{\text{mental age}}{\text{chronological age}} \times 100$$

Binet argued that intelligence was not wholly innate, since it was strongly affected by the individual's experiences. In developing a set of tasks to measure intelligence, he tried to devise tasks that would tap commonsense, everyday knowledge or practical understanding rather than knowledge that had been acquired through formal instruction. He was very concerned that his test might be used to rank students in terms of their 'mental worth' (Gould, 1981, p. 152). He did not want the test to be used to label particular children 'dull' or 'stupid', because he feared such labels would become self-fulfilling prophecies. In later years, Binet developed a series of exercises designed to raise the intelligence of children with intellectual disabilities.

FIGURE 7.5 Binet's interest in children, and particularly those with intellectual disabilities, led to him devising an intelligence test that became a model for subsequent tests.

Binet and Simon developed a test involving 30 items that tapped (measured) practical knowledge and skills. Test items required children to name objects in pictures, define words, repeat a set of digits, copy a simple shape, tell the time on an analogue clock, and cut a shape from a piece of folded paper and tell what the shape would be when unfolded. The test was standardised (that is, the test's norms, procedures and scoring were established) using 50 children who were judged to be of 'normal' intelligence and 45 people who were judged as having varying degrees of intellectual impairment. In 1916, Lewis Terman at Stanford University adapted and renamed Binet and Simon's test for use in the USA. The revised test came to be known as the Stanford-Binet Intelligence Scale and continues to be widely used in assessment of children (aged from 2 years) and adults.

The original meaning of **intelligence quotient (IQ)**, as developed by psychometricians such as Binet, was 'mental age divided by chronological age and multiplied by 100'. If you are 10 years of age, but perform on an intelligence test at the mental age of 12, you have an IQ of 120. This is how the original IQ score was calculated. The procedure is satisfactory when applied to children's scores (although people sometimes make the mistake of assuming that a child with an IQ of 120 will behave like a 12-year-old). However, the formula is only applicable when children's ability to answer questions on an IQ test (that is, their **mental age**) continues to increase steadily with their chronological age. The concept of mental age cannot be used to determine adults' test results because intelligence does not continue to increase during adulthood in the same way it does over the childhood years. A different method of calculating IQ is needed.

Wechsler's intelligence scales

David Wechsler (1939) found a solution to the problem of calculating adult IQs: the **deviation IQ**. He proposed that IQ should be determined in terms of the number of correct items someone scored on a test (that is, the test score) in relation to the expected average score obtained by people of the same age; that is, 'actual test score divided by expected test score and multiplied by 100'. The deviation IQ is a measure of how far a par-

7.6 More about the Binet and Stanford-Binet Intelligence Scale

intelligence quotient (IQ)
A score on an intelligence test that permits an individual's performance to be compared with the average performance on the test

mental age
The chronological age that typically corresponds with a particular performance level on an intelligence test

deviation IQ
An IQ score that compares an individual's performance on a test with the expected average performance of someone in the same age group

ticular test score is above or below the mean (or average) score of the relevant age cohort. It provides a method for rank-ordering individuals in terms of their performance on a test.

To collect the information needed to establish mean scores for different age groups, Wechsler's intelligence tests (such as the Wechsler Adult Intelligence Scale (WAIS); the Wechsler Intelligence Scale for Children – Version III (WISC-III); and the Wechsler Preschool and Primary Scale of Intelligence Third Edition (WPPSI-III)) were administered to very large samples of adults and children. These samples were carefully selected to be representative of demographic characteristics such as age, gender and social class. Age groups were subdivided into ranges of 5–10-year spans. Information derived from the representative group of adults and children (called the 'standardisation sample'), such as scores that would be expected for individuals of a certain age and gender, are provided in the test manual and are used by psychologists when interpreting individual scores.

Administering intelligence tests

Tests such as the Stanford-Binet Intelligence Scale and the WAIS, WISC-III and WPPSI-III are administered individually, in a one-to-one situation, by a trained psychologist. Other tests of intelligence, such as the Draw a Person Test (Goodenough, 1926; Naglieri, 1988) and the Peabody Picture Vocabulary Test-R (Dunn & Dunn, 1981), can be administered to children individually or in groups by an experienced teacher or other professional. Tests administered individually usually include an array of verbal tasks that involve answering questions by giving information or pointing, and performance tasks that involve sorting, matching or arranging blocks, beads or geometric shapes. Group tests are limited to 'paper and pencil' tasks. Tests administered individually are more expensive to use than group tests but have higher reliability (that is, the same response is obtained on successive occasions) and validity (that is, the tests measure what they are designed to measure). Group tests are mainly used for screening purposes, to identify exceptionally gifted students or those who may need extra help as a result of intellectual disability. See Chapter 11 for a more comprehensive discussion of tests and assessment procedures.

Interpreting IQ scores

Most intelligence tests are designed to have a mean score of 100, with a 'standard deviation' of approximately 15 or 16 (see Figure 7.6 opposite). The **frequency distribution**, or number of times each score occurs, is usually represented as a **bell-shaped curve** (or **normal distribution**). Someone's IQ score gives an indication of that individual's position, in relation to others, on a distribution of IQ scores; that is, where their score is located on the bell-shaped curve.

Notice that across the base of the normal curve in Figure 7.6 the scaling is in terms of 'standard deviation' units. The **standard deviation (SD)** is a measure of how much scores differ on average from the mean. For example, on a test with 25 questions each worth 1 point, scores from two groups of 8 students may have the same mean (10) but one set of scores might be spread out across the range of possible scores (9, 12, 10, 15, 21, 2, 7, 4), while the other set might cluster together (7, 8, 14, 10, 9, 12, 13, 7). The SD (of 6) in scores among those students in the first group is much larger than the SD (of 3) in scores among those students in the second group, reflecting greater spread or variability in the scores of the first group compared with those of the second. Intelligence tests such as the Stanford-Binet Intelligence Scales have a mean of 100; thus, two-thirds (68%) of scores obtained from the population used to standardise the tests fall between one SD below (85) and one SD above (115) that mean. Students with an IQ of 84 on a Stanford-Binet Intelligence Scale have therefore performed better on the test than almost 16% of their age group, whereas those with an IQ of 116 have performed better on the test than more than 84% of their age group.

---

frequency distribution
The number of times each score occurs in a range of possible scores

normal distribution (bell-shaped curve)
A representation of test scores, showing their natural tendency to cluster around the middle (mean) of the distribution and taper off at either side

standard deviation (SD)
A measure of how much test scores vary from the mean of the sample

FIGURE 7.6 The normal curve shows the tendency for most scores to cluster around the middle or mean test score, with smaller numbers of scores at either end of the curve. (Source: Sattler, 1988, p. 17, Figure 2-1.)

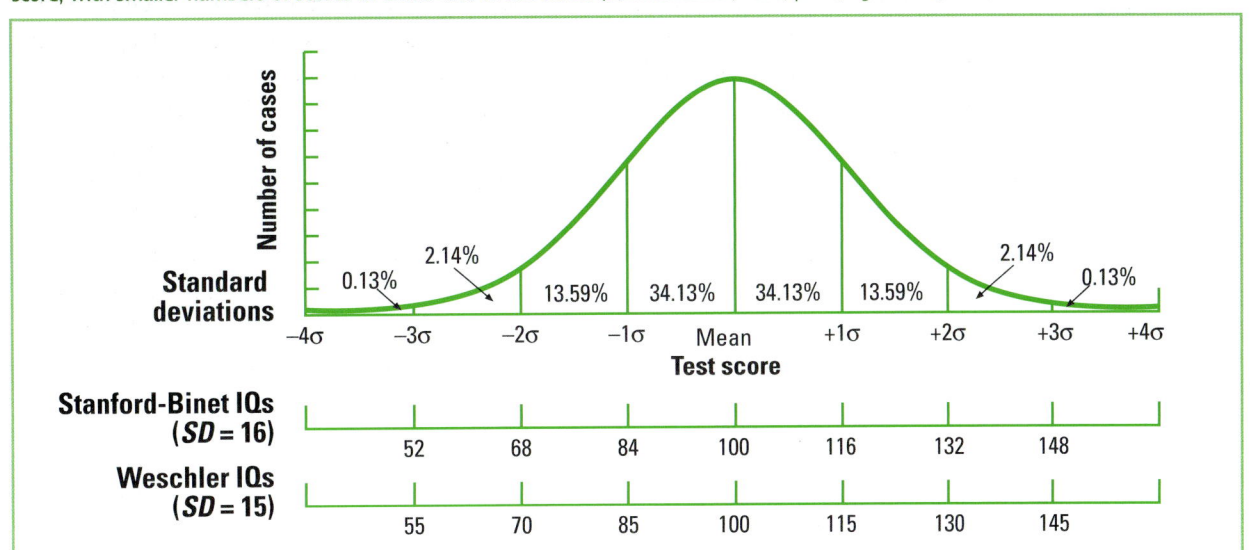

Experience in using IQ test results in schools has shown that this range (that is, one SD below and one SD above the mean) represents roughly the range of scores for children who can progress satisfactorily in the regular school system. The scores of students who are gifted and talented usually fall within the top 2% of the normal distribution curve – that is, these students have an IQ of more than 130 (Braggett, 2002, p. 292); while the scores of students with mild and moderate-to-severe intellectual disabilities typically have scores falling in the bottom 2% of the curve, in the range below 70 points (Elkins, 2002, p. 80), and these students may require a high level of additional support at school (see Chapter 8).

While many older people will remember being given a group intelligence test at school, younger people are less likely to recall such an experience. Most schools in countries like Australia and New Zealand phased out IQ tests in the early 1980s. Before that time, children were routinely tested in grades 4 and 6 (ages 9–10 and 11–12 years respectively). Since the 1980s, intelligence tests have generally been used only in special circumstances, such as for entry to a program for gifted students or for the identification of students who need some form of special help in the classroom (see Chapter 11).

Box 7.6 shows some typical items you might expect to find in an intelligence test.

Box 7.6 RESEARCH LINKS

Typical items in intelligence tests

Tests of intelligence typically include items tapping a variety of skills, including:
- *general knowledge* – 'How many days are there in a leap year?'
- *verbal knowledge* (see below) – 'Which picture shows *furniture*?' 
- *logical reasoning* – 'Three sisters were walking downstairs. Jen came downstairs first. The youngest sister followed her. Sue followed Jude. Sue is the middle sister. Who is the oldest?'
- *abstract thinking* (see below) – 'Which of these things does not belong with the others?'

- *number patterns* – 'Which is the next number? 4, 5, 7, 10, …'
- *spatial visualisation* (see below) – 'Which is a rotation of A?'

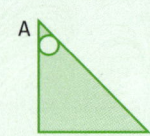

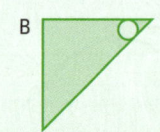

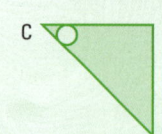

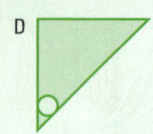

Some tests try to limit cultural bias by avoiding verbal components in visual and performance items. Items may require the individual to complete a pattern, draw a figure, put a puzzle together or sequence some pictures.

The nature–nurture debate

What is the origin of intelligence in humans? Is it a product of genetic inheritance, or is it an outcome of environmental factors such as the way parents talk to infants, the types of toys available in the home, experiences at school, or socioeconomic status? Which has primacy: 'nature' or 'nurture'? This question is often referred to as the 'hereditary versus environment' or **nature–nurture debate** (mentioned in Chapter 1). This debate over the relative influence on human development of inherited characteristics (nature) and the role of environmental factors (nurture) has a long history. Most recently, research fuelling the debate has been highly influenced by the Human Genome Project, a massive research program based in the USA (Bodmer & McKie, 1997). Researchers from all over the world are involved in this project, which has resulted in rapid increases in our understanding of genes and how they work. The goal of the project is to improve our knowledge of human genes by mapping them to DNA sequences, or the long ladder-like molecules that store genetic information in cells (Berk, 2000, p. 72). Research arising from the Human Genome Project is leading to exciting new discoveries about the relationship between heredity and intelligence. For example, it is now known that there are a number of naturally occurring genes (segments of the DNA molecules) on the X chromosome that affect lower-level cognitive skills, accounting for familial intellectual impairment and dyslexia in a small number of children (Fagerheim, Raeymaekers, Tonnesson, Pedersen, Tranebjaerg, & Lubs, 1999; Geez & Mulley, 2000).

One outcome of the human genome studies has been to provide new evidence to support the 'nature' side of the nature–nurture debate on the origins of intelligence. Following a period of growing acceptance regarding the influence of environmental factors on human development (see Chapter 8), the human genome studies' findings mean questions are again being asked about whether or not intelligence is fixed by genes, and whether intelligence is inherited. For example, is it determined by position 25 on gene x (the 'nature' position); or is it determined by how a child is raised, not just within the family, but at wider community and social level (the 'nurture' position)? Or does the answer lie somewhere between these two options? Conclusions derived from research suggest that the compromise position may be correct. You should watch for any new information reported from this rapidly developing area of research.

The heritability of intelligence

Clearly, 'the true heritability of intelligence in human populations is almost certainly above zero' (Howe, 1997, p. 122). Indeed, there is evidence that in relation to general cognitive ability, the abilities of biological parents and their children are closely linked with the degree of association, increasing steadily from early childhood, when the level of similarity is less than 20%, to as much as 40% by late adolescence (Plomin, 1999). Data reported from a Swedish twin study shows that genetic influences continue to affect cognitive ability, even into old age (Peterson, Plomin, Nesselroade, & McClearn, 1992). However, intellectual

nature–nurture debate
Controversy over the relative influence that inherent characteristics and environmental factors have on development

7.7 More about the nature-nurture debate

development is also dependent on a number of non-genetic factors. These include biological factors associated with prenatal, perinatal and postnatal events, diet (that is, inadequate nourishment, vitamin and mineral deficiencies), exposure to lead, and the occurrence of major illness or disability (see, for example, Brody, 1992; Guesry, 1998; Walker, Grantham-McGregor, Powell, & Chang, 2000). It also includes factors associated with a child's physical and social environment, such as the child's position in the family (for example, first- or second-born), size of family, and parental education, occupation and income.

Strengths and limitations of intelligence tests

Strengths

Intelligence tests are useful for identifying students who may be at risk of problems in learning as a result of impaired intellectual abilities, and for planning appropriate educational programs for such students. Intelligence tests may also be useful for identifying students who are intellectually gifted.

Limitations

Limitations to the use of intelligence tests are associated with questions concerning the reliability and validity of scores derived from group tests in particular. There is also a risk that information about individual students' performance on an intelligence test will lead to expectations about particular students' future level of achievement that have an adverse effect on achievement and self-concept.

Some issues that need to be considered by educators when using information from intelligence tests are outlined in Box 7.7.

Box 7.7 — IMPLICATIONS FOR EDUCATORS

Issues to consider when using intelligence tests scores

When considering information derived from intelligence tests, teachers need to be aware that:
- Knowledge of students' scores on an intelligence test can lead to unconscious expectations about some students' future progress.
- Scores from intelligence tests are influenced by inherited and environmental factors.
- Data derived from intelligence tests administered individually to children by trained examiners have higher levels of reliability and validity than scores from intelligence tests administered to children in groups.
- Information from intelligence tests can be useful in identifying students who may need extra help or a special program, and also students who are intellectually gifted.
- Teachers need to know how to interpret scores derived from intelligence tests.

Learners with exceptional abilities

In 2001, the youngest students taking undertaking an HSC course were a 13-year-old boy from Sydney's eastern suburbs (studying mathematics extensions 1 and 2 and School Certificate English) and a 13-year-old girl from the northern suburbs studying Japanese and Latin.

(NSW Board of Studies, 2001, p. 12)

One outcome of the focus on developing effective tools for measuring intelligence has been an interest in individuals who score at the extreme ends of the IQ distribution; that is, those who score very low on an IQ test and those who perform in the very high range. Because of the developmental and learning difficulties experienced by children who are at the very low end of the continuum, considerable attention has been paid to this group, particularly by those working in the field of special education (see Chapter 8). However, interest has also focused on children at the other end of the continuum, whose scores on tests of intelligence and ability are markedly higher than those of their peers. Such children are often labelled as 'gifted', 'talented' or 'creative'. Other terms used include 'high ability', 'genius' and 'prodigy'. However, in some contexts these children are described as 'underachievers', 'educationally disadvantaged' or 'special needs', on the grounds that schools fail to provide the programs such children need to ensure that they achieve their full potential (see Farmer, 1993). Gross (1993, p. 35) claims that 'the majority of academically gifted students underachieve significantly in the regular classroom and many are seriously de-motivated by the time they have passed through the first few years of elementary school'. So who are these children and how should they be educated?

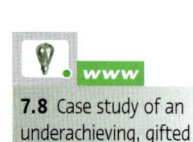

7.8 Case study of an underachieving, gifted student

Concepts of giftedness, talent and creativity

The term **gifted** has traditionally been used to refer to individuals with high general intellectual ability (Detterman, 1993). Such ability is usually considered to be innate. The concepts of **talent** and **creativity** are often viewed as subsets of 'gifted', although these words are also used separately and in combination. Examples of different usage of such terms can be seen in policy statements concerning 'gifted' students in Victoria (Department of Education, Victoria, 2001), and 'gifted and talented' students in Western Australia (Western Australian Department of Education, 2001) and in New Zealand (New Zealand Ministry of Education, 2000). Creativity is usually subsumed within policies for gifted and talented students. It is claimed (see, for example, Sternberg, 1999), that creativity is associated with (at least) 'above average' intellectual abilities as measured by conventional tests of intelligence. As might be expected, the association between creativity and intelligence is highest on tests that include a range of relatively novel items.

gifted
Exceptional general aptitude or ability

talent
Exceptional achievement in one or more areas of endeavour

creativity
Exceptional ability to produce novel or original ideas or outcomes

Apart from intellectual abilities, other influences including personal qualities (persistence, imagination) and environmental factors (such as parental attitudes, opportunities to learn and practise a particular skill) have been found to be associated with demonstrated giftedness and in particular talented and creative achievement. For example, Tannenbaum (1983; 1997) defines giftedness in terms of five interrelated factors. These include:

7.9 More about giftedness, talent and creativity

- general intelligence
- special abilities within a particular area of achievement; these may be identified during the early years or in later childhood and adolescence
- non-intellectual factors; for example, motivation, a positive self-concept, and the ability to stay 'on task' and to defer short-term rewards for long-term achievements
- environmental factors; for example, supportive and facilitative influences associated with family, peer group, school, community, and social, economic, legal and political institutions
- chance factors; for example, encounters with sympathetic teachers and role models or mentors, opportunities to learn, health status, financial situation.

Identifying gifted, talented and creative learners

Intelligence tests, such as those developed by Binet and Wechsler, have traditionally been used to identify children who are gifted; that is, those who are in the top 2% on a distribution of IQ scores (or IQ 130+) for their age group. Scores from such tests were used in longitudinal studies of giftedness (see, for example, Gottfried, Gottfried, Bathurst, & Guerin, 1994; Holahan & Sears, 1995; Hollingworth, 1926, 1942; Terman, 1925–1929; Terman & Oden, 1947) on the basis that they provided a 'reliable, valid and stable measure' of intelligence (Gottfried et al., 1994). Indeed, very high general intelligence continues to be seen as one characteristic of gifted children (Feldhusen, 2001), and tests of general ability are still used in many school systems to identify such students (Milgram, 2000; Pendarvis, Howley, & Howley, 1990).

Changes in concepts of intelligence are evident among psychologists, educators and others through the increasing level of interest in the multifaceted theories of intelligence proposed by Guilford (1967), Gardner (1983) and Sternberg (1988). For example, Meecker and Meecker (1985) developed a test based on 26 of the 120 subtests in Guilford's (1967) structure-of-intellect model. A child who scored very highly on 10 or more subtests was judged to be 'gifted' (Piirto, 1999, p. 18). Sternberg (1990) proposed five practical criteria for identifying gifted individuals, based on the kinds of (implicit) judgements that people make in everyday situations to identify outstanding abilities (see Table 7.3). These criteria could also be used as guidelines for developing educational programs for children with unusual talents.

TABLE 7.3 Sternberg's criteria for identifying giftedness

Criterion	Description
Excellence	Superiority to peers in some dimension or set of dimensions
Rarity	High level of an attribute that is rare among peers
Productivity	The dimension on which an individual is superior leads to productivity, or potential for productivity
Demonstrability	Superiority is demonstrable through valid assessments
Value	Superior performance must be in an area that is prized by the society

Source: Adapted from Sternberg (1993, pp. 6–9).

How can creativity be identified (see Figure 7.7)? According to Gardner (1993; Policastro & Gardner, 1999), creativity has three elements:

- the *creative individual*; for example, someone who has the capacity to produce and an interest in producing innovative work (such as an artist)
- the *field of endeavour*; for example, the creation of pictures and sculpture using scraps of wood or other discarded materials
- *recognition by a set of judges from that field*; for example, recognition by other artists and art critics of the quality and innovative nature of the work produced.

Without the motivation to be innovative, an artist's work is simply a demonstration of expertise; and without the judgement of experts, the work may be viewed as eccentric rather than creative (Gardner, 1993, p. 177). Other ways of identifying creative individuals include the factors identified by Guilford (1967) and Torrance (1966, 1990), which are:

FIGURE 7.7 Creativity is difficult to assess because of the subjective nature of judgements about creative work. Do you think the artwork pictured is creative? On what basis do you make your judgement?

- *fluency* – the ability to generate many ideas
- *flexibility* – being open to change, and able to change thought patterns and establish new perspectives
- *originality* – the capability to generate new or unexpected ideas
- *elaboration* – the ability to extend ideas, see details and assess consequences (Porter, 1999, p.27).

Tests such as those developed by Torrance (1966, 1990) use simple situations to explore how successfully individuals can generate unusual or interesting ideas. For example, test items might include the following:

1. Write down how many uses you can think of for a box. (uses)
2. What would the consequences be if all the clouds had strings attached to them? (consequences)

Alternatively, children could be shown a soft toy and asked what changes could be made to improve it, or given a page of circles and asked to make as many pictures as possible from the circles. Difficulties associated with the use of tests of creativity are mainly concerned with establishing criteria for scoring responses in terms of measuring the level of fluency, flexibility, originality and elaboration. Plucker and Renzulli (1999, p. 48) cite a comment by Cattell and Butcher (1968, pp. 285–286) that highlights the problems inherent in this task:

> Seldom has psychology been asked to undertake so ambitious a task as that of defining the creativity criterion. If getting a reliable criterion for 'success as a bus driver' has its difficulties, it will be evident that obtaining a criterion score on 'creativity' to check the predictive power of our tests is going to present formidable conceptual and practical problems.

Educational programs and provisions for gifted students

Selective secondary schools and special opportunity classrooms (OC) in primary schools have been a feature of the provision for gifted students in some Australian states, such as New South Wales since the 1930s (see Box 7.8). Special primary classes were also established in Tasmania and Western Australia, but were later discontinued (Senate Select Committee, 1988). Until 1988 there was little formal recognition of gifted students in New Zealand, although the New Zealand government subsequently introduced policies and programs designed to extend and challenge students who are gifted and talented (Riley, 2001, 2002).

Box 7.8 CLASSROOM LINKS

Opportunity knocks for the cream of the classroom

Julia Baird, Education writer

There was tension in the classroom as almost 11 000 Year 4 students competed yesterday for highly prized places in the opportunity classes almost guaranteed to shoehorn them into the selective school system.

S. H. Primary school pupils had mixed feelings about the test, which covered mathematics, English and general ability.

Laura M., 9, said she was so nervous her legs were shaking under the table. 'I wouldn't want to do it again,' she said.

However, she was keen to get into an opportunity class (OC) even though it means lots of work and having to be really good.

Nicole C., 9, said she tried hard because she wanted to be a doctor who cared for people and needed good marks in the HSC. She also wanted to get into a selective high school.

Claire B., who hates tests, said she did not want to get into OC because you get the same teacher for two years. 'If you get a yucky teacher you would have to stay with her for two years and that wouldn't be nice.'

Alex J. said it did not matter how he went because he wanted to go to a private boy's school.

However, he had heard the opportunity classes went to the art gallery every week.

Josef H. said the test was fun: 'My mum will like it if

I get into the opportunity class.'

There are just over 100 Year 5 opportunity classes spread across 69 NSW public schools.

However, the president of the NSW P & C Associations said she believed creaming off students to go to opportunity classes at a select group of schools was full of problems.

'It's dangerous because it steals people away from the other schools, takes them out of their peer group and says to them they are extra special. When the hormones kick in and the other kids catch up they don't feel special any more and that's really dangerous for kids.'

Source: *Sydney Morning Herald* (17 August 2001, p. 7).

Activity

Think about the advantages and disadvantages of providing separate special classes for children identified as gifted and talented:

1 Should students who score at the upper limits of intelligence tests be educated with their average-achieving peers, or should they be placed in a special class where they can receive an enriched educational program? What advantages and disadvantages do you see for the schools involved in alternative approaches?

2 How would you reply to this question if you were a parent of a very bright child? Would you respond differently if you were a teacher?

For an extensive review of OC classes and alternative programs for gifted and talented students in NSW schools, see Braggett (2002) and Farmer (1993).

In 1975, many Australian educators attended the First World Conference on Gifted Children in London, and in the next few years a number of initiatives occurred in the area of gifted education. Ministerial committees and taskforces were established to explore the specific needs of gifted and talented students. Subsequent developments have tended to focus on teacher training and on developing resources that schools can use to provide appropriate programs for students with exceptional gifts and talents. Two other influences that have affected the provision of programs for gifted and talented children are the trend towards inclusion for children with special needs in regular classrooms (see Chapter 8) and the increasing democratisation of schooling, demonstrated in the gradual replacement of selective secondary schools with comprehensive schools. Within this framework, schools rely on parents and teachers to identify students with unusual gifts and talents. This may involve identifying the special needs of a child whose development is exceptionally advanced. It may also involve teachers using norm-referenced or criterion-based tests of ability and achievement (see Chapter 11) to identify students who may benefit from some form of special provision.

Strengths and limitations of programs for gifted, talented and creative students

Strengths

Policies and programs designed to cater for students who are exceptionally gifted, talented or creative help to ensure that such students' needs are recognised and that opportunities are provided for their unusual abilities to be realised. Without such provision, there is a risk that these students will underachieve and fail to reach their full potential.

Limitations

Limitations associated with programs for students with exceptional abilities concern uncertainty about the type of programs that are most effective for students in this group. Questions that need to be asked include whether or not the regular curriculum should be enriched or whether students should be allowed to progress more quickly than usual through the regular school grades. There is also uncertainty about how special programs should be delivered. Should students with exceptional abilities be gathered into a group with a specialised program and a highly trained teacher, or should such students' needs be provided for within the regular classroom?

Box 7.9 outlines some strategies for fostering student ability in the classroom.

7.10 More about education for gifted children

Box 7.9 IMPLICATIONS FOR EDUCATORS

Strategies for fostering student ability in your classroom

It is now generally accepted that schools need to provide opportunities within the curriculum to enable the outstanding abilities and talents of a small number of students to emerge. Braggett (1998) identifies some of the strategies used by teachers to achieve this goal:

- *learning or interest centres* in early childhood and primary classrooms so children can spend time in activities associated with their particular abilities and interests
- *contracts* to allow students to work independently and at their own pace
- *use of expertise from parents and community* to provide an array of interests or specialised knowledge
- *mentor assistance* for students with highly specialised skills
- *grouping of children with similar abilities and interests* when appropriate
- *individualised programs* to encourage independent work that has a specific purpose
- *discussion and debate* of new topics, problems or challenging issues
- *open-ended activities* that require divergent thought and production
- *intellectual challenges*, which encourage students to pursue activities at a higher level of cognitive operation (see also Piaget's notion of 'cognitive challenge', discussed in Chapter 2)
- *training in study and research skills*, including library skills and independent study
- *a broad curriculum* that encourages work outside traditional subject areas.

Source: Adapted from Braggett (1998, p. 267).

Cautionary note: When teaching students who have special learning needs associated with giftedness and special talents, it is important that they be allowed (and assisted) to work more quickly or more deeply on set tasks or on activities associated with their own interests (Braggett, 2002). However, teachers need to avoid giving such students who complete set work quickly 'more of the same' or 'busy work', since this will be seen by these students as a punishment rather than a reward. Similarly, being asked to help other students, or to read while the rest of the class catches up, can become boring and a waste of time when it happens too often (Coote, 2000).

Motivation

> When I was young my main motivating thing was I had to improve, I had to do my personal best time ... when I was in primary school, probably no more than ten or eleven years old, I'd just come last in this race by ... a couple of metres and I jumped out of the pool and ran into the stand with a huge grin on my face and all I said to Mum and Dad was ... 'Is that my best time?' and that's been my philosophy, it's been what's driven me from when I was that young right up until now, it's still the standard that I use, have I done my best?
>
> (Perkins, 2002a, p. 1)

One of the great moments in Australian sporting history was the final of the 1500 metres freestyle swimming event at the 1996 Olympic Games in Atlanta. Kieren Perkins (see Figure 7.8) only just qualified for the final race and many people did not expect him to repeat his previous Olympic triumph and win a second gold medal in the 1500 metre event. Sports psychologists would say

FIGURE 7.8 Kieren Perkins is motivated by the question 'Have I done my best?'

Perkins was highly motivated to succeed in the pool. Perkins (2002b, p. 2) attributes his success in swimming to his fierce determination to better his own best time:

> I guess in the last five or six years when … I've broken world records and won Olympic Gold medals, a lot of those races … I've won by five, ten, fifteen, twenty seconds and to be in that situation you're not racing anyone but yourself and I always have raced myself, I've always wanted to get the best out of myself and do my best.

Among the many attributes that characterise individuals, the most important for learning is motivation. 'Motivation' is a term very widely used in such diverse contexts as marketing and the sporting field. At the individual or team level, it is used to explain success, or more often failure. Implicit in our society seems to be the assumption that it is difficult to do well if you are not highly motivated. But is this so, and what is motivation?

Motivation can be thought of as an internal process that activates, guides and maintains behaviour over time. Each of these components is important. 'Activation' starts you off, gets you going. 'Guidance' determines what you do, what choices you make or what interests you pursue; while 'maintenance' ensures that this activity continues over time. Note that the concept of motivation is linked closely to other constructs in education and psychology, such as the constructs of attention, needs, goals and interests (see chapters 4, 5 and 6), in that all contribute to stimulating students' interest in learning and their intention to engage in particular activities and achieve various goals. However, other ways of identifying motivation can also be found. For example, motivation can be seen as concerned with the choices you make — such as the length of time that elapses between when you decide to do an activity and when you commence it — and your intensity or level of absorption in what you are doing. Motivation is also involved in what causes you to persist with a task, or to give up, as well as influencing what you think or feel (for example, anxiety) while doing the task.

> *motivation*
> An internal process that activates, guides and maintains behaviour over time

Arousal, anxiety and motivation

Anxiety as a state (that is, feelings of tension, uneasiness and apprehension about a particular task or event) is generally thought to have a negative impact on children's motivation to learn and level of achievement. Performers such as pianists, dancers, swimmers and golfers say that some anxiety or high **arousal** (alertness) is good, provided it does not reach the level where it impedes performance (Hanton & Connaughton, 2002). Performance on any task is usually best when accompanied by a level of arousal appropriate for the activity, such as high arousal before performing or before taking a test, and lower levels for tasks such as reading for pleasure or watching television. Excessive arousal is associated with anxiety, leading to poor academic achievement, ineffective study skills, low self-esteem, general unhappiness at school and even **school phobia** (refusal to attend school) (Barrett & Turner, 2001). This effect is most evident in **test anxiety** (a fear of performing poorly in tests), which is experienced at some time by as many as 40% of children in the upper primary levels (Years 3–6) (Beidel, Turner, & Taylor-Ferreira, 1999).

> *anxiety*
> Feelings of tension, uneasiness and apprehension
>
> *arousal*
> Alertness and attentiveness
>
> *school phobia*
> Refusal to attend school
>
> *test anxiety*
> Fear of performing poorly in tests

In a school setting there are many different types of anxieties, and they can be easily related to Maslow's hierarchy of needs. For example, anxiety in students who are starting at a new school is often triggered by something unfamiliar, such as a new playground situation, a new classroom and/or large numbers of unfamiliar people. Familiarisation programs are designed to avoid this, such as when groups of students are taken to look at a new classroom complex or preschoolers are invited to visit their new school a few months before they enrol. 'Buddy' programs are also used to smooth anxieties associated with the transition from one school setting to another.

Safety needs can also cause anxiety at school, such as when one child dislikes another and bullying occurs (see Chapter 12). Self-esteem can be threatened by another student or by a teacher. Some students become very anxious about a particular subject, for example experiencing anxiety about writing or mathematics. These types of anxieties can usually be addressed by individual teachers within their classrooms or by schoolwide intervention programs. For example, Barrett and Turner (2001) reported a study where an intervention program for children who were at risk of experiencing anxiety problems at school was implemented with 6th-grade students in ten primary schools in the metropolitan Brisbane area. The schools were randomly divided into three groups. In the first group of schools, a cognitive-behavioural intervention program designed to help children cope with anxiety was implemented by a trained clinical psychologist over 10 weeks, involving one 75-minute session per week. In another third of the schools, a regular classroom teacher who had participated in a one-day training workshop implemented the same intervention program, while the remaining schools followed the usual social-studies curriculum. The intervention, called Friends for Children and based on the Coping Koala program (Barrett, Lowry-Webster, & Holmes, 1999), included instruction in topics such as relaxation, cognitive self-instruction, and family and peer support. The students' level of anxiety was assessed before and after the intervention, using a self-report questionnaire that asked about cognitive, affective and behavioural signs of depression. The questionnaire was administered by a trained psychologist who helped students read and understand the questions. Results collected at the end of the study suggested that all the students in the psychologist-led and teacher-led intervention groups showed improvements in their reported levels of anxiety, while students who did not receive the intervention showed no change in reported levels. The researchers plan to monitor the effects of the intervention over time to see if the initial improvements in anxiety levels are maintained.

It is easy to see why motivation is a huge topic of research. Everyone is motivated, unless they are 'clinically withdrawn' (that is, depressed and uninterested in any activity). It cannot be said that students are 'unmotivated'. They may be unmotivated to do what they are expected or required to do, but they will be highly motivated about other aspects of their lives, such as about being popular or doing well in sport. Motivating students to do what teachers want them to do, rather than what the students themselves want, is often a major problem in education.

Motivation in adolescence

Poor motivation is one of the chief contributors to low achievement among adolescents at secondary school, and low-achieving students at all grade levels are frequently the source of tremendous problems in classroom management. When children first begin at school, they are generally very enthusiastic to learn, and not anxious. However, there is evidence that as they progress through school, children become less interested, less intrinsically motivated and more anxious. For many students, this is a general anxiety that is demonstrated in a lack motivation for school as a whole. However, for some students, the anxiety and lack of motivation is subject-specific. The reasons for this anxiety are complex. For example, there is evidence that younger children attribute success at school to effort, believing that the harder they try, the better they will do. They even believe that working harder will increase their ability: 'Studying harder makes your brain bigger' (Harari & Covington, 1981, as cited by Covington, 1998, p. 82). However, the belief that ability can be improved by increased effort gradually changes to a belief that increased effort can compensate for low ability.

By the early years of adolescence, students begin to believe that ability is not only distinct from effort, but is also fixed (Covington, 1998). Now, motivation to work hard diminishes, since students assume that success at school is determined by ability. Effort is judged to have little impact on outcome. Achievement tends to be seen by students as the result of ability, while doing poorly is supposed to result from many causes. Uncertainty about the

FIGURE 7.9
Hands-on activities such as this construction of a lung help to maintain classroom motivation in secondary students.

causes of failure protects the failing student's self-image by putting the blame for lack of success on factors other than ability. However, a sense of the inevitability of failure can also lead to a loss of hope, to depression and to learned helplessness (Galloway et al., 1998).

In part, changes in student motivation with age can be explained in terms of the structure of school programs in the higher grades. Classroom organisation becomes increasingly formal, and there is more whole-class instruction and greater use of 'normative' forms of assessment involving comparison with the performance of others (see Chapter 11). Classes are more often 'streamed', with students grouped in terms of achievement level. Subject content becomes more abstract and there are fewer activities designed to be fun. Because adolescents are expected to be able to deal with abstract conceptual materials (see Chapter 2), there are fewer of the more enjoyable 'hands-on' activities (see Figure 7.9 above). At the same time, there is an increasing emphasis on the wide coverage of curriculum areas in preparation for final exams, which results in superficial rather than 'deep' learning.

Students are less likely to be intrinsically motivated when they lack the time and freedom to study a subject in depth (intrinsic motivation is more likely to occur in lower grade-levels, where students are not under as much pressure as those in higher grade-levels to cover a prescribed curriculum). While highly motivated students usually have both learning and performance goals, where there is a competitive exam structure performance goals will dominate. Interestingly, more general lower-level units in final competitive examinations such as the Higher School Certificate in New South Wales and the Victorian Certificate of Education are useful for poorly motivated students because such units are often more interesting than higher-level units, which are designed as preparation for further study.

Key concepts in motivation

There are several key concepts that need to be distinguished when considering motivation. The first pair of concepts is important and involves asking whether motivation is a 'trait' or a 'state'. The second pair of concepts, 'intrinsic' and 'extrinsic' motivation, is most often encountered in discussion of behavioural theories of learning (see Chapter 4). The third pair of concepts is concerned with students' orientation towards either 'performance goals' or 'mastery goals' in their learning.

Traits and states

Traits are stable, lasting dispositions that motivate us to behave in certain ways. They may be innate (for example, instinctive sex and exploratory drives) or learned (for example, the

trait
An enduring characteristic

need for achievement or power in personal relationships). Traits that are learned become part of an individual's personality and can be displayed across a range of situations. More temporary forms of motivation can be described as **state**s. They are usually short-term conditions or feelings, although they can recur and are often innate (for example, hunger and thirst). Test anxiety is learned, but is best described as a state because it is associated with specific situations.

state
A temporary condition or feeling

Extrinsic and intrinsic motivation

One of the most powerful means teachers can use to stimulate learning or encourage students to perform in a particular way is to use **extrinsic motivation**; that is, motivation arising from the use of external rewards or bribes such as food, praise, free time, money or points towards an activity (see the discussion of operant conditioning theory in Chapter 4). These incentives are all external, in that they are separate from the individual and the task. Students who are extrinsically motivated use the task as a means to get something they want (such as praise), or as a means of avoiding something unpleasant (such as punishment or a loss of privileges).

extrinsic motivation
Motivation arising from the use of external rewards such as food or praise

Intrinsic motivation refers to motivation arising from internal factors such as a child's natural feelings of curiosity, excitement, confidence and satisfaction when performing a task (for example, such as when using Paddle Pop sticks to make a model of an opening bridge or when assembling the ingredients to make and decorate a birthday cake). Here, simply undertaking the task is its own reward. Intrinsic motivation is the ultimate goal in education at every level. Students who love what they are doing and who learn for the sake of learning are said to be intrinsically motivated.

intrinsic motivation
Motivation arising from internal sources, such as an individual's feelings of curiosity, excitement and satisfaction

Performance goals and mastery goals

The term 'goal orientation' identifies a critical factor that can have an impact on students' learning. It refers to the reasons that motivate individuals to engage in particular activities. In thinking about students' goals within a classroom situation, a distinction is often made between 'performance goals' and 'mastery goals' (sometimes called 'learning goals' or 'task goals'). Students motivated by **performance goal**s – that is, students whose personal objective is to perform well in an area – are more interested in doing better than others, in winning approval and in avoiding negative feedback about their achievement. Students motivated by **mastery goal**s – that is, students whose personal objective is to achieve mastery or control of a task or skill – are concerned with increasing their competence and expertise. Performance-oriented students tend to be more self-oriented, whereas mastery-oriented students are task-oriented (Butler, 1995; Stipek, 1998). Goal orientation is not necessarily fixed across situations, however, since mastery goals may dominate during the acquisition of a new skill, while performance goals become important for maintaining interest once the basic skill is acquired (Zimmerman & Kitsantas, 1999).

performance goal
A personal objective to perform well in an area of achievement

mastery goal
A personal objective to achieve mastery of a task or skill

7.11 About performance and mastery goals

Research into the impact of goal orientation on student achievement suggests that links can be seen between students' motivation in learning situations and how they interpret the outcomes of their efforts. For example, students oriented towards mastery goals will persist when they encounter problems, assessing their competence in terms of the amount of effort invested and the level of mastery achieved (Stipek, 1998). When those who are interested in performance goals encounter obstructions, they will persist if they are extremely confident about their abilities. Examples of such performance-oriented motivation can be found among athletes striving to reach Olympic standards. But students who are oriented towards performance goals will become discouraged if their confidence in their own abilities is low, leading in extreme cases to **learned helplessness** (Dweck, 1986), or an expectation of failure. There is also some evidence that performance-oriented students tend to believe ability is fixed and cannot be altered, whereas mastery-oriented students believe ability is a

learned helplessness
An expectation, based on previous experience, that learning efforts will lead to failure

function of effort and can be changed. It is useful to remember that there are often other goals, apart from performance and mastery, that influence student behaviour. For example, both inside and outside the classroom, goals associated with children's social activities – sometimes referred to as 'social responsibility goals' or 'social approval goals' – can also have a powerful influence on achievement (Wentzel, 1996).

Strengths and limitations of motivational factors in the classroom

Strengths

Research into motivation and its impact on behaviour has made a valuable contribution to education by highlighting the importance of motivation in the learning process and also the different ways in which students' motivation can affect their achievement. The issue for educators is to ensure that students are motivated to do what is required of them.

Limitations

Limitations are associated with recognising the motives that underlie student behaviour, understanding the changes that occur in children's motivation as they mature, and minimising the impact of factors (such as anxiety) that can have a negative impact on students' motivation to learn and their achievement of educationally appropriate goals.

Box 7.10 outlines the impact of motivational factors in the classroom.

Box 7.10 IMPLICATIONS FOR EDUCATORS

Understanding the impact of motivational factors in the classroom

Research into the impact of motivational factors on learning suggests that educators should be aware of the following implications:

- A moderate level of anxiety and some level of arousal can have a positive effect on student motivation and achievement, but a high level of anxiety or extreme arousal has a negative effect on students' progress at school.
- Students' anxiety concerning their personal safety and aspects of the classroom program can be addressed through intervention programs. Their anxiety regarding a new program or attending a new school can be minimised through familiarisation programs.
- Adolescent students' motivation may be compromised in the higher school levels by the pressure to perform well academically, by more formalised and less enjoyable learning activities, and by a common belief that ability is fixed and that extra effort will not compensate for low ability.
- Problems in classroom management at the secondary level may relate to poor student motivation.
- While external rewards can be useful in motivating students, intrinsic motivation – which can arise from engaging students' natural feelings and interests – is the ultimate goal of education. Students who are intrinsically motivated enjoy learning for its own sake, so instruction should aim to arouse students' interest and stimulate their curiosity.
- Mastery goals are useful when a new skill is being acquired. Students who are motivated by mastery goals or a personal objective to achieve expertise in a task or skill tend to be concerned with increasing their level of competence and doing well in an area of achievement.
- Performance goals are useful for maintaining student interest once basic competency in an activity has been acquired. Students motivated by performance goals tend to be self-oriented and interested in doing better than others. Continual failure to achieve performance-oriented goals can lead to loss of confidence and, in extreme cases, learned helplessness.
- Student anxiety about success or failure can be avoided by motivating students with mastery goals rather than performance goals.
- Students' behaviour may be influenced by goals associated with their social activities, which can have a powerful influence – both positive and negative – on learning.

CRITICAL REFLECTIONS

- Before reading further, review the key concepts in motivation discussed earlier and consider how these apply to you.
- In the course you are studying at the moment, are you primarily intrinsically or extrinsically motivated, or a combination of both? Discuss this with a tutorial/study group member.
- Can you identify if and how your motivation changes over time in a given subject or unit of study? What factors have made a difference to your motivation to read, study and attend or listen to lectures in the past few weeks? Are these internal or external factors? What strategies do you use when you feel unmotivated to study?
- Would you say you are primarily motivated by performance or mastery goals in your study? Do these goals vary across subjects or tasks? Discuss this in your group.

Theories of motivation

Some students are highly motivated to learn, and this interest continues throughout their years at school. Others, particularly adolescents, see what happens at school as having no functional relevance to their lives. They become increasingly bored, particularly with academic tasks, and are generally uninterested in anything that happens in the classroom. Teachers recognise that there is tremendous variation in the level of energy and interest students bring to classroom activities. Some students are easy to teach because they are excited about learning and responsive to the teacher's ideas. Others are completely unmotivated by what happens in the classroom and have no interest in schoolwork.

Early explanations of motivation focused on instincts or innate patterns of activity (see, for example, James, 1890; McDougall, 1923). However, there were problems in explaining the relationship between instincts and learning. (This raises some of the issues associated with the nature–nurture debate, discussed earlier in this chapter, and the question 'Is motivation the product of instinct or is it learned?') Freud (1933/1966) suggested that motivation is a form of 'psychic energy', or psychological pressure. In Freud's model, where needs are not satisfied, psychic energy is repressed and the energy is expressed in other, sometimes unexpected, ways. Such explanations offer little for educators, since by emphasising the role of inner, often unconscious forces in motivation, they make no provision for other factors' contribution to student learning, both internal (such as needs, goals and expectations) and external (such as rewards) (Pintrich & Schunk, 1996).

Teachers explain the differing motivational levels among their students in ways that reflect their own personal philosophy of learning and teaching. Some focus on the place of rewards and punishment in motivating students to learn. Others are more concerned with students' expectations of success, or the way in which they attribute failure (is it one's own fault or someone else's?). Factors that can also influence students' motivation to learn include their observation of peers achieving success or failure, their ability to regulate their own behaviour (for example, finish homework on time, or follow instructions in class) and their need for personal fulfilment.

7.12 More about theories of motivation

Behavioural explanations

According to the behaviourist view of learning, when children are rewarded with praise and a gold star for doing their sums correctly, they look forward to the next mathematics lesson, anticipating further rewards. When Pavlov taught his dog to salivate to the sound of a bell (see Chapter 4), he was motivating the dog by associating a pleasant event (eating) with the bell ringing. Associations such as these are present whenever students anticipate some form of positive feedback or reward as an outcome of learning. At some time in the past, they must have been rewarded for similar achievements and this experience acts as a motivator for future learning of a similar type. For behaviourists, motivation is simply the product of effective contingent reinforcement, so behaviourists emphasise the use of extrinsic reinforcement to stimulate students' task engagement. Past experience of such reinforcement motivates students to further engagement in such tasks. Reinforcement can take the form of praise, a smile, an early mark or loss of privileges such as missing out on sport. Almost all teachers use extrinsic reinforcement in some form to motivate students, although they may not realise they are doing so and may not always use such reinforcement effectively (Brody, 1992).

Cognitive explanations

Cognitive explanations of motivation generally accept that children are innately active learners, so there is little need to focus on the place of motivation in the classroom (Pintrich & Schunk, 1996). However, studies of children who are experiencing problems in learning (see, for example, Galloway, Rogers, Armstrong, & Leo, 1998) have led some researchers to explore the impact that personal characteristics such as expectations of success or failure have on achievement. McClelland, Atkinson, Clark and Lowell (1953) used the term 'achievement motivation' to refer to this process. Others, such as Weiner (1992) were more interested in the way in which people attribute their success and failure to specific factors, such as the effort they put into exam preparation, or the lucky shirt they wore to the exam.

Atkinson and achievement motivation

John Atkinson and David McClelland described the need for achievement, or **achievement motivation**, as a stable personality characteristic that drives some individuals to strive for success (McClelland et al., 1953). Students who have a high need for achievement are motivated to become involved in an activity if they believe they will be successful. They are moderate risk-takers and tend to be attracted to tasks where the chances of success are fifty-fifty, since there is a good chance they will be successful. They like to attempt a task, but not if they know there is a substantial risk of failure. Such students tend to hold mastery or learning goals and are motivated to learn.

On the other hand, students who have a need to avoid failure, rather than a need to achieve success, will look for tasks that are either very easy and have little risk of failure, or very difficult so that failure is not their fault (Atkinson, 1964). The students who cannot risk failure will avoid an activity over which their anxiety about failure is greater than their need for success.

The important point here is to recognise that students do not always try to be successful. For some students, and in some situations, the risk of attempting a difficult task can be too great as a result of an overwhelming need to avoid failure (Biggs & Moore, 1993; Galloway et al., 1998).

achievement motivation
The need to strive for success

7.13 Strategies for developing achievement motivation

Weiner and attribution theory

What happens when students in the high- and low-achieving groups experience success and failure? How do they explain these different outcomes? Students who have a high need to achieve tend to attribute their success or failure to their own internal factors such as ability, hard work (in the case of success) or inadequate preparation and lack of effort (in the case of failure). Students who are low achievers and need to avoid failure are likely to attribute their success or failure to factors external to themselves, such as 'good luck' (in the case of success), or a 'very difficult exam paper' (in the case of failure). Attribution theory provides a framework for explaining these different responses.

attribution theories
Theories concerned with the way in which an individual's explanations of success and failure influence subsequent motivation and behaviour

locus of control
A tendency to attribute success or failure to internal (controllable) or external (uncontrollable) factors

Explanations of motivation based on **attribution theories** are concerned with the way in which an individual's explanations of success and failure influence that individual's subsequent motivation and behaviour. Learners may attribute success or failure to different causes, depending on their beliefs about who or what 'controls' their success and failure. There are three important elements to note regarding the way in which students interpret the causes of behavioural outcomes. First, the factors to which a learner attributes success or failure may be internal or external to the learner. When learners consistently attribute success or failure to internal factors such as their own ability or effort, they are said to have an 'internal' **locus of control**. Those with an 'external' orientation (or 'external' locus of control), however, are more likely to attribute success or failure to external causes such as luck, task difficulty, a noisy classroom or perhaps poor teaching. Second, the causal factors that learners believe contribute to success or failure may be stable (such as aptitude) or unstable (such as mood). The third element concerns the controllability of the influence of these two factors on performance. This might involve the amount of effort expended on a task (controllable), and content, degree of difficulty and time of day of an examination (uncontrollable) (Weiner, 1992). Research indicates that students who are internally oriented tend to be more achievement oriented and drive towards mastery of their learning tasks (Hill & Huntley, 1998). These students are also more likely than externally oriented students to be viewed positively by their teachers (Schraw & Aplin, 1998). Classroom studies have demonstrated that teachers' expectations can, in turn, have a profound effect on student behaviour, as demonstrated in classroom studies of self-fulfilling prophecies (Wigfield & Harold, 1992) (see also Box 7.11).

Box 7.11 RESEARCH LINKS

Pygmalion in the classroom

A now-famous study (*Pygmalion in the Classroom*, Rosenthal & Jacobson, 1968) demonstrated the effects of teacher expectations on children's performance. In this study, researchers gave students in grades 1 to 6 a non-verbal test of intelligence. Teachers were then informed that the test results showed that some of the students had shown considerable potential for development in the coming year. Researchers randomly selected 20% of the students and gave their names to the teachers, indicating that these were the children who were expected to 'bloom' intellectually during the year. When the students were retested at the end of the school year, results showed that there were significant differences between the IQ scores of the 'bloomers' and those of the other children.

Rosenthal and Jacobson concluded from the results of their study that teachers' expectations are effectively self-fulfilling prophecies, because student achievement begins to reflect such expectations. However, there were many criticisms of these findings, particularly in relation to concerns about the methodology of the study (see, for example, Snow, 1995; Weinberg, 1989). For example, the differences in achievement observed were most marked among the children in grades 1 and 2, although students from grades 3 to 6 had also participated in the study. In addition, the gains that were reported primarily involved just five children whose scores changed dramatically, while differences observed between other children were quite small.

Subsequent attempts to replicate the study's findings have generally not succeeded (Cooper & Good, 1983). The original findings have been explained, in part, in terms of the close relationship that often exists between teacher and students in the early school years. This level of personal contact usually diminishes as children move into higher grades. It is also possible that any effects from teacher expectations are more likely to become evident in scores on curriculum-related areas of learning, such as reading and mathematics, than in more indirect measures such as the non-verbal test of intelligence used in Rosenthal and Jacobson's study.

There is evidence that teacher expectations are influenced by the information available to them about their students, including IQ scores, gender, ethnicity, physical characteristics, socioeconomic background, previous academic history, performance of siblings and behaviour of the student (Good & Brophy, 1997; Pintrick & Schunk, 1996). In general, teachers are likely to dismiss information that is not consistent with their own observation.

A key feature of the attribution model is its recognition of both cognitive and emotional influences on motivation (see Chapter 3 for more information regarding the connections between cognitive and emotional development). In particular, the attribution model links the impact of emotions with internal perceptions of causality, such as when students feel pride when they think a success is due to their own efforts. Bernard Weiner (1992) showed that students are most likely to feel satisfied when they reach goals they have set themselves, rather than when they reach goals set by others. Aspirations tend to be based on prior experiences, with people who have previously been successful having higher expectations, as well as trying harder and working longer, than those who have previously experienced failure.

There is variation among groups in typical patterns of attribution, reflecting the contributions of culture and feedback from others in the formation of a particular orientation. For example, females are more likely than males to attribute failure to ability, and success to luck (see Chapter 9). In a study that compared Chinese and Japanese students with American students, Stevenson and Lee (1990) found that the Americans were more likely to attribute academic success to ability, while the Chinese and Japanese tended to emphasise effort as a cause of success.

There is some evidence that students' attributions, particularly when they are maladaptive and negative, can be modified (see, for example, Borkowski, Weyhing, & Carr, 1988; Foersterling, 1985), but these methods have been used primarily in settings that involve students with special needs, and particularly in situations involving learned helplessness. There is also evidence that the use of learning or mastery goals, focusing on students' increasing competence and achieving mastery of a topic, are more effective in terms of motivation than are self- and success-oriented performance goals. This effect is attributed in part to the disruptive effect of the anxiety associated with striving to achieve success and avoid failure (Helmke, 1988). However, there is also evidence of positive links between performance goals and students' interest and achievement in a learning area (Tauer & Harachiewicz, 1999). Performance-related goals lead students to strive to achieve competence, and this can in turn lead to increased interest and involvement in the task, thus enhancing intrinsic motivation.

Social learning theory explanations

For social learning theorists such as Bandura (1986, see Chapter 4 for more on social learning theory), motivation is conceived as goal-directed behaviour that is closely linked to feelings of personal effectiveness. Those who often experience success are more likely to positively value their own competence than those who regularly experience failure. However, this relationship does not always occur, since individuals sometimes attribute success to forces that are out of their control (such as good luck or chance), while failure is explained by bad luck rather than personal inadequacies. Another influence on self-evaluation, particularly for children, involves observation of others, particularly peers, and comparison with their achievements. Such comparison occurs frequently in competitive school situations.

Persuasion can also influence self-evaluation ('You can do it!'), as can high arousal in a challenging or frightening situation. Pintrich and Schunk (1996, p. 156) cited the example of a 5-year-old boy who saved a 6-year-old girl from choking by applying a life-saving technique he had seen performed on television. The boy had never previously practised the technique but was motivated to try it because of the danger of the situation, and because he had previously observed it to be effective in a similar situation. So for social learning theorists, motivation contributes to behaviour through the influence of judgements about personal efficacy (see Chapter 3 for more on self-efficacy).

7.14 More about social learning theory

Humanist explanations

The humanist theory of motivation is interesting because it is not only linked to achievement and education, but also has implications for students' welfare and wellbeing through its concern with basic needs. Maslow (1954) perceived motivation in terms of a hierarchy of needs (see Chapter 6) that can also be conceived as 'motives'. According to Maslow's model, once basic physiological needs have been satisfied, efforts are directed towards achieving needs associated with safety, love and belonging, and then self-esteem (see Figure 6.3 on page 174). As discussed in Chapter 6, Maslow called these deficit needs (or D-needs) and claimed that the challenges arising from them led to healthy self-esteem and motivation to further achievement and self-actualisation. Since, for most people, the latter state is never reached, motivation to achieve the fullest development of talents and capacities is never satisfied, continuing with an increasing level of intensity throughout life.

Carl Rogers's ideas (see Chapter 6) were also influential in discussions about the nature of motivation and its impact on human lives. As did Bandura, Rogers argued that behaviour was influenced by the individual's *perception* of both personal and environmental factors. Rogers argued that people should listen to their 'inner voices', or innate capacity to judge what was good for themselves, rather than relying on feedback from external sources.

Strengths and limitations of motivation theories

Strengths

Motivational theories highlight the positive impact of motivation on students' achievement, self-confidence and independence as learners. Such theories also draw attention to the need for educators to recognise the range of student needs, including those associated with physical and personal well-being, with students' attributions of personal success and failure, and with students' perception of the links between effort and success.

Limitations

Some aspects of motivational theories may have a limiting impact on learners. These include the encouragement of surface rather than deep learning, the provision of extrinsic rather than intrinsic rewards, and a resultant fear of failure in some students that may lead to them avoiding difficult or challenging tasks. Other limitations are associated with a lack of clarity in concepts such as 'self-actualisation', and a lack of research to support the efficacy of some approaches.

Table 7.4 summarises the different theoretical approaches to motivation discussed in this section, while Box 7.12 opposite looks at their application in the classroom.

TABLE 7.4	Theories of motivation			
Theories	**Behavioural**	**Cognitive**	**Social learning**	**Humanist**
Key theorists	Skinner	Atkinson and Weiner	Bandura	Maslow
Major focus	Achievement of 'on task' or desired behaviour through external rewards and reinforcement	Cognitive processes and emotions, achievement needs, and beliefs about causes of success and failure	Learning through observation of others, and self-regulation (self-talk) leading to personal standards and a sense of self-efficacy	Satisfying basic needs and achieving self-actualisation
Classroom applications	Use of contingent rewards and punishment	Need for teachers to be aware of their own and students' attributions for success or failure, and provide accurate/credible feedback	Need to ensure students are successful in new learning and that they perceive links between effort and success	Need to be aware of students' needs inside and outside the classroom, and to have positive expectations for each student

Theories	Behavioural	Cognitive	Social learning	Humanist
Strengths	Can have positive impact on motivation	Focuses on individual's interpretation of learning situations and on perception of own ability as a cause of learning	Increases independence and self-confidence	Identifies hierarchy of human needs that influence behaviour; school programs (e.g. nutrition and health) are designed to satisfy deficiency needs
Weaknesses	Can encourage surface learning for extrinsic rewards	Can lead to avoidance of challenging tasks through fear of failure	May be time-consuming for teachers to implement, particularly in regular classroom settings; evidence of efficacy needed	Concept like self-actualisation is difficult to define; problems in using needs to explain behaviour; research evidence lacking

Box 7.12 IMPLICATIONS FOR EDUCATORS

Motivation in the classroom

Behavioural approaches

To apply behavioural approaches to motivation in classroom settings, teachers need to:
- contingently reinforce students' achievements to ensure that desired behaviour is repeated
- remember that reinforcement to increase desired behaviour motivates further learning of this type
- recognise that student motivation is shaped by previous reinforcing experiences
- know that students' maladaptive attribution of success and failure, including learned helplessness, can be modified

Cognitive approaches

Implications of the cognitive view of motivation concern the need for teachers to:
- understand the underlying factors in students' behaviour, studying students carefully and using a variety of information sources to discover why students behave as they do
- accept that students are not always motivated to be successful, and that the risk of attempting to succeed may be overwhelmed by the need to avoid failure
- realise that motivating students by focusing on increasing mastery is more effective than emphasising performance goals
- be aware of their own biases and how these might affect the way they attribute success and failure in individual students
- recognise that feedback given to students can have a significant impact on the ways students attribute their performance on a learning task.

Social learning approaches

The social learning approach suggests that teachers need to:
- ensure that learners experience success, not just failure
- remember that self-evaluation is influenced by observing others' achievements, and by persuasion and high arousal in challenging situations
- recognise that motivation is affected by learners' judgements about their own efficacy.

Humanist approaches

To apply humanist ideas in classrooms, teachers need to:
- become more concerned with the wider implications of student welfare, not just with students' education
- be aware that some students are more concerned with feelings of safety, belonging and self-esteem than with the demands of the school curriculum
- understand that students who feel a strong need for group belonging will experience difficulties and lack motivation to learn if a teacher acts in ways that conflict with group mores
- recognise that students with low self-esteem will not be motivated to strive for higher levels of achievement (see Chapter 3)
- acknowledge that their own beliefs and values can have a major impact on student motivation
- know that teachers are more likely to have positive expectations about their students where there are clear learning goals, an emphasis on personal and social relationships, and a shared ethos among staff that is set out in a mission statement for the whole school.

7.15 About classroom climate and student behaviour

Concluding comments

The topics covered in this chapter – intelligence and motivation – represent critical elements in the learning–teaching process. Both elements have a powerful effect on children's progress at school and on their experiences in adult life. Intelligence provides potential for learning that can be realised if appropriate opportunities are provided within educational programs. Motivation provides an energy that can direct learners' interests into educationally valued activities. Educators' task is to motivate learners to realise their potential by engaging them in intellectually challenging learning experiences. Educators must also provide the necessary support and stimulation to ensure that unusual or exceptional gifts and talents are realised and expressed and that students' motivation to achieve is maintained and enhanced. Failure to achieve these goals leaves the whole community poorer.

Chapter review

- Intelligence is described as a complex, multifaceted cluster of abilities that have a major impact on all aspects of human activity, but particularly on learning at school.
- Early models of intelligence include Spearman's general mental capacity ('g') plus specific mental abilities ('s') and Thurstone's seven primary mental abilities, while later models include Guilford's structure-of-intellect model, Gardner's multiple intelligences and Sternberg's triarchic model.
- Teaching programs based on Guilford's, Gardner's and Sternberg's models of intelligence need to provide a range of academic and non-academic experiences.
- Tests and other assessment procedures designed to measure intelligence need to reflect diverse areas.
- There is debate about the extent to which intellectual abilities are the product of inherited characteristics or environmental influences.
- Giftedness is seen as a potential for exceptional development and achievement, and is considered to be innate in some children.
- Talent and creativity involve high levels of achievement in areas that are culturally valued, and are a product of personal and environmental factors. Their realisation is associated with strong motivation to excel, as well as mastery of relevant knowledge and skills.
- Motivation is an internal process that activates, guides and maintains behaviour over time. It can take the form of a state or trait, and can be stimulated externally or internally.
- Poor motivation frequently leads to low achievement at school and, for teachers, problems in classroom management. Learned helplessness occurs when students come to believe they will fail no matter how hard they try.

You make the connections:

Questions and activities for self-assessment and discussion

1. List some of the characteristics that are usually included in Western definitions of intelligence. Give an example of characteristics that might be used in a non-Western definition.
2. Ask some of your friends and family to give the meaning of 'intelligence', then ask them to describe some examples of intelligent behaviour. Try to get people of different ages and with different interests. Can you explain similarities and differences in their responses?
3. What is the nature–nurture debate? What answers are currently being proposed? Give some examples of research.
4. How can gifted, talented and creative children be identified? What types of programs can help children's special abilities emerge?
5. Within your own personal philosophy of teaching, what is your view of giftedness, talent and creativity? Do you think that children who have outstanding or unusual

abilities should be identified and provided with special programs? How would you provide for such children in your classroom?

6 Comment on how the key concepts relating to motivation in this chapter might influence your practice as a teacher.

Key terms

intelligence
general mental capacity (g)
specific mental abilities (s)
primary mental abilities (PMA)
Guilford's structure-of-intellect model
multiple intelligences (MI)
emotional intelligence
triarchic model of intelligence
intelligence quotient (IQ)
mental age
deviation IQ

frequency distribution
normal distribution (bell-shaped curve)
standard deviation (SD)
nature–nurture debate
gifted
talent
creativity
motivation
anxiety
arousal
school phobia

text anxiety
trait
state
extrinsic motivation
intrinsic motivation
performance goal
mastery goal
learned helplessness
achievement motivation
attribution theories
locus of control

Recommended reading

Anderson, M. (1992). *Intelligence and development: A cognitive theory*. Oxford: Blackwell.
Braggett, E. J. (2002). Gifted and talented children and their education. In A. Ashman & J. Elkins (Eds.) *Educating children with diverse abilities*, Chapter 7. Sydney: Prentice-Hall.
Farmer, D. (Ed.). *Gifted children need help? A guide for parents and teachers*. Strathfield, NSW: NSW Association for Gifted and Talented Children.
Gross, M. U. M. (1993). *Exceptionally gifted children*. London: Routledge.
Howe, M. J. A. (1997). *IQ in question: The truth about intelligence*. London: Sage.
Mackintosh, N. J. (1998). *IQ and human intelligence*. Oxford: Oxford University Press.
Piirto, J. (1999). *Talented children and adults: Their development and education* (2nd ed.). Columbus, OH: Merrill.
Pintrich, P. R., & Schunk, D. H. (1996). *Motivation in Education: Theory, research and applications*. Englewood Cliffs, NJ: Prentice-Hall.
Porter, L. (1999). *Gifted young children: A guide for teachers and parents*. St Leonards, NSW: Allen & Unwin.
Sternberg, R. J. (1990). *Metaphors of mind: Conceptions of the nature of intelligence*. Cambridge: Cambridge University Press.
Stipek, D. (1998). *Motivation to learn* (3rd ed.). London: Allyn & Bacon.

Make some online visits

More about intelligence testing: <www.indiana.edu/~intell/index.html>
Resources for teaching students who are gifted and talented: <www.nswagtc.org.au/info/articles> and <www.sofweb.vic.edu.au/futures/bfpolicy.htm>
New Zealand Ministry of Education Online Learning Centre: <www.tki.org.nz>

FIGURE 8.1 Chapter 8 concept map.

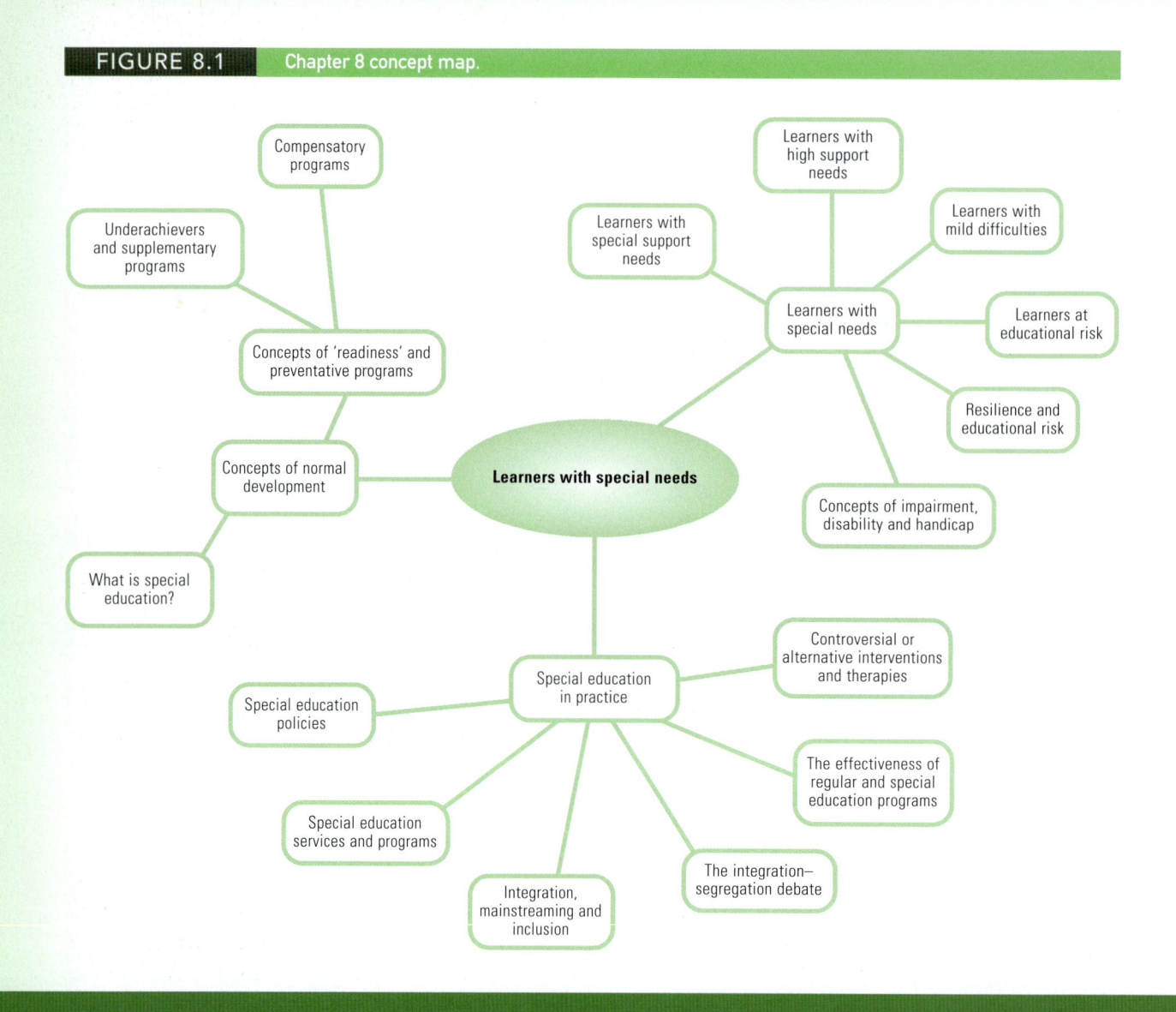

Learners with special needs

- Compensatory programs
- Underachievers and supplementary programs
- Concepts of 'readiness' and preventative programs
- Concepts of normal development
- What is special education?
- Learners with special support needs
  - Learners with high support needs
  - Learners with mild difficulties
  - Learners at educational risk
  - Resilience and educational risk
  - Concepts of impairment, disability and handicap
- Special education in practice
  - Controversial or alternative interventions and therapies
  - The effectiveness of regular and special education programs
  - The integration–segregation debate
  - Integration, mainstreaming and inclusion
  - Special education services and programs
  - Special education policies

CHAPTER OBJECTIVES

After reading this chapter you should be able to:

- define the term 'special education'
- identify the main purpose of compensatory programs for children at educational risk
- distinguish between educational risk, vulnerability and resilience in children
- comment on the impact of a non-categorical view of disability on the programs and services provided for children with special support needs
- describe the main aspects of a continuum of special education services and outline an alternative model for educating children with special learning needs
- critically evaluate the main arguments used to support the full inclusion of children with disabilities and special support needs.

CHAPTER 8

Learners with special needs

Introduction

Think back to when you were at school. Remember one of the classes you were in. Who was in that class? Were some of the students very bright? Were some of the students slower than the rest, struggling all the time to keep up with everyone else? Were you aware of other children the same age as you who went to another school that catered for children who were profoundly deaf, or could not walk without help, or had Down syndrome? Were there any children with problems like that in your class? This chapter is about the large numbers of children who are 'at risk' at school as a result of a range of problems that include disability and difficulties in learning.

special education
The system of programs and services provided in most education systems for children who have difficulties learning within the regular classroom context

What is special education?

In every group of children who turn five in a given year, there will be a small number who, as a result of some form of disability or delay in their development, will not enter the regular first class at school with their peers. And if they do start off in a regular classroom, many will encounter problems in an aspect of learning that leads to them being provided with some form of extra assistance or being placed in a special program. The term **special education** is used to refer to the system of programs and services provided in most education systems for children who have difficulties learning within the context of a regular classroom. Such children need specialised help or extra resources in order to progress satisfactorily at school. They are sometimes described as 'exceptional'. They are also described as having 'special needs'.

Concepts of normal development

In the early part of the 20th century, large-scale studies of children's development were carried out for the purpose of documenting the average chronological age at which different cognitive, social, motor and language milestones were reached. Charles Darwin (1877) had contributed to the beginnings of this process by keeping a diary of the first 3 years of his infant son's life. Alfred Binet (see Chapter 7) also had this research focus when he worked with Theodore Simon to develop a test of children's intelligence. G. Stanley Hall (1904) and his student, Arnold Gesell (Gesell & Ilg, 1943), continued the tradition of large-scale studies of children's development by refining the methods used to collect data on changes in the early-childhood development period (birth to 5 years). Their normative approach to information gathering, involving very large numbers of children, enabled them to identify both a predictable sequence and a timetable for achievements such as 'first steps' and 'first words'. More recently, books like *Dr Spock's Baby and Child Care* (Spock & Rothenberg, 1985) and other similar publications (see, for example, Leach, 1997) have given parents practical information about the development of their children and the age at which major milestones might be reached.

Concepts of 'readiness' and preventative programs

Parents and professionals often use terms like 'normal development', 'normal behaviour' or 'the average child' when thinking about children whose development seems to be slower than expected. Such children are sometimes identified when they enter school because, although of school age, they seem not yet 'ready'. In Chapter 2, the term **readiness** was used in a Piagetian sense, and here it is used in a similar way to describe a child who has the prior knowledge or experiences needed to make a link between the known and the unknown. For example, lack of readiness for school is demonstrated by a lack of development of prerequisite skills such as familiarity with books and print, knowledge of the alphabet, recognising one's own name, counting to ten, following verbal instructions or keeping track of one's own possessions. Children who lack these early 'readiness' skills are sometimes described as 'struggling learners' or 'hard-to-teach' (O'Connor, 1995, p. 63). Their problems are often mild in nature and not recognised in the first 2 or 3 years at school (O'Connor, 1995, p. 61). Many manage to keep up with their peers, while others become underachievers who need extra support to keep up in the classroom.

Often described as educationally 'at risk', these children can be helped through preventative, supplementary or compensatory programs provided either prior to school entry or within the regular school program. Examples of **preventative programs** include the **early intervention programs** developed to help children with developmental delays and disabilities, such as First Steps (Pieterse & Treloar, 1989), EPIC (Clunies Ross, 1988) and early reading programs such as SWELL (Center, Freeman, & Robertson, 2001). The aim of such programs is to provide support at a critical point in children's development in order to prevent delays and difficulties in learning.

Underachievers and supplementary programs

Daniel had been in school for 2 years and had fallen well behind most of the others in his class in reading. His teacher decided Daniel should join a small group of children who had also progressed very little in reading after a year of formal instruction (although their progress in other areas of the curriculum was satisfactory). The children were to spend about 30 minutes each day working individually with a specially trained teacher who would give them supplementary assistance with their reading. Daniel's parents were informed that their son was to take part in Reading Recovery, a program based on the work of Marie Clay, an eminent authority in reading from New Zealand (Clay, 1993; Center, Wheldall, Freeman, Outhred, & McNaught, 1995). Daniel's parents watched, with interest and some anxiety, their son's progress in reading during the year he spent in Reading Recovery, hoping it would help him 'catch up'.

Schools routinely provide **supplementary programs** to help children who are **underachievers**; that is, those who are not working to their expected level, based on assessment of classroom performance coupled with teacher and parental expectations and, in some cases, the results of intelligence or scholastic aptitude tests. Supplementary programs include Reading Recovery (Clay, 1993) and the use of volunteer parents (Bastiani, 1989; Woolley & Hay, 1999) and peers (or older students) (see, for example, Center & Beaman,

---

readiness
Used to describe a child who has the prior knowledge or experiences needed to make a link between the known and the unknown

preventative programs
Educational programs designed to support children's development in order to prevent delays and difficulties in learning

early intervention programs
Programs designed to enhance development of infants and young children who are developmentally delayed or at risk of delay

8.1 More about students at educational risk

supplementary programs
Procedures, used in schools, to help children who are underachieving

underachievers
Students whose progress at school is not as good as expected, based on perceptions of ability

1991; Jenkins, Jewell, Leicester, O'Connor, Jenkins, & Trounter, 1994) to act as tutors in the classroom by listening to children read. The types of student difficulties of concern here are usually associated with a specific aspect of the curriculum, such as memorising number facts or decoding written symbols in the early stages of reading. Such problems generally disappear once the specific learning task is achieved.

Compensatory programs

An example of the type of **compensatory program** provided to offset the limitations associated with educational disadvantage or difference is the massive Head Start program in the USA. Introduced by the US federal government in 1965, this program was part of a US 'War on Poverty', which had begun in 1964 when the US Congress gave the Office of Economic Opportunity (OEO) 'the equivalent of wartime emergency powers' to implement it (Zigler & Muenchow, 1992, p. 2). Although funds were initially directed to a Community Action Program designed to give employment assistance to economically disadvantaged adults, the focus shifted to a national program that sought to offset the disadvantage experienced by children whose families were trapped in a poverty cycle (Zigler & Styfco, 2000; Zigler & Valentine, 1979), and to give such children 'a running head start' (Zigler & Muenchow, 1992, p. 6).

compensatory programs Educational programs designed to offset the limitations associated with educational disadvantage or difference

Head Start provided 3- to 4-year-old children with one to two years' preschool education, meals and basic health screening. It sought to prepare children for school and to give them positive experiences to offset the more negative school experiences encountered in many cases by their parents. Through the program, children were given opportunities to experience success and to build self-confidence so as to create an expectation of further success at school. Health care included a nutritional component and screening for visual and hearing problems. Most unusually for a program begun in the early 1960s, parents were involved to ensure that the program goals carried over into other parts of children's lives.

Head Start proved to be a highly successful social and educational program in terms of quantifiable data such as achievement-test scores, cognitive skills, school-absenteeism levels, and grade-repetition and school drop-out rates. Qualitative data such as reports by parents, teachers and others also supported Head Start's positive impact on children and their families (Barnett, 1992; Lazar & Darlington, 1982; Lee, Brooks-Gunn, Schnur, & Liaw, 1999; Lee & Loeb, 1995). A program based on the Head Start model was established in the early 1980s in an outer-metropolitan area of Sydney (Braithwaite, 1983).

The Disadvantaged Schools program (Schools Commission, 1975), introduced by the Commonwealth Government of Australia in 1974–1975, is another example of a compensatory program. It provided additional resources to schools serving children from the most economically disadvantaged neighbourhoods (that is, children living in poverty) and to those with large numbers of children who were experiencing difficulties as a result of belonging to a minority group (ethnic, linguistic, cultural or religious). The program also made provision for other educationally disadvantaged groups such as children living in rural areas, girls, migrant groups (that is, those with language backgrounds other than English (LBOTE)) and Aboriginal children.

Compensatory programs and special education

The aim of compensatory programs for students who are disadvantaged or different is to accelerate their learning so that they can both 'catch up' and 'keep up' with their peers. This can be contrasted with special education that provides programs for children who cannot achieve academically or in other aspects of learning without special help or extra resources. However, there is often considerable overlap in the groups of children who participate in compensatory and special education programs. Children from minority backgrounds are usually over-represented in special education programs, in part because it can be difficult to determine if learning problems result from factors such as lack of English-language skills or from some degree of intellectual impairment. In some cases children experience a 'double disability', when low socioeconomic background or membership of a minority group is compounded by a disability such as mild intellectual impairment or hearing loss.

According to Allington and McGill-Franzen (1995), a long-term study of secondary students in US special education programs (Wagner, 1995) found that 'both poor and minority students were represented among special education students at rates higher than they occurred in the general population. Children from low-income families ... were substantially over-represented, while economically more advantaged children were under-represented' (Allington & McGill-Franzen, 1995, p. 26). Allington and McGill-Franzen pointed out that while some minority groups – in this case African-Americans – are over-represented in special education, poor families are also over-represented in these groups, which suggests that poverty rather than ethnicity may be the key factor for placement in special education programs (see Chapter 9).

Box 8.1 looks at those children who might benefit from preventative, supplementary or compensatory programs.

Box 8.1 IMPLICATIONS FOR EDUCATORS

Implementing preventative, supplementary and compensatory programs at school

Educators need to be aware that, in the early school years and even before school entry, children who experience difficulties can often be helped in the following ways:

- Children who have a disability, who are developmentally delayed or who are at risk of developmental delay and are not yet ready for school can be helped through preventative or early intervention programs provided prior to school entry.
- Children who are underachieving or not working at the level expected by teachers and parents need to be given supplementary or extra assistance within the classroom in those curriculum areas in which they experience difficulties.
- Children who are educationally disadvantaged as a result of poverty, gender, location in a rural area, language background other than English, Aboriginality and/or membership of a minority group can be assisted through the provision of compensatory programs designed to offset the disadvantage they experience.

8.2 More about compensatory programs for disadvantaged students

Down syndrome
A chromosomal disorder associated with intellectual impairment and distinctive facial characteristics

spina bifida
A congenital defect associated with mobility problems and resulting from the spinal column's failure to close completely prior to birth

cerebral palsy
An outcome of brain damage prior to birth, resulting in disorders of movement and posture

Learners with special needs

Learners with special support needs

If you look at any group of children (see Figure 8.2 opposite), such as those born in Canberra on 29 February 2000, you will probably find that the group includes a very small number who are exceptionally gifted in terms of academic, musical, artistic, sporting or other attributes. (Data reported at the census taken around 2015 or 2020 should confirm this claim.) There will also be a small number who have a disabling condition that affects some aspect of their development. In some cases, the disability is relatively rare in the general population but its impact on the child's development is serious (that is, 'high severity – low incidence') (Levine, Carey, Croker, & Gross, 1983). Such problems are usually identified at or soon after birth by parents, doctors or others. Children with **Down syndrome**, **spina bifida** and **cerebral palsy** are usually identified quickly because these conditions have physical characteristics that are easily recognised.

Learners with high support needs

Children whose disabilities are serious in nature are sometimes described as having **high support needs**, meaning that they will need considerable assistance in their learning at school. Their difficulties are both serious and enduring. For some, help is provided in a regular classroom by skilful teachers who are able to access appropriate resources and support. Alternatively, assistance may be provided by a suitably qualified teacher who is familiar with specialised teaching programs and technologies; for example, a teacher who has received training in working with children with severe hearing impairments. Sometimes this type of help is available from a 'visiting' teacher within a regular classroom. In other situations, it is provided in a special unit or class located within a regular school, or in a learning unit or **special school** that is physically separate from the regular school.

high support needs
A need for considerable assistance to participate at school and in daily life

special school
A separate school that caters for a specific group of students with special learning needs

Learners with mild difficulties

Other problems, such as those associated with mild to moderate hearing impairment or a learning difficulty, may be much less severe in terms of their impact on children's development, although their rate of occurrence in the general population is high (that is, low severity – high incidence). Difficulties of this type may not be recognised until there is a delay in, for example, the development of language or the acquisition of a skill, such as reading. Children who experience such problems are sometimes described as having **learning difficulties** or 'learning disabilities'. If such children have the necessary attributes, disposition and resilience – such as maturity, above-average intelligence or high verbal-communication skills (Werner & Smith, 1992) – and if their home (and/or school) environment is very supportive and appropriate assistance is available when needed, they may not need special education services.

learning difficulties
Marked problems in achievement at school

FIGURE 8.2
Which of these children might have disabilities that affect their learning?

Learners at educational risk

In its *Plan for Government School Education 1998–2000*, the Western Australian Education Department described students at educational risk as 'underachieving' or 'not achieving their full potential' (Education Department of Western Australia, 2002). Any child, at any time, can be at **educational risk** as a result of problems at home, illness, a learning difficulty or unrecognised giftedness. Werner and Smith (1977), in a study of children growing up in the Hawaiian island of Kauai, found a combination of economic disadvantage and delayed development to be associated with later poor achievement at school. According to Swanson (1999, p. 199), a number of factors are associated with risk in learners. In terms of the home environment such factors include:

- belonging to an impoverished family
- parental unemployment
- mental illness
- being situated in an unsafe and unhealthy neighbourhood.

Risk factors associated with the school environment include:

- low academic achievement
- few resources
- low expectations for achievement
- large numbers of students from poor or minority families
- inadequate teaching staff
- poor leadership
- an unsafe school
- large class sizes
- too little time devoted to instruction
- negative labelling of students with special needs.

A briefing for the New Zealand Incoming Minister of Education (NZ Ministry of Education, 2001, p. 1) identified the following as being associated with students thought to be at risk of poor school achievement:

- truancy
- suspensions and exclusions
- a demand for non-mainstream educational opportunities to be provided for the most at-risk students
- bullying and violence in schools.

Zubrick and Silburn (1997), in a study of Western Australian children's education, health and competence, identified the following three areas of student limitation as associated with the risk of low academic competence:

- low verbal and non-verbal ability
- difficulties with speech and language
- poor mental health.

In addition, attention problems and difficulties in social relationships are associated with low academic achievement. Zubrick and Silburn concluded that a combination of heredity, genetics, and social and environmental factors contributes to these students' difficulties.

Since children spend so much time at school, parents need to be alert for any signs that their children are having problems there. Parents need to be prepared to work with the school to ensure their children's problems are addressed and resolved. Signs that can indicate to parents, teachers and others that a child is at educational risk are set out in Box 8.2 (opposite).

---

educational risk
Students in danger of failure at school as a result of underachievement

Box 8.2 CLASSROOM LINKS

Indicators of educational risk

A child's progress may depend on a parent or teacher noticing significant changes in that child's behaviour, so parents and teachers need to be aware of signs that a child is experiencing difficulties. While some children express their problems in the form of disruptive behaviour or even truancy, signs of vulnerability at school are also expressed in less obvious ways.

According to the Education Department of Western Australia (2002), signs that a child is 'at educational risk' include:

- significant changes in behaviour and performance
- anxious or unhappy appearance
- not attending or participating in school
- not getting along with teachers and friends, and noticeable changes in achievement level or rate of progress, or marked difference from peers.

Teachers need to keep such indicators of vulnerability in mind when working with groups of children.

Resilience and educational risk

According to Werner and Smith (1992), **resilience** is associated with better-than-expected outcomes in children, or 'successful adaptation in spite of childhood adversity' (Werner & Smith, 1992, p. 4). Here, 'childhood adversity' may involve premature birth, extremely low birth weight, delayed language development, learning difficulties and behaviour problems. Hamilton, Anderson, Frater-Mathieson, Loewen and Moore (2001), in a study of refugee children in New Zealand schools, identified experience as a refugee as a risk factor for school success.

Factors within the child and the child's home environment that are associated with resilience or successful adaptation to adverse childhood conditions include academic achievement, school satisfaction, adequate income, a two-parent family, degree of parental education, quality of family relationships, opportunities for children to learn at home and family support for the child's education. Within the classroom, resilience in children is positively associated with the quality and quantity of teacher–student interactions, the amount of interaction with teachers and other adults at school, the quantity of time devoted to instruction, classroom climate, the use of goal-setting and other strategies for self-regulated learning, and the use of techniques to build self-esteem (Swanson, 1999, p. 199).

Miller (1996, pp. 267–268) suggested a series of interventions that may help increase resilience in at-risk groups. Such interventions might include:

- *family involvement* through activities designed to enhance cohesion and communication between parents and schools
- *a united collaborative approach* involving teachers, parents and students sharing and communicating ideas to bolster student success, leading to resilience
- *taking action* to ensure that students take an active part in activities rather than avoiding such involvement
- *involvement alongside others*, since participating with others in activities that require time and energy may lead to feelings of accomplishment and success, while also enhancing resilience
- *self-understanding*, since acknowledging and confronting one's own learning problems appears to be an important element in building resilience
- *generating alternatives* or ways of compensating for difficulties, which appears to contribute to the development of resilience
- *reframing* or reinterpreting the self in a more positive way, leading to conscious decision-making and taking charge of one's own life

resilience
Possessed by students who succeed at school in spite of adverse life experiences

- *accepting and using others' support,* or knowing how and being willing to accept the assistance others offer
- *accentuating areas of accomplishment* such as hobbies and areas of interest where the student has experienced success, particularly in group situations where a sense of accomplishment can be shared with others.

CRITICAL REFLECTIONS

Think about the information about resilience and educational risk reviewed here:
- From your own experience, can you think of any students who demonstrated resilience in the face of educational risk?
- What factors contributed to their initial difficulties and what led to the resilience they demonstrated?

Children who are vulnerable or at educational risk as a result of even relatively minor impairments may encounter problems if they do not receive the support they need at critical times (Zubrick & Silburn, 1997). For example, young children with minimal or intermittent hearing loss (for example, as a result of 'glue ear' or otitis media – see Chapter 9) often have difficulty learning to talk and may have problems later in learning to read and spell because they have not been hearing all the speech sounds. Some of these children, particularly those whose problems are less severe in nature, may be able to cope in a regular classroom without any extra help apart from that provided routinely by schools for underachievers or at home by parents and family. However, others – particularly those who are more vulnerable as a result of additional risk factors or adversities (Wang & Haertel, 1995, pp.199–200) – need some form of additional help or specialised assistance that may include services identified as 'special education' (see the case study in Box 8.3). Issues of risk and resilience are also addressed further in Chapter 9.

Box 8.3 CASE STUDY

Educational risk

When Ellis first came to the school he was taller than the other boys in his class. He was very thin, with a bright, alert face and a ready grin. Ellis had been a state ward most of his life and had experienced a number of changes in his foster-family placement, with reported physical and sexual abuse in at least two of his placements. He was now living in a leafy part of the town with a minister of religion and the minister's wife.

Although nearly 10, Ellis read like a child in Year 1. His other skills were just as poor. The school had a support teacher (learning difficulties) who began to help Ellis, taking him to a quiet corner of the classroom for daily instruction with several others who were struggling with their reading. Ellis seemed to profit from this help, and his reading performance in particular improved rapidly. However, it was reported that he was in trouble at home. Neighbours complained of him stealing small amounts of money. The driver on Ellis's school bus also reported the petty theft of cash, and said he suspected Ellis was the culprit. The classroom teacher talked with Ellis, trying to help him realise the problems he was causing for himself. Eventually Ellis seemed to settle down: he worked steadily for the rest of the year. In the new year he was moved to a new foster family, and teachers at the school lost sight of him.

About 5 years later, the support teacher visited a remand centre as part of a review team. Ellis was there, much taller and still good-looking, but less happy about his current predicament. His reading and number skills were still very poor. The teacher asked what support was available for students like Ellis. The director of the centre replied that there was little need for additional support, as the main priority was to make sure such students attended classes each day and behaved appropriately.

> **Activity**
>
> This case study concerns a boy who is educationally at risk and who has learning difficulties as a result of adverse conditions in his home and possibly his school environment. Think about Ellis's background and his experiences at home and at school. Imagine you have an opportunity over a 6-month period to spend time regularly in Ellis's remand-centre classroom:
> 1. What would you do to help Ellis and others like him at the centre?
> 2. Make a plan identifying your goals for the 6-month period and also possible teaching strategies that could be used to improve Ellis's reading and number skills.
> 3. What difficulties might you encounter in implementing your plan? How might these be overcome?

8.3 Another case study of an 'at risk' child

Concepts of impairment, disability and handicap

A distinction that needs to be made when thinking about people with disabilities concerns differences in the meaning of words like **impairment** on the one hand, and **disability** on the other. According to the *Macquarie Dictionary*, 'impairment' implies that something has been damaged or diminished in value, while 'disability' implies a lack of competence, or incapacity. So the term impairment refers to something that is imperfect but that may still be useful (that is, it is still functional), while the term disability refers to something that is damaged (that is, no longer functional).

The meaning of another word needs to be considered. When talking about people who have a disability, the word 'handicap' is often also used. The *Macquarie Dictionary* meaning of 'handicap' is in terms of a race in which 'certain disadvantages ... of weight, distance [and] time ... are placed upon competitors to equalise their chances of winning' (Delbridge, Bernard, Blair, Butler, Perters, & Yallop, 1997, p. 969). An additional meaning (p. 969) refers to 'any encumbrance or disadvantage that makes success more difficult'. In the field of special education, the word **handicap** is used to refer to a limitation or barrier within the environment that has the effect of impeding or interfering with the activities of a person with a disability. Examples of such an environmental interference or barrier include the railway station without a ramp for people who need wheelchair access, and the art gallery or library with poor lighting for people who have limited vision. Note that these examples refer to restrictions that are imposed externally and that limit the capacity of people with disabilities to function adequately. Sometimes such barriers take the form of negative attitudes that discourage or prevent people with a disability from taking part in a preferred activity. The important distinction is that, for the individual concerned, a 'disability' refers to an *internal* condition, while a 'handicap' refers to an *external* condition (Slee, 1995).

impairment
Implies that something is damaged but still functional

disability
A restriction resulting from something that is damaged and no longer functional

handicap
A restriction that limits a person's capacity to function normally

Disability incidence rates

Determining the exact number of children in a community who have a disability and the precise nature of that condition is an almost impossible task. Data on the number of people living in a community at a specific time can, however, be obtained through a census. This involves distributing a questionnaire or administering a set of questions to all households and other establishments such as hospitals, prisons and boarding schools on a specified 'census day'.

Attempts have been made to use census data to determine the prevalence of impairment or disability within a population. However, these efforts have generally been unsuccessful because of inconsistencies in people's understanding of terms such as 'blind', 'deaf' and 'intellectually impaired', and in their perception of the impact of a disabling condition on the daily life of the individual concerned. Some people who identify themselves as having a disability may not satisfy the criteria set by government agencies to determine eligibility for support, while others whom these the criteria would define as 'disabled' do not identify themselves in this way (see Box 8.4). Many different scales and tests have been developed to identify and assess people's level of disability and their need for services or support (see Madden, Black, & Wen, 1995), and these are continually being reviewed and revised in the light of new research findings and changing social conditions.

Box 8.4 RESEARCH LINKS

Perceptions of disability

At a workshop on the need for accurate information about the prevalence of disabilities among Indigenous people, Louis Ariotti (1998) used his experiences during a 12-month study of Aboriginal communities in the Warburton and Ernabella area in a discussion of how perceptions of disability affect the way we define terms like 'disability' and 'handicap'. Ariotti (p. 81) recounted the story of an old woman who had a physical-motor impairment but who did not view herself as disabled and who was not considered as having a disability by her community:

> People called her *tjirara wiya* – the one with no legs. She sits for hours in her camp making artefacts. She often goes hunting by being unceremoniously lifted into the back of a Toyota. When ... [we] offered to provide her with aids to assist her mobility and lessen the hardship, she refused them – all she wanted was hot water in her shower.

Source: Adapted from Ariotti (1998).

CRITICAL REFLECTION

■ Which areas of schooling might prove a handicap to children with particular disabilities? How could you reduce this handicap for these children?

Disability in Australia

In 1993, an Australian survey of disability, ageing and carers conducted by the Australian Bureau of Statistics (ABS) using a sample of 15 000 households found that 29% of the Australian population, or just over 5 million people, had one or more impairments or long-term health conditions. However, only 18% of the population (or a little over three million people) were disabled by their impairment, and only 14% (2.5 million people) were handicapped by their disability (ABS, 1993). More than half the people with a disability (57%) had a physical impairment, and more than one-third (37%) had a sensory impairment. Other, less common impairments included psychological (18%) and intellectual (9%) impairments. The relationship among conditions resulting in impairment, disability and handicap within the Australian population in 1993 is represented in Figure 8.3. Box 8.5 opposite explores the ABS 1993 survey results in more detail.

FIGURE 8.3

The relationship between conditions, impairment, disability and handicap in the Australian population, 1993.

(Source: Australian Bureau of Statistics, 1993, p. 1.)

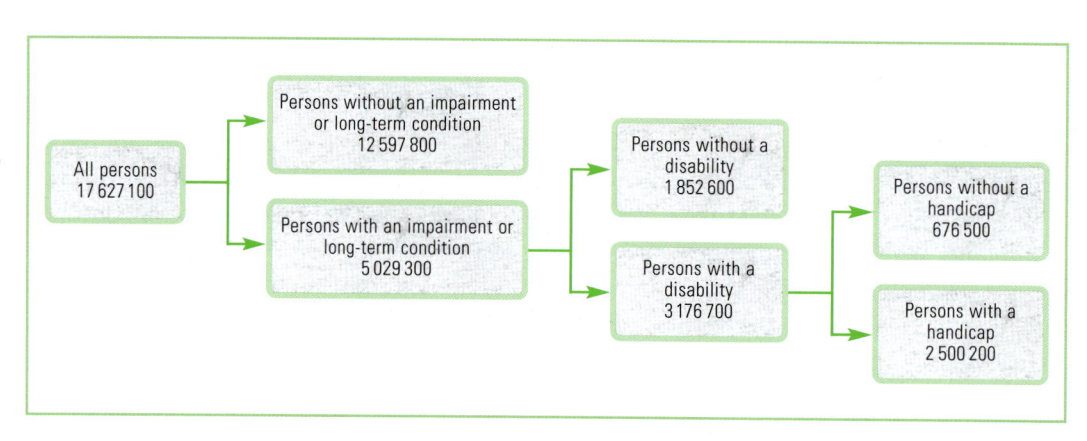

All persons 17 627 100
→ Persons without an impairment or long-term condition 12 597 800
→ Persons with an impairment or long-term condition 5 029 300
  → Persons without a disability 1 852 600
  → Persons with a disability 3 176 700
    → Persons without a handicap 676 500
    → Persons with a handicap 2 500 200

CHAPTER 8 LEARNERS WITH SPECIAL NEEDS 241

Box 8.5 RESEARCH LINKS

A survey of disability, ageing and carers

A 1993 survey of disability, ageing and carers conducted by the Australian Bureau of Statistics (ABS) using a sample of 15 000 households found that very few children in the 0–4 years age group had a disability, and among those who did, most were not handicapped by the condition, meaning their lives were not restricted in any way (see Table 8.1 below).

Among the 10% of children (0–4 years) with a disabling condition that had the potential to restrict their lives, the most common conditions were classified as 'physical'. However, for many of the children, the impact of these problems was not serious, and in Table 8.1 the disability status of these children is classified 'no disability'.

Respiratory diseases were common among the children, and mainly involved asthma; however, most of the children were not restricted in daily activities as a result of their asthma (see Table 8.1). Conditions that affected vision and hearing, neurological conditions such as epilepsy and cerebral palsy, or congenital abnormalities such as Down syndrome were generally disabling in their impact on the children involved. The prevalence in children aged 0–4 years of these different conditions (that is, the number of individuals affected by them within a population at a given time) when the ABS Disability and Disabling Conditions Survey was conducted in Australia in 1993 is set out in Table 8.1.

TABLE 8.1 Australian children aged 0–4 years in 1993: Main disabling condition by gender and disability status

Main disabling condition	Males '000	Females '000	Total '000	Disability† '000	No disability '000	Total '000
Mental disorders	**1.1	*2.2	*3.3	*3.3	—	*3.3
Physical conditions						
■ Disorders of eye and ear	*2.9	*5.2	8.1	*6.8	**1.3	8.1
■ Nervous system diseases	*3.2	**1.8	*5.0	*4.7	**0.3	*5.0
■ Respiratory diseases	48.2	28.3	76.5	14.9	61.6	76.5
■ Congenital anomalies	*2.5	*4.7	*7.2	*6.1	**1.0	*7.2
■ Speech disorders	*5.4	*2.0	*7.3	*7.3	—	*7.3
■ All other diseases/conditions	11.7	9.8	21.4	13.3	8.2	21.4
Total children aged 0–4 years with physical conditions	73.8	51.7	125.5	53.1	72.4	125.5
Total children aged 0–4 years ('000)	662.3	628.8	1291.1	56.4	1234.7	1291.1

* and ** indicate that there are standard errors in some of the results reported, and that these specific results should be viewed with caution.
† The term 'disability' indicates the presence of a restriction resulting from a disabling condition.

Source: Adapted from the Australian Bureau of Statistics (1993, tables 27 and 28, p. 35).

When considering the occurrence and nature of disability among children in the age range 0–14 years, it is apparent that slowness in learning or understanding and problems in speech are most prevalent. Data on the prevalence of these and other conditions in children (0–14 years) and young people (15–24 years) from the 1993 ABS survey are set out in Table 8.2 below.

TABLE 8.2 Australian children 0–14 years and 15–24 years in 1993: Prevalence of impairments and conditions

Impairments and conditions	Males (%)		Females (%)		All Australians (%)		
	0–14 years	15–24 years	0–14 years	15–24 years	0–14 years	15–24 years	All ages
Loss of sight or hearing	1.4	1.8	1.3	1.3	1.3	1.5	6.7
Speech problems	2.3	1.0	1.0	0.6	1.7	0.8	1.2

(Continued over page)

Impairments and conditions	Males (%)		Females (%)		All Australians (%)		
	0–14 years	15–24 years	0–14 years	15–24 years	0–14 years	15–24 years	All ages
Slow at learning or understanding	3.0	1.8	1.4	1.7	2.2	1.8	1.7
Restricted in physical activities	1.6	2.2	1.1	2.6	1.3	2.4	8.9
Nervous condition (fits or mental illness)	1.0	1.3	1.0	2.1	1.0	1.7	3.2
Disfigurement or deformity	0.4	0.6	0.6	*0.5	0.5	0.6	1.0
Head injury, stroke or brain damage	0.5	0.7	*0.4	0.8	0.5	0.8	1.4
Treated long-term restricting condition (asthma, diabetes)*	2.3	1.8	1.6	2.3	1.9	2.1	6.7
Other long-term restricting condition	1.0	0.6	0.9	1.4	0.9	1.0	3.7
Total persons ('000)	1 964.6	1 403.5	1 864.0	1 348.2	3 828.7	2 751.7	17 627.1**

*Long-term restricting conditions include arthritis, asthma, and circulatory conditions such as high blood pressure.
**See Figure 8.3 on page 240.

Source: Adapted from the Australian Bureau of Statistics (1993, Table 2, p. 14).

Activities

1 Which of the conditions listed in Table 8.1 have the least impact on the children involved in the 0–4 years age range? Which conditions are most disabling for children in this age range? What are the implications of this information for early childhood educators regarding the prevalence of disabling conditions among children aged 0–4 years?

2 Identify any patterns in the prevalence of impairments and long-term conditions in the total data reported for the age groups of 0–14 years and 15–24 years, and for all persons in Table 8.2. Can you explain any trends you see? What are the implications of this for schools?

3 According to the tables, which conditions decrease in prevalence with increasing age for all young people in the age ranges 0–14 years and 15–24 years? Is this pattern of change the same for males as it is for females? Can you explain any differences?

Labels and labelling

An important characteristic of all social groups, and one of the means by which groups establish a group identity, is the tendency to categorise and label people in terms of attributes that are significant for the group. For example, someone who is widely admired in public life is called a 'great statesman' or a 'champ'. At a more personal level, there is 'a real friend' or 'a true mate'. Negative terms, such as 'fool', 'idiot' and 'traitor', are used to identify those who cannot contribute to the welfare of the group or who are perceived as threatening its survival.

In the 19th century, when access to schools was limited to children from the wealthy and middle classes, those who were categorised negatively – whether as a result of a handicap or because of membership of a minority group – were generally denied access to education. Where some form of care was required, such children were placed in asylums for the insane or infirm (see Figure 8.4 opposite), where no provision for education was made. It is generally acknowledged that the provision of educational programs for children with disabilities can be traced to the work of Jean-Marc-Gaspard Itard (see Box 8.6 opposite).

FIGURE 8.4 Until the last quarter of the 20th century, most children with severe disabilities spent their lives in residential institutions like this one, the Mayday Hills Mental Hospital at Beechworth, Victoria.

Box 8.6 ABOUT JEAN-MARC-GASPARD ITARD

Jean-Marc-Gaspard Itard (1775–1838) joined the army during the French Revolution and trained as an assistant surgeon at a military hospital in Toulon. He later moved to Paris where he received formal training in surgery, and from 1800 to 1838 was Chief Physician at the National Institute for Deaf-Mutes in Paris. Itard, who was known for his work on ear disease, also worked as a teacher at the Institute, and developed new methods for teaching children who were deaf and mute. It was his interest in deaf education that led to his involvement with the 'Wild Boy of Aveyron' (Plucker, 2002).

The Wild Boy had been found in 1799 running wild in the woods outside Aveyron in the south of France. He was about 12 years old, and it was assumed he had been abandoned by his parents or had become lost in the woods, where he had survived on roots, berries and anything he could catch. The boy had no spoken language and his behaviour and appearance were animal-like. He drank lying flat on the floor, often walked on all fours and did not respond normally to sounds (Ashman & Elkins, 2002, p. 54). He was put in a local woman's care, but later escaped and returned to the woods. He was caught again the following year and taken to Paris to be studied as an example of a primitive human mind.

Victor was examined by a group of physicians and by Philippe Pinel, a famous psychiatrist and the director of an asylum in Paris who believed that learning was dependent on inherited characteristics. They declared that Victor was not wild, but intellectually impaired and therefore incapable of benefiting from any form of systematic instruction. Itard also examined the boy: he disagreed with his colleagues' pessimistic view, and argued that Victor was intellectually retarded as a result of neglect and social isolation. From 1800 to 1804, Itard worked intensively with the boy, being the one to name him Victor. In collaboration with a housekeeper, Madame Guerin, Itard developed an educational program that was primarily concerned with Victor's sensory, cognitive and emotional development.

Itard's efforts did not succeed in overcoming the effects on Victor of at least five years in the woods. However, the boy did acquire limited speech,

FIGURE 8.5 Itard's intensive work with Victor, the Wild Boy of Aveyron, is considered to have been the beginning of special education.

learned to read a few words, could follow simple instructions, and showed evidence of social and emotional development. Yet Victor's development remained limited, and he died in his mid-40s, still in Madame Guerin's care (Kenner, 1964; Winzer, 2002).

Itard's work with Victor was important in challenging the belief that people with intellectual impairments were ineducable. Itard demonstrated that such people were capable of learning and that provision of an enriched environment could compensate for early environmental deprivation. Itard's work with Victor, the Wild Boy of Aveyron, is considered to be the starting point for special education.

Itard's ideas, which concerned the use of sensory-motor training to rehabilitate children with intellectual disabilities, were further developed by the French physician Eduard Séguin (1812–1888) and by the Italian educator Maria Montessori (1870–1951). Séguin opened a school for children with intellectual disabilities in France in the mid-1850s. He used positive reinforcement and highly structured teaching methods. Instruction was based on individual assessment and included training in self-help and daily-living skills. Eventually, Séguin moved to the USA, where his work was already known and where several schools were implementing his teaching methods (Plucker, 2002). He had a profound influence on the development of US programs for educating and training children with intellectual disabilities (Winzer, 1993, p. 216). Montessori was influenced by Séguin's work with children with sensory disabilities. She established educational programs in Italy for children with intellectual disabilities, supplying the children with a carefully structured environment that provided experiences to help them lead fuller and more meaningful lives (Winzer, 2002).

In developed countries there is a long tradition, dating back to the second half of the 18th century, of special schools and classes for children with vision and hearing impairments (Ashman & Elkins, 2002, p. 54). Yet other children who lacked the competencies needed to survive in a regular classroom, or who were stigmatised for some reason, were either excluded from regular schools or only accepted into special schools. Such schools were often operated by voluntary or charitable organisations (for example, the New Zealand Crippled Children Society). When children who lacked the necessary skills for survival at school or who had been stigmatised did attend a regular school, teachers often found them difficult to teach, and they were labelled 'laggards', 'unmanageables' and 'defectives' (Allington, 1994). At the same time, the children attending special schools were referred to as 'idiots', 'imbeciles' and 'morons'. Increasing acceptance of schooling for children with disabilities saw such terminology change from highly stigmatised terms such as 'feeble minded', 'mentally defective' and 'subnormal' to more neutral terms such as 'intellectually impaired', 'learning disabled' and 'developmentally delayed'. 'Mongolism' was replaced by 'Down syndrome'; 'deaf-blind' and 'deaf and dumb' by 'hearing impaired'; and 'spasticity' by 'cerebral palsy'.

In addition to changes over time in the terms used to refer to specific categories of disability, there has also been increasing pressure from educators, other professionals and people with disabilities for disability to be viewed as something that has a direct impact on the daily life and experiences of an individual, rather than it being seen strictly as a medical condition. Special education was initially predominantly made up of services that were designed to assist groups of children with disabling conditions such as deafness or blindness that were considered to be organically based and identifiable in terms of a specific medical model. However, other difficulties children experience are less easily identified using available, medically based assessment procedures. Examples of such problems that have been the subject of considerable debate in relation to identification and assessment include learning disability (LD), attention deficit hyperactivity disorder (ADHD) and emotional disorder (ED). These labels have often served a useful purpose by drawing attention and financial resources to groups of students who are not receiving appropriate services. However, problems can arise when attempts are made to fit a child into an identified category such as LD or ADHD when the definition of the category is hazy and the child's characteristics do not precisely fit that particular label. Students who are refugees, and who as a result of that experience have special learning needs, illustrate the problems inherent in providing special education services on the basis of an identified disability category (Hamilton et al., 2001).

In the final decade of the 20th century there was a major shift in the way disabilities were labelled. This followed increasing community acceptance of people with disabilities, and the introduction of the concept of **normalisation**, with its pressures to allow people with disabilities to have access to the experiences of normal daily life (see also the discussion of the integration–segregation debate on page 249). The concept of normalisation was also associated with pressure to use 'politically correct' language when referring to minority or marginalised groups in the community. These changes are still particularly evident in the UK, the USA, Australia and New Zealand in the terms used to refer to people with intellectual impairments. In the UK, the term 'learning disability' is used to refer to such people, in response to the preferences of those with the disability; whereas in the USA, professional pressure has resulted in the term 'mentally retarded' being retained (Scheerenberger, 1987). In Australia and New Zealand, the term 'intellectual disabilities' is used. Another change concerns the shift from identifying people with an impairment in terms of the impairment, to referring to an impairment as but one of an individual's characteristics. Examples include 'the blind' or 'a Down's child' rephrased as 'an 8-year-old boy who has severe vision impairment' and 'a child with Down syndrome' (see Box 8.7).

normalisation
Giving people with disabilities access to the daily experiences and activities available to those in the community who do not have a disability

Box 8.7 CLASSROOM LINKS

Labelling

During the last decade of the 20th century, there was considerable debate about using 'politically correct' language or the need to avoid using expressions that are offensive to some groups in society. In particular, there was pressure to use language that was gender neutral, as in the substitution of 'flight attendant' for 'air hostess', and 'actor' for 'actress'. The words we use influence the way we think about people, objects and events. The way we think about those who are abnormal or different from the norm in some way can lead to negative valuations, discrimination and stereotyping (Goffman, 1968). We may react to the deviant person with embarrassment, rejection or over-zealous acceptance, but whatever the response, we are reacting to the deviance rather than to the person as a whole. When thinking about individuals with disabilities and other negatively valued characteristics, it is important to remember that they are people first, and that any impairment or unusual characteristics are secondary.

Activity

Read the following statements and rephrase them to avoid negative, discriminatory or stereotypic language:
1. Epileptics go to this doctor
2. This school has mentally retarded children
3. I have a diabetic friend
4. She is a dwarf
5. He is wheelchair-bound
6. My sister has a Mongol baby
7. This is a bus shelter for the blind
8. She went spastic when she found out
9. Mum had a fit when I told her
10. What a dumb child

Source: Adapted from Foreman (1996, p. 17).

A non-categorical view of disability

Doubts about the adequacy of the categorical system (based, as it is, on a medical model) to identify and classify disabilities have led to questions about the relevance of a system of special education that is based on such classifications. This problem has been particularly acute in systems such as that operating in the USA, where children's disabilities must be medically assessed and formally identified before children become eligible for special services. It is not a major problem in Australia and New Zealand because there are no legal requirements in those countries for formal diagnosis by a medical specialist or psychologist prior to accessing a special education program. However, as a way of overcoming problems associated with obtaining an accurate diagnosis, as well as coping with the needs of children who have difficulties that do not fit neatly into a currently available diagnostic category, 'non-categorical' educational services are increasingly being provided. Here, the focus is on providing a curriculum suited to the functional needs of each child (such as help in learning to hold a pencil) rather than on a program designed for a group of children who have a specific disabling condition such as autism (or impairments in social interaction and communication together with ritualistic behaviour). A non-categorical approach, with resources directed to a particular child rather than to a program, is particularly appropriate as school systems begin to implement procedures to support the integration and inclusion of children with disabilities into the regular school system.

Box 8.8 looks at the implications of resilience, educational risk and the identification of students' special learning and support needs for educators.

8.4 The Apgar Scale

Box 8.8 IMPLICATIONS FOR EDUCATORS

Resilience and educational risk

Educators need to be aware that:
- Any child can be at risk of problems in learning, and steps can be taken to help such children.
- Children can be at educational risk as a result of internal factors, home factors and factors within the school environment.
- Teachers, parents and others need to be aware of the signs that children are at risk, and need to take steps to ensure such children achieve their full potential.
- Some children succeed at school (that is, display resilience) in spite of childhood adversity. Teachers, parents and others can take steps to increase resilience in children at risk.
- Some children who experience problems at school may require assistance in the form of a special program or service.

Identifying students with special learning and support needs

In working with students with special learning and support needs, educators need to be aware of issues that might arise from the identification of these students, such as:
- Students with severe disabilities generally need a high level of support in at least some aspects of schooling.
- Students with mild difficulties may only need additional assistance when they encounter a particular problem in some aspect of schooling.
- The identification of students with a disability can be problematic, reflecting inconsistencies in people's perceptions of disability, and also changing social and environmental conditions.
- Extreme variability in the range and nature of disabilities in the community can present problems for those who attempt to identify and classify disabilities, particularly when a given instance of a disability is mild in nature and when an individual has multiple disabilities.
- The concept of normalisation has led to a focus on individuals' specific needs rather than on categories of impairment.
- The negative connotations carried by some labels used to identify specific disabilities have led to some terms being changed.
- Changing views of disability have led to people with a disability being identified first as people and then as having a disability (among other personal characteristics).
- A recognition of negative aspects of using disability categories and labels to identify people with disabilities and special learning needs has led to a non-categorical view of disability, with a focus on the functional needs of individuals.

Special education in practice

It is now generally accepted that all children, including those with disabilities, have an equal right to free and appropriate education. But this was not always so. Until Jean-Marc Gaspard Itard demonstrated through his efforts with the Wild Boy of Aveyron (see Box 8.6 on page 243) that children considered to be 'mentally retarded' could be educated, it was assumed that children with disabilities, particularly those with intellectual disabilities, were ineducable.

During the 19th century, voluntary organisations established institutions for children who were deaf, dumb and blind; and from the middle of the century, for children described as 'feebleminded' (Winzer, 1993). As mentioned earlier in this chapter, children who were mentally retarded or mentally disturbed were cared for in hospitals for the insane, with no provision made for their education until late in the century (Andrews, Elkins, Berry, & Burge, 1979).

During the 20th century, there was a steady increase in the provision of educational services for children with disabilities, mainly through the establishment of separate day schools and classes. In Australia, the first special class for 'defective' (subnormal) children was established in Western Australia in 1910, and the first government special school for the retarded opened in Victoria in 1913 (Andrews et al., 1979, p. 15). In New Zealand, a special school for backward boys was set up in Otekaike, Otago, in 1908, and a special class for backward children commenced at the Auckland Normal School in 1917 (Mitchell, 1987, p. 34). The major development in special education in Australia and New Zealand during the mid-20th century concerned the provision of government-funded services for children with mild intellectual impairments. The establishment of programs for children with more severe disabilities was generally left to non-government and, in many cases, parent-based organisations. In Australia in the 1970s, responsibility for many of the parent-based schools was assumed by state departments of education, as a result of initiatives in special education undertaken by the Commonwealth Schools Commission, which the Federal government established in 1973.

Special education policies

At about the same time as the Australian government was implementing initiatives in special education, major developments in the provision of special education services were also taking place in the UK and the USA. The Warnock Report (Warnock, 1978) provided the first major review of special education provision in the UK, followed by the Education Act (1981). One outcome of the Warnock Report was to shift the focus of special education away from a 'deficit' (or medical) model, which assumed that the 'deficiency' was within the child, to a model more concerned with children's specific needs.

In the USA, enactment of federal laws such as Public law 94-142, the Education for all Handicapped Children Act, 1975, ensured that all children with disabilities – including the very young – received an appropriate public education. These US Acts included provisions for each child to be given an **Individual Education Program (IEP)** (that is, a planned program of instruction tailored to an individual student) and to be educated in what is called the **least restrictive environment (LRE)**, which means the setting that is as close as possible to that experienced by children who do not have disabilities. These developments strongly influenced the provision of educational programs and services for students with special learning needs in Australia and New Zealand. For example, in Australia, preparation of an IEP is expected, while in New Zealand it is an administrative requirement (Ashman & Elkins, 2002, p. 63).

Individual Education Plan (IEP)
A planned program of instruction for an individual student, based on assessed needs, strengths and interests

least restrictive environment (LRE)
The setting that is as close as possible to that experienced by children who do not have disabilities

According to the definition of LRE proposed by the American Council for Exceptional Children (cited by Cole & Chan, 1990, p. 28), children with disabilities should be educated in a setting where adequate provision can be made for their educational and related needs. This concept recognises that:

- Students with disabilities have a range of educational needs that vary in intensity and duration.
- There are a range of educational settings that are, at a given time, appropriate for the needs of a particular student.
- As far as possible, students with disabilities should be educated with their peers in regular classrooms.
- Students with disabilities should only be placed in segregated special classes or schools when their needs cannot be satisfied in a regular classroom, even where supplementary aids and services are provided.

In Australia and New Zealand, services for children with disabilities or for those with special learning needs are provided at the discretion of state and territory governments. Government policies are formulated to conform with national or state legislation, reflecting factors relevant to each specific area. As a result there are variations in the way special education services are provided in the different states and territories, although all policy documents acknowledge the responsibility of government departments of education to provide an appropriate educational program for all students, regardless of disability or special learning needs.

Special education services and programs

The type of help that children with disabilities and special support needs receive at school varies widely, depending on the nature and severity of their disability; the availability of programs and services; and the preferences of the children, their parents and concerned professionals and advisers. For example, children with limited vision may need intensive individual or group instruction from teachers with special expertise in teaching students with visual impairments. This may involve such children attending a special school that is separate from a regular school, an Educational Support School, or a support class located in a regular school. It may involve instruction in Braille or access to computers that have been adapted to enable the children to write, or in some cases also communicate with the teacher or other students. It may also involve training in orientation (knowing one's position in space) and mobility (being able to move about safely). For all students who have been identified as needing the highest level of support, it will involve preparation of an IEP by a team that includes a visiting teacher or other specialist adviser. The IEP will include a statement about the student's current progress, short- and long-term goals, any supplementary services that are to be provided, and specific criteria and evaluation procedures that will be used to assess progress at an annual review. Additional advice may also be provided from government sources such as a program support group (in Victoria), a student services team (in Western Australia), an advisory visiting teacher (in Queensland), a learning support team (in New South Wales) or an IEP team (in New Zealand). In each case, all stakeholders (parents and carers, teachers, therapists and other specialists) contribute to identifying appropriate educational goals for each child.

In practice, most school systems provide a range of special education services and resources to support the learning and related needs of students with disabilities. The manner in which these services are provided is often described as a 'cascade' (Deno, 1970; Reynolds, 1962) or continuum ranging from fully segregated special schools, **special class**es and **resource room**s, to regular classrooms with the teacher supported by a specialist consultant or expert. Figure 8.6 sets out an example of a cascade model from the

8.5 More about IEP and LRE

special class
An alternative placement for students whose needs cannot be met in a regular classroom

resource room
A specific-purpose room in a regular school, where one-to-one or small-group instruction is provided for students experiencing difficulties

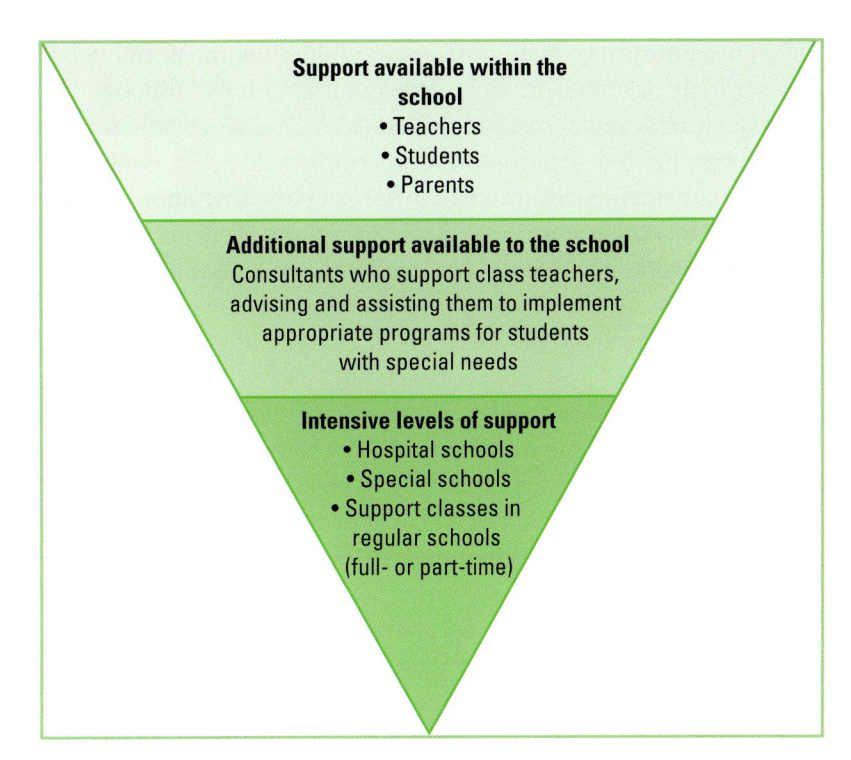

FIGURE 8.6
A cascade model of special education service delivery from New South Wales. Note that the services listed move gradually from fully integrated (the local school and its community) to segregated (special schools).
(Source: Adapted from NSW Department of Education and Training, 1998, pp. 2–3.)

Support available within the school
- Teachers
- Students
- Parents

Additional support available to the school
Consultants who support class teachers, advising and assisting them to implement appropriate programs for students with special needs

Intensive levels of support
- Hospital schools
- Special schools
- Support classes in regular schools (full- or part-time)

New South Wales school system. The cascade model continues to operate in many special education systems, but with an increasing emphasis on maintaining children as close as possible to the regular classroom.

Integration, mainstreaming and inclusion

Traditionally, most children with severe disabilities have been educated in special schools that operate independently of regular schools. Here, class sizes are smaller than in regular classrooms, teachers have usually received special training, and appropriate resources and additional services (for example, physiotherapy and occupational therapy) are sometimes available, according to student needs. However, since the 1980s there has been a trend towards providing support for children with special needs through a range of services and special arrangements within, or as close as possible to, the context of a regular school. Terms used to describe this process include 'integration', 'mainstreaming' and 'inclusion', where:

- **integration** refers to the process of moving students from a more to a less segregated setting
- **mainstreaming** involves teaching children with special needs in regular classrooms for all or part of the school day
- **inclusion** is the idea that all students should be educated in regular classrooms, regardless of the type or level of severity of their disabilities.

Note that use of the terms 'integration' (or 'full integration') and 'mainstreaming' varies across educational systems. The terms are sometimes used interchangeably to refer to students with special needs who are placed in regular classrooms. The key factor here is that children are educated in a regular classroom, or in settings that are as close as possible to that of a regular classroom, with any necessary additional support or resources provided in that setting rather than in a more segregated special class or school. The idea of inclusion requires curriculum modification, changes in attitudes to disability and impairment, additional professional development for teachers, and the provision of specialised resources. It must also be acknowledged that some children lack the capabilities required for inclusion in a regular classroom, and that some parents reject this option for their children.

integration
The process of transferring students from a more to a less segregated setting

mainstreaming
Teaching children with special needs in regular classrooms for all or part of the day

inclusion
The idea that all students should be educated in regular classrooms, regardless of the type or level of severity of their disabilities

At the beginning of the 21st century, the push to maintain children with special needs within regular classrooms is widely accepted in most developed countries, although the extent to which this goal has been achieved in practice varies widely. Younger teachers have generally received some, often very limited, exposure to the learning needs of students with disabilities as part of their initial training. Structures within schools, including support teachers and members of the school community (see Figure 8.6 on the previous page), are generally in place to help teachers working in their classrooms with students who have special learning needs. However, access to these services depends on factors such as the current economic climate, school policies and priorities in educational programs (Ashman & Elkins, 2002; Elkins, 2002).

Within schools, the reality of inclusion varies widely. It reflects differences in the preferences of students and their families – not all students with disabilities want to attend a regular school (Foreman, 1994). It also reflects the attitudes and skills of classroom teachers and other members of a school community, in that not all have the necessary competencies, or the desire, to teach students with special learning needs (Center et al., 1989; Forlin, Douglas, & Hattie, 1996).

Appropriate programs, resources and support services are not always available (Dempsey & Foreman, 1997). Dempsey and Foreman (1995, 1997) reviewed Australian data on the provision of special education services for students with special needs. They concluded that, by the end of the 20th century, the services that were being provided in special segregated classes and schools were, primarily, intended for students needing the most intensive levels of support, particularly those with multiple disabilities, difficult behaviour or emotional disturbance.

Alternative schools

One type of school does not suit all students. For some students, a more diversified school system is needed. Alternative schools, such as those described in Chapter 6, may provide a more appropriate educational experience for some students. In a review of the characteristics of alternative schools for both general and special education students, Tobin and Sprague (2000) identified a set of teaching strategies and practices that have proved to be effective for students 'at risk of school failure, dropout, delinquency, and violence' (p. 137), including small class size, highly structured classroom management, positive rather than punitive behaviour management, adult mentors, individualised behavioural interventions based on functional assessment of behaviour, social skill instruction, effective academic instruction and parent involvement.

Tobin and Sprague (2000) suggest that alternative educational programs should be made available for marginal students who have emotional, behavioural and interpersonal problems, these being students who are at risk of dropping out of school or leaving school early. They argue that traditional schools are effective for most students and may be even more effective if disruptive or unsuccessful students have access to alternative programs that serve their specific needs more effectively.

CRITICAL REFLECTIONS

- Can you think of students you have known who would have benefited from attending an alternative school, with more personalised programs, smaller class sizes and a structured school environment?

- What options are available for students who are not successful at a traditional, academically oriented school?

The integration–segregation debate

Arguments about the advantages and disadvantages of integration/inclusion and segregation have increasingly dominated the field of special education since the principle of normalisation was defined by Nirje (1985) and Wolfensberger (1972). The normalisation movement arose from concerns about the human rights of extremely deprived and neglected people who were refugees from World War II (Nirje, 1985). It was also the product of a growing awareness of and concern for the plight of children and adults with disabilities who were living in large-scale residential institutions (see, for example, Blatt & Kaplan, 1973). In drawing attention to the needs of these two groups, Nirje and Wolfensberger highlighted the right of all people to experience a normal daily life.

8.6 More about normalisation

As community acceptance of normalisation increased, and as the number of special but segregated programs and services provided for children with special education needs grew, doubts began to be raised about the policy of educating such children in segregated settings, separate from those of their non-handicapped peers. From the 1950s, more optimistic ideas were emerging about the capacity of children with disabilities to learn. Particularly influential were studies reported by Kirk (1958), Dennis and Narjarian (1957), Skeels and Dye (1939) and Skeels (1966), which explored the educability of socially and educationally disadvantaged and disabled children. Questions were also asked by researchers such as Hunt (1961), Kagan (1971) and Skinner (1957) about the impact of environmental factors on early development, and about the malleability of intelligence. An influential paper by Dunn (1968) raised doubts about the effectiveness of the special education programs being provided for children with disabilities and special support needs at the time. A subsequent review of the outcomes of special class placement (Carlberg & Kavale, 1980, cited by Kavale & Forness, 2000) found that the type of class that children with special learning needs were placed in was less important than what went on, instructionally and socially, within such classrooms.

By the end of the 20th century, integration of students with special needs had not been widely implemented in Australia or New Zealand. When integration did occur, it often took the form of partial rather than full-time placement in a regular classroom. For partial integration, arrangements were made for students from special schools and classes to spend all or part of a day in a regular classroom. In addition, students often had to attend a school not of their choice because the specialised programs and resources they needed were only provided at selected schools. This limited form of integration was, in part, an outcome of economic pressures. The situation for students with special needs seeking full inclusion was more positive in New Zealand than in Australia (Elkins, 2002, p. 77).

The Regular Education Initiative (REI)

While the cascade model of special education remains the preferred mode for delivery of special education services in many educational systems, pressures have grown within some community groups for more radical arrangements to be introduced. For example, arguments have been made to support the **Regular Education Initiative** (REI) (Davis, 1989; Wang, Reynolds, & Walberg, 1995a,b), or full inclusion of all students in regular classrooms regardless of the type and degree of severity of their disabilities. Wang, Reynolds and Walberg (1995a, p. 451) suggest that, to a large extent, special education programs are simply 'a more intensive version of what is good education for all students'.

Regular Education Initiative (REI)
A movement that advocates merging special and regular education into a single, unified program

Regular class, special class or special school?

Various claims about the relative efficacy of different types of special education provision have been made over many years. Decisions about how such services will be delivered are generally based on one of four main arguments:

8.7 More about the REI

1 *natural justice* (equality and fairness)
2 *the rights of the child* (the right to an appropriate education)
3 *needs* (the personal needs of each child)
4 *potential cost/benefits* (judgements about the relative efficacy and potential benefits of each setting against likely costs).

Ultimately, the decision made by parents about the best placement for a child with a disability or learning problem will be made in the light of the parents' goals (academic achievement, social acceptance, friendships, independence) for the child, and the alternatives available. Some parents will try to have their child educated in a fully inclusive setting, while others will prefer the relative safety of a special class or school. How can the academic, social, emotional and vocational needs of students with disabilities and special learning needs best be met? A parent might ask *where* these students are to be taught: in a regular classroom or in a support class or special school? Another question might be *how* students should be instructed.

In a naturalistic study of the integration of children with disabilities into regular schools in New South Wales, Center et al. (1989, see Box 8.9) concluded that decisions about where children with disabilities are taught should be governed by:

1 *the child's needs* (rather than the child's disabling condition)
2 *assessment of the proposed class and available resources*
3 *the attitudes of the school and the class teacher.*

Box 8.9 CASE STUDIES

Effective teaching

The two case studies set out below are from schools in New South Wales. In a research study of integration, Center et al. (1989) reported that 65% of the 69 students who were intensively observed during the second phase of the integration study were considered to be successfully integrated. Of the remaining students, the integration of 17% was judged to be ineffective; while for the other 18%, the success of the integration was judged to be marginal or uncertain. Two case studies of students who were considered to be successfully integrated are set out below. As you read the case studies, look for evidence that explains the effectiveness of the integration process for these students.

Case study 1: Annie

Disability: Annie has a profound hearing disability.
School: Moderate-sized school in an inner suburb of a small provincial city.
Grade: 5
Classroom: A class of 32 students. Annie's desk is in the front row, with her special friends on either side. The teacher's desk is to the left. Annie can lip-read, but the teacher speaks clearly in her direction anyway. Occasionally the teacher asks one of Annie's friends to convey information to her.
Teacher: Mrs James has 24 years' experience but no special education training. She has no discipline problems in this class. She usually addresses the class by standing at the front and speaking in Annie's direction, using a loud, clear voice. When asked if Annie's presence in the class increases her workload, Mrs James said that the only additional task was that oral tests have to be written out for her.

Peer acceptance: Observation showed that Annie is completely accepted by her peers, both in the playground and in the classroom. If Annie's special friend is absent from school, others make sure she has help in the classroom and that she catches her bus after school.

Parental attitudes: Annie's parents do not treat their daughter as a deaf child and, according to her mother, Annie does not consider herself 'deaf'. Her parents are very happy with her progress, and praise the teachers and the school.

Use of resources: The itinerant support teacher comes for one hour after recess on Mondays and Wednesdays, withdrawing Annie for lessons in speech, vocabulary and comprehension, and working in consultation with Mrs James to reinforce work already done in class. The support teacher feels the integration is successful because of Annie's zeal for perfection, the sympathetic staff at the school, caring friends and the no-nonsense attitude of Annie's family.

Comment: There was no difficulty in integrating

Annie because she has always attended this school. The only concern, voiced by the itinerant teacher, is that Annie may rely too much on the child sitting next to her in class, since Annie is dependent on that child relaying information correctly. Occasionally, Annie's friend has been observed to pass her the answer as well as the question.

Academically, Annie is under pressure to keep up in the classroom. Socially and emotionally, her integration seems to be a complete success.

Source: Adapted from Center et al. (1989, pp. i–iii).

Case Study 2: Brendon

Disability: Brendon has a moderate intellectual disability.

School: A moderate-sized school in a seaside suburb of a large city. The local community is closely knit, and Brendon's family are well known and accepted. The principal is new at the school this year, but highly supportive of integration. He has a background in special education and is able to give programming support and advice to Brendon's teacher.

Grade: 3

Classroom: There are 22 children in Brendon's class. Desks are arranged in a rectangle, with Brendon's desk in the front row, close to the teacher, Mr Allan. Apart from Brendon, there are three other children in the class who need special attention as a result of learning difficulties. No resource assistance is available for these children, but Brendon works every morning with a teacher's aide (special), one-to-one, in a nearby room.

Teacher: Mr Allan has 10 years' teaching experience and is currently completing a post-graduate qualification in special education. He was granted two days' release time earlier in the year to visit a nearby support class for students with moderate intellectual disabilities in order to obtain advice on the best possible programs and resources.

His approach to teaching is highly structured, well organised and efficient. A lesson plan is always prepared and he is actively involved with the students during seatwork, giving feedback and correcting work. Individual attention is given to the slower children.

Peer acceptance: Brendon is very popular with his classmates, which has been confirmed by his obtaining the highest score of any child in the class on a sociogram (a measure of acceptance within a group). Playground observation confirmed that he is able to play happily with a group of children; last year he could only play successfully with one child at a time. His mother confirms the extension of his friendships beyond the school, including visits to friends' houses and birthday parties.

Parental attitudes: Brendon's parents are happy with his overall progress and the quality and quantity of support provided for their son. Brendon's mother hopes he can remain at this school but is concerned he might become a burden for the teachers.

Use of resources: The 10 hours a week of teacher's aide (special) time is supported with Commonwealth Government funding.

Comment: The newly appointed principal with a background in special education, and the particularly effective class teacher contributed to the success of Brendon's integration. This year, the gap between his academic achievements and those of his classmates has widened, but his social and academic integration has improved. Mr Allan individualises all instructions for him, and he now works on the same subject as the others, using the same materials. All concerned agree that Brendon should continue to attend this school throughout his primary years.

Source: Adapted from Center et al. (1989, pp. xi–xv).

Activities

1. Can you identify the key factors that contributed to Annie and Brendon's successful integration? Try to identify factors associated with the school, the classroom and the home.
2. What changes in current arrangements or other factors might undermine the success of Annie and Brendon's integration?

Apparently it is important that attitudes to disability are positive in the school and that all those involved in the instruction process (that is, teachers and aides) have received appropriate training (Center et al., 1989, pp. 6–7). Commenting on the relative effectiveness of support classes in comparison with placement in regular classrooms, Center et al. noted that for students with moderate intellectual disabilities, a special class appears to have some advantages over a regular class, provided the teacher in charge is highly competent. However, the examples of such classes observed in Center et al.'s study generally had large numbers of students, non-specialist teachers and many disruptive students (confirming the data reported by Dempsey and Foreman, 1995). Center et al. concluded that special classes may be more effective if they take the form of resource rooms that students attend for short periods of intense instruction before returning to a regular classroom for the remainder of the day. In summarising their findings, Center et al. (1989, p. 6) noted that:

> [G]iven a favourable combination of child and parent characteristics and optimal support, few children with the disabilities studied [children with physical, intellectual, multiple, sensory and learning disabilities] cannot be effectively mainstreamed. Most of the factors that predict success are modifiable and lie outside the child. The issue is basically one of structured teaching methods, appropriate resource provision and positive attitudes.

The effectiveness of regular and special education programs

In an attempt to assess the relative efficacy of special and regular education programs, Swanson (1999) conducted a **meta-analysis**, or quantitative summary of the findings, of studies published in the USA between 1963 and 1997 that reported on the outcomes of interventions involving students with 'learning disabilities'. Students described as 'learning disabled' were found to comprise the largest group of students with special learning needs. In 1994 they comprised 50% of all special education placements in the USA, according to data published by the US Office of Education in 1994 (cited by Swanson, 1999, p. 6).

meta-analysis
A statistical technique used to obtain a quantitative summary of findings across a large number of research studies

In his review of published studies, Swanson (1999) explored the relative effectiveness of full inclusion with or without specialist help, and placement in a resource room, based on students' level of academic achievement in these settings. He found that the most positive effect on academic achievement was demonstrated in studies where special education services were delivered in resource rooms. Possible explanation of these findings include the excessive demands placed on teachers in regular classrooms from the increasing numbers of students with special needs in their class groups, and the level of teachers' skills in accommodating the diversity of their students' needs. This is a particular problem in increasingly multicultural communities where there are growing numbers of economically deprived families (Swanson, 1999).

Swanson concluded that there was no evidence to support changing the range of special education services available within a 'cascade model'. He argued that until evidence becomes available to support a full inclusion model, special education options – including (in particular) the resource room model – should be maintained. However, in spite of findings such as those reported by Center et al. (1989) and Swanson (1999), debate about the relative advantages of these different models for the delivery of special education is likely to continue. These discussions are fuelled by concerns about cost/benefits; access to appropriate levels of funding and specialist staff; and beliefs about children's needs and rights, and about natural justice.

What teaching methods are most appropriate for students with disabilities and special needs? Center et al. (1989, p. 71) concluded that it is critical for teachers to use structured teaching methods that include:

- clear teaching objectives
- well-sequenced curriculums
- regular monitoring of progress
- a teacher-directed approach to instruction in basic skills.

In a similar vein, Swanson (1999) suggested that the focus be on instructional strategies that the research literature has identified as effective. Examples of effective instructional strategies to use with students with special learning needs and disabilities are listed in Box 8.10.

Box 8.10 CLASSROOM LINKS

Components of effective instructional strategies

Some of the components of effective strategy instruction identified by Swanson (1999) include:

- *advance organisers* that provide students with 'mental scaffolding' upon which to build new understandings by tapping information already in students' minds and giving them new concepts to help them organise it
- *organisation*, where information questions are directed to students from time to time so that they stop and assess their understanding
- *elaboration*, where material to be learned is thought about in a way that connects it to information or ideas already in students' minds
- *generative learning*, where learners make sense of what they are learning by summarising it
- *general study strategies*, where students use underlining, note-taking, asking questions, outlining and working in pairs to summarise sections of material
- *thinking about and controlling one's thinking processes*, where students use metacognition
- *attributions*, where students evaluate a strategy's effectiveness.

The most successful programs taught a few strategies in depth as opposed to superficially, taught students to self-monitor their performance, and taught students when and where to use strategies to enhance generalisation. Strategy use also needed to be integrated as part of an existing curriculum, and there needed to be a great deal of supervised student feedback and practice.

Source: Adapted from Swanson (1999, p. 242).

Activities

1. How could you use these ideas to help students like Ellis in the case study in Box 8.3 (see page 238)?
2. Which of these strategies would be most appropriate for students in the upper primary level? Which would be most appropriate at the secondary level?

Controversial or alternative interventions and therapies

One of the main characteristics of special education is that its development is based on a search for effective procedures that will enhance educational outcomes for students who have experienced difficulties in learning. A particular focus of special education is on students who either have been refused enrolment in a regular classroom or have failed to progress at an expected rate within such a setting.

Over the years, many different interventions have been trialled, using a variety of educational and non-educational procedures. Some of these procedures are described as 'alternative' or 'non-traditional'. A few have proved highly controversial, as parents, teachers and other specialists who are committed to a new intervention or therapy defend it against critics who question its efficacy. Critics are often concerned by emerging interventions' reliance on qualitative, often highly personal accounts of efficacy rather than on evidence derived from well-designed research studies. Problems have also arisen from attempts to transplant programs that have been developed in response to identified needs in one social, political, cultural and economic setting, to different settings. One example of a controversial therapy is 'sensory integration' (Ayres, 1979), which was designed to modify, through stimulation of the senses, the neurological functioning of 'clumsy' children who have problems with the coordination and control of large and small muscle movements: the efficacy of Ayres' methods has not been supported by research (Arendt, MacLean, & Baumeister, 1988). Another example is 'conductive education' (Hari & Akos, 1988), which was developed in Hungary for children with impairments of motor functioning such as cerebral palsy (Hari & Akos, 1988): the success of its transplantation to other settings has been questioned (Bairstow, Cochrane, & Hur, 1993; Bochner, Center, Chapparo, & Donelly, 1996). Examples of other controversial interventions include 'auditory integration training' (Berard, 1993), 'perceptual-motor training' (see, for example, Doman, Delacarto, & Doman, 1964), special

8.8 More about controversial therapies

diets (see, for example, Feingold, 1975), megavitamins, tinted lenses, herbal medicines, homeopathy, iron supplements and neurofeedback (see Brue & Oakland, 1994; Porter, 1997; Rowe & Rowe, 1994; Silver, 1995).

Attention deficit hyperactivity disorder (ADHD)

Together with stimulant medication such as Ritalin, most of the more controversial interventions have been designed to help children identified as 'hyperactive' or as demonstrating the effects of **attention deficit hyperactivity disorder (ADHD)**. The term 'ADHD' is most often used to refer to children of school age who have problems in behaviour and learning. Depending on the methods used to identify ADHD in children, the prevalence rate in Australia has been reported as ranging from 2.3% to 6%, with more boys than girls affected (NHMRC, 2002). Children are generally considered to have ADHD when they demonstrate very high levels of activity, impulsivity, short attention span, learning difficulties and poor social skills. Formal diagnosis is usually done by a medical practitioner, who relies on information about a child's medical, developmental, behavioural, educational and family background. The cause of ADHD is generally not known, although cognitive, environmental and genetic factors are thought to be involved.

attention deficit hyperactivity disorder (ADHD) High levels of activity, impulsivity, short attention span, learning difficulties and poor social skills

A major difficulty with ADHD concerns its accurate diagnosis. Many children appear to their parents or teachers to be overactive and highly distractible. However, these characteristics are common in children, particularly during the early- and middle-childhood years. Not all children who display hyperactivity can be described as having ADHD, or their inattentiveness ascribed to the related attention deficit disorder (ADD). Appropriate behaviour management may be needed, both at home and at school, to help children begin to control inappropriately high levels of activity and distractibility, and to help them behave in more socially desirable ways. However, there are undoubtedly small numbers of children whose behaviour satisfies all of the criteria required for a diagnosis of ADHD.

Once the diagnosis of ADHD is confirmed, management may involve stimulant medication, behaviour management, family counselling, educational support or a combination of these methods (Forness & Kavale, 2001; NIMH, 2002; NHMRC, 2002). Progress needs to be monitored carefully and checks made for any adverse side-effects from medication, such as reduced appetite, lack of sleep, disrupted growth, anxiety and aggression (Canadian Paediatric Society, 2000; NHMRC, 2002).

Over the years that ADHD has attracted the attention of parents, educators and physicians, many non-standard treatments have been proposed and trialled by anxious parents and their advisers (Stubberfield, Wray, & Parry, 1999). One such treatment, the Feingold diet, was devised by Benjamin Feingold (1975), a Californian paediatric allergist, who suggested that **hyperactivity** – that is, excessive movement, restlessness and distractibility – is caused by an allergic reaction to salicylates (a salt), and artificial colours, flavours and preservatives. The Feingold diet seeks to avoid these chemicals. Doubts have been raised about the efficacy of the diet, and research into the diet has yielded mixed results, with some studies supporting the diet and others discrediting Feingold's ideas (Barrett, 2002; Brue & Oakland, 1994; Rowe & Rowe, 1994).

hyperactivity Excessive movement, restlessness and distractibility

Uncertainty about the efficacy of alternative, unproven or controversial procedures is based on a number of concerns. These include the possibility that the treatment will have a negative impact on the children involved, or, at best, no impact apart from a delay in the children's access to more proven intervention methods. Sometimes programs – or aspects of them – conflict with local practices or are inconsistent with local beliefs and values; for example, there might be differing assumptions about the role of play in children's development or about methods of handling inappropriate behaviour. In many cases, alternative therapies have a period of popularity and are then dropped as the expected improvements fail to appear and new 'cures' are identified.

Informed decision-making

When considering the use of an alternative or controversial treatment for a child with a disability or a learning problem, professionals and parents need to make informed decisions based on available information. Nickel and Gerlach (2001) suggested that information should be sought in relation to the following key issues:

- *Efficacy*, or information about the likelihood that the treatment will have the desired outcomes. What trials have been conducted and what were the results? What information should be collected to monitor expected changes in a child after a new drug is taken for a period of time? How long should it take for expected changes to become evident? How long should a drug be taken to avoid any undesirable long-term impact? Look for impartial sources of information, such as government documents and reports by university researchers and professional groups. Is the information located confirmed by multiple sources? Is it from local sources? (Note that there is a tendency for a different pattern of drugs to be used in countries such as Australia and the USA (NHMRC, 2002).)
- *Safety*, or the possibility of undesirable outcomes or side-effects from treatment, or unwanted interaction or interference with other treatments. Are guidelines available? What procedures will be followed if something undesirable or unexpected occurs? What warning or danger signs have been tagged?
- *Cost*, including the actual cost incurred in accessing the treatment, as well as additional costs such as travel to a distant location, accommodation while away, frequency of treatment sessions, length of treatment period (days, weeks or years). Account also needs to be taken of costs arising from any special equipment needed, the effort required by family and friends, and possible neglect of other members of the family, particularly siblings. Other hidden costs include the impact, for the child, arising from withdrawal from a more conventional but proven intervention program.

Parents and professionals need to be very well informed about all aspects of a new treatment before they commit themselves, and, more importantly, a child, to a non-traditional, controversial or alternative intervention program.

Implications for educators regarding special education are set out in Box 8.11.

Box 8.11 IMPLICATIONS FOR EDUCATORS

Special education in the classroom

Teachers involved in instructing students with special needs and disabilities in regular and special education settings need to be aware of current issues and developments in special education, such as:

- The problems experienced by children with special support needs vary widely in their level of severity and rate of occurrence, with the incidence of high support needs being relatively low in children and the incidence of mild problems being relatively high.
- Students who are not achieving at their full potential may be at risk of school failure, while other students may demonstrate 'resilience' by overcoming adverse childhood conditions.
- Thinking about children with disabilities and special support needs has shifted from a deficit model that focuses on each child's 'problem' or 'deficiency' as something existing within the child, to considering the specific needs of children while they are at school. The type of assistance students with special needs require at school varies widely depending on the nature and severity of their problems.
- The principle of normalisation is expressed in the educational context in terms of the 'least restrictive environment' (LRE); that is, the setting closest to that experienced by children without disabilities. Individual Educational Plans (IEPs) need to be prepared by teachers, parents, therapists and other specialists for students who have high support needs.
- Educational services for students with disabilities and special support needs are provided in Australia and New Zealand within a cascade model, with services ranging from full integration in a regular classroom to complete segregation in a special school or residential facility.

- There is increasing pressure to integrate (or 'mainstream') students with special learning needs in regular classrooms or in settings as close as possible to regular classrooms rather than in the more segregated special classes or special schools. The idea of inclusion is a more controversial integration model, in that it requires extensive changes to current educational practices.
- The regular education initiative is concerned with merging regular and special education services, or full inclusion in the regular school system of students with special learning needs. Research suggests that placement in a regular classroom may be more effective for some students with special needs provided that teachers use instructional procedures that research has demonstrated to be effective.
- Alternative schools may provide a suitable option for educating students who are at risk of failure, dropping out or exclusion as a result of emotional, behavioural or interpersonal problems.
- Alternative or controversial interventions and therapies include those that are not supported by well-designed research studies.
- The decision to use an alternative or controversial intervention or therapy should be based on available information about the efficacy, safety and cost of the procedure for both child and family.

Concluding comments

In considering the processes that have gradually led to the increasing inclusion of students with disabilities in regular schools, Ainscow (1999, p. 219) suggested a series of propositions that could serve as guidelines for educators attempting to make schools more effective for all students:

- use existing practices and knowledge as starting points for development
- see differences among students as opportunities for learning rather than problems to be fixed
- scrutinise barriers to pupil participation
- make effective use of available resources to support learning
- create conditions in schools that encourage a degree of risk-taking.

Principles such as those defined by Ainscow should ensure that schools become more effective for all students, including those with disabilities and special learning needs.

Chapter review

- Special education refers to the system of programs and services provided for children who have difficulties learning within the context of a regular classroom as a result of a disability or learning difficulty.
- Special education should be distinguished from the supplementary arrangements and compensatory programs that schools provide to help children who are underachievers or who are 'at risk' of educational failure, and those experiencing problems as a result of educational disadvantage and/or difference.
- The nature and degree of severity of the problems experienced by children who need special education services vary widely, with problems differing in terms of prevalence (low or high incidence rate) and degree of severity (mild to severe).
- Special education services are increasingly being provided in regular settings, with additional support provided for classroom teachers, in resource rooms, in special classes located in regular schools and in segregated special schools.
- There is evidence that provided the characteristics of both child and parents are favourable, and with good support, most children with disabilities can be educated in regular school settings. The key factors here include:
  - the use of structured teaching methods
  - availability of appropriate resources
  - positive attitudes to the integration process from all concerned
  - for those students not able to be integrated successfully, a cascade of services should be available.

You make the connections:
Questions and activities for self-assessment and discussion

1. Define and distinguish between 'impairment', 'disability' and 'handicap'. Give examples.
2. Explain the difference between children described as 'educationally disadvantaged' and those with 'special learning needs'.
3. Correct the following newspaper headlines to avoid stereotyping and negative attitudes:
   a. Wheelchair girl fights school
   b. Deaf to appeal judgement
   c. Angry anorexic attacks authorities
   d. Blind twins boycott Olympics
   d. Blind school wins appeal
4. Which of the following statements reflects a non-categorical philosophy in providing special education services?
   a. The program is designed for students with moderate intellectual impairments.
   b. The curriculum is suited to the functional needs of each child.
   c. Classroom activities are at the appropriate grade level.
   d. The teacher is very sympathetic to the problems experienced by children with disabilities.
5. Identify three advantages and three disadvantages of integration for students with and without disabilities.
6. Distinguish between the types of special education programs and services that might be provided by a special school, special (support) class, resource room, itinerant teacher and regular classroom teacher. What types of programs and services are available in the school district where you live? How do they fit within the cascade model?

Key terms

special education	high support needs	special class
readiness	special school	resource room
preventative programs	learning difficulties	integration
early intervention programs	educational risk	mainstreaming
underachievers	resilience	inclusion
supplementary programs	impairment	Regular Education Initiative
compensatory programs	disability	meta-analysis
individual education program	handicap	attention deficit hyperactivity disorder (ADHD)
Down syndrome	normalisation	hyperactivity
spina bifida	Individual Education Plan	
cerebral palsy	least restrictive environment	

Recommended reading

Ashman, A., & Elkins, J. (Eds.) (2002). *Educating children with diverse abilities.* French's Forest: Pearson.
The Australasian Journal of Special Education.
Cole, P., & Chan, L. (1990). *Methods and strategies for special education.* Sydney: Prentice-Hall.
Foreman, P. (Ed.) (1996). *Integration and inclusion in action.* Marrickville, NSW: Harcourt Brace.
International Journal of Disability, Development and Education.
Journal of Intellectual and Developmental Disability.

Make some online visits

<www.minedu.govt.nz/index.cmf>
<inclusion.uwe.ac.uk/esie/soc-edjust.htm>
<www.health.gov.au/nhmrc/publications/adhd/sum.htm>
<sofweb.vic.edu.au/disabil/csf>
<eddept.wa.edu.au/SAER/policy/intendis.htm>
<www.dest.gov.au/schools/guidelines/quadrennial>

FIGURE 9.1 Chapter 9 concept map.

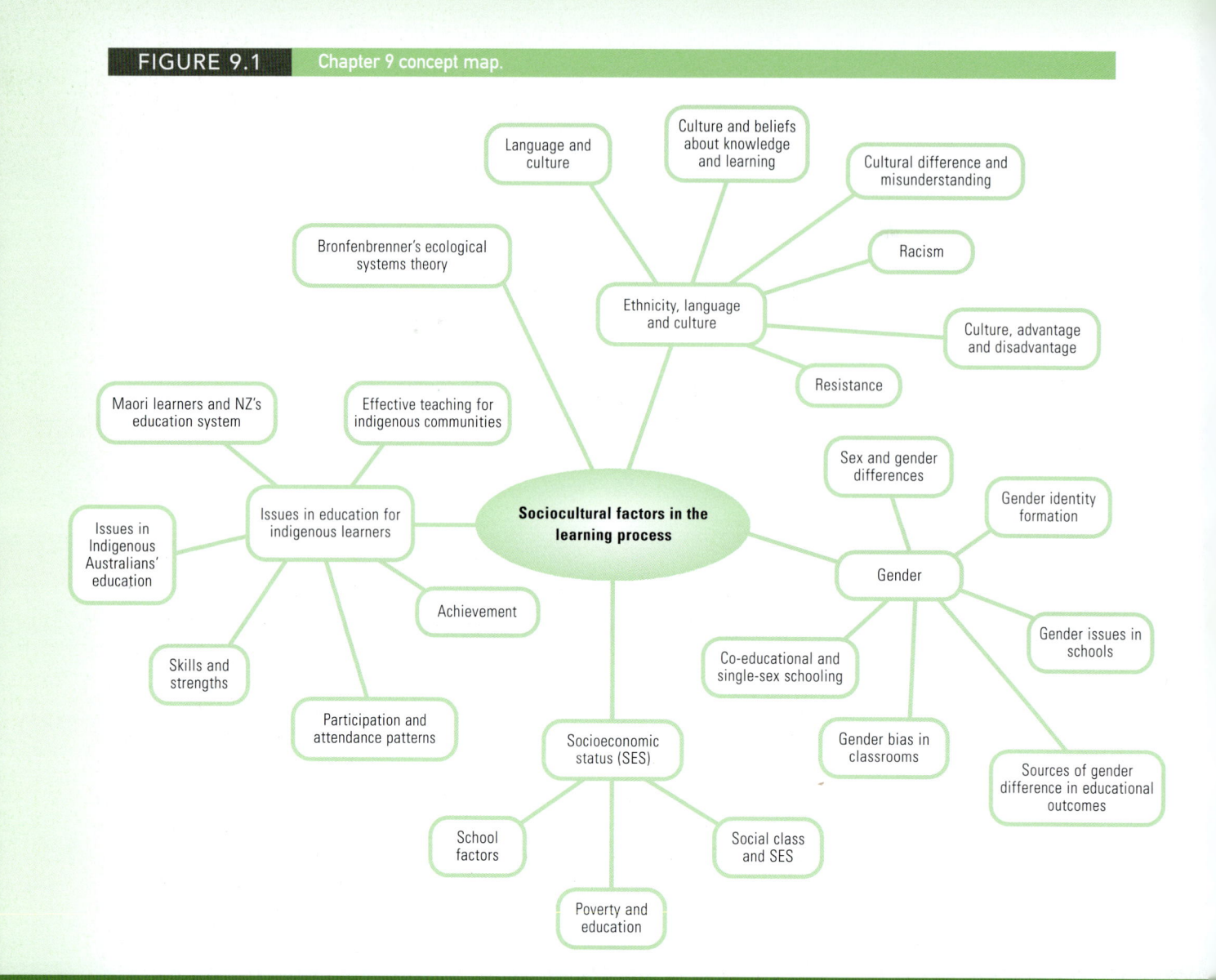

Sociocultural factors in the learning process

- Ethnicity, language and culture
  - Language and culture
  - Culture and beliefs about knowledge and learning
  - Cultural difference and misunderstanding
  - Racism
  - Culture, advantage and disadvantage
  - Resistance
- Bronfenbrenner's ecological systems theory
- Issues in education for indigenous learners
  - Maori learners and NZ's education system
  - Effective teaching for indigenous communities
  - Issues in Indigenous Australians' education
  - Skills and strengths
  - Achievement
  - Participation and attendance patterns
- Gender
  - Sex and gender differences
  - Gender identity formation
  - Gender issues in schools
  - Sources of gender difference in educational outcomes
  - Gender bias in classrooms
  - Co-educational and single-sex schooling
- Socioeconomic status (SES)
  - School factors
  - Social class and SES
  - Poverty and education

CHAPTER OBJECTIVES

After reading this chapter you should be able to:

- describe how culture influences education and its outcomes
- explain the importance of considering differences within as well as among groups of students
- give examples of ways in which poverty may have an impact on students' life chances
- argue why teachers should be aware of gender issues in their classrooms
- give some reasons why indigenous students in Australia and New Zealand continue to experience educational inequality, and suggest possible strategies for addressing this.

CHAPTER 9

Sociocultural factors in the learning process

Introduction

sociocultural factors
Factors contributing to individual difference, which have a basis in society and culture

Sociocultural factors are those that have a basis in society and culture. While previous chapters in this module focused on sources of difference that lie in the individual, in this chapter we consider some of the social and cultural contexts in which we live, learn and develop, and the ways in which these can contribute to differences among individuals. These factors are particularly important to an understanding of equity in education. In an egalitarian society, we expect that all should have the same opportunities. Yet, as we will see, some groups do not achieve equal outcomes in terms of achievement and participation in education, which suggests that opportunities are not equally available to all. Where these differences in outcomes have their basis in social or cultural aspects of society, we must ask what role teachers and schools can play in equalising individuals' ability to make use of the educational opportunities available to them.

In considering sociocultural sources of difference, we examine culture, gender, socioeconomic status and indigenous issues in education. Although this chapter deals with each topic in a separate section, it is important to recognise that factors interact, and that individuals participate in a number of contexts that they influence and are influenced by. Because of this complex interaction of contexts, which varies from individual to individual, considerable variation exists in the experiences and outcomes of members of any group.

Bronfenbrenner's ecological systems theory

Urie Bronfenbrenner (1979, 1989; also Bronfenbrenner & Morris, 1998) proposed a theory describing the various contexts in which individuals exist as interacting with individual factors in development. While some theories of development you have studied restrict themselves to individuals, or at most those individuals' family context, Bronfenbrenner described a series of contexts that have an impact upon individuals and that in turn are influenced by them.

Bronfenbrenner suggested that the environment can be conceptualised in terms of a series of concentric circles, each representing a different contextual system that interacts with features of the individual to impact upon development. An important principle of the theory is that individuals' characteristics and behaviour can affect the environment, as well as the environment influencing the individual's development. Consider a child with ADHD (described in Chapter 8): this disorder is associated with behaviour that can place considerable stress on the parents and teachers who care for the child. This will influence parenting and teaching behaviour, which in turn affects the child.

Starting from the innermost circle and working outwards (see Figure 9.2 below), the systems making up the models are the:

- microsystem
- mesosystem
- exosystem
- macrosystem
- chronosystem.

FIGURE 9.2 Bronfenbrenner's ecological systems theory.

microsystem Interactions and activities in the child's immediate environment

mesosystem Connections between settings involving the child

exosystem Settings in which the child is not involved, but which nonetheless influence the child's development

macrosystem Societal and cultural influences on development

chronosystem Changes in environments and processes over time, which influence development

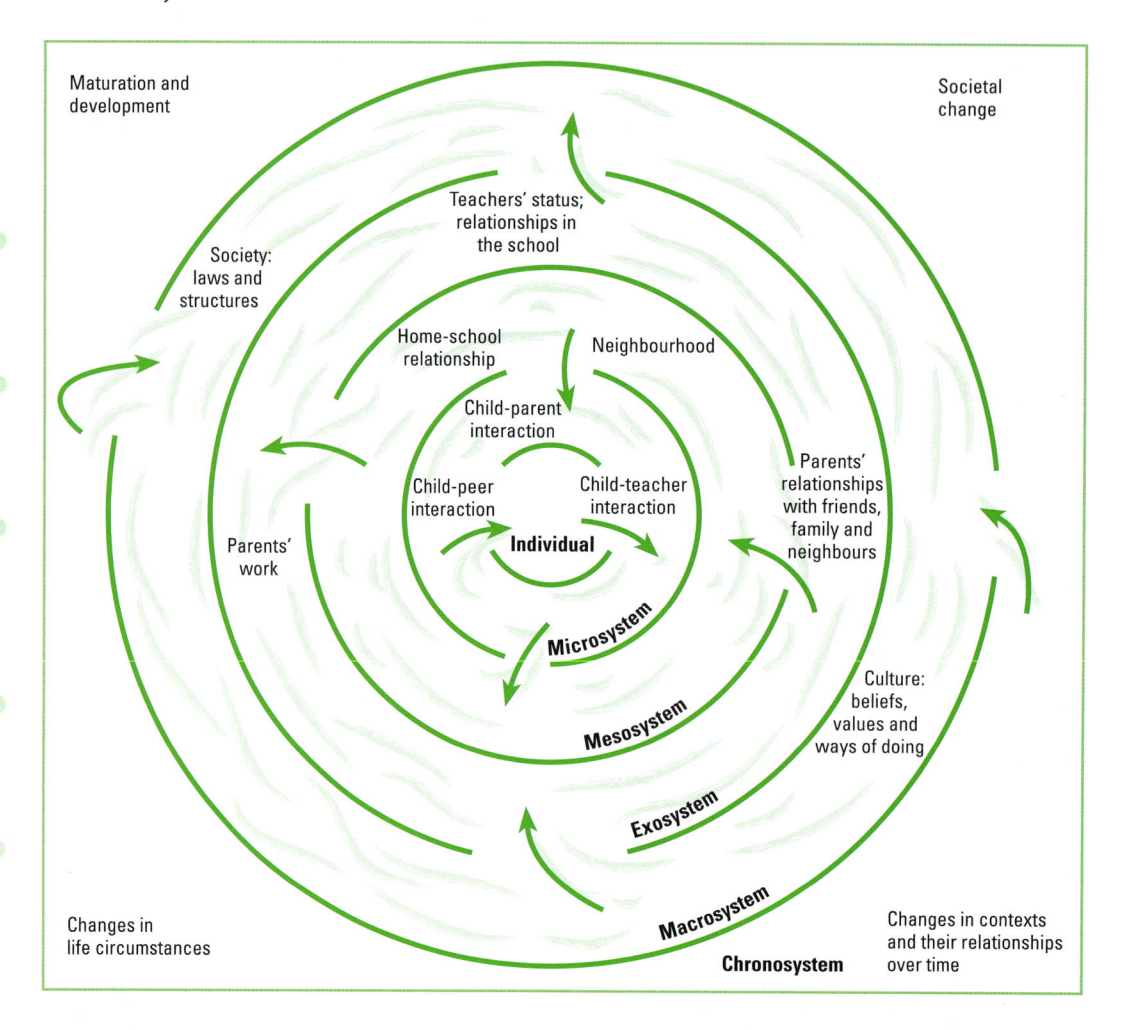

The **microsystem** describes interactions in the child's immediate environment. Interactions in which the individual is involved (parent–child, child–teacher, and peer or sibling interactions) and those between significant others (such as quality of marital relationships) can affect and be affected by the individual.

The **mesosystem** involves connections between settings. The relationships between home and school are an important example. Later in this chapter we argue that home–school and school–community relationships are the key to effectively addressing sociocultural difference.

The **exosystem** describes settings in which the child is not directly involved, but which nonetheless affect that child. Parents' work can affect children in terms of the amount of time and energy it leaves for parenting, and in shaping the goals parents hold for their children (Kohn, 1977). Parents' relationships with friends and family are another example: the support these relationships offer can impact upon parental efficacy.

The **macrosystem** concerns societal and cultural practices and norms that have an impact on children's development by setting expectations for parent and child behaviour, and by shaping the other settings. Some macrosystem influences are described in the discussion of ethnicity and culture that follows this section.

Finally, the **chronosystem** is the influence of time on each of the settings and interactions in the system. While the illustration in Figure 9.2 (see opposite page) is static, you can think of the effect of the chronosystem as transforming it into a hologram, with the size and shape of the circles shifting with time. As children develop, different settings and systems have differing effects, and impact in different ways. Compare the nature of the home–school relationship in early primary and secondary school. Parents make different use of the home–school relationship in response to difficulties their children experience, depending on the age of the student. In primary school, parents may go to the school to help in the classroom and work with the teacher, whereas in secondary school a difficulty is more likely to be dealt with separately, at home and at school, with fewer connections between them. Over time, the systems and settings (that is, the contexts for interaction) themselves also change. The discussion of risk and resilience later in this chapter (see the section on poverty) gives an example of this.

Ethnicity, language and culture

'Ethnicity' is a term sometimes used interchangeably with 'culture'. **Ethnicity** is just one source of culture, however. It refers to a group of people with a common race, nationality or religious background. In Australia and New Zealand, people commonly refer to being of Aboriginal, Torres Strait Islander, Maori, Anglo-Australian, Samoan, Tongan, Lebanese, Chinese, Vietnamese, Greek or Italian background, among many others. These all refer to ethnicity.

There are many different conceptions of the term 'culture', and its definition has been widely debated. The multicultural nature of Australian and New Zealand society means that people living in both countries are aware of others who have a cultural background different from their own, and so sometimes think of culture as something exotic. 'Culture', however, is something that defines all of us, shaping our view of the world and the ways in which we think and behave. It is much more than the visible, tangible signs we sometimes think of as cultural markers (see Figure 9.3) – dances, language, costumes and food. In fact, culture tends to reside in facets of ourselves of which we are largely unconscious, such as habitual ways of thinking, speaking and acting.

ethnicity
Membership of a group according to race, nationality or religious background

FIGURE 9.3
Some aspects of culture are obvious. Other aspects, such as beliefs and behaviours, are less visible but are also important in defining who we are.

culture
Systems of knowledge, beliefs, values and behaviour shared by a group of people

socialisation
The passing of cultural beliefs, knowledge, values and behaviour among members of a group

In this text, **culture** refers to the systems of knowledge, beliefs, values and behaviour shared by a group of people. It is shared by members of a group because of their shared history, and because they identify themselves as members of that group. The sharing of cultural understandings between members of a group is important because of the ways these understandings help group members interpret one another's behaviour and decide how to behave. Culture is learned, transmitted and constructed by each of us. Just as in other aspects of development, we are active in making sense of the world around us (constructing culture) from our experiences. The **socialisation** of individuals is the process of ensuring that those meanings are shared – passing down culture from one generation to the next, and passing culture among individuals. It is a constant process, in which we are all involved, but education plays a particularly strong role. We are involved in the socialisation of one another (transmitting culture) by the ways we interact. For example, when I take a step back, I signal that the person I am speaking to is standing too close, thus socialising them in a cultural understanding about personal space. In school, encouraging children to ask questions socialises them in a cultural understanding about knowledge and the nature of learning. The constant process of socialisation means that culture is not static, but dynamic and continually being reconstructed by its members.

Cultural differences can exist between people of different ethnic backgrounds, but also between those of different social classes and different genders. The culture of a school can differ from the home cultures of many of its students, presenting a challenge for students who have to move between cultures as they move from home to school and back again. There is overlap, too, between various cultures within a society, partly because of the movement of people between cultural settings. This overlap means that cultural variation exists within as well as across particular groups. In this chapter, we see numerous examples of such variation as we examine the large groupings of social class, gender, Indigenous Australians and New Zealand Maori people.

Language and culture

One of the main ways in which culture is transmitted is through language. You may recall from Chapter 2 that Vygotsky described language as a cultural tool, socialising children in the society's ways of thinking about the world. This happens through the words and phrases used, as well as in less obvious ways.

Like culture, any language has visible and hidden characteristics: the visible features are the vocabulary and grammar. Less visible are the **sociolinguistic features of language**; that is, conventions about language use such as how and of whom questions are asked, use of eye contact, what can be spoken about, how adults and children interact, turntaking in conversation, and how topics are organised. Both visible and invisible sets of language features are important to its task of expressing culture.

sociolinguistic features of language
Cultural conventions directing the use of language

The importance of language in culture has several implications in the classroom:

- Using and supporting students' first language in the classroom conveys respect for students' culture and ethnic identity. Box 1.6 on page 23 gives some strategies for doing this.
- Some students may share some or all of the visible features of English, while having very different rules about how it is used. Later in this chapter, we discuss Aboriginal English, which is sometimes not recognised as a language distinct from English because of the features the two languages share. Nonetheless, Aboriginal English has been defined as a language in its own right (Malcolm et al., 1999).
- Teachers and others being aware of and where possible making use of students' sociolinguistic conventions can minimise miscommunication in the classroom.

- Teaching English as a second language (ESL) involves more than teaching the visible features of English: it is also important to make explicit the invisible rules for using English in Western settings such as schools.

The following paragraphs look at some examples of sociolinguistic conventions that are linked to cultural beliefs about knowledge and learning, some of which can cause misunderstanding and even conflict in the classroom.

Culture and beliefs about knowledge and learning

As we saw in Chapter 7, cultures differ in their understanding of intelligence and what constitutes intelligent behaviour. Differences also exist in definitions of knowledge and learning. Such differences are more than ideas: they relate to ways of behaving, parents' goals for their children and childrearing practices. Students arrive at school with understandings about knowledge and learning, and behaviours relating to these understandings, which may match the understandings of the school to varying degrees.

Teachers and schools typically transmit the beliefs of the mainstream culture, sometimes referred to as the '**hidden curriculum**'. This is transmitted in a number of ways. Mehan (1979) described how teachers control classroom interaction so that students' ability to communicate their knowledge appropriately (raising your hand if you want to give the answer, listening and not interrupting when the teacher is instructing) is just as important to academic success as the knowledge itself. Students who do not know the implicit rules of interaction of the classroom, or whose own styles of interaction are not recognised by the teacher, may miss out. For example, Grossman and Grossman (1994) suggested that rather than interrupting at the first pause, girls in science and maths classes are more likely to participate when teachers wait longer for student contributions.

hidden curriculum
Understandings, values and attitudes that are implicit in school structures and in the way material is taught

Practices such as assessment and reporting influence students' and society's learning priorities and attitudes. Greenfield and Suzuki (1998) argued that when children are evaluated and rewarded according to individual achievement, we should expect a tendency towards competitiveness to prevail. This tendency might be strengthened by norm-referenced assessment and reporting systems that compare individuals (see Chapter 11).

Teaching resources such as textbooks also contain implicit and explicit messages. A history of Australia or New Zealand that gave a limited place to women and non-Anglo (that is, people not of Anglo-Celtic background) groups would relay messages about the relative importance of women and men, and of particular ethnic groups in the society and in society's formation.

Cultural difference and misunderstanding

Difficulties may arise for students when the beliefs of the home and school differ. When an individual's behaviour is interpreted from a cultural perspective different from that of the individual in question, misunderstandings and conflict can result. In Western Anglo culture, looking people in the eye when you speak to them is a mark of respect, and shows you are attending to them. However, in many other cultures, including some Aboriginal and Asian groups, this would be a mark of disrespect – particularly if done by a younger person to someone in a position of authority. Without this understanding, teachers might assume that students from cultures that do not favour eye contact are not listening or are not interested. Similarly, teachers who insist on eye contact without explaining that it denotes respect in their culture risk some students and parents assuming that those teachers do not want to be respected.

A second example of culturally based misunderstanding is in students asking questions. For middle-class Anglo groups, asking questions is an important learning strategy and is also interpreted by teachers as demonstrating curiosity and active engagement with the topic. For other cultures, however, asking questions of a teacher is considered rude, implying doubt about the teacher's willingness to share information. Eades (1993) described this belief-behaviour pattern of Aboriginal people in south-eastern Queensland: unlike in Anglo Australia, knowledge is 'owned' by individuals, and some kinds of knowledge should not be shared with certain groups (such as in mixed company), so questions are inappropriate. Eades explained that in Aboriginal English, hinting or triggering statements may be used rather than direct questions. Silence is also an important feature of Australian Aboriginal interaction.

CRITICAL REFLECTIONS

- How might teachers and students misunderstand each other where there are differences in cultural beliefs about questioning?
- How could you, as a teacher, make the value of questioning explicit to the students in your classroom?

Racism

Racism is a form of discrimination based on race or ethnicity. Underlying racism are attitudes of prejudice and cultural stereotypes (that is, assumptions applied to whole groups of people). Because these attitudes reflect beliefs, they influence the way individuals behave and the way they perceive and interpret others' actions. For this reason, combating racism involves targeting beliefs – or the prejudices underlying racist actions – as much as dealing with the actions themselves.

In schools, racism can be experienced by students and teachers directly, through harassment, abuse and discrimination; or indirectly, such as when students' or teachers' cultural beliefs and practices are not recognised, when others have prejudicial attitudes (such as low expectations) or when cultural stereotypes are promoted. Institutional racism occurs when schools are organised and managed in ways that disadvantage some groups. For Aboriginal people and Torres Strait Islanders in Australia, and Maoris in New Zealand, racism is reflected in the poorer educational outcomes these groups experience when compared with others (we discuss this issue in detail later in this chapter).

Treating indigenous students – or any other group – identically, as a response to a stereotype of indigenous culture, is a form of racism. Malin (1998) recommended that teachers get to know the community in which they are working, and that they view any student in three ways: as a learner, as a cultural being and as an individual person.

Although committing, inciting or permitting racist acts is illegal in Australia, racism is a daily experience for many school students. Anyone can experience or display racism, but it is more likely to be experienced by some groups than by others. 'Kids' Helpline', an Australian children's telephone-counselling service, reported in 1999 that students from Aboriginal and Torres Strait Islander backgrounds, and those of a language background other than English (**LBOTE**), were more likely to report bullying than were other groups of students.

Racism is destructive to individuals, affecting educational outcomes, emotions, identity and behaviour. It also has wide-reaching effects on school climate and school–community relations. Racism works against effective classroom communication, limiting some students' contributions, and promoting tension and conflict. In addition, racism is an important source of playground violence, both as racist harassment and as a reaction to it.

The website for the Australian educational initiative 'Racism. No way!' in 2003 identified the following potential consequences for students experiencing racist behaviour: reduced

---

racism
Discrimination based on race or ethnicity

LBOTE
Language background other than English

self-esteem and self-confidence, loss of identity, conflict with parents resulting from rejection of their cultural background, development of a 'resistance' culture (discussed later in this chapter), frustration, fear and withdrawal, dropping out, loss of concentration and non-participation.

Teachers can intervene by taking racism seriously rather than by dismissing as minor difficulties things like name-calling, teasing and exclusion. Teachers may need to examine their own prejudices or the cultural stereotypes they hold, asking of themselves: 'Are there some groups of which I would have lower expectations than others?', 'Do I treat all students the same regardless of background?', 'Are my classroom and curriculum built around the ideas and practices I am comfortable with?'

As Figure 9.4 on page 271 illustrates, culturally sensitive education involves dismantling student prejudice and stereotypes as well as examining teaching practices, curriculum, resources and schools as institutions. Culturally sensitive education also involves including other cultural viewpoints across the curriculum, such as investigating indigenous and other non-Anglo views of history alongside Anglo histories, looking at mathematical systems across cultures and reading literature translated from a number of languages. This conveys to students that cultures other than the dominant culture in the society are valued, and helps students develop an understanding of other cultures – including those of their peers – as a step towards breaking down negative stereotypes.

Cooperative learning approaches such as Jigsaw (described in Chapter 6) have been effective in reducing prejudice in the classroom (Wilkinson, 1989). An important element of Jigsaw's success is that it establishes a common goal for the group and helps students recognise one another's strengths and the contributions different individuals make to achieving the goal.

Culture, advantage and disadvantage

The beliefs and practices of some cultural groups fit well with our schooling system, while those of other groups do not. Thus in Australia, Vietnamese students tend to do well, with some studies showing better participation rates in tertiary education than for mainstream Anglo-Australian students (Parr & Mok, 1995; Birrell, Calderon, Dobson, & Smith, 2000). This occurs despite considerable barriers to success that have been linked to poorer academic outcomes, such as LBOTE, difference in culture, disrupted early education for those who were refugees, and low socioeconomic status (SES). Other migrant groups do not show the same results, even though the barriers to success could be said to be similar. In the section on poverty later in this chapter, we discuss risk and resilience, which goes some way to explaining these differences. Another explanation, around the concept of 'resistance', is set out below.

Resistance

Ogbu (1987, 1997) developed a theory to explain why some minority groups within a particular society succeed educationally, while others do not. Based on groups in the USA, he described different types of minority groups, defining them by the history of their contact with the majority group. **Voluntary minority group**s are those such as refugees and other migrants who have chosen to move to a new society in the hope of improving their lives in some way. For such groups, differences can be seen as barriers to be overcome in striving to succeed in the new society. The strategies these groups develop to deal with barriers tend to be adaptive.

Involuntary minority groups, by contrast, are those such as indigenous peoples, who did not choose to be brought into the society, and whose relationship with the majority has been marked by oppression and/or opposition. For such groups, differences are important

voluntary minority group
A group of people who have at some point chosen to migrate in search of a better life

involuntary minority group
A group of people who have at some point been brought into a society against their will

markers to be maintained. Educational success in countries such as the USA, Australia and New Zealand may even be seen as 'becoming White' and as rejecting indigenous culture and identity. This is particularly so when the school is strongly tied to non-indigenous culture. Folds (1987) described this resistance process in schools in the Pitjantjatjara lands of South Australia (see Box 9.1). He identified absenteeism, ridicule, disruption and the 'wall of silence' as common resistance tactics practised by students.

Box 9.1 CLASSROOM LINKS

Resistance

Folds (1987) described a kind of vicious circle perpetuated by students' resistance and teachers' forceful responses (which are offensive to Pitjantjatjara culture) leading to continued and escalated student resistance. The following example was recorded in a senior boys' classroom.

[The teacher is working on a motor bike. Four of the small class of six boys (another five are absent) are seated on a work bench observing him. Chris and Ken are 'too tired to watch'. They are 'resting', stretched out on the floor at the back of the classroom.]

Teacher: *Pitja* (come) Chris, Ken. I want you to see how I fix this bike. [A few moments pass.]

Teacher: Chris *ninti* (smart) come on – no rides on the bikes today until we fix them. [A few more moments pass.]

Teacher: Don't you boys want to ride on the motor bikes today? [With studied slowness Chris and Ken raise themselves from the floor and slowly move towards the teacher.]

Teacher: *Palya* (OK) it was the distributor after all.

Teacher: OK boys! This [bike] is going to go better than ever before. Let's finish working on the BMXs, then pack up the tools and we'll have a ten minute ride on the motor bikes. [Chris, Ken and another boy start to play a game.]

Teacher: *Wiya* (no). I said fix the BMXs first then put the tools away. [The boys ignore him.]

Teacher: Fix those bikes.

Chris: *Wiya* (no) [laughing].

Teacher [mildly angry]: Get on with it. [A few minutes later Chris and the others begin to put the wheel on. Ken now picks up a heavy hammer and proceeds to give the wheel of the bike a series of resounding blows.]

Teacher: *Wanti* (stop) What are you doing? [Ken gives the wheel a final heavy blow and stops.]

Teacher [angrily]: That's no way to do it. [The teacher snatches the hammer away and proceeds to put the wheel on himself.]

Ken [angrily]: You no good.

Teacher: OK boys, let's pack up. Have you put your tools away Chris? [No reply.]

Teacher [loudly]: Have you put your tools away? [No reply – it is clear that the boys do not intend to communicate.]

Teacher [to observer]: Good grief – now they're not talking to me.

Source: Folds (1987, p. 39).

Activities

1. Can you identify the forms of resistance in this classroom?
2. Is there anything the teacher could have done differently to avoid or respond to the resistance?
3. Peer groups can also develop a resistance culture, particularly during adolescence. Can you remember such a group in your high school? Share with your tutorial group how different teachers dealt with this, and how it affected the rest of the class.

Folds and others such as the MCEETYA Taskforce on Indigenous Education (2001) in Australia have recommended overcoming resistance by creating schools with strong links to the community, such that local ways of teaching as well as curriculum content are evident.

Culture is more than visible aspects such as food or costumes, so multicultural education must go beyond these. Banks and Banks (2001) proposed a model of multicultural education that identified the range of aspects to be considered (see Figure 9.4). Teaching style, implicit beliefs, content, students' attitudes, and the school culture and structure must all be considered.

Box 9.2 gives some strategies for educators to use in multicultural classrooms.

FIGURE 9.4 The dimensions of multicultural education. (Source: Banks and Banks, 2001, Figure 1.4.)

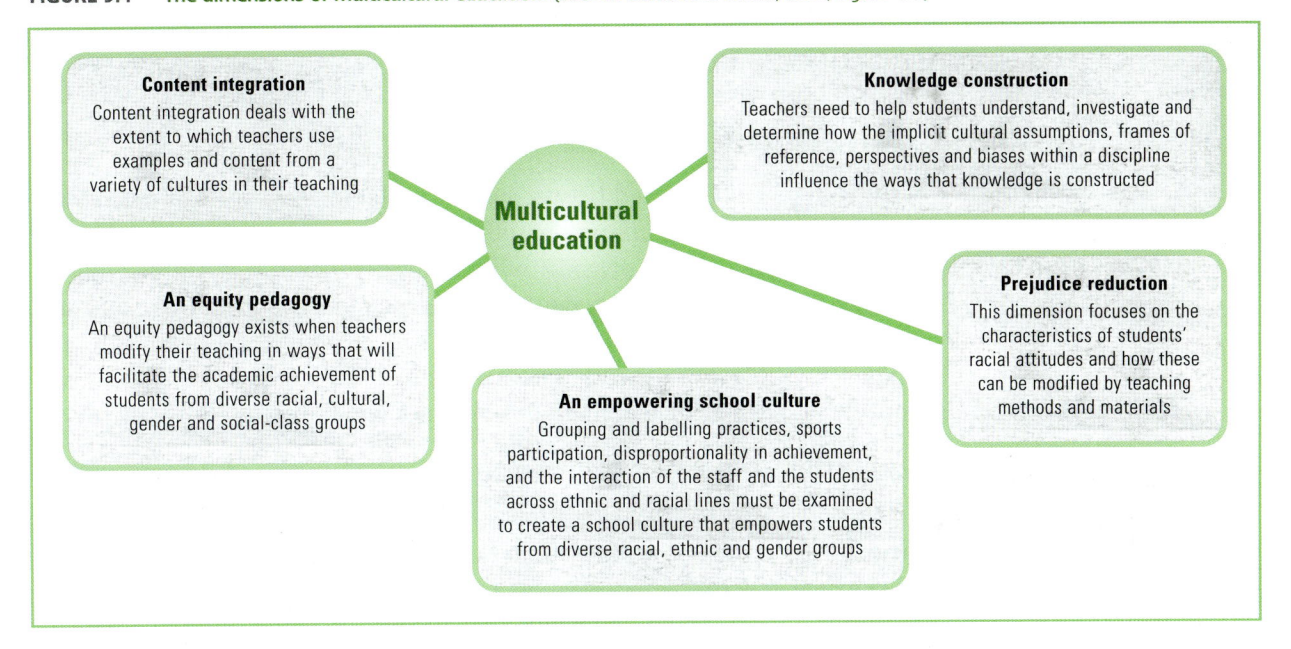

Multicultural education

- **Content integration**: Content integration deals with the extent to which teachers use examples and content from a variety of cultures in their teaching
- **Knowledge construction**: Teachers need to help students understand, investigate and determine how the implicit cultural assumptions, frames of reference, perspectives and biases within a discipline influence the ways that knowledge is constructed
- **An equity pedagogy**: An equity pedagogy exists when teachers modify their teaching in ways that will facilitate the academic achievement of students from diverse racial, cultural, gender and social-class groups
- **Prejudice reduction**: This dimension focuses on the characteristics of students' racial attitudes and how these can be modified by teaching methods and materials
- **An empowering school culture**: Grouping and labelling practices, sports participation, disproportionality in achievement, and the interaction of the staff and the students across ethnic and racial lines must be examined to create a school culture that empowers students from diverse racial, ethnic and gender groups

Box 9.2 IMPLICATIONS FOR EDUCATORS

Multicultural classrooms
- 'Invisible' aspects of culture can be difficult for teachers and students to identify. Teachers must therefore:
  - be self-aware of the cultural views they hold, and that are implicit in their teaching
  - be aware of the cultural models of the students they teach
  - teach cultural differences explicitly, in order to make the invisible visible.
- Some common ways of doing things in classrooms might need to be explained to students and/or changed to accommodate their practices. These include raising your hand to speak, one person talking at a time, looking at the teacher when the teacher is talking, staying in your seat until work is finished, and the use of questions (by teachers to assess learning, and by students to investigate).
- Understanding your own culture necessitates reflection and discussion with others.
- Understanding the cultures of your students will require interaction with the community, both inside and outside the school. For this to be effective, you will need to be careful to look at the strengths represented by the differences you encounter, rather than regarding another way of doing things as 'wrong' or as a source of difficulty.
- Other implications relate to the content of your teaching, such as examining the curriculum and resources to eliminate bias or stereotypes regarding particular groups. Students can be involved in this process so they are actively involved in detecting and dismantling stereotypes and bias inside and outside the classroom.

Gender

Look around you. If your education class is typical, there will be many more women than men. Why is it that women tend to choose education in larger numbers than men do? Why are there more women at university than men?

When discussing differences between males and females, we can talk about sex-related differences and gender differences. The use of these terms has been widely debated. Traditionally, 'sex' has been used to refer to aspects of masculinity or femininity that have a biological basis, while 'gender' has referred to the cultural aspects of masculinity and femininity. In reality, of course, we are biological *and* cultural beings, so the two sets of factors are difficult to separate. In this text we use the term **gender** as an inclusive term that encompasses biological and cultural influences, and that recognises the interdependence of biological and cultural sources of difference.

> **gender**
> Those aspects of an individual that relate to the individual's sex, including biological and cultural influences

Sex and gender differences

While many of the differences observed between males and females – such as a gendered preference for pink or blue – have a cultural basis, some appear to be relatively stable and to have a biological component. The physical differences described in Chapter 2 are an obvious example. The trend has been for gender differences in behaviour, emotion and cognition to decrease over time, however, which suggests that environmental factors are also involved (Feingold, 1993). Most of the differences described in this chapter are small, and there are also individual differences within groups of males and females.

The role of cognition in gender difference

McGuinness (1998), in a meta-analysis of studies of differences in cognition, found the largest differences to be in spatial processing, where males outperformed females. The smallest differences were in verbal abilities, where this pattern was reversed and women did better than men. Performance in mathematics was higher for either males or females depending on the type of task and the age of the subjects. Gender differences in mathematics performance appear to have been growing smaller over the last 2 or 3 decades. In general, boys are more likely than girls to excel in mathematics, and this difference in the top group of mathematics performers appears to have persisted.

The role of emotion in gender difference

Males are more likely for a combination of biological and sociological reasons to show aggression than are females, while females are more likely to show empathy (although the difference between males and females in the latter area is not as great as in the former) (Crozier, 1997). In Britain, boys present with emotional and behavioural problems at roughly twice the rate of girls, with the largest difference between the two groups being between rates of antisocial behaviour (Chazan, Laing, & Davies, 1994). Girls, however, are more likely to be anxious about failure, while boys are more likely to take risks (Saarni, 1993). This has implications for motivation (see Chapter 7).

Gender identity formation

How do we form our beliefs about what it is to be male or female? Walk into your local department store. Who is shopping, and what are they buying? What are the predominant colours in the boys' and girls' clothing and toy sections? How are items for men and women advertised? **Gender schema theory** suggests that children form a gender schema (or concept) for their sex from the messages about typical gender preferences and behaviours that are present in their environment. These messages come from people with whom they interact, such as parents, peers and others, as well as from their observations of the environment. As they organise their experiences, children sort objects or actions into 'male' and 'female', and with an awareness of their own sex apply these labels to themselves or to others (see Figure 9.5 opposite). Those objects or actions that are classed as being gender appropriate are more likely to be remembered or persisted with (Liben & Signorella, 1993).

> **gender schema theory**
> A theory proposing that children's schemas or understandings about gender influence the way they process information and their choices

FIGURE 9.5 Gender identity is formed through direct and indirect experiences. It is particularly strong and often stereotypic in the preschool years.

The formation of gender identity is not without conflict. Gender identity is typically more inflexible among preschoolers, who may be heard to say, 'Your dad can't be a nurse, he's a man' or 'He isn't a nurse, he's a doctor.' As adolescents explore their gender identity, conflicts may sometimes arise for those who are homosexually oriented and who find themselves in predominantly heterosexist schools and communities (Smith & Smith, 1998). The process of 'coming out' and identifying as a gay or lesbian adolescent often has seriously negative effects on students' family lives and peer relationships (Anderson, 1993–1994). This experience may also have a long-term negative impact on the self-concept and self-esteem of such young people (Uribe & Harbeck, 1991). Research indicates that homosexual adolescents experience feelings of isolation, fear and confusion (Ginsberg, 1997), and may be stigmatised by their school communities (Sanelli, 1999) as they seek to come to terms with their sexual orientation and gender identity.

Gender issues in schools

Gender differences in schooling have been an issue in Australian education since the publication of a report from the Commonwealth Schools Commission in 1975, entitled 'Girls, School and Society'. The report identified the poorer achievement and participation of girls in education, particularly in traditional 'male' subjects such as mathematics and science. It led to the development of a Girls' Education Strategy that has proven effective, with girls' participation and results improving to the point where girls are now achieving as well as or better than boys in traditional and non-traditional subjects. More recently, boys have become the focus for similar initiatives, as girls were perceived to be achieving higher results in a number of areas. In 2000, three reports (DETYA, 2000; Collins, Kenway, & McLeod, 2000; and Cortis & Newmarch, 2000) commented on the differences between the schooling outcomes of girls and boys in Australia. Their findings are summarised in Table 9.1. The Australian story is repeated in countries such as New Zealand, the USA and the UK (DETYA, 2000).

TABLE 9.1 Gender differences in educational outcomes in Australia

Area of difference	Nature of difference
Literacy	■ In tests of basic literacy, boys achieve consistently lower scores than do girls. These differences appear during the primary years and persist through secondary school ■ The gap between boys and girls in literacy appears to have widened over time (Marks & Ainley, 1997), with a suggestion that boys' skills have declined, while girls' skills have remained stable

(Continued over page)

Area of difference	Nature of difference
Numeracy	■ No significant differences were found between boys and girls in numeracy tests in the primary years
Learning difficulties	■ Boys outnumber girls in learning difficulties at a ratio of between 2:1 and 5:1
School attendance	■ Boys are less likely to complete secondary school ■ Suspension and expulsion rates are higher for boys than for girls
Subject choice	■ Boys tend to study a narrower range of subjects while at school, focusing on traditional areas such as mathematics, physical sciences and technology ■ Girls are more likely than boys to study subjects across the KLAs, but are less likely to study ICT ■ Girls' patterns of subject choice are less likely than boys' patterns to translate into employability
Achievement	■ Average Year 12 scores are lower for boys than for girls across a majority of subjects
Post-school education	■ Females are more likely to participate in tertiary education (figures include mature-age students as well as school leavers) ■ Males are more likely than females to participate in TAFE courses

Tables such as Table 9.1 tend to focus attention on overall differences between large groups of people. It is important to recognise that *within* the groups of boys and girls there are also large differences, some more significant than those *between* the sexes. Many boys experience success at school and have good literacy skills, just as a number of girls experience difficulties in literacy and do not achieve highly. Collins et al. (2000) argued that gender affects educational disadvantage when it is combined with other factors such as SES, rural and remote location or indigenous background. Focusing on males or females without looking at other factors means we miss a large part of the picture.

Particular groups of boys and girls are at greater risk of poor educational outcomes than boys or girls in general. For example:

- Boys in rural areas are more likely to leave school early than are any other group (girls in rural or urban areas, and boys in urban areas) (Cortis & Newmarch, 2000).
- Students from low SES groups are less likely to complete Year 12 or to achieve highly in literacy (Cortis & Newmarch, 2000). Gender differences in literacy are greater in students from low SES groups (DETYA, 1997).
- Those students from LBOTE tend to have lower scores in literacy (Marks & Ainley, 1997).
- Indigenous boys have lower school-attendance rates than their counterparts.
- There are differences among Australian states. For example, Collins et al. (2000) reported that the Australian Capital Territory and Queensland, with no external examinations, have better participation and performance results for boys than states (such as New South Wales) that make use of external examinations.

Sources of gender difference in educational outcomes

There have been a number of explanations for group variations in outcomes, drawing from studies of differences between males and females. Once again, group generalisations are just that, and we should be aware of individual differences within groups of boys or girls.

Post-school pathways

While girls may appear to be doing better than boys during school, this does not appear to translate to better employment opportunities after school (Foster, 1999). With limited employment opportunities for girls, it is not surprising that they should stay at school longer and aspire to higher education. Boys tend to move from education to training and/or employment, whereas this pathway is less available to girls (Teese, 2000). Teese suggested that this pattern is reflected in higher numbers of boys enrolling in TAFE courses, while girls tend to enrol in university programs. Related to this is the pattern of subject choice, which is more likely to translate to employability for boys, but not girls.

Sex differences

It has been argued that boys develop behind girls in language, and that this might explain girls' better performance in language-related skills such as literacy. Note, however, that the differences in literacy are not observed in the preschool years, but only appear in primary school, meaning this explanation is not supported (DETYA, 2000). Rowe and Rowe (2002) cited a number of studies showing that boys are more likely than girls to have auditory-processing problems, which can affect literacy learning and behaviour. They suggested that an implication of this research is the need for an early focus on literacy- and communication-skills development. Brain research shows differences in the structures of male and female brains. Gurian and Henley (2001) suggested that traditional schooling might 'suit' female brains. This explanation needs to be treated with caution, however, since girls have only been achieving better than boys in the past 25 years, which suggests a social rather than a purely biological basis for the differences. It is likely that the curriculum – which has shown an increasing emphasis on language and literacy skills across many subject areas – and assessment favour girls (Rowe & Rowe, 2002).

Compounded disadvantage

Collins et al. (2000) suggested that boys may dominate the lowest groups of achievers because they tend to form the majority of children with disabilities relating to education, including mental health, intellectual and physical or sensory disabilities.

Activity patterns

Boys and girls show different reading patterns, with boys mainly reading at school, while girls do more reading at home (Millard, 1997). Of course, this might be a consequence of boys' poorer literacy as much as a factor contributing to it.

School structures

It may be that schools really are structured in ways that favour girls' typical learning preferences. Once again, such arguments are difficult to sustain if we take a long-term view of the relative performance of boys and girls. Girls' participation and achievement patterns have only risen to their current levels fairly recently. Nevertheless, two structural aspects of schooling have been identified that impact differently on boys and girls.

Learning preferences

Boys tend on the whole to benefit more from competitive learning arrangements, while girls do better with cooperative learning (Gurian & Henley, 2001). Boys are also better at practical tests and at providing explanations for effects, while girls are better at looking at an issue from a number of perspectives (DETYA, 2000). Once again, these are generalisations that are based on results from large groups. It is worth restating that individual differences in learning preference exist. Traditionally, schools have emphasised passive learning, which is unlikely to suit those boys whose style is more interactive and experiential (Head, 1999).

Types of assessment

Particularly in the later years of school, assessment tends to favour those with advanced literacy skills, and so is more likely to benefit girls than boys. Head (1999) reported that boys tend to be better at short answers, while girls excel in extended writing tasks. It is interesting to note that in those states without external exams, boys have better participation and achievement.

Male and female roles

Differences in the roles men and women take in relation to schooling may influence the formation of children's gender schemas (see earlier). If women are predominantly associated with schooling children, whether at home or at school, then education could be seen as the domain of girls and women. Media reports emphasising girls doing better than boys at school can reinforce this picture.

At home, mothers and fathers have been found to take different roles in relation to children's schoolwork, with mothers more likely to be involved in literacy (Breen, Louden, Barratt-Pugh, Rivalland, Rohl, Rhydwen et al., 1994).

A feature of the school context is the feminisation of schooling, where teachers are increasingly likely to be women, particularly in primary schools (see Figure 9.6). At Sydney's Macquarie University in 2001, a class of 165 students undertaking training in primary education contained just 21 males.

FIGURE 9.6
Females as a proportion of Australian teachers, 1998 and 1999.
(Source: ABS, 2000.)

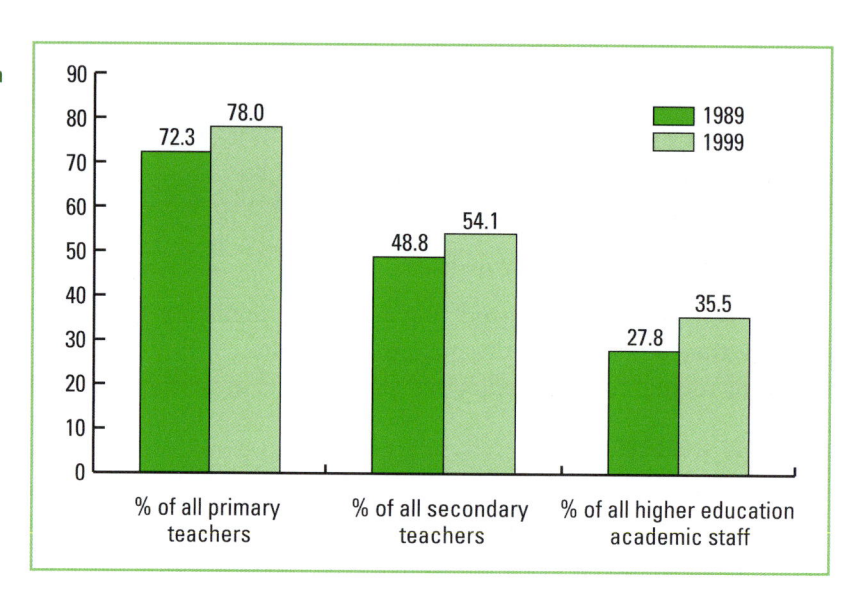

	1989	1999
% of all primary teachers	72.3	78.0
% of all secondary teachers	48.8	54.1
% of all higher education academic staff	27.8	35.5

In schools, men tend to be in roles of authority and discipline, while women are more likely to have roles that relate to student welfare and support (Cortis & Newmarch, 2000). Buckingham (2000) pointed out, however, that as male teachers are more likely to uphold gender stereotypes, increasing the number of male teachers might not be the simple answer it appears. Others have argued that an emphasis on obedience, neatness and quietness reinforces girls more than boys (Fagot, 1985).

Male and female roles are often determined by cultural factors. In communities or peer groups where masculinity is associated with bravado and sporting prowess, achieving highly in school may not be valued, particularly in subjects that are seen as 'feminine', such as English. Fletcher (1997) proposed that male culture needs to be directly addressed in schools if boys are to improve their attitudes, participation, behaviour and achievement (see Figure 9.7 opposite).

Gender bias in classrooms

Reinforcement of gender roles

While some argue that schools are intrinsically feminine institutions, discouraging assertiveness and encouraging obedience (Fagot, 1985), girls and boys tend to be treated at school in ways that reinforce traditional gender roles. Girls are more likely to be interrupted by parents and teachers than are boys, which encourages passivity in girls and social dominance

FIGURE 9.7
Some writers attribute boys' poorer educational outcomes (when compared with those of girls) to schools failing to consider and cater for boys' culture.

in boys (Hendrick & Stange, 1991). Boys tend to be praised for knowledge, and girls for obedience (Good & Brophy, 1996).

Aggression and bad behaviour has been found to be dealt with more often and more strongly in boys than in girls (Good & Brophy, 1996). Boys are more likely than girls to be referred to special education programs (Cline & Ertubey, 1997). Different experiences of boys and girls in school are reflected in their different perceptions and attitudes. Tatar (1998) surveyed secondary school students in Israel about the characteristics of significant teachers – that is, those who had had an important influence on students, whether good or bad. Girls were more likely to describe significant teachers as facilitating learning and relationships, while boys were more likely to see significant teachers as obstructing their personal development.

Patterns of teacher–student interaction

In a meta-analysis, Kelly (1988) reviewed studies from a number of countries – and with a range of ages and subject groups – concerning gender differences in teacher–student interaction. She found that boys consistently received more teacher attention than girls. This was true whether the attention involved criticism or praise, and irrespective of teachers' intentions to treat boys and girls the same. In fact, teachers tended not to be aware that boys were receiving more attention than girls. It should be noted that parents have also been found to give more attention to boys than to girls, so it may be that teachers are continuing a bias that exists in society (Weiner, 1994). Studies of teacher training in awareness have shown some success in equalising attention given to boys and girls (Kelly, 1988).

Do boys demand more attention? Kelly found that girls and boys were equally likely to put up their hand to answer questions or to participate, but that boys were more likely to receive teacher attention – that is, to be chosen. French and French (1984) warned that it may not be *all* boys but rather a particular subgroup that receives more attention. Given that boys are more likely to have special education needs, for example, one might expect those boys to receive greater teacher attention.

Is the greater attention given to boys focused on their behaviour? Boys are more likely to call out and to misbehave in class (Sadker & Sadker, 1993). However, when studies of teacher criticism looked at its target, they found that boys were more likely to be criticised for their behaviour than for academic work, but compared to girls still received more criticism of both kinds (remember they also received more praise). When girls are praised, it is more likely to be for good behaviour and neat work (Arnot & Weiner, 1987). Parsons, Kaczala and Meece (1982) suggested that criticism of academic work may convey a message to boys of high teacher expectations, which is our next topic.

Teacher expectations

Arnot and Weiner (1987) found that teachers have lower expectations of girls, and make more demands of boys intellectually. Teachers' attributions of boys' and girls' success and failure in male-stereotyped tasks also differ. For boys, success in subjects such as mathematics and science is attributed to high ability, and failure to low effort or bad luck. For girls, success is attributed to effort, and failure to lack of ability (Swim & Sanna, 1996). Swim and Sanna pointed out that it is unsurprising that girls then view those subjects as difficult and tend not to participate in them. Walden and Walkerdine (1982) looked at this phenomenon in mathematics. Teachers explained girls' good performance as a result of ard work, dismissing their ability despite evidence to the contrary. Boys' poor performance, on the other hand, was attributed to bad classroom behaviour and lack of concentration: a hidden ability was assumed, once again despite contrary evidence.

These patterns of attribution influence students' attitudes to particular subjects and also their beliefs about success and failure. Girls are more likely to show learned helplessness (Licht & Dweck, 1983) (see Chapter 7), perhaps because of their tendency to attribute success to luck and failure to ability. In comparison, boys tend to show more confidence in approaching tasks, attributing success to ability and failure to lack of effort (Sadker & Sadker, 1993).

Many of the studies concerning what happens to boys and girls in classrooms were conducted in the 1980s, but more recent ethnographic work (that is, studies of classroom interaction) suggests that the processes described have continued. Warrington and Younger (2000) looked at 20 schools in the UK. They found that boys dominated the classrooms, and that more than half the teachers had lower expectations of girls and found boys more stimulating to teach. They found differences between teacher expectations and actual performance of boys and girls similar to those described earlier, from Walden and Walkerdine's 1982 study.

Undoubtedly, gender-based differences exist in students' experiences and outcomes of schooling. Yet it is reassuring to note Rowe's (2002) finding that quality teaching has a far larger effect on academic outcomes than does gender. Box 9.3 gives some strategies for teachers that effectively address the needs of boys and girls.

Box 9.3 CLASSROOM LINKS

Promoting boys' and girls' achievement

In New Zealand, the Educational Review Office surveyed a number of schools to identify successful practice in maximising boys' achievement, culminating in a report published in 1999. Their findings emphasised that successful programs address both boys' and girls' needs, and encompass:

- quality behaviour management and discipline
- an environment that supports and encourages personal responsibility
- the provision of positive role models
- variety in the programs offered, including subjects of interest to boys.

According to the 1999 report, schools that are effective in meeting the learning needs of boys:

- consider differences in learning needs within groups of boys and girls
- set appropriate goals and expectations for boys and girls
- have assessment and reporting systems that target students' achievements and attitudes
- identify students who are not achieving to their potential
- examine the curriculum to maximise the use and development of boys' and girls' strengths
- make use, in classroom practice, of current research about preferred learning styles of boys and girls
- have a variety of strategies that address gender issues, including sometimes grouping boys and girls together, and sometimes separating them, depending on the activity
- do not focus on boys' needs to the exclusion or neglect of girls' needs
- celebrate boys' and girls' achievements.

Source: Adapted from the Education Review Office (2000), New Zealand.

In Australia, the Gender Equity Framework (MCEETYA, 1997) similarly argued that schools need to consider the needs of boys and girls, rather than focusing on one group alone. The Framework can be accessed at: <www.curriculum.edu.au/mceetya/public/genderequity.htm>

Activities

1. Think about why effective practice in meeting boys' needs would consider girls' needs also. How might this issue be addressed in single-sex schools?
2. Look up the websites to investigate this report further, plus one that followed, on promoting boys' achievement, at:
<www.ero.govt.nz/Publications/eers1999/Boys/boys1.htm>
<www.ero.govt.nz/Publications/pubs2000/promoting%20boys%20achmt.htm>

Co-educational and single-sex schooling

One response to gender differences in outcomes of schooling has been a call for single-sex education in schools. It has been argued that boys and girls in single-sex schools face less gender polarisation, with less stereotyping of subjects as 'belonging' to boys or girls (Lawrie & Brown, 1982). Single-sex schools may also enable teachers to focus on those strategies or topics that are more appropriate to one gender. But does segregating or mixing the sexes make a difference to educational outcomes?

Rowe (2000) found that quality of teaching made the most difference to educational outcomes, being more important than school type. In other words, a good co-educational school is better than a weak girls' or boys' school, and individual teachers within the school are more important in determining student outcomes than is the school itself. However, Rowe also found that boys and girls in single-sex schools reported more positive experiences of school and performed better than their peers in co-education. The effects were strongest in the middle and senior years. Similarly, a New Zealand study found that children from all socioeconomic backgrounds attending single-sex schools achieved higher examination results than those at co-educational schools (Fergusson & Horwood, 1997). Sukhnandan (2000) found that in the UK girls in single-sex classes showed greater classroom confidence, while boys reported better relationships with teachers in those contexts.

Single-sex classes in co-education

A counter-argument to the call for single-sex schools has been the need for boys and girls to interact with one another. It could be argued that separating the sexes may lead to entrenched attitudes, without giving students the means to challenge stereotypes. Some schools have responded by arranging single-sex classes, usually in mathematics and science, within a co-educational school (see Box 9.4).

Box 9.4 CLASSROOM LINKS

Boys' own adventure
Single-sex classes trialled at primary

By Miranda Wood

A NSW public primary school is trialling single-sex classes in an attempt to improve the academic performance of boys.

The head of a national inquiry into boys' education, Kerry Bartlett, who visited Griffith Public School in south-west NSW last week, said the classes showed promise.

'I was impressed mainly because it's a genuine attempt to trial a different approach,' he said.

'The teachers were very positive about the way it was working and they thought it had made it easier for them to relate to the different learning styles and to the class dynamics of the groups in single-sex classes.'

Pupils in Year 5 at Griffith Public School are in the second year of a two-year trial, having separate classes in the morning and rejoining for lessons in the afternoon.

The classes have been developed to improve boys' literacy skills at an early age. Teachers have been using a variety of reading materials, including rugby league results and motorbike and farm machinery magazines, to encourage boys to read more.

Charles Sturt University will evaluate the results of the new single-sex classes with the outcomes to be published early next year.*

Feedback from teachers during the national inquiry has found the poor literacy skills of boys are affecting their performances in assessments. Many boys struggle to understand and answer exam questions correctly including at Higher School Certificate level.

Another Griffith school, Wade High School, is conducting single-sex English classes to help students perform better in the HSC.

Mr Bartlett said the special classes were also designed to close the literacy gap between boys and girls. 'There are some promising indications coming out of single-sex classes,' he said.

'They are not the single answer and it would only be part of a number of strategies.'

Mr Bartlett said changes in teaching methods and assessment techniques over the past two decades were responsible for the declining performance of boys at school.

He said other causes are social changes including the impact of negative peer pressure, fewer positive male role models and a lack of male teachers.

Only 25 per cent of teachers at Australian primary schools are male.

For literacy levels tested at Year 3 and 5, the national average showed that 5pc fewer boys reach the benchmark than girls.

In NSW the difference was less at more than 3pc.

Also, more than 78pc of girls complete high school compared with 66pc of boys, while results for the HSC show the gap is widening.

In 1981 the difference in HSC aggregates between boys and girls was less than 1pc while it is now almost 20pc.

The recommendations from the national inquiry into boys' education, which is a Federal Government initiative, is expected to be released in June.

Source: *Sun-Herald*, 21 April 2002, p. 5.

* The trial found that literacy scores for boys and girls improved, and that the gap between them narrowed (*Sun-Herald*, 11 May 2003, p. 3).

Effective teaching considers all students, and is flexible so as to cater to students' differing needs. This applies to gender differences as much as to cultural differences. Box 9.5 gives some suggestions for inclusive teaching practices that are relevant to the gender issues discussed in this section.

Box 9.5 IMPLICATIONS FOR EDUCATORS

Gender in the classroom

- From the findings reviewed in this chapter, it appears that boys and girls can experience gender-related advantages and disadvantages at school. Effective programs consider the needs of boys as well as girls, rather than targeting one group (see Box 9.4).
- Particular groups of boys and girls appear to be particularly vulnerable to gender-based effects; for example, boys in special education programs, girls who leave school seeking employment, and boys and girls in lower socioeconomic groups. The needs of each of these groups are different from the needs of boys and girls overall.
- One key to avoiding gender bias appears to be variety; that is, ensuring that students are offered a mixture of cooperative and competitive approaches to learning, in individual and group work, and offering a choice of assessment modes and study topics.
- Participation is a second component of effective, inclusive teaching, ensuring that all students have a chance to participate in all activities. This may involve structuring activities to ensure that all students have chances to try – and succeed – in a range of tasks. Some authors have suggested that waiting longer for student responses and establishing procedures for turn-taking can encourage girls to participate in male-dominated subjects, and may also be advantageous to students of language backgrounds other than English (LBOTE) (Grossman & Grossman, 1994).
- Being aware of possible gender bias in your teaching and resources can help you limit it by taking active steps to be even-handed in your treatment of boys and girls. Try videotaping your class and observing your interactions for gender bias.

Socioeconomic status (SES)

CRITICAL REFLECTION

■ Think of someone you know who is worse off than you. What has contributed to the difference? How have your different circumstances affected your opportunities, your attitudes?

While our education system is based on equality of access for all Australians, there are differences in the educational outcomes of people from different social classes in Australia (see Figure 9.8). In addressing why these differences occur, and what might be done to even them out, a number of explanations have been proposed relating to the nature of the home background, the nature of the school, relationships between home and school, and sociocultural factors. We now explore each of these sets of factors.

Social class and SES

Social class is often discussed as consisting of three categories: upper class, middle class and working (or lower) class. A family's social class is generally evaluated in terms of **socioeconomic status (SES)** – typically a combined measure of parents' education, occupation and income. This recognises that there are economic and educational factors affecting parenting, and that parents' situation affects children's outcomes.

SES is not a magical factor that determines educational outcomes any more than do the other factors discussed in this chapter. Differences in achievement are positively correlated with SES because of particular environmental and social factors, experiences, behaviours and beliefs enacted as a result of a family's social and economic situation. While many members of the same social class may share these beliefs and behaviours, others will not. (Think of your neighbours: they are likely to share your SES, but how many differences can you think of in your belief systems, your experiences, or in the ways you live?). In a study of the literacy practices of families from a number of different communities, Breen et al. (1994) identified middle-class families with practices that fitted the typical working-class pattern, as well as working-class families with typically middle-class practices (see Box 9.6 over the page). The authors of the report made the point that SES is not static but flexible, and that families may move in and out of particular SES groups, and in and out of typical patterns of behaviour and experience associated with their SES.

socioeconomic status (SES)
A measure of social and economic position in society; typically a combination of education, occupation and income

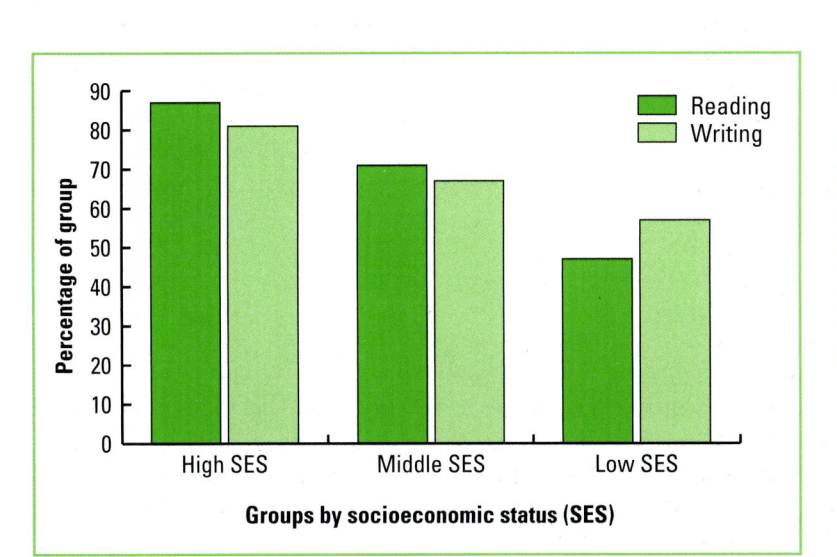

FIGURE 9.8
Percentage of Year 5 students meeting National Literacy Standards, by SES grouping. While studies typically compare the highest and lowest social class groups, SES represents a continuum affecting the educational outcomes of all students.
(Source: ACER, 1996.)

Box 9.6 CASE STUDIES

Four families

The Caravaggios are tertiary educated, employed and prosperous. Their children attend a school which is not entitled to additional funding through the Disadvantaged Schools Program. The literacy practices of the Caravaggio families closely resemble the kinds of activities valued by schools. They buy books when they travel to the city or to a larger town on the coast, borrow books from the library, read *The Bulletin* and *The Weekend Australian* and read aloud to their youngest child. They help out at school through the Parents and Citizens Association and Ann is involved in the school's mathematics and library classes, and provide effective academic assistance to their oldest child.

The adults in the Scott/Clay/Bailey family work in blue-collar occupations, left school at the end of the compulsory years, live in rented housing provided by the state housing authority, and their children attend a Disadvantaged Schools Program school. The Scott/Clay/Bailey family owns encyclopaedias but makes more use of puzzle and crossword books, they make little use of their libraries, Anne Scott is involved with the school canteen but not the school's academic program. She energetically supervises homework but cannot assist Millie with some academic tasks sent home by the school.

* * *

The Long family would be considered working class in terms of parents' education, income, or occupation. They live in a neighbourhood where many of the houses are rented from the state housing authority, and their children attend a Disadvantaged Schools Program school. Their family literacy practices, however, seem very similar to those of the Caravaggios. They provide a home environment conducive to learning, they participate in shared reading activities and read aloud to their younger child, they provide academic assistance for their children, and they are involved in the academic life of the school. Like the Caravaggios, they are well informed about their children's school performance and they regard school success as important for their children. When they help their children with school work, they do so in a way that echoes school attitudes and practices. Their daughter is a weak reader, but rather than correcting their daughter's reading syllable by syllable, Mrs Long uses a shared reading strategy and focuses firmly on making meaning from the text.

The Waugh family, on the other hand, combines significant financial resources with literacy practices more reminiscent of the Scott/Clay/Bailey family. Their home provides a relatively narrow range of print materials, they are not involved in the school's academic program, and when Amanda Waugh listened to Christopher read aloud her efforts to assist him led to a focus on sounding out words and the loss of meaning. The Waugh family would like their children to do well at school if that is what the children choose, but would be equally happy if the boys learned a trade that would *give them something to fall back on* if farm incomes were to drop.

Source: Breen et al. (1994, vol. 1, pp. 19–20).

Activities

1. What differences do you note between the families in this case study? Is there a relationship between SES and literacy practices?
2. How could you encourage the Waugh and Scott/Clay/Bailey families to develop more effective literacy practices?
3. Read the full report of this study – *Literacy in its Place: Literacy Practices in Urban and Rural Communities* – then interview a sample of families from a school you know. Note the variation between different families at a single school, and comment on any patterns you discover.

Poverty and education

Research examining the relationships between SES and educational outcomes has typically contrasted individuals in the top group with those at the bottom. The focus is therefore commonly on those who are doing worst – that is, those in poverty – although Connell, White and Johnston (1991) pointed out that the curve is incremental, in that those in the next bracket up from the poorest do better, and those in the next bracket do better still.

Poverty is associated with a number of health, cognitive and socioemotional outcomes for children, each of which can in turn affect educational outcomes. Some of the explanations regarding the relationship between poverty and educational outcomes are particular to poverty: poor nutrition or multiple stressors, for example, might be experienced in poor families but are less likely to explain why those in the highest SES bracket do better than those in a middle bracket.

It is helpful, however, to understand how poverty impacts upon education. Some more general models of the relationship between SES and education, considering societal and school factors, are discussed later in the chapter.

Health factors

In Chapter 1 we saw that children's development can be affected by environmental factors. Poor nutrition, inadequate access to health care, and exposure to particular environmental hazards such as high lead-levels can all have an impact on education, both directly and indirectly. At very poor levels, nutrition affects brain growth, physical growth, protection against disease, and cognitive functions such as long-term memory. Inadequate nutrition can also result in lethargy, which affects motivation. Environmental hazards may include overcrowded, substandard housing, and poor air quality. Children living in some outer suburbs of Sydney, for example, are at higher risk of asthma than those living in other parts of the city, and may have been exposed to high levels of lead through car emissions. This may result in school absence due to illness, and in a lowering of cognitive functioning (McLoyd, 1998). Lack of access to health care is an important factor in the high rates of otitis media (see page 294) and associated deafness in Australian Aboriginal children. Similarly, in New Zealand, hearing-loss problems in Maori children are detected later than those in Anglo children, and Maori children have higher rates of hospitalisation for asthma. These differences have been attributed to Maori people having less access than Anglo people to health care (Ministry of Health, 1998).

Parenting factors

As we saw in Module I, parents are important agents in children's development. Bradley and Corwyn (2002) reviewed a number of studies reporting a link between poverty, low levels of parental education, and lower levels of school achievement in children. Parental education appears to be a strong predictor of student performance. In a study for the Smith Family (a large Australian welfare agency), Zàppala and Parker (2000) found that even within the lowest socioeconomic group, parents' education level was strongly associated with student academic outcomes.

One explanation of the importance of parents' education is in its effect on what parents do with their children at home, and the ways in which they interact with them. Researchers Hart and Risley (1995) illustrated the relationship between SES and parenting behaviour in language when they found that parents from the poorest families in their study used only a third of the spoken language that other parents in the study used when talking to their children, meaning that the children in the poorest families had more limited parental input when learning language. Parental input is important in children's language development, which is related to cognitive development. Language is also very important to learning and displaying knowledge at school.

Providing cognitively stimulating experiences such as trips to museums, libraries, concerts and the zoo, and learning experiences such as specialist classes in gymnastics or music, is financially within the reach of some parents but not others. Bradley and Corwyn (1999) reported that such experiences provide learning opportunities and motivation for continued learning, while their lack can limit cognitive growth and reduce children's ability to benefit from school.

Parents' experiences of education influence how they interact with their children, their ability to prepare their children for school, their expectations and how they view schooling. Connell, White and Johnston (1991) pointed out that while parents from lower socioeconomic groups value education, they may not expect that their children will succeed at school. Low parental expectations are linked to children's attendance and participation patterns (Battin-Pearson, Newcomb, Abbott, Hill, Catalano, & Hawkins, 2000); for example, if parents' expectations are low, students are unlikely to extend their participation beyond compulsory schooling, as they are unlikely to perceive this as resulting in any benefit. Parents' educational experiences may also affect their view of school itself. Is it seen as a place where their child will be extended and nurtured, or where their child will be misunderstood and mistreated? While most parents value schooling as important, their experiences influence how effectively they express this value to their children (Connell, Ashenden, Kessler, & Dowsett, 1982).

Stress factors

One of the major models of the relationship between poverty and education involves the impact of stress on families and children (Bradley & Corwyn, 2002). Consider some of the likely sources of stress people living in poverty could encounter: employment uncertainty, lack of financial security, having to move house often, and living in neighbourhoods with high levels of violence, overcrowding and substandard housing conditions are all potential stressors associated with poverty. Stress, uncertainty and low social standing have all been correlated with low self-esteem, feelings of powerlessness and learned helplessness (McLoyd, 1990). These attitudes, in turn, are linked to poorer-than-average relationship quality (including parent–child relationships) (Brody, Flor, & Gibson, 1999). In particular, the stress associated with poverty is tied to maladaptive parenting behaviours such as overuse of negative control strategies ('do it or you'll get a smack'), low levels of warmth and responsiveness, and a lack of child-monitoring (McLoyd, 1990). We need to be careful when generalising such findings, however. Such behaviours have been shown to be maladaptive in Western communities, where they might express to children low expectations and a lack of care. McLoyd reported that children may respond with low self-esteem, poor ability to adapt, and (in adolescence) bonding with peers rather than parents. In other communities, however, a number of such parenting behaviours – such as a lack of child monitoring and the use of negative control strategies – might express confidence in children and a belief in children's independence, and so would have quite different consequences in terms of children's response. This belief-behaviour system, linked to beliefs about children's competence and independence, has been described in regard to Australian Aboriginal groups (Malin, 1998).

Risk and resilience

In interpreting models of the relationship between poverty and educational outcomes, we need to be careful not to generalise negative outcomes to all families in poverty. The notion of risk and resilience was introduced in Chapter 8. The factors just outlined (from the heading 'Poverty and education' onwards) constitute **risk factor**s – or factors associated with negative outcomes – that exist for children and families in poverty. They do not inevitably lead to poor outcomes. Bowes and Hayes (1999) pointed out that risk factors change over time, so families and children may move in and out of being at risk. There are also factors that engender resilience (see Chapter 8) to such risks, which helps some families and children overcome difficulties such as those described earlier. What provides an individual or a family with resilience can also change over time, and exists in balance with risk factors.

Garmezy (1993) identifies three groups of factors that provide resilience for children at risk through poverty:

risk factor
A factor associated with negative outcomes

1. *Personality characteristics.* Examples include self-esteem, belief in personal control, mastery motivation (the belief that difficulties can be overcome and that effort leads to success) and persistence; plus humour, adaptive coping strategies and optimism (for example, remaining optimistic in the face of poverty can make it less likely that negative parenting will result (Brody, Stoneman, Flor, McCrary, Hastings, & Conyers, 1994)).
2. *Family characteristics.* These include cohesion, shared values, patience and the presence of supportive adults. The considerable success of some refugee groups despite their living in poverty has been attributed to such characteristics (Caplan, Whitmore, & Choy, 1989).
3. *Availability of external support systems.* Having support from others outside the family can mitigate the effects of poverty by providing access to resources beyond the means of the family, by reducing some causes and consequences of stress, and by providing help to cope with stress as it occurs. The Smith Family's 'Learning for Life' program recognises the importance of external support by providing mentors for students (see Box 9.7).

CRITICAL REFLECTION

How could schools contribute to resilience factors in students considered as being at risk?

9.1 More on resilience and educational risk

Box 9.7 RESEARCH LINKS

Learning for Life

In 1988 TSF [The Smith Family] commenced a pilot project called EDU-CATE with the aim of providing scholarships to 60 students aged between 12 and 16 across the Sydney area. The students received cash assistance and advice and support from workers …

In 1999, the program, which since 1997 has been known as *Learning for Life*, was supporting almost 7000 students. Overall, 15 000 students have been assisted throughout the duration of the program.

The key objectives of the program to date have been to:

- ensure that students from financially disadvantaged families are able to take part in all mainstream school activities
- provide information to the parents which may help them secure a better education for their children
- encourage students to stay at school and to undertake tertiary education or provide them with information regarding other vocational training options
- provide any further information and support to parents and students which may help them develop their confidence and self-esteem
- provide a range of support activities for students to assist them in their learning
- build up research information about problems which students from disadvantaged backgrounds experience in the school system.

The key value implicit in the program has been that by giving children from economically disadvantaged backgrounds the opportunity to participate more fully in the educational process, their life opportunities and self-esteem will be improved and they will have a better chance of not falling into a cycle of disadvantage.

The LFL program now provides 'scholarships' for students from financially disadvantaged families from the primary through to tertiary level of education, and operates in NSW, Victoria, Queensland, South Australia and the ACT.

Source: Zàppala & Parker (2000, pp. 6–7).

9.2 More about the Smith Family's research

School factors

In light of research reviewed in this chapter, it might be tempting to attribute the lower achievement of children from low SES groups to home background, and even to form lower expectations of those children than of others. But schools also contribute to unequal educational outcomes in important ways, and (as we have seen) can also contribute to resilience.

So far in this chapter we have focused on the contribution that environmental and family factors associated with poverty make to negative outcomes. Yet there are a number of factors based in the school and in its interactions with the family that explain differences in educational outcomes across the broad spectrum of SES groups. Of course, we should recognise that individual schools sit within a society, and that broader forces are also at work. Our focus here, however, is on the difference that individual teachers and schools can make.

Teacher expectations

McLoyd (1998) suggested that, in terms of academic ability and behaviour, teachers tend to perceive students from lower socioeconomic backgrounds more negatively than they do students from higher socioeconomic backgrounds. Poor children are likely to receive less positive attention and less reinforcement for academic achievement, which is perhaps in line with teachers' lower expectations of these students.

In Australia, there is reported to be a widespread pattern of low teacher expectations concerning the success of students who belong to particular socioeconomic or ethnic groups, as well as a pattern of 'giving up' on such students succeeding academically (Freebody & Ludwig, 1995). In responding to this view, the National Literacy and Numeracy Plan (1998, p. 2) stated that:

> Within the National Literacy and Numeracy Plan, it is no longer accepted as inevitable that a significant proportion of students will not achieve literacy skills at the minimum level. The Plan sets unambiguous goals for all children, so that no child will be prevented from making progress at school because of inadequate competence in literacy.

Home and school difference

Some ways in which a given school may contribute to educational disadvantage are linked to the relationship between school and community. Related to this is the 'closeness of fit' between home and school practices. While some policymakers have seen this as a problem of the home, others look to the school to accommodate student differences, whether these differences originate from ethnicity, gender, social class or individual characteristics.

Following are some of the key ways in which home and school can interact to contribute to educational disadvantage. You may recognise some recurring themes that run through this chapter. Sources of individual difference are important issues for educators because of the need to consider how these differences impact on, and are impacted by, education.

- *Schools advantage children whose home experiences fit the school 'style'* (Breen et al., 1994). Because schools (like the teachers who work within them) tend to be White, Anglo, middle-class institutions, they tend to favour students who come from such backgrounds. One important example is in the use of language. Language – particularly decontextualised language (that is, language that discusses something not present in the current context) – is central to the work of schools. Studies of the language patterns of different social groups show that the way language is used in schools tends to mirror the language patterns of the middle class (Heath, 1983).
- *Establishing or maintaining a home–school divide*. The values and practices of the school and home may differ. Schools that ignore this difference or denigrate the home values set up a divide between home and school. Eckermann (1994) suggests teaching about

differences explicitly and helping students to judge when one set of values or behaviours applies, and when another would be more useful.
- *Differing communication styles of home and school.* While the language spoken at home and at school may be the same superficially, differences in communication styles used at home and at school can lead to misunderstandings and conflict.
- *Perceptions of and about minority groups.* As described earlier in this chapter, minority groups may see schools as the 'opposition' – something to be distrusted at best, and resisted at worst. This is related to societal forces beyond the school, but may be exacerbated by particular practices that reject the minority students' beliefs and behaviours. Negative perceptions may be minimised by involving the community in the school, and the school in the community.

CRITICAL REFLECTION

- Can you think of other ways in which differences between home and school could influence students' educational outcomes?

The home–school relationship

The nature of the home–school relationship also varies across social classes. Lareau (1989) compared the home–school relationships of families in working-class and middle-class schools in the USA. She found that working-class parents' involvement was characterised by the separation of family and school, a lack of knowledge of school and educational processes, fulfilment of the school's demands without going beyond them, and experiences of generic rather than customised schooling. This contrasted with upper-middle-class parents, whose relationship with the school was characterised by interconnectedness between home and school, a belief in education as a shared responsibility, experiences of customised schooling (schooling that fits the child's perceived needs), and participation in educational decision-making. Duchesne (1996) similarly found, in Australia, that working-class Anglo parents were most likely to be involved in maintenance and fundraising activities rather than in decision-making, and that their involvement was characterised by distrust of the school and concern for their children's happiness and welfare. Such differences can relate to parents' attitudes and prior school experience, as well as to school personnel's attitudes and practices.

Box 9.8 discusses some issues schools should consider in addressing socioeconomic differences. Again, you will recognise some strategies common to considering other sources of difference discussed in this chapter.

Box 9.8 IMPLICATIONS FOR EDUCATORS

Socioeconomic differences in the classroom

While schools are not wholly responsible for producing the inequities in society, they can make a contribution, as we have seen, to either perpetuating or reducing disadvantage. We focus here on the home–school relationship as a key to addressing socioeconomic difference in schools in the following ways:
- Traditional models of educational disadvantage, and the programs derived from them, have focused on either home or school factors (Eckermann, 1994). Connell, White and Johnston (1990) pointed out that the interplay of home and school factors is more likely to be important in terms of:
  - how flexible are school curriculums in taking account of students' prior knowledge and interests?
  - how closely do school, student and parent goals match?
  - how much social distance is there between the home and the school?

- Many of these questions involve the individual teacher investigating student and community concerns. Information evenings held at the start of each year often convey to parents what a teacher's goal and approach will be, but could equally be a forum for asking about parents' concerns and expectations.
- An important implication of the research reviewed in this chapter is the need to consider children as members of families and communities, not just as school students. How will your classroom support and reflect students' home experiences?
- School, home and community interaction is important in understanding the causes of educational disadvantage, and in dealing with it. The participation of parents and community members in the school, and of the school in the community, are important strategies, as we saw in the section on culture, and as we see again in the section on issues for indigenous people in education.
- Effective parent or community participation means more than token attendance at open days, and requires real two-way communication and parental involvement in decision-making (Epstein, 1995). The school needs to inform parents about school programs in ways they can access and understand, and also to provide them with a variety of ways to contribute to decision-making at classroom and schoolwide levels. Possible strategies include:
  - displays
  - newsletters with parental input
  - open classrooms where parents are given roles in order to participate
  - inviting particular groups of parents, as well as the whole school community, to discuss particular issues, and making use of key parents to communicate information and ideas between the school and other parents
  - varying meeting times to suit working parents, and providing childcare at meetings
  - involving parents as members of committees looking at curriculum areas, not just in extra-curricular areas such as canteen and fundraising.

Issues in education for indigenous learners

Indigenous people in a number of countries worldwide are educationally disadvantaged; that is, they experience poorer educational outcomes than their non-indigenous counterparts in terms of achievement, participation, attendance and experience of school. This is true of Native Americans, the Inuit in Canada, Maoris in New Zealand, and Aboriginal people and Torres Strait Islanders in Australia.

A complex interaction of factors – historical, social, political and economic – contributes to this situation, added to by factors tied more directly to education. For example, many indigenous people experience the poverty-related factors described in the previous section. In a review of Australian Indigenous people's education in the Northern Territory, Collins (1999) pointed out that education is linked to housing, health and policing issues. In New Zealand, income has been shown to be an important factor in the differences between Maori and Anglo (Pakeha) people's educational outcomes. Over a number of years, when Maori incomes rose, the gap between Maori and Anglo participation and achievement narrowed, and when Maori incomes dropped, the gap widened (Chapple, Jefferies, & Walker, 1997). In this text, we focus on those aspects of Australian and New Zealand indigenous people's experiences that are directly related to learning and teaching. It is important, however, to remember the wider sociocultural context, as this also has a direct impact.

Achievement

The Adelaide Declaration on National Goals for Schooling in the 21st Century states that, for schooling to be socially just, the learning outcomes of all students should be equal. This is not the case in Australia, with Aboriginal and Torres Strait Islander students experiencing the worst outcomes of any group (see Figure 9.9). In New Zealand, the Ministry of Education has set goals over a number of years to improve Maori children's participation and achievement in education so it matches that of the wider population (NZ Ministry of Education, 2002).

Although equality of outcomes for all students has improved in Australia and New Zealand in recent years, disparities remain. Referring to a recent comparative study, the New Zealand Ministry of Education (2002) describes Australia and New Zealand as having 'high performance, and low social equity' in education when compared with other countries in the OECD.

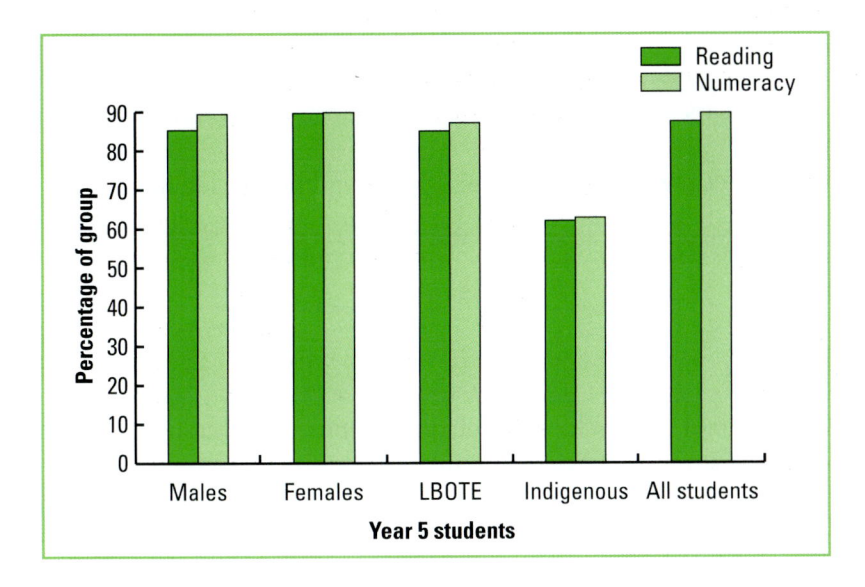

FIGURE 9.9
Percentage of Australian Year 5 students achieving national benchmarks in reading and numeracy, 2000. Relative differences in educational outcomes between different groups highlight inequalities in educational opportunity.
(Source: ACER, 2000.)

It is important not to dismiss these outcomes as 'natural' or unavoidable. Schools have a responsibility to improve opportunities for indigenous students, and to the extent that these students do not experience the same outcomes as other students, Australian or New Zealand schools have failed them (Parliament of Australia, Senate Committee, 1999; MCEETYA, 2000). Literacy and numeracy are important skills for future learning, as well as for success in the wider society. They are also skills that are widely named by indigenous people as important outcomes of education.

Many indigenous students also face issues of poverty and of having a LBOTE when accessing education. However, these elements alone cannot account for the poorer performance of indigenous students when compared to that of general student populations. For example, groups of students with LBOTE and students of low SES background were both reported as performing better than Indigenous Australian students in the Australian Council of Educational Research's (ACER's) National School English Literacy Survey (ACER, 1996).

Significant improvements have been made relatively recently in indigenous people's achievement patterns in Australia and New Zealand. In 1996 in Australia, less than 20% of Year 3 Indigenous Australian students sampled by the National School English Literacy Survey met the benchmark in reading, and less than 30% met the benchmark in writing. In 1999, this figure rose to 66% of Indigenous Australian students meeting the benchmark in reading; in 2000, the figure was 76.9%. When these results are compared with those of non-Indigenous Australian students, however, it is obvious that more work needs to be done, since in 2000, 92.5% of all Australian students met the reading benchmark. Similarly, in New Zealand there have been improvements in the relative performance of Maori students in recent years. The New Zealand Ministry of Education (2001) attributes these improvements to a focus on Maori assessment, a focus on literacy and numeracy, the integration of Maori language into the (English) science curriculum, and the increasing involvement of schools in communities and communities in schools.

Participation and attendance patterns

Participation and attendance are both contributors to and outcomes of educational disadvantage. Irrespective of teaching-program quality, if students do not attend school regularly they cannot benefit. Seeing education as relevant and achievable is necessary for regular participation, and attendance is necessary for success. A Commonwealth-funded project in 2000 found high levels of absenteeism among Indigenous Australians that far exceeded absenteeism levels among non-Indigenous Australian students (Bourke, Rigby, & Burden, 2000). In New Zealand, Maori students have higher suspension and 'stand-down' (temporary suspension) rates than those in the general population. In both Australia and New Zealand, indigenous students are less likely than non-indigenous students to stay on in the senior years of secondary school (NZ Ministry of Education, 2001; Bourke et al., 2000).

Attendance is affected by multiple factors, including poverty and health, family mobility, cultural and social obligations (such as attendance at funerals or community ceremonies), and past and present experiences of education. It is also limited in remote areas by the availability of educational facilities.

9.3 Family mobility and other factors' influence on participation and attendance patterns

Skills and strengths

Numerous authors have described the world views of various indigenous groups (Harris, 1990), and have sought to link these to learning preferences. Others have cautioned against assuming that all indigenous people have the same learning style, claiming that there will be differences in individuals' preferences as well as across different groups (Groome, 1995).

Many indigenous students are skilled in a number of areas – including spatial, observational and kinaesthetic domains – but the presence and depth of skills depend on a student's early experiences. Malin (1998) recommended observing students inside and outside school in order to discover their learning strengths and preferences. To help in this process, Groome (1995) suggested that Gardner's theory of multiple intelligences (see Chapter 7) might be useful in catering for different preferences and for assessing the learning strengths of individuals, while taking culture into account.

Issues in Indigenous Australians' education

While Indigenous Australian students bring many strengths to school, some of these constitute differences from the mainstream Western experience in which Australian schools are typically grounded. As we saw in the section on culture earlier, students can be disadvantaged educationally when there is a mismatch between their culture and that of the school, since school culture tends to favour those whose experience matches it closely. In this discussion we look first at educational outcomes for Indigenous Australian students, then at some of the strengths such students may bring to the learning–teaching process.

Diversity and commonality

Indigenous Australians – that is, Aboriginal people and Torres Strait Islanders – are not a homogeneous group. Important differences exist among different peoples and language groups, and among Indigenous Australians in urban, rural and remote locations. Kooris living in inner-city Sydney are no less Aboriginal than Yolngu people living in 'traditional' communities in the Northern Territory, notwithstanding large differences in lifestyle, language and beliefs. In addition, different individuals and communities may have differing experiences of education. Each state or territory in Australia has its own education practices and policies regarding Indigenous Australians. For example, the schools in the Torres Strait employ Indigenous teachers and principals in much higher proportions than is the case in many other areas of Australia.

Such diversity in practices and policies across Australia is complicated by individuals or groups moving between states. It is also complicated by individuals moving between urban and rural, and between 'traditional' and 'non-traditional' locations. In one school there may be students from a number of different groups; individuals within any group, too, differ in aspirations, attitudes and values. There are also differences in different communities' aspirations and their goals for education. While the majority of Indigenous Australians place a high priority on education (DEET, 1989), what they seek from that education may differ. Skills in English literacy and numeracy are important to many, as is maintaining Indigenous culture and language, but the relative importance of these two goals is different for different communities. Families living in remote communities may place less importance in learning 'White' skills and greater emphasis on the teaching of their own culture. Others might not entrust the teaching of their culture and language to the school, preferring to maintain that function within the community. For still other groups, learning the skills of literacy and numeracy is seen as an essential outcome of schooling, and such groups are concerned that this process might be compromised if too much emphasis is placed on the learning of culture (Nakata, 1995). Once again, listening to the concerns and needs of a particular community is important in ensuring a match between community and school goals.

Notwithstanding Indigenous Australians' diversity, there are commonalities among the different peoples in terms of status in society and exposure to institutional racism, and regarding issues of school attendance, participation and achievement. Commonalities have also been identified among Aboriginal groups across Australia in terms of values, ways of relating and ways of using language (Bourke et al., 2000).

Independence

The child-rearing style of many Australian Indigenous communities affords children greater independence and responsibility than typically results from Western child-rearing practices. This means that Indigenous Australian students may respond better to adult-education models than to the usual model used in schools that sees students as dependent on and, in terms of role, subordinate to the teacher. The Human Rights and Equal Opportunities Commission Report (HREOC 2000b, p. 10) quoted one submission, from Brewarrina in NSW:

> Independence is a wonderful thing and it's probably something that the school system doesn't recognise. Some of those kids are independent from the moment they walk. And self-sufficient in a lot of ways. That independence is sometimes at loggerheads with the school system. It's early days in education for Aboriginal kids I believe.

This independence may also mean parents take a different role and approach in terms of encouraging children to attend school. For example, they may be reluctant to compel children to attend.

Interdependence

Cultures that emphasise relationships over tasks (Harris, 1990) lend themselves to collaborative and cooperative learning models (see chapters 5 and 6 for examples of these approaches). Group work may be favoured over independent tasks, and cooperation over competition, although Ulstrup (1994, as cited in Groome, 1995) reported a strong preference for competition held alongside cohesion and cooperative learning preferences. Greenfield and Suzuki (1998) likewise suggested that children from cultures that emphasise relationships tend to be cooperative with groups of which they are members, and competitive with groups of which they are not members.

Language and linguistic competence

Many Indigenous Australian students are competent in several languages, and can switch between various languages and dialects when talking in different contexts. This language skill represents a strong understanding of language and how it works, which can be harnessed in English language and literacy learning. The HREOC's inquiry into rural and remote education (HREOC, 2000a, E4.2) quoted a submission revealing that such language skills can go unrecognised in Indigenous Australian students:

> My sister teaches gifted children and if she gets a kid who walks in and can speak two languages in grade one or two they are absolutely ecstatic, they have a genius on their hands. Out in the community schools they have kids that speak five or six languages fluently, none of them being English. We sit them in a classroom, teach them English and then say these kids are a bit thick and off the mark.

The majority of Indigenous Australians come to school speaking a language other than **Standard Australian English (SAE)** (Bourke et al., 2000). They may speak a language completely distinct from English, a 'creole' (that is, an amalgam of English vocabulary and Indigenous structure that exists as a new language) or a form of **Aboriginal English**.

It is important to recognise that Aboriginal English is a language in its own right, different in every aspect of language from SAE (Malcolm, Haig, Konigsberg, Rochecouste, Collard, Hill, & Cahill, 1999). Aboriginal English has many different forms across different localities; 'strong' and 'weak' forms may be used within one community, depending on the context. Although SAE and the Aboriginal English spoken in some areas may be mutually intelligible, Aboriginal English remains an important marker of Aboriginal identity. Like all languages, it bears important aspects of its speakers' culture and world view. Its similarity to SAE may cause difficulties when people – Indigenous and non-Indigenous Australians – fail to recognise its legitimacy and distinction as a separate language. Malcolm et al. described how students' use of Aboriginal English may not be accepted. Teachers who are unaware of this issue may correct students' use of Aboriginal English as being incorrect speech or writing, rather than recognising its source and explicitly teaching students about the differences between Aboriginal English and SAE, when to use SAE, and when to use Aboriginal English. The New South Wales Board of Studies (cited in Malcolm et al., 1999, p. 21) quoted an Aboriginal student as saying: 'Teachers are always correcting what we say or how we say. They say it is bad English. It makes us feel bad.'

Some Indigenous people may discourage the use of Aboriginal English out of a desire for their children to succeed in the wider society. Another example is given by Malcolm et al. (1999) from earlier research done by Eagleson, Kaldor and Malcolm (1982, p. 237):

> [M]y mother and father, uncles and aunties would constantly tell me not to use Aboriginal English and to speak far more slowly than I did and to speak in standard English. ... you had to because you went to a white school I would imagine and the whites were the people that you had to sort of mimic and be like.

The concern of Indigenous parents over their children acquiring the literacy and numeracy skills needed for survival and success in Australian society has been reported by Harris (1990). The challenge remains how to provide these skills for Indigenous Australian children without degrading or eliminating their own language and culture. One approach to dealing with this challenge has been the development of 'two-ways' (or 'both-ways') schooling (see Box 9.9 opposite), which seeks to teach Western and traditional Aboriginal content and methodology side by side (Harris, 1990).

Standard Australian English
The language of mainstream Australia, and 'standard' in the sense that it does not vary significantly across communities

Aboriginal English
A language distinct from Standard Australian English, and having many variants in different Aboriginal communities

Box 9.9 — CLASSROOM LINKS

Two-way education

Yipirinya Primary school, in Alice Springs, was established in 1978 as a community-controlled school because of concerns in the local Aboriginal community about Aboriginal schoolchildren facing a loss of language and culture, having teachers who were non-family and non-community members, teasing from non-Aboriginal children, racism and poor attendance.

The school's aims, quoted in Cook and Buzzacott (2000, p. 3), are:

- To produce people who can move freely with knowledge and confidence in both Aboriginal and non-Aboriginal societies. Yipirinya teaches the children English and other non-Aboriginal knowledge as well as maintaining and reinforcing Arrernte, Luritja and Warlpiri knowledge.
- To develop and extend children's oral language and literacy skills as well as reinforcing their Aboriginal identity, cultural knowledge, values and spirituality.
- To provide a familiar and open environment that fosters control of Yipirinya by the school community.
- To promote management of the school that reflects traditional Arrernte, Luritja and Warlpiri structures. The idea of 'two-way' education is hollow if it is not supported by a system of management which supports this philosophy.
- To promote Aboriginalisation of the school's teaching, administrative and other staff.
- To produce vernacular literature that integrates language teaching into a number of curriculum areas (e.g. mathematics, arts, crafts, cultural studies, etc.).

The school draws from families living in the town of Alice Springs, as well as from a number of camps around the town. A number of Aboriginal languages are spoken, including Central Arrernte, Western Arrernte, Luritja and Warlpiri, as well as English. Many people are bilingual or even multilingual.

Classes are arranged in language groups, with age grouping within classes. Children are taught initially in their first language, then introduced to English as a second language.

The policy is to teach equal proportions of first language and English, with each language taught separately, in different areas of the classroom, with themes across the curriculum that are particular to the language. For example, the younger group in the Western Arrernte class might explore basic mathematical concepts in Western Arrernte, while the older group extends their mathematical understanding in English. In science, students might study echidnas in Western Arrernte, and transport in English. In addition, each class takes part once a week in the culture program, which may involve days spent 'out bush', or community members coming into the school.

In a senior class for students 11 years and older, students from all language groups are combined and taught solely in English to focus on further developing English literacy and numeracy skills as preparation for secondary school.

There is a deliberate aim not to mix the languages: Aboriginal teachers only use the language they teach, and non-Aboriginal teachers speak only English in class, without translation. Each class is taught by an Aboriginal vernacular language teacher, an Aboriginal assistant teacher and a non-Aboriginal teacher.

The school is supported by a Literacy and Culture Centre, which produces and collects resources in the languages of the school. A teacher-linguist helps with curriculum planning and teacher inservice, while literacy workers in each language also work with teachers and in developing materials. The school has links with the University of South Australia, through which staff development is maintained.

Source: Adapted from Cook and Buzzacott (2000, Case Study 6).

Activities

1. Compare the above approach with the approach to Maori medium-schooling described in Box 9.13 on page 297. What common elements do you notice?
2. See Marika (1998), which is available at <www.aiatsis.gov.au/lbry/dig_prgm/wentworth/a318678_a.pdf>. Compare Yipirinya's approach to that of Yirrkala, another Aboriginal school applying two-way learning. What benefits do you see in each approach? Can you see any difficulties?

A rich cultural heritage

Recognising the richness of Indigenous Australians' cultural heritage involves being aware of contemporary culture as well as that of the past, and recognising different ways of viewing history, time, land and relationships. Students living in traditional communities might have considerable knowledge of the land, of the Dreaming, and of traditional dance, music and painting particular to their community. Those in urban communities might have a very different cultural heritage. Nonetheless, it is helpful to return to our earlier discussion of culture, remembering that this often involves more than visible characteristics. Students' cultural heritage also influences how they view learning, teachers and fellow students.

Box 9.10 outlines an Aboriginal pedagogy devised by Blitner, Dobson, Gibson, Martin, Oldfield, Oliver et al. (2000).

Box 9.10 CLASSROOM LINKS

What might an Aboriginal pedagogy look like?

A group of teachers training at the Batchelor Institute of Indigenous Tertiary Education identified the following 11 principles of Aboriginal pedagogy that affect teaching, learning and classroom management:

1 *Relationships drive teaching and learning*
2 *Continuous teaching, learning and assessment.* Those who wrote the principles recognised the connection between learning at different points in life, as well as the connections between learning that takes place in and out of school.
3 *A community of learners.* Students are grouped in family groups so that the older students help the younger. The input of community elders is also valued.
4 *Independence and respect.* Students take responsibility for themselves and for others.
5 *Use of real-life experience.* This contrasts with the decontextualised learning common in mainstream schooling.
6 *Exploration, play and informal learning experiences*
7 *High expectations of achievement for all children*
8 *Teachers model behaviour for children*
9 *The ability to be flexible and adaptable*
10 *All learning is integrated.* Integration applies to content and to age- and ability-groups, as well as to community integration with the school.
11 *Teaching through many forms and texts*

Source: Adapted from Blitner et al. (2000).

CRITICAL REFLECTIONS

- Which of these principles (if any) is different from the pedagogy with which you are familiar?
- How might the application of these principles vary with different groups of children?

Heath issues: Otitis media

While Indigenous Australian students may suffer a range of health problems, one that affects the learning of a great number of students is associated with hearing. **Otitis media** is a disease involving inflammation of the middle ear, and commonly afflicts infants and young children.

The effects of otitis media range from temporary, recurring loss of hearing, to auditory-processing disorders and permanent hearing damage. Secondary effects are learning disabilities, as when children are frequently sick they can miss a lot of school. And even if children are able to attend school, if they cannot hear clearly it becomes difficult for them to learn, particularly in the early years when learning leans heavily on language. Noise in the classroom can make this process even more difficult. In addition, when children are

otitis media
A disease of the middle ear that affects hearing

learning in a second language, difficulties with hearing limit their capacity to learn that language and to learn the curriculum content. Skills such as learning to read may be affected, which then influences further learning in later years. Box 9.11 describes some common indicators of otitis media, and strategies that can help to minimise its effects.

Box 9.11 CLASSROOM LINKS

Otitis media in the classroom

Higgins (1997) identifies a number of linguistic and behavioural indicators of otitis media, along with strategies for teachers of children who have hearing difficulties.

Indicators
- Rubbing or tugging at ears
- Looking blank, especially when the room is noisy
- Difficult-to-understand speech
- Not answering when called upon by the teacher or peers
- Difficulty learning English, reading and writing

Strategies
- Use simple language; summarise and repeat information often.
- Maintain routines to support students' understanding of what is going on and what is expected.
- Place more importance on non-verbal communication. Using gestures, sign-language, facial expressions and intonation mirrors the strategies used in Aboriginal communities to communicate with hearing-impaired children.
- Encourage observation as a learning strategy by modelling and by having peers demonstrate tasks (once again, this makes use of an Aboriginal learning strategy).
- Encourage students with fluctuating hearing loss to sit close to the teacher. Using eye contact, getting a child's attention before speaking, speaking clearly and ensuring good lighting to facilitate lip-reading are all important.
- The use of small groups and one-to-one instruction can assist hearing and enable children to monitor the non-verbal cues and responses of their peers.
- Avoid grouping students who have hearing loss, as this removes their access to hearing peers (as models), assistants and fellow learners.
- Use a buddy system to provide support from peers.
- Minimise classroom noise by using carpet, wall coverings, and rubber stoppers on tables and chairs. Air-conditioning is another frequent source of ambient noise.

Source: Adapted from Higgins (1997).

Patterns of teacher employment

Indigenous Australian children tend to be enrolled in schools with a high turnover of teaching staff, and where teachers are frequently in their first year of teaching and have little or no experience in Indigenous education (Bourke et al., 2000). This has implications in terms of teaching quality and the degree of knowledge teachers have about the community of which the school is a part.

Ideally, Indigenous Australian children would be taught by members of their own communities. In practice, Australia has few fully trained Indigenous teachers relative to the size of the Indigenous school population. One way this gap has been bridged is by employing Aboriginal and Islander Education Workers (AIEWs), who work alongside non-Indigenous teachers in the classroom. This provides an opportunity for non-Indigenous teachers to gain understanding and insight into issues relevant to their Indigenous students. AIEWs often liaise between the school and the community to make the school a welcoming place for Indigenous families. An AIEW can also function as an important role model for the children and families involved in the school. Other roles for AIEWs include assisting teachers and students, monitoring students' attendance and behaviour, counselling or advising students, and providing induction for new teachers (HREOC, 2000a). In some states, AIEWs are assisted to study to become teachers.

9.4 A description of the roles of Indigenous community members in schools

Box 9.12 discusses strategies for enhancing the school experiences of Indigenous Australian students.

Box 9.12 RESEARCH LINKS

Enhancing Indigenous Australian students' experiences

The school climate and its familiarity to students play an important role in students' experiences at school. A 2000 report entitled *What has worked (and will again)* identified a number of successful strategies for enhancing Indigenous Australian students' experiences in schools, advocating:

- The establishment of closer and less formal personal relationships between teachers and students. ('The opportunity to express what you think.' 'They talk to me as a person.')
- The establishment of a more informal and less regimented climate. ('They chat away and wander round, but they get things done.')
- The provision of a larger role for students in negotiation of work. ('You can have a say in what you do, create stuff that you decide.')
- Teaching so that success can be regularly and obviously achieved ... this can take the form of displays, performances and so on.

In addition, teachers are advised to accept Aboriginal English as a valid language, and to teach explicitly about the differences between Aboriginal English and SAE, and about when each can be most useful.

Source: McRae, Ainsworth, Cumming, Hughes, Mackay, Price, et al. (2000, p. 12).

Maori learners and New Zealand's education system

While some of the educational outcomes look similar for indigenous people across the world, the position of Maori people in New Zealand is quite different from that of Aboriginal people in Australia, for instance, and this difference flows through to the education system. Maoris make up approximately one-fifth of all New Zealand students, and the majority attend mainstream schools (ERO, 2002a). Maori words are used in curriculum documents and are commonly understood.

The common culture and language shared by Maori communities across New Zealand means the task of developing resources, training teachers in the language and culture, and appropriately shaping the curriculum is less problematic than that faced by education departments in Australia. At the same time, it can mean that Maori students are stereotyped, without consideration for differences between rural and urban, or traditional and non-traditional communities (Bishop & Glynn, 1999).

Bishop and Glynn (1999) stress that appropriate approaches to Maori education maximise outcomes such as participation by ensuring Maori community involvement in every stage of development, implementation and evaluation. This ensures that Maori aspirations, preferences and practices take central place. Maori medium-preschools (*Te Kohanga Reo*), primary schools (*Kura Kaupapa Maori* – see Box 9.13 opposite), secondary schools (*Wharekura*) and tertiary institutions (*Whare Waananga Maori*) have been successful not just because education is offered in *Te Reo Maori* (Maori language), but also because of the links between language and culture described earlier in this chapter. Maori ways of interacting, roles for teachers and students, and learning patterns such as looking, listening, imitating and storytelling are used. Importantly, too, ongoing community involvement ensures that these elements are dynamic, adapting to changes in the aspirations, preferences and practices of the community, and resisting stereotype.

Box 9.13 CLASSROOM LINKS

Kura Kaupapa Maori

While the majority of Maori students are enrolled in mainstream schools, a small number attend *kura kaupapa Maori* – Maori-language immersion schools – in which the focus is on maintaining *te reo Maori* (Maori language) and culture.

Te reo Maori is the principal language of instruction, and the curriculum is based on Maori principles and practices, as expressed in *Te Aho Matua*. This has been described as a set of evaluation criteria for *kura kaupapa Maori* by the Education Review Office (ERO), in consultation with Maori elders governing the schools.

Te Aho Matua

Te Ira Tangata

1 The whänau* practises [a] holistic approach to children's development based on Mäori cultural and spiritual values and beliefs.
2 The whänau honours all people and respects the uniqueness of the individual [criteria include modelling love, tolerance and care of others].

Te Reo

1 The whänau ensures the language will be, for the most part, exclusively Mäori.
2 The whänau achieves full competency in Mäori and English.
3 The whänau respects all languages.

Ngä Iwi

1 The whänau nurtures children to be secure in the knowledge of themselves and their own people.
2 The whänau ensures that children acknowledge and learn about others and their societies.
3 The whänau ensures all members play an integral part in children's learning and in the learning of the wider whänau.
4 The whänau affirms collective ownership and responsibility for the *kura*.**

Te Ao

1 The whänau ensures that children will be secure in their knowledge about the Mäori world and enable them to participate in the wider world.
2 The whänau ensures that children will explore the physical and natural world while maintaining their link to ancestral knowledge.

Ahuatanga Ako

1 The whänau operates a warm, loving and intellectually stimulating learning environment.
2 The whänau ensures that the importance of the learning environment will be emphasised.
3 The whänau includes strong education leadership and capable teachers.

Nga Tino Uaratanga

1 The whänau ensures that each child's abilities are successfully nurtured including their academic skills, bilingualism, natural talents, creativity, enthusiasm for learning and life, ability to retain knowledge, leadership qualities, independence, joy, spirituality balanced with physical pursuits, their links to ancestral domains and their pride of place within their *iwi*.#

Source: ERO (2002a).

* *Whänau* = family (in this context referring to the school community)
** *Kura* = school
\# *Iwi* = people or tribe

In recent years, significant progress has been made in improving the educational outcomes of Maori students. The Ministry of Education attributes this change to a number of factors, including a focus on Maori assessment, the integration of Maori language in the mainstream science curriculum, a focus on developing literacy and numeracy skills, and an increasing involvement of schools in communities and communities in schools (NZ Ministry of Education, 2001). In 2002, the ERO surveyed schools to identify successful practices in improving outcomes for Maori students. Their findings are summarised in Box 9.14.

Box 9.14 RESEARCH LINKS

Maori students: Schools making a difference

The Education Review Office (ERO, 2002) surveyed mainstream schools and identified a set of approaches common to schools in which Maori students experienced good educational outcomes. They found that 'good-practice' schools:
- are effective for all students
- have a vision shared by the board, principal and teachers, which focuses on improving Maori students' achievement
- cater for a range of learning styles with varied teaching approaches
- make use of assessment systems that give

detailed information about Maori students' achievement
- incorporate traditional and contemporary Maori language, culture and knowledge into the curriculum and daily operations of the school
- support Maori students through:
  - developing environments in which students can be proud to be Maori
  - focusing on Maori students' success at school
  - promoting positive behaviour
  - creating physical environments that include Maori cultural elements
  - supporting Maori students and their families
  - encouraging Maori students to develop leadership skills
  - promoting positive Maori role models
- work to consult with the Maori community, are involved in the Maori community and take steps to encourage Maori *whānau* (extended family) to be involved in their children's education.

Source: Adapted from ERO (2002a).

The strength of the Maori people's position, however, has meant that the needs of some other ethnic groups have not been considered. A recent report looked at the education of Pacific students, given that these students make up approximately 8% of all students in New Zealand schools (ERO, 2002b). As a group, Pacific students are concentrated in relatively few schools and show poorer educational outcomes than non-Pacific students. The report found that 'schools don't yet have a clear focus on reducing disparities in achievement between Pacific and non-Pacific students', and indeed that most schools do not even know how the two groups of students compare. Those schools that were working effectively with their Pacific communities, involving them in the school, were identified in the report as having greater success.

Effective teaching for indigenous communities

Many of the strategies for effective teaching discussed earlier in this text apply equally to the teaching of indigenous students; however, some specific suggestions have also been put forward in the literature. These are discussed in Box 9.15.

Box 9.15 IMPLICATIONS FOR EDUCATORS

Strategies for enhancing indigenous students' learning

- Some parents may feel wary of school and reluctant to participate, meaning the school has a particular responsibility to bridge the gap by going to parents in formal and informal ways, both to celebrate successes and to resolve difficulties.
- Community involvement in the school is invaluable. Support it by inviting parents and elders to be involved in classroom teaching and in educational decision-making. If inviting people into the school to teach, let them choose content and methodology. Their choices may help you understand more about community priorities and methods of teaching and learning.
- Community involvement in the school needs to be matched by school involvement in the community. Benefits include establishing links between school and community, increasing the school's understanding of the community and demonstrating the school's commitment to the community. It gives teachers an opportunity to get to know those in the community – their concerns and their goals for education.
- Know your students, and build on their strengths and learning preferences.
- Include indigenous perspectives in mainstream curriculums.
- Teach students how to recognise and dismantle stereotypes.
- Consider using cooperative methods (such as Jigsaw) as a way of reducing racial tension and developing tolerance in students.
- Ensure that the curriculum is relevant to students' needs and interests so as to encourage their participation.

Concluding comments

In this chapter we have examined a number of examples of differences among groups as well as diversity within groups. We have seen examples of factors in students' physical environment, family, culture, school and teachers that all have an impact on students' educational outcomes. It is worth recalling the finding from Rowe's (2002) research that individual teachers make a larger contribution to differences in student outcomes than do SES, ethnicity or gender alone. Effective teachers are aware of, and cater for, student difference and its sociocultural bases. A common element of effective programs that address individual difference is their focus on the *individual* as a learner as well as a member of a group.

> 9.5 A recent report detailing ways indigenous parents can be involved in the school

Chapter review

- Bronfenbrenner's Ecological Systems Theory proposed a number of interconnecting contexts that influence and are influenced by the individual in development. This mutual influence contributes to considerable individual difference between members of groups. The contexts range from the immediate interactions within the family and outwards to the wider culture.
- Culture is learned, transmitted and constructed by all of us, and includes the beliefs and behaviours shared by a group and passed on to new members through a constant process of socialisation.
- Cultural differences between groups in society can create misunderstandings and conflict. In the school context, such differences can be sociolinguistic, as well as relating to broader beliefs about learning and understandings of roles. Effective, inclusive teaching involves understanding such cultural differences and teaching about them explicitly.
- Racism is felt directly and indirectly by many students in school. Teachers have a responsibility to deal directly with acts of racism and to target attitudes of prejudice that underlie it.
- Gender differences exist in cognition, emotion and educational achievement, although such differences tend to be small, with larger differences occurring within groups than among them.
- Explanations of gender differences in educational outcomes include a differential focus on employment prospects, biological differences, school structures, and male and female roles in school and society.
- Ethnographic research of classrooms has revealed differences in teacher–student interaction, reinforcement of gender roles, and differences in teacher expectations of boys and girls. Educators can minimise gender bias by offering a variety of modes of learning and assessment, and by enacting strategies to ensure wide participation of students in all activities.
- Poverty is associated with poor educational outcomes, as well as a number of other related characteristics including health, parenting factors and stress. These characteristics constitute risks for poor outcomes, but there are also resilience factors that help individuals to overcome or withstand such difficulties.
- Schools can contribute to educational inequality through teacher expectations, differences between home and school, and the nature of a less-than-satisfactory home–school relationship. Considering children not only as school students but as members of families and communities, and involving those communities in the school, are important strategies in addressing educational inequality.
- Indigenous people worldwide, as a group, are educationally disadvantaged, which shows itself in achievement and in participation and attendance patterns.
- Indigenous people can bring a number of strengths to school, including independence, interdependence, linguistic competence, a rich cultural heritage, and skills across a number of areas.
- In Australia, there is considerable variety in culture, language and goals for education. There are also commonalities in experiences of education. Aboriginals and Torres Strait Islanders may face a number of difficulties at school, among them difficulties associated

- with language, health, high teacher mobility, racism, and poor attendance and participation.
- Maori people in New Zealand share a common language and culture, which has enabled the Ministry of Education to adapt curriculums to be more relevant to Maori students. Other ethnic groups' needs have tended not to be addressed until quite recently.
- Community involvement in the school, and school involvement in the community are key strategies for improving Indigenous students' educational outcomes.

You make the connections:
Questions and activities for self-assessment and discussion

1. Working from Bronfenbrenner's model in Figure 9.2 (see page 264), build up a bank of examples of ways in which different contexts can affect students. For example, how does the family affect students who are its members? What influences interactions at this level? Environment? Poverty/wealth?

2. Describe your own culture:
   a. What are the key beliefs?
   b. How do these key beliefs explain why you behave as you do?
   c. Which beliefs or behaviours are shared with your peers?
   d. Which beliefs or behaviours are particular to you?
   e. Discuss you responses with other members of your class, noting any differences.

3. Develop a pedagogy of education that fits your personal culture. How would you communicate your ideas to students and their parents who were from a cultural background different from your own?

4. Talk to your parents about their experiences of education, and how that might have influenced their parenting and also their goals for your education.

5. Review the list of possible explanations of gender differences in education (see pages 274–276). Evaluate the explanations' validity in terms of your own experience, and in terms of the research evidence presented.

6. Give as many examples as you can of differences within groups of people. Do these differences discount the differences reported among groups? Why/why not?

7. This chapter reports some groups of students as having lower levels of achievement compared with other groups. List some explanations for differences in achievement. How should your approach to dealing with these differences vary? Are there some common elements?

Key terms

- sociocultural factors
- microsystem
- mesosystem
- exosystem
- macrosystem
- chronosystem
- ethnicity
- culture
- socialisation
- sociolinguistic features of language
- hidden curriculum
- racism
- LBOTE
- voluntary minority group
- involuntary minority group
- gender
- gender schema theory
- socioeconomic status (SES)
- risk factor
- Standard Australian English
- Aboriginal English
- otitis media

Recommended reading

Banks, J. A., & Banks, C. A. (2001). *Multicultural education: Issues and perspectives*. New York: John Wiley & Sons.

Bradley, R. H., & Corwyn, R. F. (2002). Socioeconomic status and child development. *Annual Review of Psychology, 53*: 371–399. Available online: <//psych.annualreviews.org/cgi/content/full/53/1/371>.

Gender and Education (journal).

Harris, S., & Malin, M. (1994). *Aboriginal kids in urban classrooms*. Wentworth Falls, NSW: Social Science Press.

Partington, G. (Ed.) (1998). *Perspectives on Aboriginal and Torres Strait Islander education*. Katoomba, NSW: Social Science Press.

Make some online visits

The following government bodies have written or commissioned extensive reports on gender, poverty and Indigenous education, which can be accessed from their websites:

- DETYA: <www.detya.gov.au/>
- MCEETYA: <www.curriculum.edu.au/mceetya/>

Advice for teachers when conducting units of work involving Aboriginal themes:
<www.sofweb.vic.edu.au/arts/matters/pdsite/indig/indig-2.asp>.

Check your state Department of Education's website also, to look at current policies and support in these areas.

Search the Web for definitions of culture:
<www.ero.govt.nz>
<www.mindu.govt.nz>

Access the 'Racism. No way!' website:
<www.racismnoway.com.au>

Find out more about otitis media:
<www.nexus.edu.au/TeachStud/arera/Otitis>

FIGURE MIV Module IV concept map.

- ICT in learning and teaching
- Assessment and reporting
- Educational psychology in the inclusive classroom
- Managing behaviour and classrooms

MODULE CONTENTS

- **Chapter 10** ICT in learning and teaching

MODULE IV

Educational psychology in the inclusive classroom

Core question: *How can educational psychology help us address key learning and teaching issues?*

Educational psychology plays a central role in equipping educators to deal with the sorts of issues they confront in the learning environment. This final module considers how the theories and principles of educational psychology can help teachers in the 21st century address three significant areas, which are:
- using information and communication technology (ICT) in learning and teaching
- assessing students' learning, and reporting assessments to others
- managing the classroom and the diverse range of students who comprise a teacher's learning community.

Chapter 10 examines ways in which an understanding of learning theories and principles of development can guide the successful integration of ICTs into the learning–teaching process. Chapter 11 looks at assessment, which lies at the core of effective teaching and which is influenced by teachers' understanding of student development (see Module I), their understanding of how students learn (see Module II) and their understanding of student differences in such areas as ability, motivation and background experiences (see Module III). Chapter 12 deals with managing the inclusive classroom, and discusses how teachers manage themselves, their students, their resources, their time and their energies in the learning environment. This final chapter presents theories and strategies for classroom implementation.

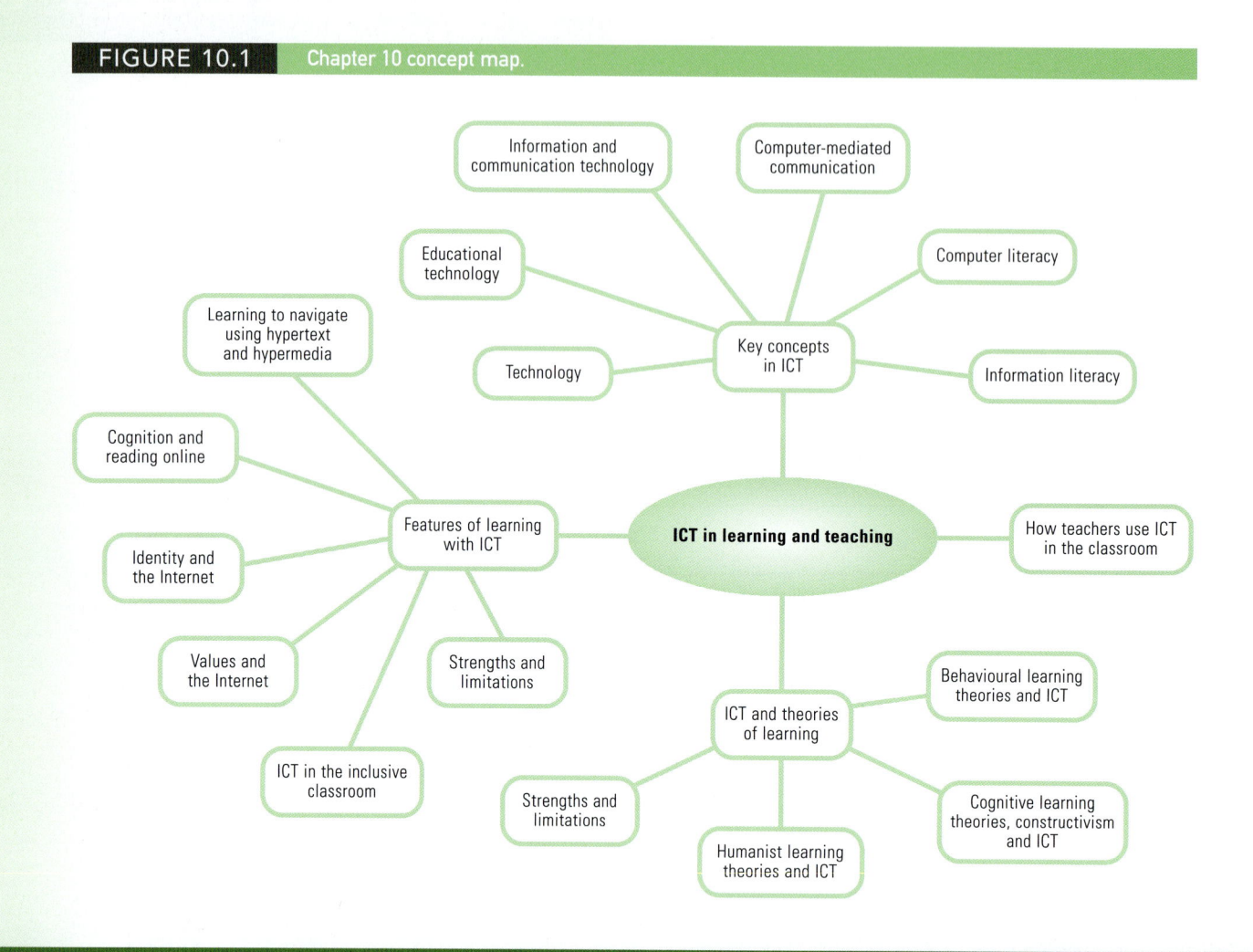

FIGURE 10.1 Chapter 10 concept map.

```
                    Information and              Computer-mediated
              communication technology            communication

                      Educational                          Computer literacy
                      technology
    Learning to navigate
    using hypertext                          Key concepts
    and hypermedia        Technology           in ICT          Information literacy

  Cognition and
  reading online
                      Features of learning
  Identity and         with ICT            ICT in learning and teaching    How teachers use ICT
  the Internet                                                              in the classroom

  Values and          Strengths and
  the Internet        limitations                     Behavioural learning
                                        ICT and theories  theories and ICT
                                        of learning
       ICT in the inclusive                                 Cognitive learning
       classroom          Strengths and                    theories, constructivism
                          limitations                       and ICT
                                 Humanist learning
                                 theories and ICT
```

CHAPTER OBJECTIVES

After reading this chapter you should be able to:

- explain the term 'information and communication technology' (ICT), and name examples of it

- give examples of how behavioural, cognitive, constructivist and humanist theories of learning influence the use of computers in education

- comment on how ICTs are changing traditional teacher-centred classrooms

- identify ways in which using computer technologies may contribute to inequities among learners, and discuss strategies for addressing these in your teaching

- critically evaluate the use of computers in the learning–teaching process.

CHAPTER 10

ICT in learning and teaching

Introduction

When did you first use a computer? Were you in primary school or high school? Perhaps you have just recently developed your computer skills so you can complete assignments or access course materials on the Web. You may be sharing lectures or tutorials with students who seem to be much more comfortable around computers than you are, or the reverse may be true. No matter what computer skills you have, you can be certain that you will need these and many more skills in the educational context in which you work. You will also need to be able to adapt these skills to changing learning environments as technology progresses and is used in different ways (Meredyth, Russell, Blackwood, Thomas, & Wise, 1999). This is the essence of lifelong learning.

This chapter is about more than information and communication technology (ICT) and computer skills alone. It addresses broader issues that challenge you to think about why and how to use computer technology in the learning–teaching process. The chapter also aims to encourage you to consider the impact of computers on the quality of students' learning and your approaches to teaching.

Key concepts in ICT

One of the more confusing aspects of electronic and computer technologies is the wide range of terms used. Some of these terms have existed for many years (for example, do you remember when you first 'saved a file on the hard drive', 'emailed an attachment' or 'transferred a folder to the zip drive'?), while new words and phrases are constantly being coined. The Internet, too, has its own jargon. Have you visited a 'cybrary' (cyber library) to use a 'webopedia' (web encyclopedia) recently? When did you last 'LOL' (laugh out loud) as you stepped 'AFK' (away from the keyboard) after saying 'B4N' ('bye for now) to your virtual chatroom friends? And are you feeling :-) (happy) or ;-((sad) today?

All these words, phrases and symbols are examples of how computer technologies and the Internet have radically altered our language. Printed books cannot keep pace with the rapid changes in language, but there are a few key terms you need to be familiar with as you study the role of computer technologies in education.

Technology

The term 'technology' is most commonly associated with computers, but it has a wider application. **Technology** can be defined as the use of tools, materials and processes to perform tasks efficiently, to improve quality of life, and to meet human needs and wants (see Williams & Williams, 1996). The New Zealand Curriculum statement (New Zealand Ministry of Education, 1993b) defined technology as the creative and purposeful use of human knowledge, skills and physical resources to solve practical problems. Technology is more than tools or products: it is also a process that helps people make or achieve something.

> **technology**
> The use of tools, materials and processes to perform tasks efficiently, to improve quality of life, and to meet human needs and wants

Educational technology

Using technology in education is not a new concept. It can be traced back to when tribal priests systematically organised bodies of knowledge and early cultures (such as those of Ancient Greece and Ancient Egypt) used complex systems of symbols and signs to record and transmit information (Roblyer, Edwards, & Havriluk, 1997). In the context of formal schooling, some of the best-known examples of **educational technology** – or learning technology – used in teaching and learning are blackboard and chalk, pens, paper, and textbooks. You would be familiar with other forms of technology used widely in schools, including overhead projectors, video-cassette recorders, slide projectors, and compact disc (CD) and digital video disc (DVD) players. Effective teaching is about choosing the best combination of these technological tools to enhance learning.

> **educational technology**
> The use of tools, materials and processes to enhance learning – includes blackboard, chalk and computers

Information and communication technology

One form of educational technology is **information technology (IT)**. This is the term most commonly used to describe the use of computers and their educational applications. More recently, the broader term **information and communication technology (ICT)** (sometimes used in the plural form 'ICTs') has been coined to refer to the vast array of technologies and forms of communication computers facilitate. ICT encompasses electronic hardware, software and network connectivity (Moran, Thompson, & Arthur, 1999; Toomey, 2001), of which IT forms a smaller part. Examples of electronic hardware – the physical parts of the computer – include computers, scanners, printers and compact disc read-only memory (CD-ROM) burners. Software refers to the programs that operate computers. These include computer programs such as the widely used Microsoft® Word or Excel, games and CD-ROMs and videos. Network connectivity refers to the linking or networking of computers so that users can communicate with one another and share resources such as printers and documents. This form of connectivity is perhaps best illustrated in the use of the Internet, a vast global network that facilitates the use of electronic mail (email), and of the World Wide Web ('the Web'), which is a part of the Internet that consists of millions of pages of text and images published by anyone with access to computers and the appropriate software. Technologies such as computer- and video-conferencing also depend on network connectivity for their success.

> **information and communication technology (ICT)**
> An array of technologies including electronic hardware, software and network connectivity
>
> **information technology (IT)**
> Refers to computers and their applications and is part of the larger group of ICTs

The broader term 'ICT' encompasses terms such as 'electronic technologies', 'online technologies' and 'computer technologies'. As the name suggests, ICT has three key functions, which pertain to:

- *information* – its access, storage, retrieval and manipulation
- *communication* – between and among users
- *knowledge creation and adaptation, skills, learning products and information sources* (Moran et al., 1999, p. 5).

ICT has the potential to facilitate innovative ways of using and manipulating information. It promotes new ways of communicating, knowing and understanding.

Computer-mediated communication

As the term 'ICT' indicates, communicating using computer technologies is a feature of life in the 21st century. There are two main types of **computer-mediated communication (CMC)**. **Asynchronous communication** is communication that takes place between two or more individuals at different times. One person may send an electronic message at 9 a.m. on Monday, and the recipient may read it on Tuesday evening. Email, messaging programs, **newsgroup**s and **listserv** (automatic mailing list) discussion groups are the most common examples of asynchronous communication. **Synchronous communication** occurs between individuals who interact simultaneously in 'real time' (that is, the actual time during which a process occurs). Examples include videoconferencing (where computers relay video images and audio connections to facilitate meetings between people around the world), and **Internet relay chat (IRC**, where people in disparate locations can have live, real-time discussions by means of the Internet), which often takes place in **Internet chatroom**s (virtual rooms in which 'chat sessions' take place).

A unique feature of CMC is the use of the types of abbreviations mentioned earlier (for example, 'ROFL', meaning 'rolling on the floor laughing') and 'emoticons' (symbols or icons that indicate emotions).

Computer literacy

What does it mean to be computer literate? **Computer literacy** involves developing basic computer skills, such as knowing how to switch on a computer, and how to use a mouse and a keyboard, as well as knowing how to use computer applications and touch-type smoothly (Rothstein, 1997). Being computer literate means being at ease with using computers and their applications, and having a basic understanding of what a computer is and how it can be used as a resource for different purposes (Nichols, 1998).

The International Computer Driving License (ICDL) is an example of an internationally recognised computer literacy training program. The program focuses on developing fundamental skills needed for everyday computer use and provides people with an internationally recognised certificate (or 'computer driver's licence') stating their level of skill at using word processors, spreadsheets, email, databases (a program for organising information on a computer in searchable form), the Internet, graphics and other software applications (Csapo, 2002).

Information literacy

While computer literacy definitions tend to focus on basic computer skills, **information literacy** extends beyond technical skills and may be defined as the ability to locate, evaluate and use information to become an independent lifelong learner (Meredyth et al., 1999). Information literacy extends beyond knowledge and skills to include values and attitudes about knowledge and how it is used and shared (Langford, 2000). To be information literate, you need technical skills, but these are not an end in themselves. Rather, they provide access to information and facilitate critical reflection on the nature of information, the way it is organised and communicated, and the impact of sociocultural and philosophical influences on that information and how it is presented (Shapiro & Hughes, 1996). While information literacy encompasses the use of print and electronic resources, it is largely centred on the use of ICTs.

Information-literate learners are able to search for information strategically (McLean, 2000), using a range of complex search strategies. Once information has been found, these learners are able to sift through it, using the higher-order cognitive skills of analysis and evaluation, and making judgements about its relative value and reliability. Information literacy

---

computer-mediated communication (CMC)
The use of computer technologies to communicate

asynchronous communication
Electronic communication between individuals who are not talking in real time (such as in email and listserv discussion groups)

newsgroup
An online discussion on a particular topic, with newsgroup messages posted electronically using a 'newsreader' program to connect users to the Internet

listserv
An online communication tool allowing individuals to email contributions to a mailing list that automatically makes available all messages to everyone on the list

synchronous communication
Communication between individuals who interact in real time in a call-and-response format (for example, video conferencing or Internet chatrooms)

Internet relay chat (IRC)
A chat system that enables Internet-connected individuals anywhere to join live, real-time discussions

Internet chatroom
A virtual (computer-generated) 'room' in which individuals 'chat' with others online

computer literacy
Basic computer skills; having an understanding of what a computer is and how to use it

information literacy
The ability to locate, evaluate and use information; extends beyond technical skills

also involves selecting the most relevant information, and perhaps deciding how to publish and disseminate it. Such skills develop over time and are influenced by a learner's developmental stage and level of experience in computer use.

The Internet is a highly visual medium, using combinations of colourful text, icons, videos and graphics in ways that traditional paper-based texts do not. Another dimension of information literacy is therefore that of being able to 'read' a website (a page or set of pages on the Web) or database. This means being able to 'navigate' (move around) a site without getting lost or losing track of the initial aim of the information search. Skill in being able to critically evaluate a site's worth is also essential. In order to navigate and evaluate websites, learners need 'visual literacy' – the ability to create, use and understand visual images.

Box 10.1 below outlines several strategies for integrating information literacy skills into your teaching. Box 10.2 opposite looks at what teachers might consider when using ICT in the classroom.

Box 10.1 CLASSROOM LINKS

The 'Big6 Skills Approach' to information problem solving

The following six-step outline is designed to help teachers develop their students' information-literacy skills. The six steps guide collection, use and evaluation of information for the purposes of solving a problem or completing a task. The skills are designed to be integrated into the content area you are teaching, and may be adapted to suit a range of age groups and contexts.

1 Task definition
   1.1 Define the task (the information problem)
   1.2 Identify the information needed in order to complete the task

In step 1, students need to recognise that they require information to solve a problem. They need to identify the type and amount of information they require, and perhaps communicate with teachers about assignments, use email, participate in online discussions and be involved in desktop teleconferencing.

2 Information-seeking strategies
   2.1 Brainstorm all possible sources
   2.2 Select the best sources

In step 2, students consider all possible information sources and develop a search plan. For example, a student might assess the value of various types of electronic resources – including databases, CD-ROM resources, commercial and Internet online resources – for the purposes of data gathering. Here, students determine their priorities for information seeking.

3 Location and access
   3.1 Locate sources
   3.2 Find information within the source

In step 3, students locate and access information. For example, they might use the Internet commercial computer networks to contact experts as well as help and referral services.

4 Use of information
   4.1 Engage with the source (read, hear, view, touch)
   4.2 Extract relevant information

In step 4, students engage with information, perhaps by recording electronic information sources and locating such sources in order to cite them in footnotes, endnotes or bibliographies. Here they might analyse and filter electronic information in relation to the task, rejecting irrelevant information.

5 Synthesis
   5.1 Organise information from multiple sources
   5.2 Present the information

In step 5, students organise and communicate information through email or by using presentation software to create electronic slide shows.

6 Evaluation
   6.1 Judge the process (efficiency)
   6.2 Judge the product (effectiveness)

In step 6, students need to judge how well the final product meets the original task requirements, and how efficiently the problem-solving process occurred. Students may evaluate their own work or be evaluated by others.

Source: Adapted from Eisenberg and Johnson (2002).

10.1 Information literacy in student learning

CRITICAL REFLECTIONS

- What types of information literacy skills have you used in the past week?
- 'Ability to access, manage and manipulate information is fast distinguishing the information rich from the information poor.' To what extent do you agree with this view? What difference will your information literacy skills make to the way you teach?

Box 10.2 IMPLICATIONS FOR EDUCATORS

Technology in the classroom

- *Remember that technology is a tool for you to use in your teaching.* Like other educational technologies – such as pens, paper or whiteboards – computers are vehicles to help students learn. Integrate computers and their wide-ranging applications into your lessons at the planning stage, rather than adding them as an afterthought to your teaching-resources repertoire.
- *Make the most of students' willingness to experiment with computer technologies.* Some students will always know more than you do about using computers, so encourage the more capable students to demonstrate their skills and to help you and their peers where appropriate. Try to find out about the latest computer programs and ask students what they have discovered recently. This will help students to feel valued and will keep you up to date with their computer interests.
- *Make the most of ICTs' communication capacity.* Use computer technologies to encourage students to communicate with learners in other countries and from other cultures. Design projects that involve collaborations between students in your classroom and those in rural areas, other cities or other countries. Discuss 'netiquette' (Internet etiquette) and sociocultural differences that may emerge from crosscultural interactions online.
- *Go beyond skills-based computer literacy.* Help students to explore their attitudes, values and judgement-making abilities by developing their information literacy. Students need time to search and evaluate the Internet in meaningful ways, so provide scaffolding to help them do this step by step. Encourage critical thinking and the analysis of electronic information. Give students every opportunity to apply their learning by encouraging them to publish their own websites.

How teachers use ICT in the classroom

An anonymous contributor cited in Moran et al. (1999, p. 9) said: 'Put Florence Nightingale in a modern hospital and she'd be struck dumb. Put a modern teacher into an 1890s school and they'd pick up the chalk and keep teaching.' Is this true? Will new electronic technologies make any difference to the way you think about education or to the way you teach in the future? It has been said that 'technologies do not teach – people do' (Ingram, 1996, p. 31). It is worth noting that while computer skills are important, the most critical skill for teachers is to know *how*, *when* and *why* to use ICT to optimise learning experiences. Computers have the potential to facilitate student-centred learning and to structure learning environments in innovative ways (NSW Department of Education and Training, 1999), but the key to success is how the technologies are used. In chapters 5 and 6 you learned about cooperative and collaborative learning, and the value of encouraging learners to actively construct their learning and to make meaning for themselves: ICT provides a useful set of tools for achieving this. In order to guide teachers' use of ICT, countries like Australia and New Zealand have developed national goal statements identifying broad sets of skills, attitudes and values that students should develop as a result of their experiences with ICT in schools. Selections from these national statements are included in Box 10.3.

Box 10.3 CLASSROOM LINKS

National goals for ICT use in schools

Australia and New Zealand both have national goal statements relating to students' competence and understandings in the area of ICT.

Australia

In Australia, the broad goal (Goal 1.6, MCEETYA, 1999) is that:

> [W]hen students leave schools they should ... be confident, creative and productive users of new technologies, particularly information and communication technologies, and understand the impact of those technologies on society.

New Zealand

The New Zealand Ministry of Education (1993b) states that:

> Students will develop an understanding of the ways in which technology both shapes and is shaped by society. They will learn how technology has influenced the lives of people of different cultures, backgrounds, and times, and how people have developed and used technologies to meet human needs. They will develop an awareness of the impact of technology on the environment and the workplace. Students will be helped to make informed decisions about the use of technology in relation to society, the environment, and the economy. They will learn to appraise the potential costs and benefits of various technological applications. ... They will develop confidence and competence in a range of technologies and the adaptability to use new technologies.

New Zealand students are also expected to:

- 'become competent in using new information and communication technologies, including augmented communication for people with disabilities' (New Zealand Ministry of Education, 1993c)
- 'use a range of information-retrieval and information-processing technologies confidently and competently' (New Zealand Ministry of Education, 1993c).

According to a study of IT skills among Australian school students (Meredyth, Russell, Blackwood, Thomas, & Wise, 1999), teachers and students reported that computer technologies were most frequently used in their classrooms for information purposes (such as accessing information from CD-ROMs and using computerised library catalogues) and for creative purposes (such as using computers to make music or create pictures), followed by educational programs and games. Neither teachers nor students made much use of ICT for communicating with others (see Table 10.1).

TABLE 10.1 Student and teacher use of ICT in Australian schools

IT curriculum domains	Students %	Teachers %
Using information	62	70
Creative uses	56	50
Educational programs and games	45	43
Communicating with people	12	10

The way teachers use ICT depends on a number of factors including their familiarity with the technology, the resources and support that are available to them, and the learning outcomes they aim to achieve. Australian school teachers reported that a low level of confidence regarding their computer skills was a factor in their decision-making about the use of ICT in their teaching (Meredyth, Russell, Blackwood, Thomas, & Wise, 1999) (see Box 10.4 opposite).

Box 10.5 opposite outlines several ways teachers might make use of computers in the classroom context.

Box 10.4 RESEARCH LINKS

Student and teacher computer competence

Meredyth and colleagues (1999) reported a study in which a representative sample of 400 schools from all Australian states and territories was surveyed to establish baseline information about students' and teachers' experience and skills in computer use. The survey provided information from 6213 students, 1258 primary and secondary school teachers and 222 principals.

Although the teachers surveyed reported that computer technology was very important for their students and for their own professional development, and that it was important to integrate technology into the curriculum, significant issues were identified that were associated with teachers' pre-service preparation and ongoing professional development. Teachers identified barriers to using computer technologies in the classroom, reported low levels of confidence about their ability to keep themselves informed of technological developments, and reported low levels of support for professional development in terms of computer technology in teaching.

Activities

1. Survey, formally or informally, a sample of teachers. Your sample might come from the school you attended, your child's or sibling's school, or the school where you are doing your teaching practicum. Your survey may include some of the following items, but add your own as well:
   - 'Rate your computer skills on a scale of 1 to 10.'
   - 'How comfortable do you feel about using computers in your classroom teaching? Why/why not?'
   - 'Where and how did you first develop your computer skills?'
   - 'How often do you use computers as a teaching resource?'
   - 'How do you cope with students who know more about computers than you do?'
2. After surveying your sample, report back to your tutorial group and discuss your results.
3. List strategies for integrating computers into your teaching as a tool rather than as an afterthought.

Box 10.5 IMPLICATIONS FOR EDUCATORS

Using computers in the classroom

Computers may be used in several ways in the classroom. Four of the main uses are:
- *creative uses* – including use of computers across the curriculum to write or create stories, poems, scripts, pictures, graphics, slide shows, animations, music or sound
- *informational uses* – including research activities (such as obtaining information from a CD-ROM or using the Web); and mathematics, science, social science applications (such as creating graphs or diagrams and using spreadsheets or databases)
- *communication uses* – including sending and receiving email, and taking part in email discussions, Internet relay chat, video conferencing or communicating with other schools
- *educational programs and games* – including skill-building applications (such as learning programs).

Source: Adapted from Meredyth, Russell, Blackwood, Thomas and Wise (1999, p. 110).

ICT and theories of learning

One factor that helps determine an individual teacher's use of ICT is that teacher's philosophy of learning and teaching, including understandings of how students learn best. Module II outlined several theories of learning that we revisit in this chapter. They provide a useful framework for understanding different approaches to ICT use in education.

The way learners interact with ICT has changed over time, reflecting different learning theories in action. Early use of computers in classrooms tended to be restricted to drill and practice applications or word processing (Morrison, Lowther, & DeMeulle, 1999). In the early 1980s, emphasis was placed on learning how to program computers using computer languages such as Logo (see Maddux, Johnson, & Willis, 2001; Papert, 1980). More recently there have been rapid developments in Internet and Web use, and a relative improvement in teachers' and students' skill levels in using ICTs. As a result, there has been an increase in creative and interactive applications, Internet-based learning activities, web-page design and electronic publishing. Each of these ICT uses has merit, depending on the goals of the learning experience, and each is informed by learning theories as outlined in this section. Before reading further, you may benefit from reviewing the theories presented in Module II.

Behavioural learning theories and ICT

Behaviourism argues that learning takes place through the association of stimulus and response (see Chapter 4). Learning is mastering subject matter and achieving behavioural objectives. Computers are particularly useful for this purpose. Before the era of computers, B. F. Skinner himself supported the use of teaching machines as a way of providing immediate reinforcement to promote learning and to respond to individual learner needs (Skinner, 1968; O'Donohue & Ferguson, 2001). In the context of ICT, behavioural learning exponents advocate using computer software to tutor students (Gardner, 2000). Using behavioural principles of stimulus–response, and reward–punishment, the computer and its software operate as a tutor, teaching the user through **computer-assisted instruction (CAI)**, which is also known as 'computer-based instruction' (CBI), or 'computer-assisted learning' (CAL). (Note that these differ from 'computer-mediated instruction' (CMI, or distributed learning), which is discussed on page 318.)

With the computer as tutor, the teaching process is computer-driven, using the following pattern of interaction (see Figure 10.2 for an illustration of this process):

- the computer presents information
- the user is asked to respond to a question or problem
- the computer evaluates the user's response using pre-programmed criteria
- the computer responds to the user (for example, if users enter a correct response, the program allows them to move to the next stage (or equivalent), and if responses are inappropriate or incorrect, the computer program may take the users back to repeat an exercise until they are able to provide the correct response).

computer-assisted instruction (CAI)
Where a computer and its software operate as a tutor; also known as 'computer-based instruction' (CBI), or 'computer-assisted learning' (CAL)

10.2 More about the computer as tool, tutor and tutee

FIGURE 10.2 Using the computer as a tutor.

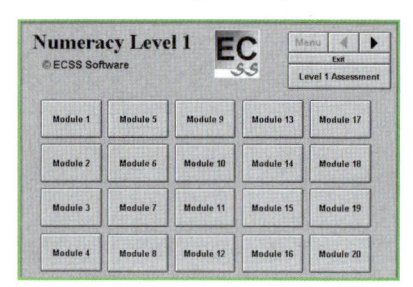

a Students select modules that are sequentially arranged to develop numeracy skills. Learning is self-paced and tasks are at different levels of difficulty. (Source: Rod Krause, ECSS.)

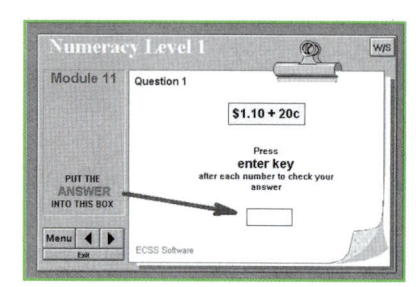

b Instructions are given and students enter their response. (Source: Rod Krause, ECSS.)

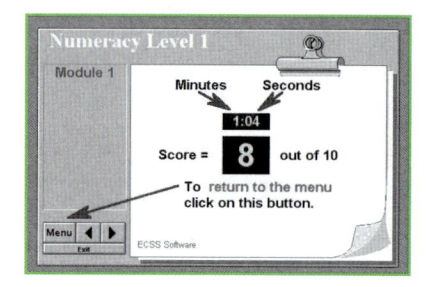

c An advantage of the computer as tutor is that students' time on task can be measured, and scores provided instantly. (Source: Rod Krause, ECSS.)

Some examples of tutor applications include drill-and-practice applications, problem-solving applications and games (Merrill, Hammons, Vincent, Reynolds, Christensen, & Tolman, 1996). Drill-and-practice applications are used widely to help students with numeracy skills. A typical drill-and-practice routine is illustrated in Figure 10.2, where the student has multiple opportunities to practise a particular problem and provide the correct answer. In some computer programs students are given additional instruction when they enter incorrect responses; if not, teachers may provide such support.

Drill-and-practice applications are based on the principle of mastery learning which contends that everyone can learn given the right circumstances and sufficient practice (see Chapter 7 for more on mastery goals). The software demonstrated in Figure 10.2 illustrates some of the distinctive capabilities of CAI: the learning is self-paced, the program has an inbuilt stopwatch so students have direct feedback on their level of accuracy and the time they have taken, and students may go back over problems and repeat them to achieve mastery of the skills. In addition, the computer can be programmed to randomly generate new problems of the same type, so no two students will do the same set of questions, and retesting is meaningful.

Computer games are another example of the-computer-as-tutor applications. Many of your students will have grown up on Nintendo, Pokémon, Sony PlayStation or computer chess. All of these provide examples of competitive play between a user (or users) and the computer, with instant feedback and often an associated high level of interest and motivation. The Nelson dog (see Figure 10.3) is an animated cartoon character who appears in a series of games developed by Nelson Thomson Learning Company in Australia. These games provide a variation on drill and practice, but with a game element that rewards young players who spell simple words, match rhyming words and learn the alphabet. Such games combine bright colours and animation to motivate and stimulate young learners.

There is some evidence to suggest that CAI can enhance achievement because it leads to automaticity of lower-level skills through extended practice (Merrill et al., 1996; Vockell & Schwartz, 1992). Kulik (1994) concludes that students usually learn more and in less time with computer-based instruction. One of the advantages of computers is that they are capable of repeating the same task and generating random examples or activities that provide learners with plenty of practice and opportunities to master their skills (as shown in Figure 10.2 earlier). In the tutorial form of CAI, the computer provides additional information to the learner if an incorrect answer is supplied. This continues until the learner is successful.

FIGURE 10.3 The Nelson dog – using computer games to teach spelling.

CRITICAL REFLECTIONS

- Can you see any benefits in using computers for drill-and-practice activities in your teaching area?
- Discuss the following statement with your tutorial or study group: 'Computers enable the teacher to be in the machine. Eventually computers will replace teachers.'

Cognitive learning theories, constructivism and ICT

ICTs play a significant role in promoting cognitive learning principles in classrooms. Cognitive theorists such as Piaget emphasised active problem-solving and meaning-making on the part of the learner. Piaget and Vygotsky (see Chapter 2) pointed out the importance of social interaction in learning. One of the key characteristics of ICTs is interactivity (Pachler, 2001), both between machine and user, and between users.

Computer technologies, particularly web-based technologies, have been called 'mindtools' (Jonassen, 1996, p. 9) because of their interactive nature and information-processing capabilities. Computers have the capacity to function as 'intellectual partners' to promote critical thinking and higher-order cognitive processing. Text, voice, music, graphics, photos, animation and video are combined to promote thinking and encourage learners to accomplish creative, higher-level tasks (Maddux et al., 2001). According to Bagley and Hunter (1992), ICTs empower learners and encourage them to spend more time actively constructing knowledge. ICTs provide a range of resources for students to use in problem solving, thinking, reflecting and collaborating with others within physical classrooms and across the globe in virtual learning contexts. It is also argued that ICTs, with their potential for interactivity, are more conducive to active and engaged learning than to more traditional teacher-centred approaches (see Figure 10.4). They also assist in meeting the individual learner's needs and interests (Bruce & Levin, 1997).

FIGURE 10.4 ICTs can be effective tools for encouraging students to interact and collaborate with each other around the computer.

In a constructivist learning environment, ICT plays a purposeful role in day-to-day activities, but does not become the object of instruction (McClintock, 1992). According to its advocates, the constructivist classroom that integrates ICT provides students with a complex laboratory in which to observe, question, practise and validate knowledge. In such classrooms, the emphasis is on learning *with*, not from or about, ICTs.

Computers can be particularly useful for teachers interested in understanding learners' cognitive and thinking processes, since computers can make students' thinking processes visible for teachers in a way that other methods of learning cannot (Means & Olson, 1997). For instance, students' choices about how to use a particular computer application can reveal their thinking and problem-solving strategies: word processing applications facilitate learners revising and editing on screen, while records of students' Internet search strategies are easily reviewed. Teachers can observe students working with computers, monitor their progress, stop and ask about students' goals and make suggestions for revision or the use of different strategies.

ICTs can be integrated into constructivist learning environments in a range of ways. According to Dimock and Boethel (1999), these learning environments are characterised by teachers who seek to:

- learn more about students' prior knowledge, understanding and beliefs
- tap into learners' interests and enhance motivation for learning
- base classroom discussion on authentic, real-world problems
- provide a variety of experiences, opportunities to experiment and a non-threatening environment in which learners can negotiate meaning for themselves
- take on the role of facilitator
- enhance students' ability to test multiple scenarios, and thus challenge preconceived notions or misconceptions

- broaden the circle of social interaction to include students' peers and also experts beyond the classroom, the school and the community.

Research supports the value of ICT in constructivist classrooms, as discussed in Box 10.6 at the base of this page.

Vygotsky's zone of proximal development and ICT

One of the many advantages of computer-based learning resources is their capacity for facilitating individualised learning. This is evident in behaviourist-type drill-and-practice programs, but computers may also function as scaffolds that identify a learner's 'zone of proximal development' (see Chapter 2) and foster their cognitive development (Salomon, Perkins, & Globerson, 1991). Vygotsky argued that in order for cognitive development to come about, partners should work together to solve problems. Computers may function as useful partners in some instances. For example, some computer programs test students to see what they can achieve independently and by means of assistance when needed. In this way, computers and their applications serve as a useful scaffolding device, but this process does not occur in isolation. The teacher needs to monitor student progress carefully, selecting the most appropriate resources and using the technology only when it is most appropriate – never as a substitute for effective class teaching or group interaction.

Simulations and authentic learning

As you will recall from Chapter 5, constructivism examines the ways in which learners make meaning from experience. Rather than viewing learning as the transmission of knowledge, constructivists see it as an internal process of interpretation. Constructivists value 'authentic' or 'situated' learning, where learners take part in activities that are directly relevant to the application of learning and that take place within a culture similar to the applied setting (Brown, Collins, &, Duguid, 1989; McLellan, 1996). ICTs are a valuable means of increasing student involvement with complex, authentic tasks (Means, Blando, Olson, Middleton, Morocco, Remz et al., 1993; Squires, 1999; see Box 10.6). These authentic tasks enable learners to experience problem solving in real-world contexts. An example of computer technology that encourages students to solve problems in an 'authentic' environment is a computer simulation.

10.3 OzProjects: authentic projects online

Box 10.6 RESEARCH LINKS

ICT in constructivist classrooms

Means and Olson (1997) investigated 17 constructivist learning environments where teachers were using ICTs to enhance student learning and to encourage cooperative learning among students. Students were involved in authentic projects using real-world examples and issues such as those they might find on the Web. Provision was also made for students to specialise in different aspects of technology use according to individual or group interests.

The researchers interviewed teachers about the impact of ICT on their students. The results are summarised in Table 10.2 below.

TABLE 10.2 Teacher-reported effects of technology on students	
Observed effect	**Number reporting***
Improvements in student performance	
Technical skills	15
Accomplishment of more complex tasks	14
Increased use of outside information resources	10
Enhanced creativity	9

(Continued over page)

Observed effect	Number reporting*
Improvements in student performance	
Improved design skills; ability to present information better	7
Improved understanding of audience needs	7
Higher-quality products	7
Increased likelihood of editing own writing; better editing skills	4
Greater consideration of multiple perspectives	3
Improved oral communication skills	2
Motivational effects	
Increased motivation	16
Heightened self-esteem	11
Improved behaviour, such as attendance, time on task	5
Changes in student and teacher roles	
More collaboration with peers; peer teaching	13
Better self-regulation of own learning	11
Students teaching teachers	5

*Out of 17 case-study teachers

Apart from reporting improvements in students' academic performance and technical skills, teachers said that the use of ICTs had positive effects on students' motivation, self-esteem and, in some cases, their behaviour in class. Teachers also found that ICTs could be used to encourage student collaboration with peers.

Simulations

Simulations are a unique form of tutoring facilitated by computer technology. A computer simulation represents a model of a real system or phenomenon. Simulations make use of **hypermedia**, a system that links pieces of information such as text, graphics, sound and video elements in an online virtual environment. These simulations offer an imaginary environment that is realistic enough to provide meaningful issues and consequences and to encourage learners to confront authentic problems and make decisions (Knapp & Glenn, 1996). For example, students learning geography may see a computer-simulated volcanic eruption. They may analyse conditions and practise their analytical skills without actually visiting a volcano. A stock-market simulation enables students to buy and sell and to practise their problem-solving skills without putting real money at risk. Simulations can be beneficial, since they allow users to experience certain phenomena vicariously and with less risk and cost (Merrill et al., 1996).

It is widely acknowledged that people learn best through direct experience and experimentation (Felix, 2002; Hovelynck, 2001; Lamb & Nunan, 2001; Powell & Wells, 2002), yet many things children would benefit from participating in are not available to them. Simulation software has the potential to challenge learners' existing ideas by encouraging them to manipulate variables and observe the effects of those manipulations on physical objects. Problem-solving skills are also developed as learners generate hypotheses based on observations and then test them, providing further opportunities for challenging students' ideas (Powell, 1994).

Simulation software offers an opportunity for uncovering and examining learners' prior knowledge. Students take an active part in interacting with a simulation, and prior knowledge

---

simulation
A model of a real system or phenomenon

hypermedia
A system that links pieces of information such as text, sound, visual images, animation and video in electronic environments

guides the choices they make. Observing a student's choices and discussing reasons for them provides a rich opportunity for teacher and student to explore the student's prior knowledge (Dimock & Boethel, 1999). In the computer simulation *SimCity*, created by Maxis, Inc., users 'build' a city of the future, which behaves according to the complex dynamics of current cities (see Figure 10.5). The *Ollie Saves the Planet* CD-ROM is a fun children's game, developed by Australian government and industry groups, that introduces players to the concept of sustainability, using simulations to focus on such issues as waste, water, energy, air and biodiversity (see Figure 10.6). Various Australian characters guide players by introducing them to problems, suggesting solutions and providing encouragement along the way.

A study examining students' use of computer simulations found evidence that students were motivated by the relevance and realism of a task that allowed for multiple solutions (as many simulations do) (Teague & Teague, 1995).

Authentic learning experiences

Authentic learning experiences are also facilitated by Internet communication tools such as newsgroups, IRC, 'MUDs' and 'MOOs'. **Multiple-user domains (MUDs)** are simulated electronic 'rooms' in which users communicate using synchronous, text-based conversations in real time (Bruckman & Resnick, 1995; Resnick, 1996). **Multiple-user object-oriented (domains) (MOOs)** expand the text-based context of MUDs by adding visual objects with which participants can interact. In these object-oriented environments, doors can be opened, chairs can be moved and point of view can be altered. Participants can also create their own objects to add to the virtual environment (Dillenbourg & Schneider, 1995). Both MUDs and MOOs allow learners to participate in authentic, virtual worlds. These electronic spaces can replicate real-world environments and problems in which students are able to test ideas and practise skills (Dimock & Boethel, 1999).

Using email also facilitates authentic learning. Email (electronic mail) provides a medium for written communication that is embedded in an authentic context — that of exchanging ideas and information with peers within the class or elsewhere, including overseas. Email and word-processing software may be used to encourage students to write for a real audience, such as peers or community members, about topics that affect them (Maddux et al., 2001). There are several benefits of such authentic learning and assessment experiences supported by computers (Gallini & Helman, 1993), which include an increase in students' motivation for learning as they come to appreciate the relevance of their learning in real-world contexts. In many classes, authentic learning and assessment tasks also encourage collaboration between learners, and they become more active constructors and interpreters of their learning.

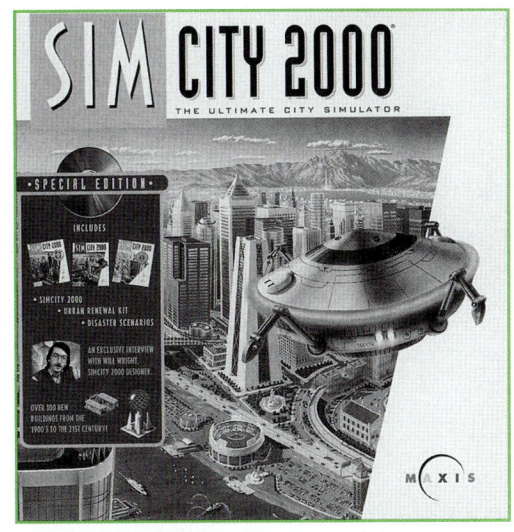

FIGURE 10.5 *SimCity* – computer simulations encourage creative problem-solving in real and imagined worlds.

FIGURE 10.6 *Ollie Saves the Planet* — simulation and problem-solving online.

multiple-user domain (MUD)
A simulated electronic 'room' in which synchronous, text-based conversations occur between users in real time, using text-based messages

multiple-user object-oriented (domain) (MOO)
Simulated electronic environments that expand the text-based context of MUDs by adding visual objects with which participants can interact

Collaboration and social interaction

Collaboration among learners is another defining characteristic of constructivist classrooms (Jonassen, 1994). The Web has strong potential for social interactivity and for supporting collaboration and student-centred learning (Light, 1993; Mercer, 1996). For example, it is possible for virtual communities of learners on the Internet to work in small collaborative groups to achieve a common goal (Dillenbourg & Schneider, 1995). Collaboration can also be encouraged as learners sit around the computer and work on problem-solving or interactive activities as a group. Teachers need to be careful when forming such groups, as students may need assistance in maintaining task focus and in sharing responsibilities among group members. In the case of computers in particular, there may be a tendency for more-competent and confident computer users to dominate. Nevertheless, the heterogeneous grouping of learners around computer-related tasks can assist in creating zones of proximal development (Walker & Lambert, 1996; see also Chapter 2) and be beneficial for all students.

ICT provides opportunities for students to build shared meaning and to collaborate as they use technology. For example, when students are arranged in groups around computers, they often act as peer coaches for one another, offering advice to those having difficulty with computers or software applications (Means & Olson, 1997; Roschelle, 1996). Sivin-Kachala and Bialo (1997) found that collaborative technologies such as interactive brainstorming programs, interactive writing programs, telecommunication links and Internet access contributed significantly to peer collaboration and required less teacher direction of classroom learning. This collaboration can be fostered through electronic networks such as online discussion or bulletin boards that support ongoing dialogues and the exchange of information (Bagley & Hunter, 1992; Resnick, 1994; Riel, 1994).

ICTs facilitate global collaboration, as the circle of social interaction is enlarged beyond student peers in the classroom to students and experts across the school, the larger community and the globe. Through the introduction of a variety of perspectives and increased opportunities to interact with others, learners are challenged to think laterally and to consider other cultural and community perspectives. In the process, they construct new knowledge for themselves in a context that is meaningful to them (Duffy & Cunningham, 1996).

Distributed learning

distributed learning (computer-mediated instruction, or CMI)
Where teachers, students and learning resources can be in different locations so learning and teaching occur independently of time and place

One way in which ICTs facilitate collaboration is through **distributed learning (computer-mediated instruction, or CMI)**, which allows teachers, students and learning resources to be in different locations so that teaching and learning can occur independent of time and place. This is particularly useful when learners are in isolated or remote areas, such as in rural Australia. Regular face-to-face interaction with peers and teachers may be impossible, yet distributed learning and teaching means that students may learn by means of technology such as video- or audio-conferencing, email, satellite broadcasting or the Web.

Distributed learning and teaching has a learner-centred focus and emphasises interaction and communication among learners and teachers. The Internet connects teachers and learners to people outside the school environment, providing access to expertise not available locally (Harasim, Hiltz, Teles, & Turoff, 1995; Wighton, 1993). Web-based videos or photographs provide visual stimuli for learning, hyperlinks expand the information resources available to learners, and online discussion forums and email facilitate collaborative learning activities. Digital technologies also allow learners to distribute and publish their own material in a range of creative ways.

There are several approaches to distributed learning. One is Electronic Learning Circles (Riel, 1996), a global project where teachers and learners from classes in diverse geographical locations choose a learning task collaboratively. Students exchange their work and receive guidance from their own teacher as well as from teachers in other locations and from the learning circle facilitator. A single publication is created from the work of all the students in the learning circle. A reflection about the activity, the product and the learning that took place closes the learning circle. An Australian-based example of distributed learning in action is shown in Box 10.7 opposite.

Box 10.7 CLASSROOM LINKS

Distributed learning in action: The Ozone Monitoring Network

The Ozone Monitoring Network involves a group of Victorian secondary schools that have worked with Australian and international bodies since 1995. The project involves monitoring ozone levels in the stratosphere and troposphere, and sharing results with a global community of schools. It involves students from years 3 to 12, who work in close collaboration with the Australian Bureau of Meteorology, the Environment Protection Authority (EPA) and a US-based organisation called Vistanomics.

As part of the project, students measure ozone pollution levels and the size of the ozone hole across Victoria. All results are entered into a spreadsheet program that graphs and maps the results. The results are published on the Network's webpage and are compared to the EPA and Bureau of Meteorology's results.

For more information visit: <www.netspace.net.au/~vicozone/>.

Activities

1. What elements of distributed learning can you identify in the Ozone Monitoring Network project?
2. What are the advantages of involving learners in such projects?
3. Can you identify any potential limitations of distributed learning in online environments?

Distributed cognition

Related to distributed learning is the concept of **distributed cognition**, which argues that cognition is not limited to individuals but is something shared by individuals who form communities and share cultural tools. Salomon (1993, p. xiii) stated that: 'people think in conjunction and partnership with others and with the help of culturally provided tools and implements.' Technological tools such as CMC (computer-mediated communication, discussed earlier) and the Internet have fostered the study and understanding of distributed cognition, reminding us that human cognition is situated in a complex sociocultural world by which it is significantly affected (Hollan, Hutchins, & Kirsh, 2000; Hutchins, 1995).

ICTs have a significant role to play in enhancing student learning in constructivist classrooms. A 'WebQuest' is an online activity that illustrates many constructivist principles. WebQuests are inquiry activities that present students with a challenging task, provide access to a range of resources (most often accessed through the Internet) and scaffold the learning process to promote higher-order thinking (March, 2001). WebQuests are an example of online activities that help students to learn and think collaboratively while capitalising on the possibilities of using the Internet to facilitate distributed cognition. The reason that the Web is so critical in WebQuest activities is because it offers the breadth of perspectives and viewpoints that is usually needed to construct meaning on complex topics. Students benefit from being linked to a wide variety of Web resources, including learners from other cultures and countries, so that they can explore and make sense of the issues involved in each challenge.

Humanist learning theories and ICT

Humanist theories of learning draw attention to the more personal, social and qualitative aspects of learning. They emphasise holistic learning and the development of human potential (Joyce & Weil, 1996; see also Chapter 6). Some might argue that humanism and technology are incompatible, yet technology can still provide opportunities for connecting students to others across the globe, for fostering self-understanding and for engendering a greater awareness and appreciation of students' own culture and that of others. Tapscott (1998) argued that the 'Net Generation' is a generation that combines the values of humanism

---

10.4 More about Web Quests

distributed cognition
The notion that cognition is shared by individuals who make up communities and who share cultural tools

with societal and technical dimensions. By enabling connectivity and interaction with others from diverse cultures and backgrounds, ICT can play an important role in raising learners' awareness of the interrelationships between themselves and their community, both locally and globally (Aphek, 2002). When educators select and use ICTs with care, such technologies may be used to shape educational experiences that help learners understand themselves better, take responsibility for their learning, and learn to reach beyond their current development to reach their full potential.

An example of humanist theory at work in the world of ICT was Williams' (2001) proposal for ICFT: 'information, communication and *friendship* technology'. He proposed (p. 49) that:

> If, eventually, every school across the world learns to use the internet to link pupils of all ages, races, cultures and religions, so that they can respect and celebrate the rich diversity of other people's lives, then ... each project, each email message, each image, each music file, each database file, each videoconference, each shared website, is contributing something, however small and seemingly insignificant in itself, to that larger goal of world peace.

Strengths and limitations of different approaches to learning with ICT

ICT can do much to foster learners' construction of meaning and their own learning experiences, whether they are working at their own pace or in collaboration with others. However, if not informed by sound educational principles and theories, computer-based learning resources can impede learning, waste valuable learning time, and become a distraction rather than an asset (Preece & Davies, 1992).

There are obvious limitations to the behavioural approach to learning, as outlined in Chapter 4. These limitations apply equally in the context of ICT use, for since behavioural theory relies almost exclusively on observable behaviour and does not account for individual thought processes, the role of behaviourism in learning is limited to the types of learning that can be easily observed (such as factual recall), rather than less-defined learning that involves conceptual change within the learner. Jonassen (2000) found that 85% of available education software across several countries surveyed fell into the category of drill-and-practice materials. In light of the limited, skills-based focus of the drill-and-practice format, this is of serious concern.

While constructivist classrooms offer much to promote student-centred learning, teaching that is based on constructivist principles is extremely demanding of the teacher (Borko & Putnam, 1995), particularly when technology is involved. It takes time to locate appropriate resources, plan activities, arrange the classroom so as to promote collaboration, and at the same time ensure quality time on task. Another problem may be that some of the most appealing software websites may provide realistic representations of content by using video that may be slow to download. Bandwidth issues and limited computer resources in some schools or remote locations can also work against the creative use of ICT.

Despite these limitations, ICTs provide a valuable means of teaching students to question, think critically, analyse, interpret for themselves in an informed way, be flexible, adapt, and apply skills in new contexts. The use of word-processing software or email so students can share understandings with peers as well as teachers has been demonstrated to improve writing skills, produce more and better ideas for decision-making, and increase motivation (Center for Applied Special Technology, 1996; Chun, 1994; Honey & Henriquez, 1996; Olaniran, 1994). These are important skills and principles that promote lifelong learning and the ability to communicate with people on a local and global scale.

Using ICTs in classrooms has implications for classroom management (see Chapter 12), assessment (see Chapter 11) and the ways in which teachers approach their work. A number of strategies for using ICTs in your classroom are presented in Box 10.8 opposite.

Box 10.8 IMPLICATIONS FOR EDUCATORS

Strategies for using ICT in classrooms

- *Decide your aims for the lesson/unit and select software and online resources accordingly.* Be guided by what you know about how students learn best. If you want to focus on developing students' basic skills, use software that promotes mastery learning. If you want to encourage discovery learning, allow time for students to explore the Internet or CD-ROMs, but provide appropriate scaffolding and guidance to avoid time-wasting.

- *Motivate students and develop their interests.* Databases of information that is available on CD-ROM or on the Internet allow students to examine a multitude of topics to find those of individual interest.

- *Build on students' background knowledge.* As students use computer applications, observe their problem-solving strategies and how they interact with the content. This will give you an indication of what students know. Ask questions about why students have chosen to explore a particular website or used a certain application. This gives opportunities for interaction and for dialogue about students' understandings and knowledge.

- *Encourage different approaches to problem solving on the computer.* 'Microworlds' (similar to simulations but limited to exploring conditions that exist in the real world), simulations, virtual environments and links to resources that extend well beyond the classroom all expand students' options for learning and pose problems that engage students' interest, provide complex challenges and offer rich, meaningful contexts for application (Bednar, Cunningham, Duffy, & Perry, 1992).

- *Foster active learning.* When students use technology as a tool or as a means of communicating with others, they take an active role rather than passively receiving information that has been transmitted by a teacher, textbook or television. The student actively makes choices about how to generate, obtain, manipulate or display information (Means & Olson, 1997, p. 125).

- *Support learners as the classroom structure and organisation change.* When technology is used to enhance learning environments, student roles change. Learners often become peer mentors and mentors for their teachers as well. Sometimes this is difficult for teachers and students. Students need help in learning how to function in such roles.

  The Cognition and Technology Group (1992, p. 117) observed that many students they studied believed that: (a) problems are something presented by teachers rather than discovered by good learners, (b) good learners almost instantly know the answer to all problems, and (c) if they cannot solve a problem in 5 minutes, then they will never solve it. These perceptions need to be challenged. Learners and teachers need to support one another in adapting to changes in roles and expectations.

- *Adapt your classroom-management techniques.* Issues such as abuse of expensive equipment and student access to unacceptable material on the Internet must be addressed by teachers and schools as they change their practices. Managing group collaboration around computers and encouraging individualised learning using computers all require careful planning.

10.5 Sample lesson plans integrating ICTs

Features of learning with ICT

There are several unique characteristics of learning with ICT that are changing the way students learn and interact with others. When computers are used in learning environments, teachers need to consider a number of aspects, including:

- how to prepare learners to navigate the Web using hypertext
- what skills learners need in order to read electronic texts
- the role of ICTs in learners' identity development
- how the use of ICTs might contribute to or reinforce inequities in a classroom.

Features of learning with ICTs include the need to become familiar with hypertext and hypermedia, hyperlinks and non-linearity, and cognitive issues that arise from learners having to read computer screens.

navigation
To move around an electronic environment (specifically the Web) by following hyperlinked paths

hypertext
A system of computer coding that links pieces of information online

hyperlink
Text (that is, words or symbols) that when activated by a mouse click allow the user access to the relevant linked information

Learning to navigate using hypertext and hypermedia

The term **navigation** is used to describe how ICT users move around virtual environments. **Hypertext** is the primary means of navigating through these virtual environments, being a way of linking pieces of online information and of using these links to access related pieces of information. Hypertext usually refers to text linking (or **hyperlink**s) in the form of a word or a phrase that, when clicked on with the computer mouse, provides access to the relevant material. Hypertext may also include other linked media such as graphics, video, sound and animation (Nielsen, 1995). Hypermedia (see Glossary) refers to the combination of these hypertext items in an electronic environment that allows users to move through text, images and sound.

One of the main features of hyptertext is the way it differs from traditional Western text models, which involve readers moving from left to right and top to bottom on a page. Traditional texts also typically have an obvious opening, a middle section and a conclusion. Hypertexts, on the other hand, are characteristically non-linear, in that they do not follow a 'straight line' from beginning to end, but may be read or navigated in a range of ways depending on which links the user clicks. Pages and chunks of text are often linked in 'information webs' through which those reading on computer screens must determine their own paths (Pachler, 2001, p. 23).

Navigating using hypertext and hyperlinks allows for exploration and discovery but also has potential problems. It can be very time-consuming to work through hypertext, as there are many opportunities for clicking on hyperlinks. Students need to learn how to read and process hypertext effectively and efficiently. They may be familiar with hypermedia environments as a result of playing computer games or surfing the Web, yet they may lack the necessary skills to focus on a search task, ignore irrelevant hyperlinks or return to the task after becoming sidetracked by hyperlinks that might take them far from their original goal. The teacher's role is to support learners by selecting appropriate activities and by providing and modelling strategies to help learners make the transition from familiar linear formats of reading and writing to non-linear formats (Leader & Klein, 1996; Mayer & Moreno, 1998).

Table 10.3 outlines some features of hypertext and how it differs from paper-based text.

10.6 Bunyip: a hypermedia environment

TABLE 10.3 Differences between hypertext and paper-based text

Hypertext	Paper-based text
■ Interlinked pieces of text or other information are stored electronically	■ Printed on paper
■ Non-linear	■ Linear in Western print traditions
■ Through hyperlinks, readers can move around the document as they wish: no single order determines the sequence of information to be read	■ The text sequence is predetermined by the writer
■ Readers have control over which links to pursue: they move through hypertext by browsing or navigating, both of which emphasise how readers must actively determine their path through the network	■ Readers tend to have limited control over how they will process and move through a linear text
■ Readers may be easily disoriented and lose track of their location within a document	■ In a linear structure, it is easier than in a non-linear structure to keep track of your reading and to review content covered
■ Context is often lost in hypertext documents: readers may find a passage but have no concept of its context	■ In a book, it is possible to read the paragraph or chapter before and after, or to check the index to establish context and meaning

Source: Adapted from Troffer (2000).

Cognition and reading online

There are a number of differences between screen and print reading (Thurstun, 2000), and screen reading makes particular demands on computer users. These demands relate to ways in which learners process information. Studies show that reading from a computer screen is about 30% slower than reading from paper (Nielsen, 1995, p. 154). Screen reading may present difficulties for the following reasons (Allstetter, 1998; Troffer, 2000):

- Screen size can be smaller than a page of printed material.
- Screen resolution is low compared to printed material.
- Screen glare can impair reading.
- Letters on a computer screen appear coarse to the eye.
- Screen reading can cause eyestrain (Horton, 1994).
- Processing text online requires spatial and relational processing abilities (Wenger & Payne, 1996).
- Desktop computers are not portable and can be less convenient to use than printed material, and laptop computers may have very small screens.

Schriver (1997) notes that documents not designed for the screen are often posted online with no consideration for the particular needs of screen readers.

CRITICAL REFLECTIONS

- What steps will you take to help your students overcome some of the challenges of screen reading?
- Identify benefits and limitations of hyperlinking and of the non-linearity of the Internet.
- What difficulties have you had with navigating the Internet?
- Have you ever become 'lost in cyberspace'? What strategies do you use to make sure you do not get sidetracked or 'lost' when searching the Internet?

Identity and the Internet

An important part of effective ICT use involves understanding their role in young learners' development in a range of areas. We have seen that computer technologies may be used to enhance learners' cognitive development by providing opportunities to solve problems with the help of scaffolding from the computer. Further, there are opportunities for students to interact with others through computer technology (for example, using email) or to interact with their peers or teachers as they sit in groups at a computer and work through tasks. ICTs also have the potential to play a role in the personal, social and moral development of learners in the 21st century, depending on the extent of their involvement with the technology. The psychology of the Internet is a growing area of study (Joinson, 2002; Riva & Galimberti, 2001a; Suler, 2002) because of the possibilities of Internet communication and because of the potential for identity experimentation such communications offer.

It has been said that the Internet represents a new psychosocial space that fosters social relationships and that allows individuals to play different roles and possibly develop a new sense of self (Murray, 2000; Riva & Galimberti, 2001b). Cyberspace brings with it anonymity, which tends to provide people with a safe place to try out different roles, voices and identities (Suler, 2002). As quoted in Murray (2000, p. 17): 'It's sort of like training wheels for the self you want to bring out in real life.' This anonymity may prove problematic if, as Joinson (1998) suggested, it leads to disinhibition, where Internet users feel free to reveal excessive

10.7 The construction of identity in adolescents' personal homepages

amounts about themselves online and find it increasingly attractive to inhabit virtual space, rather than the real world. On the other hand, the Internet can provide positive opportunities for self-explanation and presentation, from searching and emailing to chatting or creating a 'homepage' on the Web (Joinson, 2001; Turkle, 1994, 1997). For many adolescents, the chance to represent themselves through developing a webpage or perhaps by assuming a new identity in Internet chatrooms is particularly appealing.

CRITICAL REFLECTION

- Discuss the advantages and disadvantages of the Internet as a new psychosocial space that fosters social relationships and allows individuals to play different roles.

Values and the Internet

In Chapter 3 we discussed how learners develop morally over time and the importance of developing values as part of the learning–teaching process. The rapid growth and use of ICTs in all aspects of our lives raises significant issues relating to equity, intellectual property, commercial exploitation, privacy and the impact of the Internet on cultural heritage and personal identity (Hoekstra, Gordon, & Donald, 1999). These issues are closely bound to the values we hold, and provide opportunities for learners and teachers to make values more 'visible' by taking time to discuss them. Here is a selection of values-based questions (adapted from Hoekstra, Gordon, & Donald, 1999, p. 13) for you to consider and discuss in your own learning–teaching context:

- Are we teaching students to be discerning users of ICT? Can they make informed judgements about the merits of various pieces of software or Internet sites?
- Will ICT result in reduced intellectual competence? Are we relying too heavily on computers to do our work for us?
- Will computers alter our perceptions of reality? How do we prevent people from becoming so engrossed in Internet chatrooms that they confuse these with the reality of face-to-face contact? Is ICT redefining what it means to be human? Is Internet addiction a potential problem for some?
- What effect will ICT have on society? We already have a 'digital divide' between those who have ready access to technology and all it brings, and those who do not. How do we prevent this divide from widening?

There is scope for teachers to address these and other questions as they consider ways in which ICTs might be used to promote learners' critical thinking and values systems. Box 10.9 looks at some values-based issues regarding ICT in the classroom.

Box 10.9 CLASSROOM LINKS

Values-based issues associated with ICT in the classroom

The Values Star is a strategy developed for VITAL, and is short for 'values in information technology and learning' (Hoekstra, Gordon, & Donald, 1999, p. 7). It is one way of classifying values-based issues under the general headings of spiritual, personal, ethical, economic, environmental, cultural and social issues. Each issue forms one point of the star (see Figure 10.7 opposite), and specific examples of each issue are added to the star as they arise in the classroom. In this way, values are made 'visible' and ICT provides a helpful vehicle for exploring some of these values-related issues.

FIGURE 10.7 The VITAL star. (Source: Commonwealth of Australia.)

Ethical issues
Ethics is a system of moral principles by which human actions and proposals may be judged good or bad, right or wrong. We must assess the authority and credibility of what is communicated
★ ICT issues include: copyright, plagiarism, intellectual property, security, privacy and a sense of right and wrong

Spiritual issues
Questions of ultimate meaning and destiny are spiritual issues. To what extent does ICT allow users to appreciate and explore what it is to be human?
★ ICT issues include: communication, research and the nature of reality

Personal issues
Issues of self-esteem and self-image are dealt with here. To what extent is ICT an extension of oneself, enhancing a sense of personal competence and fulfilment, and to what extent is it an invasion of privacy?
★ ICT issues include: independence, self-directed learning and the use of email and Internet relationships

Cultural issues
ICT language and visual impact are of particular cultural interest. Cultural issues may overlap with social issues
★ ICT issues include: literacy, visual literacy, spelling, jargon, gender and organisation

Values in ICT and learning

Social issues
Social issues are those that relate to the communities or societies in which we live
★ ICT issues include: health, gender, status, aesthetics, timeliness, bias, censorship, distance education and community control/development

Economic issues
Economic advantage for some may result in educational disadvantage for others. Economic rationalism and the impact of ICT on employment are also key issues
★ ICT issues include: outlay and running costs, upgrading, obsolescence and employment

Environmental issues
Environmental issues are of great interest to young people. Societies are increasingly aware of the need to adopt environmentally sustainable practices
★ ICT issues include: waste, energy usage, planned obsolescence, recycling and production processes

Activities

The following activities, adapted from Hoekstra, Gordon and Donald (1999, p. 108), will need to be modified according to your students' age group, background and abilities:
1 Hold a class discussion about ICTs and their impact on our society. Consider the uses of ICTs and their possible relationship to values-based issues such as honesty, equity, justice, responsibility and respect.
2 Discuss the following questions:
   a Are people with computers advantaged over those without?
   b Do people with computer skills have better access to employment than those without?
   c What could be done to address inequities?
   d How do you think ICTs are affecting our society at the moment?

ICT in the inclusive classroom

Research indicates that students' ICT skills are at least partly dependent on access to and opportunities to use computers at school (Meredyth et al., 1999). This raises important questions about digital equity issues. The rest of this chapter looks at relevant factors, such as equity of access, gender, special learning needs, culture and remote location, to help you consider how to best support all learners as you integrate ICTs into your particular educational context.

10.8 The digital divide

Access to ICT

Lack of access or inequitable access to technology is a significant issue that influences the quality of student learning and learning outcomes. Learners' socioeconomic status and the financial resources of the schools they attend play a significant role in determining access to quality learning resources. This is particularly apparent in the area of ICT, since computer technology can be costly and there are complex access issues related to Internet use (Boyd, 2002; Palmer, 1998). The term 'digital divide' was coined to highlight the inequitable distribution of ICT resources and Internet access across groups (National Telecommunications and Information Administration (NTIA), 2000; Smolenski, 2000). Venezky (2000, p. 63) outlines three groups of students who suffer as a result of the digital divide. These include:

- students in remote rural or poor inner-urban areas where telecommunications are limited and/or expensive, and students who have disabilities
- student groups who find the technology isolating and mechanical, for example some females and minority groups who have had little or no exposure to ICT
- students from low-SES homes lacking ICT resources.

In making decisions about how and to what extent to integrate ICT into the learning process, teachers need to consider factors such as students' access to computer resources at home, and the potential disadvantages lack of access may cause. Wiburg (1995) noted that the ways in which ICTs, particularly computers, are integrated into educational settings have the potential to either change or reinforce existing inequalities.

Equitable access to ICTs means that all learners have equal access to ICTs regardless of socioeconomic background, gender, ability level, geographic location, ethnicity or language background. This may involve providing a variety of adaptive devices designed to enable learners with disabilities to take full advantage of the power of technology to enhance personal freedom (Roblyer & Edwards, 2000, p. 21). Or it may involve using a range of innovative resources to extend the more able students' learning. All learners should have the opportunity to use ICTs for the full range of purposes for which they were designed, including information access and communication through a range of technologies.

The rate at which equipment is purchased by schools or other educational institutions has an impact on individuals' ability to access information technologies, especially in an educational setting (Marginson, 1993, pp. 91–101). The unequal distribution of ICT resources among schools, individual students and home environments is a significant barrier to equitable educational practice and the development of ICT skills across all student groups. Disadvantage is further compounded by such factors as the priority parents and families give to computer use, the value attached to education and the availability of home-based ICT resources. The notion of compounded disadvantage (see Chapter 9) is illustrated in a study of the digital divide in New Zealand. The researchers noted that low-income families, Maori and Pacific Nations people, and those living in isolated rural regions typically had telephone-connection rates lower than those for the general population and therefore had less access to the Internet (Maharey & Swain, 2000).

Gender and ICT use

Particular groups of students are more likely than others to experience disadvantage with the introduction of ICT into the classroom. Existing studies suggest that female students, for example, may not receive the benefits of ICT in the classroom to the same extent as their male peers (Comber, Colley, Hargreaves, & Dorn, 1997; Fletcher-Flinn & Suddendorf, 1996; Meredyth et al., 1999). The findings of a 1997 international study (Reinen & Plomp) supported the proposition that females 'know less about information technology, enjoy using the computer less than male students, and perceive more problems with software' (p. 65), and these differences were evident inside and outside school. Based on analyses of the results, the authors concluded that reasons for the disparity in the experiences of ICT between the sexes might include the level of parental support, students' access to computers (in terms of availability and use), a relative lack of female role models (Silverman & Pritchard, 1993) and the types of activities carried out with computers in schools (Bransgrove, 1994; Greenhill, 1998). Gender differences in computer use may not be as significant as this in some schools – an obvious example is in single-sex girls' schools (Littleton, Light, Joiner, Messer, & Barnes, 1998) – however, if you are concerned about increasing female learners' use of computers, Box 10.10 offers a selection of strategies.

Box 10.10 CLASSROOM LINKS

Encouraging female learners to use computers

- Provide computer-use role models including women and men. Draw attention to interesting projects being done by women *and* men, emphasising that technology is used by people who have varying roles and responsibilities.
- Provide female mentors and guest speakers.
- Design instruction using computers that appeals to both sexes.
- Make a conscious effort to encourage female learners to use computers. In class, call on them more often, even if they do not volunteer. Ask them challenging questions that require higher-order thinking. Try to find time for girls to be on computers when boys are not around. Choose a girl to help set up new hardware or software.
- Start a computer club designed to appeal to girls.
- Make sure girls take the highest level of computing offered in high school settings.
- For young girls, purchase games that appeal to them. The more time a young child can spend on a computer, the more confident she will become with the technology.
- In class, collaborate more; compete less. In general, girls respond better to collaborative rather than competitive projects. Encourage collaboration and team work.
- Give girls equal access to learning: do not let boys dominate the computers.
- If a girl is struggling with an answer, do not call on a boy to finish it for her.
- Do not do for girls what you would not do for boys.
- Use email as a way of reducing the impact of stereotypes based on gender and appearance.
- Talk to counsellors, parents, and other teachers to enlist their help in encouraging the girls in your school into the highest levels of computer science.
- Be reflective: look at your own attitudes and behaviours regarding male and female roles.

Source: Adapted from <math.rice.edu/~lanius/club/girls.html#Tips> and <www.cew.wisc.edu/equity/gender_equity_in_classroom_compu.htm>

Research indicates that boys tend to use computers in the classroom more often than girls do (Scott, 1996) (see Figure 10.8), and that girls typically have less positive attitudes towards computers than do boys (Ayersman & Reed, 1996; Sacks, Bellisimo, & Mergendoller, 1994). Attitudes and perceptions regarding computers play a significant role in the ways males and females approach them, and these may be apparent at an early age (Bernhard, 1992; Fletcher-Finn & Suddendorf, 1996). Collis and Williams (1987) found that adolescent males in China and Canada believed females were less proficient computer users than males, while Makrakis (1992) found that adolescent males in Sweden and Japan had more positive attitudes about the suitability of computers for males than females did for their own gender (see also

FIGURE 10.8 Boys may dominate computer use in coeducational classrooms. What strategies would you use to prevent this from happening in your classroom?

Martin, 1991). Boys have been found more likely than girls to have access to a computer at home that they could 'play around on' and experiment with (Robertson, Calder, Fung, Jones, & O'Shea, 1995). On the other hand, girls do not tend to view computers as toys, and are less likely than boys to 'play around' with computers in order to find out how they work. Girls may be disadvantaged by this prevailing attitude to computers as a more functional tool, since the process of experimenting with technology typically contributes to self-efficacy (Whitley, 1997) and to a sense of mastery over the computer.

ICT for learners with different abilities

With its potential for addressing the needs of students on an individual basis, ICT can be particularly useful for extending students with high academic abilities, and catering for those with special learning needs.

10.9 Using ICT to support learners with diverse abilities and needs

Learners with high academic abilities

For high achievers, ICT may be helpful for extension work and encouraging students to work beyond the specified curriculum (Gross, 1993). There are several examples of this practice working well in mainstream schools. For example, the TalentEd Virtual Enrichment Program (Smith, 2000) uses computer technology to provide enrichment courses in various subjects and topics to students of high ability across all age groups. Course notes are provided on the Internet, and students communicate with their course-leader by email. Collaborative learning among students is encouraged using chatrooms and online forums. Students may do the course either as part of a school subject or from home. In this program, the Internet provides enrichment for students who may not otherwise have such opportunities because of social or geographic isolation, or because of a physical disability. In another innovative Australian program, Year 10 students of high ability from remote Victorian country schools are joined with 'virtual mentors' among undergraduate students at the University of Melbourne. Most of the communication occurs through email, and the program is designed to extend each student's ability to conduct independent research in an area of interest negotiated by student and mentor.

Learners with special learning needs

ICTs are used in a range of ways to support students with special learning needs through the use of technologies to assist learning (Cormack, Couch, & McColl, 2000; Curriculum Corporation, 1994; Pressman & Blackstone, 1997). Computers with assistive devices have the potential to support learners with physical disabilities, including those with cerebral palsy, spinal cord injuries and muscular dystrophy (Pell, Gillies, & Carss, 1999), providing them with learning opportunities that were previously unavailable.

Box 10.11 presents a case study from South Australia that demonstrates the advantages of ICT use in teaching students with learning disabilities. Drawn from a national Australian study into the use of computer-based technologies among students of differing disabilities and needs, it illustrates some principles for integrating ICTs into classrooms with students who have disabilities.

Box 10.11 CASE STUDY

Introducing technology into a classroom of learners with disabilities

Particularly when introducing new methods of computer access, teachers taught a number of sub-skills before attempting to teach the whole class. Depending upon students' needs and the complexity of the task, teachers and support staff used modelling, intermittent verbal prompts and one-to-one or small group instruction to introduce technology.

Students benefited from practising their new skills, especially in the early stages of the programs. In particular, students with severe multiple disabilities required continual revision and repetition. Teachers found that the more familiar the program, the more the students could achieve. Even for students with less significant need, one teacher noted that regular work on the computer encouraged its acceptance as an integral part of classroom activities. The graded approach of some software programs encouraged each student to progress as appropriate. Many were also motivated by bright computer graphics accompanied by sound. [A classroom teacher commented]:

> If they are asked to construct a sentence, 'Here is the dog', repeatedly over a six-month period until they've got it, they are likely to switch off. However, if they can construct, 'Here is the . . .' and the gap asks them to insert an item (sometimes using Intellikeys) from their current text, they are much more interested in activities. The item used from text is always supported by a graphic or picture so that the student is not expected to read the text only, but to interpret the picture.

* * *

In a few case studies [documented in this report], the introduction of new technology resulted in heightened stress for teachers and/or students. In these instances, teachers with primary responsibility for the programs monitored stress levels and the use of technology was relaxed from time to time to alleviate its effect on the student, family and staff. Another strategy for minimising stress was to alternate difficult and simple tasks in classroom activities.

Teachers emphasised that accommodating individual interests and learning styles increased student motivation in computer-based activities ... In this study, the health and mood of many students with disabilities affected their daily routines. A flexible approach to technology-based learning helped reduce frustration or unacceptable behaviour. If the computer was used on days when students were not receptive, it was not as effective in achieving stated objectives. As one teacher explained:

> Sometimes, it was just incredibly hard to get done what I wanted to do and the mood of the students would be different or the students would be a bit ratty that day and you can't push through these kids. You just have to accept and say, 'Oh, right, you know, they're just not going to get there today'. So being realistic about your planning, that probably helped. I would just think, 'OK, I may only get two interesting technology aspects covered this week rather than the five that I've planned'.

Source: Ministerial Advisory Committee: Students with Disabilities (2000).

Activity

This case study raises several issues relating to using technology with students who have disabilities.
1 What are these issues?
2 Can you think of any other issues that are not covered in this excerpt?
3 Are any of these issues relevant to the use of ICT in regular classrooms? Discuss your views.

Potential cultural biases of ICT

Much of the Internet and educational software is dominated by Western (primarily US-based) cultural values and the English language (Moran, Thompson, & Arthur, 1999), although this is changing rapidly; for example, the Chinese uptake of Internet connections has expanded enormously relative to what it was in the last years of the 20th century (Press, Foster, Wolcott, & McHenry, 2002). Nevertheless, such cultural biases send messages to learners about the type and form of information that is valued (Greenhill, Fletcher, & von Hellens, 1999). When selecting software or integrating ICT into your teaching program, you need to be aware of potential sources of cultural bias.

ICTs have been used to help learners from non-English-speaking backgrounds improve their English-language acquisition, to encourage learner dependence and to foster communication skills (Adkins-Bowling, Brown, & Mitchell, 2001; Meskill, Mossop, & Bates, 1999; Reichhardt, 1996). Where this technology has been used effectively, it has encouraged learners from non-English-speaking backgrounds (NESBs) to take risks in practising their English and has fostered increased cross-cultural understandings among students (Ryan, 1997). Yet while the use of innovative computer-assisted teaching practices may assist students' acquisition of language skills, care needs to be taken in selecting software for NESB learners. Some practitioners and researchers have questioned the quality of such software (Kersteen, Linn, Clancy, & Hardyck, 1988), but before dismissing these computer resources it is worth evaluating them and determining their benefits and limitations. In Australia, for example, sites such as that of the National Centre for English Language Teaching and Research at Macquarie University (<www.nceltr.mq.edu.au/eslnet.htm>) promote critical analysis of software and Internet resources related to English-language teaching.

One study of students with limited English proficiency (LEP) who used CD-ROMs as part of instruction over a 3-year period reported that the students undertaking the instruction had significantly stronger agreement with statements such as: 'I like my science class', 'We do fun things in science', 'My friends like science' and 'I would like to take more science' than LEP students in conventional classrooms (Barrutia, Bissell, Rodriguez, & Scarcella, 1993).

In addition to supporting students' language learning, ICTs – with their capacity to connect learners across the globe – can help young people celebrate cultural diversity and develop cultural awareness and tolerance. The First Peoples' Project was developed by the International Education and Resource Network (iEARN), a global network of teachers and students dedicated to using ICTs to encourage young people in different parts of the world to work collaboratively and to share their understanding of one another's cultures (see <www.learn.org.au/fo/efphome.htm>). The First Peoples' Project draws together indigenous students (of all ages in the K–12 range) from around the world to work together on collaborative projects (visit <www.iearn.org.au/fp/>). Students can be involved in writing exchanges, art exchanges and discussion about issues relating to indigenous students. Students can also be involved in the Humanitarian Effort. The First Peoples' Project links Koori students in Victorian schools with other indigenous students in Australia and around the world in an exchange of writing, art and discussion. There are indigenous students involved from Australia, the USA, Thailand, Mexico, Guatemala and Argentina. Each year a calendar is produced representing artwork from each national group. A magazine is also produced that features writing, artwork and photographs from each group. Communication between the participants is by way of email and online newsgroups. The schools involved in the First Peoples' Project endeavour to involve their local indigenous community in all aspects of the project.

ICT and students in rural or remote areas

ICT has the potential to transform the schooling experiences of children living in rural and remote areas by providing them with access to resources and connections to people and information that they would otherwise not have. Children living on rural properties or attending small or isolated schools have the opportunity to access an expanded range of courses through a combination of ICT and distance education. Access to the Internet and communication technologies helps develop students' global awareness and an understanding of Australia's role in a global context (NSW DET, 2002). For example, Wilsmore (2001) reported on a small one-teacher school in north-western New South Wales that is 200 km from the state capital, yet the teacher is using ICTs to enthuse students and enhance their learning by connecting them to knowledge and people on a global scale.

However, not all children in rural and remote areas benefit from access to new technology and improved communications infrastructures. Australian researchers (see, for example, Hatton & Elliott, 1998; Sidoti, 2000) observed that students and teachers in rural areas in Australia are suffering from inequities in access to and use of ICTs. Excessive distances can make it difficult for students to access necessary ICT resources. Moreover, the disadvantage brought about by remoteness of location is often compounded by the low socioeconomic status of some students' families and by limited funding for computers in rural schools.

CRITICAL REFLECTIONS

- Have you seen evidence of the 'digital divide' in your educational experience?
- What strategies will you put in place to minimise disadvantage brought about by ICT use?
- What disadvantages might there be in giving students the option of completing all their assignments on computer? Do you think there is merit in asking that all students submit at least one assignment in handwritten form, rather than in word-processed form?

Strengths and limitations of using ICT in the classroom

ICT promises a future that is faster, more exciting and better than anything that has gone before. But the mere presence of a computer in a classroom does not automatically guarantee improved learning and teaching. Recent studies indicate that the use of computer-based instruction when compared with conventional instruction has a moderate positive effect on student outcomes and on their attitudes to computers and learning (Means & Olson, 1997; Cuttance, 2001; Steketee, Herrington, & Oliver, 2001). However, these results should be interpreted with caution, as the quality of computer-based instructional materials varies widely, as do the skills with which teachers are able to integrate ICTs into their teaching. Some of the benefits listed in the following material are adapted from Roblyer et al. (1997, p. 29).

10.10 The Internet's impact on teacher practice and classroom culture

Strengths of using ICT in the classroom

Enhanced motivation

The use of computers in classrooms has been found to enhance motivation and self-esteem (Musker, 2000), particularly when students observe a tangible improvement in the quality of their work presentation (see also Deal, 1995; Ferneding-Lenert & Harris, 1994; Lowry, Koneman, Osmand-Jouchoux, & Wilson, 1994; Ryser, Beeler, & McKenzie, 1995; Sandholtz, Ringstaff, & Dwyer, 1997; Williams, 1995). ICTs may contribute to enhanced student motivation (see Figure 10.9), since their use in classrooms has been found to:

- engage learners (Jonassen, Carr, & Yueh, 1998; Volker, 1992)
- encourage self-regulation and control over learning (Arnone & Grabowski, 1992; Relan, 1992)
- improve attendance and enhance students' attitudes toward learning (Charp, 1998; King, 1997; Newhouse, 1998).

FIGURE 10.9
ICTs may enhance motivation in students, improving their attendance and attitudes towards learning.

Promoting student engagement

ICTs are thought to promote student engagement through:

- linking learners to information sources through hyperlinks and hypertext systems (Kozma, 1991, 1994)
- catering for different cognitive styles; for example, helping visual learners 'see' problems and solutions through interactive visual media
- tracking learner progress (for self and reporting to others)
- linking learners to learning tools because ICT can cover long distances, support instruction and enhance learning (Hauser & Malouf, 1996; Roblyer, 1990, 1999)
- increasing physical involvement and engagement with learning, in that computer users engage by using the mouse to control movements and actions, and by selecting courses of action or search strategies for themselves
- facilitating cooperative learning in small groups or with others in virtual communities; for example, with hypermedia products and Logo programs, and research projects using online and offline databases
- enabling distributed learning and cognition, which may broaden students' experiences and perspectives.

Improved learning outcomes

Improved learning outcomes from ICTs may occur through:

- facilitating student-centred learning, which allows students a degree of autonomy and self-management, and which offers some choice and flexibility in content and delivery (Alonso & Norman, 1996; Means et al., 1993; Mercer, 1996; Saye, 1997)
- encouraging independent learning among students, particularly those who are not high achievers in traditional book-based learning (School of Education, James Cook University, 1998)
- developing learners' metacognitive skills in a computer environment (Clements, 1999)
- offering a wider range of options through using online and digital delivery methods and establishing links with external experts in certain fields (this is particularly relevant for smaller schools with limited curriculum offerings, or for students in remote areas).

Box 10.12 discusses an online collaborative project that illustrates many of the advantages of using ICTs to teach in an authentic learning environment so as to connect students to learning and encourage collaboration.

Box 10.12 CASE STUDY

Connecting learners to the Web and the world

The Environmental Mystery Competition (EMC) was a very successful Global Classroom Project for years 4 to 8. Developed and coordinated by David Francis of Kyneton Secondary College in Victoria, the online collaborative project ran as a series of competitions between 1997 and 2000.

The mystery competition unfolded in parts on the Web over a period of 6 to 8 weeks, with students attempting to solve it. The website (<www.kynsec.vic.edu.au/emc/> included sequential story parts and provided a list of all participants, their contact details and what they contributed to solving the mystery. Student participants could ask questions of the coordinating team and submit artwork and other presentations for inclusion on the website.

Involvement levels with EMC varied. Where one class might limit itself to downloading and discussing part 1 of the story from the EMC website, another class might coordinate the submission of possible solutions to the mystery. Submitting possible solutions could be done using email, by corresponding with others involved in the project and even by generating websites and hardcopy publications associated with the themes of the mystery unfolding.

The project catered for different levels of commitment, technology and skill, allowing students to develop areas of interest and to collaborate with others. Students from all over the world participated, with involvement levels ranging from individual students working on the project to whole classes submitting their responses. Classes with access to only one online computer participated by 'rotating' the different roles required within the project.

Online projects do not begin with technology use. Simply, the technology enables the extension of curriculum that teachers and students value.

10.11 What do students think of learning with ICTs?

Limitations of using ICT in the classroom

Equity issues

ICT has the potential to reinforce differences between economically advantaged and disadvantaged schools and students, and to entrench existing inequities. It costs a great deal to maintain adequate computer equipment and software in schools, and this contributes further to inequities. There are often disparities between students in terms of the types of ICT resources they have, and have access to, at home. Several other potential sources of disadvantage — such as gender, language background and disability — have been discussed in this chapter. Inequitable access to ICTs may compromise the quality of learning experiences for students from any disadvantaged group, both at school and later in life.

Classroom-management issues

Computers can be used as an effective classroom-management tool to encourage students to collaborate on computer-related tasks, with a focus on student-centred activities using computers (Pisapia, Knutson, & Coukos, 1999). However, for many teachers — particularly those new to teaching — integrating computers into the curriculum may present several practical classroom-management challenges. For instance, there are often insufficient computers for individualised use, which means students may need to be grouped around computers. If groups are not effectively arranged, if students are not used to working collaboratively or if they do not have specified roles in their group, they may become distracted as they surf the Web or waste time talking. Time on task may suffer and this may cause undue noise and disruption in the classroom. If students are working online, there may be technical difficulties — such as computers crashing or networks going down — that could mean the planned task cannot be accomplished. In this case, teachers need to have contingency plans and alternative activities organised. Such classroom-management issues can be addressed, but they can also cause frustration and stress for both teachers and learners. Moran and colleagues (1999, p. 55) noted that teachers regularly request professional development in class-management techniques relating to ICTs.

Psychosocial issues: alienation, anxiety and addiction

A survey of online databases such as PsycINFO and ERIC (Educational Resources Information Center) reveals a growing research interest in psychological aspects of computer use and specifically Internet use. While the Internet has the potential to offer support and connections with other people through such features as online chatrooms and discussion boards, the potential for overusing or misusing the technology is an important issue for educators. Some have likened Internet addiction (IA) to a behavioural addiction like pathological gambling. This also has implications for associated addictions such as cybersex addiction and cyber-relationship addiction (Hansen, 2002; Pratarelli & Browne, 2002).

Heavy Internet users may become alienated from their regular social connections as they become increasingly involved in online cyber-relationships (Amichai-Hamburger & Ben-Artzi, 2003). Shyness and anxiety levels may contribute to individuals using electronic forms of communication and entertainment to avoid making face-to-face contact with others (Scealy, Phillips, & Stevenson, 2002). If taken to the extreme, this may contribute to unhealthy behaviours and attitudes. A study of 753 Taiwanese adolescents (Lin & Tsai, 2002) found that those classified as Internet-dependent reported that excessive use of the Internet had a negative impact on their daily routines, school performance and relationships with their parents.

Despite the apparently widespread use of computers, anxieties and phobias about their use remain among some teachers (Bradley & Russell, 1997) and learners, particularly those classified as non-users (Ayersman & Reed, 1996; Maurer, 1994; Murero, 2002). One researcher referred to computer-related anxiety as 'technostress' (Genco, 2000). Technostress is related to perceived technical competence, and continues to have an impact on ways in which ICTs are integrated into teaching and learning experiences. In terms of computer use among teachers, a national study of IT skill-levels among Australian schoolteachers indicated that teachers' self-perceptions regarding computer skills are strongly related to age, with younger teachers consistently reporting higher skill-levels than older teachers (Meredyth et al., 1999).

Ethical issues

The use of ICTs poses several ethical issues for educators. These include the potential for:

- plagiarism of Web materials
- breach of copyright rules through downloading Web resources such as music, videos and graphics
- exposure to obscene or harmful materials (such as pornography) on the Web
- exposure to online interactions that may prove harmful (such as with online stalkers, see Spitzberg & Hoobler, 2002)
- exposure to paedophiles who may have access to young people through online chatrooms and the like.

In a national survey of Australian teachers from a wide range of primary and secondary schools, Meredyth and colleagues (1999) found that the majority of teachers (58%) in the sample were not confident that they could prevent students from plagiarising Internet sources, nor did they feel they knew enough about copyright to guide their students' use of the Web (53%). Almost half of the teacher respondents (46%) expressed a lack of confidence in their ability to restrict students' access to obscene or harmful material online. Issues regarding student access to ICTs are of particular concern, as these technologies are increasingly integrated into student learning experiences.

Resource issues

There are many resource limitations that threaten the effective and widespread adoption and integration of ICTs into the curriculum. Devising ways of integrating ICTs into teaching programs and developing resources that are appropriate to learners' needs is a time-consuming task that requires skill on the teacher's part (Boethel, 1996) as well as support for teachers in the form of professional development, technical support and access to resources. The cost of purchasing hardware and software, arranging for professional development and funding resources and support for staff may be prohibitive for some schools. In other situations, the physical layout of school buildings restricts network placement and computer location (Moran, Thompson, & Arthur, 1999). These are just some of the potential limitations to using ICTs creatively and successfully in schools.

CRITICAL REFLECTIONS

- In your experience, have the advantages of ICT use outweighed the disadvantages?
- How do you plan to integrate ICTs in your teaching in light of the benefits and limitations outlined in this chapter?

Box 10.13 lists some characteristics of leading educational practice in ICT use in schools. (Note that IT is distinguished from ICT in the list, and refers specifically to computer technologies.)

10.12 ICT supporting reflective learning and teaching

Box 10.13 IMPLICATIONS FOR EDUCATORS

Characteristics of good ICT practice in teaching

[An] ICT Leading Practice ... should be one that:
- interests and motivates students for greater learning and promotes independent thought
- is interactive, relevant and inclusive
- is based on sound pedagogical principles
- caters for a wide range of learning abilities and styles
- develops students' IT and ICT abilities
- enhances lifelong learning skills such as critical thinking, problem solving, research and analytical skills
- involves both teachers and students in learning and facilitation, and is dependent on teachers' ICT professional development and vision.

Source: EdNA Online (2002). (ICT Leading Practice site: <leadingpractice.edna.edu.au.criteria.html>).

Activities

1. Observe a class group (of any age) who are using ICTs as part of a learning experience:
    a Can you see evidence in the activity of at least three of the ICT leading-practice characteristics?
    b Document the evidence and discuss it with your tutorial group.
    c How do you think the activity might be improved to better reflect ICT leading practice?
2. How would you summarise your vision for using ICT in your teaching? Share your views with your tutorial group.

Concluding comments

In deciding when, how, why – and perhaps if – you will integrate ICTs into your educational setting, the most important message is that, as research indicates, technology on its own is of little value. It does not, on its own, improve teaching and learning, unless it is used as part of a planned, integrated approach to foster student learning (Sivin-Kachala & Bialo, 1996) and unless educators are supported in using it in the classroom (Australian Council for Computers in Education, 2000). Moreover, to be most effective, ICTs require teachers and school communities to rethink issues such as school design, timetabling, curriculum, and the traditional rules, roles and relationships of educational contexts (Morrison & Goldberg, 1996; Seaton, 1998). As we emphasised at the beginning of this chapter, ICT is a vehicle that may enhance learning and teaching, but only when used in an informed and reflective way as part of a carefully planned strategy that incorporates all the best teaching tools.

Chapter review

- Information and communication technology (ICT) encompasses information technology (computer technology) and communications technologies including videoconferencing and the World Wide Web's capacity to facilitate both synchronous (real-time) and asynchronous (virtual time) communication.
- Computer literacy focuses on computer skills, while information literacy is the ability to manipulate information in critically reflective ways.
- ICTs have the potential to change teaching practices, but many teachers do not yet feel confident about their ability to integrate ICT into their curriculum.
- How teachers incorporate ICT into their teaching will depend on what and how they want students to learn.
- ICT use may be informed by behavioural learning theories, which see the computer as a tutor and emphasise drill-and-practice activities.
- Cognitive and constructivist theories emphasise the interactive potential of ICTs and their role in scaffolding learning and promoting collaboration.
- From the point of view of humanist learning theory, ICT may be a useful tool for helping learners understand other cultures, for promoting awareness of the self and one's place in a global society, and for promoting tolerance and peace through understanding and communication.
- ICTs may play a role in learners' personal and social development by giving them opportunities to experiment with different roles in electronic environments.
- There is the opportunity for teachers to use ICTs to promote development of students' values systems.
- New technologies have the potential to enhance the learning opportunities of students from a range of backgrounds, including those of different abilities and needs, and those in remote and rural areas. However, ICTs are also potential sources of inequity.
- Benefits of ICTs in education include enhanced motivation, increased student engagement and improved learning outcomes. These need to be balanced by considering limitations such as the potential for inequity, technical and resource constraints, time and cost issues, and the anxiety that some people have regarding computer use.
- Computers and their applications are tools that are only as effective as the teachers who integrate them and who make decisions about how, when, and why to use them to enhance learning.

You make the connections:

Questions for self-assessment and discussion

1. Explain the meaning of the term 'information and communication technology'.
2. Distinguish between 'computer literacy' and 'information literacy'.
3. Comment critically on how behavioural, cognitive, constructivist and humanist theories of learning influence the ways in which ICTs are used in education.
4. Define 'hypertext' and explain how it differs from paper-based text.
5. Identify and discuss at least three potential sources of inequity in the use of ICTs.
6. Critically evaluate the benefits and limitations of using ICTs in educational contexts.
7. Ingram (1996, p. 31) said: 'Technologies do not teach – people do.' Do you agree? What role do you think ICTs, including computers, should play in the classroom of the 21st century?

Key terms

technology	synchronous communication	multiple-user object-oriented (domain) (MOO)
educational technology	Internet relay chat (IRC)	distributed learning (computer-mediated instruction, or CMI)
information and communication technology (ICT)	Internet chatroom	
	computer literacy	
information technology (IT)	information literacy	distributed cognition
computer-mediated communication (CMC)	computer-assisted instruction (CAI)	navigation
asynchronous communication	simulation	hypertext
newsgroup	hypermedia	hyperlink
listserv	multiple-user domain (MUD)	hypermedia

Recommended reading

Bryant, M. H. (1996). *Integrating technology into the curriculum.* Highett, Victoria: Hawker Brownlow Education.

Grabe, M. (1998). *Integrating technology for meaningful learning.* Boston, MA: Houghton Mifflin Company.

Heinich, R. (1999). *Instructional media and technologies for learning* (6th ed.). Upper Saddle River, NJ: Merrill.

Jonassen, D. H., Peck, K. L., & Wilson, B. G. (1999). *Learning with technology: A constructivist perspective.* Upper Saddle River, NJ: Merrill.

Maier, P. (1998). *Using technology in teaching and learning.* London: Kogan Page.

Monteith, M. (Ed.) (1998). *IT for learning enhancement.* Exton, PA: Swets & Zeitlinger Publishers.

Ross, T. W., & Bailey, G. O. (1997). *Technology-based learning: A handbook for teachers and technology leaders* (Rev. ed.). Cheltenham, Victoria: Hawker Brownlow Education.

Make some online visits

New Zealand schools' experiences with technology: <www.cwa.co.nz/eduweb/stories/stories.html>
Learn more about cyberpsychology: <ess.ntu.ac.uk/miller/cyberpsych/>
The 'digital divide' – ICT and equity issues: <www.ctcnet.org/access.html>
Values in ICT and learning: <www.vital.nsw.edu.au/>
Examples of ICT projects in Australian schools: <leadingpractice.edna.edu.au>
Australian Council for Computers in Education: <www.acce.edu.au/>
Evaluating online materials: How to critically analyse information sources:
   <www.library.cornell.edu/okuref/research/skill26.htm>
Evaluating what really matters in computer-based education:
   <www.educationau.edu.au/archives/cp/reeves.htm>

FIGURE 11.1 Chapter 11 concept map.

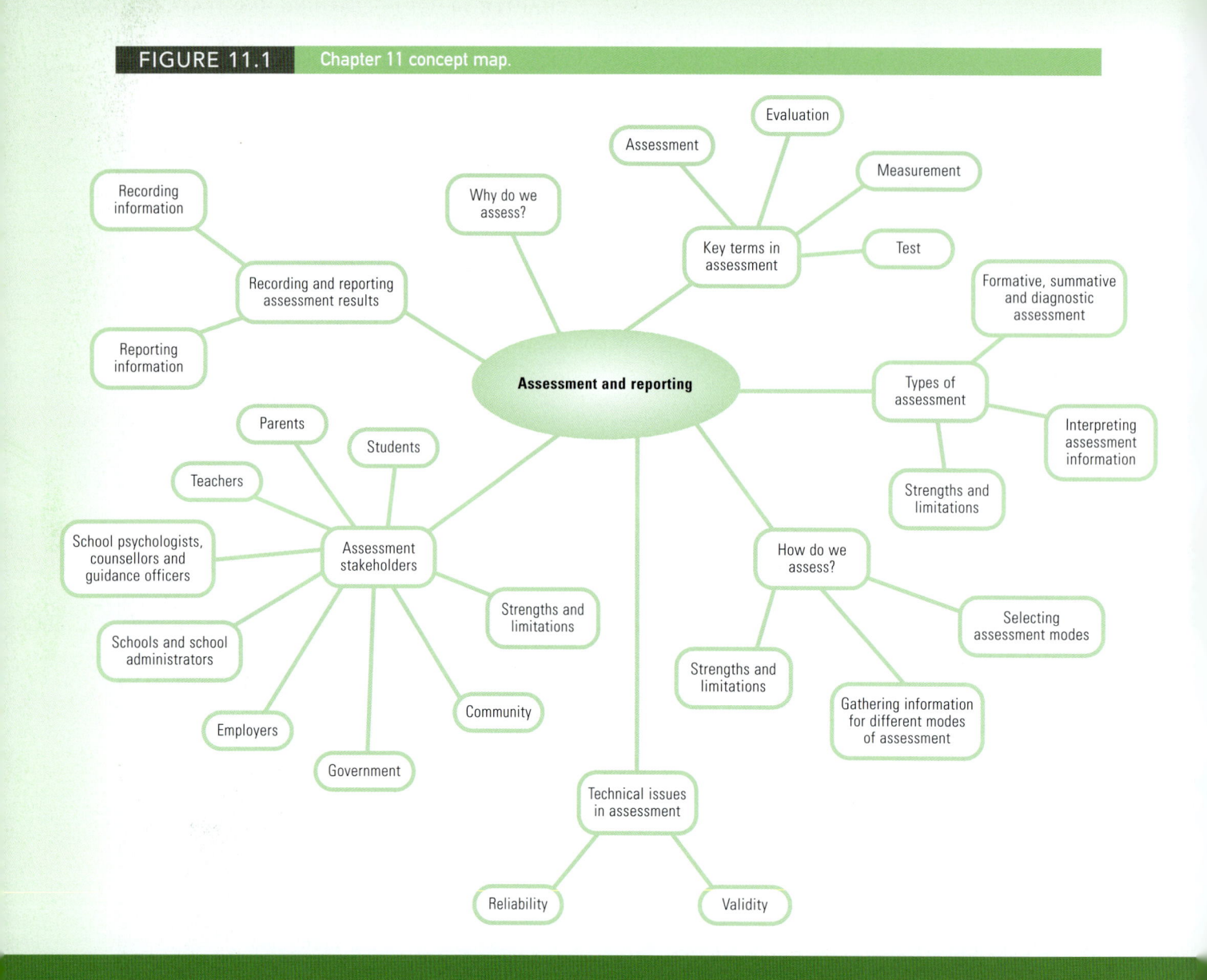

- **Assessment and reporting**
  - Why do we assess?
  - Key terms in assessment
    - Assessment
    - Evaluation
    - Measurement
    - Test
  - Types of assessment
    - Formative, summative and diagnostic assessment
    - Interpreting assessment information
    - Strengths and limitations
  - How do we assess?
    - Selecting assessment modes
    - Gathering information for different modes of assessment
    - Strengths and limitations
  - Technical issues in assessment
    - Reliability
    - Validity
  - Assessment stakeholders
    - Parents
    - Students
    - Teachers
    - School psychologists, counsellors and guidance officers
    - Schools and school administrators
    - Employers
    - Government
    - Community
    - Strengths and limitations
  - Recording and reporting assessment results
    - Recording information
    - Reporting information

CHAPTER OBJECTIVES

After reading this chapter you should be able to:

- identify some of the main forms of assessment teachers use for instructional purposes

- describe some key similarities and differences between norm-referenced and criterion-referenced assessments

- explain the development of non-traditional forms of assessment as alternatives to more traditional measures

- identify the forms of assessment that will provide the most useful information for giving feedback to students, parents and prospective employers

- discuss the implications, for teachers, of introducing curriculum profiles to the student assessment and reporting process.

CHAPTER 11

Assessment and reporting

Introduction

Anna moved to her new school in the middle of the year. It seems much the same as her old school, but she feels confused when at the end of a social studies unit on government, instead of giving her a test the teacher gives her a form to fill in called a 'Learning Review' (Cumming, 1998, p. 26). The teacher says Anna is to use the form to assess her own progress. Anna has never been given a test like this before and is confused. Is the Learning Review a test, or will the real test be given tomorrow, or next week? What kinds of tests are used at this school? What will Anna's parents think if she does not come in the top three or four in the class like she did at the last school?

This chapter is about assessment and the way teachers report the outcomes of assessment to students, parents and others. We could also have used the terms 'evaluation', 'measurement' or other related terms such as 'testing', 'grading' and 'appraising', to describe the assessment process.

Why do we assess?

Traditionally, most assessment has taken the form of a test, usually set by a classroom teacher who wants to find out how much each student has learned in a specific area of the curriculum over a set time period. Marks are allocated for each question in the test, and a final score calculated by adding these marks. The final scores are then used to rank students in terms of their score, or how much they have learned. Those with the highest scores are praised, and those with the lowest scores are urged to 'work harder next time'. However, in the final decades of the 20th century, questions began to be asked about the way education was organised and, in particular, the way educational outcomes were assessed. The value of traditional testing of student knowledge was questioned as a result of growing awareness of the need for decisions about curriculum content and educational outcomes to be based on assessment information. Reviews of literacy and numeracy teaching in primary schools led to discussion of the most effective strategies for instruction in these key curriculum areas and the need to assess learning outcomes in more varied ways, including informal teacher-made tests as well as the more formal tests set by external examiners. Such pressures for change can be traced to diverse groups' specific interests; for example, governments are concerned about the efficient use of funds, business is concerned about access to a skilled workforce, and there has been growing community awareness of the need for well-educated citizens (Brady & Kennedy, 2001).

One outcome of changes in ideas about education's purpose and how it can best be delivered has been a major shift in approaches to assessment in schools. Traditional 'input-driven' programs that are subject-based and involve comparison of individual performance with the performance of others on the same test are being broadened to include 'outcomes-based' assessment that involves comparison of individual achievements with a specified criterion or standard, or at a system level, rate of retention of students beyond the compulsory years of schooling or percentage of students proceeding to post-school training or tertiary studies (Griffin, 1998). There is also increased monitoring of student progress in literacy and numeracy at local, national and international levels (see, for example, WA Department of Education and Training, 2003). In this chapter, the process of assessment is considered in the context of these changing ideas about education and how educational outcomes are measured.

Key terms in assessment

What do you think of when you hear the word 'assessment'? Are you reminded of the examinations that you took at the end of your final year at school? Or do you think of the weekly spelling or number-facts tests your teachers gave you in primary school? What about terms such as 'measurement' and 'evaluation': do you think of them as having a precise meaning, or can they be used interchangeably with 'test' and 'assessment'?

Assessment

Most people would regard assessment as the process by which we judge the relative value of something, such as a painting, a bottle of wine, a new variety of tomato or a pedigree puppy. Here, 'assessment' is a general term that incorporates aspects of *evaluation* ('Is this the best puppy in the litter?') and *measurement* ('How long is the puppy's nose?'). However, for teachers, assessment is concerned with the process of describing student progress, such as whether teaching objectives have been met (Griffin & Nix, 1991).

'Assessment' refers to the procedures used in appraising student learning. It incorporates both evaluation and measurement and is concerned with the processes involved in describing and reporting on the outcomes of learning and teaching. Assessment can be both qualitative and quantitative and may occur at any time during or at the end of a unit of instruction. It can cover a broad range of learning outcomes – cognitive, affective, social – from the simplest to the most complex (Bloom, 1956).

What distinguishes assessment from other types of activity undertaken by teachers? Griffin and Nix (1991) define **assessment** and reporting as the collection, analysis, recording and communicating information about the outcomes of learning and teaching. The processes referred to are concerned with collecting and explaining information that is related to learning and teaching outcomes. Notice that both *quantitative* and *qualitative* activities are identified, and that assessment and reporting are seen as two parts of the same process. Assessing learning, and communicating the outcomes of such assessment to stakeholders, is a significant part of the educative process.

assessment
The purposeful gathering, interpreting, recording and communicating of information about student achievement

Evaluation

When you evaluate something, you ask: 'What is this worth?' You are generally interested in the relative value or worth of something, such as a ring, a painting, an old manuscript or an idea. In education, **evaluation** is concerned with making judgements about the relative or absolute worth of entities as varied as an essay, a dance performance, a class project, a specific curriculum, a new teaching method or a statewide school system. For example,

evaluation
The process of making judgements about relative or absolute worth

evaluating a student's painting or sculpture involves making a qualitative judgement about the work in terms of a predetermined set of criteria. The evaluation process involves making subjective judgements and for this reason is relatively imprecise.

Measurement

Measurement is involved when we seek information regarding the extent to which an individual demonstrates a particular characteristic or behaviour (Linn & Gronlund, 1995, p. 6). A test is used for measurement when numerical values in the form of scores are attached to the tasks or test items used to assess student performance. The numerical values used may be based on a count of the number of test items answered correctly by a student; for example, 'Sam answered 11 out of 20 number problems correctly.' Alternatively, a measurement value may be obtained by comparing one student's performance with an explicit or implicit criterion; for example, 'Lindsay has a score of 5 for calculator use because he observed 5 of the 10 rules set for this task', and 'Anna has a score of 7 for her painting because she reached the standard set for Level 7 in Art.'

> *measurement*
> A test of student performance that involves the use of numerical values in the form of scores

Test

A **test** comprises any assessment procedure used systematically to measure a sample of behaviour provided the test is administered in a formal setting such as a classroom, laboratory or gymnasium, with standardised (uniform) procedures for administration and marking. Results should be able to be compared with other assessment data that can include outcomes achieved by other students and within a specific curriculum area. Teachers tend to devise most of the tests that are used in their own classroom; however, many tests designed by teams of experts in a curriculum area are also available commercially.

> *test*
> Any assessment procedure that is used systematically to measure a sample of behaviour

Table 11.1 lists and gives examples for key terms in assessment, including the four terms already covered. Remember that some of the terms overlap and that there is disagreement among experts about the way in which some of the terms are defined.

TABLE 11.1 Key terms in assessment

Term	Definition	Example
Assessment	Gathering, interpreting, recording and communicating information about student achievement	Planned observation, description and reporting of Year 2 students' performance on a set reading task
Evaluation	Making judgements about relative or absolute worth	Judging the quality (in terms of a standard or set of criteria) of a sculpture submitted as part of a final examination in visual arts
Measurement	Testing student performance using numerical values in the form of scores	Counting the number of correct answers given by Year 2 students in a test of number facts, and assigning a numerical value
Test	An assessment procedure used systematically to measure a sample of behaviour	On Friday, students in Year 6 will be required to complete 20 questions based on material covered in this week's mathematics lessons
Aim	A very general description of a long-term intent: an 'aspiration'	Developing in young people an understanding of the philosophy and underlying principles of democratic government
Goal	A general description of a medium-term intent: a 'direction'	Teaching a 12-year-old boy with a moderate intellectual disability to travel to school independently by bus
Objective	A specific statement of a short-term plan: an 'intention'	When asked to count to ten, the student can count correctly to ten with no errors over three consecutive trials

(Continued over page)

Term	Definition	Example
Outcome	Changes in behaviour following instruction: a 'demonstration'	Students can recall number facts when given no more than 5 seconds to answer
Criterion	A defined level on a continuum: a 'threshhold'	Students can correctly read between 70% and 80% of words on a list of 10 consonant–vowel–consonant words
Standard	A predetermined or approved level of achievement or performance: a 'requirement'	Students demonstrate an understanding of addition, subtraction, multiplication and division
Benchmark	A reference point: a 'touchstone'	For concepts of print: • holds book the right way up • turns pages from front to back • indicates the title of the book
Target	A specific point at which to aim in the medium-to-long term: a 'destination'	By 2005, 80% of 10 year olds will have completed at least one term's study of a language other than English
Reliability	An assessment that obtains the same result on successive occasions: a 'dependable' measure	Josh gets the same six sums correct on the number test when it is given on Wednesday and again the following Monday
Validity	An assessment task that measures what it is designed to measure: a 'true' measure	Alyce is assessed at Level 7 in Language skills on a book evaluation task and at Level 7 on a task requiring accurate recall of information from a newspaper clipping

CRITICAL REFLECTIONS

- What forms of assessment were used most widely when you were at school?
- What lasting impressions do you have of the way your progress was assessed? Do you think your progress was fairly assessed? Is there anything you would try to do differently in your own classroom? Why?

Types of assessment

Think about the different kinds of assessment you experienced at school. You should be able to remember classroom tests that were given at regular times, such as at the end of the week or at the end of a curriculum unit. You will remember the major formal examinations held towards the end of the school year, and the formal public examination at the end of your final year at school. What was the purpose of these different assessments, and what was done with the results obtained?

Traditionally, assessment has focused almost exclusively on testing students as a means of determining 'how much' they have learned, and has often featured tests that do not measure what the students have actually learned. However, there has been a major broadening of assessment away from traditional forms of testing in schools and other educational institutions towards procedures that combine instruction and assessment. These changing assessment procedures are reflected in the increasing use of tests described as 'formative' or 'diagnostic' that contribute to the learning–teaching process, rather than to tests described as 'summative' that are concerned with the final outcomes of instruction. Changes in assessment practices are also evident in the way test data are interpreted. Comparisons are made with a predetermined outcome in the form of a standard or criterion ('criterion-referenced' assessment) or curriculum objectives ('curriculum-based' assessment) rather than the more traditional procedure of comparing test data with the average performance of other students on the same test ('norm-referenced' assessment). Changes in assessment practices also reflect the beliefs of particular groups of stakeholders – such as parents, employers and the government – about the purpose of assessment in the 21st century (see page 361).

11.1 The purpose and function of assessment

There is a close association between the purpose of assessment and the type of assessment procedures used, whether the assessment is done for the purpose of providing feedback to students and teachers, accreditation or the development of government policy initiatives. For example, the types of assessments used most often by classroom teachers, particularly at the primary school level, are informal and designed to give quick feedback about the immediate outcomes of learning. Such assessment may involve ongoing observation of work done during a classroom activity, or a test at the end of a unit. The focus may be on processes such as communicating, cooperating in a group or problem solving, or on products such as an essay, a science report, artwork or a dance performance. However, by the time students enter secondary school, their focus and that of their teachers is firmly on the 'high stakes' assessment of Year 12 examinations. And although students' final school results are based on a combination of school-based and end-of-school assessments, the purpose and form of the final examination has a significant impact on teachers' practices in terms of what they teach and how they assess student learning (Barnes, Clark, & Stephens, 2000).

Formative, summative and diagnostic assessment

Among the differing purposes of assessment, the distinction between 'formative', 'summative' and 'diagnostic' assessment is particularly important for classroom teachers. While these three types of assessment are concerned with collecting information about student progress, they do this in very different ways.

Formative assessment

Formative assessment is where assessment comprises part of the teaching process. It consists of teachers providing students with feedback on their progress, and also guides teachers' further instruction. Most informal assessment is formative.

Think about the 'grazing' teacher who moves about the classroom, looks at what students are doing as they work and provides them with immediate feedback. Think also about the informal tests or skill checks teachers use, such as question-and-answer sessions, where no formal record is made of what has been observed. What is the teacher's purpose? In most cases it is to assess how students are progressing at that moment in time on a small piece of work. Any problems identified can be solved immediately, and learning can continue. This type of classroom activity provides immediate feedback, with no grade or report required. Such assessment has an immediate impact on student learning, and also influences what will be taught next, although it has no impact on the curriculum as a whole. Griffin and Nix (1991) noted that the effectiveness of formative assessment depends on the teacher's skills and on the teacher–student rapport. Most classroom assessments are of this type.

formative assessment
Informal checks that are designed to give feedback about the immediate outcomes of learning, and to guide further instruction

Summative assessment

You will have taken 'final' examinations at different stages in your educational career. Such examinations usually occur at the end of a school year or at the completion of a stage of schooling (such as with the examinations held at the end of each school year for middle- and final-secondary-years students). Most formal assessment is summative, and is used to document student achievement when a topic of work or a section of schooling is completed. **Summative assessment** is conducted as a check on learning outcomes at the end of a teaching program, and is also used outside the classroom for administrative purposes such as certification and selection (Griffin & Nix, 1991, p. 27).

Summative assessment looks back to see if students have achieved the expected outcomes. More formal tasks are often used in such assessments, with marks, grades, or in

summative assessment
Formal checks of learning outcomes that are conducted at the end of a teaching program

some cases certificates, diplomas and degrees awarded on the basis of assessment results. Data derived from summative examinations such as the Victorian Certificate of Education (VCE) or the National Certificate of Educational Achievement (NCEA) in New Zealand are used for certification, selection and accountability (or justification of expenditure) purposes.

Diagnostic assessment

A teacher finds that students are having problems in 2-digit subtraction in mathematics. Does the problem stem from students not understanding the concept of 'place value' or from students not knowing their number facts? While wandering around a class, the teacher notices some odd answers to sums, such as:

$$21 - 19 = 18$$
$$33 - 25 = 12$$

The teacher thinks about these answers and begins to understand some of the procedures the students are using. In this case, the students are following a rule that states: 'when subtracting, always take the smaller number away from the larger'. Using this rule to answer the sum '21 take away 19', students give the answer '18'. Why? If you try to take the 9 in '19' away from the 1 in '21', it cannot be done. But if you reverse the numbers in order to follow the rule and take the 1 away from 9, you get 8, and the 1 in '19' taken away from the 2 in '21' gives 1. So the answer is 18. Once the teacher understands the way in which students are applying the rule to achieve their answers – that is, once the teacher makes a 'diagnostic assessment' – further instruction can be given in using the rule correctly.

'Diagnostic' is generally understood to be a medical term, since doctors diagnose disease. Teachers, however, use **diagnostic assessment** to pinpoint exactly what a student knows and does not know in a particular area of teaching. Teachers using diagnostic assessment are attempting to find out not what the students can or cannot do, but why they make particular mistakes. Diagnostic assessment is particularly useful in literacy and numeracy instruction for pinpointing areas of student difficulty.

Tests used for diagnostic purposes cover a narrow range of skills, and sample these skills in some depth. They often take the form of mastery tests, focusing on the degree to which specific learning outcomes have been achieved or 'mastered'. Understanding the cause of student difficulties is an important first step in helping students overcome them. Mastery tests can also indicate the need for tests of hearing, vision and general health, or alert teachers to problem behaviour and related social- and family-background factors (see chapters 8 and 9).

diagnostic assessment
Checks made to determine why students make particular mistakes

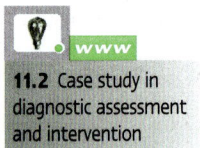

11.2 Case study in diagnostic assessment and intervention

CRITICAL REFLECTIONS

- Think about the forms of assessment being used to assess your progress at university this year. Can you identify an example of formative, summative and diagnostic assessment in each subject?
- Do you think forms of assessment vary depending on age, ability level or subject area?
- Which forms of assessment help you learn most effectively? Why?

Interpreting assessment information

How should assessment information be interpreted? Traditionally, test results have been interpreted by comparing them with the average performance of other students on the same test, with results reported in the form of a grade (such as 'A', 'B' and 'C'). This procedure 'places' each student in relation to other students ('norm-referenced' assessment). However, the shift from using traditional summative forms of assessment to using formative and diagnostic assessment procedures has given rise to alternative approaches to test-result interpretation. For example, comparison with a predetermined standard or criterion (referred to as 'criterion-referenced' assessment) is used, as is comparison with a curriculum (known as 'curriculum-based' assessment). Alternatively, test results are sometimes compared with the student's own previous performance ('ipsative' assessment).

Norm-referenced assessment

If teachers need to collect information about their students' progress in relation to others in the class, the school or region, they use 'norm-referenced' (or 'normative') assessment procedures. **Norm-referenced assessment** occurs when one student's score on a test is compared with the average score gained on the test by students of similar age and learning background. In this situation, the mean (or average score) of students who have taken the test provides a standard of performance, or **norm**, against which the scores of individual students on the same test can be compared. Teachers use information from norm-referenced tests to find out if a student has done better than other comparable students and is thus above the norm, or if the student has done worse than other students and is thus below the norm. The focus of attention in this type of assessment is on how well the student has done on a test in comparison with other students. Norms can be based on student scores drawn from a class, a school, a school district or a wider area.

Most tests of achievement used in classrooms are prepared by teachers and are norm-referenced with norms based on the scores of the whole class. However, norm-referenced tests can also be designed for use with larger groups, with norms based on the scores of a large group of students who are similar to those taking the test, such as students aged around 14 years who have studied biology for a year. Many of the norm-referenced tests used in schools in Australia and New Zealand were developed by specialist psychometricians (psychology-test designers) and are published by agencies such as the Australian Council for Educational Research (ACER) and the New Zealand Council for Educational Research (NZCER). These tests are sometimes described as **standardised test**s because they have been designed according to strict rules, must be administered under uniform conditions as specified in the test manual, and have standard procedures for scoring and interpreting results and comparing these with the test norms (Griffin & Nix, 1991). The main feature of norm-referenced assessment, whether the tests are standardised or not, is that they provide information about individual students' level of achievement when compared with students of similar age and educational background in a specific area of learning.

Criterion-referenced assessment

If a teacher's main interest is to pinpoint how well students have mastered a particular skill, the most appropriate form of assessment may be **criterion-referenced assessment**.

The growing democratisation of education in Western societies culminated, in the final decades of the 20th century, in increasing pressure for schools to provide appropriate education programs for all students regardless of their social, religious or ethnic background, and regardless of disability. As a result, educators' focus shifted from normative evaluation of student achievement by means of peer comparison, to evaluation based on an identified standard or according to prescribed curriculum goals. Norm-referenced tests have been gradually supplemented or replaced with criterion-referenced tests that compare individual performance on a set of test items with a specified level of performance that is typical of students who are competent on these items (Piper, 1997; Ward & Murray-Ward, 1999). Performance levels are usually organised sequentially in terms of a developmental hierarchy, with student progress measured in terms of achieving progressively higher levels in the sequence.

Examples of such changes can be found in the Curriculum and Standards Framework (CSF and CSF II) introduced into Victorian schools in 1995 by the Board of Studies

---

norm-referenced assessment
Used to compare the performance of individuals or groups with the performance of a comparable group on the same task

norm
The mean or average performance of a group of people

11.3 More about norm-referenced tests used in schools

standardised test
A test designed in accordance with set rules, administered under uniform conditions, and scored and interpreted in terms of identified norms

criterion-referenced assessment
Where achievement is compared against a specified criterion or standard

11.4 Using criterion-referenced assessment

(Victorian Curriculum and Assessment Authority, 2001), the South Australian Curriculum Standards and Accountability (SACSA) Framework introduced into South Australian schools in 2001 (SA Curriculum Policy Directorate, 2000) and in the National Certificate of Educational Achievement (NCEA) introduced into New Zealand schools (New Zealand Ministry of Education, 2002c). The Victorian CSF and CSFII provide a clear set of indicators that teachers can use to judge whether students have achieved required standards. Teachers are free to design their own programs, according to their students' specific needs, but use a common set of goals and content in preparing such programs. The CSF II 'describes what students in Victorian schools should know and be able to do at progressive levels from Prep to Year 10 – in other words, it describes standards' (Victorian Curriculum and Assessment Authority, 2001, p. 1). In New Zealand, the NCEA has replaced the Sixth Form Certificate, which used norm-referenced assessment based on a school's results from the previous year. The new assessment has not involved a change in the content of school education, but rather makes clearer the standards students need to achieve. In addition, practical skills such as laboratory work in science are now included in student assessment in New Zealand, where the former system used only examination-based test results (New Zealand Ministry of Education, 2002a). The advantage of using criterion-referenced assessment is that the standards used remain constant over time and place (Lambert, 2001). This can be contrasted with norm-referenced assessment, where norms can vary depending on the achievement level of the group of students on which the norms are based.

Curriculum-based assessment

If teachers want to how much of a specific curriculum area has been achieved, assessment will be curriculum-based, or concerned with the extent to which teaching objectives have been reached.

Assessments derived from the curriculum and carried out as part of the teaching process give vital information about what students have learned and how effective teaching has been. Such **curriculum-based assessment**s can be used to diagnose students' strengths and weaknesses, and to plan future teaching programs (Arthur, 1996). This type of assessment is usually carried out by a classroom teacher for the purpose of:

- obtaining information about the level of students' entry skills so as to decide where to place them within the curriculum
- defining and planning appropriate teaching objectives
- determining the degree to which these objectives are met by monitoring students' progress through an instructional sequence
- evaluating and refining teaching techniques.

The type of assessment used by teachers in curriculum-based assessment varies widely. It can include the weekly spelling test of 20 words compiled by the class teacher, or a checklist of gross motor skills for kindergarten children (for example, 'hop in a straight line', 'ascend and descend stairs using alternate feet', 'kick a ball'). It often involves task analysis of a curriculum area and the preparation of a scope-and-sequence chart. The Curriculum Bands and associated learning areas (Curriculum Scope) and outcomes (Standards) in the South Australian Curriculum Standards and Accountability (SACSA) Framework are examples of this process. Curriculum **profile**s provide teachers with an ordered sequence or continuum of descriptors of learning outcomes that they can use to chart students' progress. Data derived from profiles provide information about what students need to know and the logical order of this material.

The main advantages of curriculum-based assessment are that it provides for:

- direct monitoring of the content being taught
- precise feedback about the effectiveness of teaching
- frequent modification of teaching strategies in response to student performance

---

curriculum-based assessment
Assessment that compares individual students' performance with curriculum goals

profile
An ordered sequence or continuum of learning descriptors that can be used to chart progress

www
11.5 Developing subject profiles, and a case study of curriculum-based assessment

- a sensitive measure of change
- the possibility of repeated administrations, which can yield more information than could be generalised from a single administration.

Ipsative assessment

If the interest is in how much progress an individual student has made, then 'ipsative assessment' is used. Employed most often to assess performance skills outside a school setting (such as in sports like swimming or skiing), **ipsative assessment** can also be used in educational contexts, where it involves an individual's performance in a particular aspect of learning being compared with that person's previous performance. When people talk about their 'personal best', or their 'best performance', they are referring to ipsative assessment. This type of assessment is concerned with an individual's own performance and whether this has improved or deteriorated over time.

The procedures used to collect the information required for ipsative assessment can include formal paper-and-pencil tests, or informal methods such as direct observation, checklists and rating scales, interviews, and appraisal of work samples (written, performed or created). Information derived from such sources can be used to compile profiles of student achievement, as part of both ongoing and final assessment.

ipsative assessment
Assessment that compares an individual's current achievement with previous achievement

---

CRITICAL REFLECTIONS

- How do you think that knowing the difference between norm-referenced, criterion-referenced, curriculum-based and ipsative forms of assessment will help make you a better teacher?
- What connections do you see between effective assessment and student motivation (see Chapter 7) and self-esteem (see Chapter 3)?

Strengths and limitations of different types of assessment

Strengths and limitations of formative, summative and diagnostic assessment

When teachers decide on the type of assessment they will use during and at the end of a unit of instruction, they need to consider the purpose of the assessment and the way in which information derived from the assessment process will be used. Traditionally, assessment has been conducted at the end of instruction to find out how much students have learned. Summative assessment (discussed earlier) is useful for decision-making about the next stage in a student's educational program or placement in a specific educational program. It is also useful for employers for job-selection purposes. Information from summative assessments can be used to give feedback about student progress to teachers, students and parents. However, since such assessment is conducted at the end of instruction, any feedback cannot be used to improve student performance or overcome weaknesses. Formative assessment, implemented for the purpose of improving learning outcomes, is the most useful type of assessment for teachers and students. Formative assessments can take any form and are conducted during the period of instruction so that relevant information can be used to shape the teaching process. They may involve additional time and planning by the teacher but can be quite informal in nature, and implemented as part of instruction. Diagnostic assessment is useful for pinpointing the errors that students are making, especially when students encounter problems in a specific part of the curriculum. One limitation of conducting diagnostic assessment is that it can be time-consuming and may require specialist skills, so this type of assessment may be more appropriately carried out by a specialist, resource or support teacher.

Strengths and limitations of interpretation procedures

Traditionally, assessment data have been interpreted by means of norm-referenced assessment, a method that is useful for describing individual or group performance relative to that of other, similar individuals or groups. Norm-referenced assessment is generally understood in the community and widely used by teachers in classroom practice; however, it has the disadvantage that it does not always provide information about what individuals have learned or what they can and cannot do. The overall level of ability of different groups can also vary widely, meaning that one student's performance on a norm-referenced test may be considered outstanding if comparison is made with a low-ability group, or poor if comparison is made with a high-ability group. Tests that combine norm-referenced and criterion-referenced characteristics, such as the Basic Skills Tests, overcome some of these weaknesses.

Interpreting data in criterion-referenced assessment has the advantage of focusing attention on individual students' performance. Those who fail to demonstrate 'mastery' of a specified level of performance can readily be identified and provided with further opportunities for learning. However, a risk with criterion-referenced assessment is that developing a coherently ordered set of tasks to represent the achievement sequence for proficiency in a particular area or in line with a curriculum can be a difficult task, requiring skills that may be outside an individual teacher's competency. Widespread implementation of criterion-referenced assessment depends on the availability of such sequenced materials in relevant curriculum areas.

The strength of curriculum-based assessment is its concern with direct assessment of student performance on a set of identified, sequentially ordered objectives that are derived from the curriculum. Assessment occurs frequently and takes place in the classroom as part of daily instruction. Assessment tasks given to each student are derived from the point in the instructional sequence that the student is currently working on, meaning each assessment is tied directly to the student's current learning goals. Information derived from such assessments helps teachers identify exactly what a given student can and cannot do, and teaching can then be tailored to the student's current needs. Curriculum-based assessment is particularly useful for students who are at risk of experiencing problems in some aspect of learning. A limitation of curriculum-based assessment is that it can be time-consuming in terms of collecting assessment data (students can be involved in this task), recording and interpreting the data, and planning specific teaching objectives to ensure student progress.

Ipsative assessment is useful for helping students to become motivated and independent learners. Strategies such as setting personal goals, deciding what needs to be done and monitoring personal progress have been shown to have a positive impact on achievement levels. Students learn to use their own frame of reference in assessment. The process of ipsative assessment is concerned not with common goals shared by other students, but with personal goals and with students 'learning to learn' (Griffin & Nix, 1991, p. 94).

Some issues that educators need to consider when designing an assessment program are set out in Box 11.1.

Box 11.1 IMPLICATIONS FOR EDUCATORS

Putting effective assessment into practice

- There has been a broadening from forms of assessment that are only weakly related to students' actual learning experiences to forms that are closely linked to the curriculum.

- Changes in assessment philosophy are demonstrated in the gradual shift from assessment practices described as 'summative', which are implemented at the end of a period of learning; towards procedures labelled 'formative', which function as part of the curriculum and which

- provide feedback to teachers and students that contributes to modifications and improvements to teaching.
- Changes in assessment philosophy are also evident in increased 'blending' of assessment and teaching (Griffin & Nix, 1991), leading to reform in assessment and reporting procedures.
- Such changes in the types of assessment used have been encouraged and supported by universities, state education departments and agencies such as the Queensland Assessment and Reporting Taskforce, the Victorian Curriculum and Assessment Authority, the New South Wales Board of Studies, the South Australian Curriculum Policy Directorate, the Australian Curriculum Studies Association, the Australian Council for Educational Research (ACER), the Australian Ministerial Council on Education, Employment, Training and Youth Affairs, and the New Zealand Ministry of Education.

How do we assess?

Selecting assessment modes

At the beginning of any school year, and indeed at many times during the year, most teachers have to make a number of important decisions about the teaching program, the instructional procedures they will use and how they will assess student learning. These decisions will vary widely, depending on a teacher's particular situation, the students in the class, factors associated with the school as a whole, parental needs and expectations, and so on.

Lin and Gronlund (1995) emphasised the need for teachers to collect different types of information about student learning, ranging from informal observation to formal tests of achievement. The various modes of assessment used by teachers can be categorised in terms of a number of dimensions (adapted from Lambert, 2001, p. 2):

- *informal* – carried out by most teachers as part of daily teaching or learning activities
- *formal* – carried out as a discrete, structured information-gathering task
- *continuous* – happening throughout a term, semester, year or stage
- *final* – happening at the end of a term, semester, year or stage
- *coursework* – what the student does or produces during a period of instruction, which may involve completion of set tasks
- *examination* – what the student does or produces in response to set tasks, at a set time and under particular conditions
- *process-oriented* – a focus on *what* is done (for example, participating, talking, moving), and assessed in 'real time'
- *product-oriented* – a focus on *what* is produced, involving tangible, concrete evidence (such as written texts, artwork and projects)
- *internal* – assessed by someone within the teaching situation, usually the classroom teacher
- *external* – assessed by a person or people outside the teaching situation, or through tasks set outside the school.

The teacher must make choices in terms of these dimensions each time an assessment procedure is planned. The data-collection process also involves choices being made between different modes of assessment (see Box 11.2).

Box 11.2 CLASSROOM LINKS

Designing an assessment program

Lin and Gronlund (1995) listed the main questions teachers might ask themselves when designing an assessment program, and also the types of assessment practices teachers might use to answer such questions.

From Table 11.2 on the next page, it is evident that Lin and Gronlund highlighted the need for teachers to collect a number of different types of information about their students across a variety of content areas, ranging from informal observations to highly formalised tests of aptitude and achievement.

TABLE 11.2 Issues to consider when designing an assessment program

Issues in instruction	Appropriate assessment type
How realistic are my teaching plans for this particular group of students?	■ Scholastic aptitude tests ■ Past records of achievement
How should the students be grouped for more effective learning?	■ Teacher-constructed tests ■ Past records of achievement ■ Observation
To what extent are the students ready for the next learning experience?	■ Pretests of needed skills ■ Past records of achievement
To what extent are students attaining the learning goals of the course?	■ Teacher-constructed tests ■ Class projects ■ Oral questioning ■ Observation
To what extent are students progressing beyond the minimum essentials?	■ Teacher-constructed tests ■ General achievement tests ■ Class projects ■ Observation
At what point would a review be most beneficial?	■ Periodic quizzes ■ Oral questioning ■ Observation
What types of learning difficulties are students encountering?	■ Diagnostic tests ■ Observation ■ Oral questioning ■ Student conferences
Which students should be referred to counselling, special classes or remedial programs?	■ Scholastic aptitude tests ■ Achievement tests ■ Diagnostic tests ■ Observation
Which students have poor self-understanding?	■ Self-ratings ■ Student conferences
Which school grade should be assigned to each student?	■ Review of portfolio of all assessment data
How effective was my teaching?	■ Achievement tests ■ Student ratings ■ Supervisor's comments

Source: Adapted from Lin and Gronlund (1995, pp. 4–5).

Gathering information for different modes of assessment

When we think of assessment, it is generally in terms of paper-and-pencil tests. Most students are familiar with such tests, but these are not the only type of assessment. Other methods used to document student achievement include observing and recording learning directly, and mapping progress through student work products using portfolios that contain examples of essays, stories, poems, paintings, models and so on. Anecdotal records, interviews and recollections can also provide useful information to supplement data from **direct assessment** procedures such as tests that assess specific, clearly defined content.

direct assessment
Criterion-referenced or mastery tests that assess specific content from a clearly defined curriculum

Direct observation

An example of direct observation is when a teacher scans a classroom, looks purposefully at what students are doing, listens to what they are saying and provides immediate feedback. **Direct observation** – or purposeful, focused looking and listening – is a most effective form of assessment. It is particularly useful for aspects of learning that the teacher cannot access through products such as essays, written examinations, projects or homework assignments (Forster & Masters, 1996a, b; Masters & Forster, 1996) (see Figure 11.2). It is also useful for verifying assessment data collected in other ways (see Box 11.3).

direct observation
Purposeful, focused looking and listening

11.6 More about observation in assessment

FIGURE 11.2 Direct observation is a powerful form of assessment. What might this teacher observe about her students?

Box 11.3 CLASSROOM LINKS

Using direct observation in the classroom

- Direct observation is a practical way to collect information about student behaviour in natural settings, although care needs to be taken to ensure that data collection is not haphazard, unsystematic or subjective.
- Procedures used to collect data can be quite informal, with the observer simply watching ongoing events and observing more carefully anything that attracts attention.
- When used as part of an assessment process, observation is usually more structured and purposeful, with behaviour observed more systematically.
- To use direct observation in a classroom, begin by watching some children and noting anything that seems interesting or unusual.
- To understand what is happening in the classroom, focus on individual students, on a small group of students or on a specific aspect of classroom activity.
- Forster and Masters (1996a, p. 9) suggest that 'spotlighting' or watching just a few aspects of behaviour helps to focus on 'significant events as they relate to relevant learning outcomes'.
- Information derived from direct observation can be recorded in the form of anecdotal records, diaries, checklists, rating scales or an A-B-C record (antecedent-behaviour-consequence, see Chapter 4).
- The recording system should be organised, easy to use and time-efficient (Forster & Masters, 1996a, p. 11).

Activity

Teachers often have difficulty in knowing how well children function in problem-solving situations. Simply asking children how they solved a problem may under- or overestimate how much they contributed to the solution, whereas observation can provide a large amount of detailed information. Try the following activity, adapted from Siegler (1976).
1 Set a Piagetian formal operations task, such as the balance-scale problem (Siegler, 1976, p. 482) or the pendulum problem (Wadsworth, 1996, pp. 116–117) (see Chapter 2), for a group of 11- to 12-year-olds.

2 Have an observer rate each child on factors such as:
- leadership
- cooperation
- focus on the task
- identification of rules to solve the problem
- originality and relevance of ideas
- willingness to listen to others' ideas.

Portfolios

portfolio
A collection of samples of student work

A **portfolio** is a collection of samples of a student's work that can be used to assess students' progress over a term or year by comparing, after the fact, samples of work taken from different stages throughout the given period. Portfolios are often used for self-assessment, parent–teacher conferences and parent–teacher–child conferences.

Portfolios can be built up in different ways. A teacher can say 'Today's work is for your portfolio' or over a period of about a month students can choose samples of their work for inclusion in their portfolio (Forster & Masters, 1996b). Building a portfolio involves the purposeful collection of work samples that reflect a prescribed curriculum standard or criterion, that show evidence of the learner being able to apply knowledge in innovative ways, and that give the learner opportunities to reflect and self-evaluate when selecting work to be included.

Performance assessment

performance assessment
A mode of assessment that requires a student to engage in a complex task

Performance assessment is used to assess the progress of students who engage in complex tasks in curriculum areas such as dance (see Figure 11.3), drama, music, visual and creative arts, physical education (PE), and technology and design. Performance assessment involves on-the-spot evaluation of students demonstrating their mastery of a task (Forster & Masters, 1996a, p. 1). This assessment mode is used where activities cannot be assessed easily using more traditional methods, and provides a measure of achievement that is closer to real life than are more traditional forms of assessment tasks (Broadfoot, 1995).

The use of portfolios and performance for assessment raises some interesting and problematic technical issues, including (Nuttall, 1992):

- time needed to conduct such assessments
- scoring of students, since without appropriate training there is little consistency among teachers in the way they score the same portfolios and performances
- level of reliability of such assessments.

FIGURE 11.3
Performance assessment can be problematic. How can the reliability of the assessment of this dancer be improved?

Overall, methods that rely on the professional judgement of teachers need to be based on (Lambert, 2001):
- more than a single performance
- achievement in more than one context
- reliable data acquired in a fair and challenging environment.

Authentic assessment

When tasks students are given during instruction are meaningful and involve applying higher-order thinking and problem-solving skills to real-life situations, they are said to be examples of **authentic assessment** (Avery, 1999; Goodwin & MacDonald, 1997). Portfolios and performance assessment are sometimes called authentic assessment (Brady & Kennedy, 2001). The tasks developed in England and Wales as part of assessment for the National Curriculum (see Box 11.4) are an example of this type of assessment. Authentic assessment is a feature of constructivist classrooms (see Chapter 5), which emphasises the importance of students constructing their own knowledge and meaning within real-world contexts.

authentic assessment
A mode of assessment that uses tasks similar to those performed in the real world

11.7 Rich tasks and Education Queensland's New Basics Project

Box 11.4 RESEARCH LINKS

Implementing authentic assessment

The Standard Assessment tasks piloted in 1991 as part of the National Curriculum tests in England and Wales are an example of authentic assessment. The following steps were followed in implementing this assessment (Nuttall, 1992):

1. The tests were sent out to schools well before the assessment period so teachers could become familiar with them and integrate the tests into their own teaching program.
2. There were no standardised instructions, so teachers could introduce the tasks in their own words with small groups of children or individually in a one-to-one situation.
3. It was estimated that the tests would take about three weeks to administer, or about 30 hours of teacher time.
4. Experience with the tests showed that the children enjoyed doing the tasks.
5. Teachers reported that while they gained new insights into their students' attainments, administering the tests was time-consuming and on average involved about 44 hours for them to prepare, administer and grade. In addition, most teachers needed extra help to look after the rest of the class while administering the tests.

The National Curriculum tests were eventually redesigned, following complaints from teachers about excessive demands on their time, and from other critics who believed that the tests were not sufficiently rigorous. New, simpler paper-and-pencil tests were prepared that could be administered by teachers to the whole class at the same time.

Here is an adapted example of one of the original science tests:

The task, for 7-year-olds, commences with a long list of materials the teacher might need, including containers of water for floating and sinking investigations. Instructions to teachers are as follows:
- Set up the apparatus and give each student four objects including:
  - an object with some features that are easier to see using a hand lens (a twig, for example)
  - at least two objects that will float (a twig and an apple, for example)
  - at least one object that will sink (a stone, for example)
  - at least one heavy object that will float (a piece of fruit, for example).
- Ask students to find out as much as they can about why some objects float and why some sink.
- Ask students to tell you what they think will happen – and why – if one of their objects is placed in a container of water.
- Ask students to draw each object, weigh it and make a prediction regarding whether it will float or sink, then have students test each object to see whether their predictions are correct. Have students record predictions, the test outcomes, and each object's weight.
- Ask students to draw each object without using a hand lens and then have them finish the detail of each drawing with the aid of a hand lens.
- When students have completed their activity, ask for each student's findings about why some objects floated and some sank, and see if students can collate information from the chart.

If students meet the standards for the average level, they can proceed to the next level, where they will investigate the hypothesis that heavy objects sink.

Source: Adapted from Nuttall (1992).

> ### Activities
> 1. Can you think of an example of 'authentic assessment' from your own experiences at school?
> 2. What do you think are the advantages of this type of assessment?
> 3. Do you see any disadvantages in this type of assessment? How could these be overcome?

Anecdotal records

Anecdotal records are objective descriptions of behaviour at a particular time and place, recorded as soon as possible after the behaviour has occurred. Teachers often find it helpful to keep brief notes about any unusual or significant occurrences during the school day, sometimes in a journal or diary. Such notes can be useful in documenting the actions of a particular child whose behaviour is causing concern, as a first step in designing some form of intervention or as a basis for report writing or discussions with parents. Anecdotal records are most often used in early-childhood settings and in situations involving children who are having social, emotional or behavioural problems. Similar records can also be kept to document parent or teacher behaviour.

anecdotal record
Objective description of behaviour at a particular time and place, recorded as soon as possible after the behaviour has occurred

11.8 Anecdotal record of Kim's first days at school

Checklists

A **checklist** comprises a list of descriptions of specific behaviours that can be systematically identified and tallied by observers as they occur ('event sampling') or during a specified time period ('time sampling'). Checklists are often used by teachers to collect information about easily observed behaviours such as motor skills ('can hop on one leg for 5 seconds') or literacy skills ('can find a word in a dictionary'). Checklists are a simple and useful tool for recording observations of a range of behaviours with a number of students.

checklist
A set of descriptions of specific behaviours that an observer records as present or not present

Rating scales

Rating scales are used to record the degree to which a particular skill has been achieved, or the strength of a particular trait or personality characteristic in terms of a particular dimension. Rating scales are similar to checklists in that they provide a method for recording the degree to which a specific behaviour or characteristic is present, but they have the added advantage of including a quantitative component in the resulting judgement. Instead of simply recording the occurrence of a specified behaviour (yes/no), a value judgement is also made about the behaviour as the record is compiled ('On a scale of 1 to 10, I would rate John as 5, Mary as 3 and Ken as 9'). Rating scales can take a numerical form, as in the example just cited; or can be graphic, as in the 'semantic differential', where the judgement is recorded by placing a mark on a point between two opposing descriptors (such as 'honest–dishonest', 'brave–cowardly') to indicate the relative strength of that characteristic in the individual being assessed (Osgood, Suci, & Tannenbaum, 1957).

Box 11.5 gives some examples of the different types of rating scale used in assessment.

rating scale
A procedure for recording the degree to which a specific behaviour or characteristic is present

Box 11.5 CLASSROOM LINKS

Examples of rating scale formats

When designing a rating scale, decisions must be made about the way ratings will be done. The dimensions on the scale can be defined by using words or numbers (such as '1', '2' and '3') to represent highest to lowest. Observers are required to select a position on a dimension to best represent their judgement about the relative strength or weakness of the characteristic being assessed. The advantage of this procedure is that the format highlights the continuous nature of the variable being assessed. Disadvantages are associated with the degree of error that can occur in the judgements that are made when selecting the appropriate point on the scale.

Examples of possible formats are shown below.
- Judgement using numbers, for example:

Appearance	1*	2	3	4	5
Punctuality	1	2	3	4	5
Reliability	1	2	3	4	5
Flexibility	1	2	3	4	5

* Student characteristic (circle): 1 = very poor; 5 = very good

- Judgement using words, for example:

Characteristic	Very poor**	Poor	Average	Good	Very good
Leadership					
Approachability					
Friendliness					
Tolerance					

** Indicate choice with a tick

- Judgement using semantic differential (adapted from Osgood, Suci, & Tannembaum, 1957), for example:

Good† ___ ___ ___ ___ ___ ___ Bad
Happy ___ ___ ___ ___ ___ ___ Sad
Fast   ___ ___ ___ ___ ___ ___ Slow
Strong ___ ___ ___ ___ ___ ___ Weak
Clean ___ ___ ___ ___ ___ ___ Dirty

† Indicate choice with a cross ('✗')

11.9 Example of a holistic rating scale format

Activity

Many end-of-term report forms use rating scales to give parents information about the achievements of their children in comparison with the rest of the class:
1. What type of information is best conveyed using a rating scale?
2. What are the advantages for parents of this method of reporting?
3. What are the disadvantages, and how could these be overcome?

Interviews

An interview is a form of observational assessment. Interviews may be formal or informal, structured or unstructured. A formal or a structured interview using a defined procedure and a prepared set of questions is used in many intelligence tests where respondents are given precise instructions about the procedure to be followed. An informal or an unstructured interview has no set procedure or questions, and the interviewer is free to interact with the interviewee in a natural, conversational way. Piaget used an informal interview technique to collect information about the way children think and solve problems (see Chapter 2) and teachers use interviews to place students in the Victorian Early Years Numeracy Program. Interviews are probably most effective when used with older students who are familiar with the rules of conversation and who can respond successfully to the questions asked. The interview method tends to be less successful with younger students and with students from cultural backgrounds that have different rules about adult–child verbal interaction (Siegal, 1991).

11.10 Piaget's free conversation or clinical method

Sociograms

Sociograms are linked to a form of questioning sometimes used by teachers to assess a class group's social structure. For example, children can be asked to write down the name of their best friend(s) or the child they would like to sit next to, work with, play with or ask to a birthday party. Choices can be depicted graphically, in the form of a **sociogram**.

A sociogram is a quick way of finding out how individual members of a group feel about each other. It is a useful technique for examining the social status or level of acceptance of children considered to be at risk in terms of their social position in a class group. One difficulty is that as the number of individuals in a social group increases, so does the time taken to construct the sociogram (although using a computer makes the task much easier). The

sociogram
A graphical depiction of the pattern of interactions among group members

FIGURE 11.4 A sociogram showing responses from 8–9-year-old tennis-club members who were asked to nominate the person they would *most* like to invite home and the person they would *least* like to invite home.

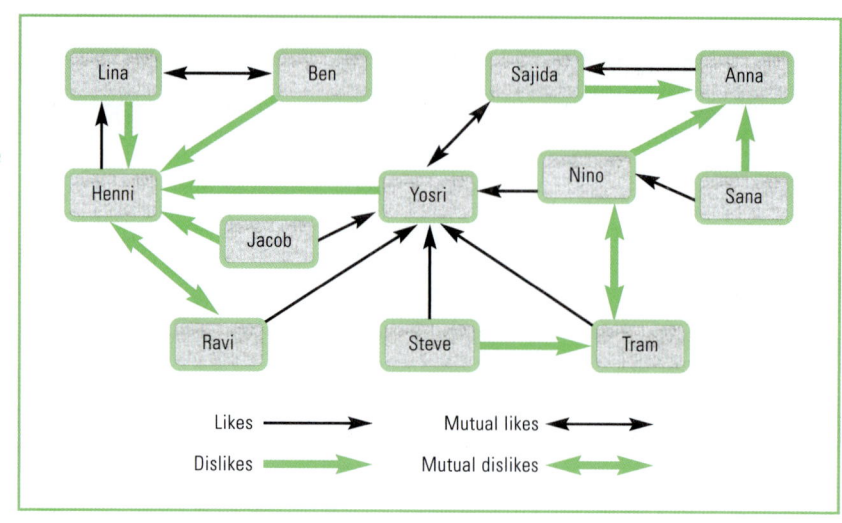

sociogram in Figure 11.4 illustrates the type of pattern that might emerge if one asked a small group of 8–9-year-olds in a tennis club to nominate the person they would most like to invite home and the person they would least like to invite home.

The results of children's sociometric choices need to be interpreted with care, as the same questions asked in different ways can lead to different results. For example, children's responses to the question 'Who is your best friend?' might change if they are asked who they would most like to sit next to in class (a best friend might not be able to help with reading or maths) or the person they would most like to invite to their party (a best friend's mother might not buy good presents).

Self-assessment

Encouraging students to assess their own work is a good way to increase their motivation and to help them gain insight into their own learning (D'Urso, 1996; van Kraayenoord & Paris, 1997). However, Sadler (1989, p.119), suggested that, for self-assessment to be fully effective, students need to have:

- an understanding and appreciation of what constitutes high-quality work
- the evaluative skills needed to compare the quality of their own work with a higher standard
- a set of strategies that can be used to modify their own work.

According to guidelines set out by the New South Wales Department of School Education (1996, p. 50), student self-assessment is useful because it provides an additional source of information to supplement more conventional assessment information for instruction planning, while enabling realistic outcomes to be targeted and providing an insight into individual students' learning styles. Self-assessment enables students to become aware of their own strengths, weaknesses and needs; allows them to take an active part in the assessment process; and contributes to improving self-esteem and realistic notions about self-worth. It involves honesty from students, as well as a trusting relationship between students and teacher (Griffin & Nix, 1991). Participation in building up a portfolio is a form of self-assessment. Examples of different forms of self-assessment are presented in Box 11.6.

Box 11.6 CLASSROOM LINKS

Self-assessment

Self-assessment (and peer assessment) by students is an important component of an *outcomes approach* to learning. It ensures that students are aware of instruction goals and that they learn to monitor their own progress towards achieving these goals.

Examples of self-assessment formats include:

Student self-assessment sheet

Name _____ Date _____

By doing this work I learned _____

I had some trouble with _____

I needed some help with _____

because _____

I think I could improve if _____

I enjoyed doing _____

Time and work management

I finished on time ❑
I left my area tidy ❑
I chose the right equipment ❑
I used the equipment safely ❑
I worked cooperatively ❑

Source: Adapted from NSW Department of School Education (1996, pp. 51–52).

11.11 Another example of self-assessment

Activities

1. The sample self-assessment sheet above is designed for use in primary school settings. Design a similar self-assessment form that can be used with students in the lower secondary level in a curriculum area of your choice.
2. Have you ever been required to use a self-assessment instrument in a learning context? If so, how effective was it for you?
3. As a teacher, would you include student self-assessment in your own teaching program?
4. As a parent, how would you view this procedure's value?

CRITICAL REFLECTIONS

- What advantages and disadvantages can you identify in each of the information gathering techniques just discussed?
- Are there any assessment methods listed that you definitely would not use in your classroom? Why?
- Some modes of assessment focus on numerical values and scores for achievement. Are there some forms of learning you cannot measure? How do you deal with this problem in teaching?

Strengths and limitations of different assessment modes

Assessment in schools is often concerned with giving teachers, students and parents quantitative or norm-referenced information about a given student's performance in particular aspects of the curriculum during the school year. This has resulted in frequent use of assessment strategies that provide a grade or score, since students and more particularly parents usually understand this type of information most easily. Yet an increasing trend towards using more qualitative forms of assessment has drawn attention to alternative methods for gathering information about student learning. These methods tend to focus directly on classroom activities and may involve the observation of a student at work in class, the collection of work samples, demonstrations of skill mastery, informal records, checklists, rating scales, interviews, sociograms and the use of self-assessment.

The strength of these alternative approaches to assessment lies in their increased validity, in that the process of assessment is more closely tied to the real-life performance of the task or skill being assessed. Weaknesses in these non-traditional modes of assessment arise from the additional time and skill required to design and implement such procedures. In addition, it needs to be acknowledged that there is variability in the level of reliability attained from assessments that are based on procedures such as student-performance observation and review of work samples. Such variability needs to be compensated for by using information from multiple rather than single sources.

Issues that might affect educators' decisions regarding modes of assessment are set out in Box 11.7.

Box 11.7 — IMPLICATIONS FOR EDUCATORS

Deciding on a mode of assessment

When deciding on a mode of assessment, teachers need to consider the following:
- The mode should be appropriate for a particular teaching program.
- A range of assessment practices can be used.
- Information should be gathered from a variety of sources ranging from formal examinations to direct observation of students engaged in an activity.
- The modes of assessment to be used in a unit of instruction should be preplanned.
- Any resources required for specific assessment procedures should be prepared beforehand.
- Teachers should endeavour to develop the competencies required to document and interpret assessment results.

Technical issues in assessment

In deciding the type of assessment to use and the way in which data will be collected, educators need to be aware of technical aspects of the assessment modes they employ. In a classroom situation, teachers need to ensure that the procedures they use are reliable, valid and fair (Brady & Kennedy, 2001). This section discusses the concepts 'reliability' and 'validity' and how these apply to assessment methods and procedures.

Reliability

Those who use test results need to know that such results are not the product of chance. **Reliability** is concerned with an assessment result's dependability. If an assessment were to be repeated, either by giving a test a second time or by re-marking test protocols, the assessment procedure's reliability would be demonstrated if the same results were obtained on both occasions.

Further, for a test or assessment method to be considered reliable it needs to yield the same results not only if given on separate occasions (also known as 'test-retest reliability'), but also if different people mark or score it ('scorer reliability'). That is, if the same piece of work is given to two independent markers, they should produce much the same result – they should both give an 'A' to the same essay, for instance. Multiple-choice tests, which measure single skills or content identified from a specific program of instruction, are an objective form of assessment that should be 100% reliable because correct answers are invariable and are identified at the time the test is constructed, with items being 'framed' to

reliability
The extent to which a test or measurement device obtains the same result when used on successive occasions

allow students to select the best option from an array of alternatives. However, forms of assessment that require more subjective judgements (such as essays or portfolios) tend to be affected by examiner judgement, so marks can vary widely. A reliable system for marking an essay or portfolio therefore requires two independent markers, with neither marker being aware of the grade given by the other. The two marks are then averaged to achieve a improved level of scorer reliability.

A single test or assessment task can never measure every aspect of a skill, domain or theoretical construct unless the scope of that skill, domain or construct is very restricted. This means results from separate tests that measure different aspects or elements of the same skill, domain or construct need to be comparable for such tests to be considered reliable measures. In the same way, results of tests that are purported to be of comparable difficulty – whether or not they measure content from the same or different areas – should also be comparable for the tests to be considered reliable measures of that degree of difficulty.

Chance factors can still affect test results and compromise the reliability of a test or assessment method. Such factors include those associated with (Sax, 1997, p. 272):

- *the examinee* – fatigue, boredom, lack of motivation, carelessness
- *characteristics of the test* – ambiguous items, trick questions, poorly worded directions, unfamiliar format
- *conditions of test-taking and marking* – poor examination conditions, excessive heat or cold, carelessness in marking, disregard or lack of clear standards for scoring, computational errors.

Validity

A second technical aspect of assessment concerns the notion of **validity**, or truthfulness. A test or assessment procedure's validity relates to its purpose: does the test or procedure measure what it is designed to measure? Several kinds of validity are desirable in any test or assessment. **Face validity** is achieved if a test *appears* to measure what it is intended to measure. A test is said to have **content validity** if it can be demonstrably linked to relevant curriculum objectives. **Construct validity** is demonstrated if a test measures the knowledge, attitudes and skills (the 'constructs') that underlie the curriculum objectives.

A valid assessment allows students to demonstrate broad understanding of the curriculum area being assessed, rather than simply recording their performance on a specific set of tasks. In addition, assessments that are valid can have social consequences by improving student performance in a curriculum area – a form of validity known as **consequential validity** (Wiggins, 1993) – not just monitoring it. A test's consequential validity is demonstrated if students find an assessment 'challenging and engaging' (Brady & Kennedy, 2001, p. 96), and if it leads to an increased motivation or interest in learning.

Validity is a crucial aspect of assessment. In practical terms, if you give a test of number facts, is it only students' knowledge of number facts that influences their performance on the test, or are other factors involved? An example of validity problems occurred in the first version of the number facts section of the Basic Skills Tests given to New South Wales years 3 and 5 primary school students in 1988. The test contained glossy stimulus documents, and students had to solve problems based on information in the material, using their knowledge of basic number (Bochner, Cooney, & Outhred, 1989). Before students could solve the problems, however, they had to read the stimulus material, meaning the test was 'tapping' reading skills as well as skills in basic number facts. This first use of the Basic Skills Tests in numeracy was widely criticised on the basis that the tests were invalid because a poor level of performance might indicate poor reading skills rather than a low level of skill in number facts.

validity
The extent to which a test or measurement device measures what it purports to measure

face validity
The degree to which a test appears to measure what it is intended to measure

content validity
A measure of the link between a test and relevant curriculum objectives

construct validity
A measure of the link between a test and underlying knowledge, attitudes and skills

consequential validity
A test that has the effect of improving student performance in a curriculum area

Test bias

When judging an assessment procedure's validity, attention needs to be given to its fairness, or lack of 'test bias'. **Test bias** occurs when an unfair advantage is given to some students. This might occur when the knowledge or skills required to do well on a test are likely to be found more in particular groups of test-takers – such as boys, children living in urban areas or children who come from a particular religious background – than in other groups. Lack of bias is established in a test if it can be shown that neither the test content nor the interpretation of its results disadvantages specific groups of students. For example, students who have reading problems will be at a disadvantage in text-based assessments but not in assessments where no reading is required.

test bias
Where particular groups are disadvantaged by factors associated with a test's content and the interpretation of results

Culture-sensitive and culture-fair tests

In developing the first intelligence test, Binet and Simon created items that tapped the practical knowledge of children living in Paris at the end of the 19th century (see Chapter 7). The test was later adapted for use in the USA. Subsequent use of the Stanford-Binet Intelligence Scale and similar tests of intelligence with children from other cultural backgrounds (for example, the children of immigrants who moved to the USA at the beginning of the 20th century) highlighted the inappropriateness of many of the test items for some children. Apart from language differences, the immigrant children often lacked knowledge about objects familiar to American children, such as postage stamps, telephones, pianos or mirrors (Anastasi, 1976). For these children, intelligence tests such as the Stanford-Binet were neither **culture-sensitive** nor **culture-fair test**s. Children from socially disadvantaged or minority-group backgrounds may thus experience difficulties with tests that include items requiring culturally based knowledge.

culture-sensitive or culture-fair test
A test that does not require culturally based knowledge

It is important to note that each technical aspect of a test or assessment procedure – such as reliability, validity, test bias and cultural bias – needs to be evaluated separately because, for example, a test can be highly reliable but lack validity. The implications for educators that may arise from technical issues in the different modes of assessment are summarised in Box 11.8 at the base of this page.

11.12 More about validity

CRITICAL REFLECTION

■ How will you check to make sure assessment methods are reliable and valid in your classroom?

Box 11.8 IMPLICATIONS FOR EDUCATORS

Technical issues in assessment

In using different modes of assessment to monitor student learning, teachers need to be aware of issues associated with reliability and validity; for example:
- Attention needs to be paid to the reliability of an assessment procedure, with provision made to improve reliability if it is judged unacceptable.
- The reliability of an assessment can include factors associated with the examinee, characteristics of the assessment procedure, and the conditions under which the assessment is administered and marked.
- An assessment procedure can be judged to have validity if the consequences of its use are as expected.
- Indications of validity in a test include the absence of test bias and content that is culture-sensitive.

Assessment stakeholders

Who might need information from assessment results? At the most immediate level, such information will be of interest to those involved directly – students and their parents. Tests that provide information for these groups are part of the teaching process. The types of assessments used are usually informal rather than formal, and formative rather than summative in nature. Feedback, particularly for students, is often immediate and given to the student personally. Others who may have an interest – particularly in the results of more formal assessments – include school administrators, potential employers and in some cases politicians. These groups require information from tests for administrative purposes such as determining eligibility for a special program, in job selection and in government policy formulation. Reporting of this type of test information tends to be impersonal and by means of official documents and publications, with interested groups often remote from the assessment process. Figure 11.5 shows who assessment stakeholders might be and what information they might require.

FIGURE 11.5 Stakeholders and their information needs. (Source: Adapted from Griffin & Nix, 1991, p. 35.)

Stakeholders	Information needs	Assessment and reporting methods
Students	Feedback from teachers	Informal, personal, immediate, formative, instructional
Parents	Feedback on performance of their child in context of performance of other children in the class	
Teachers	Feedback on teaching and student performance; diagnosis of student strengths and weaknesses	
Psychologists	Information on student strengths and weaknesses for programming, placement, advising and counselling purposes	
School administrators	Information for screening, eligibility and certification purposes	
Employers	Information about skills and personal characteristics	
Government	Information about standards	
Community	General information on operation of schools	Formal, impersonal, remote, summative, administrative

Students

What is the first thing you look at, as a student, when you collect an assignment? For most students it is the mark or grade. This indicates how well you did in the task. After that, what do you look at? If the assignment is a piece of written work, you will look for comments. If the grade is good, you will probably get few comments, but if it is poor, there are likely to be more comments; that is, feedback is usually given on perceived strengths and weaknesses, as seen by the marker, who pays greater attention to weaknesses than to strengths. The marker's aim is to have an impact on the student's next piece of work. This is most likely to occur if the feedback is given to students so that it (Black & Wiliam, 1998; Linn & Gronlund, 1995, p. 334):

- clearly sets out planned instructional outcomes
- identifies student strengths and weaknesses
- gives full feedback on specific errors and poor strategies, with suggestions for how to improve
- contributes to student motivation.

11.13 Reporting to parents

Parents

What do parents want from the assessment process? Most parents would say 'Good marks'! They want to know what their child can and cannot do. Parents also want to know where their child comes in class; that is, where the child ranks in relation to others; that is, they prefer norm-referenced assessment. There is a good reason for this. A good mark may seem high, but may not really be so compared with the marks of others in class. Most parents want to see their child's performance not just in terms of a single score or grade, but in the broader context of the class as a whole. They need to have such information reported in a form that is understandable and meaningful. Remember that most parents understand norm-referenced assessment procedures because that is what they remember from their own experiences at school. They often need assistance in understanding information from other types of assessment.

Teachers

For teachers, one of the main purposes of student assessment is to obtain feedback on their teaching. It is also used to guide the teacher's decisions regarding the next piece of work. On the basis of assessment results, study topics are changed, materials that have been covered but not yet fully understood are revised, or a current topic that has been adequately covered is abandoned in order to begin the next.

Criterion-referenced or curriculum-based assessments carried out as part of the instructional process give teachers vital information about what students have learned and how effective their teaching has been. Such data can be used to diagnose students' strengths and weaknesses, and to plan future teaching programs. This type of assessment begins with the careful analysis of a specific area of teaching in order to identify the skills and subskills that must be mastered by all students who study it. The level of students' entry skills can be measured at the beginning of a new program to decide where to place each student within the curriculum. Assessment data are used to identify appropriate teaching objectives, and ongoing assessment provides a basis for monitoring individual students' progress through a learning sequence. At the end of the learning sequence, student achievement is assessed and the results are used to evaluate and refine teaching methods.

School psychologists, counsellors and guidance officers

Most schools have access to the services of an educational psychologist or school counsellor who is trained to administer and interpret standardised tests of intelligence, aptitude (talent) and personality (see Chapter 7). These tests are often administered to students individually, and results are used to make decisions about future school placements or to develop classroom management plans. Information derived from such tests is used to advise and support teachers, parents and students in making informed decisions about instructional programs, behaviour management, student placement and other issues related to learning and teaching.

11.14 Assessing a Year 1 child

Schools and school administrators

For teachers and parents, the primary focus of assessment is on the individual student. However, at the school level, information from assessment gives important feedback about the curriculum as a whole and about overall progress in learning and teaching within and across grades, and within and across subject areas. At another level, some analyses of school-wide assessment data, particularly at a secondary level, are used to examine the relative performance of different subject departments to see if one department is more effective than others. Other information of interest to schools is obtained from more formal testing programs such as the annual statewide testing of basic skills in years 3 and 5 in New South

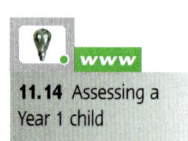

Wales and Victoria, and the assessment of essential learning areas and skills in a sample (around 3%) of 8-year-olds and 12-year-olds every four years in New Zealand. These programs provide comparative information about one school's performance in relation to other schools in the district or state. There is a competitive element in such programs, but they provide valuable information for schools about the relative standard of their students.

Information from often large-scale assessment programs is used by schools and school systems for such varied purposes as screening, selection, classification, placement, eligibility and certification. Screening, for instance, may involve a quick, simple check of large numbers of students to identify specific characteristics or conditions. This information might then be used to find students who have the potential to become Olympic-style rowers or champion chess players, those with sensory impairments, or those who are exceptionally gifted in areas such as mathematics, languages, art, music or dance.

Employers

There are two main issues in student assessment that are of interest to prospective employers: what can students do, and are they employable? Employers want to know about basic skills such as whether or not recent graduates know the basic number facts, or how well they can spell. Employers also want to know about students' personal characteristics.

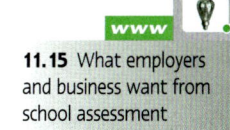

11.15 What employers and business want from school assessment

Government

What does the government want out of student assessment? Data from state-based or national assessments provide information about school standards across each of the states and/or across the nation. An example in Australia is the annual national collection of benchmark data in reading and numeracy by MCEETYA. Such information may be needed in order to decide funding priorities, or to identify areas where outstanding progress has been achieved or where special initiatives need to be taken. Alternatively, towards the end of a period in office, a government may want to be able to claim that standards have risen so voters will continue to support it. Many of the changes in testing seen over the last decades of the 20th century were related to the needs and interests of all levels of government. For example, an Australian Federal Government Department of Education, Science and Training initiative in the areas of early literacy and numeracy can be traced to concern about levels of literacy and numeracy in the workforce (DEETYA, 1998).

Community

How do you find out what the community wants from student assessment or from other information related to education? Look at the daily newspapers and weekly magazines and monitor the amount and type of information given to the community at large about the operation of their schools. Education is likely to figure most often during key times in the school year, such as at the start of a school year or during administration of Basic Skills Tests. Other times when education-related issues receive heightened public attention are during the period preceding an election and at times of major change, such as the introduction of the new HSC in New South Wales (NSW Board of Studies, 2001a) or the NCEA in New Zealand (NZ Ministry of Education, 2002c).

CRITICAL REFLECTIONS

- Do you see any difficulties in there being so many stakeholders in the assessment process?
- As a teacher, do you think it will be possible to meet the needs of all these stakeholders? If so, how can this best be achieved? If not, which stakeholders will be your main priority when you plan your assessment? Why?

Strengths and limitations of stakeholders' interest in assessment information

Strengths

Information from assessments is particularly important for students and their teachers because it gives feedback about learning and teaching either during or at the completion of a unit or instruction phase. Students need to know if they are progressing as expected or if they are failing to meet educational goals. Teachers use assessment data to evaluate their own teaching, to monitor students' achievement of learning objectives and to plan further instruction. Assessment information is also very important for school psychologists and counsellors, since a large part of their role in schools requires knowledge and understanding of particular students' needs and of the classroom situations in which those students are placed.

Limitations

The main limitation of providing information about assessment results to different stakeholders is associated with large-scale testing. There is a risk that information may be used inappropriately; for example, for making comparisons between individual teachers, classes, schools and school districts. Efforts need to be made to ensure that assessment results are used for the purpose for which they were intended, and that where appropriate the confidentiality of assessment data is ensured.

Box 11.9 discusses some implications stakeholders' assessment-information needs may have for educators.

Box 11.9 IMPLICATIONS FOR EDUCATORS

Stakeholders' assessment needs

In thinking about assessment and the specific needs of different stakeholders, educators need to remember that:

- For students, assessment feedback is motivating, helps identify strengths and weaknesses, highlights specific errors and indicates areas for improvement.
- Parents want information about student performance that they can understand and that compares individual results with those achieved by other students.
- Teachers want information about instruction outcomes so as to evaluate their own teaching, monitor student learning, identify appropriate teaching objectives and plan further instruction.
- School psychologists, counsellors and guidance officers use assessment information to support teachers, design behaviour management strategies and make decisions about program placement.
- Schools and school administrators use assessment information to monitor teaching and learning progress within and across grades and curriculum areas. Data from large-scale assessment programs are used for purposes such as screening, selection and certification.
- Employers are interested in assessments that provide information on school leavers' basic competencies and personal characteristics.
- Government bodies are interested in the outcomes of large-scale assessment when this gives comparative information about school standards. Such information helps identify areas where there has been progress and areas where special initiatives are needed.
- The community is interested in assessment results when major changes are introduced or when education becomes a focus of political interest.

Recording and reporting assessment results

Having decided what should be assessed and how this information will be collected, the next task is to decide how the results of assessment should be recorded and then reported to students, their parents and other interested stakeholders. Changes in the way that assessment information is collected, together with developments in technology, have resulted in an array of strategies being available for recording assessment data, together with a range of formats for reporting results.

Issues to consider in the collection of information concerning students include privacy and consent. Teachers must be alert to students' and parents' right to privacy in relation to personal information. While children are at school, school staff function as parent substitutes (*in loco parentis*) (Sax, 1997, p. 310), and teachers' decisions about collecting and using information regarding the children in their care must be made in terms of this responsibility. In addition, parents and students (aged 16 years or older) must be informed in writing of any procedure that involves collecting or disseminating personal information or information about a student that is not directly relevant or essential to the student's school program. The written consent of parents or older students indicating that they understand the purpose of the procedure and how it will be carried out (**informed consent**) must be obtained.

informed consent
Agreement given by a parent or student for the collection and/or dissemination of information not directly relevant to the student's school program

11.16 Principles for recording assessment information

Recording information

Once data on student performance have been collected, decisions must be made about the way in which this information is recorded so it can be easily retrieved and used at a later date. The time that elapses between collection and later use, and the type of use to which data are put can vary widely, so some care needs to be taken in designing such records.

The type of information collected for assessment purposes may be statistical; including, for example, marks, grades, records of attendance and standardised test scores. Informal notes, checklists or anecdotal records of unusual classroom behaviour, exceptional achievements, notes from home or from other professionals about significant personal crises or important events may also be collected and recorded in some way (see Box 11.10). Other information collected for assessment purposes may include reports from previous teachers, and students' self-assessments in the form of reflective writing, diaries, log books, work samples and lists of completed tasks. These different types of information will be collected at different times of the school year, so a timetable may need to be set up for the completion of specific assessment tasks. Decisions will also have to be made about who will complete each assessment, where and how data will be recorded and by whom. Relevant materials may be assembled into a portfolio (Forster & Masters, 1996b), or a record of achievement can be created (Broadfoot, 1986), containing detailed information about all aspects of a student's life at school.

Box 11.10 CLASSROOM LINKS

Teachers' 'in-the-head' knowledge and record-keeping

Teachers carry information about their students' performance 'in the head', and draw upon such information when making informal judgements about, for example, the quality of a piece of work or the amount of effort that went into completing it. Students can be involved in this process. Withers (1991, p. 35) suggested that some schools involve students in the process of record-keeping, particularly when assessment concerns monitoring the completion of goal-based or required work. He cited the example of a science course that used a

record sheet for each topic. Work to be undertaken was listed and students and teacher recorded details of work completed, together with details and dates of any student–teacher negotiations. Some of the benefits for students in this involvement with record-keeping are that students:
- have some say in what and how they learn
- learn how to honestly assess their own performance
- show an ability to work independently and to take initiative with their work
- develop study and examination skills
- come to a realistic appreciation of their strengths and weaknesses.

Source: Adapted from Withers (1991, p.35).

Activities

Think of a unit of study you are currently undertaking:
1 Design a plan you can use to keep track of the tasks required for the unit.
2 Include all relevant activities in your plan, such as:
  i a timetable for completion of tasks
  ii details of resources that may be useful for specific tasks
  iii periods when intensive preparation is needed for the completion of an assignment or preparation for a test.
3 Include a space for personal assessment of your performance on each task.
4 Try using the plan for the rest of the unit. See if it helps you plan your study more effectively and whether your overall performance improves. Note in particular any effects from the self-assessment component of the activity.

Technology-based record-keeping systems

Schools are increasingly using technology-based record-keeping systems to solve the problem of how data will be recorded and where they will be stored. Examples of such systems supported by educational authorities include KIDMAP 2001 (Mercator Software, 2001) in Victoria and, in New South Wales, the Motorised Markbook (Board of Studies NSW, 2002). KIDMAP is designed to be used in conjunction with outcome-based developmental approaches to instruction, such as the CSF II standards and indicators for achievement of students across the eight key learning areas. The Motorised Markbook provides a software package that teachers who lack mathematical skills can use to record and statistically analyse assessment data.

Once student assessment data have been recorded, issues of access, security and confidentiality must be considered. Who will be allowed to examine these data? Will parents be free to look at any material being held about their children? Can students see their own records? Should parents' or students' consent be necessary for other teachers in the school, or agencies outside the school, to access a student's records? If a child moves to another school, what information will be passed on to the new school? In addition, care must be taken to ensure that assessment files are securely stored and that access to computer records is strictly controlled.

Access to the results of individual children on tests such as the Basic Skills Tests is generally restricted to students and their parents, the classroom teacher, the school administrators and, for government schools, the appropriate state and federal departments.

Reporting information

How assessment information is reported is influenced by the report's purpose and audience. The main consumers of information about student achievement are teachers, students themselves and students' parents. Most assessment information that teachers collect is part of the teaching process. Students and parents are interested in information about individual patterns of achievement. According to studies cited by Griffin and Nix (1991, p. 143), parents get most of their information about their child and the school itself from:

- the child
- school newsletters
- regular parent–teacher conferences
- report cards
- notes, telephone calls and personal visits to the school.

Linn and Gronlund (1995, p. 354) suggested that the assessment information communicated to parents should include:

- *description* of what has been measured, such as 'rate, accuracy and comprehension' in a reading test or 'computation and problem solving' for a maths test
- *explanation* of the meaning of scores, such as 'In reading, Anna scored higher than 75% of the students in her class' or 'Geoffrey's score on the history test was below the class average'
- *clarification* of score accuracy, as in 'Peter's maths score (8) is higher than his English score (6) but the difference is not great and he was away for several days with a cold just before the English exam'
- *discussion* of test-result use, as in a teacher's comment 'I'll check on whether Jan should be moved to another group for Science, as her poor marks might be the result of working in a rather disorganised group.'

The New South Wales Department of School Education (1997) identified **three-way reporting** (involving teacher, student and parent input) (see Figure 11.6) as a useful strategy for reviewing student achievement. Such reporting may be in the form of students taking home examples of their work that has already been assessed and commented on by the teacher and student. Parents can then respond in turn with their own comments on their child's work. Alternatively, teachers, students and parents can meet and review a portfolio of work.

When developing a school policy for reporting on student progress to parents, it is a good idea to involve parents in the planning stage. Box 11.11 over the page lists some guidelines that schools in New South Wales use for reporting to parents.

three-way reporting
Reporting that involves student, teacher and parent input

FIGURE 11.6 Students, parents and teachers require different information from assessment. What might each of these people bring to the three-way reporting process?

11.17 Designing a user-friendly format for school reports

Box 11.11 — IMPLICATIONS FOR EDUCATORS

Developing a school reporting policy

Much of a school's success depends on communicating effectively with parents regarding their children's progress. Parents need to understand what is happening at the school and be involved in their children's education (Griffin & Nix, 1991). Most schools provide written reports to parents at least twice a year regarding their children's progress and educational needs. In New South Wales, schools are expected to design procedures for reporting to parents in terms of the following checklist (NSW Department of School Education, 1997, p. 57):

- The parent community was consulted in the development of the report.
- The report informs parents of the progress and educational needs of their children through an appropriately written format that is maintained at least twice per year.
- The report was developed through a planned and coordinated whole school approach.
- The report is informed by well considered class/grade/faculty/school assessment practices that reflect an outcomes-approach.
- The report clearly conveys what the student knows and how that compares with the standard expected by the syllabuses.
- The report is manageable for teachers.
- The report is sensitive to the self esteem and general well-being of students, providing honest and constructive feedback.
- Values and attitude outcomes are reported where appropriate.
- The report considers issues related to curriculum, class groupings, timetabling, programming and resource allocation.

Concluding comments

This chapter has raised some rather technical issues, and we encourage you to reread the more complex sections and discuss them in your tutorial or lecture groups. Effective assessment and reporting is a key to promoting quality learning and teaching, so your choice of assessment strategies should be guided by your knowledge and understanding of your students' needs. This chapter should be viewed in light of the development and learning theories presented earlier in this text. For instance, how might an outcome-based approach to instruction or the use of collaborative learning strategies lead to the use of different forms of assessment? Consider also how you might use assessment to promote students' low self-esteem (Chapter 3) or enhance their motivation (Chapter 7). Or think about how you might vary your assessment strategies depending on such factors as the way learning experiences are organised (chapters 5 and 6), gender distribution in the class, students' language backgrounds (Chapter 9) or students' abilities (chapters 7 and 8). Also reflect on how your style of assessment and reporting might be influenced by your philosophy of teaching and your view of how students learn best (Module II).

Chapter review

- Assessment, evaluation and measurement are some of the terms used to refer to the process of collecting, interpreting, recording and reporting information about student achievement.
- Information derived from the assessment process is of immediate interest to teachers and students who want feedback on their teaching and learning and to parents who want to know how their children are progressing at school.
- School psychologists use assessment to make decisions about school placements and to assist teachers to develop classroom management plans
- School principals and other administrators use this type of information for screening, selection, classification, placement, eligibility and certification.
- The *primary purposes of assessment* are
  - *formative* (providing feedback for students on their progress in learning and teachers on the effectiveness of their instruction),
  - *summative* (providing information on learning outcomes) and
  - *diagnostic* (pinpointing exactly what students know and do not know in a particular area of instruction).
- The procedures used in assessment can take many forms, depending on the purpose of assessment, including traditional tests and examinations (summative information), direct observation and anecdotal records, portfolios containing examples of student work, the direct assessment of performance and student self-assessment (formative information);
- Assessment outcomes need to be systematically recorded and reported in an appropriate manner (oral and/or written) to interested stakeholders, including, in particular, students and their parents.
- Technology-based recording procedures are increasingly being used in schools and reporting procedures have been modified to reflect the outcome-based procedures used in assessment.
- Interested agencies, both government and non-government, have supported these changes through the formulation of new policies and practices, the design of new assessment resources and the provision of relevant professional development programs for teachers and educators.

You make the connections:
Questions for self-assessment and discussion

1. What were some of the main changes that occurred in the last decades of the 20th century regarding the assessment of learning?
2. Identify the main groups who are interested in the outcomes of assessment in schools. Distinguish between the types of information they are interested in.
3. You are on the staff of a school that has traditionally used norm-referenced testing (using marks and grades) for all assessments, and you would like to use a criterion-based strategy in your classroom. Set up a debate in a tutorial or workshop and have different students take each side of the question: 'Are norm-referenced assessment procedures more effective than criterion-referenced procedures in this school?'
4. What are some strengths of the direct observation method for assessing student learning? What are some limitations and how can these be avoided?
5. Devise a set of procedures for reporting assessment information to parents.
6. Imagine you are teaching a class of very hard-working students. However, you are worried about one student who seems to have no interest in classroom activities and who has done poorly in recent tests. How will you report this information to the student's parents? What procedures will you follow to communicate your concerns?

Key terms

assessment	profile	validity
evaluation	ipsative assessment	face validity
measurement	direct assessment	content validity
test	direct observation	construct validity
formative assessment	portfolio	consequential validity
summative assessment	performance assessment	test bias
diagnostic assessment	authentic assessment	culture-sensitive or culture-fair test
norm-referenced assessment	anecdotal record	
norm	checklist	informed consent
standardised test	rating scale	three-way reporting
criterion-referenced assessment	sociogram	
curriculum-based assessment	reliability	

Recommended reading

Black, P., & Wiliam, D. (1998). Assessment and classroom learning. *Assessment in Education, 5,* 7–74.
Brady, L., & Kennedy, K. (2001). *Celebrating student achievement: Assessment and reporting.* French's Forest, NSW: Pearson Education.
Broadfoot, P. (1987). *Introducing profiling.* Basingstoke, UK: Macmillan Education.
Cumming, J. (Ed.) (1998). *Outcome-based education: Resources for implementation.* Canberra: Australian Curriculum Studies Association.
Forster, M., & Masters, G. (1996). *Performances: Assessment resource kit.* Camberwell, Victoria: ACER.
Forster M., & Masters, G. (1996). *Portfolios: Assessment and resource kit.* Camberwell, Victoria: ACER.
Griffin, P., & Nix, P. (1991). *Educational assessment and reporting: A new approach.* Sydney: Harcourt Brace Jovanovich.
Lambert, P. (2001). *Standards-referenced assessment in primary schools.* Retrieved 11.17.01 from <www.bosnsw-k6.nsw.edu.au/parents/k6standards_assess.html>.
Linn, R. L., & Gronlund, N. E. (1995). *Measurement and assessment in teaching* (7th ed.). Englewood Cliffs, NJ: Prentice-Hall.
Masters, G., & Forster, M. (1996). *Developmental assessment: Resource development kit.* Camberwell, Victoria: ACER.
NSW Board of Studies (2001a). *Establishing explicit standards for the new Higher School Certificate.* Sydney: Board of Studies NSW.
Piper, K. (1997). *Riders in the Chariot: Curriculum reform and the national interest 1965–1995.* Melbourne: ACER.
Withers, G. (1991). *From marks to profiles and 'Records of Achievement'.* Geelong: Deakin University.

Make some online visits

Australian Council for Educational Research (ACER): <www.acer.edu.au>
Australian Curriculum Studies Association: <www.acsa.edu.au/policies/studass.htm>
Education Queensland: <education.qld.gov.au/public_media/reports/curriculum-framework/html/p4_ap.html>
New Zealand Council for Educational Research: <www.nzcer.org.nz>
New Zealand Ministry of Education: <www.minedu.govt.nz>
NSW Board of Studies: <www.boardofstudies.nsw.edu.au>

South Australian Department for Education and Children's Services :
  <www.nexus.edu.au/publicat/Policies/Ass_Rep.html>
Tasmanian Department of Education: <www.education.tas.gov.au/about/curriculum.htm>
Victorian Curriculum and Assessment Authority: <www.vcaa.vic.edu.au/csf/infopar.htm>
Western Australian Department of Education and Training: <www.eddept.wa.edu.au>

FIGURE 12.1 Chapter 12 concept map.

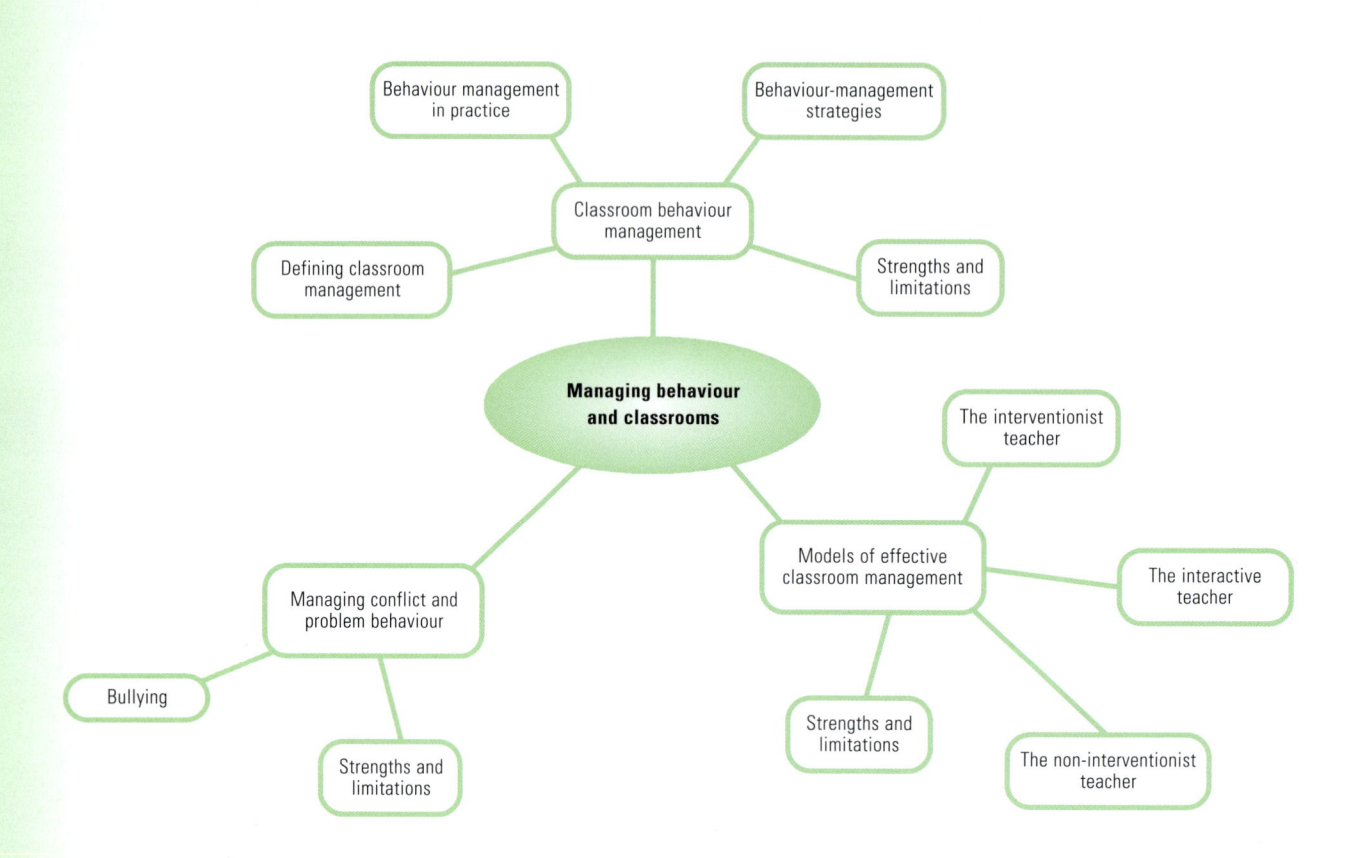

- Managing behaviour and classrooms
  - Classroom behaviour management
    - Behaviour management in practice
    - Behaviour-management strategies
    - Defining classroom management
    - Strengths and limitations
  - Managing conflict and problem behaviour
    - Bullying
    - Strengths and limitations
  - Models of effective classroom management
    - The interventionist teacher
    - The interactive teacher
    - The non-interventionist teacher
    - Strengths and limitations

CHAPTER OBJECTIVES

After reading this chapter you should be able to:

- define classroom management
- identify different views of what constitutes an effective learning environment for children
- compare and contrast alternative models for managing student behaviour
- recognise your own philosophical approach to classroom management
- give examples of different approaches to reducing bullying.

CHAPTER 12

Managing behaviour and classrooms

Introduction

Two students sitting at the back of a Year 7 History lesson are whispering together about the birthday party they are to attend on the weekend. The teacher, aware of what is going on at the back of the class, walks slowly in their direction, continuing with the lesson and not looking at the two students. They see her approach, stop their chatter and begin to pay attention. What has happened here? What has the teacher done and why have the students reacted as they have? If we think about the teacher's role in a classroom, two functions seem dominant: the first is concerned with the *content of education*, or subject matter to be learned; the second is concerned with the *process of instruction*, or how children learn, their attitudes to learning, the resources and technology needed to support such learning, and the context in which it occurs. This chapter is concerned with the second of these two aspects of learning; that is, issues associated with the instruction process. The chapter focuses in particular on how teachers manage classroom activities and the strategies they use to ensure that classrooms provide a context to support and facilitate rather than inhibit learning.

pedagogy
The art of teaching and instruction

Classroom behaviour management

What makes an effective school and classroom? How important is behaviour management in the context of effective schooling? What part of **pedagogy**, or the art of teaching and instruction, is concerned with behaviour management? To what extent is effective teaching the product of classroom order? What other factors are relevant (see Figure 12.2)?

FIGURE 12.2
What sort of teacher would you want to have if you were a primary-level student? What about if you were at high school? What sort of teacher would you want to *be*? Why?

Defining classroom management

If you ask someone in the general community what classroom management means, they will probably talk about discipline and controlling disruptive students. But is this what classroom management is about? Does it simply refer to controlling behaviour in instructional settings, or is it more than that? **Classroom management** is certainly concerned with behaviour, but it can also be defined more broadly as involving the planning, organisation and control of learners, the learning process and the classroom environment to create and maintain an effective learning experience in which expected pedagogical outcomes are achieved. Within this definition, 'learners' include students and teachers, since in an effective classroom both gain in knowledge and understanding. The 'learning process' includes classroom activities and the teaching strategies that teachers use. The 'classroom environment' provides a context for learning and includes not only the physical space, furnishings, resources and materials, but also the class atmosphere, participants' attitudes and emotions, and the social dynamics of the learning experience. The teacher's role in this setting is complex, reflecting the heterogeneous nature of the classroom environment, which must be managed successfully if learning is to occur. Doyle (1986, p. 394) suggested that teachers face the following two main instructional tasks:

- *a teaching goal* that must be achieved, involving maximising opportunities for students to learn through the use of effective instructional strategies and classroom organisation procedures, and also involving tasks that are well prepared, motivating and at an appropriate level in terms of students' needs and prior learning
- *a problem space* that must be managed, encompassing the set of participants or learners, the learning activities that are the focus of the lesson, available materials and resources, and a physical space.

The critical task for teachers is to achieve their stated goals through effective use of all the different elements that are present in the complex setting of a conventional classroom. As you consider approaches to managing students' behaviour, think about the context in which learning happens and the many factors that may influence how students behave in a classroom.

Behaviour management in practice

The teacher asks Ozturk a question at the beginning of Science class, and when Ozturk gives a funny reply, all the students laugh. The teacher becomes very angry. After that, whenever that teacher asks Ozturk a question, everyone giggles. What can the teacher do to stop this behaviour?

In most classrooms, students' behaviour is generally appropriate and does not present a challenge to the teacher. However, there are sometimes a few children whose behaviour is at times inappropriate or a nuisance. Occasionally, teachers also encounter students whose behaviour is so disturbed or difficult to manage that teachers need to seek additional help from experts, either to develop better strategies for coping with particular students or to find some other solution. An important element of the classroom-management process concerns the range of behaviours that may be present in a particular group of students, and the identification and implementation of appropriate strategies for handling these behaviours.

Behaviour management in effective schools and classrooms

In a study of what makes an effective school in Australia, McGaw, Piper, Banks and Evans (1993, p. 174) reported that problems in **discipline** and behaviour management did not appear to be major barriers to school effectiveness and improvement. Such problems were mentioned by some of the participants surveyed in the study but were not of great concern

---

classroom management
The planning, organisation and control of learners, the learning process and the classroom environment to create and maintain an effective learning experience

discipline
A system of rewards and punishments for managing behaviour

to them. Only 12% referred to the need for an effective school to have an environment that was 'safe and congenial' (p. 124). Discipline was mentioned by 6% of participants, but they were mainly concerned that schools should have clear discipline policies that were well known to students and consistently applied. A few emphasised the need for students to accept authority and submit to school discipline, and some also referred to the importance of self-discipline. Only a small number (1%) commented on the difficulties presented by disruptive students, arguing that schools should have clear and effective strategies for removing such students so that teachers' attention was not distracted and so other students could get on with their work. Studies of school effectiveness reported by Rutter, Maughan, Mortimore and Ouston (1979), Mortimore, Sammons, Stoll, Lewis and Ecob (1988) and Slee (1995a) suggested that an important component of discipline consists of a system of rewards and punishments, with an emphasis on praise and rewards.

Defining and identifying disruptive and disturbed behaviour

Every teacher experiences, at some time, problems in classroom management and instruction that are the outcome of a student's disruptive or disturbed behaviour (see Figure 12.3). Over time, most teachers develop strategies for responding to disturbances caused by such behaviour (Block, Oakar, & Hurt, 2002). All school systems have policies that address difficulties associated with **inappropriate behaviour** – that is, behaviour that interferes with a student's own learning and/or disrupts the class – in school settings. Such policies usually set out general guidelines for student management, welfare and discipline, although individual school communities are often encouraged to develop policies and programs suited to their students' particular needs. Issues addressed in school policy documents include guidelines for creating safe, caring, orderly and productive learning environments, and a code of conduct that sets out expectations for appropriate behaviour, plus procedures to be followed when the code is disregarded. Other issues addressed in policy documents include bullying, harassment, violence, and the processes involved in student suspension and exclusion.

Doyle (1986) used the term 'problematic' to refer to any behaviour perceived as inappropriate for a given activity. Such behaviour may range from daydreaming and mild interruptions, to unnecessary and excessive movement, shouting, swearing, fighting and so on. According to Doyle (1986), problematic behaviours tend to occur most often during passive individual activities such as silent reading and seated work. Such behaviours are less likely to occur during small-group and whole-class activities where, paradoxically, individual students

inappropriate behaviour
A behaviour that interferes with a student's own learning and/or disrupts the class

FIGURE 12.3
Which of these behaviours would you consider disruptive? Which would require immediate attention?

Labels: Feet on desk; Moving around the classroom; Daydreaming; Talking; Flicking paper; Flying a paper aeroplane; Sleeping

disruptive behaviour
Behaviour that is problematic or inappropriate in the context of a given activity or for a certain teacher

behaviour disturbance
Significant abnormalities in the behaviour of an individual who does not have a diagnosable psychiatric illness

emotional disturbance
Evident from inappropriate behaviours that require psychiatric treatment in the form of ongoing therapy

receive a higher level of teacher attention compared with that received during solitary work on individual tasks (Galton, Hargreaves, Comber, Wall, & Pell, 1999).

Galloway, Ball, Bloomfield and Seyd (1982) suggested that children's behaviour at school can be seen in terms of a continuum ranging from extremely cooperative to totally unacceptable. Few children's behaviour is consistently at the same point on such a continuum. Changes will occur with age increases, different teachers, different learning areas, different classrooms and so on. Some teachers may be unaffected by a behaviour that others find irritating or disruptive. **Disruptive behaviour** is any behaviour that appears problematic or inappropriate in the context of a given activity or to a certain teacher. Doyle (1986) also distinguished between behaviours that minimise learning in an individual student – such as daydreaming, drowsiness and wriggling; and those that disrupt the flow of activity for the whole group – such as calling out, arguing and excessive movement. Terms used to distinguish different types of behaviour – in addition to the terms 'inappropriate behaviour' and 'disruptive behaviour' already discussed – include **behaviour disturbance** and **emotional disturbance**. The distinction between all these descriptors is a matter of degree, and classroom teachers can have problems in distinguishing between them. It is little wonder that when faced with a student whose behaviour they find inappropriate, disruptive or disturbed, teachers are often uncertain about the exact nature of the problem they are dealing with, and what action should be taken (see Box 12.1).

Box 12.1 CASE STUDY

A difficult child

Lachlan was 5 years of age when he was referred to a withdrawal unit for children with language and communication difficulties, which was located on the campus of a metropolitan university. Lachlan was small, fair-haired, looked angelic and had delayed language. He was reported to exhibit frequent episodes of disruptive, even destructive behaviour, which had been noted in a psychologist's report.

At first Lachlan was playful and interacted successfully with the other children in his unit classroom, although there was evidence of disruptive behaviour during his first weeks in the class. Over time, as Lachlan's language and communication skills showed signs of improvement, his behaviour began to deteriorate. The teacher and classroom aide had to focus increasingly on controlling Lachlan's behaviour and protecting the other children from his destructive and aggressive outbursts. After about 4 months they asked the school principal for help. It was decided Lachlan should be referred to a school psychologist for further assessment.

The psychologist visited the school and talked at length to Lachlan's teacher and the classroom aide. He observed the boy over an extended period and, after widespread consultation, everyone involved with Lachlan's case – including his parents – felt that Lachlan should be moved to a nearby residential support unit that could provide a behaviour-management program and counselling for parents and child.

Lachlan entered the residential unit and a behaviour-management program was instituted. His destructive and aggressive behaviour was eventually controlled. It was also established that his delayed development, particularly in the area of language and communication, was associated with mild intellectual impairment that had been difficult to identify earlier because of his communication problems coupled with extremely disturbed behaviour. Lachlan's relationship with his parents broke down during this period, and he was eventually declared a state ward.

Activities

1. How would you describe Lachlan's behaviour?
2. Should greater efforts have been made to retain Lachlan in the unit? Why/why not?
3. What could have been done to help Lachlan and his family once he entered the residential unit?

What behaviours do teachers see as disruptive?

Behaviours that teachers see as disruptive vary across cultures. For example, in a study of teachers in the USA, Duke and Meckel (1984) reported that teachers regarded absenteeism and lateness as having the most disruptive effect on their teaching. In the UK, Wheldall and Merrett (1988) found that, for teachers at primary and secondary levels, the most troublesome behaviours were students talking out of turn and hindering other students. Wheldall and Merrett's study found that boys were most often the source of these irritating and time-wasting disruptions. Behaviours identified as particularly annoying included disobedience and slowness or idleness. Physical violence and verbal abuse were rarely cited as being among the behaviours that annoyed teachers, probably because these behaviours' occurrence was less frequent (Wheldall & Merrett, 1988).

Australian study findings are consistent with the data reported in studies of British schools. For example, Hyde and Robinson (1982, unpublished, cited by Louden, 1985) reported that 40% of suspensions from schools in Western Australia were for behaviours classified as persistent disobedience, refusal to obey instructions, and insolence. Galloway and Barrett (1984) found a similar pattern in New Zealand. Field (1986), in a small study of Australian primary teachers, found that distractibility was cited most often and concluded that acting-out or highly disruptive behaviours occurred only rarely in these classrooms. Stephenson, Linfoot and Martin (2000) also reported that, in western Sydney, 130 teachers of children aged five to eight from 21 schools who were confident of their classroom-management skills were most concerned about aggressive behaviour and about their need for support in dealing with distractibility. Less confident teachers were concerned about aggression, distractibility and disobedience, and also needed assistance with distractibility and disobedience. Bor, Presland, Lavery, Christie and Watson (1992) cited inattentiveness and, to a lesser extent, aggression, as the most commonly reported problems for students in primary and lower-secondary school levels. Aggression was most common in students who were experiencing more serious problems in adjusting to school life. Inattentiveness and aggression were both more common in boys than in girls, and declined in frequency in the upper-secondary level (possibly because some students have left school). The most severe but less frequent problems identified in Bor et al.'s study included social withdrawal, anxiety, depression and self-destructiveness. This is a reminder that undesirable behaviour can be directed internally, affecting an individual child but causing no disturbance to classroom activities (Chazan, Laing, Davies, & Phillips, 1998).

12.1 Problem behaviours identified by teachers in Queensland state schools

CRITICAL REFLECTIONS

- What behaviours do you categorise as disruptive or problematic in classrooms?
- Compare your list with those of others in your group and discuss strategies for dealing with disruptive or problematic behaviours.
- Do you have concerns about managing disruptive behaviour in your classroom? If so, share these with your group and identify ways of addressing your concerns.

The influence of home and school

According to Louden (1985), there was a shift during the latter part of the 20th century in thinking about the home–school relationship and the occurrence of troublesome or disturbed behaviour. For many years it was assumed that the school's influence was less significant than the home's in relation to student behaviour and achievement. But while the home is still seen as crucial – primarily in relation to providing a secure base for social, emotional and intellectual development, and because parental expectations have an important influence on student achievement and behaviour – school-related factors are also important, particularly in terms of student behaviour that is a product of interplay between the individual and the environment (Bronfenbrenner, 1979). Hemphill (1996, p. 113) identified three risk factors implicated in children developing conduct disorders, these being maladaptive family interaction and communication, a high level of family stress, and socioeconomic disadvantage. On the other hand, Kauffman (2001, p. 262) noted seven school-based factors that can contribute to inappropriate and disturbed behaviour in students. These include:

- insensitivity to students' individuality from teachers, school administrators and peers
- inappropriate teacher expectations of students
- inconsistent teacher management of student behaviour
- instruction in non-functional or irrelevant skills
- ineffective instruction in critical skills
- use of inappropriate reinforcement contingencies
- provision by teachers and peers of inappropriate or undesirable behavioural models.

Studies of school effectiveness, such as that reported by Rutter et al. (1979), show that children's behaviour at school – as well as their examination results, attendance and chances of getting into trouble with the police – are influenced by social background and by the school they attend. So while problem behaviour was once seen as a product of the child's heredity and home environment, it is increasingly viewed as a product of interaction between experiences children bring to school and their experiences within the school context. See also Box 12.2 on factors within the classroom environment that can affect student behaviour.

Box 12.2 CLASSROOM LINKS

Classroom environment factors

A number of factors have an impact on activities that take place within a classroom setting, regardless of the activity's nature or participants. Doyle (1986) identified some of the critical elements that are shared by all classrooms as:

TABLE 12.1 Factors affecting the classroom environment

Classroom environment factors	Implications for teachers
Multidimensionality: The wide range of players and events that are present in a classroom	■ Develop strategies for addressing the wide range of ability levels; preferences; and social, emotional, cultural and linguistic backgrounds of students in your classroom
Simultaneity: Many different things happen at the same time in a classroom	■ Be aware of what is happening at every level, including that of individual students, small groups and the class as a whole ■ Learn to have 'eyes in the back of your head' ■ The challenge of simultaneity may contribute to high levels of stress and burn-out unless you develop coping strategies (see, for example, Brouwers & Tomic, 1999)
Immediacy: The speed at which events in a classroom unfold	■ Manage time at both micro and macro levels ■ Give immediate feedback to students during face-to-face interaction ■ Learn to allocate time appropriately for planned learning activities ■ Behavioural problems are most likely to arise when students' attention, interest and motivation begin to ebb as a result of poor timing ■ Be alert to ongoing events in a busy classroom setting
Unpredictability: Carefully planned classroom activities do not always proceed as planned	■ Be flexible ■ Respond appropriately when the unexpected occurs ■ Where possible, take advantage of surprising or unanticipated events
Publicness: Many people, often students, witness what teachers do, or learn about a teacher's actions from other witnesses	■ Be aware that what you do and say is observed and may be discussed outside the classroom ■ Use this as an opportunity to model appropriate or desirable behaviour for students

Classroom environment factors	Implications for teachers
History: Class groups continue to meet regularly over extended periods of time	■ Consider the effect of accumulated memories of previous experiences when developing plans for classroom activities

Source: Adapted from Doyle (1986, pp. 394–395).

Incidence rates of disruptive behaviour in schools

Bor et al. (1992) reported that the teachers they studied perceived almost 17% of students as experiencing adjustment difficulties (6.3% mild, 7% moderate and 3.7% severe). Zubrick, Silburn, Gurrin, Teoh, Shepherd, Carlton and Laurence (1997) reported similar incidence rates in a study of child health conducted in Western Australia. In this case, school principals reported that within the previous 6 months they had been informed of emotional and behavioural problems in 16% of students in their schools.

Information has also been reported regarding the number of students who exhibit the more disruptive and disturbing behaviours, with percentages of such children in the general school-aged population in Australia and New Zealand ranging from around 3% (Andrews, Elkins, Berry, & Burge, 1979; Doherty, 1982; Pickering & Dickens, 1992; Quinn, Sultmann, & Elkins, 1988; Norman, Sritheran, & Ridding, 1984) to 6–8% (Barrie & Tomlinson, 1985; Mitchell, 1985). Studies of Catholic schools in Queensland (Quinn, Sultmann, & Elkins, 1988) and Victoria (Pickering & Dickens, 1992) cited rates of less than 4% in Catholic primary and secondary schools. In a national study of special education in Australia, Andrews et al. (1979) found rates of 3.4% for behavioural difficulties among students in all regular and special primary and secondary government and non-government schools (primary 3.0%, secondary 3.4%); while for all New South Wales schools, Doherty (1982) cited incidence rates for students who are behaviourally disturbed at 3.2%. In New Zealand, Norman, Sritheran and Ridding (1984) suggested that 2–3% of children were judged to be '[s]ocially/behaviourally maladjusted' (cited by Wotherspoon, 1987, p. 272).

It should be noted that the information on incidence rates reported here is based on studies that have used highly varied samples, different terminology and different criteria to identify and categorise their subjects. However, the figures of around 16% to 17% for students with difficulties in adjustment and 3 to 4% for more serious behavioural problems in countries such as Australia and New Zealand are consistent with data reported in overseas studies (Conway, 1998).

12.2 Classroom management over time

Behaviour-management strategies: Alternatives to corporal punishment

Managing student behaviour is clearly a complex process. Teachers must be multiskilled, talented and able to deal with a range of behaviours. Different behaviour-management strategies were used in classrooms during the 19th and 20th centuries. The last two decades of the 20th century saw schools shifting from using corporal punishment in Australian and New Zealand classrooms, to using suspension and exclusion as a means of last resort (Slee, 1995a, p. 166).

In Australia and New Zealand, corporal punishment is not allowed in government schools nor in most non-government schools (Association of Professional Teachers, 2001; Youthlaw, 2003). Registration requirements for non-government schools require each to have a behaviour-management policy which states that corporal punishment will only be used as a last resort. In addition, a register of corporal punishment incidents must be maintained (Slee, 1995a).

Corporal punishment has been replaced by alternative forms of discipline, which range from detention, extra written work, time out, removal of privileges, behaviour contracts or agreements, in-school suspension and community service to exclusion and expulsion (Youthlaw, 2003). Classroom teachers have been given additional training on alternative methods of school discipline and have access to specialist itinerant teachers or support teachers whose purpose is to assist regular classroom teachers to maintain control in their classrooms and to cope with students who exhibit disturbed behaviour. In addition, some special-class arrangements and special units and schools for students with behavioural disturbance have been established (Conway, 2002; Dempsey & Foreman, 1997).

There have been objections regarding the use of suspension and exclusion as viable alternatives to other methods of student discipline. The Burdekin Report into homeless youth (HREOC, 1989) demonstrated links between school suspension, exclusion and the drift towards juvenile crime, homelessness and long-term dependency on welfare agencies (Slee, 1995a, p. 149). In 1999, the New Zealand government introduced an alternative educational program for young people from 13-and-a-half to 15 years old who have been alienated from school. The program includes young people who have been out of school for two terms or more, who have been excluded from school on multiple occasions or who have a history of dropping out of school. The initiative is seen as a response to the problems presented by students whose needs are not adequately provided for within the regular school system due to demographic and social change (NZ Ministry of Education, 2002a).

Strengths and limitations of classroom behaviour management

While there are problems associated with using labels to identify a particular cluster of behaviours (see the discussion of labelling in Chapter 8), finding an appropriate label to describe the range of behaviours that a particular student exhibits can be an important first step in obtaining help. However, one of the problems associated with the guidelines provided for teachers who need to manage inappropriate or disruptive behaviour concerns the confusing way in which key terms are defined. This lack of clarity can cause problems for teachers and others who try to find a label that is appropriate for the array of behaviours a particular student presents. This uncertainty can also lead to difficulties in finding an appropriate solution.

Although the types of problems teachers see as disruptive tend to be mild in nature, teachers need an array of options for responding to difficult classroom behaviour. The move away from corporal punishment to using alternatives such as extra work and time out – together with the possibility of access to specialist support – gives teachers more humane options for handling inappropriate behaviour. This move is also consistent with ideas concerning the rights of children. However, suspension or exclusion from school may have a more long-lasting and negative impact on students than do the more traditional forms of punishment.

Strategies that teachers can use as a first step in managing classrooms are listed in Box 12.3.

12.3 More about identifying behavioural disturbance or disorder

Box 12.3 IMPLICATIONS FOR EDUCATORS

Managing behaviour in the classroom
- Be prepared:
  - devote time to planning
  - have a clear, well-considered plan for managing your classroom and student behaviour
  - plan to provide a variety of tasks
  - plan how you will motivate students whose interest seems to wane
  - plan how students will spend time on task and how you will manage disruptive behaviour.
- Be organised:
  - decide before teaching begins what

procedures you will follow in establishing and maintaining discipline in classrooms so your reactions to classroom-management problems can be quick, consistent and congruent with your underlying values
- organise your time, resources and classroom.
• Develop a classroom-management plan:
  - decide on preventative measures ahead of time
  - consider what verbal and non-verbal cues you will use
  - encourage students to take responsibility for their actions.
• Be guided by your personal philosophy of teaching and learning. Think about:
  - what you want your students to learn
  - how you would like your students to learn
  - how you will foster such learning.
• Know your students:
  - be aware of their needs (they may have special learning needs) and individual differences
  - monitor, circulate, and assess students' progress regularly.
• Know how your school operates:
  - ensure your classroom-management plan is consistent with policies and procedures followed in the whole-school policy
  - any classroom-management and discipline plan needs back-up support from colleagues and the wider school community.
• Be aware of the power relations in your classroom:
  - a critical feature of an individual teacher's classroom-management plan is the extent to which power is held by the teacher, or shared in a relatively equal way between teacher and students
  - differences in the ways power is managed are a major factor in distinguishing between different approaches to classroom management.
• Be positive – enjoy your teaching!
• Be enthusiastic – establish an atmosphere of cooperation, balance and mutual respect.

Source: Adapted from Girard and Koch (1996, p. 107).

Models of effective classroom management

To survive in the classroom, every teacher needs to have a clear, well-thought-out plan that provides an effective framework for maintaining discipline. Such a plan will involve a set of beliefs about the instruction process, and also about the organisation and management of the environment in which instruction occurs. To create such a plan, a teacher needs to understand the psychology of learning and development (as discussed in modules I and II) and the factors that play a role in learning (see Module III). This understanding informs your personal philosophy of learning, or beliefs about how children learn and what constitutes an effective learning environment. Such beliefs provide guidelines for establishing an effective learning environment in a classroom, as well as strategies for coping with inappropriate or disruptive behaviour.

Teachers' ideas about managing classrooms can be thought of in terms of the degree of balance between the teacher's and the students' power (Porter, 2000). In a traditional classroom, the teacher's role is to retain firm control of all aspects of teaching and learning. However, as is evident in earlier chapters in this book, there has been a steady shift towards allowing students to have some level of control over what happens during instruction. Examples of this development can be seen in the discussions of cooperative learning in Chapter 6 and of self-assessment in Chapter 11.

The extent to which teachers retain or devolve some of their authority to students is influenced by a given teacher's personal philosophy of classroom management. Wolfgang (1995) used the terms 'interventionist', 'interactive' and 'non-interventionist' to describe teaching and discipline styles that differ in regard to their emphasis on teachers' and students' relative power. We discuss each of these styles in turn in this section.

The interventionist teacher

interventionist teacher
Sees children's development as an outcome of external factors

The **interventionist teacher** is guided by the view that children's development is an outcome of external factors. Frederic H. Jones (1987) is a psychologist who spent many hours in classrooms as a teacher and as a researcher. He also has a background in child psychotherapy, family therapy in a humanistic framework and parent training within an operant-conditioning framework (see Chapter 4 for a discussion of operant conditioning). In his work on classroom discipline, Jones emphasises the need for teachers to maintain firm control through the following four aspects of classroom organisation (Wolfgang, 1995, p. 197):

- limit setting through body language
- responsibility training
- back-up system (supported by policies at the school level)
- classroom structure.

Limit setting through body language

limit-setting strategies
Strategies that establish boundaries in regard to children's activities

According to Jones, teachers need to set limits on students' behaviour that are simple, practical and, once mastered, easy to use. Responses to disruption should be physical, using body language, and employ a minimal number of words, such as when a teacher stands beside a student and points to the student's workbook to indicate that the set task is to be completed. Teachers need to move around the classroom, using eye contact and proximity to maintain students' engagement with their work. The ultimate effect of these **limit-setting strategies** is to reduce the teacher's workload (see Table 12.2).

TABLE 12.2 Sequence of strategies for limit-setting in the classroom

Strategy	Method
1 Eyes in the back of your head	Teachers need 'with-it-ness' so they can see everything that is happening around them
2 Terminate instruction	Discipline comes before instruction, so instruction must cease when disruption occurs
3 Turn, walk to the edge of the student's desk, prompt	The teacher must turn to face the offending student squarely, make unwavering eye contact, maintain a flat expression (no smiles), walk slowly to the front of the student's desk and prompt the action required from the student (e.g. completion of a set of sums)
4 Palms	If further intervention is required, the teacher places both hands, palms down, on each side of the student's work
5 Camping out in front	If necessary, the teacher puts weight on one elbow on the edge of the desk, still maintaining eye contact, and waits for compliance
6 Camping out from behind	If two neighbouring students are creating the disruption, the teacher can move between the two desks, keeping elbow, body and eye contact with one of the offending students while placing a wall between them. Once the first student resumes work, the teacher can begin to move out, first thanking that student for the compliance, then turning to hold eye contact with the second student until the second student resumes work, when that student can be thanked and the process of class instruction resumed

Source: Adapted from Wolfgang (1995, pp. 203–215).

Responsibility training

responsibility training
The use of an incentive system to elicit new behaviours or maintain existing ones

In Jones's view, teachers need a system that is simple to implement and that ensures students will do anything the teacher requires at any time, with almost no effort on the part of the teacher. **Responsibility training** involves providing incentives through a group reward, through 'preferred activity time' ('PAT'), or through periods of free or play time. Students can win time by working quickly and well, but can also lose time by dawdling, talking or playing up. According to Jones (1987), with this system in place, the teacher is in control and students learn to conform and to complete required tasks. These strategies are discussed in Chapter 4 in the section on Skinner and operant conditioning.

Back-up system

A **back-up system** is a set of hierarchically ordered penalties for misbehaviour, ranging from a simple warning given privately to an individual student or group of students, to a conference with the student, time out, detention, a conference with a parent and, as a last resort, suspension or expulsion. To implement such a system, support is required at the school level, both professionally and in the form of appropriate policies, procedures and resources.

Classroom structure

Classroom structure encompasses the rules that are established in classrooms, daily routines and the way classroom furniture is organised, since all affect what happens in a classroom. Students achieve a sense of predictability and security when they know how their classroom is organised and managed. Jones (1987) argued that students should be taught the rules, routines and standards of behaviour that are critical aspects of successful classroom operation. This instruction should begin at the start of a school year and be retaught periodically during the year. Classroom furniture should be arranged to maximise the teacher's mobility, physical access and proximity to students.

Jones's (1987) ideas about classroom management included a plan for arranging desks so as to allow the teacher space to move around the classroom. A teacher's walking path enables the teacher to supervise students through proximity (1–3 metres) and eye contact. An example of a classroom arranged to provide a walking path for the teacher is set out in Figure 12.4.

Box 12.4 discusses some classroom-environment issues teachers need to consider.

> **backup system**
> A set of hierarchically ordered penalties for misbehaviour
>
> **classroom structure**
> The rules, daily routines and physical organisation and environment of a classroom
>
> **12.4** Example of the steps in a limit-setting scenario

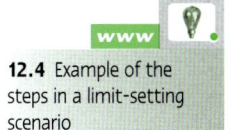

FIGURE 12.4 The teacher's walking path as an interior loop.
(Source: Wolfgang, 1995, Figure 8-4.)

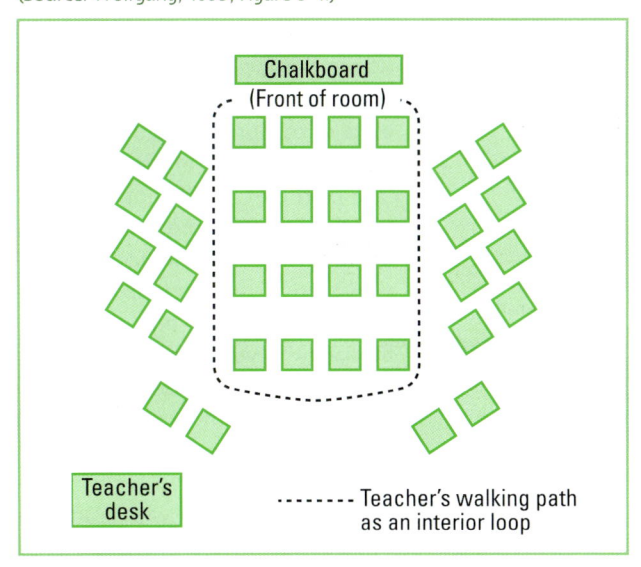

Box 12.4 CLASSROOM LINKS

Time and space in classroom management

It is generally accepted that schools should provide both a quality education and a caring, safe and orderly environment for all students. These aims can be achieved if schools and classrooms have effective behaviour-management plans and well-designed physical environments in classroom and playground (Clark, Glew, Kelly, Lander, Lawlor, & Scott, n.d.).

Many aspects of the classroom physical environment are likely to have an impact on student achievement. For example, sufficient seating and appropriate placement of students must be considered, with students who are least likely to annoy or distract each other seated together and distractible students seated away from possible distracters. Lighting should be appropriate and noise levels should not interfere with effective communication. Classroom rules and routines should be posted around the room for easy reference. Student work should be displayed to add colour and interest to the space, since dull and uninteresting classrooms can contribute to lower levels of motivation and disruptive behaviour (Weinstein & Mignano, 1993). Storage areas for classroom resources and student possessions should be well organised and easily accessible to students and the teacher (Gordon, Arthur, & Butterfield, 1996).

Wragg (1993) identified time and space as important considerations in classroom management. Issues here include decisions about using particular teaching and work patterns (such as cooperative learning or peer tutoring) for the whole class, for small groups or for individuals, with all having identifiable advantages and disadvantages. Similarly, the way furniture and resources are arranged in a classroom can have an impact on teacher decisions to introduce small-group or whole-class activities.

Activities

1. On a square piece of paper, draw the plan of a classroom you are familiar with (such as rectangular or L-shaped). Assume that:
   - there are 52 square metres of available space
   - there may be 24–30 students present at any time
   - one student at a single desk will need about 1–1.25 square metres of floor space
   - six students sitting around a circular table will need 4–5 square metres of floor space
   - three students sitting at a rectangular or square table will need about 2–2.25 square metres of floor space
   - at least 2 square metres of teacher's storage space will be required
   - each square on your plan represents 1 square metre
   - [optional] your school has an open plan or has paired classrooms with moveable walls, and you share resources and activity areas with another class or classes.
2. On your classroom plan, show:
   a where the students will sit and work
   b where the facilities you would like to have (such as a sink and power outlets) are located
   c any other resources or facilities you would like located in a shared 10 square metres per class of resource area that is shared with other teachers.
3. When your plan is complete, check that it allows for your preferred way of working. Indicate on the plan that it will allow:
   a freedom of movement for the teacher and students
   b flexibility for students to work alone or in groups
   c provision for you to work with the class as a whole
   d proper display of work
   e flexibility to vary activities from day to day or lesson to lesson with minimal disruption.
4. Finally, in looking at any management problems that may arise, identify:
   a where movement by students or the teacher might be difficult
   b whether the teacher will be able to see all that is happening in the room, or whether there are blind spots
   c how you would deal with students working independently in the shared resource area – that is, rules you would establish, whether permission would be required to go there, whether students would have to report back and so on
   d whether the arrangements you have made would enhance or inhibit learning
   e whether you have made the best possible use of the space available to you and your class.

Source: Activities adapted from Wragg (1993, pp. 43 and 45).

The interactive teacher

interactive teacher
Sees children's development as an interaction between internal and external factors

The **interactive teacher** sees children's development as a product of interaction between internal and external factors. Alfred Adler (1930), Rudolf Dreikurs (1968) and Maurice Balson (1992) exemplify theorists who emphasised the role of the school in preparing students to live in a democratic society through the sharing of power between teachers and students.

Adler was a Viennese psychiatrist who argued that human beings are essentially social creatures whose basic psychological characteristics enable them to live in democratic way. Dreikurs was an associate of Adler's who emigrated to the USA in the late 1930s (see Box 12.5 opposite).

Box 12.5 ABOUT RUDOLF DREIKURS

Rudolf Dreikurs (1897–1972) spent his early years in Vienna, Austria. He graduated in Medicine from the University of Vienna and worked for a time with Alfred Adler.

Dreikurs emigrated to the USA in 1937, obtaining a position as Director of the Alfred Adler Institute in Chicago (Edwards, 1997). His primary interest was in child and family counselling and this work led to an interest in classroom management. Influenced by Adler's ideas about children's behaviour, Dreikurs argued that behaviour is always purposeful and directed towards social goals such as gaining status, attracting attention and achieving a sense of belonging through membership of a social group. These ideas are set out in Dreikurs's key publications *Psychology in the classroom: A manual for teachers* (Dreikurs, 1968), *A new approach to discipline* (Dreikurs & Grey, 1968) and *Discipline without tears* (Dreikurs & Cassel, 1990). In Australia and New Zealand, Dreikurs's ideas are evident in Maurice Balson's work (1992).

FIGURE 12.6 Dreikurs believed that in order to live in a democracy, children need to learn that freedom implies order and responsibility.

Dreikurs and Balson shared the neo-Adlerian idea that humans are social beings whose main desire is to belong. From these basic premises, they have argued that children have a basic need to be accepted and to belong, and in order to achieve this, human behaviour is orderly, purposeful and directed towards achieving social recognition. Misbehaviour in students is perceived to be caused by mistaken goals and misperceptions that lead to distortions in their relationships with others. Faced with such behaviour, teachers need to look not at the actual behaviour but at students' underlying motives (see Box 12.6). Teachers can also use techniques such as a sociogram (see Figure 11.4 on page 356) to study the social makeup of a class, identifying students who are socially successful and, more importantly, those who are ignored or socially rejected.

Box 12.6 CLASSROOM LINKS

Understanding student misbehaviour

According to neo-Adlerian research, children's misbehaviour is generally motivated by four possible hierarchically organised goals. Children may misbehave in order to:

- *gain attention* – using any means, both active and passive, constructive and destructive (Dreikurs, Grunwald, & Pepper, 1982)
- *overcome feelings of inferiority* – real or imagined, by exercising power and control to become model students through exaggerated conscientiousness or by competing hard to gain praise or recognition
- *exact revenge* – attempting to overcome feelings of unequal status and lack of attention by lashing out at others, destroying property, hitting other children and/or insulting the teacher
- *display feelings of inadequacy and failure* – becoming discouraged, avoiding participation in group activities, giving up to feelings of helplessness (Edwards, 1997) and appearing to others as inadequate.

A teacher's response to such behaviour in a student should be to observe the student carefully in order to identify the underlying goal motivating the behaviour. Conclusions can be verified by further observation and by questioning the student. Teachers should also examine their own reactions to the student's behaviour as well as the student's responses to correction, as these will help explain the student's underlying motives (see Table 12.3 following).

TABLE 12.3 Responses to student misbehaviour

Student's goals	Teacher's feelings	Student's reaction to correction
Seeking attention	Feels minor annoyance	Behaviour temporarily stops
Seeking power	Feels personally challenged	Behaviour persists
Seeking revenge	Feels deeply hurt	Behaviour intensifies
Displaying inadequacy	Feels like giving up	Disinterest remains

Source: Adapted from Balson (1992, p. 31).

Activities

1. Are these ideas on student misbehaviour consistent with your own beliefs about the causes of inappropriate or disturbing behaviour?
2. Observe a group of children interacting with a teacher or other adult:
   a. How does the adult respond to inappropriate behaviour?
   b. How do the children react to the adult's actions?
   c. What else could the adult do when a child behaves inappropriately?
   d. What would you do?

12.5 More about natural and logical consequences

natural consequences
Outcomes that occur without interference

logical consequences
Outcomes contrived to influence behaviour

Teachers' responses to the different motives that underlie student behaviour should include the use of both encouragement and natural or logical consequences that follow the behaviour. Procedures that can be used to encourage students include recognising and building on their strengths while minimising any weaknesses, and emphasising engagement in an activity rather than the result that is achieved (Balson, 1992). Examples include comments such as 'You seem to really enjoy your art' and 'I can tell you worked hard to prepare for your exam', rather than praise such as 'Your artwork is excellent' and 'You have the highest mark in the exam' (Edwards, 1997, p. 110). **Natural consequences** are outcomes that occur without intervention, while **logical consequences** are contrived to influence behaviour. In each case, the focus is on allowing students to experience the consequences of their actions (see Figure 12.6). For example, Balson (1992) gives the following examples of a natural consequence:

- students who do not put their equipment away in the correct place and cannot find it the next time they need it
- students who do not study for a test and then get poor marks on the test.

FIGURE 12.6
In some situations, natural consequences may not be the best option. (Source: Martin in Ward, Bochner, Center et al., 1987, p. 159.)

Examples of a logical consequence include:
- students who forget to bring required materials to a class and as a result miss out on an activity
- students who draw on a wall and then have to clean their marks off the wall.

The non-interventionist teacher

Non-interventionist teachers allow the process of development to occur naturally. The work of William Glasser (1992) and William ('Bill') Rogers (1998) represents a model of classroom management and discipline in which power is shared more equally between teacher and students than in the interventionist and interactive approaches just discussed, with greater weight on students' roles and responsibilities. A more extreme example of a non-interventionist model can be found in the form of Summerhill, A. S. Neill's school (see Box 6.6, on page 180).

William Glasser, a psychiatrist known for 'reality therapy' (Glasser, 1965) and 'control theory' (1969, 1992), became interested in behaviour management in classrooms as a result of his work with young delinquent girls in a residential institution in California (Gordon, Arthur, & Butterfield, 1996) (see Box 12.7). His educational ideas described in *Schools without failure* (Glasser, 1969) are a blend of humanist and behavioural principles. The focus is on teachers helping students to become more responsible for their own behaviour, leading to students' increased social acceptance and enhanced status among peers.

non-interventionist teacher Allows children's development to occur naturally

Box 12.7 ABOUT WILLIAM GLASSER

William Glasser (1925–) was born in Cleveland, Ohio. He gained an MA in Clinical Psychology in 1948, an MD in Psychiatry in 1953 and subsequently worked as a psychiatrist in private practice, lecturing widely on his ideas. His most influential publications include *Reality therapy* (Glasser, 1965), in which he rejected Freudian psychoanalysis for a more behaviourist approach to correcting behavioural problems; and *Control theory in the classroom* (Glasser, 1986), an extension of his ideas on reality therapy but more concerned with preventing rather than correcting discipline problems. A later book, *The quality school* (Glasser, 1992), reflects the influence of industrial-management expert W. Edwards Denning's (1982) ideas on Glasser's thinking about managing schools. Denning's ideas, which involved introducing democratic practices to Japanese factories, are considered to have contributed significantly to the success of Japanese industry after World War II. Glasser (1992) suggested that there were many similarities between traditional factory management practices and the way schools and classrooms were managed, arguing that a democratic model that values students and provides a supportive work environment is more effective, in terms of outcomes, than a hierarchical system with teachers in control and students given apparently meaningless tasks over which they have no control.

Glasser's ideas have been highly influential among educators in Australia and New Zealand. In 1989, the William Glasser Institute was established in Australia, an extension of a similar Institute in California. The influence of Glasser's approach to school discipline can be found in management and discipline policies in Australian and New Zealand schools (for example, see Balmain High School, 2003) and in the teaching and publications of Bill Rogers (1989, 1998).

FIGURE 12.7 Glasser's ideas have significantly influenced ideas about classroom management and discipline in Australia and New Zealand.

Bill Rogers (1998) sees discipline as a teacher-directed activity that seeks to 'lead, guide, direct, manage, or confront a student about behaviour that disrupts the rights of others, be they teachers or students' (Rogers, 1998, p. 11). Here, the focus is on causes of behaviour difficulties and the teacher's responsibility to guide students towards enhanced self-control, self-esteem and personal accountability for their own behaviour.

Glasser and Rogers have both argued that students misbehave because schools fail to fulfil their basic needs. These needs, clearly reflecting elements of Maslow's hierarchy of needs (see Chapter 6), include:

- *belonging* – security, comfort and group membership
- *power* – importance, status and being taken into account by others
- *freedom* – being free from the control of others, being able to choose, being self-directed and having responsibility for one's own actions
- *fun* – having satisfying and enjoyable experiences.

In helping children to meet these needs, teachers should be caring. They should help children develop friendships, give them tasks that enhance their status in the group, and allow choices that encourage self-direction and responsibility. At the same time, learning should be fun (Rogers, 1998).

Teachers as leaders

Glasser (1992) argued that teachers need to become 'lead-managers', not 'boss-managers'. To achieve this change, schools should provide the necessary tools (curriculum and resources) and atmosphere (non-coercive and cooperative). The way in which curriculum material is presented should emphasise quality schoolwork, with skills developed rather than facts learned, and achievement tests should be replaced by student self-evaluation. When disruptive behaviour occurs, Glasser proposed that teachers should try to stop the misbehaviour through use of reality therapy techniques (see Box 12.8). This approach is based on the belief that, to feel worthwhile, students must maintain a satisfactory standard of behaviour. The emphasis is on intrinsic motivation, cooperative learning strategies and, for students, the recognition of class and school rules and their own rights and responsibilities.

Box 12.8 CLASSROOM LINKS

Reality therapy techniques

Gordon, et al. (1996) suggested that to implement reality therapy in a classroom, teachers need to:
- first get to know students
- provide students with experiences that are meaningful and that satisfy their basic needs
- help students identify their inappropriate behaviour
- encourage students to evaluate their misbehaviour and its consequences
- assist students to make and stick to a plan to eliminate the problem behaviour
- avoid punishment or criticism
- meet with students and give them an opportunity to evaluate their school experiences and make any necessary changes.

Rules, rights and responsibilities

A major focus of Rogers's ideas is on the fundamental place of rules, rights and responsibilities in the operation of classroom communities. While the curriculum is a critical element in classroom management and discipline, teachers' primary goal is to develop self-control and self-discipline in students through the establishment of fair rules, coupled with understanding of personal rights and responsibilities within the framework of these rules.

Early in a school year, teachers need to discuss with students the fundamental rights that all people in the school should expect, these being:
- the right to feel safe
- the right to be treated with dignity and respect
- the right to learn and teach.

Rules are the other side of rights, and function to safeguard rights. Individual responsibility for actions at school and in the classroom ensures that rules are followed and rights are respected. When misbehaviour occurs, Rogers (1998) suggested teachers use strategies that move from least to most intrusive, depending on the seriousness of the disruption and the degree to which others' basic rights are being infringed.

12.6 More about Glasser-based school management and discipline

Strengths and limitations of classroom-management models

Strengths and limitations of the interventionist model

In the interventionist model of teaching described by Jones (1987), classroom management involves, at the class level, limit setting and responsibility training. At the school level, effective backup systems are required. In addition, teachers need to establish a well-organised classroom structure that incorporates clear rules and efficient arrangement of available space. The main strength of Jones's approach is in the detail of the procedures he identified for maximising classroom management and organisation. The main weakness, for some educators, is in the high level of control retained by the teacher, which may be intimidating for students and may lead to violent student reactions (Edwards, 1997).

Strengths and limitations of the interactionist model

One of the main strengths of the neo-Adlerian approach described by Dreikurs (1968) and Balson (1992) is its focus on students understanding why they behave as they do and the consequences of their behaviour. The interactionist approach tends to encourage a high degree of student autonomy, as well as respect between teachers and students (Edwards, 1997). One of the main weaknesses of this approach is that teachers often have difficulty recognising the motives that underlie student behaviour. Moreover, it is probably too simplistic to explain student behaviour in terms of four basic goals, and teachers may have difficulty in identifying and implementing easily understood and acceptable consequences for inappropriate behaviour.

Strengths and limitations of the non-interventionist model

The strength of the non-interventionist position presented by Glasser (1992) and Rogers (1998) is in the degree of autonomy and responsibility it gives to students, allowing them to see the consequences of their behaviour and to determine possible solutions (Gordon et al., 1996). Weaknesses concern the difficulties teachers may have in giving students increased autonomy and responsibility without at the same time feeling threatened by loss of control. It can be difficult, too, for teachers to help students who do not wish to cooperate in this approach. Solving discipline problems through class meetings can also be very time-consuming (Edwards, 1997).

Box 12.9 over the page lists some points about different classroom-management models that educators need to consider when planning classroom-management strategies.

CRITICAL REFLECTIONS

- Which of the three management styles discussed are you most familiar with from your experiences as a student and as a teacher?
- Which classroom-management style would you prefer to use as a teacher? Why?

Box 12.9 IMPLICATIONS FOR EDUCATORS

Models of classroom management in strategy planning

When planning classroom management strategies, educators need to be aware that:
- In an interventionist model, effective classroom management strategies include limit-setting, responsibility training and a well-organised classroom structure that includes clear rules and efficient use of available space, with backup support available at the school level.
- In an interactionist model, students need to understand the consequences of their behaviour and as well have a high degree of autonomy and responsibility.
- In a non-interventionist model, students need opportunities to make choices. This model encourages self-direction and responsibility in students, and includes students recognising class rules and their own rights and responsibilities.

12.7 Linking preferred classroom-management style to personal philosophy

Managing conflict and problem behaviour

Most classroom disruptions that teachers face are minor, concerning student inattention, excessive talking, unnecessary movements and so on. However, teachers are also required at times to handle more challenging behaviours in their students. Examples of such behaviours include bullying and harassment, alcohol and drug abuse, violence, stealing, truancy, racism, sexism and prejudice. Interventions designed to assist in managing such problems are in many cases primarily concerned with developing more effective prosocial behaviour and also the skills required for successful conflict resolution. Examples of the types of strategies that have been developed for school use include anger management, assertiveness training, conflict resolution and peer mediation.

Bullying

Bullying is one type of problem behaviour that teachers often have to manage in a classroom. It is a particularly vicious form of aggressive behaviour and is present to some extent in all schools. The problem of bullying in schools has been reported in Scandinavia (Olweus, 1978), Japan (Morita, 1996) and Europe (Smith & Morita, 1999) and is now recognised as an international problem for teachers and students in schools (Smith, Morita, Junger-Tas, Olweus, Catalano, & Slee, 1999). **Bullying** is an abuse of power that takes the form of ongoing aggression involving words or actions by individuals or groups and directed towards particular victims who are unable to defend themselves (Eisenberg, 1998; Smith & Morita, 1999). Bullies take advantage of situations where they can victimise others who may be physically smaller, younger, less strong, outnumbered or simply unable to defend themselves. Rubin, Bukowski & Parker (1998, p. 639) identified several defining characteristics of bullies. Typically, they have:

- strong tendencies towards aggressive behaviour
- relatively weak control over their aggressive impulses
- relatively high tolerance for aggressive behaviour.

Bullying can take place in any situation that involves a power relationship. It is a particular problem in hierarchically organised institutions such as schools. Since attendance at school is now compulsory in most countries, and many years are spent at school, most children are likely to be involved in bullying at some time during their school years, whether as perpetrator, victim or onlooker.

bullying
Ongoing aggression involving words or actions by individuals or groups and directed towards particular victims who are unable to defend themselves

The incidence of bullying

Rigby and Slee (1999, p. 326) reported data from an Australian study (Rigby, 1997) that suggested as many as one child in six or seven (20% of boys and 16% of girls) are bullied at least once a week. Another Australian study (Parada, Marsh, & Yeung, 1999) found that up to 10% of students reported being an active bully. Teachers and parents in a Western Australian study (Zubrick et al., 1997) claimed that one child in nine (11%) had been bullied during the previous 6 months, with the incidence highest among 10- to 11-year-olds and among boys rather than girls. Canadian data (see, for example, Bentley & Li, 1995; Harachi, Catalano, & Hawkins, 1999) are similar to those reported in other countries. For example, Bentley and Li found that 21% of 8- to 12-year-olds were bullied while 12% bullied other children. Very high rates of bullying have been reported in New Zealand (Lind & Maxwell, 1996; Sullivan, 1999), and bullying – together with truancy, suspensions and exclusions – has been identified as a factor associated with poor achievement of at-risk students in that country (NZ Ministry of Education, 2001a). Whitney and Smith (1993) reported that 27% of primary school students in England and Wales claim to have been bullied at least *sometimes* and an additional 10% have been bullied once a week or more often.

Gender and age are strongly associated with reported incidents of bullying (see tables 12.4, 12.5 and 12.6 in Box 12.10 below). Rates are generally higher among children aged around 8 to 9 years, increasing in the first year of secondary school for boys and then decreasing steadily in the later secondary years. For girls, bullying occurs most frequently at around 8 years of age, decreasing steadily after that. Students from minority group backgrounds and those with disabilities are particularly vulnerable to bullying (Smith, Sharp, & Cowie, 1994; Whitney, Smith, & Thompson, 1994).

12.8 More data on the incidence of bullying in schools

Box 12.10 RESEARCH LINKS

Bullying in schools

Finding out how much bullying occurs in schools can be difficult. Rigby (1996) reports that the Peer Relations Questionnaire (PRQ) (Rigby & Slee, 1995) has been used in a number of studies to obtain information from students about bullying at school (see Rigby & Slee, 1999). The questionnaire is anonymous (no names are given) and is administered in a group situation. Rigby (1996) reports that the PRQ's reliability is demonstrated by the consistency of students' answers to questions that are similar in content. The PRQ's validity is demonstrated in the close agreement among answers to questions that ask students to nominate others who are bullies or the victims of bullies, and self-reports about the experience of bullying or being bullied (Rigby, 1996, p. 32).

Tables 12.4, 12.5 and 12.6 give examples from data derived through administering the PRQ in 1993 and 1994 to over 6000 male and 2500 female students attending 16 schools in South Australia, Victoria, New South Wales and Queensland.

TABLE 12.4 Forms of bullying experienced 'often' during the school year

Reported experience	Percentages Boys	Girls
Being called hurtful names	12.6	11.5
Being teased in an unpleasant manner	11.3	10.6
Being left out of things on purpose	5.8	9.5
Being hit or kicked	5.9	2.9
Being threatened with harm	5.4	3.2

Source: Rigby (1996, Table 2.1).

TABLE 12.5	Incidence of reported victimisation among school children		
		Percentages	
		Boys	**Girls**
Every day		1.8	0.9
Most days		4.4	3.8
Once or twice a week		6.8	5.2
Once a week		6.3	5.1
Less than once a week		29.2	27.6
Never		51.4	57.4

Source: Rigby and Slee (1995; reproduced in Rigby, 1996, Table 2.2).

TABLE 12.6	Gender of the bully or bullies – percentages in each category			
		Reported bullies		
		Always a boy	Always a girl	Sometimes a boy, sometimes a girl
Boys reporting being victimised		69.0	3.9	27.1
Girls reporting being victimised		24.1	24.5	51.4

Source: Rigby (1996, Table 2.5).

Activities

1. What trends can you identify from tables 12.4, 12.5 and 12.6 in relation to the gender of students who are victims of bullying?
2. What forms of bullying do boys experience most often? What about girls? Can you explain any differences? What is the relationship of gender to being a bully and to being bullied?
3. What methods might someone use to collect information about the incidence of bullying in schools? What might be the strengths and limitations of these methods?
4. How might information like that in tables 12.4, 12.5 and 12.6 be used by educators in planning an anti-bullying program for a school?
5. Think about a classroom, scout group, soccer team, after-school-care group or any other group of children you are familiar with. Are you aware of any form of bullying or victimisation within this group? What procedures might you use to find out if any form of victimisation and bullying was occurring in the group?

Forms of bullying

It is generally agreed that bullying can take many forms (see Table 12.4). These include:
- *verbal forms,* such as ridicule and sexual harassment that involves name calling
- *psychological forms,* such as being isolated or subject to gossip and hurtful rumours
- *physical forms,* such as being hit or physically threatened, or having property damaged or stolen.

Bullying occurs as often in one-on-one situations as it does in group encounters, with the term 'mobbing' used to describe bullying that involves groups (Porter, 2000). Most bullying occurs in the playground, particularly at the primary level, with less than half occurring as children travel between home and school (Smith & Morita, 1999). Boys are usually seen as involved more often than girls in bullying incidents, both as aggressors and victims (Smith & Morita, 1999). Girls are more likely to use and experience indirect or psychological forms of aggression (Björkqvist, Lagerspetz, & Kaukiaöinen, 1992; Björkqvist & Osterman, 1999; Owens & McMullin, 1995). However, gender-based variations in aggressive behaviour at school may simply reflect age-related differences in development, with more sophisticated, indirect aggressive strategies used first by girls, who generally mature earlier than boys (Owens, 1996). Whatever the form of bullying, it always involves a problem in the relative power among those involved in such incidents.

Effects of bullying

Student responses to bullying vary widely, with a study by Rigby and Slee (1999) finding about half (55% of boys and 40% of girls) reporting that bullying did not really worry them – although these percentages almost halved when the frequency of bullying was at least once a week (Rigby & Slee, 1999). Boys were more likely to report that bullying made them angry, while girls reported that it tended to make them sad. Zubrick and colleagues (1997) found that students who are bullied are more likely to have poor academic performance, high rates of absenteeism, low self-esteem and significant mental health problems when compared with students who are not bullied (see also Forero, McLellan, Rissel, & Bauman, 1999; Perry, Perry & Kennedy, 1992; Rigby, 1994; Slee, 1995a, 1995b). Victims of bullying also tend to be anxious, insecure and isolated from their peer groups (Olweus, 1993). Research findings on the effects of bullying on aggression levels are equivocal: some researchers have found that victims are less likely to be aggressive (Olweus, 1993), while others indicate that bullying victims typically demonstrate high levels of aggression themselves (Perry et al., 1992).

While victims of bullying typically experience low self-esteem, aggressive adolescents and bullies who repeatedly victimise others have been found to have high self-esteem (Olweus, 1997). Those who bully others also score high on measures of social and physical self-concept, and typically overestimate their levels of social competence and the quality of their relationships with significant others (Edens, 1999). Few students tell their teachers about bullying incidents (reporting occurs more often at the primary level). However, girls in particular sometimes tell parents, and more often friends. This can sometimes lead to the situation improving, mainly where younger students are involved. It seems that older students, particularly boys, are less likely to inform others because they have little faith in any positive outcome from this action (Harachi et al., 1999; Neuman, Murray, & Lussier, 2001; Rigby & Slee, 1999; Whitney & Smith, 1993).

12.9 The impact of bullying on victims

FIGURE 12.8
Bullying can involve groups as well as individuals. How might you intervene to prevent this situation occurring?

Interventions to reduce bullying

Traditionally, schools have tended to ignore bullying (Zubrick et al., 1997). Children are loath to report incidents to adults, and teachers underestimate or disbelieve estimates of the prevalence of bullying and its effects on those involved (see Figure 12.8). Research cited by Johnson and Johnson (1996) suggested that students left to resolve conflict without assistance or training in peer mediation or conflict resolution tend to:

- leave the conflict unresolved
- ask an adult to help resolve the conflict
- achieve resolution through one of the protagonists 'winning'.

Failure to report bullying is often an outcome of loyalty to those who are accused as perpetrators rather than to those who are the victims, who are often seen as weak, unable to protect themselves and not to be believed. Programs to counteract bullying, with associated funding and resources, have attracted community attention in the past decade, and a number of intervention models have been developed (see, for example, Berne, 1996; Rigby, 1996, 2001; Slee, 1996; Suckling & Temple, 2001).

Classroom arrangements that provide opportunities for students to work together in cooperative groups have also been used as a means of reducing the incidence of bullying. Cowie, Smith, Boulton and Laver (1994), reported a case study concerning the use of a cooperative group-learning strategy ('cooperative group work', or 'CGW') in a class of 8- to 9-year-old middle-school students in an ethnically mixed (Asian and Caucasian) school in northern England. The study was conducted over 2 school years, and aimed to improve ethnic and social relationships within the class (see Box 12.11, which is based on material reported by teachers, together with the results of quantitative and qualitative assessment of students' academic achievement, social experiences and attitudes towards ethnic groups).

Box 12.11 CASE STUDY

Case study of a bully

At the beginning of the project, Mark was 9 years old, tall for his age and physically fit. One of his hobbies was practising karate. It seemed that he tended to view the world as a threatening place and thought it necessary to be ready to defend himself.

* * *

Mark had bullied other children since he was in first school. He could recall, without apparent emotion, an incident from the past when he acted aggressively towards Ali:

Mark: When it was my ball, I brought it to school. He goes, 'I'll pop it,' and I said, 'I'll pop *your* brain!' Then he popped it and I gave him one ... [pauses] he had a broken nose. I broke his nose!

Interviewer: You broke his nose?

Mark: He was on the floor before it got broken. I just stamped on it like that.

Interviewer: You stamped on his nose? Were you sorry afterwards?

Mark: No ... He admitted that he started the fight ...

This pattern of responding to other children with a strong counter-attack persisted throughout the first year of the project. He usually showed no remorse for his overreactions and always seemed convinced that the victim deserved all he got, even when there was no obvious provocation. Here is how Shoukat, a boy nominated by 75% of his classmates as a victim, described his experience of being with Mark:

When I'm doing good work, Mark and Yussef start confusing me, like calling me nasty names and pushing my chair. Or they get a piece of paper and tear it and tell Miss I did it. That's what they did today. I think why they're doing it is just that they are jealous. Like they got hold of my chair and started pushing it. I said 'Stop it!' but they wouldn't so I moved my chair to the other side of the table so they couldn't push it, and then Miss moved them, because they were messing about.

At that time, other children tried confronting Mark with specific examples of aggressive behaviour but he did not then find it easy to listen to honest feedback and reacted angrily to any hint of criticism from others ... During the first year of the project no one, it seemed, had been able to challenge Mark.

* * *

[By the end of the first year] Mark seemed to be a little more able to deal with the interactions within his group and was certainly less physically aggressive towards the others. However, he still showed very little capacity to be supportive towards others and a continuing tendency to use insults towards his peers, some of which appeared to be racist.

[At the start of the new year] Mark had become subdued. He was no longer having so many outbursts but was complaining of being bullied himself. This was confirmed by peer nominations towards the end of the year ...

Mark remained acutely aware of the dominance hierarchies within the class and was unable to benefit greatly from the potential for power-sharing and collaboration [that cooperative group work] can offer.

Source: Cowie et al. (1994, pp. 166–170).

Activities

1 Would you consider the strategy used with Mark to have been successful?
2 What further steps would be needed to avoid further inappropriate or bullying behaviour?
3 How would you help Mark become more fully and positively integrated with his peer group?

Bullying is generally seen as a school-based problem rather than as something intrinsic to the particular children involved, so intervention programs typically take a school-wide approach. This is supported by the inclusion of bullying as a specific focus in policy statements at the levels of school system and individual school. Freedom from any form of violence, including bullying and harassment, is generally part of a school's discipline policy, and often appears as an element in policy concerned with student safety in schools. Strategies introduced to counteract school bullying include modifying school curriculum to increase awareness of bullying, introducing exercises that promote alternative forms of social interaction so as to avoid conflict, changing school environments to reduce bullying opportunities, peer counselling, assertiveness training, anger-management training and instruction on conflict resolution.

Conflict or dispute-resolution procedures used in schools include peer conferencing or peer mediation (Johnson & Johnson, 1996; Van der Kley & Burn, 1993). Here, students are left to settle their disagreements between themselves, assisted by peer mediators who arrange for the disputing parties to meet and who help in drawing up agreements or contracts to settle the dispute. A Dutch program called Rock and Water has been used in some Australian schools as a means of reducing bullying and enhancing self-esteem (Tabakoff, 2002, see Box 12.12 below). Other approaches include anger management, assertiveness training and conflict resolution (Girard & Koch, 1996; Ransom, 2001, see Box 12.13 over the page). An anti-violence curriculum has been proposed by Jenkin (1996). With the wider introduction of such procedures in schools, it may be possible to reduce the incidence of bullying and other aggressive and violent behaviours, and make schools safer, happier and more effective places for students and teachers.

CRITICAL REFLECTIONS

- Have you observed or been affected by bullying at school? How was it dealt with, if at all?
- Discuss your experiences and observations with others in your group.

12.10 More examples of anti-bullying programs

Box 12.12 CLASSROOM LINKS

The Rock and Water program

Tabakoff (2002), in a newspaper series on 'class acts' in schools, reported that some high schools are using the Rock and Water approach to overcome problems in bullying and aggression among students. One school explained that 'Year 8 was our target group for boys because they were the ones who were most aggressive.'

Tabakoff went on to say:

> One popular exercise is known as Chinese boxing, a hand-tapping exercise in which one boy tries to knock another off balance using techniques such as feinting, ducking or stepping back unexpectedly. The person who wins is the one who retains balance, so it is important for boys to maintain calm and equilibrium. The 'rock' technique of hitting is no guarantee of victory.

Boys are encouraged to view confrontation in a rock and water way, weighing up when a co-operative or passive approach might work best.

Tabakoff reported a teacher involved in implementing the program as commenting that 'A lot of these boys realised that being angry and macho was actually a negative, and that being calm in a crisis or a difficult situation was a lot more rewarding.'

Tabakoff quoted a student who had done the program as saying: 'It changed the way I thought about people who thought it was fun to pick on you … You can sit back and think, "They're only doing it for attention really".' Tabakoff reported another student as saying: 'Some people at school think they are the hard-cores. But if you think about it, the ones who can walk away from a fight are the strong ones.'

Source: Adapted from Tabakoff (2002, p. 4).

Box 12.13 CLASSROOM LINKS

Implementing a conflict-resolution strategy

An early example of training in conflict-resolution skills was implemented in a Quaker Education Unit in New York in 1972 (Johnson & Johnson, 1996, p. 459). Children were taught that the strength of a non-violent response to conflict lay in 'justice, caring and personal integrity' (p. 460). Similar programs have been developed to teach non-violence as a response to conflict through the use of conflict-resolution skills.

Examples of tasks used in such training are set out below. Students given these problems are expected to find a resolution through working with a mediator and using strategies such as exchanging information, explaining major concerns about the conflict situation, negotiating alternative actions and problem solving.

Conflict situations

1. A student has a **teacher** who speaks English well, but with an accent. The student mimics the teacher during class.
2. A student with an Aboriginal background is called an 'Abo' by an Anglo-Australian student during an angry exchange over the use of a computer. The **teacher** is unsure what to do.
3. At lunchtime, Jake and Joey are playing with others on a slippery-slide in the school playground. Both boys know the school rule about only one child being allowed on the slide at a time. Jake sits at the top of the slide and shouts out that he is king of the castle and will not come down. Joey shouts at him, calling him a crude name. The **teacher** on playground duty sees them fighting.
4. A **parent** comes to the school to see her child's teacher. The teacher thinks the child is very badly behaved. The parent thinks the child can do no wrong.
5. A student in Grade 5 is told by her **teacher** to stop talking and sit down. The student tells the teacher to shut up and refuses to sit down. The rest of the class looks on in silence.
6. Year 10 students are given an exercise that requires cooperation and planning within a **group**. It also requires a group presentation to the class and is part of the assessment for that class. A student in one of the groups will not cooperate with group members. The uncooperative student gives a very sloppy and inadequate presentation with the result that the group gets a poor mark.

Source: Adapted from Girard and Koch (1996, p. 49).

Activities

1. Form groups of at least 4 people and consider the six conflict situations. For each situation, consider what the person in **bold** should do. One person in your group should role-play the target teacher or parent, another should take the role of the mediator, and the rest of the group should represent students or observers. Role-play each scenario and try to answer the following questions:
   a. What is the conflict about?
   b. Who needs to be involved in resolving the conflict?
   c. Should the conflict be dealt with through direct action or intervention?
   d. Is negotiation or mediation appropriate?
   e. Would a consensus process, where agreement is sought within the group as a whole, be appropriate? (See Box 12.14 opposite.)
2. For this activity, it is a good idea to work in a small group or with a partner. The steps are as follows:
   a. Find a definition for 'conflict' that everyone in the group accepts. Note that conflict is neither positive nor negative.
   b. Still within the group, think of some metaphors for conflict, such as 'a clenched fist', 'a battle' or 'an onion' (many layers).
   c. Consider ways in which conflict might be managed using the metaphors as a framework.
   d. Decide how metaphorical solutions might be translated into practical solutions (for example, using a white flag from the battle metaphor to represent a sign of peace in one of the six scenarios).

Strengths and limitations of conflict- and problem-behaviour-management interventions

Strengths

Following training, the number of students who resolve their conflicts by discussion and agreement increases, and teachers report that students use conflict-resolution skills spontaneously (Johnson & Johnson, 1996). In addition, there is evidence that training in conflict resolution when conducted in the context of curriculum areas such as English literature and history can increase students' academic achievement.

Training in skills such as peer mediation and conflict resolution has the potential to reduce the number of student conflicts occurring in school. This in turn should lead to a reduction in the number of students suspended and excluded from school.

Limitations

Limitations that have been reported regarding the efficacy of interventions such as peer mediation and conflict resolution suggest that skills students learn in such training programs may not be maintained over time, nor may they generalise into other situations, either at school or at home. This lack of sustainment and generalisation may continue to be a factor until more is known about how conflicts develop and how students manage such conflicts, with and without others' help.

Some strategies that can be used in situations of classroom conflict are set out in Box 12.14.

Box 12.14 IMPLICATIONS FOR EDUCATORS

Strategies for consensus building

1. *Prepare for a meeting to reach consensus about a problem.* Consult group members to identify possible solutions; develop an agenda from among the group and prioritise these items.
2. *Begin the meeting.* Get everyone's attention, agree on the goals for the meeting, and explain the consensus-building process.
3. *Define the issues and set an agenda.* Have one person introduce the first item and the issues it raises. Ask for others to comment, raise additional issues or reframe the issues.
4. *Uncover hidden interests.* Ask participants what elements must be present or what interests satisfied. Try to get group members to agree that they will accept those elements as the criteria that a solution must meet.
5. *Generate options.* Ask for ideas about possible solutions or options that might satisfy stated interests. Use brainstorming, open discussion, what others have done, private thinking and trial-and-error suggestions.
6. *Assess options.* Review interests, needs and concerns. Discuss and evaluate proposed solutions. Have participants state 'What I like about …'
7. *Reach an agreement.* Eliminate solutions that do not meet the criteria or are unacceptable. Combine options that meet all participants' needs. Test for agreement by restating the proposed solution. If no agreement is reached, go back to an earlier step to rework the issues. When agreement is reached, restate and confirm agreement to the solution.
8. *Implement the agreement.* Review it, then identify and agree upon the steps that are needed to implement it.
9. *Monitor implementation.* Make sure all agreements, implementation steps and monitoring procedures are in writing. Design a monitoring procedure.
10. *Evaluate the meeting.* Determine what went well and what could be done to improve the consensus-building process.

Source: Adapted from Girard and Koch (1996, p. 107).

CRITICAL REFLECTIONS

- Do you consider consensus building a viable alternative in managing classroom disagreements and conflicts?
- In what types of situation do you think consensus building would be most useful?
- Identify some of the main strengths and weaknesses of consensus building.

Concluding comments

The classroom is a complex microcosm of society in which many new relationships are formed. Within this context, the learning process needs to be carefully planned and managed in order for it to be meaningful and to meet the needs of a diverse range of students. As a teacher, your task is to find a philosophical approach to classroom management and organisation that is congruent with your personal values and beliefs, and that will support the development and learning of students from different cultural and socioeconomic backgrounds, as well as that of students with different attitudes, motivations and life experiences. The challenge of learning how to manage student behaviour and provide a safe and effective learning environment is one that even experienced teachers can find daunting. When the challenge is met successfully, learning becomes a satisfying and enjoyable experience. Then, the classroom has an atmosphere of cooperation, balance and mutual trust, and teachers are positive and enthusiastic about their teaching.

Chapter review

- Classroom management is concerned with the planning, organisation and control of learners; the learning process, including learning goals and the strategies used to reach them; and a learning space that includes a physical setting, furniture and resources, and participants' emotions, attitudes and social dynamics.
- All teachers encounter challenges with classroom management and discipline, and over time develop strategies for responding to these situations. Schools usually have policies that set out general guidelines for student management, welfare and discipline.
- Most of the discipline difficulties teachers face in their classrooms involve minor disruptions such as unnecessary talking, inattentiveness and disobedience. Serious behaviours, such as physical violence, are more rare.
- Procedures for handling disruptive behaviour in the classroom have changed over time, from widespread use of corporal punishment to a greater focus on curriculum and an array of classroom-based options, including suspension and exclusion as a last resort.
- Classroom teachers need to identify their own set of beliefs about how children learn and how classrooms should be managed.
- Philosophies that teachers can follow include the interventionist, interactionist and non-interventionist model of teaching. Each involves a different level of control being exercised by the teacher over a class.
- Bullying, involving the abuse of power, is a serious form of inappropriate behaviour in schools.
- Bullying is generally more common among boys, and in children aged around 8–9 years, than among those in other age groups. It decreases in frequency through the secondary years.
- Strategies used to combat bullying include anger management, assertiveness training, conflict resolution and peer mediation.

You make the connections:

Questions and activities for self-assessment and discussion

1. Identify some of the characteristics of classroom environments that influence teaching and learning. What can teachers do to control these factors' effects on classroom activities?
2. Set up a debate with your tutorial group on the topic: 'Disruptive and inappropriate behaviour at school is the product of a child's home background.'
3. Ask some teachers to identify the classroom behaviours they find most difficult and disruptive. What strategies do they use to manage such behaviours? Can you identify the type of management philosophy each teacher is using? To what extent are these philosophies eclectic?
4. Think about a classroom you are familiar with. Redesign the space, arranging the teacher's and students' desks and chairs, storage cupboards and activity centres to suit your teaching philosophy. Repeat this task in your tutorial group. Are there basic elements of classroom design that you all agree on? In what ways do your plans differ?
5. Identify some of the main philosophies of classroom management. What are the key factors that distinguish these different models? In what ways are the models different?
6. Define 'bullying' and outline some of the steps that can be taken to eliminate it.

Key terms

pedagogy	emotional disturbance	interactive teacher
classroom management	interventionist teacher	natural consequences
discipline	limit-setting strategies	logical consequences
inappropriate behaviour	responsibility training	non-interventionist teacher
disruptive behaviour	backup system	bullying
behaviour disturbance	classroom structure	

Recommended reading

Balson, M. (1992). *Understanding classroom behaviour* (3rd ed.). Melbourne: ACER.
Conway, R. (1998). Meeting the needs of students with behavioural and emotional disorders. In A. Ashman and J. Elkins (Eds.), *Educating children with special needs* (3rd ed.). Sydney: Prentice-Hall.
Gordon, C., Arthur, M., & Butterfield, N. (1996). *Promoting positive behaviour: An Australian guide to classroom management*. Melbourne: Nelson.
Olweus, D. (1993). *Bullying in schools*. Oxford: Blackwell.
Porter, L. (2000). *Student behaviour: Theory and practice for teachers*. St Leonards, NSW: Allen & Unwin.
Rigby, K. (2002). *Stop the bullying: A handbook for schools*. Melbourne: ACER.
Rigby, K. (2002). *A meta-evaluation of methods and approaches to reducing bullying in pre-schools and early primary schools in Australia*. Barton, ACT: National Crime Authority, <www.ncp.gov.au/Publications/meta.pdf>.
Rogers, W. A. (1998). *'You know the fair rule' and much more: Strategies for making the hard job of discipline and behaviour management in school easier*. Melbourne: ACER.
Slee, R. (1995). *Changing theories and practices of discipline*. London: Falmer Press.

Suckling, A., & Temple, C. (2001). *Bullying: A whole school approach*. Melbourne: ACER.
Van der Kley, M., & Burn, W. (1993). *The positive playground: How to improve school discipline and enhance school tone*. Christchurch, New Zealand: Van der Kley.
Wragg, E. C. (1993). *Classroom management*. London: Routledge.

Make some online visits

Kids Helpline Australia on Bullying: <www.kidshelp.com.au/info7/Bully.htm>
Bullying in schools and what to do about it: <www.education.unisa.edu.au/bullying/>
Balmain High School Discipline Document:
   <www2.edfac.usyd.edu.au/LocalResource/schooldocs/balmain.html>
State of Victoria (Department of Education and Training):
   <www.eduweb.vic.gov.au/bullying/index.htm>
YouthLaw Tino Rangatiratanga Taitamariki: <www.youthlaw.co.nz/school_B6.html>
NZ Ministry of Education:
   <www.mimedu.govt.nz/index.cfm?layout=document&document=6912&data=1>

Glossary

A

Aboriginal English   A language distinct from Standard Australian English, and having many variants in different Aboriginal communities

accommodation   Using fresh information to form a new mental model or scheme

achievement motivation   The need to strive for success

active listening   Attending purposefully to the meaning and intention of what another person is saying

adaptation   The process of adjusting to new situations and experiences through the modification of existing schemes (assimilation) or the creation of new schemes (accommodation)

adolescence   The period between childhood and adulthood

adolescent egocentrism   The tendency in adolescence to assume that others share one's thoughts and feelings

affect   Attitudes and feelings, such as happiness or resentment

anecdotal record   Objective description of behaviour at a particular time and place, recorded as soon as possible after the behaviour has occurred

antecedent   An event that precedes a behaviour

antecedent-behaviour-consequence (A-B-C)   Behaviour represented as an ongoing chain of activity involving events that immediately precede the behaviour and that follow it

anxiety   Feelings of tension, uneasiness and apprehension

applied behaviour analysis (ABA)   The use of behavioural principles to change behaviour

aptitude-treatment interaction   The relationship between learner characteristics and the characteristics of the learning situation

arousal   Alertness and attentiveness

assessment   The purposeful gathering, interpreting, recording and communicating of information about student achievement

assimilation   Adjusting an existing mental model or scheme to fit a new experience

associationism   An explanation of learning as the formation of connections between stimuli and responses

asynchronous communication   Electronic communication between individuals who are not talking in real time (such as in email and listserv discussion groups)

attention deficit hyperactivity disorder (ADHD)   High levels of activity, impulsivity, short attention span, learning difficulties and poor social skills

attribution theories   Theories concerned with the way in which an individual's explanations of success and failure influence subsequent motivation and behaviour

authentic assessment   A mode of assessment that uses tasks similar to those performed in the real world

autonomous morality   Moral reasoning that appreciates the perspectives of others and the motives behind their words and actions

axon   The long 'arm' of a neuron that carries messages to other cells by means of electrical impulses

B

backup system   A set of hierarchically ordered penalties for misbehaviour

basic emotions   Babies are born with the ability to express basic emotions such as happiness, sadness, anger and fear

basic needs   Lower-level or deficit needs, such as the need for food, safety, love and respect

behaviour   Actions that are observable and measurable

behaviour disturbance   Significant abnormalities in the behaviour of an individual who does not have a diagnosable psychiatric illness

behavioural objectives   An instructional goal stated in terms of observable and measurable behaviour

being needs (B-needs)   Growth needs that motivate individuals to achieve personal fulfilment and self-actualisation

bottom-up approaches   Teaching approaches that emphasise the development of individual skills that can be built up towards competence in the overall task

British Infant Schools   Classes for children aged 5 to 8 years in British schools, usually providing an informal, open approach to learning with student-selected activities

bullying   Ongoing aggression involving words or actions by individuals or groups and directed towards particular victims who are unable to defend themselves

C

cardinality   The principle that when counting, the last number counted represents the total

centration   Concentrating attention on one aspect of a stimulus while ignoring other features

cerebral cortex   The outer layer of the brain, which is responsible for human intelligence

cerebral palsy   An outcome of brain damage prior to birth, resulting in disorders of movement and posture

chaining   When one action functions both as a reinforcer for the previous action and as a stimulus for the next

character education   An approach to education based on the philosophy that values can be conveyed to students through discipline and modelling

checklist   A set of descriptions of specific behaviours that an observer records as present or not present

child-directed speech   A type of speech directed to young children, characterised by high pitch, short and well-spaced sentences, simple vocabulary, and exaggerated intonation

chronosystem   Changes in environments and processes over time, which influence development

class inclusion   Understanding that a number of small collections can be combined in different ways to form a larger collection

classical conditioning   The association of an automatic response with a new stimulus

classification   The ability to mentally group objects in terms of similar characteristics; for example, pansies, daffodils and roses are all 'flowers'

classroom management   The planning, organisation and control of learners, the learning process and the classroom environment to create and maintain an effective learning experience

classroom structure   The rules, daily routines and physical organisation and environment of a classroom

clique A group whose members associate regularly on the basis of affection, common interests and shared identity

cognition The mental processes involved in perceiving, attending to, understanding and recalling information

cognitive apprenticeship An 'apprentice' learner or novice is guided by an expert

cognitive behaviour modification Use of behavioural strategies and cognitive processes to change behaviour

cognitive learning theory Concerned with internal mental processes and how learners manipulate information during learning

cognitive style The way an individual tends to perceive and process information

collectivistic culture Typically group-centred, viewing individuals in terms of their relationships, roles and responsibilities in the community

compensation The ability to see that an increase in one dimension (such as height) is compensated for by a decrease in another dimension (such as width)

compensatory programs Educational programs designed to offset the limitations associated with educational disadvantage or difference

computer literacy Basic computer skills; having an understanding of what a computer is and how to use it

computer-assisted instruction (CAI) Where a computer and its software operate as a tutor; also known as 'computer-based instruction' (CBI), or 'computer-assisted learning' (CAL)

computer-mediated communication (CMC) The use of computer technologies to communicate

concrete operations stage Piaget's third stage, in which a child is able to mentally manipulate and think logically about objects that are present

conditional knowledge *Knowing when and how* to use different types of knowledge

conditioned response (CR) A response evoked by a conditioned stimulus

conditioned stimulus (CS) A previously neutral stimulus that elicits a conditioned response after pairing with an unconditioned stimulus

conditioning The establishment of a new association between a stimulus and a response

connectionist model Views the brain as a complex network of interconnected units of information, with information stored in patterns of connectivity

consequence An event that follows a behaviour

consequential validity A test that has the effect of improving student performance in a curriculum area

conservation The ability to see that certain characteristics (size, height, length, amount) of an object do not change with changes in the object's physical appearance

construct validity A measure of the link between a test and underlying knowledge, attitudes and skills

constructivism An explanation of learning that views it as a self-regulated process that builds on learners' existing knowledge and in which learners are active participants

content validity A measure of the link between a test and relevant curriculum objectives

contiguity The association of two events that are always closely paired or that repeatedly occur at about the same time

contingency Reinforcement that is only given when the target behaviour is produced

conventional morality Being a good member of society and helping those close to you is a priority

cooperative learning The organisation of classroom activities so that students must cooperate in order to gain contingent rewards

creativity Exceptional ability to produce novel or original ideas or outcomes

criterion-referenced assessment Where achievement is compared against a specified criterion or standard

critical reflection Analysing what we are thinking and learning by questioning assumptions, perspectives and values related to our thoughts or to new information

cueing Using a specific stimulus to elicit a desired response

culture Systems of knowledge, beliefs, values and behaviour shared by a group of people

culture-sensitive or culture-fair test A test that does not require culturally based knowledge

curriculum-based assessment Assessment that compares individual students' performance with curriculum goals

D

declarative knowledge *Knowing that* certain facts, information and experiences exist and are real

deductive reasoning Using rules or general principles to find general solutions to specific problems

deferred imitation Actions copied from models no longer present, the actions having previously been observed and remembered

deficit needs (D-needs) Basic needs that motivate individuals to action in order to reduce or eliminate the need

dendrites Branch-like protrusions from a neuron that receive messages from other cells

deviation IQ An IQ score that compares an individual's performance on a test with the expected average performance of someone in the same age group

diagnostic assessment Checks made to determine why students make particular mistakes

direct assessment Criterion-referenced or mastery tests that assess specific content from a clearly defined curriculum

direct observation Purposeful, focused looking and listening

disability A restriction resulting from something that is damaged and no longer functional

discipline A system of rewards and punishments for managing behaviour

discovery learning The learner actively manipulates materials or ideas in the learning environment and discovers connections between them

discrimination Learning that it is appropriate to respond to some stimuli but not to others

disequilibrium Cognitive imbalance resulting from inconsistency between what is known and expected, and something strange and unexpected

disruptive behaviour Behaviour that is problematic or inappropriate in the context of a given activity or for a certain teacher

distributed cognition The notion that cognition is shared by individuals who make up communities and who share cultural tools

distributed learning (computer-mediated instruction, or CMI) Where teachers, students and learning resources can be in different locations so learning and teaching occur independently of time and place

Down syndrome A chromosomal disorder associated with intellectual impairment and distinctive facial characteristics

E

early intervention programs Programs designed to enhance development of infants and young children who are developmentally delayed or at risk of delay

educational psychology A branch of psychology concerned with studying how people learn and the implications for teaching

educational risk Students in danger of failure at school as a result of underachievement

educational technology The use of tools, materials and processes to enhance learning – includes blackboard, chalk and computers

egocentrism An individual's belief that everyone sees the world in exactly the same way as that individual

emergent literacy Understandings about and attitudes towards reading and writing, which are the precursors of acquiring those skills

emotion Occurs when we evaluate an event as relevant to our concerns or goals. Usually experienced as a mental state, emotion is closely connected to behaviour

emotional disturbance Evident from inappropriate behaviours that require psychiatric treatment in the form of ongoing therapy

emotional intelligence The ability to recognise and understand emotions

episodic memory Memory for personal events in our lives

equilibration Achieving cognitive balance between what is familiar and known, and what is new or unfamiliar, through the processes of assimilation and accommodation

ethnicity Membership of a group according to race, nationality or religious background

evaluation The process of making judgements about relative or absolute worth

exosystem Settings in which the child is not involved, but which nonetheless influence the child's development

expansion Parents' tendency to respond to young children's utterances by restating them in a more elaborate form

extinction Reduction and cessation of a response following the withdrawal of reinforcement

extrinsic motivation Motivation arising from the use of external rewards such as food or praise

F

face validity The degree to which a test appears to measure what it is intended to measure

field dependence A cognitive style related to perceiving items, events or information as an integral part of a broader context (or 'field')

field independence The tendency to perceive individual items, events or pieces of information analytically, and as distinct from the broader context (or 'field')

fine motor skills Movement skills using small muscle groups

formal operations stage Piaget's fourth stage, in which the individual is now able to think abstractly and logically, to form hypotheses and to solve problems systematically

formative assessment Informal checks that are designed to give feedback about the immediate outcomes of learning, and to guide further instruction

frequency distribution The number of times each score occurs in a range of possible scores

friendship A voluntary relationship, characterised by reciprocity of affection

functional-organisational approach An approach that views emotions as shaping and organising thoughts and behaviours

G

gender Those aspects of an individual that relate to the individual's sex, including biological and cultural influences

gender schema theory A theory proposing that children's schemas or understandings about gender influence the way they process information and their choices

general mental capacity (g) Basic intellectual capacity

generalisation Learning to respond to stimuli that are similar to but not the same as those that previously triggered a response

gifted Exceptional general aptitude or ability

goal-directed or intentional action A sequence of acts produced intentionally to achieve a desired outcome

gross motor skills Movement skills using large muscle groups

group An exchange involving several interacting individuals who have formed a relationship and who have some degree of reciprocal influence over one another

growth needs Higher-level, or 'being' needs, such as the need for self-actualisation

Guilford's structure-of-intellect model Classification of intellectual abilities as mental operation (process), type of stimulus material (content) and form (product)

H

handicap A restriction that limits a person's capacity to function normally

heteronomous morality Moral decisions based on the rules of authority figures such as parents

hidden curriculum Understandings, values and attitudes that are implicit in school structures and in the way material is taught

high support needs A need for considerable assistance to participate at school and in daily life

horizontal decalage Gradual development within a cognitive stage, as demonstrated in the gradual attainment of the different aspects of conservation within the concrete operations stage

humanism An orientation or philosophy that is primarily concerned with human rather than spiritual matters

hyperactivity Excessive movement, restlessness and distractibility

hyperlink Text (that is, words or symbols) that when activated by a mouse click allow the user access to the relevant linked information

hypermedia A system that links pieces of information such as text, sound, visual images, animation and video in electronic environments

hypertext A system of computer coding that links pieces of information online

I

identity An internal self-structure in which we organise our beliefs, abilities, needs and self-perceptions

identity achievement Occurs when adolescents explore several identity roles, but resolve conflicts and feel comfortable with who they are and who they hope to be

identity diffusion Occurs when young people have little direction, their life and career goals are unclear, and they do not know who they are or who they want to be

identity foreclosure Describes adolescents who typically form their identity by adopting the occupational and ideological goals of significant others, often their parents

impairment Implies that something is damaged but still functional

impulsivity Having a cognitive preference for rapid problem solving

inappropriate behaviour A behaviour that interferes with a student's own learning and/or disrupts the class

inclusion The idea that all students should be educated in regular classrooms, regardless of the type or level of severity of their disabilities

Individual Education Plan (IEP) A planned program of instruction for an individual student, based on assessed needs, strengths and interests

individualistic culture Focuses on the self as an autonomous individual; successful pursuit of individual goals is valued

inductive reasoning Inducing general rules or principles from observation of specific examples

information and communication technology (ICT) An array of technologies including electronic hardware, software and network connectivity

information literacy The ability to locate, evaluate and use information; extends beyond technical skills

information processing model Likens the human mind to a computer that interprets, stores and retrieves information

information technology (IT) Refers to computers and their applications and is part of the larger group of ICTs

informed consent Agreement given by a parent or student for the collection and/or dissemination of information not directly relevant to the student's school program

integration The process of transferring students from a more to a less segregated setting

intelligence A general aptitude and capacity for understanding and learning

intelligence quotient (IQ) A score on an intelligence test that permits an individual's performance to be compared with the average performance on the test

interaction A first-order (or superficial) social exchange between two or more individuals, with little emotional commitment

interactive teacher Sees children's development as an interaction between internal and external factors

Internet chatroom A virtual (computer-generated) 'room' in which individuals 'chat' with each other online

Internet relay chat (IRC) A chat system that enables Internet-connected individuals anywhere to join live, real-time discussions

interpersonal skills Awareness of and sensitivity to others' attitudes, intentions, feelings, needs and motivations

interval schedules When a reward is given after a set period of time

interventionist teacher Sees children's development as an outcome of external factors

intrinsic motivation Motivation arising from internal sources, such as an individual's feelings of curiosity, excitement and satisfaction

involuntary minority group A group of people who have at some point been brought into a society against their will

ipsative assessment Assessment that compares an individual's current achievement with previous achievement

J

Jigsaw A form of cooperative learning where each group member works individually on components of the one task

joint attention When carer and child together attend to a stimulus, such as when reading books or playing peekaboo games

L

lateralisation The specialisation of functions in the two hemispheres of the cerebral cortex

law of effect Responses that have a satisfying outcome are likely to be strengthened and repeated

law of exercise Connections between actions and new consequences are strengthened the more they are repeated

LBOTE Language background other than English

learned helplessness An expectation, based on previous experience, that learning efforts will lead to failure

learning difficulties Marked problems in achievement at school

learning style Learner preferences for types of learning and teaching activities

least restrictive environment (LRE) The setting that is as close as possible to that experienced by children who do not have disabilities

levels of processing model A process-oriented approach that attaches most importance to the type and depth of processing taking place

limit-setting strategies Strategies that establish boundaries in regard to children's activities

listserv An online communication tool allowing individuals to email contributions to a mailing list that automatically makes available all messages to everyone on the list

literacy The ability to read and use written information, and to write appropriately in a range of contexts

locus of control A tendency to attribute success or failure to internal (controllable) or external (uncontrollable) factors

logical consequences Outcomes contrived to influence behaviour

long-term memory A permanent storage facility for information

M

macrosystem Societal and cultural influences on development

mainstreaming Teaching children with special needs in regular classrooms for all or part of the day

maintenance The continued performance of a learned action after instruction has ceased

mastery goal A personal objective to achieve mastery of a task or skill

measurement A test of student performance that involves the use of numerical values in the form of scores

mental age The chronological age that typically corresponds with a particular performance level on an intelligence test

mesosystem Connections between settings involving the child

meta-analysis A statistical technique used to obtain a quantitative summary of findings across a large number of research studies

metacognition Knowledge about knowledge

metalinguistic awareness Awareness of and understandings about language

microsystem Interactions and activities in the child's immediate environment

modelling A form of prompting that involves demonstrating a desired response for someone to imitate

moral dilemma A moral problem requiring individual judgements and moral reasoning

morality The fundamental questions of right and wrong, justice, fairness and basic human rights

moratorium Refers to the state of adolescents who postpone making a definitive commitment to a single identity or set of values

morphology The combination of units of meaning in words, e.g. listen + ed = past tense of 'listen'

motivation An internal process that activates, guides and maintains behaviour over time

multiple intelligences (MI) Seven or more domains of intellectual functioning

multiple-user domain (MUD) A simulated electronic 'room' in which synchronous, text-based conversations occur between users in real time, using text-based messages

multiple-user object-oriented (domain) (MOO) Simulated electronic environments that expand the text-based context of MUDs by adding visual objects with which participants can interact

multistore model Depicts how information is processed and stored in memory in a sequence of stages

myelination The process whereby axons are insulated with a sheath of fatty cells, which improves the speed and efficiency of message transmission

N

natural consequences Outcomes that occur without interference

nature–nurture debate Controversy over the relative influence that inherent characteristics and environmental factors have on development

navigation To move around an electronic environment (specifically the Web) by following hyperlinked paths

negative reinforcement Increasing the likelihood of a behaviour being repeated by contingently removing an aversive object or activity

neo-Piagetians Theorists who retained many of Piaget's ideas while conceptualising children's thinking in terms of information-processing

neuron A nerve cell

neurotransmitter A chemical substance that carries messages between neurons across the synapse

neutral stimulus (NS) An event or happening that has no effect on an organism

newsgroup An online discussion on a particular topic, with newsgroup messages posted electronically using a 'newsreader' program to connect users to the Internet

non-directive teaching Teaching in which the teacher is a facilitator, guiding students and nurturing their learning

non-interventionist teacher Allows children's development to occur naturally

norm The mean or average performance of a group of people

norm-referenced assessment Used to compare the performance of individuals or groups with the performance of a comparable group on the same task

normal distribution (bell-shaped curve) A representation of test scores, showing their natural tendency to cluster around the middle (mean) of the distribution and taper off at either side

normalisation Giving people with disabilities access to the daily experiences and activities available to those in the community who do not have a disability

numeracy The ability to use mathematics effectively and with confidence in a range of contexts

O

object permanence Piagetian term used to refer to children's understanding that objects continue to exist even when they are out of sight

one-to-one correspondence The principle that each item in a group is counted only once

open education A model of learning and teaching that provides a warm, caring environment, and that builds on children's interests and experiences and actively involves them in the learning process

operant conditioning The use of positive and negative consequences to strengthen or weaken voluntary behaviour

operants Voluntary actions, usually goal-directed

operations Actions that are governed by rules and logic, and that are performed mentally rather than physically

order The principle that numbers are counted in a fixed order

otitis media A disease of the middle ear that affects hearing

overextension Inappropriate use of a word for a class of things rather than for one particular thing

overregularisation Application of a grammatical rule, ignoring its exceptions

P

pedagogy The art of teaching and instruction

performance assessment A mode of assessment that requires a student to engage in a complex task

performance goal A personal objective to perform well in an area of achievement

perspective-taking The ability to imagine the self in another's position and to understand others' feelings

phonology The sound system of language

portfolio A collection of samples of student work

positive reinforcement Increasing the likelihood of a behaviour occurring, by contingent presentation of a reward immediately following it

postconventional morality Individuals move beyond the conventional rules of their community to focus more broadly on what is best for society at large, and on ways of promoting justice in society

pragmatics Rules for the appropriate use of language in social contexts

preconventional morality Morality is seen as a set of rules handed down by adults

prejudice A preconceived, uninformed opinion

Premack principle (Grandma's rule) Any behaviour that is enjoyed and that occurs often can be used to reinforce behaviours that are not enjoyed and that do not occur often

preoperational stage Piaget's second stage, in which a child is not yet able to 'operate' or carry out logical physical actions mentally, but is reliant on manipulating real materials

preventative programs Educational programs designed to support children's development in order to prevent delays and difficulties in learning

primary mental abilities (PMA) The separate abilities that comprise intelligence

primary reinforcer An unconditioned (unlearned) stimulus that is innately rewarding

private speech Silent speech used by adults to guide their thinking and actions

procedural knowledge *Knowing how* to perform an action or sequence of actions

procedural memory Memory about steps or procedures for performing a skill

profile An ordered sequence or continuum of learning descriptors that can be used to chart progress

progressive education A child-centred approach to education based on a commitment to democratic ideals

prompting Providing an additional stimulus to elicit a desired response

prosocial behaviour Voluntary behaviour intended to benefit others

psychological constructivism Focuses on individual learners and how they construct their own knowledge, beliefs and identity

psychosocial crisis A 'turning point', where individuals experience a temporary state of conflict and disequilibrium

psychosocial development Psychological development in a social context

puberty The biological changes associated with sexual maturity

punishment Weakening or reducing behaviour through contingent use of aversive objects or events

R

racism Discrimination based on race or ethnicity

rating scale A procedure for recording the degree to which a specific behaviour or characteristic is present

ratio schedules When a reward is given in a predetermined ratio to the number of responses

readiness Used to describe a child who has the prior knowledge or experiences needed to make a link between the known and the unknown

recasting Parents' tendency to respond to children's utterances by restating them in the correct grammatical form

reciprocal determinism The interactive, complementary system formed by people and environments

reciprocal teaching Adopts the principles of collaborative learning, where peers assist each other under the guidance of an expert who facilitates group thinking processes

reflectivity Having a cognitive preference for taking time to solve problems and to analyse oneself and the context

Reggio Emilia A system of education for the early childhood years (under 6 years of age)

Regular Education Initiative (REI) A movement that advocates merging special and regular education into a single, unified program

reinforcement Increasing or strengthening the likelihood of a behaviour recurring through use of contingent feedback

reinforcer Any event that strengthens the behaviour it follows

relationship An exchange between two or more people, resulting from several interactions and taking on emotional significance

reliability The extent to which a test or measurement device obtains the same result when used on successive occasions

resilience Possessed by students who succeed at school in spite of adverse life experiences

resource room A specific-purpose room in a regular school, where one-to-one or small-group instruction is provided for students experiencing difficulties

respondents Elicited or reflex reactions to a specific stimulus

response An observable reaction to a known (or unknown) stimulus

responsibility training The use of an incentive system to elicit new behaviours or maintain existing ones

reversibility The ability to mentally reverse thought, such as adding back something that has been taken away or remoulding something to its original shape

risk factor A factor associated with negative outcomes

S

scaffolding The support provided to learners to enable a task to be done successfully and a student to work more independently

scheme A mental image or cluster of related ideas used to organise existing knowledge and to make sense of new experiences

school phobia Refusal to attend school

secondary reinforcer A conditioned (learned) stimulus that functions as a reward

self Who we are, what makes us unique and who we believe ourselves to be

self-actualisation The achievement of one's full potential

self-concept A collection of information, ideas, attitudes and beliefs we have about ourselves

self-conscious emotions Higher-order emotions (such as pride and shame) that require advanced cognitive processes and a capacity to understand how the self might be harmed or enhanced

self-efficacy An individual's sense of being able to manage a task effectively and successfully in a particular domain

self-esteem The level of satisfaction and pride that individuals have in the self

self-monitoring A metacognitive activity that involves monitoring how well we are understanding and remembering

self-regulation A metacognitive activity that involves planning, directing and evaluating one's cognitive processes

semantic memory Memory about language and the world around us

semantics The system of meanings associated with language

sensorimotor stage The earliest of Piaget's developmental stages, characterised by object permanence, intentional or goal-directed behaviour, and deferred imitation

sensory register New information enters the sensory register through the five senses and is stored for less than one second

seriation The ability to mentally arrange objects or elements in terms of a dimension such as length, weight or volume

shaping Reinforcement of gradual approximations of the target behaviour

short-term memory A temporary storage place with a limited capacity to store approximately seven items

simulation A model of a real system or phenomenon

social constructivism Emphasises the role of social and cultural factors in shaping learning

social emotions Cultural constructions determining what individuals feel and how they should demonstrate these feelings in public

social interaction (social transmission) The interactions with others (parents, peers, teachers etc.) that contribute to children's learning experiences

socialisation The passing of cultural beliefs, knowledge, values and behaviour among members of a group

sociocultural factors Factors contributing to individual difference, which have a basis in society and culture

socioeconomic status A measure of social and economic position in society; typically a combination of education, occupation and income

socioemotional development Emotional development in a social context

sociogram A graphical depiction of the pattern of interactions among group members

sociolinguistic features of language Cultural conventions directing the use of language

special class An alternative placement for students whose needs cannot be met in a regular classroom

special education The system of programs and services provided in most education systems for children who have difficulties learning within the regular classroom context

special school A separate school that caters for a specific group of students with special learning needs

specific mental abilities (s) A collection of distinct intellectual abilities

spina bifida A congenital defect associated with mobility problems and resulting from the spinal column's failure to close completely prior to birth

Standard Australian English The language of mainstream Australia, and 'standard' in the sense that it does not vary significantly across communities

standard deviation (SD) A measure of how much test scores vary from the mean of the sample

standardised test A test designed in accordance with set rules, administered under uniform conditions, and scored and interpreted in terms of identified norms

state A temporary condition or feeling

stimulus An environmental condition or event that activates the senses

summative assessment Formal checks of learning outcomes that are conducted at the end of a teaching program

supplementary programs Procedures, used in schools, to help children who are under-achieving

symbolic thought The ability to represent objects and events mentally

synapse The gap between the axon and dendrites of two neurons

synchronous communication Communication between individuals who interact in real time in a call-and-response format (for example, video conferencing or Internet chatrooms)

syntax The grammatical system that orders the construction of sentences

T

talent Exceptional achievement in one or more areas of endeavour

task analysis Breaking a task into a series of manageable steps so as to assist learning

technology The use of tools, materials and processes to perform tasks efficiently, to improve quality of life, and to meet human needs and wants

telegraphic speech Communication using two-word sentences, leaving out smaller words

test Any assessment procedure that is used systematically to measure a sample of behaviour

test anxiety Fear of performing poorly in tests

test bias Where particular groups are disadvantaged by factors associated with a test's content and the interpretation of results

three-way reporting Reporting that involves student, teacher and parent input

top-down approaches Teaching approaches (such as the whole-language approach) that emphasise task presentation and skill development within real contexts that involve whole-skill development

trait An enduring characteristic

trial-and-error learning An explanation of learning that states when an individual is placed in a problem-solving situation, the correct response will be learned through being reinforced

triarchic model of intelligence Intelligence defined as thinking (analytic), responding to new experiences (creative) and coping with everyday situations (practical)

U

unconditioned response (UR) An action triggered spontaneously by a stimulus

unconditioned stimulus (US) An object, event or happening in the physical environment that causes spontaneous activity in an organism

underachievers Students whose progress at school is not as good as expected, based on perceptions of ability

underextension Inappropriate use of a word for one thing rather than for a class of things

V

validity The extent to which a test or measurement device measures what it purports to measure

values Ideals that individuals hold regarding what is of worth

vertical decalage Unevenness in cognitive development, as demonstrated by advanced development in one area compared to development in other areas

voluntary minority group A group of people who have at some point chosen to migrate in search of a better life

Z

zone of proximal development The distance between children's current level of competence on a task and the level they can achieve with support or guidance

References

Abrami. P. C., Chambers, B., Poulsen, C., De Simone, C., D'Apollonia, S., & Howden, W. (1995). *Classroom connections: Understanding and using cooperative learning.* Toronto: Harcourt Brace.

ACER (Australian Council for Educational Research) (1996). *National School English Literacy Survey.* Melbourne: ACER.

Ackard, D. M., & Neumark-Sztainer, D. (2002). Date violence and date rape among adolescents: Associations with disordered eating behaviors and psychological health. *Child Abuse and Neglect, 26*(5), 455–473.

Adkins-Bowling, T., Brown, S., & Mitchell, T. L. (2001). *The utilization of instructional technology and cooperative learning to effectively enhance the academic success of students with English-as-a-second-language.* Paper presented at the Biennial Meeting of Kappa Delta Pi, Orlando, FL. (ERIC Document Reproduction Service No. ED458208).

Adler, A. (1930). *The education of children.* Chicago: Gateway.

Aichele, D. B., & Coxford, A. F. (Eds.). (1994). *Professional development for teachers of mathematics.* Reston, VA: National Council of Teachers of Mathematics.

Ainscow, M. (1999). *Understanding the development of inclusive schools.* London: Falmer Press.

Alberto, P. A., & Troutman, A. C. (1999). *Applied behaviour analysis for teachers* (5th ed.). Columbus, OH: Merrill.

Allen, J. (Ed.). (1998). *Sociology of education: Policies and practices.* Katoomba: Social Science Press.

Allington, R. L. (1994). What's special about special programs for children who find learning to read difficult? *Journal of Reading Behaviour, 26,* 1–21.

Allington, R. L., & McGill-Franzen, A. (Eds.). (1995). Individualised planning. In M. C. Wang, M. C. Reynolds & H. J. Walberg (Eds.), *Handbook of special education and remedial education: Research and practice* (pp. 5–35). Oxford: Elsevier Science.

Allport, G. W. (1954). *The nature of prejudice.* Cambridge, MA: Addison-Wesley.

Allport, G. W. (1961). *Pattern and growth in personality.* Oxford: Holt, Reinhart & Winston.

Allstetter, W. (1998). That mess on your web site. *MIT's Technology Review, 101*(5), 72–76.

Alonso, D. L., & Norman, K. L. (1996). Forms of control and interaction as determinants of lecture effectiveness in the electronic classroom. *Computers and Education, 27*(3/4), 205–214.

Alves-Martins, M., Peixoto, F., Gouveia-Pereira, M., Amaral, V., & Pedro, I. (2002). Self-esteem and academic achievement among adolescents. *Educational Psychology, 22*(1), 51–62.

Amichai-Hamburger, Y., & Ben-Artzi, E. (2003). Loneliness and internet use. *Computers and Human Behavior, 19*(1), 71–80.

Anastasi, A. (1976). *Psychological testing* (4th ed.). New York: Macmillan.

Anderson, D. A. (1994). Lesbian and gay adolescents: Social and developmental considerations. *High School Journal, 77* (1–2), 13–19.

Anderson, M. (1999). Project development – the shape of things to come. In M. Anderson (Ed.), *The development of intelligence* (pp. 3–15). Hove, East Sussex: Psychology Press.

Anderson, R., Wilson, P., & Fielding, L. (1988). Growth in reading and how children spend their time outside of school. *Reading Research Quarterly, 23,* 285–303.

Andrews, R. J., Elkins, J., Berry, P. B., & Burge, J. A. (1979). *A survey of special education in Australia: Provisions, needs and priorities in the education of children with handicaps and learning difficulties.* St Lucia, Queensland: Fred and Eleanor Schonell Educational Research Centre.

Anglin, J. M. (1993). Vocabulary development: A morphological analysis. *Monographs of the Society for Research in Child Development, 58*(10, Serial No. 238), 1–165.

Anonymous (2000). *Ananda Marga River School: Aims and ideals.* Retrieved 14 November, 2000, from http://www.suncoast.com.au/Maleny/AnandaMargaRiverSchool/aims.html

Anonymous (2001). *Brisbane Independent School.* Retrieved 1 February, 2001, from http://www.geocities.com/Heartland/Lane/1078/

Antell, S., & Keating, D. (1983). Perception of numerical invariance in neonates. *Child Development, 54,* 595–701.

Antil, L. R., Jenkins, J. R., Wayne, S. K., & Vadesy, P. F. (1998). Cooperative learning: Prevalence, conceptualizations, and the relation between research and practice. *American Educational Research Journal, 35,* 419–454.

Aphek, E. (2002). Children, computers and reading skills. *Turkish Online Journal of Distance Education, 4*(1). Retrieved 2 June, 2003, from http:// tojde.anadolu.edu.tr/tojde8/notes_for_editor/aphek.htm

Arendt, R., MacLean, W., & Baumeister, A. (1988). Critique of sensory integration therapy and its application in mental retardation. *American Journal of Mental Retardation, 92,* 401–411.

Ariotti, L. (1998). Do/how to/should definitions of disability incorporate indigenous perceptions of disability? In Australian Institute of Health and Welfare, *Indigenous disability data: Report on proceedings of the Canberra workshop,* April 1998 (pp. 79–84). Canberra: Australian Bureau of Statistics.

Armstrong, S. J. (2000). The influence of individual cognitive style on performance in management education. *Educational Psychology, 20*(3), 323–340.

Arnone, M. P., & Grabowski, B. L. (1992). Effects on children's achievement and curiosity of variations in learner control over an interactive video lesson. *Educational Technology Research and Development, 40*(1), 15–27.

Arnot, M., & Weiner, G. (Eds.). (1987). *Gender and the politics of schooling.* London: Hutchinson in association with the Open University.

Aronfeed, J. (1968). *Conduct and conscience: The socialization of internalized control over behavior.* New York: Academic Press.

Aronson, E., Blaney, N., Stephen, C., Sikes, J., & Snapp, M. (1978). *The jigsaw classroom.* Beverley Hills, CA: Sage.

Arsenio, W., & Kramer, R. (1992). Victimizers and their victims: Children's conceptions of the mixed emotional consequences of moral transgressions. *Child Development, 63,* 915–927.

Arsenio, W., & Lover, A. (1995). Children's conceptions of sociomoral affect: Happy victimizers, mixed emotions, and other expectancies. In M. Killen & D. Hart (Eds.),

Morality in everyday life: Developmental perspectives. Cambridge studies in social and emotional development, (pp. 87–128). New York: Cambridge University Press.

Arthur, M. (1996). Designing effective teaching interventions. In P. Foreman (Ed.), *Integration and inclusion in action* (pp. 115–143). Sydney: Harcourt Brace.

Ashman, A., & Conway, R. N. F. (1993). *Using cognitive methods in the classroom.* London: Routledge.

Ashman, A., & Elkins, J. (2002). Rights and learning opportunities. In A. Ashman & J. Elkins (Eds.), *Educating children with diverse abilities* (pp. 41–72). French's Forest, NSW: Pearson.

Association of Professional Teachers (2001). *Professional advice leaflet: Discipline and physical contact.* Retrieved 29 January, 2003, from http://www.apt.org.au/advice_leaflets/discipline_and_physical_contact.html

Atkinson, J. W. (1964). *An introduction to motivation.* Princeton, NJ: Van Nostrand.

Atkinson, R. C., & Shiffrin, R. M. (1968). Human memory: A proposed system and its control processes. In K. W. Spence & J. T. Spence (Eds.), *The psychology of learning and motivation* (Vol. 2). London: Academic Press.

Australia Parliament Senate Employment, Workplace Relations, Small Business and Education References Committee (2000). *Katu kalpa: Report on the inquiry into the effectiveness of education and training programs for indigenous Australians.* Canberra, ACT: Senate Employment, Workplace Relations, Small Business and Education References Committee.

Australian Association of Mathematics Teachers (1997). *Numeracy = Everyone's Business. Report of the Numeracy Education Strategy Development Conference May 1997.* Adelaide: Association of Mathematics Teachers.

Australian Broadcasting Authority (1996). *Families and electronic media.* Monograph Number 6. Retrieved 3 May, 2003, from http://www.aba.gov.au/tv/research/projects/families.htm

Australian Bureau of Statistics (1993). *Disability, ageing and carers: Summary of findings.* No. 4430.0. Canberra: Commonwealth Government Printer.

Australian Bureau of Statistics (1997). *Participation in sport and physical activities, 1995–1996.* ABS cat. no. 4177.0. Canberra: ABS.

Australian Bureau of Statistics (2000). *Australian social trends 2000.* ABS cat. no. 4102.0. Canberra: ABS.

Australian Council for Computers in Education (2000). *Teacher learning technologies competencies project: Background paper.* Canberra: Australian Council for Computers in Education. Retrieved 4 April, 2003, from http://www.acce.edu.au/tltc/a-contents.asp

Australian Sports Commission (1999). *How to include women and girls in sport, recreation and physical activity: Strategies and good practice.* Canberra: Australian Sports Commission.

Ausubel, D. P. (1977). The facilitation of meaningful verbal learning in the classroom. *Educational Psychologist, 12*, 162–178.

Ausubel, D. P. (1978). In defense of advance organizers: A reply to the critics. *Review of Educational Research, 48*, 251–258.

Avery, P. G. (1999). Authentic assessment and instruction. *Social Education, 63*, 368–373.

Ayersman, D., & Reed, M. (1996). Effects of learning styles, programming, and gender on computer anxiety. *Journal of Research on Computing in Education, 28*(2), 148–161.

Ayres, J. (1979). *Sensory integration and the child.* Los Angeles: Western Psychological Services.

Azmitia, M., & Montgomery, R. (1993). Friendship, transactive dialogues, and the development of scientific reasoning. *Social Development, 2*, 202–221.

Baddeley, A. (1986). *Working memory.* Oxford: Oxford University Press.

Baer, D. M., Wolf, M. M., & Risley, T. R. (1968). Some current dimensions of applied behaviour analysis. *Journal of Applied Behaviour Analysis, 1*, 91–97.

Bagley, C., & Hunter, B. (1992). Restructuring constructivism and technology: Forging a new relationship. *Educational Technology, 32*(7), 22–27.

Bagwell, C. L., Newcomb, A. F., & Bukowski, W. M. (2000). Preadolescent friendship and peer rejection as predictors of adult adjustment. In W. Craig (Ed.), *Childhood social development: The essential readings* (pp. 86–112). Malden, MA: Blackwell Publishers.

Bai, D. L., & Bertenthal, B. I. (1992). Locomotor status and the development of spatial search skills. *Child Development, 63*, 215–226.

Baillargeon, R. (1991). Object permanence in young infants: Further evidence. *Child Development, 62*, 1227–1246.

Baillargeon, R., Pascual-Leone, J., & Roncadin, C. (1998). Mental-attentional capacity: Does cognitive style make a difference? *Journal of Experimental Child Psychology, 70*, 143–166.

Bairstow, P., Cochrane, R., & Hur, J. (1993). *Evaluation of conductive education for children with cerebral palsy* (Final report, Part 1). London: HMSO.

Ball, D. L., & Bass, H. (2000). Making believe: The collective construction of public mathematical knowledge in the elementary classroom. In D. C. Phillips (Ed.), *Constructivism in education: Opinions and second opinions on controversial issues* (pp. 193–224). Chicago: The National Society for the Study of Education.

Balmain High School (2003). *Balmain High School.* Retrieved 26 January, 2003, from http://www2.edfac.usyd.edu.au/LocalResource/schooldoes/balmain.html

Balson, M. (1992). *Understanding classroom behaviour* (3rd ed.). Melbourne: ACER.

Bandura, A. (1969). *Principles of behavior modification.* New York: Holt, Rinehart & Winston.

Bandura, A. (1977). *Social learning theory.* Oxford: Prentice Hall.

Bandura, A. (1994). Self-efficacy. In V. S. Ramachaudran (Ed.), *Encyclopedia of human behavior* (Vol. 4, pp. 71–81). New York: Academic Press.

Bandura, A. (1995). Exercise of personal and collective self-efficacy in changing societies. In A. Bandura (Ed.), *Self-efficacy in changing societies* (pp. 1–45). Cambridge: Cambridge University Press.

Bandura, A. (1997). *Self-efficacy: The exercise of control.* New York: W. H. Freeman.

Bandura, A., Ross, D., & Ross, S. (1961). Transmission of aggression through imitation of aggressive models. *Journal of Abnormal and Social Psychology, 63*, 575–582.

Bandura, A., & Walters, R. H. (1959). *Adolescent aggression.* New York: Ronald Press.

Banks, J. A. & Banks, C. M. (Eds.). (2001). *Multicultural

education: Issues and perspectives (4th ed.). New York: John Wiley.

Barcan, A. (1980). *A history of Australian education*. Melbourne: Oxford University Press.

Barnes, M., Clarke, D., & Stephens, M. (2000). Assessment: The engine of systematic reform? *Journal of Curriculum Studies, 32*, 623–650.

Barnett, W. S. (1993). Benefit-cost analysis of preschool education: Findings from a 25-year follow-up. *American Journal of Orthopsychiatry, 63*, 500–508.

Baroody, A. J. (1987). *Children's mathematical thinking*. New York: Teachers College Press.

Barrett, K. (2000). The development of the self-in-relationships. In R. Mills & S. Duck (Eds.), *The developmental psychology of personal relationships* (pp. 91–107). Chichester: Wiley.

Barrett, K. C., & Campos, J. J. (1987). Perspectives on emotional development II: A functionalist approach to emotions. In J. D. Osofsky (Ed.), *Handbook of infant development* (2nd ed., pp. 555–578). New York: Wiley.

Barrett, P., Lowry-Webster, H., & Holmes, J. (1999). *Friends for children participant workbook* (2nd ed.). Brisbane: Australian Academic Press.

Barrett, P., & Turner, C. (2001). Prevention of anxiety symptoms in primary school children: Preliminary results from a universal school-based trial. *British Journal of Clinical Psychology, 40*, 399–410.

Barrett, S. (2002). *The Feingold diet: Dubious benefits, subtle risks*. Retrieved 22 March, 2002, from http://www.quackwatch.com/01QuackeryRelatedTopics/feingold.html

Barrie, J., & Tomlinson, D. (1985). *Handicapped children in rural areas: A pilot study of the Eastern goldfields region* (Research Series No. 3). Nedlands, WA: Centre for Research on Rural Education (University of Western Australia).

Barrutia, R., Bissell, J., Rodriguez, E., & Scarcella, R. (1993). *The language and cognitive development of Hispanic middle school students*. Final report submitted to the University of California Linguistic Minority Research Institute. Irvine, CA: Department of Education, University of California, Irvine.

Basseches, M. (1984). *Dialectical thinking and adult development*. Norwood, NJ: Ablex.

Bastiani, J. (1989). *Working with parents: A whole school approach*. London: NFER Nelson.

Bates, E., & Goodman, J. (1999). On the emergence of grammar from the lexicon. In B. MacWhinney (Ed.), *The emergence of language*. Mahwah, NJ: Erlbaum.

Battin-Pearson, S., Newcomb, M. D., Abbott, R. D., Hill, K. G., Catalano, R. F., & Hawkins, J. D. (2000). Predictors of early high school drop-out: A test of five theories. *Journal of Educational Psychology, 92*, 568–582.

Baum, S. M., Renzulli, J. S., & Herbert, T. P. (1995). Reversing underchievement: Creative productivity as a systematic intervention. *Gifted Child Quarterly, 39*, 224–235.

Beasley, F., & Shayer, M. (1990). Learning potential assessment through Feuerstein's LPAD: Can quantitative results be achieved? *International Journal of Dynamic Assessment and Instruction, 1*, 37–48.

Bednar, A. K., Cunningham, D., Duffy, T. M., & Perry, J. D. (1992). Theory into practice: How do we link? In T. M. Duffy & D. H. Jonassen (Eds.), *Constructivism and the technology of instruction: A conversation* (pp. 17–34). Hillsdale, NJ: Lawrence Erlbaum Associates.

Beidel, D. C., Turner, S. M., & Taylor-Ferreira, J. C. (1999). Teaching study skills and test-taking strategies to elementary school students: The Testbusters program. *Behavior Modification, 23*(4), 630–646.

Beilin, H. (1978). Inducing conservation through training. In G. Steiner (Ed.), *Psychology of the 20th century, Vol. 7: Piaget and beyond* (pp. 260–289). Zurich: Kindler.

Beilin, H. (1992). Piagetian theory. In R. Vasta (Ed.), *Six theories of child development: Revised formulations and current issues* (pp. 85–131). London: Jessica Kingsley.

Bell, M. A., & Fox, N. A. (1997). Individual differences in object permanence performance at 8 months: Locomotor experience and brain electrical activity. *Developmental Psychobiology, 31*(4), 287–297.

Bennett, N., Andreae, J., Hegarty, P., & Wade, B. (1980). *Open plan schools: Teaching, curriculum, design*. Windsor, Berks.: NFER Publishing.

Bentley, K. M., & Li, A. K. F. (1995). Bully and victim problems in elementary schools and students' beliefs about aggression. *Canadian Journal of School Psychology, 11*, 153–165.

Berard, G. (1993). *Hearing equals behaviour*. New Canaan, CT: Keats.

Bergstrome, S. E. (2002). The relative importance of academic achievement in determining self-esteem of students in rural British Columbia: An empirical examination of students in grades 6, 8, 10 and 12. *Dissertation Abstracts International, 62*(10–A), 3291.

Berk, L. (2003). *Child Development* (6th ed.). Needham Heights, MA: Allyn & Bacon.

Berndt, T. J. (1992). Friendship and friends' influence in adolescence. *Current Directions in Psychological Science, 1*(5), 156–159.

Berndt, T. J. (1998). Friendship and friends' influence in adolescence. In R. E. Muuss & H. D. Porton (Eds.), *Adolescent behaviour and society* (5th ed., pp. 170–174). Boston: McGraw-Hill College.

Berndt, T. J., & Burgy, L. (1996). Social self-concept. B. Bracken (Ed.), *Handbook of self-concept* (pp. 171–209). New York: Wiley.

Berne, S. (1996). *Bully-proof your child*. Melbourne: Lothian.

Bernhard, J. K. (1992). Gender-related attitudes and the development of computer skills: A preschool intervention. *The Alberta Journal of Educational Research, 38*, 177–188.

Berninger, V. A., Abbott, R. D., Abbott, S. P., Graham, S., & Richards, T. (2002). Writing and reading: Connections between language by hand and language by eye. *Journal of Learning Disabilities, 35*(1), 39–56.

Bertenthal, B. I., Campos, J. J., & Barrett, K (1984). Self-produced locomotion: An organiser of emotional, cognitive and social development in infancy. In R. Emde & R. Harmon (Eds.), *Continuities and discontinuities in development* (pp.174–210). New York: Plenum.

Bevevino, M. M., Dengel, J., & Adams, K. (1999). Constructivist theory in the classroom: Internalizing concepts through inquiry learning. *The Clearing House, 72*, 275–278.

Bierman, K. L., & Greenberg, M. T. (1996). Social skills training in the Fast Track program. In R. D. Peters & R. J. McMahon (Eds.), *Preventing childhood disorders,*

substance abuse, and delinquency (pp. 65–89). Thousand Oaks, CA: Sage.
Biesheuval, S. (1969). Psychological tests and their application to non-European peoples. In D. R. Price-Williams (Ed.), *Cross-cultural studies: Selected readings* (pp. 57–75). Harmondsworth: Penguin.
Biggs, J. B. (1987a). *Student approaches to learning and studying*. Hawthorn, Victoria: ACER.
Biggs, J. B. (1987b). *The Learning Process Questionnaire: Users manual*. Hawthorn, Victoria: ACER.
Biggs, J. B. (1996). Approaches to learning of Asian students: A multiple paradox. In J. Pandey, D. Sinha & D. P. S. Bhawuk (Eds.), *Asian contributions to cross cultural psychology* (pp. 180–199). Thousand Oaks, CA: Sage.
Biggs, J. B. (2001). Teaching across cultures. In F. Salili (Ed.), *Student motivation: The culture and context of learning* (pp. 293–308). New York: Kluwer.
Biggs, J. B., & Collis, K. F. (1982). *Evalauating the quality of learning: The SOLO taxonomy*. New York: Academic Press.
Biggs, J. B., & Moore, P. J. (1993). *The process of learning* (3rd ed.). Sydney: Prentice-Hall.
Birrell, B., Calderon, A., Dobson, I. R., & Smith, T. F. (2000). Equity in access to higher education revisited. *People & Place*, 8(1), 50–61.
Bishop, R., & Glynn, T. (1999). *Culture counts: Changing power relations in education*. Palmerston North, NZ: Dunmore Press.
Bjork, D. W. (1993). *B. F. Skinner: A life*. New York: Basic Books.
Bjorkqvist, K., Lagerspetz, K. M. J., & Kaukiaainen, A. (1992). Do girls manipulate and boys fight? Developmental trends regarding direct and indirect aggression. *Aggressive Behaviour*, 18, 117–127.
Bjorkqvist, K., & Osterman, K. (1999). Finland. In P. K. Smith, Y. Morita, J. Junger-Tas, D. Olweus, R. Catalano, & P. Slee (Eds.), *The nature of school bullying: A cross-national perspective* (pp. 56–67). London: Routledge.
Black, P., & Wiliam, D. (1998). Assessment and classroom learning. *Assessment in Education*, 5, 7–74.
Blatt, B., & Kaplan, F. (1967). *Christmas in purgatory*. Boston: Allyn & Bacon.
Blatt, B., & Kaplan, F. (1973). *Souls in extremis: An anthology on victims and victimizers*. Boston: Allyn & Bacon.
Blitner, S., Dobson, V., Gibson, F., Martin, B., Oldfield, N., Oliver, R., Palmer, I., & Riley, R. (2000). *Strong voices*. Batchelor, NT: Batchelor Institute of Indigenous Tertiary Education.
Block, C. C., Oakar, M., & Hurt, N. (2002). The expertise of literacy teachers: A continuum from preschool to grade 5. *Reading Research Quarterly*, 37, 178–206.
Bloom, B. S. (Ed.). (1956). *Taxonomy of educational objectives: Handbook 1. Cognitive domain*. London: Longmans.
Bloom, L. (1998). Language acquisition in its developmental context. In D. Kuhn & R. S. Siegler (Eds.), *Handbook of Child Psychology* (Vol. 2, 5th ed.). New York: J. Wiley.
Blumenfeld, P. C., Marx, R., Soloway, E., & Krajcik, J. (1997). Learning with peers: From small group cooperation to collaborative communities. *Educational Researcher*, 25, 37–40.
Blyth, D. A., Simmons, R. G., & Zakin, D. F. (1985). Satisfaction with body image for early adolescent females: The impact of pubertal timing within different school environments. *Journal of Youth and Adolescence*, 14, 207–225.
Bochner, S., Center, Y., Chapparo, C., & Donelly, M. (1996). Implementing conductive education in Australia: A question of programme transplantation. *Educational Psychology*, 16, 181–192.
Bochner, S., Cooney, G., & Outhred, L. (1989). *Review of the Basic Skills Test Program*. Sydney: School of Education, Macquarie University.
Bochner, S., & Freeman, L. (2002). *Bridging the gap: Improving literacy outcomes for Aboriginal students. Project report*. Macquarie University, Sydney: School of Education.
Bochner, S., & Jones, J. (2003). *Child language development: Learning to talk* (2nd ed.). London: Whurr.
Bochner, S., Price, P., Salamon, L., Yeend, G., & Orr, E. (1980). Language intervention: A classroom report. *British Journal of Disorders in Communication*, 15, 87–102.
Bodmer, W., & McKie, R. (1997). *The book of man: The Human Genome Project and the quest to discover our genetic heritage*. Oxford: Oxford University Press.
Bodrova, E., & Leong, D. J. (1996). *Tools of the mind: The Vygotskian approach to early childhood education*. Englewood Cliffs, NJ: Merrill.
Boekaerts, M. (1997). Self-regulated learning: A new concept enhanced by researchers, policy makers, educators, teachers, and students. *Learning and Instruction*, 7(2), 161–186.
Boeree, C. (2000). *Abraham Maslow: 1908–1970*. Retrieved 11 March, 2000, from http://www.ship.edu/~cgboeree/maslow.html
Boethel, M. F. (1996, November). *The promise and challenges of constructivist professional development: A review of the literature and of the SCIMAST approach*. Unpublished draft. Austin, TX: Southwest Educational Development Laboratory.
Boice, R. (1994). *How writers journey to comfort and fluency: A psychological adventure*. Westport, CT: Praeger Publishers/Greenwood Publishing Group.
Bor, W., Presland, I., Lavery, B., Christie, R., & Watson, K. (1992). Teachers' perceptions of students' adjustment difficulties. In J. Elkins & J. Izard (Eds.), *Student behaviour problems: Context, initiatives, programs* (pp. 77–92). Melbourne: ACER.
Borkowski, J. G., Carr, M., Rellinger, E., & Pressley, M. (1990). Self-regulated cognition: Interdependence of metacognition, attributions, and self-esteem. In B. F. Jones & L. Idol (Eds.), *Dimensions of thinking and cognitive instruction* (pp. 53–92). Hillsdale, NJ: Erlbaum.
Borkowski, J. G., & Muthukrishna, N. (1992). Moving metacognition into the classroom: 'Working models' and effective strategy teaching. In M. Pressley, K. R. Harris, & J. T. Guthrie (Eds.), *Promoting academic competence and literacy in school* (pp. 477–501). San Diego, CA: Academic.
Borkowski, J. G., Weyhing, R. S., & Carr, M. (1988). Effects of attributional retraining on strategy-based reading comprehension of learning-disabled students. *Journal of Educational Psychology*, 80, 46–53.
Bossert, S. (1988). Cooperative activities in the classroom. In E. Rothkopf (Ed.), *Review of research in education* (Vol. 15, pp. 225–250). Washington, DC: American Educational Research Association.

Bourke, C. J., Rigby, K., & Burden, J. (2000). *Better practice in school attendance. Improving the school attendance of Indigenous students.* Canberra: DETYA.

Bower, B. (1989). Co-operative multiple ability groupwork: A curricular response to tracking in the social studies. *Social Studies Review, 28,* 69–73.

Bower, T. (1989). The perceptual world of the new-born child. In A. Slater & G. Bremner (Eds.), *Infant development* (pp. 85–96). Hove: Lawrence Erlbaum.

Bowes, J. M., & Hayes, A. (Eds.). (1999). *Children, families and communities: Contexts and consequences.* Melbourne: Oxford University Press.

Boyd, S. (2002). *Literature review for the evaluation of the digital opportunities projects: Report to the Ministry of Education.* Wellington: NZ Council for Educational Research.

Bradley, G., & Russell, G. (1997). Computer experience, school support, and computer anxiety. *Educational Psychology: An International Journal of Experimental Psychology, 17*(3), 267–284.

Bradley, R. H., & Corwyn, R. F. (1999). Parenting. In C. Tamis-leMonda & L. Balter (Eds.), *Child psychology: A handbook of contemporary issues* (pp. 339–362). New York: Psychology Press.

Bradley, R. H., & Corwyn, R. F. (2002). Socioeconomic status and child development. *Annual Reviews Psychology, 53*(1), 371–399.

Brady, L., & Kennedy, K. (2001). *Celebrating student achievement: Assessment and reporting.* French's Forest, NSW: Pearson Education.

Braggett, E. J. (1998). Gifted children. In A. Ashman & J. Elkins (Eds.), *Educating children with special needs* (3rd ed., pp. 229–281). Sydney: Prentice Hall.

Braggett, E. J. (2002). Gifted and talented children and their education. In A. Ashman & J. Elkins (Eds.), *Educating children with diverse abilities* (pp. 286–348). Sydney: Prentice Hall.

Brainerd, C. J. (1996). Piaget: A centennial celebration. *Psychological Science, 7,* 191–195.

Braio, A., Dunn, R., Beasley, T. M., Quinn, P. & Buchanan, K. (1997). Incremental implementation of learning style strategies among urban low achievers. *Journal of Educational Research, 91,* 15–25.

Braithwaite, J. (1983). *Explorations in early childhood education.* Hawthorn, Victoria: ACER.

Bransgrove, E. (1994). Teachers' understanding of gender implications for learning with computers. *Australian Educational Computing, 9,* 23–27.

Breen, M. P., Louden, W., Barratt-Pugh, C., Rivalland, J., Rohl, M., Rhydwen, M., Lloyd, S., & Carr, T. (1994). *Literacy in its place: Literacy practices in urban and rural communities.* Perth: School of Language Education, Edith Cowan University.

Brennan, C. (1998). 'Why isn't it being implemented?' Race, racism and Indigenous education. In G. Partington (Ed.), *Perspectives on Aboriginal and Torres Strait Islander education.* Katoomba, NSW: Social Science Press.

Broadfoot, P. (1995). Performance assessment in perspective: International trends and current English experience. In H. Torrance (Ed.), *Evaluating authentic assessment: Problems and possibilities in new approaches to assessment* (pp. 9–43). Buckingham: Open University Press.

Broadfoot, P. (Ed.). (1986). *Profiles and records of achievement: A review of issues and practice.* London: Cassell.

Brockett, R. G. (2000). *Humanism as an instructional paradigm.* Retrieved 2 November, 2000, from http://www-distance.syr.edu/romira 1&.html

Brody, G. H., Flor, D., & Gibson, N. M. (1999). Linking maternal efficacy beliefs, developmental goals, parenting practices, and child competence in rural single-parent African-American families. *Child Development, 70,* 1197–1208.

Brody, G. H., Stoneman, Z., Flor, D., McCrary, C., Hastings, L., & Conyers, O. (1994). Financial resources, parent psychological functioning, parent co-caregiving, and early adolescent competence in rural two-parent African-American families. *Child Development, 65,* 590–605.

Brody, N. (1992). *Intelligence* (2nd ed.). San Diego: Academic Press.

Bronfenbrenner, U. (1979). *The ecology of human development: Experiments by nature and design.* Cambridge, MA: Harvard University Press.

Bronfenbrenner, U. (1989). Ecological systems theory. In R. Vasta (Ed.), *Annals of child development* (Vol. 6, pp. 187–251). Greenwich, CN: JAI.

Bronfenbrenner, U., & Morris, P. A. (1998). The ecology of developmental processes. In R. M. Lerner (Ed.), *Handbook of child psychology, Vol. 1: Theoretical models of human development* (5th ed., pp. 535–584). New York: Wiley.

Brooks-Gunn, J. (1988). Antecedents and consequences of variations in girls' maturational timing. *Journal of Adolescent Health Care, 9,* 365–373.

Brooks-Gunn, J., & Warren, M. P. (1989). Biological and social contributions to negative affect in young adolescent girls. *Child Development, 60*(1), 40–55.

Brophy, J. (1981). Teacher praise: A functional analysis. *Review of Educational Research, 51,* 5–21.

Brophy, J. (1998). *Failure Syndrome Students.* Report no. EDO-PS-98-2. (Eric Document Repoduction Service ED419625.)

Brown, A. I., Metz, K. E., & Campione, J. C. (1996). Social interaction and individual understanding in a community of learners: The influence of Piaget and Vygostky. In A. Tryphon & J. Voneche (Eds.), *Piaget–Vygotsky: The social genesis of thought* (pp. 145–170). London: Psychology Press.

Brown, A. L., & Palincsar, A. S. (1989). Guided, cooperative learning and individual knowledge acquisition. In L. B. Resnick (Ed.), *Knowing, learning, and instruction: Essays in honor of Robert Glaser* (pp. 393–451). Hillsdale, NJ: Erlbaum.

Brown, D. F., & Rose, T. D. (1995). Self-reported classroom impact of teachers' theories about learning and obstacles to implementation. *Action in Teacher Education, 17*(1), 20–29.

Brown, J. D. (1993). Self-esteem and self-evaluation: Feeling is believing. In J. M. Suls (Ed.), *The self in social perspective. Psychological perspectives on the self* (Vol. 4, pp. 27–58). Hillsdale, NJ: Lawrence Erlbaum Associates.

Brown, J. S., Collins, A., & Duguid, P. (1989). Situated cognition and the culture of learning. *Educational Researcher, 18*(1), 32–41.

Brown, R. J., & Turner, J. (1981). Interpersonal and intergroup behaviour. In J. C. Turner & H. Giles (Eds.), *Intergroup behaviour* (pp. 33–65). Oxford: Blackwell.

Bruce, B. C., & Levin, J. A. (1997). Educational technology: Media for inquiry, communication, construction, and expression. *Journal of Educational Computing Research, 17*(1), 79–102.

Bruce, M., & Robinson, G. L. (2001, July). *The clever kid's reading program: Metacognition and reciprocal teaching*. Paper presented at the 12th Annual European Conference on Reading, Dublin, Ireland, 1–4 July 2001.

Bruckman, A., & Resnick, M. (1995). The MediaMOO Project: Constructivism and professional community. *Convergence, 1*(1), 94–109.

Brue, A. W., & Oakland, T. D. (1994). *Attention deficit hyperactivity disorder*. National Institute of Mental Health. Retrieved 22 March, 2002, from http://www.nimh.nih.gov/publicat/adhd.cfm

Bruer, J. T. (1999). In search of … brain-based education. *Phi Delta Kappan, 80*(9), 648–654.

Bruner, J. (1966). *Toward a theory of instruction*. Cambridge, MA: The Belknap Press of Harvard University.

Bruner, J. S. (1975). The ontogenesis of speech acts. *Journal of Child Language, 2*, 1–19.

Bruner, J. S. (1990). *Acts of meaning*. Cambridge, MA: Harvard University Press.

Bruner, J. S., & Sherwood, V. (1975). Peekaboo and the learning of rule structures. In J. S. Bruner, A. Jolly, & K. Sylva (Eds.), *Play – its role in development and evolution* (pp. 277–285). Harmondsworth, Middlesex: Penguin.

Bryant, P. E. (1974). *Perception and understanding in young children*. London: Methuen.

Bryant, P. E. (1990). Empirical evidence for causes in development. In G. Butterworth and P. Bryant (Eds.), *Causes of development: Interdisciplinary perspectives* (pp. 33–45). Hemel Hempstead, Herts: Harvester Wheatsheaf.

Bryant, P. E., Bradley, L., McClean, M., & Crossland, J. (1989). Nursery rhymes, phonological skills, and reading. *Journal of Child Language, 16*, 407–28.

Buckingham, J. (2000). *Boy troubles: Understanding rising suicide, rising crime and educational failure*. Policy monograph. St Leonards, NSW: Centre for Independent Studies.

Burks, V. S., Dodge, K. A., & Price, J. M. (1995). Models of internalizing outcomes of early rejection. *Development & Psychopathology. Special issue: Developmental processes in peer relations and psychopathology, 7*(4), 683–695.

Burns, D. E., Johnson, S. E., & Gable, R. K. (1998). Can we generalize about the learning style characteristics of high academic achievers? *Roeper Review, 20*, 276–282.

Butler, R. (1995). Motivational and informational functions and consequences of children's attention to peers' work. *Journal of Educational Psychology, 87*, 347–360.

Byrne, B. M. (1996). Academic self-concept: Its structure, measurement, and relation to academic achievement. In B. Bracken (Ed.), *Handbook of self-concept* (pp. 287–316). New York: Wiley.

Byrne, B. M., & Gavin, D. A. (1996). The Shavelson model revisited: Testing for the structure of academic self-concept across pre-, early, and late adolescents. *Journal of Educational Psychology, 88*, 215–228.

Byrne, B. M., & Shavelson, R. J. (1996). On the structure of social self-concept for pre-, early-, and late adolescents: A test of the Shavelson, Hubner, and Stanton (1976) model. *Journal of Personality and Social Psychology, 70*, 599–613.

Byrnes, J. P. (1996). *Cognitive development and learning in instructional contexts*. Boston: Allyn & Bacon.

Calderon, M., & Slavin, J. (1999). This issue. *Theory into Practice, 38*, 66.

Callan, R. (1996). Learning styles in the high school: A novel approach. *NASSP Bulletin, 80*(557), 66–71.

Cambourne, B. (1988). *The whole story: Natural learning and the acquisition of literacy in the classroom*. Auckland, NZ: Ashton Scholastic.

Campos, J. J., Barrett, K., Lamb, M., Goldsmith, H., & Stenberg, C. (1983). Socioemotional development. In M. Haith & J. J. Campos (Eds.), *Handbook of child psychology, Vol. II: Infancy and developmental psychobiology* (pp. 783–915). New York: Wiley.

Campos, J. J., Kermoian, R., & Zumbahlen, M. R. (1992). Socioemotional transformation in the family system following infant crawling onset. In N. Eisenberg & R. A. Fabes (Eds.), *New Directions for Child Development, 55*, 25–40.

Canadian Paediatric Society (2000). Use of methylphenidate for attention deficit hyperactivity disorder. *Canadian Medical Association Journal, 142*(8), 817–818.

Caplan, N. S., Whitmore, J. K., & Choy, M. H. (1989). *The boat people and achievement in America: A study of family life, hard work, and cultural values*. Ann Arbor, MI: University of Michigan Press.

Caple, C. (1996). *The effects of spaced practice and spaced review on recall and retention using computer assisted instruction*. Ann Arbor, MI: UMI.

Capon, N., & Kuhn, D. (1979). Logical reasoning in the supermarket: Adult females' use of a proportional reasoning strategy in an everyday context. *Developmental Psychology, 15*, 450–452.

Cardelle-Elaware, M. (1995). Effects of metacognitive instruction on low achievers in mathematics problems. *Teaching and Teacher Education, 11*(1), 81–95.

Carl R. Rogers Collection. (2003). HPA MSS 32, Department of Special Collections, University Library. Santa Barbara, Ca: University of California.

Carlberg, C. & Kavale, K. A. (1980). The efficacy of special versus regular class placement for exceptional children: A meta-analysis. *The Journal of Special Education, 14*, 295–309.

Carpenter, M., Nagell, K., & Tomasello, M. (1988). Social cognition, joint attention, and communicative competence from 9 to 15 months of age. *Monographs of the Society for Research in Child Development, 63*(4, Serial No. 255).

Carr, M., Alexander, J., & Folds-Bennett, T. (1994). Metacognition and mathematics strategy use. *Applied Cognitive Psychology, 8*, 583–595.

Carroll, J. B. (1996). A three-stratum theory of intelligence: Spearman's contribution. In I. Dennis & P. Tapsfield (Eds.), *Human abilities: Their nature and measurement* (pp. 1–17). Mahwah, NJ: Erlbaum.

Case, R. (1985). *Intellectual development: Birth to adulthood*. Orlando: Academic Press.

Case, R., & Okamoto, Y. (1996). Role of conceptual structures in the development of children's thought. *Society for Research in Child Development, 61*(pt 1–2).

Caspi, A. (1995). Puberty and the gender organisation of schools: How biology and social context shape the adolescent experience. In L. J. Crockett & A. C. Crouter (Eds.), *Pathways through adolescence: Individual development in relation to social contexts* (pp. 57–74). Mahwah, NJ: Erlbaum.

Cattell, R. B., & Butcher, H. J. (1968). *The prediction of achievement and creativity*. Indianapolis: Bobbs-Merrill.

Caudron, S. (1997). Can Generation Xers be trained? *Training and Development, 51*(3), 20–24.

Center for Applied Special Technology (1996). *The role of on-line communications in schools: A national study*. Retrieved 23 May, 2003, from http://www.cast.org/udl/index.cfm?i=121

Center, Y., & Beaman, R. (1991). The use of a peer-tutoring program to promote positive attitudes and outcomes for children in special (support) units. *Australian Educational and Developmental Psychologist, 8*, 8–16.

Center, Y., Ferguson, C., & Ward, J. (1988). *The integration of children with disabilities into regular classrooms (mainstreaming): A naturalistic study*. Stage 1 report. Sydney: Macquarie University.

Center, Y., & Freeman, L. (2000). *Becoming literate: Year One manual*. Sydney: Macquarie University.

Center, Y., Freeman, L., & Robertson, G. (2001). A longitudinal evaluation of the Schoolwide Early Language and Literacy Program (SWELL). In R. Slavin & N. Madden (Eds.), *Success for all* (pp. 111–148). New Jersey: Lawrence Erlbaum.

Center, Y., Ward, J., Ferguson, C., Conway, B., & Linfoot, K. (1989). *The integration of children with disabilities into regular schools: A naturalistic study: Stage 2 report*. Sydney: Macquarie University.

Center, Y., Wheldall, K., Freeman, L., Outhred, L., & McNaught, M. (1995). An evaluation of Reading Recovery. *Reading Research Quarterly, 30*, 240–263.

Cha, J. H. (1994). Aspects of individualism and collectivism in Korea. In U. Kim, H. C. Triandis, C. Kagitcibasi, S. Choi, & G. Yoon (Eds.), *Individualism and collectivism: Theory, methods, and applications* (pp. 157–174). Thousand Oaks, CA: Sage.

Chall, J. S. (1983). *Learning to read: The great debate* (Updated ed.). New York: McGraw-Hill.

Chan, C., Burtis, J., & Bereiter, C. (1997). Knowledge building as a mediator of conflict in conceptual change. *Cognitive Instruction, 15*, 1–40.

Chapple, S., Jefferies, R., & Walker, R. (1997). *Maori participation and performance in education*. Wellington: Ministry of Education.

Charp, S. (1998). Preparing the 21st century teacher. *THE Journal: Technological Horizons in Education, 26*, 6–8.

Charter, A. (1996). Integrating traditional Aboriginal teaching and learning approaches in post-secondary settings. *Issues in the North, Vol. 1*. (ERIC Document Reproduction Service: ED403091.)

Chazan, M., Laing, A. F., & Davies, D. (1994). *Emotional and behavioural difficulties in middle childhood: Identification, assessment, and intervention in school*. London: Falmer Press.

Chazan, M., Laing, A. E., Davies, D., & Phillips, R. (1998). *Helping socially withdrawn and isolated children and adolescents*. London: Cassell.

Christie, M., Harris, S., & McClay, D. (1987). *Teaching Aboriginal children: Milingimbi and beyond*. Mt Lawley, WA: Western Australian College of Advanced Education.

Chu, P. C., & Spires, E. E. (1991). Validating the computer anxiety rating scale: Effects of cognitive style and computer courses on computer anxiety. *Computers in Human Behavior, 7*, 7–21.

Chun, D. M. (1994). Using computer networking to facilitate the acquisition of interactive competence. *System, 22*(1), 17–31.

Clark, K. L., Glew, S., Kelly, F., Lander, M., Lawlor, G., & Scott, A. (n.d.). *Behaviour management in schools: Implementation package*. Perth: Perth District Education Office.

Clay, M. M. (1985). *The early detection of reading difficulties*. Exeter, NH: Heinemann.

Clay, M. M (1991). *Becoming literate: the construction of inner control*. Birkenhead, NZ: Heinemann Education.

Clay, M. M. (1993). *Reading recovery: A guidebook for teachers in training*. Portsmouth, NH: Heinemann.

Clements, D. (1999). Metacognition, learning and educational computing environments. In D. D. Shade (Ed.), *Information technology in childhood education annual* (pp. 39–59). Virginia: AACE.

Cline, T., & Ertubey, C. (1997). The impact of gender on primary teachers' evaluations of children's difficulties in school. *British Journal of Educational Psychology, 67*, 447–456.

Clunies Ross, G. G. (1988). Early education and integration for children with intellectual disabilities: Some results of a 10-year EPIC. In M. Pieterse, S. Bochner & S. Bettison (Eds.), *Early intervention for children with disabilities: The Australian experience* (pp. 97–104). Sydney: Macquarie University.

Cobb, P., & Yackel, E. (1996). Constructivist, emergent, and sociocultural perspectives in the context of developmental research. *Educational Psychologist, 31*(3–4), 175–190.

Coenen, M. E. (2002). Using gifted students as peer tutors: An effective and beneficial approach. *Gifted Child Today, 25*(1), 48–55.

Cognition and Technology Group (1992). Some thoughts about constructivism and instructional design. In T. M. Duffy and D. H. Jonassen (Eds.), *Constructivism and the technology of instruction: A conversation* (pp. 115–119). Hillsdale, NJ: Lawrence Erlbaum Associates.

Cohen, E. G. (1994). Restructuring the classroom: Conditions for productive small groups. *Review of Educational Research, 64*, 1–35.

Cohen, E. G., & Lotan, R. A. (1995). Producing equal-status interaction in the heterogeneous classroom. *American Educational Research Journal, 32*(1), 99–120.

Coker, C. A. (1995). Learning style consistency across cognitive and motor settings. *Perceptual and Motor Skills, 81*, 1023–1026.

Colby, A., Kohlberg, L., & Kauffman, K. (1987a). Theoretical introduction to the measurement of moral judgment. In A. Coby & L. Kohlberg, *The measurement of moral judgment* (Vol. 1). Cambridge: Cambridge University Press.

Colby, A., Kohlberg, L., & Kauffman, K. (1987b). Instructions for moral judgment interviewing. In A. Colby & L. Kohlberg, *The measurement of moral judgment* (Vol. 1). Cambridge: Cambridge University Press.

Cole, K. A. (1996). Structuring academic engagement in classrooms. *Dissertation Abstracts International Section A: Humanities & Social Sciences, 56*(10–A), 3885.

Cole, M., & Cole, S. R. (2001). *The development of children* (4th ed.). New York: Worth.

Cole, M., & Wertsch, J. V. (2000). *Beyond the individual–social antimony in discussions of Piaget and Vygotsky*. Retrieved 29 August, 2000, from http://www.massey.ac.nz/~ALOCK/virtyal/colevyg.htm

Cole, P., & Chan, L. (1990). *Methods and strategies for special education.* Sydney: Prentice Hall.

Coley, J. D., DePinto, R., Craig, S., & Gardner, R. (1993). From college to classroom: Three teachers' accounts of their adaptations of reciprocal teaching. *The Elementary School Journal, 94*(2), 255–267.

Colley, A. (1998). Education. In K. Trew, J. Kremer, (Eds.), *Gender and Psychology.* London: Arnold.

Collins, C., Kenway, J., & McLeod, J. (2000). *Factors influencing the educational performance of males and females in school and their initial destinations after leaving school.* Canberra: Department of Education, Employment, Training and Youth Affairs.

Collis, B. A., & Williams, R. L. (1987). Cross-cultural comparison of gender differences in adolescents' attitudes towards computers and selected school subjects. *Journal of Educational Research, 81,* 17–27.

Comber, C., Colley, A., Hargreaves, D. J., & Dorn, L. (1997). The effects of age, gender and computer experience upon computer attitudes. *Educational Research, 39*(2), 123–133.

Commonwealth Department of Education, Science and Training (1998). *Literacy for all: The challenge for Australian schools. Commonwealth Literacy Policies for Australian Schools.* Australian Schooling Monograph Series No 1/1998. Retrieved 26 May, 2003, from http://www.deet.gov.au/archive/schools/literacy&numeracy/publications/lit4all.htm

Comunian, A. L., & Gielen, U. P. (Eds.). (2000). *International perspectives on human development.* Lengerich, Germany: Pabst Science Publishers.

Connell, R. W., Ashenden, D. J., Kessler, S., & Dowsett, G. W. (1982). *Making the difference: Schools, families and social division.* Sydney: Allen & Unwin.

Connell, R. W., White, V. M., & Johnston, K. M. (1990). *Poverty, education and the Disadvantaged Schools Program (DSP): Project overview and discussion of policy questions.* Sydney: School of Behavioural Science, Macquarie University.

Connell, R. W., White, V. M., & Johnston, K. M. (Eds.). (1991). *'Running twice as hard': The Disadvantaged Schools Program in Australia.* Geelong, Victoria: Deakin University.

Conroy, J. S. (1980). Autonomy vs authority. In D. Cohen (Ed.), *Alternative education: The Currambena experience* (pp. 290–304). Sydney: David Cohen.

Conway, R. (1998). Meeting the needs of students with behavioural and emotional disorders. In A. Ashman and J. Elkins (Eds.), *Educating children with special needs* (3rd ed., pp. 148–186). Sydney: Prentice Hall.

Conway, R. (2002). Behaviour in and out of the classroom. In A. Ashman & J. Elkins (Ed.), *Educating children with diverse abilities* (pp. 172–236). French's Forest, NSW: Pearson.

Cook, L., & Buzzacott, K. (2000). Case Study 6: Yipirinya School, Alice Springs, NT. In Board of Studies (Ed.), *Teaching Aboriginal languages. Case studies* (pp. 43–54). Sydney: Board of Studies NSW. Retrieved 4 June, 2003, from http://www.boardofstudies.nsw.edu.au/aboriginal_research/pdf_doc/aborlang_casestudies.doc

Cooper, H. M., & Good, T. L. (1983). *Pygmalion grows up: Studies in the expectation communication process.* New York: Longman.

Cooper, R. P., & Aslin, R. N. (1994). Developmental differences in infant attention to the spectral properties of infant-directed speech. *Child Development, 65,* 1663–1677.

Coote, C. (2000). Special needs (gifted) in the mainstream primary classroom. *Gifted, 112,* 25–27.

Corcoran, J., & Franklin, C. (2002). Multi-systemic risk factors predicting depression, self-esteem and stress in low SES and culturally diverse adolescents. *Journal of Human Behavior in the Social Environment, 5*(2), 61–76.

Cortis, N., & Newmarch, E. (2000). *Boys in schools, what's happening?* Paper presented at Manning the Next Millennium Conference, Queensland University of Technology, 1–2 December 2000.

Cote, J. E., & Allahar, A. L. (1996). *Generation on hold: Coming of age in the late twentieth century.* New York: New York University Press.

Coupe, J., & Goldbart, J. (Eds.). (1988). *Communication before speech: Normal development and impaired communication.* London: Croom Helm.

Covington, M. V. (1998). *The will to learn: A guide for motivating young people.* Cambridge: Cambridge University Press.

Cowie, H., & Rudduck, J. (1990). *Cooperative group work: Transitions and traditions.* London: B.P. Educational Services.

Cowie, H., Smith, P., Boulton, M., & Laver, R. (1994). *Cooperation in the multi-ethnic classroom: The impact of cooperative groups work on social relationships in middle schools.* London: Fulton.

Craik, F., & Lockhart, R. (1972). Levels of processing: A framework for memory research. *Journal of Verbal Learning and Verbal Behavior, 11,* 671–684.

Crain, R. M. (1996). The influence of age, race, and gender on child and adolescent multidimensional self-concept. In B. Bracken (Ed.), *Handbook of self-concept* (pp. 395–420). New York: Wiley.

Crain, W. (2000). *Theories of development: Concepts and applications* (4th ed.). Upper Saddle River, NJ: Prentice Hall.

Crockett, L. J., & Crouter, A. C. (1995). Pathways through adolescence: An overview. In L. J. Crockett & A. C. Crouter (Eds.), *Pathways through adolescence* (pp. 1–12). Mahwah, NJ: Lawrence Erlbaum Associates.

Crozier, W. Ray (1997). *Individual learners: Personality differences in education.* London: Routledge.

Csapo, N. (2002). Certification of computer literacy. *THE Journal,* September. Retrieved 15 June, 2003, from http://www.thejournal.com/magazine/vault/A4117.cfm

Cumming, J. (Ed.). (1998). *Outcome-based education: Resources for implementation.* Canberra: Australian Curriculum Studies Association.

Cummins, J. (1979). Cognitive/academic language proficiency, linguistic interdependence, the optimal age question, and some other matters. *Working Papers in Bilingualism, 9,* 1–43.

Cunningham, C. E., Cunningham, L. J., Martorelli, V., Tran, A., Young, J., & Zacharias, R. (1998). The effects of primary division, student-mediated conflict resolution program on playground aggression. *Journal of Child Psychology and Psychiatry and Allied Disciplines, 39,* 653–662.

Curriculum Corporation (1989). *National report on schooling in Australia.* Carlton, Victoria: Curriculum Corporation.

Curriculum Corporation (1994). Technology as an area of

learning. In Australian Education Council, *A statement on technology for Australian schools*. Carlton, Victoria: Curriculum Corporation.

Curriculum Council (1998). Western Australian Curriculum Framework. Retrieved 25 June, 2003, from http://www.curriculum.wa.edu.au/pages/framework/framework000.htm

Curriculum Support Directorate, NSW Department of Education and Training (1998). *Count me in too: professional development package*. Ryde, NSW: The Directorate.

Curry, L. (1990). A critique of the research on learning styles. *Educational Leadership*, 48(2), 50–55.

Cuttance, P. (2001). Information and communication technologies. In P. Cuttance (Ed.), *School innovation: Pathway to the knowledge society* (pp. 73–100). Canberra: Department of Education, Training and Youth Affairs (DETYA). Retrieved 20 May, 2003, from http://www.dest.gov.au/schools/Publications/2001/innovation/chapter4.htm

Daiute, C., & Dalton, B. (1993). Collaboration between children learning to write: Can novices be masters? *Cognitive Instruction*, 10, 281–333.

Daiute, C., & Griffin, T. M. (1993). The social construction of written narratives. In C. Daiute (Ed.), *New directions in child development, No. 61: The development of literacy through social interaction* (pp. 97–120). San Francisco: Jossey-Bass.

Damasio, A. R. (1994). *Descartes' Error: Emotion, reason, and the human brain*. New York: G. P. Putnam.

Darling, J. (1990). Progressivism and individual needs. In N. C. Entwistle (Ed.), *Handbook of educational ideas and practices* (pp. 43–51). London: Routledge.

Darling, J. (1994). *Child-centred education and its critics*. London: Paul Chapman.

Darwin, C. (1877). Biographical sketch of an infant. *Mind*, 2, 285–294.

Dasen, P. R. (1973). Piagetian research in central Australia. In G. E. Kearney, P. R. deLacy, & G. R. Davidson (Eds.), *The psychology of Aboriginal Australia*. Sydney: Wiley.

Dasen, P. R. (Ed.). (1977). *Piagetian psychology: Cross cultural contributions*. New York: Gardner.

Davenport, P., & Howe, C. (1999). Conceptual gain and successful problem-solving in primary school mathematics. *Educational Studies*, 25(1), 55–78.

Davidson, J. E., Deuser, R., & Sternberg, R. J. (1994). The role of metacognition in problem solving. In J. Metcalfe & A. P. Shimamura (Eds.), *Metacognition: Knowing about knowing* (pp. 207–226). Cambridge, MA: MIT.

Davis, J., & Cochran, K. F. (1989). An information processing view of field dependence–independence. *Early Child Development and Care*, 43, 129–145.

Davis, W. E. (1989). The Regular Education Initiative debate: Its promises and problems. *Exceptional Children*, 55, 440–6.

De Carvalho, R. J. (1991). *The founders of humanistic psychology*. New York: Praeger.

De Vries, D. L., & Slavin, R. E. (1978). Teams-Games-Tournament: Review of ten classroom experiments. *Journal of Research and Development in Education*, 12, 28–39.

Deal, N. (1995). *Is the medium the message? Comparing student perceptions of teacher responses via written and e-mail forms*. Paper presented at the annual National Educational Computing Conference, Baltimore, MD. (ERIC Document Reproduction Service No. ED 392 432.)

Dean, R. S., & Anderson, J. L. (1997). Lateralisation of cerebral function. In A. M. Horton, Jr., D. Wedding & J. Webster (Eds.), *The neuropsychology handbook, Vol. 1: Foundations and assessment* (2nd ed., pp. 139–168). New York: Springer.

Debus, R. L. (1970). The effects of brief observation of model behaviour on conceptual tempo of impulsive children. *Developmental Psychology*, 2, 22–32.

DEET (1989). *National Aboriginal and Torres Strait Islander Education Policy: Joint policy statement*. Canberra: AGPS.

DEET (1991). *Australia's language: The Australian Language and Literacy Policy*. Canberra: AGPS.

DEETYA (1998). *Literacy for all: The challenge for Australian schools: Commonwealth literacy policies for Australian schools*. Australian Schooling Monograph Series, No. 1. Canberra: Department of Education, Employment, Training and Youth Affairs.

Delbridge, A., Bernard, J. R. L., Blair, D., Butler, S., Perters, P., & Yallop, C. (1997). *The Macquarie Dictionary* (3rd ed.). Macquarie University, Sydney: The Macquarie Dictionary.

Dempsey, I., & Foreman, P. J. (1995). Trends and influences in the integration of students with disabilities in Australia. *The Australasian Journal of Special Education*, 2, 47–53.

Dempsey, I., & Foreman, P. J. (1997). Trends in the educational placement of students with disabilities in New South Wales. *International Journal of Disability, Development and Education*, 44, 207–216.

Denning, W. E. (1982). *Out of crisis*. Cambridge, MA: Institute of Technology: Center for Advanced Engineering Study.

Dennis, W., & Najarian, P. (1957). Infant development under environmental handicap. *Psychological Monograph*, 71, 436.

Dennison, G. (1969). *The lives of children: The story of the First Street School*. Harmondsworth, Middlesex: Penguin.

Deno, E. (1970). Special education as developmental capital. *Exceptional Children*, 37, 229–237.

Department of Education (DoE), Victoria (2001). *A policy statement to support the education of gifted students*. Retrieved 3 August, 2003, from http://www.sofweb.vic.edu.au/futures/bfpolicy.htm

DeRosier, M., Kupersmidt, J. B., & Patterson, C. J. (1994). Children's academic and behavioral adjustment as a function of the chronicity and proximity of peer rejection. *Child Development*, 65(6), 1799–1813.

Detterman, D. K. (1993). Giftedness and intelligence: One and the same? In G. R. Block & K. Ackrill (Eds.), *The origins and development of high ability* (pp. 22–43). Chichester, West Sussex: Wiley.

DETYA (1997). *Mapping literacy achievement: Results of the 1996 National School English Literacy Survey*. Canberra: DETYA. Retrieved 18 April, 2003, from http://www.detya.gov.au/mla/index.htm

DETYA (2000). *The education of boys*. Submission to the House of Representatives Standing Committee on employment, education and workplace relations. Canberra: DETYA.

Dewey, J. (1916). *Democracy and education*. New York: Macmillan.

Dewey, J. (1937). *Experience and education*. New York: Macmillan.

Dillenbourg, P., & Schneider, D. (1995). Mediating the mechanisms which make collaborative learning sometimes effective. *International Journal of Educational Telecommunications, 1*(2/3), 131–146.

Dimock, V., & Boethel, M. (1999). *Constructing knowledge with technology: Technology in constructivist learning environments*. Southwest Educational Development Laboratory. Retrieved 19 May, 2003, from http://www.sedl.org/ pubs/tec27/9.html

Division of Educational Psychology, American Psychological Association (n.d.). *What is educational psychology?* Available online: http://www.cedu.niu.edu/epf/Psychology.PDF

Dixon-Krauss, L. (1996). Vygotsky's sociohistorical perspective on learning and its application to western literacy instruction. In L. Dixon-Krauss (Ed.), *Vygotsky in the classroom: Mediated literacy instruction and assessment* (pp. 7–24). White Plains, NY: Longman.

Doherty, P. (1982). *Strategies and initiatives for special education in New South Wales: A report of the working party on a plan for special education in NSW*. Sydney: NSW Department of Education.

Doman, G., Delacato, C. H., & Doman, R. (1964). *The Doman–Delacato Developmental Profile*. Philadelphia: Institute for the Achievement of Human Potential.

Donaldson, M. (1978). *Children's minds*. Glasgow: Fontana.

Dong, Q., Yang, B., & Ollendick, T. I. (1994). Fears in Chinese children and adolescents and their relations to anxiety and depression. *Journal of Child Psychology and Psychiatry, 35*, 351–363.

Donnelly, J., Ferraro, H., & Eadie, C. (2001). Effects of a health and relationship program on drug behaviors. *North American Journal of Psychology, 3*(3), 453–462.

Donovan, J. J., & Radosevich, D. J. (1999). A meta-analytic review of the distribution of practice effect: Now you see it, now you don't. *Journal of Applied Psychology, 84*(5), 795–805.

Doyle, T. (2003). *Nelson maths for Victoria: Student book*. Melbourne: Nelson.

Doyle, W. (1986). Classroom organisation and management. In M. C. Wittrock (Ed.), *Handbook of research on teaching* (3rd ed., pp. 392–431). New York: Macmillan.

Dreikurs, R. (1968). *Psychology in the classroom. A manual for teachers* (2nd ed.). New York: Harper & Row.

Dreikurs, R., & Cassel, P. (1990). *Discipline without tears* (2nd ed.). New York: Dutton.

Dreikurs, R., Grunwald, B. B., & Pepper, F. C. (1982). *Maintaining sanity in the classroom: Classroom management techniques* (2nd ed.). New York: Harper & Row.

Driver, R. (1983). *Pupil as scientist*. Milton Keynes, Bucks: Open University Press.

Duchesne, S. (1996). *Parental beliefs and behaviours in relation to schooling: A cross-cultural study of Vietnamese and Anglo-Australian families*. Unpublished manuscript, Macquarie University, Sydney.

Duckworth, E. (1987). *'The having of wonderful ideas' and other essays on teaching and learning*. New York: Teachers College Press.

Duffy, T. M., & Cunningham, D. J. (1996). Constructivism: Implications for the design and delivery of instruction. In D. H. Jonassen (Ed.), *Handbook of research for educational communications and technology* (pp. 170–198). New York: Simon Schuster Macmillan.

Duit, R., & Confrey, J. (1996). Reorganising the curriculum and teaching to improve learning in science and mathematics. In D. F. Treagust, R. Duit, & B. J. Fraser (Eds.), *Improving teaching and learning in science and mathematics* (pp. 79–93). New York and London: Teachers College Press.

Duke, D. L., & Meckel, A. M. (1984). *Teachers guide to classroom management*. New York: Random House.

Dunn, J., & Kendrick, C. (1982). *Siblings: Love, envy and understanding*. Cambridge, MA: Harvard University Press.

Dunn, L. M. (1968). Special education for the mildly retarded – is much of it justified? *Exceptional Children, 35*, 5–22.

Dunn, L. M., & Dunn, L. M. (1997). *Peabody Picture Vocabularly Test* (3rd ed.). Circle Pines, MN: American Guidance Services.

Dunn, R., Dunn, K., & Perrin, J. (1994). *Teaching young children through their individual learning styles: Practical approaches for grades K–2*. Boston: Allyn & Bacon.

Dunn, R., Dunn, K. J., & Price, G. E. (1989). *Learning Style Inventory*. Lawrence, KS: Price Systems.

Dunne, E., & Bennett, N. (1990). *Talking and learning in groups*. London: Methuen.

Dunphy, D. (1963). The social structure of urban adolescent peer groups. *Sociometry, 26*, 230–276.

Dunphy, D. (1990). Peer group socialization. In R. Muuss (Ed.), *Adolescent behavior and society: A book of readings*. New York: McGraw–Hill.

Duran, R. P. (1994). Cooperative learning for language minority students. In R. A. DeVillar, C. J. Faltis, & J. Cummins (Eds.), *Cultural diversity in schools: From rhetoric to practice* (pp. 145–159). Buffalo, NY: SUNY.

Durbrow, E. H., Schaefer, B. A., & Jimerson, S. R. (2001). Learning-related behaviors versus cognitive ability in the academic performance of Vincentian children. *British Journal of Educational Psychology, 71*(3), 471–483.

Duren, P. E., & Cherrington, A. (1992). The effects of cooperative group work versus independent practice on the learning of some problem-solving strategies. *School Science and Mathematics, 92*(2), 80–83.

Durkheim, E. (1925/1961). *Moral education: A study in the theory and application of the sociology of education*. (Foreword by Paul Fauconnet; translated from the French by Everett K. Wilson and Herman Schnurer; edited with a new introduction by Everett K. Wilson.) New York: Free Press of Glencoe.

D'Urso, J. (1996). What happens when students take part in their own assessment. *Teaching and Change, 4*, 5–19.

Duveen, G. (1997). Psychological development as a social process. In L. Smith, J. Dockrell, & P. Tomlinson (Eds.), *Piaget, Vygotsky and beyond: Future issues for developmental psychology* (pp. 67–90). Kidlington, Oxford: Routledge.

Dweck, C. S. (1986). Motivational processes affecting learning. *American Psychologist, 41*, 1040–1048.

Dwyer, P., & Wyn, J. (2001). *Youth, education and risk: Facing the future*. London: Routledge/Falmer.

Eades, D. (1993). Aboriginal English. *Primary English Notes (PEN), 93*. Sydney: Primary English Teaching Association.

Eades, D. (1997). Communication with Aboriginal speakers of English. *Australian Communication Quarterly*, Summer 96/97, 24–25.

Easton, C. E., & Watson, J. A. (1993). Spatial strategy use during Logo mastery: The impact of cognitive style and development level. *Journal of Computing in Childhood Education, 4*, 77–96.

Eccles, J. S., & Wigfield, A. (1995). In the mind of the actor: The structure of adolescents' achievement task values and expectancy-related beliefs. *Personality & Social Psychology Bulletin, 21*(3), 215–225.

Eckermann, A-K. (1994). *One classroom, many cultures: Teaching strategies for culturally different children*. St Leonards, NSW: Allen & Unwin.

Edens, J. F. (1999). Aggressive children's self-systems and the quality of their relationships with significant others. *Aggressive Violent Behaviour, 4*, 151–177.

EdNA Online (2002). *ICT Leading Practice website*. Retrieved 20 February, 2003, from http://leadingpractice.edna.edu.au/criteria.html

Education Department of Western Australia (2002). *About students at educational risk*. Retrieved 11 March, 2002, from http://www.eddept.wa.edu.au/saer/about/content.htm

Education Department of Western Australia (1999). *Students at educational risk: Making the difference*. East Perth: Education Department of Western Australia. Retrieved 26 March, 2002, from http://www.eddept.wa.edu.au/SAER/default.htm

Educational Resource Information Center (ERIC) (1980). Processing and Reference Facility. Retrieved 26 November, 2002, from http://www.ericfacility.net/extra/pub/thessearch.cfm

Edwards, B. (1981). *Drawing on the right side of the brain*. London: Souvenir.

Edwards, C. H. (1997). *Classroom discipline and management* (2nd ed.). Upper Saddle River, NJ: Prentice Hall.

Edwards, C. P., Gandini, L., & Forman, G. E. (Eds.). (1998). *The hundred languages of children: The Reggio Emilia approach – advanced reflections* (2nd ed.). Greenwich, CT: Ablex.

Edwards, J. (1991). To teach responsibility, bring back the Dalton Plan. *Phi Delta Kappan, 72*, 398–401.

Eisenberg, M. B., & Berkowitz, B. (1988). *Curriculum initiative: An agenda and strategy for library media programs*. Norwood, NJ: Ablex.

Eisenberg, M. B., & Johnson, D. (2002). Learning and teaching information technology computer skills in context. *ERIC Digest*. Retrieved 21 May, 2003, from http://ericit.org/digests/EDO-IR-2002-04.shtml

Eisenberg, N. (1998). Introduction. In N. Eisenberg (Ed.), *Handbook of child psychology Vol. 3: Social, emotional, and personality development* (5th ed., pp. 1–24). New York: Wiley.

Eisenberg, N., & Fabes, R. A. (1998). Prosocial development. In N. Eisenberg (Ed.), *Handbook of child psychology Vol. 3: Social, emotional, and personality development* (5th ed., pp. 701–778). New York: Wiley.

Elkins, J. (2002). The school context. In A. Ashman & J. Elkins (Eds.), *Educating children with diverse abilities* (pp. 73–113). French's Forest, NSW: Pearson.

Ellis, L. A., Marsh, H. W., & Richards, G. E. (2002, August). *A brief version of the Self-Description Questionnaire II*. Paper presented at the SELF Research Centre International Conference, Sydney, Australia. Retrieved 14 February, 2003, fromhttp://edweb.uws.edu.au/self/Conferences/2002_CD_Ellis,_Marsh_&_Richards.pdf

Ellis, R., & Humphreys, G. W. (Eds.). (1999). *Connectionist psychology: A text with readings*. Hove, East Sussex: Psychology Press.

Ellis, S., & Whalen, S. F. (1992). Keys to cooperative learning: 35 ways to keep kids responsible, challenged, and most of all, cooperative. *Instructor, 101*, 34–37.

Ely, R. (1997). Language and literacy in the school years. In J. Berko Gleason (Ed.), *The development of language* (4th ed.). Boston: Allyn & Bacon.

Ely, R., & McCabe, A. (1994). The language play of kindergarten children. *First Language, 14*, 19–35.

Engelbrecht, P., Natzel, S. G. (1997). Cultural variations in cognitive style: Field dependence vs field independence. *School Psychology International, 18*, 155–164.

Engle, R. W., & Oransky, N. (1999). Multi-store versus dynamic models of temporary storage in memory. In R. J. Sternberg (Ed.), *The nature of cognition* (pp. 515–556). Cambridge, MA: The MIT Press.

Entwistle, N. J. (1991). Cognitive style and learning. In K. Marjoribanks (Ed.), *The foundations of student learning* (pp. 139–146). Oxford: Pergamon.

Epstein, J. L. (1995). School/family/community partnerships: Caring for the children we share. *Phi Delta Kappan, 76*(9), 701–712.

Erdley, C., Nangle, D., Newman, J., & Carpenter, E. (2001). Children's friendship experiences and psychological adjustment: Theory and research. In D. Nangle & C. Erdley (Eds.), *The role of friendship in psychological adjustment* (pp. 5–24). San Francisco: Jossey-Bass.

Erikson, E. H. (1959). *Identity and the life cycle: Selected papers*. Oxford: International Universities Press.

Erikson, E. H. (1963). *Childhood and society* (2nd ed.). New York: W. W. Norton.

Erikson, E. H. (1964). *Insight and responsibility*. New York: W. W. Norton.

Erikson, E. H. (1975). *Life history and the historical moment*. Oxford: W. W. Norton.

Erikson, E. H. (1976). *Identity, youth and crisis*. New York: Harper.

Erikson, E. H. (1997). *The life cycle completed: Extended version*. New York: W.W. Norton.

ERO (2000). *Promoting boys' achievement*. Retrieved 22 February, 2002, from http://www.ero.govt.nz/Publications/pubs2000/promoting%20boys%20achmt.htm

ERO (Education Review Office) (2002a). *Maori students: schools making a difference*. Wellington: ERO. Retrieved 22 February, 2002, from http://www.ero.gov.nz/Publications/pubs2002/MaoriStudents.htm

ERO (2002b). *The education of Pacific students in New Zealand schools*. Wellington: ERO. Retrieved 2 March, 2003, from http://www.ero.gov.nz/Publications/pubs2002/PacificStudents.htm

ERO (2002c). *The performance of Kura Kaupapa Maori*. Wellington: ERO. Retrieved 5 March, 2003, from http://www.ero.gov.nz/Publications/pubs2002/Kura.htm

Evans, N. J., Forney, D. S., & Guido-DiBrito, F. (1998). *Student development in college: Theory, research, and practice*. San Francisco: Jossey-Bass.

Evelyth, P. B., & Tanner, J. M. (1990). *Worldwide variation in human growth* (2nd ed.). Cambridge: Cambridge University Press.

Eysenck, M. W., & Keane, M. (2000). *Cognitive psychology: A student's handbook* (4th ed.). East Sussex: Psychology Press.

Fagerheim, T., Raeymaekers, P., Tonnesson, F. E., Pedersen, M., Tranebjaerg, L., & Lubs, H. A. (1999). A new gene (DYX3) for dyslexia is located on chromosome 2. *Journal of Medical Genetics, 36*, 664–669.

Fagot, B. I. (1985). Beyond the reinforcement principle: Another step toward understanding sex role development. *Developmental Psychology, 21*(6), 1097–1104.

Fang, A., & Cox, B. E. (1999). Emergent metacognition: A study of preschoolers' literate behaviour. *Journal of Research in Childhood Education, 13*, 175–187.

Farmer, D. (Ed.). (1993). *Gifted children need help? A guide for parents and teachers*. Strathfield, NSW: NSW Association for Gifted and Talented Children.

Feingold, A. (1988). Cognitive gender differences are disappearing. *American Psychologist, 43*, 95–103.

Feingold, A. (1993). Cognitive gender differences: A developmental perspective. *Sex Roles, 29*, 91–112.

Feingold, A. (1994). Gender differences in personality: A meta-analysis. *Psychological Bulletin, 116*, 429–456.

Feingold, B. F. (1975). *Why your child is hyperactive*. New York: Random House.

Feldhusen, J. (2001). Terman, Hollingworth, and the gifted. *Roeper Review, 23*, 165.

Felix, U. (2002). The web as a vehicle for constructivist approaches in language teaching. *ReCALL: Journal of Eurocall, 14*(1), 2–15.

Fergusson, D. M., & Horwood, L. J. (1997). Gender differences in educational achievement in a New Zealand birth cohort. *New Zealand Journal of Educational Studies, 32*, 1.

Ferneding-Lenert, K. F., & Harris, J. B. (1994). Redefining expertise and reallocating roles in text-based asynchronous teaching/learning environments. *Machine Mediated Learning, 4*(2/3), 129–148.

Ferrari, M., & Sternberg, R. J. (1998). The development of mental abilities and styles. In D. Kuhn, & R. S. Siegler (Eds.), *Handbook of child psychology* (Vol. 2, 5th ed., pp. 899–946). New York: John Wiley & Sons.

Feuerstein, R., Rand, Y., & Hoffman, M. (1979). *The dynamic assessment of retarded performers: The Learning Potential Assessment Device. Theory, instruments and techniques*. Baltimore, MD: University Park Press.

Field, B. A. (1986). The nature and incidence of classroom behaviour problems and their remediation through preventative management. *Behaviour Change, 3*, 53–57.

Fine, S. (2001). They're connected, but are they learning? *Globe and Mail* newspaper (Toronto, Canada). Retrieved 23 May, 2003, from http://www.unesco.org/courier/2001_03/uk/education.htm#e1

Finke, L., & Williams, J. (1999). Alcohol and drug use of inter-city versus rural school age children. *Journal of Drug Education, 29*(3), 279–291.

Fischer, K. W., & Rose, S. P. (1995). Concurrent cycles in the dynamic development of brain and behaviour. *SRCD Newsletter, 3*–4, 15–16.

Fischer, K. W., Wang, L., Kennedy, B., & Cheng, C-L. (1998). Culture and biology in emotional development. In D. Sharma & K. W. Fischer (Eds.), *Socioemotional development across cultures* (No. 81, pp. 21–44). San Francisco: Jossey-Bass.

Flannery, K. A., & Liederman, J. (1995). Is there really a syndrome involving the co-occurrence of neurodevelopmental disorder, talent, non-right handedness and immmune disorder among children? *Cortex, 31*, 503–515.

Flavell, J. H. (1987). Speculations about the nature and development of metacognition. In F. Weinert & U. R. Kluwe (Eds.), *Metacognition, motivation, and understanding* (pp. 21–29). Hillsdale, NJ: Erlbaum.

Flavell, J. H. (1996). Piaget's legacy. *Psychological Science, 7*, 200–203.

Flavell, J. H. (1999). Cognitive development: Children's knowledge about the mind. *Annual Review of Psychology, 50*, 21–45.

Flavell, J. H., Miller, P. H., & Miller, S. A. (1993). *Cognitive development* (3rd ed.). Englewood Cliffs, NJ: Prentice Hall.

Fletcher, R. (1997). *Improving boys' education: A manual for schools*. Newcastle, NSW: Family Action Centre, University of Newcastle.

Fletcher-Flinn, C. M., & Suddendorf, T. (1996). Computer attitudes, gender and exploratory behaviour: A development study. *Journal of Educational Computing Research, 15*(4), 369–392.

Foersterling, F. (1985). Attributional retraining: A review. *Psychological Bulletin, 98*, 495–512.

Fogel, A. (1995). Relational narratives of the prelinguistic self. In P. Rochat (Ed.), *The self in infancy: Theory and research* (pp. 117–139). Amsterdam: Elsevier North Holland.

Folds, R. (1987). *Whitefella school: Education and Aboriginal resistance*. Sydney: Allen & Unwin.

Foreman, P. J. (1994). Services to children with Down Syndrome. *Australasian Journal of Special Education, 18*, 37–46.

Foreman, P. J. (1996). *Integration and inclusion in action*. Sydney: Harcourt Brace.

Forero, R., McLellan, L., Rissel, C., & Bauman, A. (1999). Bullying behaviour and psychosocial health among school students in New South Wales, Australia: A cross sectional survey. *British Medical Journal, 319*(&206), 344–348.

Forlin, C., Douglas, G., & Hattie, J. (1996). Inclusive practices: How accepting are teachers? *International Journal of Disability, Development and Education, 43*, 119–133.

Forman, E. A., Stein, M. K., Brown, C., & Larreamendy-Joerns, J. (1995). *The socialization of mathematical thinking: The role of institutional, interpersonal, and discursive contexts*. Presented at the 77th Annual Meeting of the American Educational Research Association, San Francisco.

Forness, S., & Kavale, K. A. (2001). ADHD and a return to the medical model of special education. *Education and Treatment of Children, 24*(3), 224–248.

Forster, M., & Masters, G. (1996a). *Performances: Assessment resource kit*. Camberwell: ACER.

Forster, M., & Masters, G. (1996b). *Portfolios: Assessment resource kit*. Camberwell: ACER.

Fosnot, C. (1993). Preface. In J. Grennon Brooks & M. G. Brooks, *In search of understanding: The case for constructivist classrooms* (pp. vii–viii). Alexandria, VA: Association for Supervision and Curriculum Development.

REFERENCES

Foster, V. (1999). Gender, schooling achievement and post-school pathways: Beyond statistics and populist discourse. In S. Dinham & C. Scott (Eds.), *Teaching in context*. Melbourne: ACER.

Fox, K. R. (1997). The physical self and processes in self-esteem development. In K. Fox (Ed.), *The physical self: From motivation to well-being* (pp. 111–140). Champaign, IL: Human Kinetics.

Fraiberg, S. (1977). *Insights from the blind: Comparative studies of blind infants*. New York: Basic Books.

Frank, B. M., & Keene, D. (1993). The effect of learners' field independence, cognitive strategy instruction, and inherent word-list organization on free-call memory and strategy use. *Journal of Experimental Education, 62*, 14–25.

Franzen, R. J. (2000). Self-perceptions of multiple intelligences among students from a middle school in the Midwest. *Dissertation Abstracts International Section A: Humanities & Social Sciences, 61*(1–A), 82.

Freebody, P., Ludwig, C., & Gunn, S. (1995). *Everyday literacy practices in and out of schools in low socio-economic urban communities: A descriptive and interpretive research program*. Canberra: DETYA.

French, J., & French, P. (1984). Sociolinguistics and gender divisions. In S. Acker (Ed.), *1984 world yearbook of education 1983–84: Women and education*. London: Kogan Page.

Freud, S. (1930/1963). *Civilisation and its discontents* (J. Strachey, Rev. ed., and J. Riviere, Trans.). London: Hogarth Press and the Institute of Psycho-Analysis.

Freud, S. (1933). *New introductory lectures on psychoanalysis*. New York: Norton.

Freud, S. (1966). *The complete introductory lectures on psychoanalysis* (J. Strachey, Trans.). New York: Norton.

Fridja, N. H. (1986). *The emotions*. Cambridge: Cambridge University Press.

Fuchs, L. S., Fuchs, D., Hamlett, C. L., & Karns, K. (1999). High-achieving students' interactions and performance on complex mathematical tasks as a function of homogeneous and heterogeneous pairings. *American Educational Research Journal, 35*(2), 227–268.

Fuchs, L. S., Fuchs, D., Kazdan, S. A., Karns, K., Calhoon, M. B., Hamlett, C. L., & Hewlett, S. (2000). Effects of workgroup structure and size on student productivity during collaborative work on complex tasks. *Elementary School Journal, 100*, 183–212.

Fuller, A., & Pawsey, R. (Eds.). (1994). *Young people at risk: Homeless Agencies Resource Project*. Austin and Repatriation Medical Centre: Department of Child, Adolescent and Family Psychiatry.

Gallagher, J. J. (1994). Teaching and learning: New models. *Annual Review of Psychology, 45*, 171–195.

Gallini, J., & Helman, H. (1993). *Collaborative learning in virtually expanded classrooms*. Paper presented at the annual meeting of the American Educational Research Association, Atlanta, Georgia.

Galloway, D., Ball, T., Bloomfield D., & Seyd, R. (1982). *Schools and disruptive pupils*. London: Longman.

Galloway, D. (1981). *Disruptive pupils. SET research information for teachers. 1*. Wellington: NZCER.

Galloway, D., & Barrett, C. (1984). Factors associated with suspension from New Zealand secondary schools. *Educational Review, 36*, 277–285.

Galloway, D., Rogers, C., Armstrong, D., & Leo, E. (1998). *Motivating the difficult to teach*. London: Longman.

Galton, M., Hargreaves, L., Comber, C., Wall, D., & Pell, T. (1999). Changes in patterns of teacher interaction in primary classrooms: 1976–1996. *British Educational Research Journal, 25*, 23–37.

Gardner, H. (1982). *Developmental psychology: An introduction* (5th ed.). Boston: Little, Brown.

Gardner, H. (1983). *Frames of mind: The theory of multiple intelligences*. New York: Basic Books.

Gardner, H. (1993). Early giftedness and later achievement. In G. R. Bock and K. Ackrill (Eds.), *The origins and development of high ability. Ciba Foundation Symposium 178* (pp. 175–182). Chichester, West Sussex: Wiley.

Gardner, H. (1999). Are there additional intelligences? The case for naturalistic, spiritual and existential intelligences. In J. Cain (Ed.), *Education: Information and transformation* (pp. 111–132). Englewood Cliffs, NJ: Prentice Hall.

Gardner, H. (2000). The complete tutor. *Technos: Quarterly for Education and Technology* (Fall). Retrieved 14 February, 2003, from http://www.findarticles.com/cf_0/m0HKV/3_9/66408221/print.jhtml

Gardner, H., & Sternberg, R. J. (1994). Novelty and intelligence. In R. J. Sternberg and R. K. Wagner (Eds.), *Mind in context: Interactionist perspectives on human intelligence* (pp. 38–73). Cambridge: Cambridge University Press.

Garmezy, N. (1993). Children in poverty: Resilience despite risk. *Psychiatry, 56*, 127–136.

Garmon, L. C., Bassinger, K. S., Gregg, V. R., & Gibbs, J. C. (1996). Gender differences in stage and expression of moral judgment. *Merrill-Palmer Quarterly, 42*, 418–437.

Garton, A., & Pratt, C. (1998). *Learning to be literate: The development of spoken and written language* (2nd ed.). Oxford: Blackwell.

Ge, X., Conger, R. D., & Elder, G. H., Jr. (1996). Coming of age too early: Pubertal influences on girls' vulnerability to psychological distress. *Child Development, 67*, 3386–3400.

Geez, J., & Mulley, J. (2000). Genes for cognitive function: Developments on the X. *Genome Research, 10*, 157–163.

Gelman, R., & Gallistel, C. R. (1978). *The child's understanding of number*. Cambridge, MA: Harvard University Press.

Gelman, R., & Meck, E. (1983). Preschoolers' counting: Principles before skill. *Cognition, 13*, 343–359.

Genco, P. (2000). Technostress in our schools. *Access, 14*(4), 12–13.

Gesell, A., & Ilg, F. L. (1943). *Infant and child in the culture of today: The guidance of development in home and nursery school*. London: Hamilton.

Gibbons, P. (1991). *Learning to learn in a second language*. Newtown, NSW: Primary English Teaching Association.

Gibbons, P. (2002). *Scaffolding language, scaffolding learning: Teaching second language learners in the mainstream classroom*. Portsmouth, NH: Heinemann.

Gillies, R. M., & Ashman, A. F. (2000). The effects of co-operative learning on students with learning difficulties in the lower elementary school. *Journal of Special Education, 34*, 19–27.

Gilligan, C. (1982). *In a different voice*. Cambridge, MA: Harvard University Press.

Ginsburg, H. P. (1997). Entering the child's mind: The clinical interview in psychological research.

Ginsburg, H. P., Klein, A., & Starkey, P. (1998). The development of children's mathematical thinking: Connecting research with practice. In I. E. Siegel & K. A. Renninger (Eds.), *Handbook of child psychology, Vol. 4. Cognition, perception and language* (5th ed. pp. 401–476). New York: Wiley.

Girard, K., & Koch, S. (1996). *Conflict resolution in schools: A manual for educators*. San Francisco: Jossey-Bass.

Glasser, W. (1965). *Reality therapy: A new approach to psychiatry*. New York: Harper & Row.

Glasser, W. (1969). *Schools without failure*. New York: Harper & Row.

Glasser, W. (1986). *Control theory in the classroom*. New York: Perennial Library.

Glasser, W. (1992). *The quality school: Managing students without coercion* (2nd ed.). New York: Harper-Collins.

Gleason, J. Berko (Ed.). (1997). *The development of language* (4th ed.). Needham Heights, MA: Allyn & Bacon.

Goffman, E. (1968). *Stigma: Notes on the management of spoiled identity*. Harmondsworth, Middlesex: Penguin.

Gombert, J. E. (1992). *Metalinguistic development*. Hemel Hempstead, Herts: Harvester Wheatsheaf.

Good, T. L., & Brophy, J. E. (1997). *Looking in classrooms* (7th ed.). New York: Longman.

Goodenough, F. (1926). *Measurement of intelligence by drawings*. New York: Harcourt, Brace & World.

Goodnow, J. J. (1962). A test of mileau differences with some of Piaget's tasks. *Psychological Monographs*, 76(No. 555).

Goodwin, L., & MacDonald, M. (1997). Educating the rainbow: Authentic assessment and authentic practice for diverse classrooms. In L. Goodwin (Ed.), *Assessment for equity and inclusion: Embracing all our children* (pp. 211–228). New York: Routledge.

Goodwin, M. W. (1999). Cooperative learning and social skills. What skills to teach and how to teach them. *Intervention in School and Clinic*, 35, 29–33.

Gopnick, A., & Meltzoff, A. N. (1997). *Words, thoughts and theories*. Cambridge, MA: MIT Press.

Gordon, C., Arthur, M., & Butterfield, N. (1996). *Promoting positive behaviour: An Australian guide to classroom management*. Melbourne: Nelson.

Goswami, U. (1991). Analogical reasoning: What develops? A review of research and theory. *Child Development*, 62, 1–22.

Gottfried, A. W., Gottfried, A. E., Bathurst, K., & Guerin, D. W. (1994). *Gifted IQ: Early developmental aspects: The Fullerton Longitudinal Study*. New York: Plenum Press.

Gould, S. J. (1981). *The mismeasure of man*. New York: Norton.

Graber, J. A., & Archibald, A. B. (2001). Psychosocial change at puberty and beyond: Understanding adolescent sexuality and sexual orientation. In A. R. D'Augelli & C. J. Patterson (Eds.), *Lesbian, gay, and bisexual identities and youth: Psychological perspectives* (pp. 3–26). London: Oxford University Press.

Granott, N., & Garder, H. (1994). When minds meet: Interactions, coincidence, and development in domains of ability. In R. J. Sternberg & R. K. Wagner, *Mind in context: Interactionist perspectives on human intelligence* (pp. 171–201). Cambridge: Cambridge University Press.

Grasha, A. F. (1996). *Teaching with style: A practical guide to enhancing learning by understanding teaching and learning styles*. Pittsburgh: Alliance Publishers.

Gray, P. (1991). *Psychology* (2nd ed.). New York: Wo.

Graybeal, S. S., & Stodolsky, S. S. (1985). Peer work in elementary schools. *American Journal of Educ.* 93, 409–428.

Greenfield, P. M., & Suzuki, L. K. (1998). Culture a human development: Implications for parenting, educa tion, pediatrics, and mental health. In I. E. Sigel & K. A. Renninger (Eds.), *Handbook of child psychology, Vol. 4: Child psychology in practice* (5th ed., pp. 1059–1112). New York: Wiley.

Greenhill, A. (1998). *Equity and access to information technology: Shifting the source of the problem in the 21st century*. Paper presented at TASA 98 Conference, QUT, December 1998. Retrieved 12 May, 2003, from http://www.spaceless.com/papers/9.htm

Greenhill, A., Fletcher, G., & von Hellens, L. (1999). Cultural differences and information technology skills. In D. Meredyth, N. Russell, L. Blackwood, J. Thomas, & P. Wise, *Real time: Computers, change and schooling* (pp. 287–290). Canberra: Australian Key Centre for Cultural and Media Policy, Commonwealth Department of Education, Training and Youth Affairs.

Greenway, C. (2002). The process, pitfalls and benefits of implementing a reciprocal teaching intervention to improve the reading comprehension of a group of year 6 pupils. *Educational Psychology in Practice*, 18(2), 113–137.

Greve, W., Anderson, A., & Krampen, G. (2001). Self-efficacy and externality in adolescence: Theoretical conceptions and measurement in New Zealand and German secondary school students. *Identity*, 1(4), 321–344.

Griffin, C. C., Malone, L. D., & Kameenui, E. J. (1995). Effects of graphic organizer instruction on fifth grade students. *Journal of Educational Research*, 89(2), 98–108.

Griffin, E. A., & Morrison, F. J. (1997). The unique contribution of home literacy environment to differences in early literacy skills. *Early Child Development and Care*, 127, 233–243.

Griffin, P. (1998). Outcomes and profiles: Changes in teachers' assessment practices. *Curriculum Perspectives*, 18, 9–19.

Griffin, P., & Nix, P. (1991). *Educational assessment and reporting: A new approach*. Sydney: Harcourt Brace Jovanovich.

Grigorenko, E., & Sternberg, R. J. (1995). Thinking styles. In D. H. Saklofske & M. Zeidner (Eds.), *International handbook of personality and intelligence* (pp. 205–229). New York: Plenum Press.

Groome, H. (1995). *Working purposefully with Aboriginal students*. Wentworth Falls, NSW: Social Science Press.

Gross, M. (1993). *Exceptionally gifted children*. London: Routledge.

Grossman, H., & Grossman, S. H. (1994). *Gender issues in education*. Boston: Allyn & Bacon.

Guenther, R. K. (1998). *Human cognition*. Upper Saddle River, NJ: Prentice Hall.

Guesry, P. (1998). The role of nutrition in brain development. *Preventive Medicine*, 27(2), 189–194.

Guilford, J. P. (1967). *The nature of human intelligence*. New York: McGraw-Hill.

Gurian, M., & Henley, P. (2001). *Boys and girls learn differently!: A guide for teachers and parents*. San Francisco: Jossey-Bass.

Hinde, R. A. (1995). A suggested structure for a science of relationships. *Personal Relationships*, 2, 1–15.

Hoekstra, T., Gordon, B., & Donald, H. (Eds.). (1999). *VITAL: Values in information technology and learning*. Canberra: Commonwealth of Australia. Retrieved 14 November, 2001, from http://www.vital.nsw.edu.au/

Hogan, K., Nastasi, B., & Pressley, M. (2000). Discourse patterns and collaborative scientific reasoning in peer and teacher-guided discussions. *Cognition and Instruction*, 17(4), 379–432.

Holahan, C. K., & Sears, R. R. (1995). *The gifted group in later maturity*. Stanford, CA: Stanford University Press.

Holden, M. C. (1992). Designing hypercard stacks for cooperative learning. *Computing Teacher*, 19(5), 20–22.

Hollan, J., Hutchins, E., & Kirsh, D. (2000). Distributed cognition: Toward a new foundation for human-computer interaction research. *ACM Transactions on Computer– Human Interaction*, 7(2), 174–196.

Hollingworth, L. S. (1926). *Gifted children: Their nature and nurture*. New York: Macmillan.

Hollingworth, L. S. (1942). *Children above 180 IQ (Stanford-Binet): Origin and development*. New York: World Book.

Holmbeck, G. N. (1996). A model of family relational transformations during the transition to adolescence: Parent–adolescent conflict and adaptation. In J. A. Graber, J. Brooks-Gunn, & A. C. Peterson (Eds.), *Transitions through adolescence*. Mahwah, NJ: Erlbaum.

Honey, M., & Henriquez, A. (1996). *Union City Interactive Multimedia Education Trial: 1993–95 summary report*. CCT Reports Issue No. 3. Retrieved 5 April, 2003, from http://www.edc.org/CCT/

Horton, W. (1994). *Designing and writing online documentation: Hypermedia for self-supporting products* (2nd ed.). New York: John Wiley and Sons.

Hovelynck, J. (2001). Beyond didactics: A reconnaissance of experiential learning. *Australian Journal of Outdoor Education*, 6(1), 4–12.

Howe, C., Tolmie, A., Greer, K., & McKenzie, M. (1995). Peer collaboration and conceptual growth in physics: Task influences on children's understanding of heating and cooling. *Cognition and Instruction*, 13, 483–503.

Howe, K., & Berv, J. (2000). Constructing constructivism, epistemological and pedagogical. In D. C. Phillips (Ed.), *Constructivism in education: Opinions and second opinions on controversial issues* (pp. 19–40). Chicago: The National Society for the Study of Education.

Howe, M. J. A. (1997). *IQ in question: The truth about intelligence*. London: Sage.

Howell, L. C. (2001). The effect of learning styles, preferred intelligence, and study strategies on a student's preference for condensed or distributed instruction. *Dissertation Abstracts International Section A: Humanities & Social Sciences*, 62(6–A), 2016.

Human Rights and Equal Opportunity Commission (HREOC) (1989). *Our homeless children: Report of the national inquiry into homeless children*. Canberra: AGPS.

HREOC (2000a). *Rural and Remote Education Inquiry*. Retrieved 12 February, 2003, from http://www.hreoc.gov.au/human_rights/rural_education/briefing/

HREOC (2000b). *Rural and Remote Education Inquiry: Indigenous education briefing paper E: Barriers to participation and success*. Retrieved 15 February, 2003, from http://www.hreoc.gov.au/human_rights/rural_education/briefing/indigenous_ed5.html

Hunt, J. McV. (1961). *Intelligence and experience*. New York: Ronald Press.

Hutchins, E. (1995). How a cockpit remembers its speeds. *Cognitive Science*, 19, 265–288.

Hutt, S. J., Tyler, S., Hutt, C., & Christopherson, H. (1990). *Play, exploration and learning: A natural history of the preschool*. London: Routledge.

Hymel, S., LeMare, L., Ditner, E., & Woody, E. Z. (1999). Assessing self-concept in children: Variations across self-concept domains. *Merrill-Palmer Quarterly*, 45(4), 602–623.

Ingram, A. L. (1996). Teaching with technology. *Association Management*, 48(6), 31–38.

Inhelder, B. (1968). *The diagnosis of reasoning in the mentally retarded*. New York: Chandler.

Inhelder, B., & Piaget, J. (1958). *The growth of logical thinking from childhood to adolescence: An essay on the construction of formal operational structures* (A. Parsons & S. Milgram, Trans.). London: Routledge and Kegan Paul.

Ireson, J., Hallam, S., & Plewis, I. (2001). Ability grouping in secondary schools: Effects on pupils' self-concepts. *British Journal of Educational Psychology*, 71(2), 315–326.

Irving, K. (1998). The location and arrangement of peer contacts: Links with friendship initiation knowledge in 4- to 7-year-olds. In P. T. Slee & K. Rigby (Eds.), *Children's peer relations* (pp. 164–182). London: Routledge.

Irving, L. M., Wall, M., Neumark-Sztainer, D., & Story, M. (2002). Steroid use among adolescents: Findings from Project EAT. *Journal of Adolescent Health*, 30(4, Suppl), 243–252.

Ishler, A. L., Johnson, R. T., & Johnson, D. W. (1998). Long-term effectiveness of a state-wide staff development program on cooperative teaching. *Teaching and Teacher Education*, 14, 273–281.

Izard, C. E., Fantauzzo, C. A., Castle, J. M., Haynes, O. M., Rayias, M. F., & Putnam, P. H. (1995). The ontogeny and significance of infants' facial expressions in the first 9 months of life. *Developmental Psychology*, 31, 997–1013.

Jackson, C., & Lawtyjones, M. (1996). Explaining the overlap between personality and learning style. *Personality and Individual Differences*, 20, 293–300.

Jacobs, J. E., Lanza, S., Osgood, D. W., Eccles, J. S., & Wigfield, A. (2002). Changes in children's self-competence and values: Gender and domain differences across grades one through twelve. *Child Development*, 73(2), 509–527.

Jacques, N., Wilton, K., & Townsend, M. (1998). Cooperative learning and social acceptance of children with mild intellectual disability. *Journal of Intellectual Disability Research*, 42, 29–36.

James, W. (1890). *The principles of psychology*. New York: Henry Holt.

Jenkin, J. (1996). Resolving violence through education: An anti-violence curriculum for secondary students. In J. Izard & J. Evans (Eds.), *Student behaviour: Policies, intervention and evaluation* (pp. 234–246). Hawthorn: ACER.

Jenkin, J., Jewell, M., Leicester, N., O'Connor, R., Jenkins, L., & Trounter, N. (1994). Accommodations for individual differences without classroom ability groups: An experiment in school restructuring. *Exceptional Children, 60,* 344–358.

Johnson, D. W., & Johnson, R. (1996). Conflict resolution and peer mediation programs in elementary and secondary schools – a review of the research. *Review of Educational Research, 66,* 459–506.

Johnson, D. W., & Johnson, R. T. (1989). *Cooperation and competition: Theory and research.* Edina, MN: Interaction Book Co.

Johnson, D. W., & Johnson, R. T. (1991). *Cooperative learning structures.* Edina, MN: Interaction Book Co.

Johnson, D. W., & Johnson, R. T. (1996). The role of cooperative learning in assessing and communicating student learning. In T. R. Guskey (Ed.), *ASCD yearbook 1996: Communicating student learning* (pp. 25–46). Alexandria, VA: Association for Supervision and Curriculum Development.

Johnson, D. W., & Johnson, R. T. (1999). *Learning together and alone: Cooperation, competition and individualization* (5th ed.). Boston, MA: Allyn & Bacon.

Johnson, D. W., Johnson, R. T., & Holubec, E. J. (1994). *The new circles of learning: Cooperation in the classroom and school.* Alexandria, VA: Association for Supervision and Curriculum Development.

Johnson, M., & Ward, P. (2001). Effects of classwide peer tutoring on correct performance of striking skills in 3rd grade physical education. *Journal of Teaching in Physical Education, 20*(3), 247–263.

John-Steiner, V., & Mahn, H. (1996). Sociocultural approaches to learning and development. *Educational Psychology, 31,* 191–206.

Joinson, A. N. (1998). Causes and effects of disinhibition on the Internet. In J. Gackenbach (Ed.), *The psychology of the Internet* (pp. 43–60). New York: Academic Press.

Joinson, A. N. (2001). Self-disclosure in computer-mediated communication: The role of self-awareness and visual anonymity. *European Journal of Social Psychology, 31,* 177–192.

Joinson, A. N. (2002). *Understanding the psychology of Internet behaviour: Virtual worlds, real lives.* Basingstoke: Palgrave Macmillan.

Jonassen, D. H. (1994). Thinking technology: Towards a constructivist design model. *Educational Technology, 34*(3), 34–37.

Jonassen, D. H. (1996). *Computers in the classroom: Mindtools for critical thinking.* Englewood Cliffs, NJ: Prentice Hall.

Jonassen, D. H. (2000). *Computers as mindtools for schools: Engaging critical thinking.* Columbus, OH: Prentice Hall.

Jonassen, D. H., Carr, C., & Yueh, H. P. (1998). Computers as mindtools for engaging learners in critical thinking. *TechTrends, 43*(2), 24–32. Retrieved 15 February, 2003, from http://tiger.coe.missouri.edu/~jonassen/ Mindtools.pdf

Jonassen, D. H., & Grabowski, B. L. (1993). *Handbook of individual differences, learning and instruction.* Hillsdale, NJ: Lawrence Erlbaum Associates.

Jones Diaz, C., Arthur, L., Beecher, B., & McNaught, M. (2001). *Literacies, communities and under 5s: The Early Literacy and Social Justice Project.* Ryde: NSW Department of Education and Training, Early Learning Unit.

Jones F. H. (1987). *Positive classroom discipline.* New York: McGraw-Hill.

Jones, J. E., & Davenport, M. (1996). Self-regulation in Japanese and American art education. *Art Education, 49*(1), 60–65.

Jones, M. C. (1924). The elimination of children's fears. *Journal of Experimental Psychology, 7,* 383–390.

Joyce, B., & Weil, M. (1996). *Models of teaching* (5th ed.). Boston: Allyn & Bacon.

Kagan, J. (1958). The concept of identification. *Psychological Review, 65,* 296–305.

Kagan, J. (1966). Reflection–impulsivity and reading ability in primary grade children. *Child Development, 36,* 609–628.

Kagan, J. (1971). *Change and continuity in infancy.* New York: Wiley.

Kagan, S. (1992). *Cooperative learning: Resources for teachers.* San Juan Capistrano, CA: Resources for Teachers.

Kamii, C. (2000). *Young children reinvent arithmetic: Implications of Piaget's theory* (2nd ed.). New York: Teachers College Press.

Kanerva, P. (1993). Sparse distributed memory and related models. In M. Hassoun (Ed.), *Associative neural memories: Theory and implementation.* New York: Oxford University Press.

Kaniel, S., Licht, P., & Peled, B. (2001). The influence of metacognitive instruction of reading and writing strategies. *Gifted Education International, 15*(1), 45–63.

Kauffman, J. M. (2001). *Characteristics of emotional and behavioural disorders of children and youth* (7th ed). Columbus, OH: Merrill.

Kavale, K. A., & Fortness, S. R. (2000). History, rhetoric and reality – analysis of the inclusion debate. *Remedial and Special Education, 21,* 279–296.

Kaye, K. (1982). Organism, apprentice, and person. In E. Z. Tronick (Ed.), *Social interchange in infancy: Affect, cognition and communication* (pp. 183–196). Baltimore, MD: University Park Press.

Kazdin, A. E., Siegel, T. C., & Bass, D. (1992). Cognitive problem-solving skills training and parent management training in the treatment of antisocial behavior in children. *Journal of Consulting and Clinical Psychology, 60,* 733–747.

Kearney, M., & Treagust, D. F. (2001). Constructivism as a referent in the design and development of a computer program using interactive digital video to enhance learning in physics. *Australian Journal of Educational Technology, 17*(1), 64–79.

Keating, D. (1980). Adolescent thinking. In J. Adelson (Ed.), *Handbook of adolescent psychology* (pp. 211–246). New York: Wiley.

Keefe, J. W., & Ferrell, B. G. (1990). Developing a defensible learning style paradigm. *Educational Leadership, 48,* 57–61.

Kelly, A. (1988). Gender differences in teacher–pupil interactions: A meta-analytic review. *Research in Education, 39,* 1–23.

Kenner, L. (1964). *A history of the care and study of the mentally retarded.* Springfield, IL: Charles C. Thomas.

Kersteen, Z. A., Linn, M. C., Clancy, M., & Hardyck, C. (1988). Previous experience and the learning of computer programming: The computer helps those who help themselves. *Journal of Educational Computing Research, 4,* 321–334.

Kids Helpline (2000). *Infosheet 07: Bullying*. Retrieved 15 March, 2003, from http://www.kidshelp.com.au/research/infosheets/07BULLYING.PDF

Killen, R. (1998). *Effective teaching strategies: Lessons from research and practice* (2nd ed.). Katoomba, NSW: Social Science Press.

Kindermann, T. A. (1995). Distinguishing 'buddies' from 'bystanders': The study of children's development within natural peer contexts. In T. A. Kindermann & J. Valsiner (Eds.), *Development of person–context relations* (pp. 205–226). Hillsdale, NJ: Lawrence Erlbaum Associates.

King, C. M., & Johnson, L. (1999). Constructing meaning via reciprocal teaching. *Reading Research and Instruction*, 38(3), 169–186.

King, T. (1997). *Technology in the classroom: A collection of articles*. Melbourne: Hawker Brownlow Education.

Kirk, S. A. (1958). *Early education of the mentally retarded: An experimental study*. Urbana, IL: University of Illinois Press.

Klahr, D., & MacWhinney, B. (1998). Information processing. In D. Kuhn & R. S. Siegler (Eds.), *Handbook of child psychology, Vol. 2: Cognition, perception, and language* (5th ed., pp. 631–678). New York: John Wiley & Sons.

Klassen, R. (2002). Writing in early adolescence: A review of the role of self-efficacy beliefs. *Educational Psychology Review*, 14(2), 173–203.

Klerman, L. V. (2002). Adolescent pregnancy in the United States. *International Journal of Adolescent Medicine and Health*, 14(2), 91–96.

Klingner, J. K., & Vaughn, S. (1996). Reciprocal teaching of reading comprehension strategies for students with learning disabilities who use English as a second language. *The Elementary School Journal*, 96(2), 275–294.

Kluwe, R. H. (1982). Cognitive knowledge and executive control: Metacognition. In D. R. Griffin (Ed.), *Animal mind – human mind* (pp. 201–224). New York: Springer-Verlag.

Knapp, L. R., & Glenn, A. D. (1996). *Restructuring schools with technology*. Boston: Allyn & Bacon.

Kogan, N. (1994). Cognitive styles. In R. J. Sternberg (Ed.), *Encyclopedia of intelligence* (Vol. 1, pp. 266–273). New York: Macmillan.

Kohl, H. R. (1968). *36 children*. London: Victor Gollancz.

Kohl, H. R. (1969). *The open classroom: A practical guide to a new way of teaching*. New York: Random House.

Kohlberg, L. (1963). The development of children's orientations toward a moral order. I. Sequence in the development of moral thought. *Human Development*, 6, 11–33.

Kohlberg, L. (1984). *Essays in moral development. Volume II: The psychology of moral development*. San Francisco: Harper & Row.

Kohlberg, L. (1987). The development of moral judgment and moral action. In L. Kohlberg, *Child psychology and childhood education: A cognitive-developmental view* (pp. 259–328). New York: Longman.

Kohlberg, L., Levine, C., & Hewer, A. (1983). *Moral stages: A current formulation and a response to critics*. Basel, New York: Karger.

Kohn, A. (1993). Choices for children: Why and how to let students decide. *Phi Delta Kappan*, 75, 8–21.

Kohn, A. (1994). The truth about self-esteem. *Phi Delta Kappan*, 76, 272–283.

Kohn, A. (1996). *Beyond discipline: From compliance to community*. Alexandria, VA: Association for Supervision and Curriculum Development.

Kohn, M. L. (1977). *Class and conformity: A study in values, with a reassessment* (2nd ed.). Chicago: University of Chicago Press.

Kong, C-K. (2000). Chinese students' self-concept: Structure, frame of reference, and relation with academic achievement. *Dissertation Abstracts International Section A: Humanities and Social Sciences*, 61(3–A), 880.

Koutselini, M., & Hadjiyianni, I. (1999). Intervention in metacognition and learning: A case study in the elementary school. *Curriculum and Teaching*, 14(2), 75–94.

Kozma, R. B. (1991). Learning with media. *Review of Educational Research*, 61(2), 179–211.

Kozma, R. B. (1994). Will media influence learning? Reframing the debate. *Educational Technology Research and Development*, 42(2), 7–19.

Kramer, L. A. (1996). Sex differences in self-efficacy ratings during pre and early adolescence. *Dissertation Abstracts International Section A: Humanities and Social Sciences*, 57(2–A), 0578.

Kratochwill, T. R., & Bijou, S. W. (1987). The impact of behaviorism on educational psychology. In J. A. Glover, & R. R. Ronning (Eds.), *Historical foundation of educational psychology* (pp. 131–154). New York: Plenum Press.

Krause, K. (1997). *Adolescent planning, writing apprehension and essay writing competence: A study of their interrelationships and the effects of teacher intervention*. Unpublished doctoral dissertation, Macquarie University, Sydney.

Krause, K., & O'Brien, D. (2001). Adolescent second language writers in China: A sociocultural analysis. In D. M. McInerney & S. Van Etten (Eds.), *Research on sociocultural influences on motivation and learning* (pp. 265–290). Greenwich, CT: Information Age Publishing.

Kubes, M. (1998). Adaptors and innovators in Slovakia: Cognitive style and social culture. *European Journal of Personality*, 12(3), 187–198.

Kuhn, D. (2000). Metacognitive development. *Current Directions in Psychological Science*, 9(5), 178–181.

Kulik, J. A. (1994). Meta-analytic studies of findings on computer-based instruction. In E. L. Baker & H. F. O'Neill (Eds.), *Technology assessment in education and training*. Hillsdale, NJ: Lawrence Erlbaum.

Kurtz, B. E. (1990). Cultural influences on children's cognitive and metacognitive development. In W. Schneider & F. E. Weinert (Eds.), *Interactions among aptitudes, strategies and knowledge in cognitive performance*. New York: Springer-Verlag.

Labouvie-Vief, G. (1980). Beyond formal operations: Uses and limits of pure logic in life-span development. *Human Development*, 23, 141–161.

Ladd, G. W., Kochenderfer, B. J., & Coleman, C. C. (1996). Friendship quality as a predictor of young children's early school adjustment. *Child Development*, 67(3), 1103–1118.

Lamb, C., & Nunan, D. (2001). Managing the learning process. In D. R. Hall & A. Hewings (Eds.), *Innovation in English language teaching: A reader* (pp. 27–45). London: Routledge.

Lambert, B., & Clyde, M. (2000). *Re thinking early childhood theory and practice*. Katoomba, NSW: Social Science Press.

Lambert, P. (2001). *Standards-referenced assessment in primary schools*. Retrieved 11 November, 2001, from http://www.bosnsw-k6.nsw.edu.au/parents/k6standrads_assess.html

Lane, A. M., Jones, L., & Stevens, M. J. (2002). Coping with failure: The effects of self-esteem and coping on changes in self efficacy. *Journal of Sport Behavior*, 25(4), 331–345.

Langford, L. (2000). Critical literacy: A building block towards information literacy. In L. Hay & J. Henri (Eds.), *Enter the millennium: Information services in schools: 1999 online conference proceedings* (pp. 181–187). Wagga Wagga, NSW: Centre for Studies in Teacher Librarianship, Charles Sturt University.

Langford, P. E. (1995). *Approaches to the development of moral reasoning*. Hove: Lawrence Erlbaum Associates.

Lareau, A. (1989). *Home advantage: Social class and parental intervention in elementary education*. London: Falmer Press.

Larson, R. W., Richards, M. H., Moneta, G., Holmbeck, G., & Duckett, E. (1996). Changes in adolescents' daily interactions with their families from ages 10 to 18: Disengagement and transformation. *Developmental Psychology*, 32, 744–754.

Lawrie, L., & Brown, R. (1982). Sex stereotypes, school subject preferences and career aspirations as a function of single/mixed sex schooling and presence/absence of the opposite sex sibling. *British Journal of Educational Psychology*, 62, 132–138.

Lazar, I., & Darlington, R. (1982). Lasting effects of early education: A report from the Consortium for Longitudinal Studies. *Monographs of the Society for Research in Child Development*, 47(2–3, Serial No. 195).

Lazarus, R. S. (1991). *Emotion and adaptation*. New York: Oxford University Press.

Leach, P. (1997). *Your baby and child: A new version for a new generation*. London: Penguin.

Leader, L. F., & Klein, J. D. (1996). The effects of search tool type and cognitive style on performance during hypermedia database searches. *Educational Technology Research and Development*, 44(2), 5–15.

Leaper, C. (Ed.). (1994). Childhood gender segregation: Causes and consequences. *New directions for child development, No. 65* (pp. 67–86). San Francisco, CA: Jossey-Bass/Pfeiffer.

Leary, M. R., Schreindorfer, L. S., & Haupt, A. L. (1995). The role of low self-esteem in emotional and behavioral problems: Why is low self-esteem dysfunctional? *Journal of Social and Clinical Psychology*, 14(3), 297–314.

Lederer, J. M. (2000). Reciprocal teaching of social studies in inclusive elementary classrooms. *Journal of Learning Disabilities*, 33(1), 91–107.

LeDoux, J. E. (1995). Emotion: Clues from the brain. *Annual Review of Psychology*, 46, 209–235.

Lee, M. (2001). Chaotic learning: The learning style of the Net generation? In J. Henri, L. Hay, & K. Hanson (Eds.), *New millennium, new horizons: Information services in schools: 2000 Online conference proceedings* (pp. 165–171). Wagga Wagga, NSW: Centre for Studies in Teacher Librarianship, Charles Sturt University.

Lee, V. E., Brooks-Gunn, J., Schnur, E., & Liaw, F. (1990). Are Head Start effects sustained? A longitudinal follow-up comparison of disadvantaged children attending Head Start, no preschool, and other preschools programs. *Child Development*, 61, 495–507.

Lee, V. E., & Loeb, S. (1995). Where do Head Start attendees end up? One reason preschool effects fade out. *Education Evaluation and Policy Analysis*, 17, 62–82.

LeFrancois, G. R. (1997). *Psychology for teaching* (9th ed.). Belmont, CA: Wadsworth.

Leman, P. J. (2001). The development of moral reasoning. In C. Fraser & B. Burchell (Eds.), *Introducing social psychology* (pp. 195–215). Cambridge: Polity Press.

Leming, J. S. (2000). Tell me a story: An evaluation of a literature-based character education programme. *Journal of Moral Education*, 29(4), 413–427.

Leslie, M. B., Stein, J. A., & Rotheram-Borus, M. J. (2002). Sex-specific predictors of suicidality among runaway youth. *Journal of Community Psychology*, 31(1), 27–40.

Levine, M. D., Carey, W. B., Croker, A. C., & Gross, R. T. (1983). *Developmental-behavioral pediatrics*. Philadelphia, PA: Saunders.

Lewis, A., Maras, P., & Simonds, L. (2000). Young school children working together: A measure of individualism/collectivism. *Child: Care, Health and Development*, 26(3), 229–238.

Lewis, D. H. (1972). *We, the navigators: The ancient art of landfinding in the pacific*. Canberra: ANU Press.

Lewis, E. J. (1996). *Modes of presentation of ideas, computers and learning styles in K–6 mathematics*. Unpublished Masters thesis, University of Western Sydney, Nepean, Kingswood, NSW.

Lewis, M. (1993a). The emergence of human emotions. In M. Lewis & J. Haviland (Eds.), *The handbook of emotion* (pp. 223–246). New York: Guilford Press.

Lewis, M. (1993b). Self-conscious emotions: Embarrassment, pride, shame, and guilt. In M. Lewis & J. Haviland (Eds.), *The handbook of emotion* (pp. 563–573). New York: Guilford Press.

Liben, L. S., & Signorella, M. L. (1993). Gender-schematic processing in children: The role of initial interpretations of stimuli. *Developmental Psychology*, 29, 141–149.

Licht, B. G. (1992). The achievement-related perceptions of children with learning problems: A developmental analysis. In D. H. Schunk & J. L. Meece (Eds.), *Student perceptions in the classroom* (pp. 247–264). Hillsdale, NJ: Erlbaum.

Licht, B. G., & Dweck, C. S. (1983). Sex differences in achievement orientations: Consequences for academic clones and attainments. In M. Marland (Ed.), *Sex differentiation and schooling*. London: Heinemann.

Lifter, K., & Bloom, L. (1998). Intentionality and the role of play in the transition to language. In A. M. Wetherby, S. R. Warren, & R. Reichle (Eds.), *Transitions in prelinguistic communication: Preintentional and presymbolic to symbolic* (pp. 161–195). Baltimore, MD: Paul H. Brookes.

Light, P. (1993). Collaborative learning with computers. In P. Scrimshaw (Ed.), *Language classrooms and computers* (pp. 40–56). London: Routledge.

Lightfoot, C. (1997). *The culture of adolescent risk taking*. New York: Guilford Press.

Lin, S. S. J., & Tsai, C-C. (2002). Sensation seeking and internet dependence of Taiwanese high school adolescents. *Computers in Human Behavior*, 18(4), 411–426.

Linchevski. L., & Kutscher, B. (1998). Tell me with whom you're learning, and I'll tell you how much you've learned:

Mixed-ability versus same-ability groupings in mathematics. *Journal for Research in Mathematics Education, 29,* 533–554.

Lind, J., & Maxwell, G. (1996). *Children's experiences of violence at school.* Wellington: Office of the Commissioner for Children.

Linn, R. L., & Gronlund, N. E. (1995). *Measurement and assessment in teaching* (7th ed.). Englewood Cliffs, NJ: Prentice Hall.

Lipovsek, V., Karim, A. M., Zielinsky Gutierrez, E., Magnani, R. J., & Gomez, M. (2002). Correlates of adolescent pregnancy in La Paz, Bolivia: Findings from a quantitative–qualitative study. *Adolescence, 37*(146), 335–352.

Little, Q., & Richards, D. R. T. (2000). Teaching learners – learners teaching: Using reciprocal teaching to improve comprehension strategies in challenged readers. *Reading Improvement, 37*(4), 190–194.

Littleton, K., Light, P., Joiner, R., Messer, D., & Barnes, P. (1998). Gender, task scenarios and children's computer-based problem solving. *Educational Psychology, 18*(3), 327–340.

Liu, M., & Reed, W. M. (1994). The relationship between the learning strategies and learning styles in a hypermedia environment. *Computers in Human Behaviour, 10,* 419–434.

Livson, N., & Peshkin, H. (1980). Perspectives on adolescence from longitudinal research. In J. Adelson (Ed.), *Handbook of adolescent psychology* (pp. 47–98). New York: Wiley.

Lock, A. J. (Ed.). (1978). *Action, gesture and symbol: The emergence of language.* London: Academic Press.

Lock, A. J., Service, V., Brito, A., & Chandler, P. (1989). The social structuring of infant cognition. In A. Slater & G. Bremner (Eds.), *Infant development* (pp. 243–271). Hove: Erlbaum.

Lockhart, R. S., & Craik, F. I. M. (1990). Levels of processing: A retrospective commentary on a framework for memory research. *Canadian Journal of Psychology, 44,* 87–112.

Long, M. H. (1990). Maturational constraints on language development. *Studies in Second Language Acquisition, 12*(4), 251–285.

Louden, L.W. (1985). *Disruptive behaviour in schools. Report of the Ministerial Working Party appointed by the Minister for Education and Planning in Western Australia, and chaired by Dr L. W. Louden.* Perth: Education Department of Western Australia.

Lourenco, O., & Machado, A. (1996). In defense of Piaget's theory: A reply to 10 common criticisms. *Psychological Review, 103,* 143–164.

Lowry, M., Koneman, P., Osmand-Jouchoux, R., & Wilson, B. (1994). Electronic discussion groups: Using e-mail as an instructional strategy. *Tech Trends, 39*(2), 22–24.

Lucangeli, D., Coi, G., & Bosco, P. (1997). Metacognitive awareness in good and poor math problem solvers. *Learning Disabilities Research and Practice, 12*(4), 209–212.

Luria, A. R. (1961). *The role of speech in the regulation of normal and abnormal behaviour.* New York: Pergamon Press.

Luria, A. R. (1963). Psychological studies of mental deficiency in the Soviet Union. In N. R. Ellis (Ed.), *Handbook on mental deficiency* (pp. 353–387). New York: McGraw-Hill.

Lutz, D. J., & Sternberg, R. J. (1999). Cognitive development. In M. H. Bornstein & M. E. Lamb (Eds.), *Developmental psychology: An advanced textbook* (pp. 275–311). Mahwah, NJ: Erlbaum.

MacMullin, C. (1998). Developing a social skills programme for use in school. In P. T. Slee & K. Rigby (Eds.), *Children's peer relations* (pp. 242–253). London: Routledge.

Madden, R., Black, K., & Wen, X. (1995). *The definition and categorisation of disability in Australia.* Canberra: AGPS.

Maddux, C. D., Johnson, D., & Willis, J. (2001). *Educational computing: Learning with tomorrow's technologies* (3rd ed.). Boston: Allyn & Bacon.

Maharey, S., & Swain, P. (2000). *Closing the digital divide – what do we know about the digital divide in New Zealand? A cabinet paper.* Wellington: NZ Government. Retrieved 29 January, 2003, from http://www.executive.govt.nz/minister/maharey/divide/divide1.pdf

Makin, L., Campbell, J., & Jones Diaz, C. (1995). *One childhood, many languages: Guidelines for early childhood education in Australia.* Pymble, NSW: Harper Educational.

Makrakis, V. (1992). Cross-cultural comparison of gender differences in attitude towards computers in Japan and Sweden. *Scandinavian Journal of Educational Research, 36,* 275–287.

Malcolm, I., Haig, Y., Konigsberg, P., Rochecouste, J., Collard, G., Hill, A., & Cahill, R. (1999). *Two-way English: Towards more user-friendly education for speakers of Aboriginal English.* Perth: Education Department of Western Australia.

Male, M. (1992). Cooperative learning, computers, and writing: Maximising instructional power. *Writing Notebook: Creative Word Processing in the Classroom, 9*(4), 21–22.

Malin, M. (1998). They listen and they've got respect: Cultural pedagogy. In G. Partington (Ed.), *Perspectives on Aboriginal and Torres Strait Islander education.* Katoomba, NSW: Social Science Press.

Malina, R. M. (1998). Motor development and performance. In S. J. Ulijaszek, F. E. Johnston, & M. A. Preece (Eds.), *The Cambridge encyclopedia of human growth and development* (pp. 247–250). Cambridge: Cambridge University Press.

Malott, R. W., Whaley, D. L., & Malott, M. E. (1993). *Elementary principles of behaviour* (2nd ed.). Englewood Cliffs, NJ: Prentice Hall.

Maqsud, M. (1997). Effects of metacognitive skills and nonverbal ability on academic achievement of high school pupils. *Educational Psychology, 17*(4), 387–397.

Maratsos, M. (1998). The acquisition of grammar. In W. Damon, D. Kuhn & R. S. Siegler (Eds.), *Handbook of child psychology* (Vol. 2, 5th ed., pp. 421–466). New York: Wiley.

March, T. (2001). *Working on the web for education: Theory and practice on integrating the web for learning.* Retrieved 25 October, 2002, from http://ozline.com/learning/theory.html

Marcia, J. E. (1980). Identity in adolescence. In J. Adelson (Ed.), *Handbook of adolescent psychology* (5th ed., pp. 159–187). New York: Wiley.

Marginson, S. (1993). *Education and public policy in Australia.* New York: Cambridge University Press.

Marika, R. (1998). The Wentworth lecture. *Australian Aboriginal Studies, 1999, 1*, 2–9. Retrieved 24 February, 2003, from http://www.aiatsis.gov.au/lbry/dig_prgm/wentworth/a318678_a.pdf

Marjoribanks, K. (1997). Parents' and young adults' individualism–collectivism: Ethnic group differences. *Psychological Reports, 80*(3, Pt. 1), 934–936.

Marks, G. N., & Ainley, J. (1997). *Reading comprehension and numeracy among junior secondary students in Australia. LSAY Research Report No.3.* Melbourne: ACER.

Markus, H. R., & Kitayama, S. (1991). Culture and the self: Implications for cognition, emotion, and maturation. *Psychological Review, 98*, 224–253.

Marsh, H. W. (1986). Verbal and math self-concepts: An internal/external frame of reference model. *American Educational Research Journal, 23*, 129–149.

Marsh, H. W. (1990). *Self-Description Questionnaire, II.* San Antonio, TX: The Psychological Corporation.

Marsh, H. W. (1992). Content specificity of relations between academic achievement and academic self-concept. *Journal of Educational Psychology, 84*, 35–42.

Marsh, H. W. (1993). Academic self-concept: Theory, measurement, and research. In J. Suls (Ed.), *Psychological perspectives on the self* (Vol. 4, pp. 59–98). Hillsdale, NJ: Erlbaum.

Marsh, H. W., Byrne, B. M., & Shavelson, R. (1988). A multifaceted academic self-concept: Its hierarchical structure and its relation to academic achievement. *Journal of Educational Psychology, 80*, 366–380.

Marsh, H. W., Chessor, D., Craven, R., & Roche, L. (1995). The effect of gifted and talented programs on academic self-concept: The big fish strikes again. *American Educational Research Journal, 32*(2), 285–319.

Marsh, H. W., & Craven, R. G. (1991). Self–other agreement on multiple dimensions of preadolescent self-concept: The accuracy of inferences by teachers, mothers, and fathers. *Journal of Educational Psychology, 83*, 393–404.

Marsh, H. W., Craven, R., & Debus, R. (2000). Structure, stability, and development of young children's self-concepts: A multicohort-multioccasion study. In W. Craig (Ed.), *Childhood social development: The essential readings* (pp. 223–271). Malden, MA: Blackwell Publishers.

Marsh, H. W., & Hattie, J. (1996). Theoretical perspectives on the structure of self-concept. In B. A. Bracken (Ed.), *Handbook of self-concept* (pp. 38–90). New York: Wiley.

Marsh, H. W., Hey, J., Roche, L. A., & Perry, C. (1997). Structure of physical self-concept: Elite athletes and physical education students. *Journal of Educational Psychology, 89*, 369–380.

Marsh, H. W., Kong, C-K., & Hau, K-T. (2000). Longitudinal multilevel models of the big-fish-little-pond effect on academic self-concept: Counterbalancing contrast and reflected-glory effects in Hong Kong schools. *Journal of Personality and Social Psychology, 78*(2), 337–349.

Marsh, H. W., Parada, R. H., Yeung, A. S., & Healey, J. (2001). Aggressive school troublemakers and victims: A longitudinal model examining the pivotal role of self-concept. *Journal of Educational Psychology, 93*(2), 411–419.

Marsh, H. W., & Yeung, A. S. (1998). Longitudinal structural equation models of academic self-concept and achievement: Gender differences in the development of math and English constructs. *American Educational Research Journal, 35*, 705–738.

Martin, G. (1995). *Early detection of emotional disorder with particular reference to suicidal behaviours.* Bedford Park, South Australia: Southern CAMHS, Southern Flinders Medical Centre, South Australia.

Martin, M. (1987). Managing inappropriate behaviour in the classroom. In J. Ward., S. Bochner., Y. Center, L. Outhred, & M. Pieterse (Eds.), *Educating children with special needs in regular classrooms: An Australian perspective* (pp. 159–189). Sydney: Special Education Centre, Macquarie University.

Martin, R. (1991). School children's attitudes towards computers as a function of gender, course subjects and availability of home computers. *Journal of Computer Assisted Learning, 7*, 187–194.

Marton, F. (1975). On non-verbatim learning – 1: Level of processing and level of outcome. *Scandinavian Journal of Psychology, 16*, 273–279.

Maslow, A. (1954). *Motivation and personality.* New York: Harper.

Maslow, A. (1968). *Towards a psychology of being* (2nd ed.). New York: Van Nostrand Reinhold.

Maslow, A. (1969). Existential psychology – what's in it for us? In R. May (Ed.), *Existential psychology* (2nd ed. pp. 49–57). New York: Random House.

Maslow, A. (1970). *Motivation and personality* (2nd ed.). New York: Harper & Row.

Masters, G., & Forster, M. (1996). *Developmental assessment: Resource development kit.* Camberwell: ACER.

Mastropieri, M. A., Scruggs, T., Mohler, L., Beranek, M., Spencer, V., Boon, R. T., & Talbott, E. (2001). Can middle school students with serious reading difficulties help each other and learn anything? *Learning Disabilities Research and Practice, 16*(1), 18–27.

Matthews, M. (2000). Appraising constructivism in science and mathematics education. In D. C. Phillips (Ed.), *Constructivism in education: Opinions and second opinions on controversial issues* (pp. 161–192). Chicago: The National Society for the Study of Education.

Maude, D., Wertheim, E. H., Paxton, S., Gibbons, K, & Szmukler, G. (1993). Body dissatisfaction, weight loss behaviours, and bulimic tendencies in Australian adolescents with an estimate of female data representatives. *Australian Psychologist, 28*(2), 128–132.

Maurer, M. M. (1994). Computer anxiety correlates and what they tell us: A literature review. *Computers in Human Behavior, 10*(3), 369–376.

Mayer, J. D. (2001). Emotion, intelligence, and emotional intelligence. In J. P. Forgas (Ed.), *Handbook of affect and social cognition* (pp. 410–431). Mahwah, NJ: Lawrence Erlbaum Associates.

Mayer, J. D., Caruso, D., & Salovey, P. (1999). Emotional intelligence meets traditional standards for an intelligence. *Intelligence, 27*, 267–298.

Mayer, J. D., Salovey, P., & Caruso, D. (2000). Selecting a measure of emotional intelligence: The case for ability scales. In R. Bar-On & J. D. A. Parker (Eds.), *Handbook of emotional intelligence* (pp. 35–54). San Fransisco: Jossey-Bass.

Mayer, R. E., & Moreno, R. (1998). A split-attention effect in multimedia learning: Evidence for dual processing systems in working memory. *Journal of Educational Psychology, 90*, 312–320.

McCaslin, M., & Good, T. (1996). *Listening to students*. New York: HarperCollins.

McClelland, D. C., Atkinson, J. W., Clark, R. W., & Lowell, E. L. (1953). *The achievement motive*. New York: Appleton-Century-Crofts.

McClintock, R. (1992). *Power and pedagogy: Transforming education through information technology*. New York: Institute for Learning Technologies, Teachers College Press.

McDevitt, T. M., & Ormrod, J. E. (2002). *Child development and education*. Upper Saddle River, NJ: Merrill/Prentice Hall.

McDonald, H., & Ingvarson, L. (1997). Technology: A catalyst for educational change. *Journal of Curriculum Studies*, 29(5), 513–527.

McDougall, W. (1923). *Outline of psychology* (4th ed.). London: Methuen.

McDowell, H., & Ziginskas, D. (Eds.). (1994). *Feeling stink: A resource on young people's mental health issues for those who work with them*. New Zealand: Ministry of Health.

MCEETYA (Ministerial Council on Education, Employment, Training and Youth Affairs) (1997). *Gender equity framework*. Canberra: MCEETYA. Retrieved 24 January, 2003, from http://www.curriculum.edu.au/public/genderequity.htm

MCEETYA (1999). *The Adelaide declaration on national goals for schooling in the twenty-first century*. Adelaide, 22–23 April 1999. Retrieved 4 April, 2003, from http://www.curriculum.edu.au/mceetya/nationalgoals/natgoals.htm

MCEETYA taskforce on indigenous education (2000). *Report of MCEETYA Taskforce on indigenous education*. Retrieved 4 February, 2003, from http://www.curriculum.edu.au/mctyapdf/reportm.pdf

MCEETYA taskforce on indigenous education (2001). *Effective learning issues for Indigenous children aged 0 to 8 years*. Discussion paper. Retrieved 30 January, 2003, from http://www.mceetya.gov.au

McGaw, B., Piper, K., Banks, D., & Evans, B. (1993). *Making schools more effective: Report of the Australian Effective Schools Project*. Hawthorn, Victoria: ACER.

McGuinness, C. (1998). Cognition. In K. Trew & J. Kremer (Eds.), *Gender and Psychology*. London: Arnold.

McHalick, M. (1996). *In out*. Auckland: Scholastic.

McInerney, V., McInerney, D. M., Marsh, H. W. (1997). Effects of metacognitive strategy training within a cooperative group learning context on computer achievement and anxiety: An aptitude–treatment interaction study. *Journal of Educational Psychology*, 89(4), 686–695.

McKay, P., & Scarino, A. (1991). *ESL framework of stages: An approach to ESL learning in schools, K–12*. Carlton, Victoria: Curriculum Corporation.

McLean, J. (2000). Cyberseeking: Language and the quest for information. In D. Gibbs & K. Krause (Eds.), *Cyberlines: Languages and cultures of the Internet* (pp. 79–102). Melbourne: James Nicholas Publishers.

McLelland, J. L., & Rumelhart, D. E. (1986). A distributed model of human learning and memory. In J. L. McLelland & D. E. Rumelhart (Eds.), *Parallel distributed processing: Explorations in the microstructure of cognition* (Vol. 2, pp. 170–215). Cambridge, MA: MIT Press.

McLoughlin, C., & Gower, G. (2000). *Indigenous learners on-line: A model for flexible learning in an innovative web-based environment*. Paper presented at the Australian Indigenous Education Conference, Perth, WA. Retrieved 20 June, 2003, from http://www.kk.edu.au/sub/schoola/research/confs/aiec/papers/cmclough04.htm

McLoyd, V. C. (1990). The impact of economic hardship on black families and children: Psychological distress, parenting and socioemotional development. *Child Development*, 61, 311–46.

McLoyd, V. C. (1998). Socioeconomic disadvantage and child development. *American Psychologist*, 53, 185–204.

McRae, D., Ainsworth, G., Cumming, J., Hughes, P., Mackay, P., Price, K., Rowland, M., Warhurst, J., Woods, D., & Zbar, V. (2000). *What has worked (and will again). The national coordination and evaluation report on the IESIP Strategic Results projects*. Canberra: Australian Curriculum Studies Association.

Meadows, S. (1998). Children learning to think: Learning from others? Vygotskian theory and educational psychology. *Educational and Child Psychology*, 15(2), 6–13.

Means, B., & Olson, K. (1995). *Technology's role in education reform: Findings from a national study of innovating schools*. Menlo Park, CA: SRI International.

Means, B., & Olson, K. (1997). *Technology and education reform*. Washington, DC: Office of Educational Research and Improvement, US Department of Education.

Meecker, M., & Meecker, R. (1985). *SOI-Learning Abilities test: Screening form for atypical students*. Vida, OR: M & M Enterprises.

Mehan, H. (1979). *Learning lessons: Social organization in the classroom*. Cambridge, MA: Harvard University Press.

Mehrabian, A., & Williams, M. (1971). Infant cognitive development scale. *Journal of Psycholinguistic Research*, 1, 113–126.

Meichenbaum, D. (1977). *Cognitive-behaviour modification: An integrative approach*. New York: Plenum.

Meichenbaum, D., & Goodman, J. (1971). Training impulsive children to talk to themselves. A means of developing self-control. *Journal of Abnormal Psychology*, 77, 115–126.

Mengheri, M., & Tubi, V. (1989). Sports participation and development of cognitive processes in 7 to 14 year old children. *Movimento*, 5(1), 34–35.

Menon, U. (2000). Analyzing emotions as culturally constructed scripts. *Culture and Psychology*, 6(1), 40–50.

Mercator Software (2001). KIDMAP. Available from http://www.mercator.com.au/aboutkm.html

Mercer, N. (1996). The quality of talk in children's collaborative activity in the classroom. *Learning and Instruction*, 6(4), 346–377.

Meredyth, D., Russell, N., Blackwood, L., Thomas, J., & Wise, P. (1999). *Real time: Computers, change and schooling*. Canberra: Australian Key Centre for Cultural and Media Policy, Commonwealth Department of Education, Training and Youth Affairs.

Merrill, P. F., Hammons, K., Vincent, B. R., Reynolds, P. L., Christensen, L., & Tolman, M. N. (1996). *Computers in education* (3rd ed.). Boston: Allyn & Bacon.

Meskill, C., Mossop, J., & Bates, R. (1999). *Electronic text and English as a second language environments*. (CELA Report No. CELA-RR-12012.) (ERIC Document Reproduction Service No. ED436956.)

Mevarech, Z. R., & Light, P. H. (1992). Cooperative learning with computers. *Learning and Instruction*, 2(3), 155–185.

Milgram, R. M. (2000). Identifying and enhancing talent in Israel: A high national priority. *Roeper Review, 22,* 108–110.

Millard, E. (1997). *Differently literate: Boys, girls and the schooling of literacy.* London: Falmer Press.

Miller, G. A. (1956). The magical number seven, plus or minus two: Some limits on our capacity for processing information. *The Psychological Review, 63,* 81–97. (Also available online: http://www.well.com/user/smalin/miller.html)

Miller, J. G., & Bersoff, D. M. (1992). Culture and moral judgment: How are conflicts between justice and interpersonal responsibilities resolved? *Journal of Personality and Social Psychology, 62*(4), 541–554.

Miller, M. (1996). Relevance of resilience to individuals with learning disabilities. *International Journal of Disability, Development and Education, 43,* 255–269.

Miller, P. H. (1993). *Theories of developmental psychology* (3rd ed.). New York: W. H. Freeman.

Ministerial Advisory Committee (2000). *Technology for learning: Students with disabilities.* Canberra: Commonwealth of Australia. Retrieved 23 March, 2003, from http://www.macswd.sa.gov.au/pdf/TechnologyforLearning.pdf

Ministry of Education (2002). *Briefing for the incoming minister of education.* Wellington: Ministry of Education. Retrieved from http://www.minedu.govt.nz/web/downloadable/dl7541_v1/BIM%20Education%202002.doc

Misiak, H., & Sexton, V. S. (1973). *Phenomenological, existential, and humanistic psychologies: A historical survey.* London: Grune & Stratton.

Mitchell, D. R. (1987). Special education in New Zealand: An historical perspective. In D. R. Mitchell & N. N. Singh (Eds.), *Exceptional children in New Zealand* (pp. 26–38). Palmerston North, NZ: The Dunmore Press.

Mitchell, R. (1985). *Report of the Review of Services for Behaviourally Disordered Persons in South Australia.* Adelaide: Government Printer.

Moely, B. E., Santulli, K. A., & Obach, M. S. (1995). Strategy instruction, metacognition, and motivation in the elementary school classroom. In F. E. Weinert & W. Schneider (Eds.), *Memory performance and competencies: Issues in growth and development.* Hillsdale, NJ: Erlbaum.

Moffitt, T. E., Caspi, A., Belsky, J., & Silva, P. A. (1992). Childhood experience and onset of menarche: A test of a sociobiological model. *Child Development, 63,* 47–58.

Moon, L., Meyer, P., & Grau, J. (1999). *Australia's young people: Their health and wellbeing 1999: The first report on the health of young people aged 12–24 years by the Australian Institute of Health and Welfare.* Canberra: Australian Institute of Health and Welfare.

Moon, L., Rahman, N., & Bhatia, K. (1998). *Australia's children: Their health and wellbeing 1998: The first report on children's health by the Australian Institute of Health and Welfare.* Canberra: Australian Institute of Health and Welfare.

Moran, L., Thompson, L., & Arthur, P. (1999). *Strategic analysis: Improving teaching and learning in Australian school education through the use of information and communications technologies.* A discussion paper for the Schools Advisory Group of Education Network Australis (EdNA). Canberra: Lifelong Learning Associates. Retrieved 24 October, 2002, from http://www.edna.edu.au/edna/system/11report/home.html

Morita, Y. (1996). Bullying as a contemporary behaviour problem in the context of increased 'societal privatization' in Japan. *Prospects: Quarterly Review of Comparative Education, 26,* 311–329.

Morrison, D., & Goldberg, B. (1996). Technology and whole-school educational restructuring: The Co-NECT experience. In P. Carlson & F. Makedon (Eds.), *Educational telecommunications, 1996.* World Conference on Telecommunications, Boston, June 17–22.

Morrison, G. R., Lowther, D. L., & DeMeulle, L. (1999). *Integrating computer technology into the classroom.* Upper Saddle River, NJ: Prentice Hall.

Mortimore, P., Sammons, P., Stoll, G., Lewis, D, & Ecob, R. (1988). *School matters: The junior years.* Wells: Open Books.

Mueller, J. H. (1992). Anxiety and performance. In A. P. Smith and D. M. Jones (Eds.), *Handbook of human performance* (Vol. 3, pp. 127–160). London: Academic.

Mulryan, C. M. (1995). Fifth- and sixth-graders' involvement and participation in cooperative small groups in mathematics. *The Elementary School Journal, 95*(4), 297–310.

Murero, M. (2002). E-life: Internet effects on the individual and social change. *Dissertation Abstracts International, 62*(8–A), 2615.

Murray, A. D., Johnson, J., & Peters, J. (1990). Fine tuning of utterance length to preverbal infants: Effects on later language development. *Journal of Child Language, 17,* 511–525.

Murray, B. (2000). A mirror on the self. *Monitor on Psychology, 31*(4), 17.

Musker, R. (2000). Why ICT makes a difference. *Education in Science, 186,* 4.

Naglieri, J. A. (1988). *DAP; Draw a person: A quantitative scoring system.* New York: Harcourt Brace Jovanovich.

Nakata, M. (1995). Cutting a better deal for Torres Strait Islanders, *Youth Studies Australia, 14*(4), 29–34.

National Institute of Mental Health (NIMH) (2002). *Attention deficit hyperactivity disorder.* Retrieved 22 March, 2002, from http://www.nimh.nih.gov/publicat/adhd.cfm

National Telecommunications and Information Administration (NTIA) (2000). *Falling through the net: Toward digital inclusion.* Washington DC: NTIA. Retrieved 15 March, 2003, from http://www.ntia.doc.gov/ntiahome/fttn00/contents00.html

Navarro, J. I., Aguilar, M., & Alcalde, C. (1999). Relationship of arithmetic problem solving and reflective–impulsive cognitive styles in third-grade students. *Psychological Reports, 85*(1), 179–186.

Neill, A. S. (1968). *Summerhill.* Harmondsworth, Middlesex: Penguin Books.

Neimark, E. O. (1981). Confounding with cognitive style factors: An artifact explanation for the apparent nonuniversal incidence of formal operations. In I. E. Sigel, D. M. Brodzinsky, & R. M. Golinkoff (Eds.), *New directions for Piagetian theory and practice.* Hillsdale, NJ: Erlbaum.

Nelson, T. O., & Narens, L. (1994). Why investigate metacognition? In J. Metcalfe & A. P. Shimamura (Eds.), *Metacognition – knowing about knowing.* Cambridge, MA: MIT Press.

Neuman, R. S., Murray, B., & Lussier, C. (2001). Confrontation with aggressive peers at school: Students' reluctance to seek help from the teacher. *Journal of Educational Psychology, 93*, 398–410.

New, R. S. (2000). Reggio Emilia: Some lessons for U.S. educators. ERIC Digest. Retrieved 22 November, 2002, from http://ericeece.org/pubs/digests/1993/new93.html

New Zealand Ministry of Education (1993a). *New Zealand Curriculum Framework*. Wellington: Ministry of Education.

New Zealand Ministry of Education (1993b). *New Zealand Curriculum Framework: Essential learning areas*. Retrieved 12 November, 2001, from http://www.tki.org.nz/r/governance/nzcf/ess_learning_e.php

New Zealand Ministry of Education (1993c). *New Zealand Curriculum Framework: Information skills*. Retrieved 12 November, 2001, from http://www.tki.org.nz/r/governance/nzcf/ess_skills_e.php#number

New Zealand Ministry of Education (1994). *English in the New Zealand curriculum*. Wellington: Ministry of Education.

New Zealand Ministry of Education (1999). *Health and physical education in the New Zealand curriculum*. Wellington: Ministry of Education.

New Zealand Ministry of Education (2000). *Gifted and talented students: Meeting their needs in New Zealand schools*. Wellington: Learning Media.

New Zealand Ministry of Education (2001a). *Briefing for the incoming Minister of Education 1999*. Retrieved 14 August, 2002, from http://www.minedu.govt.nz/web/document/document_page.cfm?id=373&goto=00-17

New Zealand Ministry of Education (2001b). *Curriculum Update, 45*. Wellington: Ministry of Education. Retrieved 20 August, 2002, from http://www.tki.org.nz/r/governance/curric_updates/curr_update45_e.php

New Zealand Ministry of Education (2001c). *Nga Haeata Matauranga: Annual report on Maori education 2000/ 2001 and directions for 2002*. Available from http://www.minedu.gov.nz

New Zealand Ministry of Education (2002a). *Alternative education: Literature review and report on key informants' experiences*. Retrieved 27 January, 2003, from http://www.minedu.govt.nz/index.cfm?layout=document&documentid=6912&data=1

New Zealand Ministry of Education (2002b). *Literacy leadership in New Zealand schools*. Wellington: Learning Media.

New Zealand Ministry of Education (2002c). *NCAE letter to parents: Last update: 27 Aug 2002*. Retrieved 22 January, 2003, from htttp:www.minedu.govt.nz/index.cfm?layout=documents&documentid=7523

New Zealand Ministry of Health (1998). *Our children's health*. Wellington: Ministry of Health.

Newell, F. M. (1996). Effects of a cross-age tutoring program on computer literacy learning of second-grade students. *Journal of Research on Computing in Education, 28*, 346–358.

Newhouse, P. (1998). The impact of portable computers on classroom learning environments. *Journal of the Australian Council for Educational Computer, 13*(1), 5–11.

Newman, D., Griffin, P., & Cole, M. (1989). *Construction zone: Working for cognitive change in school*. Cambridge: Cambridge University Press.

Newman, F., & Holzman, L. (1993). *Lev Vygotsky: Revolutionary scientist*. London: Routledge.

NHMRC (2002). *Attention deficit hyperactivity disorder. Part II – management*. Retrieved 25 March, 2002, from http://www.health.gov.au/nhmrc/publications/adhd/part2.htm

Nicholas, H., Lightbown, P., & Spada, N. (2001). Recasts as feedback to language learners. *Language Learning, 51*(4), 719–758.

Nichols, J. (1998). *Computer overview*. Retrieved 25 May, 2003, from http://astro.temple.edu/ ~nichols/55c1

Nickel, R. E., & Gerlach, E. K. (2001). The use of complimentary and alternative therapies by families of children with chronic conditions and disabilities. *Infants and Young Children, 14*, 67–78.

Nielsen, J. (1995). *Multimedia and hypertext: The Internet and beyond*. Boston: Academic Press.

Nirje, B. (1985). The basis and logic of the normalization principle. *Australian and New Zealand Journal of Developmental Disabilities, 11*, 65–68.

Nisbett, R. E., Peng, K., Choi, I., & Norenzayan, A. (2001). Culture and systems of thought: Holistic versus analytic cognition. *Psychological Review, 108*(2), 291–310.

Nixon, J. G., & Topping, K. J. (2001). Emergent writing: The impact of structured peer interaction. *Educational Psychology, 21*(2), 41–58.

Norman, H., Sritheran, E., & Ridding, C. (1984). *Teachers' perceptions of children with special needs: A national survey of primary school teachers concerning children with special needs in regular classes*. Wellington: Department of Education.

Northern Territory Department of Education (1999). *Learning lessons: An independent review of Indigenous education in the Northern Territory*. Darwin: Northern Territory Department of Education.

NSW Board of Studies (2000a). Geography syllabus. NSW Stages 4 and 5 Geography Syllabus. Retrieved 28 March, 2003, from http://www.boardofstudies.nsw.edu.au/syllabus_sc/geography_syl_index.html

NSW Board of Studies (2000b). K–10 Curriculum Framework. Retrieved 4 April, 2003, from http://www.boardofstudies.nsw.edu.au/manuals/pdf_doc/curriculum_fw_K10.pdf

NSW Board of Studies (2001a). *Establishing explicit standards for the new Higher School Certificate*. Sydney: Board of Studies NSW.

NSW Board of Studies (2001b). *Media guide: The new Higher School Certificate and School Certificate*. Sydney: Board of Studies NSW.

NSW Board of Studies (2002). *Motorised markbook*. Retrieved 12 April, 2003, from http://www.boardofstudies.nsw.edu.au/markbook/indix.html

NSW Department of Education and Training (1998). *Special education handbook for schools*. Sydney: NSW Department of Education and Training.

NSW Department of Education and Training (2002). *Learning at school: K–12 focus areas*. Retrieved 12 March, 2003, from http://www.schools.nsw.edu.au/learning/yrk12focusareas/distanceed/index.php

NSW Department of School Education (1997). *Strategies for assessment and reporting: Primary schools*. Ryde, NSW: Department of School Education, Assessment and Reporting Directorate.

Nucci, L. P. (2001). *Education in the moral domain*. Cambridge: Cambridge University Press.

Nuthall, G. A. (2000). The role of memory in the acquisition and retention of knowledge in science and social studies units. *Cognition and Instruction, 18*(1), 83–139.

Nuttall, D. L. (1992). Performance assessment: The message from England. *Educational Leadership, 49*, 54–57.

O'Connor, R. E (1995). Elementary school programs. In M. C. Wang, M. C. Reynolds, & H. J. Walberg (Eds.), *Handbook of special education and remedial education: Research and practice* (pp. 61–105). Oxford: Elsevier Science.

O'Donohue, W. T., & Ferguson, K. E. (2001). *The psychology of B. F. Skinner*. Thousand Oaks, CA: Academic Press.

Ogborn, J., Kress, G., Martins, I., & McGillicuddy, K. (1996). *Explaining science in the classroom*. Buckingham, Philadelphia: Open University Press.

Ogbu, J. U. (1987). Variability in minority school performance: A problem in search of an explanation. *Anthropology and Education Quarterly, 18*, 312–334.

Ogbu, J. U. (1997). Understanding the school performance of urban blacks: Some essential background knowledge. In H. J. Wallberg, O. Reyes, & R. P. Weissberg (Eds.), *Children and youth: Interdisciplinary perspectives*. Thousand Oaks, CA: Sage.

Ogbu, J. U., & Simons, H. D. (1998). Voluntary and involuntary minorities: A cultural-ecological theory of school performance with some implications for education. *Anthropology and Education Quarterly, 29*(2), 155–88.

Oglesby, F., & Suter, W. N. (1995). Matching reading styles and reading instruction. *Research in the Schools, 2*(1), 11–15.

Olaniran, B. A. (1994). Group performance in computer-mediated and face-to-face communication media. *Management Communication Quarterly, 7*(3), 256–281.

Ollendick, T. H., Weist, M. D., Borden, M. C., & Greene, R. W. (1992). Sociometric status and academic, behavioral, and psychological adjustment: A five-year longitudinal study. *Journal of Consulting and Clinical Psychology, 60*(1), 80–87.

Olweus, D. (1978). *Aggression in schools: Bullies and whipping boys*. Washington, DC: Wiley.

Olweus, D. (1993). *Bullying in schools: What we know we can do*. Oxford: Blackwell.

Olweus, D. (1997). Bully/victim problems in school: Facts and intervention. *European Journal of Psychology of Education, 12*, 495–510.

Orlick, T., Zhou, Q. Y., & Partington, J. (1990). Co-operation and conflict within Chinese and Canadian kindergarten settings. *Canadian Journal of Behavioural Science, 22*, 20–25.

Osgood, C. E., Suci, G. J., & Tannenbaum, P. H. (1957). *The measurement of meaning*. Urbana, IL: University of Chicago Press.

Owens, L. (1996). Sticks and stones and sugar and spice: Girls' and boys' aggression in schools. *Australian Journal of Guidance and Counselling, 6*, 45–55.

Owens, L., & McMullin, C. E. (1995). Gender differences in aggression in children and adolescents in South Australian schools. *International Journal of Adolescence and Youth, 6*, 21–35.

Pachler, M. (2001). Issues of ICT in school-based learning. In M. Leask (Ed.), *Issues in teaching using ICT* (pp. 15–30). London: Routledge Falmer.

Pajares, F. (1997). Current directions in self-efficacy research. In M. Maehr & P. R. Pintrich (Eds.), *Advances in motivation and achievement* (Vol. 10, pp. 1–49). Greenwich, CT: JAI Press.

Pajares, F., & Schunk, D. H. (2001). Self-beliefs and school success: Self-efficacy, self-concept, and school achievement. In R. J. Riding & S. G. Rayner (Eds.), *Self perception: International perspectives on individual differences* (Vol. 2, pp. 239–265). Westport, CT: Ablex Publishing.

Palincsar, A. S. (1982). *Improving the reading comprehension of junior high school students through the reciprocal teaching of comprehension-monitoring strategies*. Unpublished Doctoral Dissertation, University of Illinois at Urbana-Champaign.

Palincsar, A. S. (1986). The role of dialogue in providing scaffolded instruction. *Educational Psychologist, 21*, 73–98.

Palincsar, A. S. (1987). *Collaborating for collaborative learning of text comprehension*. Paper presented at the Annual Meeting of the American Educational Research Association, Washington, DC.

Palincsar, A. S. (1998). Social constructivist perspectives on teaching and learning. *Annual Review of Psychology, 49*, 345–375.

Palincsar, A. S., & Brown, A. L. (1984). Reciprocal teaching of comprehension-fostering and comprehension-monitoring activities. *Cognitive Instruction, 1*, 117–175.

Palincsar, A. S., & Brown, A. L. (1989). Classroom dialogues to promote self-regulated comprehension. In J. Brophy (Ed.), *Advances in research on teaching* (pp. 35–72). Greenwich: JAI.

Palincsar, A. S., Brown, A. L., & Campione, J. C. (1993). First grade dialogues for knowledge acquisition and use. In E. A. Forman, N. Minnick, & C. A. Stone (Eds.), *Contexts for learning: Sociocultural dynamics in children's development* (pp. 43–57). New York: Oxford University Press.

Palincsar, A. S., & Herrenkohl, L. R. (1999). Designing collaborative contexts: Lessons from three research programs. In A. M. O'Donnell & A. King (Eds.), *Cognitive perspectives on peer learning. The Rutgers invitational symposium on education series* (pp. 151–177). Mahwah, NJ: Lawrence Erlbaum Associates.

Palmer, S. (1998). Current issues and limitations in using the Internet for teaching and learning. *Australian Educational Computing, 13*(1), 12–17.

Papert, S. (1980). *Mindstorms: Children, computers, and powerful ideas*. New York: Basic Books.

Parada, R. H., Marsh, H. W., & Yeung, A-S. (1999). *Bullying in schools: Can self-concept theory shed any light?* Paper presented at the Joint Annual Conference of the Australian Association for Research in Education and New Zealand Association for Research in Education, 29 November–2 December, 1999, Melbourne.

Paris, S. G., & Winograd, P. (1990). How metacognition can promote academic learning and instruction. In B. F. Jones & L. Idol (Eds.), *Dimensions of thinking and cognitive instruction* (pp. 15–51). Hillsdale, NJ: Erlbaum.

Park, C. C. (2000). Learning style preferences of Southeast Asian students. *Urban Education, 35*, 245–268.

Parliament of Australia. Senate Employment, Workplace Relations, Small Business and Education Committee (1999). *Katu Kalpa – Report on the inquiry into the effectiveness of education and training programs for Indigenous Australians*. Canberra: Parliament of Australia. Retrieved from http://www.aph.gov.au/senate/committee/EET_CTTE/indiged/contents.htm

Parr, N., & Mok, M. (1995). Differences in the educational achievements, aspirations and values of birthplace groups in New South Wales. *People and Place*, 3(2), 1–8.

Parsons, J. E., Kaczala, C., & Meece, J. (1982). Socialisation of achievement, attitudes and beliefs: Classroom influences. *Child Development*, 53, 322–339.

Pascual-Leone, J. (1970). A mathematical model for the transition rule in Piaget's development stages. *Acta Psychologica*, 32, 301–345.

Patterson, C. H. (1973). *Humanistic education*. Englewood Cliffs, NJ: Prentice Hall.

Pavlov, I. (1928). *Lectures on conditioned reflexes* (W. Gantt, Trans.). New York: International Universities Press.

Pedersen, N. L., Plomin, R., Nesselroade, J. R., & McClearn, G. E. (1992). A quantitative genetic analysis of cognitive abilities during the second half of the life span. *Psychological Science*, 3, 346–353.

Peklaj, C., & Vodopivec, B. (1999). Effects of cooperative versus individualistic learning on cognitive, affective, metacognitive and social processes in students. *European Journal of Psychology of Education*, 14, 359–373.

Pell, S. D., Gillies, R. M., & Carss, M. (1999). Use of technology by people with physical disabilities in Australia. *Disability and Rehabilitation*, 21(2), 56–90.

Pendarvis, E. D., Howley, A. A., & Howley, C. B. (1990). *The abilities of gifted children*. Englewood Cliffs, NJ: Prentice Hall.

Perfetti, C. A. (1988). Verbal efficiency in reading ability. In M. Daneman, G. E. MacKinnon & T. G. Waller (Eds.), *Reading research: Advances in theory and practice* (Vol. 6, pp. 109–143). San Diego: Academic Press.

Perkins, K. (2002a). *Australians: Kieren Perkins*. Retrieved 7 February, 2002, from http://www.abc.net.au/btn/australians/perkins.htm

Perkins, K. (2000b). *How Kieren began swimming*. Retrieved 2 February, 2002, from http://www.kierenperkins.org/kpstart.htm

Perry, D. G., Perry, L. C., & Kennedy, E. (1992). Conflict and the development of antisocial behavior. In C. U. Shanz & W. W. Hartup (Eds.), *Conflict in child and adolescent development* (pp. 301–329). New York: Cambridge University Press.

Perry-Burney, G. D., & Takyi, B. K. (2002). Self esteem, academic achievement and moral development among adolescent girls. *Journal of Human Behavior in the Social Environment*, 5(2), 15–28.

Petersen, L. (1994). Stop and think learning: Motivating learning in social groups and individuals. In M. Tainsh & J. Izard (Eds.). *Widening horizons: New challenges, directions and achievements. Selected papers from the national conference on behaviour management and behaviour change of children and youth with emotional and behaviour problems* (pp. 70–83). Melbourne: ACER.

Petersen, L., & Gannoni, L. (1992). *Manual for social skills training in young people with parent and teacher programmes: Stop think do*. Hawthorn, Victoria: ACER.

Peterson, C. C., & Siegal, M. (1999). Representing inner worlds: Theory of mind in autistic, deaf and normal hearing children. *Psychological Science*, 10(2), 126–129.

Pfeiffer, S. I. (2001). Emotional intelligence: Popular but elusive construct. *Roeper Review*, 23, 38–42.

Phillips, D. C. (1997). How, why, what, when, and where: Perspectives on constructivism and education. *Issues in Education: Contributions from Educational Psychology*, 3, 151–194.

Phillips, D. C. (2000a). An opinionated account of the constructivist landscape. In D. C. Phillips (Ed.), *Constructivism in education: Opinions and second opinions on controversial issues* (pp. 1–18). Chicago: The National Society for the Study of Education.

Phillips, D. C. (2000b). Editor's preface. In D. C. Phillips (Ed.), *Constructivism in education: Opinions and second opinions on controversial issues* (pp. vii–ix). Chicago: The National Society for the Study of Education.

Piaget, J. (1932). *The moral judgement of the child* (M. Gabain Trans.). London: Kegan Paul, Trench, Trubner & Co.

Piaget, J. (1971). *Biology and knowledge* (B. Walsh, Trans.). Chicago: University of Chicago Press.

Piaget, J. (1972). Intellectual evolution from adolescence to adulthood. *Human Development*, 15, 1–12.

Piaget, J. (1974). *Understanding causality* (D. Miles & M. Miles, Trans.). New York: Norton.

Piaget, J., & Inhelder, B., (1969). *The psychology of the child* (H. Weaver, Trans.). London: Routledge & Kegan Paul.

Pickering, D., & Dickens, E., with Duerdoth, P. (1992). *Special schools: Students, parents, teachers*. Burwood, Victoria: Victoria College Press.

Pieterse, M., & Treloar, R. (1989). *Small steps: An early intervention program for children with developmental delays*. Sydney: Macquarie University.

Piirto, J. (1999). *Talented children and adults: Their development and education* (2nd ed.). Upper Saddle River, NJ: Merrill.

Pintrich, P. R., & DeGroot, E. V. (1990). Motivational and self-regulated learning components of classroom academic performance. *Journal of Educational Psychology*, 82, 33–40.

Pintrich, P. R., & Schunk, D. H. (1996). *Motivation in education: Theory, research and applications*. Englewood Cliffs, NJ: Prentice Hall Merrill.

Piper, K. (1997). *Riders in the chariot: Curriculum reform and the national interest 1965–1995*. Melbourne: ACER.

Pisapia, J., Knutson, K., & Coukos, E. (1999). *The impact of computers on student performance and teacher behavior*. Paper presented at the Annual Meeting of the Florida Educational Research Association, 10–12 November 1999. (ERIC Document Reproduction Service No. ED438323.)

Plomin, R. (1999). Behavioural genetics. In M. Bennett (Ed.), *Developmental psychology: Achievements and prospects* (pp. 231–252). Philadelphia, PA: Psychology Press.

Plucker, J. (2002). *Jean-Mark Gaspard Itard*. Retrieved 19 January, 2003, from http://www.indiana.edu/~intell/itard.html

Plucker, J. A., & Renzulli, J. S. (1999). Psychometric approaches to the study of human creativity. In R. J. Sternberg (Ed.), *Handbook of creativity* (pp. 35–61). Cambridge: Cambridge University Press.

Policastro, E., & Gardiner, H. (1999). From case studies to robust generalisations: An approach to the study of creativity. In R. J. Sternberg (Ed.), *Handbook of creativity* (pp. 213–225). Cambridge: Cambridge University Press.

Porter, L. (1997). Selected perspectives on ADD – attention deficit disorder – and ADHD – attention deficit hyperactivity disorder. *Australian Journal of Early Childhood*, 22, 7–14.

Porter, L. (1999). *Gifted young children: A guide for teachers and parents*. St Leonards, NSW: Allen & Unwin.

Porter, L. (2000). *Behaviour in schools: Theory and practice for teachers*. Buckingham, Open University Press.

Postman, N., & Weingartner, C. (1973). *The school book*. New York: Delacorte.

Powell, K., & Wells, M. (2002). The effectiveness of three experimental teaching approaches on student science learning in fifth-grade public school classrooms. *Journal of Environmental Education, 33*(2), 33–38.

Powell, M. J. (1994). *Equity in the reform of mathematics and science education: A look at issues and solutions*. Austin, TX: Southwest Educational Development Laboratory.

Powell, S. D., & Makin, M. (1994). Enabling pupils with learning difficulties to reflect on their own thinking. *British Educational Research Journal, 20*(5), 20–29.

Power, C., Higgins, A., & Kohlberg, L. (1989). *Lawrence Kohlberg's approach to moral education*. New York: Columbia University Press.

Pratarelli, M. E., & Browne, B. L. (2002). Confirmatory factor analysis of internet use and addiction. *CyberPsychology and Behavior, 5*(1), 53–64.

Prawat, R. (1996). Constructivisms, modern and postmodern. *Educational Psychology, 31*, 215–225.

Preece, J., & Davies, G. (1992). Multimedia: Some promises, some problems and some issues in human-systems interaction. In Promaco Conventions (Eds.), *Proceedings of the International Interactive Multimedia Symposium* (pp. 259–266). Perth: Promaco Conventions Pty Ltd.

Press, L., Foster, W., Wolcott, P., & McHenry, W. (2002). The Internet in India and China. *First Monday, 7*(10). Retrieved 26 March, 2003, from http://firstmonday.org/issues/issue7_10/press/index.html

Pressley, M. (1994). State-of-the-science primary-grades reading instruction or whole language? *Educational Psychologist, 29*, 211–215.

Pressman, H., & Blackstone, S. (1997). Technology and inclusion: Are we asking the wrong questions? In D. K. Lipsky & A. Gartner (Eds.), *Inclusion and school reform: Transforming America's classrooms*. Baltimore: Paul H. Brookes.

Pronto, N. H. (1969). *Panorama of psychology*. Belmont, CA: Wadsworth.

Purdie, N., & Hattie, J. (1996). Cultural differences in the use of strategies for self-regulated learning. *American Educational Research Journal, 33*(4), 845–871.

Purdie, N., Tripcony, P., Boulton-Lewis, G., Fanshawe, J., & Gunstone, A. (2000). *Positive self-identity for Indigenous students and its relationship to school outcomes*. Canberra: Commonwealth of Australia. Also available from http://www.detya.gov.au/schools/publications/2000/PSI_synth.pdf

Quinn, M. G., Sultmann, W. F., & Elkins, J. (1988). Exceptional students in Queensland Catholic Schools: Prevalence, priorities and future directions. *Australasian Journal of Special Education, 12*, 10–20.

Raab, V. C. (2001). Multiple risk factors in adolescent suicide: A meta-analysis of the published research. *Dissertation Abstracts International Section B: The Sciences and Engineering, 61*(12–B), 6719.

Ransom, L. (2001). Cultural diversity and conflict resolution: An interdisciplinary unit for the Californian fourth-grade classroom. *Multicultural Education, 9*, 30–37.

Ratner, C. (2000). Agency and culture. *Journal for the Theory of Social Behavior, 30*(4), 413–434.

Rees, M. (1993). Menarche when and why? *Lancet, 342*, 1375–1376.

Reeves, L. L. (1997). Minimizing writing apprehension in the learner-centered classroom. *English Journal, 86*(6), 38–45.

Reichhardt, E. (September, 1996). Internet basics in TESOL. In ELICOS Association (Ed.), *Proceedings of the 9th Annual Elicos Association Education Conference* (pp. 223–228). Pyrmont, NSW: ELICOS Association.

Reinen, I. J., & Plomp, T. (1997). Information technology and gender equity: A contradiction in terms? *Computers Education, 28*(2), 65–78.

Relan, A. (1992). *Motivational strategies in computer-based instruction: Some lessons from theories and models of motivation*. Proceedings of Selected Research Presentations at the Annual Convention of the AECT. (ERIC Document Reproduction No. ED 348 017.)

Renshaw, P. (1998). Sociocultural pegagogy for new times: Reframing new concepts. *Australian Educational Researcher, 25*, 83–100.

Resnick, M. (1994). Changing the centralized mind. *Technology Review, 97*(5), 32–41.

Resnick, M. (1996). *Distributed constructivism*. Paper presented at the International conference on the Learning Sciences Association for the Advancement of Computing in Education. Northwestern University, Evanston, Illinois. Available online at http://web.media.mit.edu/~mres/papers/Distrib-Contruc/Distrib-Construc.html

Rest, J. R. (1979). *Development in judging moral issues*. Minneapolis: University of Minnesota Press.

Rest, J. R. (1986). *Moral development: Advances in research and theory*. New York: Praeger.

Rest, J. R., & Narváez, D. (1994). *Moral development in the professions*. Hillsdale, NJ: Lawrence Erlbaum Associates.

Rest, J. R., Thomas, J., Edwards, L. (1997). Designing and validating a measure of moral judgment: Stage preference and stage consistency approaches. *Journal of Educational Psychology, 89*(1), 5–28.

Reynolds, M. C. (1962). A framework for considering some issues in special education. *Exceptional Children, 28*, 367–370.

Rich, J. M. (1992). *Foundations of education: Perspectives on American education*. New York: Merrill.

Richards, A. C., & Combs, A. (1993). Education and the humanist challenge. In F. J. Wertz (Ed.), *The humanist movement: Recovering the person in psychology* (pp. 256–273). Lake Worth, FL: Gardner Press.

Riding, R., & Cheema, I. (1991). Cognitive styles: An overview and integration. *Educational Psychology: An International Journal of Experimental Educational Psychology, 11*(3–4), 193–215.

Riding, R. J., & Al-Sanabani, S. (1998). The effect of cognitive style, age, gender, and structure on the recall of prose passages. *International Journal of Educational Research, 29*, 173–185.

Riding, R. J., & Rayner, S. G. (1998). *Cognitive style and learning strategies*. London: David Fulton Publishers.

Riel, M. (1994). Education change in a technology-rich environment. *The Journal of Research on Computing in Education, 5*, 261–274.

Riel, M. (1996). Cross-classroom-collaboration: Communication and education. In T. Koschmann (Ed.), *CSCL:*

Theory and practice of an emerging paradigm (pp. 187–207). Mahwah, NJ: Lawrence Erlbaum Associates.

Rigby, K. (1994). Family influence, peer relations and health effects among school children. In K. Oxenberry, K. Rigby, & P. T. Slee (Eds.), *Children's peer relations. Conference proceedings* (pp. 294–304). Adelaide: The Institute of Social Research, University of South Australia.

Rigby, K. (1996). *Bullying in schools: What to do about it.* Melbourne: ACER.

Rigby, K. (1997). Attitudes and beliefs of Australian schoolchildren regarding bullying in schools. *Irish Journal of Psychology, 18,* 202–220.

Rigby, K. (2001). *Stop the bullying: A handbook for schools.* Melbourne: ACER.

Rigby, K., & Slee, R. (1995). *Manual for the Peer Relations Questionnaire (PRQ).* Adelaide, SA: University of South Australia.

Rigby, K., & Slee, R. (1999). Australia. In P. K. Smith, Y. Morita, J. Junger-Tas, D. Olweus, R. Catalano, & P. Slee (Eds.), *The nature of school bullying: A cross-national perspective* (pp. 324–355). London: Routledge.

Riley, T. L. (2001). Mapping out new directions? Or using the same road map? *Gifted Child Today, 24,* 24–29.

Riley, T. L. (2002). Looking back and thinking ahead. *Gifted Child Today, 25,* 46–49.

Rittle-Johnson, B., & Alibali, M. W. (1999). Conceptual and procedural knowledge of mathematics: Does one lead to the other? *Journal of Educational Psychology, 91*(1), 175–189.

Riva, G., & Galimberti, C. (2001). Virtual communication: Social interaction and identity in an electronic environment. In G. Riva & F. Davide (Eds.), *Communications through virtual technologies, Vol. 1: Identity, community and technology in the communication age* (Chapter 2). Retrieved 27 April, 2003, from http://www.vepsy.com/communication/volume1.html

Rivers, L. (1995). *Young person suicide.* Wellington: Special Education Service.

Roberts, D., Gracey, M., & Spargo, R. M. (1988). Growth and morbidity in children in a remote Aboriginal community in north-western Australia. *The Medical Journal of Australia, 148,* 69.

Robertson, I., Calder, J., Fung, P., Jones, A., & O'Shea, T. (1995). Computer attitudes in an English secondary school. *Computers and Education, 24,* 73–81.

Robinson, A. (1990). Cooperation or exploitation? The arguments against cooperative learning for talented students. *Journal for the Education of the Gifted, 14,* 9–27.

Roblyer, M. D. (1990). The impact of microcomputer-based instruction on teaching and learning: A review of recent research. *Educational Technology, 30,* 54–55.

Roblyer, M. D. (1999). Is choice important in distance learning? A study of students' motives for taking Internet-based courses at community college and high school levels. *Journal of Research on Computing and Education, 32*(1/2), 157–171.

Roblyer, M. D., & Edwards, J. (2000). *Integrating educational technology into teaching* (2nd ed.). Upper Saddle River, NJ: Merrill.

Roblyer, M. D., Edwards, J., & Havriluk, M. A. (1997). *Integrating educational technology into teaching.* Upper Saddle River, NJ: Prentice Hall.

Rogers, C. (2000). *Carl Rogers.* Retrieved 16 November, 2002, from http://www.geocities.com/Athens/Troy/2967/Rogers.html

Rogers, C. R. (1939). *The clinical treatment of the problem child.* Boston: Houghton Mifflen.

Rogers, C. R. (1942). *Counseling and psychotherapy: New concepts in practice.* Boston: Houghton Mifflen.

Rogers, C. R. (1951). *Client-centered therapy: Its current practice, implications and theory.* Boston: Houghton Mifflen.

Rogers, C. R. (1969). *Freedom to learn.* Columbus, OH: Merrill.

Rogers, C. R. (1983). *Freedom to learn for the 80s: A view of what education might become.* Columbus, OH: Merrill.

Rogers, W. A. (1989). *Making a discipline plan: Developing classroom management skills.* Melbourne: Nelson.

Rogers, W. A (1998). *'You know the fair rule' and much more: Strategies for making the hard job of discipline and behaviour management in school easier.* Melbourne: ACER.

Rogoff, B. (1990). *Apprenticeship in thinking: Cognitive development in social context.* New York: Oxford University Press.

Rogoff, B. (1998). Cognition as a collaborative process. In D. Kuhn & R. S. Siegler (Eds.), *Handbook of child psychology* (Vol. 2, 5th ed., pp. 679–744). New York: John Wiley and Sons.

Roh, K. (1997). An understanding of higher order thinking in social studies: A naturalistic case study of a Korean middle school classroom. *Dissertation Abstracts International. Section A: Humanities and Social Sciences, Vol. 58* (6–A), 2060.

Rokx, H., Woodham, B., & Joe, M. (1999, July). *Maori programme development: He Taonga Te Mokopuna – The child is precious.* Paper presented at Children and Family Violence: Effective Interventions Now Conference, Wellington, New Zealand. Retrieved 2 June, 2003, from http://www/justice.govt.nz/pubs/reports/1999/family_conference/index.html

Roschelle, J. (1995). What should collaborative technology be? A perspective from Dewey and situated learning. Paper presented at Computer Support for Collaborative Learning '95, Indiana University, Bloomington, IN.

Rosen, L., Sears, D. C., & Weil, M. W. (1993). Treating technophobia: A longitudinal evaluation of the Computerphobia reduction program. *Computers in Human Behavior, 9,* 27–50.

Rosenberg, M., & Owens, T. J. (2001). Low self-esteem people: A collective portrait. In T. J. Owens, S. Stryker, & N. Goodman (Eds.), *Extending self-esteem theory and research: Sociological and psychological currents* (pp. 400–436). New York: Cambridge University Press.

Rosenblum, G. D., & Lewis, M. (1999). The relations among body image, physical attractiveness and body mass in adolescence. *Child Development, 70*(1), 50–64.

Rosenshine, B. (1997). Advances in research on instruction. In J. W. Lloyd, E. J. Kameenui, & D. Chard (Eds.), *Issues in educating students with disabilities* (pp. 197–221). Mahwah, NJ: Lawrence Erlbaum Associates.

Rosenshine, B., & Meister, C. (1994). Reciprocal teaching: A review of the research. *Review of Educational Research, 64*(4), 479–530.

Rosenthal, R., & Jacobson, L. (1968). *Pygmalion in the classroom.* New York: Holt, Rinehart & Winston.

Ross, H. E., & Ivis, F. (1999). Binge eating and substance use among male and female adolescents. *International*

Journal of Eating Disorders, 26(3), 245–260.

Roth, W-M., & Bowen, G. M. (1995). Knowing and interacting: A study of culture, practices and resources in a Grade 8 open-inquiry science classroom guided by a cognitive apprenticeship metaphor. *Cognition and Instruction, 13*, 73–128.

Rothschild, L. W. (1999). Using peers to teach scientific reasoning. *Dissertation Abstracts International Section A: Humanities and Social Sciences, Vol. 60*(4–A), 1014.

Rothstein, E. (1997). Gate's largesse stirs a discomfiting question: Is there indeed a computer literacy? *The New York Times*, 7 July.

Rowe, K. J. (2001). *What really matters: The 'pimple' or the 'pumpkin'? Exploring the evidence for 'real' factors affecting girls' and boys' experiences and outcomes of schooling.* Paper presented at Boys Education and Beyond conference, Fremantle, 2001. Retrieved 4 May, 2003, from http://www.acer.edu.au/library/doconline/ 116874.pdf

Rowe, K. J. (2000). *Celebrating coeducation? Maybe, but not necessarily for academic achievement! An examination of the emergent research evidence.* Keynote address to Second National Conference on Co-education. Kinroos Wollaroi School, Orange, NSW. 16–19 April 2000.

Rowe, K. J. (2002). The importance of teacher quality. *Issue Analysis, 22.* Sydney, NSW: Centre for Independent Studies. Retrieved 24 February, 2003, from http://www.cis.org.au

Rowe, K. S., & Rowe, K. J. (1994). Synthetic food coloring and behavior: A dose response effect in a double-blind, placebo-controlled, repeated measures study. *Journal of Paediatrics, 125*(5,Pt. 1), 691–698.

Rowe, K. J., & Rowe, K. S. (2002). *What matters most: Evidence-based findings of key factors affecting the educational experiences and outcomes for girls and boys throughout their primary and secondary schooling.* Supplementary submission to House of Representatives Standing Committee on Education and Training: Inquiry into the Education of Boys, May 2002. Retrieved 12 February, 2003, from http://www.aph.gov.au/house/committee/edt/Eofb/index.htm

Rubin, K. H; Booth, C., Rose-Krasnor, L., & Mills, R. S. L. (1995). Social relationships and social skills: A conceptual and empirical analysis. In S. Shulman (Ed.), *Close relationships and socioemotional development. Human development* (Vol. 7, pp. 63–94). Westport, CT: Ablex Publishing.

Rubin, K. H., Bukowski, W., & Parker, J. G. (1998). Peer interactions, relationships, and groups. In N. Eisenberg (Ed.), *Handbook of child psychology, Vol. 3: Social, emotional and personality development* (5th ed., pp. 619–700). New York: Wiley.

Rutter, M., Maughan, B., Mortimore, P., & Ouston, T. (1979). *Fifteen thousand hours: Secondary schools and their effects on children.* Cambridge, MA: Harvard University Press.

Rutter, M., & Rutter, M. (1992). *Developing minds: Challenge and continuity across the life span.* Harmondsworth, UK: Penguin.

Ryan, J. (1997). Student communities in a culturally diverse school setting: Identity, representation and association. *Discourse, 18*(1), 37–53.

Ryser, G. R., Beeler, J. E., & McKenzie, C. M. (1995). Effects of a computer-supported intentional learning environment (CSILE) on students' self-concept, self-regulatory behavior, and critical thinking ability. *Journal of Educational Computing Research, 13*(4), 375–385.

Saarni, C. (1993). Socialisation of emotion. In M. Lewis & J. M. Haviland (Eds.), *Handbook of emotions* (pp. 435–446). New York: Guilford Press.

Saarni, C., Mumme, D. L., & Campos, J. J. (1998). Emotional development: Action, communication, and understanding. In N. Eisenberg (Ed.), *Handbook of child psychology, Vol. 3: Social, emotional, and personality development* (5th ed., pp. 237–309). New York: Wiley.

Sachs, J. (2001). Communication development in infancy. In J. Berko Gleason (Ed.), *The development of language* (5th ed.). Boston: Allyn & Bacon.

Sacks, C., Bellisimo, Y., & Mergendoller, J. (1994). Attitudes towards computers and computer use: The issues of gender. *Journal of Research on Computing in Education, 26*(2), 256–269.

Sadker, D., & Sadker, M. (1993). Sex equity: Assumptions and strategies in *The international encyclopedia of education.* Oxford: Pergamon Press.

Sadler, D. R. (1989). Formative assessment and the design of instructional systems. *Instructional Science, 18*, 119–144.

Sadler-Smith, (2001). The relationship between learning style and cognitive style. *Personality and individual differences, 30*, 609–616.

Salomon, G. (1993). Editor's introduction. In G. Salomon (Ed.), *Distributed cognitions: Psychological and educational considerations* (pp. xi–xxi). New York: Cambridge University Press.

Salomon, G., Perkins, D., & Globerson, T. (1991). Partners in cognition: Extending human intelligence with intelligent technologies. *Educational Researcher, 20*(3), 2–9.

Sandholtz, J. H., Ringstaff, C., & Dwyer, D. C. (1997). *Teaching with technology: Creating student-centered classrooms.* New York: Teachers College, Columbia University.

Sanelli, M. F. (1999). Identity development of stigmatised adolescents. *Dissertation Abstracts International, 59*(12–A), 4399.

Saracho, O. (1998). Editor's introduction: Cognitive style research and its relationship to various disciplines. *International Journal of Educational Research, 29*, 169–172.

Sax, G. (1997). *Principles of educational and psychological measurement and evaluation* (4th ed.). Belmont, CA: Wadsworth.

Saye, J. (1997). Technology and educational empowerment. *Educational Technology Research and Development, 45*(2), 5–24.

Scarino, A., Vale, D., McKay, P., & Clark, J. (1988). *The Australian Language Levels (ALL) Guidelines.* Canberra: Curriculum Development Centre.

Scealy, M., Phillips, J. G., & Stevenson, R. (2002). Shyness and anxiety as predictors of patterns of internet usage. *CyberPsychology and Behavior, 5*(6), 507–515.

Scheerenberger, R. C. (1987). *A history of mental retardation: A quarter of a century of promise.* Baltimore: Paul H. Brookes.

Schloss, P. J., & Smith, M. A. (1998). *Applied behaviour analysis in the classroom* (2nd ed.). Boston, MA: Allyn & Bacon.

Schneider, B. H. (2000). *Friends and enemies: Peer relations in childhood.* London: Arnold.

Schneider, B. H., & Blonk, R. W. (1998). Children's comments about their social skills training. In P. T. Slee & K. Rigby (Eds.), *Children's peer relations* (pp. 272–287). London: Routledge.

Schneider, W., & Bjorklund, D. F. (1998). Memory. In D. Kuhn & R. S. Siegler (Eds.), *Handbook of child psychology* (Vol. 2, 5th ed., pp. 467–52). New York: John Wiley and Sons.

School of Education, James Cook University (1998). Submission No. 138, Vol. 5, p. 175 in Parliament of Australia: Senate Committee, *A class act* (Chapter 6). Canberra: Commonwealth of Australia.

School students gain virtual mentors (1997). Retrieved 12 January, 2003, from http://www.unimelb.edu.au/ExtRels/Medi/UN/archive/multimediatwo/schoolstudentsgainvirtual.html

Schools Commission (1975). *Report for the triennium, 1976–78*. Canberra: Australian Government Printer.

Schraw, G., & Aplin, B. (1998). Teacher preferences for mastery-oriented students. *Journal of Educational Research, 91*, 215–220.

Schriver, K. (1997). *Dynamics in document design*. John Wiley & Sons.

Schwarzer, R. (1998). Stress and coping from a social-cognitive perspective. In P. Csermely (Ed.), *Stress of life: From molecules to man. Annals of the New York Academy of Sciences* (Vol. 851, pp. 531–537). New York: New York Academy of Sciences.

Schwarzer, R., & Fuchs, R. (1995). Changing risk behaviours and adopting healthy behaviours: The role of self-efficacy beliefs. In A. Bandura (Ed.), *Self-efficacy in changing societies* (pp. 259–288). Cambridge: Cambridge University Press.

Scott, V. (1996). Why are girls under represented? Ten years on. *Australian Educational Computing, 11*(1), 16–21.

Seaton, A. (1998). Opening school doors to the real world: A review of literature on computer mediated communication and its role in the creation of constructivist learning environments. *Australian Educational Computing, 13*(1), 18–21.

Semel, S. (1992). *The Dalton School: Transformation of a progressive school. American University Studies* (Series XIV, Vol. 34). New York: Peter Lang.

Senate Select Committee (1988). *The education of gifted and talented children*. Canberra: AGPS.

Senechal, M., & LeFevre, J. (2001). Storybook reading and parent teaching: Links to language and literacy development. *New Directions for Child and Adolescent Development, 92*, 39–52.

Shapiro, J., & Hughes, S. (1996). Information literacy as a liberal art: Enlightenment proposals for a new curriculum. *EducomReview, 31*(2). Retrieved 28 December, 2002, from http://www.educause.edu/pub/er/review/reviewArticles/31231.html

Sharan, S. (1980). Cooperative learning in small groups: Recent methods and effects on achievement, attitudes and ethnic relations. *Review of Educational Research, 50*, 241–271.

Sharan, S. (1990). Cooperative learning and helping behaviour in the multi-ethnic classroom. In H. C. Foot, M. J. Morgan, & R. H. Shute (Eds.), *Children helping children* (pp. 151–176). Chicester, West Sussex: John Wiley and Sons.

Sharan, S., & Shachar, H. (1988). *Language and learning within the cooperative classroom*. New York: Springer-Verlag.

Sharan, Y., & Sharan, S. (1992). *Extending cooperative learning through group investigation*. New York: Teachers College Press.

Share, D. L., Jorm, A. F., Maclean, R., Matthews, R., & Waterman, B. (1983). Early reading achievement, oral language ability, and a child's home background. *Australian Psychologist, 18*(1), 75–87.

Sharples, D. (1990). Teaching styles and strategies in the open-plan primary school. In N. Entwisle (Ed.), *Handbook of educational ideas and practices* (pp. 785–793). London: Routledge.

Sharratt, P. A., & van den Heuvel, E. (1995). Metamemorial knowledge in a group of black South African school children. *South African Journal of Psychology, 25*, 59–73.

Shavelson, R. J., Hubner, J. J., & Stanton, G. C. (1976). Self-concept: Validation of construct interpretations. *Review of Educational Research, 46*, 407–441.

Shayer, M. (1997). Piaget and Vygotsky: A necessary marriage for effective educational intervention. In L. Smith, J. Dockrell, & P. Tomlinson (Eds.), *Piaget, Vygotsky and beyond: Future issues for developmental psychology and education* (pp. 36–59). London: Routledge.

Sherif, M. (1967). *Group conflict and co-operation*. London: Routledge and Kegan Paul.

Shin, M. (1998). Promoting students' self-regulation ability: Guidelines for instructional design. *Educational Technology, 38*(1), 38–44.

Shweder, R. A., & Haidt, J. (2000). The cultural psychology of the emotions: Ancient and new. In M. Lewis & J. Haviland (Eds.), *Handbook of emotions* (2nd ed., pp. 397–414). New York: Guilford.

Sidoti, C. (2000). *Access to education: A human right for every child*. Speech given at the 29th Annual Federal ICPA Conference, 3 August 2000, Griffith, NSW.

Siegal, M. (1991). *Knowing children: Experiments in conversation and cognition*. London: Erlbaum.

Siegler, R. S. (1976). Three aspects of cognitive development. *Cognitive Psychology, 8*, 481–520.

Siegler, R. S. (1998). *Children's thinking* (3rd ed.). Upper Saddle River, NJ: Prentice Hall.

Siegler, R. S., & Ellis, S. (1996). Piaget on childhood. *Psychological Science, 7*, 211–215.

Silver, L. B. (1995). Controversial therapies. *Journal of Child Neurology, 10*(Suppl. 1), S96–S100.

Silverman, S., & Pritchard, A. (1993). *Building their future: Girls in technology education in Connecticut*. Retrieved 10 October, 2002, from http://borg.lib.vt.edu/ejournals/JTE/jte-v7n2/silverman.jte-v7n2.html

Simpson, G. (2001). Learner characteristics, learning environments and constructivist epistemologies. *Australian Science Teachers Journal, 47*(2), 17–24.

Singer, D. G., & Revenson, T. A. (1996). *A Piaget primer: How a child thinks* (Rev. ed.). New York: Plume.

Sivin-Kachala, J., & Bialo, E. R. (1996). *Report on the effectiveness of technology in schools, '95–'96*. Washington, DC: Software Publishers Association.

Sivin-Kachala, J., & Bialo, E. R. (1997). *Report on the effectiveness of technology in schools, '90–'97*. Washington, DC: Software Publishers Association.

Skeels, H. M. (1966). Adult status of children with contrasting early life experiences: A follow-up study.

Monographs of the Society for Research in Child Development, 31(3), Serial No. 105.

Skeels, H. M., & Dye, H. (1939). A study of the effects of differential stimulation on mentally retarded children. *Proceedings and addresses of the Sixty-third Annual Session of the American Association on Mental Deficiency, 44,* 114–130.

Skinner, B. F. (1938). *The behavior of organisms: An experimental analysis.* New York: Appleton-Century.

Skinner, B. F. (1948). *Walden two.* New York: Macmillan.

Skinner, B. F. (1957). *Verbal behaviour.* New York: Appleton-Century-Crofts.

Skinner, B. F. (1968). *The technology of teaching.* New York: Appleton-Century-Crofts.

Skinner, B. F. (1971). *Beyond freedom and dignity.* New York: Knopf.

Slavin, R. E. (1994). *A practical guide to cooperative learning.* Boston: Allyn & Bacon.

Slavin, R. E. (1996). Research on cooperative learning and achievement: What we know, what we need to know. *Contemporary Educational Psychology, 21,* 43–69.

Slee, R. (1992). National trends in discipline policy. In J. Elkins & J. Izard (Eds.), *Student behaviour problems: Context, initiatives and programs* (pp. 1–12). Hawthorn, Victoria: ACER.

Slee, R. (1995a). *Changing theories and practices of discipline.* London: Falmer Press.

Slee, R. (1995b). Educating for all: Arguing principles or pretending agreement? *Australian Disability Review, 2,* 3–19.

Slee, J. (1996). Selective mutism: A behavioural approach to a behaviour disorder. In J. Izard & J. Evans (Eds.), *Student behaviour: Policies, interventions and evaluations* (pp. 268–281). Camberwell, Victoria: ACER.

Smetana, J. (1995). Morality in context: Abstractions, ambiguities, and applications. *Annals of Child Development, 10,* 83–130.

Smith, D. J., Sharp, S., & Cowie, H. (1994). Working directly with pupils involved in bullying situations. In P. K. Smith & S. Sharp (Eds.), *School bullying: Insights and perspectives* (pp. 193–212). London: Routledge.

Smith, H. (2000). Internet provision of enrichment opportunities to school and home. *Australian Educational Computing, 15*(2), 20–25.

Smith, J. D., & Caplan, J. (1988). Cultural differences in cognitive style development. *Developmental Psychology, 24,* 46–52.

Smith, J. D., & Nelson, D. G. (1988). Is the more impulsive child a more holistic processor? A reconsideration. *Child Development, 59,* 719–727.

Smith, L. (1993). *Necessary knowledge: Piagetian perspectives on constructivism.* Hove, UK: Lawrence Erlbaum.

Smith, M. M., & Grenyer, B. F. S. (1999). Psychosocial profile of pregnant adolescents in a large Australian regional area. *Australian Journal of Rural Health, 7*(1), 28–33.

Smith, P. K., & Morita, Y. (1999). Introduction. In P. K. Smith, Y. Morita, J. Junger-Tas, D. Olweus, R. Catalano, & P. Slee (Eds.), *The nature of school bullying: A cross-national perspective* (pp. 1–4). London: Routledge.

Smolenski, M. (2000). *The digital divide and American society.* Stamford, CT: Gartner Group. Retrieved 24 May, 2003, from http://www.gartnerweb.com/public/static/techies/digital_d/national2.html

Snarey, J. (1985). Cross-cultural universality of social-moral development: A critical review of Kohlbergian research. *Psychological Bulletin, 97*(2), 202–232.

Snow, C. E. (1995). Issues in the study of input: Fine-tuning, universality, individual and developmental differences, and necessary causes. In P. Fletcher & B. McWhinney (Eds.), *Handbook of child language.* Oxford: Blackwell.

Snow, R. E. (1991). Aptitude-treatment interaction models of teaching. In K. Marjoribanks (Ed.), *The foundations of students' learning* (pp. 183–190). Oxford: Pergamon Press.

Snow, R. E. (1995). Pygmalion and intelligence. *Current Directions in Psychological Science, 4,* 169–171.

Solomon, J. (2000). The changing perspectives of constructivism: Science wars and children's creativity. In D. C. Phillips (Ed.), *Constructivism in education: Opinions and second opinions on controversial issues* (pp. 283–307). Chicago: The National Society for the Study of Education.

Sophian, C., & Adams, N. (1987). Infants' understanding of numerical transformations. *British Journal of Developmental Psychology, 5,* 257–264.

South Australia, Ministerial Advisory Committee: Students with Disabilities (2000). *Technology for learning: Students with disabilities.* Retrieved 12 November, 2001, from http://www.macswd.sa.gov.au

South Australian Curriculum Policy Directorate (2000). *Bulletin.* Retrieved 14 May, 2003, from http://www2.nexus.edu.au/ems.sacsa.downloads/bulletin/nov2000/nov2000.html

Spearman, C. E. (1904). 'General intelligence', objectively determined and measured. *American Journal of Psychology, 15,* 201–293.

Spearman, C. E. (1927). *The abilities of man, their nature and measurement.* London: Macmillan.

Spelke, E. S., Breinlinger, K., Macomber, J., & Jacobson, K. (1992). Origins of knowledge. *Psychological Review, 99,* 605–632.

Spence, D. J., Yore, L. D., & Williams, R. L. (1995). *Explicit science reading instruction in Grade 7: Metacognitive awareness, metacognitive self-management and science reading comprehension.* (ERIC Document Service No.: ED388500.)

Spence, D. J., Yore, L. D., & Williams, R. L. (1999). The effects of explicit science reading instruction on selected Grade 7 students' metacognition and comprehension of specific science text. *Journal of Elementary Science Education, 11*(2), 15–30.

Spitzberg, B. H., & Hoobler, G. (2002). Cyberstalking and the technologies of interpersonal terrorism. *New Media and Society, 4*(1), 71–92.

Spock, B., & Rothenberg, M. B. (1985). *Dr Spock's baby and child care.* New York: Pocket Books.

Squires, D. (1999). Educational software for constructivist learning environments: Subversive use and volatile design. *Educational Technology, 39*(3), 48–54.

Sroufe, A. L. (2000). Early relationships and the development of children. *Infant Mental Health Journal, 21*(1–2), 67–74.

Stahl, G. (1997). Webguide: Guiding collaborative learning on the web with perspectives. *Journal of Interactive Media in Education, 1,* 1–53.

Stallings, J. A., & Stipek, D. (1986). Research on early childhood and elementary school teaching programs. In M. C.

Wittrock (Ed.), *Handbook of research on teaching* (3rd ed., pp. 727–753). New York: Macmillan.

Stattin, H., & Magnusson, D. (1990). *Pubertal maturation in female development*. Hillsdale, NJ: Erlbaum.

Stein, M. K., Grover, B. W., & Henningsen, M. (1996). Building student capacity for mathematical thinking and reasoning: An analysis of mathematical tasks used in reform classrooms. *American Educational Research Journal, 33*(2), 455–488.

Steinberg, L. D. (1999). *Adolescence* (5th ed.). New York: McGraw-Hill.

Steketee, C., Herrington, J., & Oliver, R. (2001). Computers as cognitive tools: Do they really enhance learning? In P. L. Jeffrey (Ed.), *Australian Association for Research in Education (AARE) 2001 conference papers*. Melbourne: Australian Association for Research in Education. Retrieved 12 January, 2003, from http://www.aare.edu.au/01pap/ste01110.htm

Stellwagen, J. B. (2001). A challenge to the learning style advocates. *Clearing House, 74*(5), 265–268.

Stephenson, J., Linfoot, K., & Martin, A. (2000). Behaviors of concern to teachers in the early years of school. *International Journal of Disability, Development and Education, 47*, 225–235.

Sternberg, R. J. (2000). *Handbook of intelligence*. Cambridge, MA: Cambridge University Press.

Sternberg, R. J. (1993). The concept of 'giftedness': A pentagonal implicit theory. In G. R. Bock & K. Ackrill (Eds.), *The origins and development of high ability* (pp. 5–31). Chicester, West Sussex: Wiley.

Sternberg, R. J. (1985). *Beyond IQ: A triarchic theory of intelligence*. New York: Cambridge University Press.

Sternberg, R. J. (1988). *The triarchic mind: A new theory of human intelligence*. New York: Viking.

Sternberg, R. J. (1990). *Metaphors of mind: Conceptions of the nature of intelligence*. Cambridge: Cambridge University Press.

Sternberg, R. J. (1997). Educating intelligence: Infusing the triarchic theory into school instruction. In R. J. Sternberg & E. L. Grigorenko (Eds.), *Intelligence, heredity and environment* (pp. 343–362). Cambridge: Cambridge University Press.

Sternberg, R. J. (1999). Looking back and looking forward on intelligence: Toward a theory of successful intelligence. In M. Bennett (Ed.), *Developmental psychology: achievements and prospects* (pp. 289–308). Philadelphia: Psychology Press.

Sternberg, R. J. (2001). Epilogue: Another mysterious affair at styles. In R. J. Sternberg & L. F. Zhang (Eds.), *Perspectives on thinking, learning, and cognitive styles* (pp. 249–252). Mahwah, NJ: Lawrence Erlbaum Associates.

Sternberg, R. J., & Grigorenko, E. L. (1995). Styles of thinking in school. *European Journal of High Ability, 6*(2), 201–219.

Sternberg, R. J., & Grigorenko, E. L. (1997). Are cognitive styles still in style? *American Psychologist, 52*(7), 700–712.

Sternberg, R. J., Torff, B., & Grigorenko, E. L. (1998). Teaching triarchically improves school achievement. *Journal of Educational Psychology, 90*, 374–384.

Stevenson, H. W. (1992). Learning from Asian schools. *Scientific American, 267*(6), 32–38.

Stevenson, H. W., & Lee, S. Y. (1990). Contexts of achievements: A study of American, Chinese and Japanese children. *Monograph of the Society for Research in Child Development, 55*(1–2, Serial No. 221).

Stipek, D. (1998). *Motivation to learn* (3rd ed.). Boston: Allyn & Bacon.

Strein, W. (1995). *Assessment of self-concept*. (ERIC Digest. Report: EDO-CG-95-14.) (ERIC Document Reproduction Service: ED389962.)

Stubberfield, T. G., Wray, J. A., & Parry, T. S. (1999). Utilization of alternative therapies in attention-deficit hyperactivity disorders. *Journal of Paediatrics and Child Health, 35*, 450–453.

Sturrock, F., & May, S. (2002). *Programme for International Student Assessment 2000 (PISA): The New Zealand context*. Wellington: Comparative Education Research Unit, Research Division, New Zealand Ministry of Education.

Suckling, A., & Temple, C. (2001). *Bullying: A whole school approach*. Melbourne: ACER.

Suedfeld, P. (2000). Cognitive styles: Personality. In A. E. Kazdin (Ed.), *Encyclopaedia of Psychology* (Vol. 2, pp. 166–169). Oxford: Oxford University Press.

Sukhnandan, L. (2000). *An investigation into gender differences in achievement, Phase 1: A review of recent research and LEA information on provision*. Slough: National Foundation for Educational Research.

Sukhnandan, L., Lee, B., & Kelleher, S. (2000). *An investigation into gender differences in achievement, Phase 2: School and classroom strategies*. Slough: National Foundation for Educational Research.

Suleiman, M. F. (1996). *Achieving congruence between learning and teaching styles in linguistically diverse environments*. Paper presented at the Annual Meeting of the National Social Science Conference, San Diego, CA. (ERIC Document Reproduction Service: ED395048.)

Suler, J. (2002). *The psychology of cyberspace*. Retrieved 25 March, 2003, from http://www.rider.edu/users/suler/psycyber/psycyber.html

Sullivan, K. (1999). Aotearoa/New Zealand. In P. K. Smith, Y. Morita, J. Junger-Tas, D. Olweus, R. Catalano, & P. Slee (Eds.), *The nature of bullying: A cross-national perspective* (pp. 340–355). London: Routledge.

Sulzer-Azaroff, B., & Mayer, G. R. (1977). *Applying behaviour-analysis procedures with children and youth*. New York: Holt, Rinehart and Winston.

Sussman, E. B. (1998). Cooperative learning: A review of factors that increase the effectiveness of cooperative computer-based instruction. *Journal of Educational Computing Research, 18*, 303–322.

Sutherland, P. (1992). *Cognitive development today: Piaget and his critics*. London: Paul Chapman.

Swanson, H. L. (1999). *Interventions for students with learning difficulties: A meta-analysis of treatment outcomes*. New York: Guilford Press.

Swim, J. K., & Sanna, L. J. (1996). He's skilled, she's lucky: A meta-analysis of observers' attributions for women's and men's successes and failures. *Personality and Social Psychology Bulletin, 22*, 507–519.

Sylva, K. (1984). A hard-headed look at the fruits of play. *Early Child Development & Care, 15*(2–3), 171–183.

Sylva, K., Roy, C., & Painter, M. (1980). *Child watching at playgroup and nursery school*. London: Grant McIntyre.

Tabakoff, J. (2002). Class acts: A Herald series. *Sydney Morning Herald*, 10 June, p. 4.

Tannenbaum, A. (1983). *Gifted children: Psychological and educational perspectives*. London: Collier-Macmillan.

Tannenbaum, A. (1997). The meaning and making of giftedness. In N. Colangelo & G. A. Davis (Eds.), *Handbook of gifted education* (2nd ed., pp. 27–42). Boston: Allyn & Bacon.

Tanner, J. M. (1990). *Foetus into man* (2nd ed.). Cambridge, MA: Harvard University Press.

Tapscott, D. (1998). *Growing up digital: The rise of the net generation*. New York: McGraw-Hill. Also available from http://www.growingupdigital.com

Taranowski, C. J. (1995). The effects of locally developed drug education on student attitudes and drug use. *Dissertation Abstracts International Section A: Humanties and Social Sciences*, 55(8–A), 2594.

Tatar, M. (1998). Teachers as significant others: Gender differences in secondary school pupils' perceptions. *British Journal of Educational Psychology*, 68, 217–227.

Tauer, J. M., & Harackiewicz, J. M. (1999). Winning isn't everything: Competition, achievement orientation, and intrinsic motivation. *Journal of Experimental Psychology*, 35, 209–238.

Taylor, J., & Cox, B. D. (1997). Microgenic analysis of group-based solution of complex two-step mathematical word problems by fourth-graders. *Journal of the Learning Sciences*, 6(2), 183–226.

Taylor, R. P. (Ed.). (1980). *The computer in the school: Tutor, tool, tutee*. New York: Columbia University, Teachers College Press.

Teague, M., & Teague, G. (1995). Planning with computers: A social studies simulation. *Learning and Leading with Technology*, 23(1), 20–22.

Teese, R. (2000). *Academic success and social power: Examinations and inequality*. Carlton, Victoria: Melbourne University Press.

Terman, L. M. (1925–1929). *Genetic Studies of Genius* (Vols. 1–4). Stanford, CA: Stanford University Press.

Terman, L. M., & Oden, M. H. (1947). *The gifted child grows up: Genetic studies of genius* (Vol. 4). Stanford, CA: Stanford University Press.

Thomas, W. P., & Collier, V. P. (1999). *Evaluation that informs school reform of programs for language minority students*. Paper presented at the American Education Research Association Conference, Montreal.

Thorndike, E. L. (1898). Animal intelligence. An experimental study of the associative process in animals. *Psychological Review Monograph, Supplement*, 2(No. 8).

Thorndike, E. L. (1911). *Animal intelligence*. New York: Macmillan.

Thorndike, E. L. (1931). *Human Learning*. New York: Appleton-Century-Crofts.

Thurstone, L. L. (1938). *Primary mental abilities*. Chicago: University of Chicago Press.

Thurstun, J. (2000). Screen reading: Challenges of the new literacy. In D. Gibbs, & K. Krause (Eds.), *Cyberlines: Languages and cultures of the Internet* (pp. 61–78). Melbourne: James Nicholas.

Tiberius, R. G. (1990). *Small group teaching: A trouble shooting guide*. Toronto, Canada: The Ontario Institute for Studies in Education. (ERIC Document ED318690.)

Tinajero, C., & Paramo, M. F. (1998). Field dependence–independence and strategic learning. *International Journal of Educational Research*, 29, 251–262.

Tobin, K. (2000). Constructivism in science education: Moving on … In D. C. Phillips (Ed.), *Constructivism in education: Opinions and second opinions on controversial issues* (pp. 227–253). Chicago: The National Society for the Study of Education.

Tobin, T., & Sprague, J. (2000). Alternative education strategies: Reducing violence in school and community. *Journal of Emotional and Behavioural Disorders*, 8, 177–186.

Toma, C. (1991). *Explicit use of others' voices for constructing arguments in Japanese classroom discourse: An analysis of the use of reported speech*. Paper presented at the Boston University Conference on Language Development, Boston.

Tomlinson, C. A., Moon, T. R., & Callahan, C. M. (1997). Use of cooperative learning at the middle level: Insights from a national survey. *Research in Middle Level Education Quarterly*, 20, 37–55.

Toomey, R. (2001). *Schooling issues digest: Information and communication technology for teaching and learning*. Sydney: Department of Education, Training and Youth Affairs (DETYA).

Torff, B., & Gardner, H. (1999). The vertical mind – the case for multiple intelligence. In M. Anderson (Ed.), *The development of intelligence* (pp. 139–159). Hove, East Sussex: The Psychology Press.

Torrance, E. P. (1966). *Torrance Tests of Creative Thinking: Norms and technical manual*. Princeton: Personal Press.

Torrance, E. P. (1990). *Torrance Tests of Creative Thinking: Norms and technical manual, figural (streamlined) forms A & B*. Bensenville, IL: Scholastic Testing Service.

Triandis, H. C., McCusker, C., Betancourt, H., Iwao, S., Leung, K., Salazar, J. M., Setiadi, B., Sinha, J. B. P., Touzard, H., & Zaleski, Z. (1993). An etic-emic analysis of individualism and collectivism. *Journal of Cross-Cultural Psychology*, 24(3), 366–383.

Troffer, A. (2000). *Writing effectively online: How to compose hypertext. Computers and composition: An international journal for teachers of writing*. Retrieved 12 November, 2001, from http://corax.cwrl.utexas.edu/cac/online/01/troffer/htintro.html

Tulving, E. (1974). Cue-dependent forgetting. *American Scientist*, 62, 74–82.

Tulving, E. (1985). How many memory systems are there? *American Psychologist*, 40, 385–398.

Turiel, E. (1983). *The development of social knowledge: Morality and convention*. Cambridge: Cambridge University Press.

Turiel, E. (1998). Moral development. In N. Eisenberg (Ed.), *Handbook of child psychology, Vol. 3: Social, emotional, and personality development* (5th ed., pp. 863–932). New York: Wiley.

Turiel, E. (2001). Foreword. In L. Nucci, *Education in the moral domain* (pp. ix–xx). Cambridge: Cambridge University Press.

Turkle, S. (1994). Constructions and reconstructions of self in virtual reality: Playing in the MUDs. *Mind, Culture, and Activity*, 1(3), 158–167.

Turkle, S. (1997). *Life on the screen: Identity in the age of the Internet*. New York: Touchstone.

Turner, J. E., Husman, J., & Schallert, D. L. (2002). The importance of students' goals in their emotional experience of academic failure: Investigating the precursors and consequences of shame. *Educational Psychologist*, 37(2), 79–89.

Uribe, V., & Harbeck, K. M. (1991). Addressing the needs of lesbian, gay and bisexual youth: The origins of PROJECT 10 and school-based intervention. *Journal of Homosexuality*, 22(3–4), 9–28.

Uzgiris, I. C., & Hunt, J. McV. (1975). *Ordinal scales of psychological development*. Urbana, IL: University of Illinois Press.

Van der Kley, M., & Burn, W. (1993). *The positive playground: How to improve school discipline and enhance school tone*. Christchurch, New Zealand: M. Van der Kley.

van Kraayenoord, G. E., & Paris, S. G. (1997). Australian students' self appraisal of their work. *The Elementary School Journal*, 5, 523–537.

Venezky, R. (2000). The digital divide within formal school education: Causes and consequences. In Organisation for Economic Cooperation and Development (OECD) (Ed.), *Learning to bridge the digital divide* (pp. 63–76). Paris: OECD. Retrieved 20 May, 2003, from http://www1.oecd.org/publications/e-book/ 9600081E.PDF

Victorian Curriculum and Assessment Authority (2001). *Information for parents*. Retrieved 7 September, 2001, from http://www.vcaa.vic.edu.au/esf/infopar.htm

Victorian Government (2002). *Federal Government Inquiry into the Education of Boys in Australian Schools: Victorian Government submission – executive summary*. Retrieved 27 April, 2003, from http://www.sofweb.vic.edu.au/gender/docs/boyseducation.doc

Vincent, J. (2001). The role of visually rich technology in facilitating children's writing. *Journal of Computer Assisted Learning*, 17(3), 242–250.

Vispoel, W. P. (1995). Self-concepts in the arts: An extension of the Shavelson model. *Journal of Educational Psychology*, 87, 134–145.

Vockell, E. L., & Schwartz, E. M. (1992). *The computer in the classroom* (2nd ed.). New York: Mitchell McGraw-Hill.

Volker, R. (1992). *Applications of constructivist theory to the use of hypermedia*. Proceedings of selected research presentations at the Annual Convention of the AECT. (ERIC Document Reproduction No. ED 348 037.)

Vosniadou, S. (1995). A cognitive psychological approach to learning. In P. Reimann & H. Spada (Eds.), *Learning in humans and machines. Towards an interdisciplinary learning science* (pp. 23–36). London: Pergamon.

Wadsworth, B. J. (1996). *Piaget's theory of cognitive and affective development* (5th ed.). White Plains, NY: Longman.

Wagner, D., Cook, G., & Friedman, J. (1998). Staying with their first impulse?: The relationship between impulsivity/reflectivity, field dependence/field independence and answer changes on a multiple-choice exam in a fifth-grade sample. *Journal of Research and Development in Education*, 31, 166–175.

Wagner, M. (1995). *The contribution of poverty and ethnic background to the participation of secondary school students in special education*. Menlo Park, CA: SRI International.

Walberg, H. J. (1986). Synthesis of research on teaching. In M. C. Wittrock (Ed.), *Handbook of research on teaching* (pp. 214–229). New York: Macmillan.

Walberg, H. J., & Haertel, G. D. (1992). Educational psychology's first century. *Journal of Educational Psychology*, 84(1), 6–19.

Walden, R., & Walkerdine, V. (1982). *Girls and mathematics: The early years. A review of literature and an account of original research*. London: University of London Institute of Education.

Walker, I., & Crogan, M. (1998). Academic performance, prejudice and the jigsaw classroom: New pieces to the puzzle. *Journal of Community and Applied Social Psychology*, 8, 381–393.

Walker, L. J. (1984). Sex differences in the development of moral reasoning: A critical review. *Child Development*, 55, 677–691.

Walker, L. J., DeVries, B., & Trevethan, S. D. (1987). Moral stages and moral orientations in real-life and hypothetical dilemmas. *Child Development*, 58, 842–858.

Walker, R. A., & Lambert, P. E. (1996). *Designing electronic learning environments to support communities of learners: A tertiary application*. Retrieved from http://walkerr.edfac.usyd.edu/henresite/aare/AARE-paper-.html

Walker, S. P., Grantham-McGregor, S. M., Powell, C. A., & Change, S. M. (2000). Effects of growth restriction in early childhood on growth, IQ, and cognition at age 11 to 12 years and the benefits of nutritional supplementation and psychological stimulation. *Journal of Pediatrics*, 137, 36–41.

Walz, G. R., & Bleuer, J. C. (Eds.). (1992). *Developing support groups for students: Helping students cope with crises*. (Report: ISBN-1-56109-040-9.) (ERIC Document Reproduction Service No. ED340986.)

Wang, M. C., & Haertel, G. D. (1995). Educational resilience. In M. C. Wang, M. C. Reynolds, & H. J. Walberg (Eds.), *Handbook of special education and remedial education: Research and practice* (pp. 159–200). Oxford: Elsevier Science.

Wang, M. C., Reynolds, M. C., & Walberg, H. J (1995a). Epilogue. In M. C. Wang, M. C. Reynolds, & H. J. Walberg (Eds.), *Handbook of special education and remedial education: Research and practice* (pp. 449–458). Oxford: Elsevier Science.

Wang, M. C., Reynolds, M. C., & Walberg, H. J. (1995b). Introduction: Inner-city students at the margins. In M. C. Wang & M. C. Reynolds (Eds.), *Making a difference for students at risk: Trends and alternatives* (pp. 1–26). Thousand Oaks, CA: Sage.

Wang, W., & Viney, L. L. (1996). A cross-cultural comparison of Eriksonian psychosocial development: Chinese and Australian children. *School Psychology International*, 17(1), 33–48.

Ward, A. W., & Murray-Ward, M. (1999). *Assessment in the classroom*. Belmont, CA: Wadsworth.

Ward, J., Bochner, S., Center, Y., Outhred, L., & Pieterse, M. (1987). *Educating children with special needs in regular classrooms: An Australian perspective*. Sydney: Macquarie University.

Warnock, H. M. (1978). *Special education needs: Report of the Committee of Enquiry into the Education of Handicapped Children and Young People*. London: HMSO.

Warrington, M., & Younger, M. (2000). The other side of the gender gap. *Gender and Education*, 12(4), 493–508.

Watson, J. A., & Brinkley, V. M. (1992). Logo mastery and spatial problem-solving by young children: Effects of

Logo language training, route strategy training, and learning styles on immediate learning and transfer. *Journal of Educational Computing Research, 8*, 521–540.

Watson, J. B. (1913). Psychology as the behaviourist views it. *Psychological Review, 20*, 158–177.

Watson, J. B. (1919). *Psychology from the standpoint of a behaviourist*. Philadelphia: Lippincott.

Watson, J. B. (1925). *Behaviourism*. New York: Norton.

Watson, J. B., & Rayner, R. (1920). Conditioned emotional reactions. *Journal of Experimental Psychology, 3*, 1–14.

Webb, N., & Farivar, S. (1994). Promoting helping behaviour in cooperative small groups in middle school mathematics. *American Educational Research Journal, 31*, 369–395.

Webb, N., & Farivar, S. (1999). Developing productive group interaction in middle school mathematics. In A. M. O'Donnell & A. King (Eds.), *Cognitive perspectives on peer learning* (pp. 117–149). Mahwah, NJ: Erlbaum.

Wechsler, D. (1966). *The measurement and appraisal of adult intelligence*. Baltimore: Williams & Wilkins.

Weinberg, R. A. (1989). Intelligence and IQ: Landmark issues and great debates. *American Psychologist, 44*, 98–104.

Weiner, B. (1992). *Human motivation: Metaphors, theories and research*. Newbury Park, CA: Sage.

Weiner, G. (1994). Gender and racial differences among students in classrooms. In T. Husen & T. N. Postlethwaite (Eds.). *International encyclopedia of education* (2nd ed.) (pp. 5822–5827). Oxford: Pergamon.

Weinert, F. E. (1987). Introduction and overview: Metacognition and motivation as determinants of effective learning and understanding. In F. E. Weinert & R. H. Kluwe (Eds.), *Metacognition, motivation, and understanding* (pp. 1–19). Hillsdale, NJ: Lawrence Erlbaum Associates.

Weinstein, C., & Mignano, A. (1993). *Elementary classroom management: Lessons from research and practice*. New York: McGraw-Hill.

Wells, G. (2000). *Dialogic inquiry in education: Building on the legacy of Vygotsky*. Ontario Institute for Studies in Education, University of Toronto. Retrieved 6 July, 2000, from http://www.oise.utoronto.ca/~gwells/NCTE.HTML

Wells, G., & Chang-Wells, G. L. (1992). *Constructing knowledge together: Classrooms as centers of inquiry and literacy*. Portsmouth, NH: Heinemann.

Wenger, M. J., & Payne, D. G. (1996). Comprehension and retention of nonlinear text: Considerations of working memory and material-appropriate processing. *American Journal of Psychology, 109*(1), 93–130.

Wentzel, K. R. (1996). Social goals and social relationships as motivators of school adjustment. In J. Juvonen & K. Wentzel (Eds.), *Social motivation: Understanding school adjustment* (pp. 226–247). New York: Cambridge University Press.

Wentzel, K. R., & Asher, S. R. (1995). The academic lives of neglected, rejected, popular, and controversial children. *Child Development, 66*(3), 754–763.

Wentzel, K. R., & Erdley, C. A. (1993). Strategies for making friends: Relations to social behaviour and peer acceptance in early adolescence. *Developmental Psychology, 29*, 801–826.

Werner, E. E., & Smith, R. S. (1977). *Kauai's children come of age*. Honolulu: University of Hawaii Press.

Werner, E. E., & Smith, R. S. (1992). *Overcoming the odds: High risk children from birth to adulthood*. Ithica, NY: Cornell University Press.

Wertsch, J. V. (1985). *Vygotsky and the social formation of mind*. Cambridge, MA: Harvard University Press.

Wertsch, J. V., McNamee, G. D., McLane, J. B., & Budwig, N. A. (1980). The adult–child dyad as a problem-solving system. *Child Development, 51*, 1215–1221.

Westera, J., & Moore, D. W. (1995). Reciprocal teaching of reading comprehension in a New Zealand high school. *Psychology in Schools, 32*(3), 225–232.

Western Australian Curriculum Council (1998). *Curriculum Framework for kindergarten to Year 12 education in Western Australia*. Retrieved 4 June, 2003, from http://www/curriculum.wa.edu.au/pages/framework/framework00.htm

Western Australian Department of Education (2001). *The education of gifted and talented students in Western Australia*. Retrieved 3 August, 2001, from http://www.eddept.wa.edu.au/centoff/gifttal/giftpol.htm

Western Australian Department of Education and Training (2003). *Western Australian literacy and numeracy assessment*. Retrieved 10 April, 2003, from <www.eddept.wa.edu.au/walna/history.html>.

Western Australian Health Department (1994). *Making a difference: Youth suicide prevention resource manual*. Perth, WA: Health Department of Western Australia and Youthlink.

Wheldall, K., & Merrett, F. (1988). Which classroom behaviours do primary school teachers say they find most troublesome? *Educational Review, 40*, 13–27.

Whicker, K. M., Bol, L., & Nunnery, J. A, (1997). Cooperative learning in the secondary mathematics class. *Journal of Educational Research, 91*, 42–48.

White, R., & Wyn, J., 2002. *Youth and society*. Sydney: Oxford University Press.

Whitley, B. E. (1997). Gender differences in computer-related attitudes and behaviour: A meta-analysis. *Computers in Human Behaviour, 13*, 1–22.

Whitney, I., & Smith, P. K. (1993). A survey of the nature and extent of bullying in junior/middle and secondary schools. *Educational Research, 35*, 3–25.

Whitney, I., Smith, P. K., & Thompson, D. (1994). Bullying and children with special education needs. In P. K. Smith and S. Sharp (Eds.), *School bullying: Insights and perspectives* (pp. 213–240). London: Routledge.

Whyte, M., Karolick, D., & Taylor, M. D. (1996). *Cognitive learning styles and their impact on curriculum development and instruction*. Proceedings of selected research and development presentations at the 1996 National Convention of the Association for Educational Communications and Technology. (ERIC Document Reproduction Service ED 397 846.)

Wiburg, K. (1995). Gender issues, personal characteristics and computing. *The Computing Teacher, 22*(4), 7–10.

Wigfield, A., & Harold, R. (1992). Teacher beliefs and children's achievement self-perceptions: A developmental perspective. In D. Schunk & J. Meece (Eds.), *Student perceptions in the classroom* (pp. 95–121). Hillsdale, NJ: Lawrence Erlbaum.

Wiggins, G. (1993). Assessment to improve performance, not just monitor it: Assessment reform in the social sciences. *Social Science Record, 30*, 5–12.

Wighton, D. J. (1993). *Telementoring: An examination of the potential for an educational network*. Retrieved 24 May, 2003, from http://mentor.creighton.edu/htm/telement.htm

Wilen, W. W., & Phillips, J. A. (1995). Teaching critical thinking: A metacognitive approach. *Social Education*, 59(3), 135–138.

Wilkinson, L. C. (1989). Grouping children for learning: Implications for kindergarten education. *Review of Research in Education, 15*, 203–50.

Willcoxson, L., & Prosser, M. (1996). Kolb's Learning Style Inventory (1985): Review and further study of validity and reliability. *British Journal of Educational Psychology, 66*, 247–257.

Williams, A. (1995). Long-distance collaboration: A case study of science teaching and learning. In Speigel, S. A., Collins, A., and Lappert, J. (Eds.), *Action research: Perspectives from teachers' classrooms* (pp. 101–116). Talahassee, FL: Southeastern Regional Vision for Education.

Williams, J., & Williams, A. (Eds.). (1996). *Technology education for teachers*. South Melbourne: Macmillan.

Williams, L. (2001). ICFT: Information, communication and friendship technology: Philosophical issues relating to use of ICT in school settings. In M. Leask (Ed.), *Issues in teaching using ICT* (pp. 49–60). London: Routledge Falmer.

Williams, L. R. T., Anshel, M. H., & Quek, J. (1997). Cognitive style in adolescent competitive athletes as a function of culture and gender. *Journal of Sport Behaviour, 20*(2), 232–245.

Williams, W. M., Blythe, T., White, N., Li, J., Sternberg, R. J., & Gardner, H. (1996). *Practical intelligence for school: A handbook for teachers of grades 5–8*. New York: HarperCollins.

Wilsmore, D. (2001). Establishing a community of learners: The use of information technology (IT) as an effective learning tool in rural primary or elementary schools. *Educational Technology and Society, 4*(3), 11–20.

Wilson, F. J. (1994). *The use of analogical reasoning as a problem solving strategy*. Unpublished Masters thesis. Queensland University of Technology.

Winitzky, N. E. (1991). Classroom organisation for social studies. In J. P. Shaver (Ed.), *Handbook of research on social studies teaching and learning*. New York: Macmillan.

Wintre, M. G., & Vallance, D. D. (1994). A developmental sequence in the comprehension of emotions: Intensity, multiple emotions, and valence. *Developmental Psychology, 30*, 509–514.

Winzer, M. A. (1993). *The history of special education: From isolation to integration*. Washington, DC: Gallaudet University Press.

Wither, D. P. (1998). *A longitudinal study of the relationship between mathematics achievement and mathematics anxiety from years 6 to 10*. Unpublished Doctoral thesis, University of Adelaide, South Australia.

Withers, G. (1991). *From marks to profiles and 'records of achievement'*. Geelong: Deakin University.

Witkin, H. A., & Goodenough, D. R. (1981). *Cognitive styles: Essence and origins*. New York: International Universities Press.

Witkin, H. A., Lewis, M., Herzman, K., Machover, P. B., Meissner, P. B., & Wapner, S. (1954). *Personality through perception*. New York: Harper.

Witt, S. D. (2000). The influence of peers on children's socialization to gender roles. *Early Child Development and Care, 162*, 1–7.

Wittrock, M. C. (1991). Generative teaching of comprehension. *The Elementary School Journal, 92*, 169–184.

Wolfensberger, W. (Ed.). (1972). *The principle of normalization in human services*. Toronto: National Institute on Mental Retardation.

Wolfgang, C. H. (1995). *Solving discipline problems: Methods and models for today's teachers* (3rd ed.). Boston: Allyn & Bacon.

Wolfgang, C. H., & Glickman, C. (1980). *Solving discipline problems*. Sydney: Allyn & Bacon.

Wong, M. S. W., & Watkins, D. (2001). Self-esteem and ability grouping: A Hong Kong investigation of the big fish little pond effect. *Educational Psychology, 21*(1), 79–87.

Wood, D., Bruner, J., & Ross, G. (1976). The role of tutoring in problem-solving. *Journal of Child Psychology and Psychiatry, 17*, 89–100.

Woolley, G., & Hay, I. (1999). Parent tutoring: Effective reading intervention approaches. In P. Westwood and W. Scott (Eds.), *Learning disabilities: Advocacy and action* (pp. 146–160). Parkville, Victoria: Australian Resource Educators Association.

Wotherspoon, T. (1987). Behaviourally maladjusted children. In D. Mitchell & N. Singh (Eds.), *Exceptional children in New Zealand* (pp. 271–282). Plamerston North: Dunmore Press.

Wragg, E. C. (1993). *Classroom management*. London: Routledge.

Wragg, J. (1989). *Talk sense to yourself: A programme for children and adolescents*. Melbourne: ACER.

Wright, D. (1992). Review of learning styles and strategies. In J. J. Kramer & J. C. Conoley (Eds.), *The Eleventh Mental Measurements Yearbook*. Lincoln, NE: The University of Nebraska Press.

Wyn, J., & White, R. (1997). *Rethinking youth*. Sydney: Allen & Unwin.

Yager, R. E., & Lutz, M. V. (1994). Integrated science: The importance of 'how' versus 'what'. *School Science and Mathematics, 94*(7), 338–345.

Youthlaw (2003). *Young people and school management: A student guide to discipline*. Retrieved 29 January, 2003, from http://youthlaw.co.nz/school_B6.html

Zahn-Waxler, C., & Radke-Yarrow, M. (1990). The origins of empathic concern. *Motivation and Emotion, 14*, 107–130.

Zahn-Waxler, C., & Robinson, J. (1995). Empathy and guilt: Early origins of feelings of responsibility. In J. P. Tangney & K. W. Fischer (Eds.), *Self-conscious emotions* (pp. 143–173). New York: Guilford.

Zàppala G. & Parker B. (2000). *The Smith Family's Learning for Life program a decade on: Poverty and educational disadvantage*. Research and Advocacy Team Background Paper No. 1, 2000.

Zhang, L. F., & Sternberg, R. J. (2000). Are learning approaches and thinking styles related? A study of two Chinese populations. *Journal of Psychology, 134*, 469–489.

Zigler, E., & Muenchow, S. (1992). *Head Start: The inside story of America's most successful educational experiment*. New York: Basic Books.

Zigler, E., & Styfco, S. J. (2000). Pioneering steps (and fumbles) in developing a federal preschool intervention. *Topics in Early Childhood Special Education, 2*, 67–70.

Zigler, E., & Valentine, J. (Eds.) (1979). *Project Head Start: A legacy of the War on Poverty*. New York: Free Press.

Zimbardo, P. (Host). (1987). *Discovering psychology: Learning (Part 8)*. Boston: W6BH, in association with the American Psychological Association.

Zimmerman, B. J. (1998). Developing self-fulfilling cycles of academic regulation: An analysis of exemplary instructional models. In D. H. Schunk & B. J. Zimmerman (Eds.), *Self-regulated learning: From teaching to self-reflective practice* (pp. 1–19). New York: The Guilford Press.

Zimmerman, B. J., & Kitsantas, A. (1999). Acquiring writing revision skill: Shifting from process to outcome self-regulatory goals. *Journal of Educational Psychology, 91*, 1–10.

Zohar, A. (1999). Teachers' metacognitive knowledge and the instruction of higher order thinking. *Teaching and Teacher Education, 15*, 413–429.

Zubrick, S. R., & Silburn, S. R. (1997). Education, health and competence. In S. R. Zubrick. *Western Australian Child Health Survey: Education, health and competence* (pp. 57–67). Perth: Australian Bureau of Statistics and the TVW Telethon Institute for Child Health Research.

Zubrick, S. R., Siburn, S. R., Gurrin, L., Teoh, H., Shepherd, C., Carlton, J., & Laurence, D. (1997). *Western Australian Child Health Survey: Education, health and competence*. Perth: Australian Bureau of Statistics and the TVW Telethon Institute for Child Health Research.

Index

A

Aboriginal English 292
Aboriginal and Islander Education Workers 295
abstract thought 41, 42, 219
    development in adolescence 20, 26
    and emotional development 88
    and self-concept 76
academic achievement and peer experiences 73, 93
academic self-concept 72–3
accommodation 54–5
achievement
    gender differences 274
    motivation 221, 223
    and self-esteem 74
'achieving approach' to learning 154
active listening 176
active participation in learning 158
active/assisted learning 65
activity and development 5, 33, 55
adaptation 54
addiction issues of ICT use 333–4
Adler, Alfred 384
adolescence
    body image 7, 8
    cognitive development 4, 7–9
    definition of 7
    developing identity 81
    egocentrism 8
    emotional development 88
    family relationships 8
    homosexuality 273
    language development 19–20, 26
    moratorium in 82
    motivation 218–19, 222
    peer relationships 8, 91, 92
    physical development 7–9
    risk-taking behaviour 8
    role confusion 81
    self-concept 76
    writing skills 26
adults
    and cognitive development 61
    and language development 20–1
affect 73
age
    and bullying 391
    and motivation 219
    and self-conscious emotions 87
aggression and vicarious learning 128–9, 130
alienation issue of ICT use 333–4
alternative schools 250
anecdotal records for assessment 350, 354
animism 46
antecedent 119
antecedent-behaviour-consequence (A-B-C) 118–19
anxiety
    and ICT use 333–4
    and motivation 217–18
applied behaviour analysis (ABA) 127
aptitude–treatment interaction 155
arousal and motivation 217
asking questions 267–8
assessment
    interpreting information 344–7
    key terms 340–2
    modes of 349–58
    program design 350
    reasons for 339–40
    recording and reporting results 365–8
    stakeholders in 361–4
    technical issues 358–60
    types of 342–8
assimilation 54–5
assisted discovery 65
associationism 110, 115
asynchronous communication 307
Atkinson, John 223, 226–7
attendance
    gender differences 274
    indigenous learners 290
attention deficit hyperactivity disorder (ADHD) 244, 245, 256
attribution theory of motivation 223–5
auditory integration training 255
auditory learners 154–5
authentic assessment 353
authentic learning 315, 317
autonomous morality 95
axons 12, 13

B

back-up system of penalties 383
backward chaining 125
Balson, Maurice 384, 385, 386
Bandura, Albert 94
    aggression studies 128, 129
    motivation 225, 226–7
    social learning theory 128–30
basic emotions 87
basic needs 174
behaviour disturbance 376
behaviour management
    bullying 217, 390–5
    see also classroom management
behavioural views of learning
    behavioural objectives 127
    classical conditioning 110–14, 117
    cognitive behaviour modification 131–3
    and ICT 312–13
    and motivation 222–3
    operant conditioning 114–28
    reciprocal determinism 128–30
    self-regulation 131–2
    social learning theory 130
being (B) needs 174, 175
benchmark of assessment 342
big-fish-little-pond effect 73
Biggs, J. B. 56
Binet, Alfred 40, 206–7, 231
    Stanford-Binet test 206–7, 209, 212, 360
bodily-kinaesthetic intelligence 201
body image
    in adolescence 7, 8
    and self-concept 8
bottom-up approach to literacy teaching 27–8
brain development
    in children 4, 12, 13–14
    and environment 14
brain structures 4, 12–14
British Infant Schools 180
Bronfenbrenner, Urie 263–5
Bruner, J.
    discovery learning 158
    Peekaboo study 61
buddy programs 217
bullying 217, 390–5

C

cardinality in numeracy 29
cascade delivery of special education 248–9, 254
cats and the puzzle box study 115
causality, understanding 16, 17
centration 46
centre of gravity and physical development 5, 6
cerebral cortex 13–14
cerebral palsy 234, 255
chaining 124, 125
chaotic learning 155
character education 101–2
checklists for assessment 354
child-directed speech 20
childhood *see* early childhood; infancy; middle childhood
chronosystem of environment 264, 265
chunking 138, 141
class-inclusion principle 49–50
classical conditioning
    in classrooms 114
    Pavlov 110–12, 113, 124, 222–3
    Skinner on 117
    strengths and limitations of 113–14
    Watson 113
classification principle 49–50
classroom
    approaches to learning 154–6
    character education 101–2

classroom (cont.)
   constructivism 158–64
   feminisation of schooling 276
   gender bias in 276–9
   language and culture 266–7
   socioeconomic differences 287–8
   teaching literacy 26–8
   teaching new behaviours 124–6
   teaching numeracy 29–31
   use of ICT 308, 309–11, 315–16, 321, 324–35
classroom management 374
   of behaviour 333, 373–98
   and classroom structure 383
   effective 374–5, 381–9
   disruptive behaviour 376–9
   and ICT use 320–1, 333
   in practice 374–9
   rules, rights and responsibilities 388–9
   strategies 379–80
clique 92
clumsy children 255
co-educational schooling 279
cognition 39
   and cerebral cortex 13–14
   in gender difference 272
   in infancy 4
   and motor activity 5
   and physical development 15
   and reading online 323
cognitive apprenticeship 67, 163
cognitive balance 55–6
cognitive behaviour modification 131–3
cognitive development 39
   in adolescence 4, 7–9
   and emotional development 88
   and language development 16
   linking Piaget and Vygotsky 66–7
   and moral development 94–100
   and peer relationships 90
   Piaget's theory of 39–59
   role of social interaction 67
   Vygotsky's sociocultural theory 60–6
cognitive explanations of learning
   cognitive learning theory 137
   cognitive style 150–7
   constructivism 157–65
   and ICT 314–19
   information processing approach 137–44
   metacognition 145–50
   and motivation 223–5
cognitive style 150–1
   and approaches to classroom learning 154–7
   conceptual tempo 152–3
   deep and surface learning 153–4
   perceptual style 151–2
   sociocultural factors 154
cognitive-development theories of
   moral development 94–100
collaborative learning 159, 161–2, 166
   and ICT 317–19
collectivistic culture 85, 86
community and student assessment 361, 363
compensation principle 48
compensatory programs 233–4
comprehension of language 16
computer games 313
computer literacy 307
computer use 155, 161
computer-assisted instruction (CAI) 312–13
computer-mediated communication (CMC) 307, 320
computer-mediated instruction (CMI) 318–19
conceptual tempo 152–3
concrete operations stage of cognitive development (Piaget)
   class inclusion 49–50
   classification 49–50
   compensation 48
   conservation 42, 47–8, 51
   developmental milestones 42
   in education 50–1, 59
   main achievements 41
   reversibility 48
   seriation 48–9
conditional knowledge 142–3
conditioned response 111, 112
conditioned stimulus 112, 113
conditioning 112
   classical 110–14
   operant 114–28
conductive education 255
connectionist model of information processing 140, 144
consequences
   punishment 119, 121–2
   reinforcement 119–24
consequential validity 359
conservation principle 42, 47–8, 51
construct validity 359
constructivism
   authentic assessment in 353
   in classroom 158–64
   forms of 157–8
   and ICT 314–19, 320
   Piaget 46, 57, 157
   principles of 158
   and social interaction 157
   strengths and limitations 165
content validity 359
contiguity 110
contingency of reinforcement 119–20
contingent rewards 183
continuous assessment 349
continuous reinforcement 123
contracts 124
conventional morality 97
cooperative learning 57, 159–60, 162–3, 166, 182–7, 269
cooperative play 92
core values 101
corporal punishment 379–80
counsellors and assessment 362, 364
coursework assessment 349
crawling 4
creative learners 212–14
criterion of assessment 342
criterion-referenced assessment 345–6, 362
'cross-age' tutoring 160
cue-dependent forgetting 141
cueing 124, 125
culture 265–6
   advantage and disadvantage 269
   and beliefs about knowledge and learning 267
   collectivistic 85, 86
   differences and misunderstanding 267–8
   and ethnicity 265–6
   heritage of Indigenous Australians 294
   and ICT 325, 329–30
   individualistic 85
   and intelligence 198
   and language 266–7
   and learning styles 155
   metacognitive strategies 148–9
   and numeracy 29
   peer experiences 93
   and self 85–6
   and self-conscious emotions 87
culture-fair tests 360
culture-sensitive tests 360
curriculum-based assessment 346–7, 348, 362

D

Dalton Plan 182
declarative knowledge 142–3
decoding and literacy 25, 28
deductive reasoning 51
deep learning 153–4
'deep' processing 139–40
deferred imitation 41, 42, 43
deficit (D) needs 174, 175, 226
Defining Issues Test 98
dendrites 12, 13
development 32–3
   influences on (Piaget) 55–6
   metacognitive 148
   and self-concept and self-esteem 76–7
   and social relationships 83–4
   see also cognitive development; physical development
developmental milestones 42
deviation IQ 207
Dewey, John 179, 187
diagnostic assessment 344, 347
direct assessment 350

direct observation for assessment 351
disability 239
    in Australia 240–2
    gender differences 275
    incidence rates 239–40
    labels and labelling 242–5
    non-categorical view 246
    normalisation 245
Disadvantaged Schools program 233
discipline
    alternatives to corporal punishment 379–80
    behaviour management 333, 373–98
discovery learning 57, 158–9, 165, 166
discrimination in stimulus response 112
disequilibrium 54
disruptive behaviour 376–9
distributed cognition 319
distributed learning (computer-mediated instruction) 318–19
Down syndrome 234
Dreikurs, Rudolf 384, 385
Durkheim, E. 94
dynamic assessment 66

E

early childhood
    language development 16–18
    motor-skill development 5
    peer interactions 90–1
    physical development in 5
    self-concept 76
early intervention programs 232
ecological systems theory 263–5
economic issues and ICT 325
educational outcomes, gender differences in 273–6
educational risk 236–8
educational technology 306
effective classroom management 374–5, 381
ego integrity 83
egocentrism
    adolescents 8
    children 45
elaboration 139, 141
electronic hardware 306
Electronic Learning Circles 318
email and authentic learning 317
emergent literacy 24
emoticons 307
emotional disorder 244
emotional disturbance 376
emotional intelligence 202
emotions
    and cerebral cortex 13
    and cognitive development 88
    functional-organisational approach to 86–7
    in gender difference 272
    in infancy 4, 87
    and socioemotional development 86–8
empathy 88
employers and assessment 361, 363
encounter groups 177
engagement and ICT use 332
English as a second language (ESL) 22, 23–4, 267
environment
    and brain development 14
    Bronfenbrenner's ecological systems theory 263–5
    and emergent literacy 24
    and ICT use 325
    and physical development 9–10, 33
episodic memory 139
equilibration and development 55–6
equity issues and ICT use 333
Erikson, Erik 77, 78
Erikson, Joan 78, 83
Erikson's theory of psychosocial development 71
    in the classroom 84–5
    Freudian links 78, 84
    overview of theory 78
    psychosocial crisis 78
    stages 78, 79–83
    strengths and limitations 83–4
ethical issues and ICT use 325, 334
ethnicity 265
evaluation, meaning of 340–1
examination assessment 349
exclusion as punishment 380
exercise involvement, gender differences in 11
existential intelligence 202
exosystem of child's environment 264
expansion of speech 20
experience, metacognitive 146–7
explicit approach to literacy teaching 28
external assessment 349
extinction 122–3
extrinsic motivation 219, 220
eye–hand coordination 5

F

face validity 359
'fair pair' 122–3
familiarisation programs 217
family relationships in adolescence 8
feminisation of schooling 276
feminist approach to moral development 100
field dependence 151–2
field independence 151–2
final assessment 349
fine motor skill development 5
First Peoples' Project 330
Foot–hand coordination 5
foreign-language learning 22
forgetting
    classroom strategies 141–2
    cue-dependent 141
    mnemonic devices 141, 142
    reasons for 140–1
formal assessment 349
formal operations stage of cognitive development (Piaget)
    abstract thought 41, 42
    deductive reasoning 51
    developmental milestones 42, 51
    in education 53, 59
    hypothetical reasoning 41, 42, 51–3
    inductive reasoning 51
    main achievements 41
    tasks 51–3
formal schooling 47
formative assessment 343, 347
forward chaining 125
Four Component Model of model behaviour 98
freedom to learn 176–8
frequency distribution 208
Freud, Sigmund 94, 172
    influence on Erikson 78, 84
    on motivation 222
friendship 89, 90
functional approach to literary teaching 28
functional-organisational approach to emotions 86–7

G

games
    and language development 16
    and motor skill development 6
    role-taking 45
    see also play
Gardner, Howard 199, 213
    multiple intelligences model 155, 199, 201–2, 205
gender
    and bullying 391–2
    definition of 272
    and learning 271–80
gender differences
    in achievement 274
    in attendance 274
    disability status 241–2
    in ICT use 326–6
    in maturity 10
    in physical development 10–11
    role of cognition in 272
    role of emotion in 272
    in self-concept 76–7
    sex and 272
    in sport involvement 10–11
gender identity formation 272–3
gender schema 272, 276
general mental capacity ('g') 199
general self-concept 72, 73
generalisation 123

generativity 82
Gesell, Arnold 231
Gibbons, P. 22, 23
gifted children *see* learners with exceptional abilities
Gilligan, Carol 100
Glasser, William 387, 388
global self-concept 72, 73
goal of assessment 341
goal-directed action 41, 42, 43
goal-oriented motivation 220–1
Goleman, Daniel 202
government and student assessment 361, 363
grammar
    development of 16–17, 18
    overgeneralisation in first- and second-language acquisition 22
Grandma's rule (Premack principle) 109, 121
Grasha–Reichmann learning styles 156–7
gross motor skill development 5
group 88, 89
    size of and cooperative learning 188
'guided discovery' learning 158–9
Guilford, J. P. 199, 213
    structure-of-intellect model of intelligence 200, 205

H

Hall, G. S. 231
handicap 239, 240
Head Start 233
health
    environmental influences on 9
    issues for Indigenous Australians 294–5
    and learning 283
hearing problems 238, 294–5
heritability of intelligence 210–11
heteronomous morality 95
hidden curriculum 267
hierarchy of human needs 120, 173–6, 217, 388
high support needs 235
higher-order emotions 87
home environment
    and disturbed behaviour 377–8
    and emergent literacy 24–5
    and learning 286–7
homosexual adolescents 273
horizontal decalage 50
Human Genome Project 210
humanism 172–3
humanist approach to learning 159, 178–9
    cooperative learning 182–7
    Dalton Plan 182
    explanations of motivation 226
    and ICT 319–20
    progressive education 179–81
    strengths and limitations 187–9
hyperactivity 256
hyperlink 322
hypermedia 316, 322
hypertext 322
hypothetical reasoning 41, 42, 51–3
hypothetical thinking 50–1

I

ICT (information and communication technology)
    features of learning with 321–35
    functions 305
    how it is used in the classroom 309–11
    key concepts in 305–9
    and theories of learning 311–21
ICT in the inclusive classroom
    access to ICT 326
    gender and ICT use 326–8
    for gifted learners 328
    potential cultural biases 329–30
    in remote areas 330
    special learning needs 328–9
    strengths and limitations 331–5
identity
    in adolescence 81
    Erikson's theory 81–2
    and the Internet 323–4
    and peer relationships 90
    and puberty 82
identity achievement 82
identity diffusion 82
identity foreclosure 82
imaginary play 92
impairment 239, 240
impulsivity of response 152–3
inappropriate behaviour 375–9
inclusion 249–50
inclusive classroom, ICT in 325–35
Indigenous Australians
    Aboriginal pedagogy 294
    cultural heritage 294
    diversity and commonality 290–1
    health issues 294–5
    independence 291
    interdependence 291
    language and linguistic competence 292
    learning styles 155
    multicultural education 170–1
    resistance 269–71
    teacher employment patterns 295
Indigenous children
    development of motor skills 5
    English as a second language 22
    health 9–10
    identity 85
    improving literacy 25
    racism 268–9
    self-efficacy and achievement 75–6
indigenous learners
    achievement 288–9
    education issues 288–98
    enhancing learning 298
    ICT use 329–30
    Indigenous Australians 290–6
    Maori children 296–8
    participation and attendance patterns 290
    skills and strengths 290
individual constructualism 157
Individual Education Plan (IEP) 247
individualistic culture 85
inductive reasoning 51
infancy
    brain structure 4
    emotional development 88
    language development 16
    peer interactions 90
    physical development in 4
informal assessment 349
information and communication technology *see* ICT
information literacy 307–8
information processing approach to cognitive learning 137–8
    connectionist model 140, 144
    forgetting 140–2
    information and knowledge 142–3
    levels of processing model 139–40, 144
    multi-store model 138–9, 143–4
    strengths and limitations 143–4
informed consent and assessment 365
Inhelder, Barbel 58
integration 249
integration–segregation debate 251–2
intelligence
    cultural influences on 198
    definition 197–8
    emotional 202
    heritability of 210–11
    nature–nurture debate 210–11
intelligence, measuring
    administering tests 208
    interpreting IQ scores 208–10
    Stanford-Binet test 206–7, 209, 212, 360
    strengths and limitations 211
    Wechsler's intelligence scales 207–8, 209
intelligence, models of
    Gardner's multiple intelligences 199, 201–2, 205
    Guilford's structure-of-intellect 155, 199, 200, 205
    Spearman and 'g' 199, 200, 205
    Sternberg's triarchic model 199, 202–3, 205
    strengths and limitations 205
    Thurstone's primary mental abilities 199–200, 205

intelligence quotient (IQ) 207
    interpreting score 208–10
intentional action 41, 42, 43
interaction 88, 89
interactive teacher 384–7
intermittent reinforcement 123–4
    interval schedules 124
    ratio schedules 124
internal assessment 349
International Computer Driving License (ICDL) 307
Internet
    chatroom 307
    and identity 323–4
    and values 324–5
Internet relay chat (IRC) 307
interpersonal intelligence 201
interpersonal skills and cooperative learning 188
interpreting assessment information 344–9
interval schedules 124
interventionist teacher 382–4
interviews for assessment 350, 355
intimacy 82
intrapersonal intelligence 201
intrinsic motivation 219, 220
involuntary minority group 269–70
ipsative assessment 347, 348
Itard, Jean-Marc-Gaspard 242–3, 247

J

jigsaw strategy 185, 186–7, 269
joining words 17
joint attention 20

K

kinesthetic learning 155
knowledge
    conditional 142–3
    declarative 142–3
    metacognitive 145–6, 147
    procedural 142–3
Kohlberg, Lawrence 95, 96
Kohlberg's theory of moral development 96
    neo-Kohlbergians 98, 99
    stages 96, 97, 99
    strengths and limitations of 98–9

L

labelling children with disabilities 242–5
language
    and abstract thought 20
    and culture 266–7
    first- and second- language acquisition 22–3
    and linguistic competence 292
    as a mental tool 62–3
    sex differences in 275
    symbolic processes 128
    window of acquisition 22–3

language development
    in adolescence 19–20, 26
    building blocks of 15–16
    and cerebral cortex 13
    and cognitive development 16
    in early childhood 13, 16–18
    during infancy 16
    in middle childhood 18–19
    role of adults 20–1
    sociolinguistic features of 266–7
lateralisation 13–14, 15
law of effect 115
law of exercise 115, 116
LBOTE (language background other than English) 268, 274, 289
learned helplessness 220
learned response 111
learners with exceptional abilities 211
    concepts of giftedness 212
    ICT for 328
    identifying 212–14
    programs for 214–16
learners with special needs 212
    compensatory programs 233–4
    disability 234, 239–46
    early intervention programs 232
    at educational risk 236–7
    high support needs 235
    ICT for 328–9
    mild difficulties 235
    non-categorical approach 246
    normal development, concepts of 231–2
    preventative programs 232, 234
    readiness for school 232
    special support needs 234–5
    supplementary programs 232–3, 234
    see also special education
learning difficulties 235, 244, 245
    gender differences 274
    and metacognition 148
learning disability 235, 244, 245
learning process
    behavioural views of 109–35, 222
    cognitive explanations of 137–69
    humanist approaches to 171–92
    sociocultural factors in 262–301
learning style 151, 154–6
learning with ICT
    cognition and reading online 323
    identity and the Internet 323–4
    in the inclusive classroom 325–32
    navigating with hypertext and hypermedia 322
    outcomes 332
    strengths and limitations of 331–5
    values and the Internet 324–5
least restrictive environment (LRE) 247–8
left-handedness 13–14
Leontiev, Alexei 60

levels of processing model 139–40, 144
limit-setting strategies 382
linguistic intelligence 201
listserv 307
literacy
    computer 307
    definition 24
    information 307
    New Zealand strategy 24
literacy development
    decoding 25, 28
    emergent literacy 24
    gender differences 273, 275
    learning to read and write 25–6
    and metalinguistic awareness 18
    teaching literacy 26–8
    writing skills in adolescence 26
Little Albert and the rat experiment 113
locus of control 224
logical consequences 386
logical-mathematical intelligence 201
long-term memory 139, 141
low self-esteem 74
Luria, Alexander 31, 60

M

macrosystem of child's environment 264, 265
mainstreaming 249
maintenance of skill 123
Maori children
    development of motor skills 5
    learners 296–8
Maslow, Abraham 173–4, 177, 179
    hierarchy of human needs 120, 173–6, 217, 388
    impact of ideas 187
    and motivation 226–7
    strengths and limitations 175
mastery goals 220
mastery learning theory 313
Matching Familiar Figures Test 153
maturity
    and development 55
    gender differences 10
    and physical development 33
McLelland, David 223
measurement
    definition of 341
    of intelligence 206–11
Meichenbaum, Donald 131
memory 138–41
menarche 7, 9
mental age 207
mental tools and cognitive development 62–3
mesosystem of child's environment 264
meta-analysis 254
metacognition
    across cultures 148–9

metacognition (*cont.*)
  development of 148
  experience 146–7
  knowledge 145–6, 147
  self-monitoring 145
  self-regulating 145
  strategies and learning 148
metalinguistics awareness 18–20
metaneeds 174
microsystem of child's environment 264
middle childhood
  emotional development 88
  language development 18–19
  motor-skill development 6
  peer relationships 91, 92
  physical development in 5–6
  self-concept 76
  writing in 26
mild difficulties 235
mind tools 314
mnemonic devices 141, 142
modelling 124, 126
Montessori, Maria 181, 244
moral development
  cognitive-development theories of 94–100
  Gilligan's feminist approach 100
  Kohlberg's theory 96–9
  and peer relationships 90
  Piaget 58, 94–6
  role of educators 101–2
  socialisation approaches 94, 100
  values 101
moral dilemma 95
moral reasoning 98, 99
moral rule 94–5
morality 94
moratorium in adolescence 82
morphology of language 15
motivation 216–17
  in adolescence 218–19, 222
  and anxiety 217–18
  and arousal 217
  in the classroom 221
  enhanced with ICT use 331
  extrinsic 219, 220
  goal orientation 220–1
  intrinsic 219, 220
  strengths and limitations 221
  traits and states 219–20
motivation, theories of
  behavioural 222–3
  in the classroom 227
  cognitive 223–5
  humanist 226
  social learning 225
  strengths and limitations 226–7
motor skill development
  and cognition development 4, 6
  in early childhood 5
  in middle childhood 6
  sex differences in 10

multicultural education 270–1
multiple-choice tests 358–9
multiple intelligences model 155, 199, 201–2
multiple-user domain (MUD) 317
multiple-user object-oriented (domain) (MOO) 317
multi-store model of information processing 138–9, 143–4
musical intelligence 201
myelination 12

N

natural consequences 386
naturalist intelligence 201
nature–nurture debate 210
navigating websites 308
navigating with hypertext and hypermedia 322
needs, hierarchy of 120, 173–6, 217, 226
negative reinforcement 120–2
Neill, A. S. 180, 387
neo-Kohlbergians 98, 99
neo-Piagetians 56
neo-Vygotskyians 154
network connectivity 306
neural network 14
neuron 12, 13
neurotransmitter 12
neutral stimulus 112
new behaviours, teaching 124–6
New Zealand
  alternative educational program 380
  assessment 344–9
  at risk children 391
  bullying 391
  children with disabilities 246
  culture 86
  discipline 380
  education system 296–8
  English as a second language 22
  gifted children 214
  Indigenous learners 288, 290, 296–8
  learners at risk 236, 391
  learning styles 155
  literacy and numeracy strategy 24
  national goals for ICT use 310
  promoting achievement 278
  special education 247, 248, 251
newsgroup 307
non-academic self-concept 73
non-directive teaching 176–8
non-interventionist teacher 387–8, 389
norm 345
normal development 231–2
normal distribution 208
normalisation 245
norm-referenced assessment 345, 348

numeracy development 28–31
  gender differences in outcomes 274

O

object permanence 4, 16, 41–3, 48
objective of assessment 341
observation (vicarious learning) 128
one-to-one correspondence in numeracy 29
open education 179–82
'open' learning 157, 158–9, 165, 166, 167
operant conditioning
  definition 115
  principles of 117–26
  Skinner 114–15, 116–17
operants 117
operations (Piaget) 44
order in numeracy 29
otitis media 238, 294–5
outcome of assessment 342
overextension of language 16–17
overregulation of grammatical forms 17
Ozone Monitoring Network 319

P

parallel play 92
parallel reinforcers 121
parent–adolescent conflict 8
parenting factors and learning 283–4
parents and assessment 361, 362
participation, indigenous learners 290
Pascual-Leone, J. 56
Pavlov, Ivan Petrovic 111, 113, 124
  dog studies 110–11, 222–3
paying attention 138
pedagogy 373
Peekaboo study 61
peer acceptance 93
peer experiences
  and academic achievement 73, 93
  across cultures 93
  in adolescence 8, 91, 92
  role of 89–90
  over time 90–2
  and socioemotional development 88–93
  types of 88–9
peer-assisted learning 160, 166
perceptual motor training 255
perceptual style of learning 151–2
performance assessment 352–3
performance goals 220–1
person knowledge 145–6
personal issues and ICT 325
perspective-taking 88
phonology 15, 18, 19, 23
physical appearance
  gender differences 77
  and self-concept 73, 77
physical bullying 392
physical development

in adolescence 7–9
and cognition 14–15
in early childhood 5
gender differences 10–11
in infancy 4
mastering sporting skills 5
in middle childhood 5–6
principles of 32–3
variations in 9–10
what contributes to 33
physiological needs 174
Piaget, Jean 39, 40–1, 158, 314
and constructivism 46, 47, 157
contribution 40, 67
on moral development 58, 94–6
Piaget's theory of cognitive development 29
accommodation 54
adaptation 54
assimilation 54
concrete operations stage 41, 42, 47–51, 59
developmental milestones 42
equilibration 55–6
formal operations stage 41, 42, 59
influences on development 55–6
linking with Vygotsky 60, 66–7
neo-Piagetians 56
preoperational stage 41, 42, 44–6, 59
schemes 53–5
sensorimotor stage 41, 42–3, 59
strengths and limitations 56–9
summary 59
transition between stages 47
pigeon experiments 116–17
play
with language 19
and symbolic thought 45
types of 91–2
playground games and motor skill development 5, 6
portfolios for assessment 352
positive reinforcement 120
postconventional morality 97
post-school education, gender differences 274–5
poverty and learning 283–5
pragmatics 15
praise 109, 120
preadolescence, peer relationships 91, 92
preconventional morality 97–8
prejudice and cooperative learning 185–7
Premack principle (Grandma's rule) 109, 121
preoperational stage of cognitive development (Piaget)
animism 46
centration 46
in the classroom 59
developmental milestones 42

in education 46, 59
egocentrism 45
language acquisition 41, 42
main achievements 41, 42
symbolic thought 44–5
pretend play 92
preventive programs 232, 234
primary mental abilities (PMA) 199–200, 205
primary reinforcer 120
private speech 62–3
problem space 374
procedural knowledge 142–3
procedural memory 139
process-oriented assessment 349
product-oriented assessment 349
profile 346–7
progressive education 179–82
prompting 124, 125–6
propositional thinking 51
prosocial behaviour 88
psychological bullying 392
psychological constructivism 157
psychologists and assessment 361, 362, 364
psychology and humanism 172–3
see also Maslow; Rogers
psychosocial crisis 78
psychosocial development (Erikson) 71, 77–85
psychosocial issues of ICT use 333–4
puberty 7–9
identity issues 82
punctuation, learning 26
punishers 121
punishment 119, 121–2

R

racism 268–9
rating scales for assessment 354–5
ratio schedules 124
readiness for school 232
reading
elaboration strategies 139
and home environment 25
information-processing approach 25
learning to 25–6
moving to silent 26, 63
online 323
and play with language 19
reality therapy 388
recasting speech 20
reciprocal determinism 128–30
reciprocal learning 65
reciprocal teaching 163–4, 166
recording assessment data 365–6
record-keeping 265–6
reflection and constructivist learning 164
reflective listening 176
reflectivity of response 152–3
refugee children 245

Reggio Emilia education system 181
Regular Education Initiative (REI) 251
rehearsal 138, 139
reinforcement 109, 115, 116, 117
contingency of 119–20
distinguishing from punishment 121
and motivation 223
negative 120
positive 120
time out from 122–3
reinforcement schedules 123–4
reinforcers 119–21
relationship 88, 89
reliability 342
reliability of assessment 342, 358–9
reporting assessment information 366–8
resilience
and educational risk 237–8, 246
and learning 284–5
resistance 269–71
resource issues of ICT use 334
resource room 248–9
respondents 117
response 110
responsibility training 382–3
Rest, J. R. 98
reversibility of principle 48
rewards 115, 116
and cooperative learning 183
risk factors and learning 284–5
risk-taking behaviour in adolescence 8
Rogers, Bill 387, 388
Rogers, Carl 173, 177, 179
active listening 176
basic needs 174
in the classroom 178
impact of ideas 187
and motivation 226
non-directive teaching and freedom to learn 176–7
strengths and limitations 178
role confusion 81
role-taking games 45
rural and remote areas, ICT use 330

S

satiation 123
scaffolding tasks 65
school administrators and assessment 361, 362–3
school factors
and classroom behaviour 377–9
in learning 286–7
school phobia 217
school-based skills
literacy development 24–8
numeracy development 28–31
second-language development 21–4
scope-and-sequence charts 126

second-language development 21–4
secondary reinforcer 120
Séguin, Eduard 244
self
    across cultures 85–6
    defining 71
    moral development 94–102
    socioemotional development 86–94
self-absorption 82
self-actualisation 174, 175
self-assessment 356–7
self-concept
    academic 72–3
    and body image 8
    defining 72
    and development 76–7
    development over time 76
    gender differences 76–7
    general 72, 73
    non-academic 73
    and physical appearance 77
self-conscious emotions 87
self-efficacy 75–6
self-esteem 73, 218
    and achievement 74
    and development 76–7
    enhancing 77
    enhancement with ICT use 331
    and metacognitive experience 146
    and peer relationships 90
self-managing behaviour 131–2
self-monitoring 145
self-questioning 164
self-regulation 128, 131–2, 145, 158
self-talk 62–3, 128, 131
semantic memory 139
semantics 15, 19
semenarche 7
sensorimotor stage of cognitive development (Piaget)
    in the classroom 59
    deferred imitation 41, 42, 43
    developmental milestones 42
    goal-directed action 41, 42, 43
    main achievements 41
    object permanence 41, 42, 43
sensory integration 255
sensory register 138
seriation principle 48–9
sex
    differences in adolescent development 10
    and gender differences 272
'shallow' processing of information 139, 140
shaping 124–5
Shayer, M. 66–7
short-term ('working') memory 138, 140
'sight vocabulary' 26
Simon, Theodore 206, 231
    Stanford-Binet test 206–7, 209, 212, 360

simulations 315, 316–17
simultaneous multiplication 49–50
single-sex schooling 279–80
situated learning 315
skill 75, 290
Skinner, B. F. 114–15, 124, 172
    on motivation 226–7
    pigeon experiments 116–17
social class and socioeconomic status 281–2
social constructivism 157–8
social emotions 87
social interaction 55
    and cognitive development 67
    in constructivism 157
    and learning 314
social issues and ICT 325
social learning theory 94, 225
'social negotiation' 160
social responsibility goals 221
socialisation 266
sociocultural factors
    and cognitive style 154
    in learning 263–99
sociocultural theory of cognitive development (Vygotsky) 60–7
socioeconomic status (SES) 281
    access to ICT 326
    in the classroom 287–8
    and educational outcomes 274
    and emergent literacy 24–5
    and language input 21
socioemotional development
    and emotions 86–8
    and peer experiences 88–93
    and physical and cognitive development 7–9
sociograms for assessment 355–6
sociolinguistic features of language 266–7
sociomoral development 100
software 306
solitary play 92
'solitary scientist' 55–7, 65
spatial intelligence 201
Spearman, Charles 199
    'g' model of intelligence 199, 200, 205
special classes 248–9, 251–2
special education
    alternative schools 250
    in the classroom 257–8
    and compensatory programs 233–4
    controversial/alternative interventions 255–7
    definition 231
    delivery of 251–4
    effectiveness 254–5
    inclusion 249–50
    integration 249
    integration–segregation debate 251

    mainstreaming 249
    policies 247–8
    services and programs 248–9
special learning needs *see* learners with special needs
special school 235, 251–2
special support needs 234
specific mental abilities 199
spelling, learning 26
spina bifida 234
spiritual intelligence 202
spiritual issues and ICT 325
sports
    activity and cognition (learning capacity) 6
    gender differences in participation 10–11
    mastering skills in early childhood 5–6
Standard Australian English 292
standard deviation (SD) 208–9
standard of assessment 342
standardised tests 345
Stanford-Binet test 206–7, 209, 212, 360
Steiner, Rudolf 181
Sternberg, Robert 199, 203
    identifying gifted children 213
    triarchic model of intelligence 199, 202–3, 205
stimulus 110
strategy knowledge 146
stress factors and learning 284
structure-of-intellect model of intelligence 200
student cooperation and cooperative learning 188
students and assessment 361, 364
subject choice, gender differences 274
summative assessment 343–4, 347
Summerhill school 180
supplementary programs 232–3, 234
surface learning 153–4
suspension as punishment 380
Swanson, H. L. 254–5
symbolic processes (language) 128, 131
symbolic thought (Piaget) 44–5
sympathy 88
synapses 12, 13, 14
synchronous communication 307
syntax 15, 19–20, 23

T

tabula rasa 110
tactile learning 155
talented learners 212–14
target of assessment 342
task analysis 124, 126
task completion and cooperative learning 188
task knowledge 146

task structure and cooperative learning 183
teachers
    and assessment 361, 362, 364–6
    expectations 278, 286
    female 276
    interventionist 382–4
    as leaders 388
    non-interventionist 387–8, 389
teacher–student interaction 277–8
teaching *see* classroom
teaching goal 374
technology 306, 309, 366
telegraphic speech 16
television, time spent watching 6
test 341
test anxiety 217
test bias 360
test–retest reliability 358
theories of learning and ICT 311–21
Thorndike, E. L. 114–16, 124, 173
three-way reporting 367
Thurstone, L. L. 199
    primary mental abilities model of intelligence 199–200, 205
time out from reinforcement 122–3
top-down approach to literacy 26–7, 28
traits 219–20
trial-and-error learning 115–16

triarchic model of intelligence 199, 202–3, 205
turning points 78
two-factor theory of intelligence 199, 205

U

unconditioned response 112
unconditioned stimulus 112
underachievers 212, 232–3, 234, 235, 238
underextension of language 16–17

V

validity of assessment 342, 359
values 101
    and the Internet 324–5
verbal bullying 392
vertical decalage 50
vicarious learning 128–9, 130
videoconferencing 307
visual conversations 16
visual learners 154
visual literacy 308
vocabulary
    increase 16, 18, 21
    'sight' 26
voluntary minority groups 269
Vygotsky, Lev Semanovich 30, 157, 158, 314
    contribution 67

    and Piaget 60, 66–7
Vygotsky's sociocultural theory of cognitive development 148
    adult–infant interaction 61, 64–5
    language as a mental tool 62–3
    neo-Vygotskyians 154
    self-regulation 131
    self-talk 62–3
    strengths and limitations 65–6
    zone of proximal development 63–5, 315

W

Warnock Report (UK) 247
Watson, John B. 113, 124
Web (World Wide Web) 306, 319
Webquest 319
website 308
Wechsler's intelligence scales 207–8, 209
Weiner, Bernard 223, 225, 226–7
    whole-language approach to literacy 26
Wild Boy of Aveyron 243–4, 247
'working' (short-term) memory 138
writing skills 26

Z

zone of proximal development 63–5, 315